Praise for *Business Process Change*

This book is a must-read for every business manager who wants to manage business process change in an e-business environment; it's a true practitioner's guidebook to the complex world of end-to-end business process management. The book not only gives an excellent introduction to all aspects of process change management (from analysis or redesign to implementation to monitoring to improvement of business processes), but also provides a comprehensive guide to state-of-the-art techniques and technologies supporting the various aspects of this process (from process design methodologies to realizing business processes via choreography of Web services).

—Steve Mill, *Senior Vice President, IBM Software Group*

Finally a book that brings it all together—background, theory, and practice—in a way that is easily digested by business and IT managers alike. This book is a must-read for anyone contemplating a business change project in order that they understand why a holistic approach is beneficial and how the work they are undertaking will impact others.

The concepts and notations presented in the book are straightforward and easy to follow and do not require either weeks of training or an army of outside consultants to help implement them. I feel sure that after reading the book, any manager will come away with two lasting impressions: first, "Now I understand where that fits . . ." and "Yes, I can do it."

—Mark McGregor, *Vice President, MEGA International*

Finally, someone has written a practical guide for those building a business for the information age.

—Bill Coleman, *Founder, Chairman, CSO, BEA Systems*

When it comes to Business Process Change, Paul Harmon's new book is a must-read. It is a great resource for performance improvement professionals.

—Dr. Roger M. Addison, *Director Performance Technologies International Society for Performance Improvement*

Business Process Change

**A Manager's Guide
to Improving, Redesigning,
and Automating Processes**

Business Process Change

A Manager's Guide to Improving, Redesigning, and Automating Processes

Paul Harmon
Senior Consultant, Business Process Trends

MORGAN KAUFMANN PUBLISHERS

An Imprint of Elsevier

AMSTERDAM   BOSTON   LONDON   NEW YORK
OXFORD   PARIS   SAN DIEGO   SAN FRANCISCO
SINGAPORE   SYDNEY   TOKYO

Acquisitions Editor	Tim Cox
Publishing Services Manager	Edward Wade
Senior Production Editor	Cheri Palmer
Editorial Coordinator	Stacie Pierce
Cover Design	Frances Baca Design
Text Design	Side by Side Studios/Mark Ong
Technical Illustration and Composition	Technologies 'N Typography
Copyeditor	Ken DellaPenta
Proofreader	Carol Leyba
Indexer	Ty Koontz
Printer	The Maple-Vail Book Manufacturing Group

Designations used by companies to distinguish their products are often claimed as trademarks or registered trademarks. In all instances in which Morgan Kaufmann Publishers is aware of a claim, the product names appear in initial capital or all capital letters. Readers, however, should contact the appropriate companies for more complete information regarding trademarks and registration.

Morgan Kaufmann Publishers
An Imprint of Elsevier
340 Pine Street, Sixth Floor
San Francisco, CA 94104–3205
www.mkp.com

07 06 05   5 4 3

Library of Congress Control Number: 2002110618
ISBN: 1-55860-758-7

This book is printed on acid-free paper.

To Celia Wolf,
my business partner and a
wise and supportive friend

Foreword

Geary A. Rummler
Founder and Chairman, Performance Design Lab

THERE HAVE BEEN SOME SIGNIFICANT changes in the world of business since Alan Brache and I first published *Improving Performance—How to Manage the White Space on the Organization Chart* in 1990. At that time we put forth a rather straightforward model for looking at organization performance and made a case for how important it was to address three levels of performance—the Organization Level, the Process Level, and the Job Level. We pointed out how critical the Process Level was to meeting both customer and shareholder needs and discussed how to improve, measure, and manage processes.

Since that time, we have seen three major forces in the business world come into vogue, drop off the radar screen, and return again, even stronger the second time:

▶ Process Improvement morphed into Process Reengineering, which then mutated into Reengineering the Corporation, and ultimately became the euphemism for corporate downsizing. The emphasis shifted from customer focus, which provided value, to cost reduction, which provided little value, resulting in process becoming a dirty word throughout corporate America. The focus on process began to disappear like all management fads before it. BUT, not so fast! "Process" is back, and this time it's here to stay.

▶ E-business and "dot-com" swept the nation. The Internet came out of nowhere, it seemed, and was going to rule the business world. CEOs of major companies decreed that 80% of their sales would be done over the Internet in 18 months, or else. Technology investment was off the charts. And then it all crashed and burned even faster than it came on the scene. The tech bubble burst and "dot-com" became another dirty word. But again, not so fast! The Internet and e-business are back and, this time, likely to remain.

▶ Under the pressure of stiff foreign competition in the 1970s and 1980s, many American firms cleaned-up their operational acts and through process improvement and wise technology investments entered the 1990s operationally sound. However, as a function of the sudden flow of investment money into high tech in the mid-1990s, and the apparent threat of a new economy, old economy companies suddenly found themselves competing with Silicon Valley for capital. A subtle shift in emphasis began—a shift from manufacturing and providing quality products and services to the manufacturing of "profits." Now corporate America is taking a major public (and investor) opinion shellacking for apparently cooking the books. Now "business" is a dirty word. But not so fast! Real profits are being demanded by investors, and that requires two things of companies: a differentiating strategy and *sound internal operations,* which combined will provide a competitive advantage. Operationally sound, competitive business organizations are on their way back.

It is no accident that these three factors—process, the Internet, profits—are all "back." They constitute a critical interdependency. Profits require sound operations that consistently meet the needs of consumers *and* investors alike. Now more than ever, sound operations that meet these requirements depend on effective and efficient processes, which are the operational spine of any organization. They also require the use of information systems, like the Internet, which function as the central nervous system of the organization. Process and the Internet form a vital synergy. Increasingly, it will be Internet technologies that drive strategy changes and simultaneously provide the technical means for integrating and automating processes. And this critical relationship between operational excellence, process, and the Internet/IT brings us to this book by Paul Harmon.

A great deal has been written about process improvement and business process reengineering, most before its presumed demise and recent resurrection. Much has been written about the Internet and e-business, most before the tech bubble. This book is "post-bust"; it is the first book to thoroughly discuss the critical link between "process," information technology, and the Internet—all things that *managers* must understand if they are to develop and manage sound internal operations that will provide *legitimate* profits. And it is the *manager's* job to do that. Some of the technical work must be done by business process consultants and IT staff, but the setting of the direction and requirements, the management of the integrating efforts, must be done by managers. That critical role cannot be delegated to the "techies." Meeting that management challenge will be made easier by this book.

Paul and I were colleagues many years ago. We both share the same "performance improvement" roots. Paul took a turn into the world of IT twenty years ago, where he has developed a worldwide reputation as a communicator about the intricacies of that field. Recently, Paul and I began to talk about the need for a book that recognized the important foundation "process" provides for operational excellence and that described how IT must interact with process to deliver on that requirement. I am very pleased that Paul has now written that book and flattered that he has used the basic systems view and process notions described in *Improving Performance* as his point of departure.

Contents

Foreword by Geary Rummler   ix
Preface   xix

Introduction   1

Business Process Change and the Manager's Job   5
The Evolution of an Organization's Understanding of Process   6
The Variety of Options   10
The Variety of Solutions   10
How This Book Is Organized   13

1 Business Process Change   19

Organizations as Systems   20
Systems and Value Chains   21
Business Process Reengineering   23
The Role of Information Technology in BPR   26
Misuses of BPR   27
Workflow and Packaged Applications   27
Software Engineering   29
The Rummler-Brache Methodology   30
ISO 9000 and the Six Sigma Methodology   32
Changes in Business and IT in the Late 1990s   33
Mergers, Acquisitions, and Globalization   34

A Quick Summary   36
Business Process Change Today   37

PART I   PROCESS MANAGEMENT   43

2   Strategy, Value Chains, and Competitive Advantage   45

Defining a Strategy   46
Porter's Model of Competition   48
Industries, Products, and Value Propositions   51
Strategies for Competing   52
The Unisys Corporate Strategy   54
Porter's Theory of Competitive Advantage   57
E-Business Strategies   64
The Evolution of the Strategic Process   65

3   Process Architecture and Organizational Alignment   67

The TeleManagement Forum's Process Framework   72
Types of Processes   78
Deciding What Kind of Process Change Effort to Undertake   80
The Process Architecture and IT Planning   84
The Process Architecture Process   87
From Strategy Statements to Models   90

PART II   MODELING ORGANIZATIONS AND PROCESSES   91

4   Modeling Organizations   93

The Traditional View of an Organization   93
The Systems View of an Organization   95
Models and Diagrams   96
Organization Diagrams   98
Organization Diagrams and Processes   105
Systems and Processes   109

5 Modeling Processes   111

Process Diagram Basics   111
More Process Notation   115
IS, COULD, and SHOULD Process Diagrams   124
Levels of Analysis   131

6 Analyzing Activities   133

Analyzing a Specific Activity   134
Analyzing the Human Performance Required for an Activity   138
Managing the Performance of Activities   144
Automating the Enter Expense Reports Activity   145
A More Complex Activity   146
Analyzing a Completely Automated Activity   149
Activities, Job Descriptions, and Applications   153

**PART III MANAGING AND IMPROVING
BUSINESS PROCESSES   157**

7 Managing and Measuring Business Processes   159

Managing Business Processes   160
The Role of a Manager   161
A Closer Look at a Manager's Job   162
How to Manage a Process   165
Goals, Measures, and Monitoring   167
The Balanced Scorecard Approach   172
Continuous Measurement, and Improvement   173
Management Redesign at Chevron   176

8 Process Improvement with Six Sigma   179

Six Sigma   179
The Six Sigma Concept   183
The Six Sigma Approach to Process Improvement   186
Six Sigma Teams   187
Phases in a Six Sigma Project   188
Alternative Approaches to Process Improvement   204

PART IV   BUSINESS PROCESS REDESIGN   207

9   A Business Process Redesign Methodology   209

Why Have a Methodology?   211
How Does It All Begin?   211
What Happens?   212
Who Makes It All Happen?   214
Phase 1: Planning for a Redesign Effort   215
Phase 2: Analysis of an Existing Process   219
Phase 3: Design of a New or Improved Process   224
Phase 4: Development of Resources for an Improved Process   228
Phase 5: Managing the Transition to a New Process   231
Summary   234

10   Process Redesign Patterns   235

Types of Process Redesign Patterns   236
The Reengineering Pattern   237
The Simplification Pattern   244
The Value-Added Analysis Pattern   247
The Gaps and Disconnects Pattern   249

PART V   BUSINESS PROCESS AUTOMATION   255

11   Workflow and XML Business Process Languages   257

Workflow Systems   257
Types of Workflow Systems   264
Two Case Studies: Anova and iJET Travel Intelligence   266
Workflow and XML   268
Generic Business Process Languages and Web Services   269
The Future of Workflow and Business Process Workflow Languages   279

12   ERP-Driven Redesign   281

Processes and Packages   282
A Closer Look at SAP   283
Implementing an ERP-Driven Design   292

Case Study: Nestlé USA Installs SAP   295

13 Software Development   299

A Little Software History   299
Application Development   302
The Requirements Interface   305
Software Analysis and UML   306
UML and Business Process Modeling   310
The Model Driven Architecture   312
Software Languages, UML Modeling Tools, and CASE   317
Process Architectures and Software Architectures   318
IDEF   321
RM-ODP   321
XML Business Process Languages   323
The Capability Maturity Model   323

PART VI   THE E-BUSINESS CHALLENGE   327

14 E-Business: Portals and Customer-Oriented Applications   329

E-Business Applications   329
A Customer Focus   333
Web Sites and Portals   334
Analyzing Customer-Oriented Processes   344
Customer-Oriented E-Business Redesign   348

15 Supplier and Internally Oriented E-Business Applications   351

Supplier-Oriented E-Business Redesign   351
How Do Companies Structure Supply Chain Applications?   354
E-Business Marketplaces   355
Directly Linked Supply Chain Systems   362
The Supply Chain Council's SCOR Approach   366
Internally Oriented E-Business Redesign   375
An E-Business Is a Network   382

PART VII   PUTTING IT ALL TOGETHER   387

16   The Ergonomic Systems Case Study   389

Ergonomic Systems, Inc.   389
An E-Business Strategy   394
Phase 1: Planning for the Redesign of the Order Process   401
Phase 2: Analyzing the Current Order Fulfillment Process   403
Phase 3: Designing the New Order Process   409
Phase 4: Resource Development   421
Phase 5: The New Order Process Goes Online   422

17   Software Tools for Business Process Development   425

Why Use Business Process Tools?   425
The Variety of Business Process Tools   426
A Professional BP Modeling Tool   429
Modeling the Ergonomics Case   431

18   Conclusions and Recommendations   445

Glossary   457
Notes and References   485
Bibliography   503
Index   507

Preface

THIS BOOK BEGAN in 2000 in a series of conversations I had with Geary Rummler. I have known Geary since I worked with him in New York in the late 1960s. Initially, I suggested that he revise *Improving Performance,* the book he had written with Alan Brache in 1990, to incorporate information on the kinds of process changes that were being driven by the Internet and e-business applications. Over the course of the next two years, we met several times to talk about these issues. Eventually, having gained many new insights from Geary and convinced that a book on business process redesign that stressed Internet concerns would be useful to business managers, I decided to write the book myself.

My starting point was the business process methodology that Geary Rummler and Alan Brache laid out in *Improvement Performance.* I believe theirs is the most comprehensive and manager-friendly approach to business process change. I have tried to update it and extend it to incorporate more about the information technologies that are so critical to today's business project efforts, but I have tried to maintain the overall approach and scope of their methodology. Anyone familiar with *Improvement Performance* will be immediately aware of how much I have borrowed from Geary's work and his writings. It's hard to sufficiently thank someone who started teaching me some thirty-five years ago and who still continues to share new ideas and techniques with me today.

In addition to Geary Rummler, I owe significant debts to many other people. Some read the entire manuscript and provided detailed critiques. Paul Fjelstra, a Principal at Bayside Consulting, Mark McGregor, Vice President of Mega International, and Sevn van der Zee, a Senior Consultant at CIBIT, all helped make this book much better than it otherwise would have been.

Brian James, Chief Methodologist of Proforma, and Chuck Faris, Director of Consulting at Popkin Software, each created a case study in their tools, provided lots of good feedback, and then allowed me to use screen shots from their versions of the application to illustrate my chapter on software modeling tools.

Many others read parts of the manuscript or simply discussed issues with me. With apologies to anyone I've omitted, this list includes: Johathan Adams (IT Consultant, IBM), Roger Addison (Director of Human Performance Technology, International Society for Performance Improvement), Paul Allen (Computer Associates, and the editor of Component Development Strategies newsletter), Michael Anthony (International Performance Group), Conrad Bock (Director of Standards, Kabira), George W. Brown (IT Industry Business Research, Intel Corporation and Chairman of the Board, Supply Chain Council), David Burke (Manager of Consulting Methodologies, J.D. Edwards and Co.), Allison Burkett (President, Lexington Associates) Magnus Christerson (Director, Product Strategy for Rational Rose, Rational Software), Bill Curtis (Chief Scientist, Teraquest) Edward Cobb (VP Architecture and Standards, BEA Systems), Bill Coleman (Founder, Chairman and Chief Strategy Officer, BEA Systems), Mark Cotteleer (Harvard Business School), J. Kenneth Feldman (VP Quality and Productivity, Bank of America), Layna Fischer (General Manager, Workflow Management Coalition), Hideshige Hasegawa (Hitachi), James Hollingsworth (ICL/Fujitsu and Chair of the Workflow Management Collotion Technical Committee), George Keeling (CaseWise), Andre Leclerc (Senior Consultant, Cutter Consortium), Antoine Lonjon (Mega International), Mike Marin (System Architect, FileNET and Board Member of BPMI), Hugh Mench (Director of Development, Proforma Corp.), Steven A Mills (SVP and Group Executive, IBM), Chris Nugent (Popkin Systems), James Odell (Consultant), Ken Orr (Ken Orr Associates), Dr. Allison Rossett (Professor, Educational Technology, San Diego State University), Georg Simon (Senior Manger of Technology Solutions, IDS Scheer), Richard Mark Soley (CEO, Object Management Group), Annette L. Steenkamp (DMIT Program Coordinator, Lawrence Technological University), Jonathan Tepper (Principal, J. Tepper Group), Petri Tottereman (HMV), Harumasa Umeda (Executive Director, Chiken Company), Steven A. White (Director of Standards, SeeBeyond and Chair of BPMI's Notation Committee), Cherie Wilkins (Consultant, Performance Design Lab).

I need to add, of course, that, in the end, I took everything everyone offered and fitted it into my own perspective and expressed it in my own words. Those who helped can take credit for the many good things they contributed, but they can hardly be blamed for the mistakes I'm sure I've introduced.

I dedicated this book to Celia Wolf but want to thank her one more time. She also critiqued the entire manuscript and kept asking insightful questions about the market, the strategies and services of the various players, and company practices, until I finally understood them and could explain them to her satisfaction. As this book was being written, she worked with me to create a new company, Business Process Trends, to provide business managers with information on business process change. As a result, readers of this book can come to our portal, *www.businessprocesstrends.com,* and sign up for our newsletter that will provide ongoing information on business process change.

Finally, I want to thank my editor, Tim Cox, his assistant, Stacie Pierce, Cheri Palmer who oversaw production, and Technologies 'N' Typography for the great job they did on some very complex graphics, and all the other people involved at Morgan Kaufmann.

Introduction

WE LIVE IN A WORLD that keeps changing faster all the time. What worked only yesterday may not work today or tomorrow. Smart managers knows that organizations that succeed do so because they adjust to keep up with the changes that are taking place. This book is about business process change. It describes how smart managers analyze, redesign, and improve the business processes they manage.

Every year dozens of books are written by management consultants to propose a great new management idea. Some of these new ideas have merit, but most are simply fads that are popular for a year or two and then gradually fade. This book is not such a book. In the first place, this book describes a variety of process change techniques that have been proven over the course of a decade. It describes how companies can achieve efficiencies by integrating and improving their business processes and by aligning those business processes with corporate strategies and goals. Companies that routinely practice business process improvement, using the techniques described in this book, are able to consistently improve the results obtained from existing processes. Companies that undertake more extensive business process redesign efforts can typically achieve improvements in excess of 20%. This isn't miraculous; it simply reflects the fact that most existing processes are less efficient than they could be and that new technologies make it possible to design much more efficient processes.

This book wasn't written to hype the idea of process change. If you need convincing or motivation, you should read one of the popular books that have been written to do just that. This book is designed to help you actually make process change happen, systematically and consistently.

The value of this book is twofold. First, it summarizes what is known about analyzing and improving business processes, presents a methodology based on the work of many successful practitioners, and offers detailed case studies to help readers understand how these methods can be used.

Second, this book offers new insights. The process redesign methodology described here has been updated to include the latest business process modeling and improvement strategies. The emphasis on management and alignment with goals, for example, is more extensive in this book than in business process books written in the early to mid-1990s. Similarly there is more on how to actually facilitate a project. Most practitioners of business process improvement have learned that management preparation and support are vital to successful efforts. Too many business process teams have created new processes and then watched, discouraged, as the company failed to actually implement the new process. The management of the transition from the old to the new process is a vital part of serious business process change efforts. The foundation for a successful transition is laid when the team first begins a project and continues throughout the project as the team designs management incentive systems into the process to assure that managers will monitor and support the steps necessary for the transition. A lot has been learned in the past few years about how to make business process change successful, and these insights have been incorporated into this book.

In addition, these new techniques and strategies are useful because most businesses have entered a new era of business process redesign. In 1995 the Internet burst on the business scene and customers began to visit company Web sites to obtain information or to buy products. Since then, companies have been struggling to determine how best to modify business processes to take advantage of the Internet. The use of the Internet and email for internal company portals has also led to significant changes in how processes are organized. A new emphasis on supply chain integration is one example. The use of data mining to improve management decisions is another. This book is a primer on business process analysis and redesign for the Internet era. It is a handbook for new managers who need to analyze and redesign business processes in an era when software systems and the Internet play a pervasive role in most business process efforts. This book offers proven techniques and heuristics for how to best apply business process techniques in the Internet era.

In 2001, we conducted a survey of some 230 organizations located throughout the world to determine what they were doing about business process change. The results of that survey, which was rather extensive, were published by the Cutter

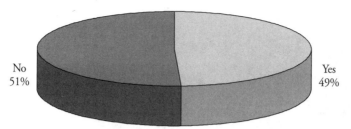

Figure I.1 Companies active in BPR in the mid-1990s.

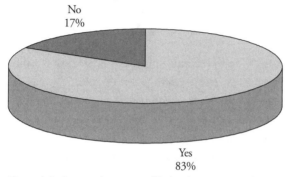

Figure I.2 Companies engaged in business process improvement or redesign today.

Consortium as a report, *Who's Profiting from Business Process Redesign.* (See the Notes and References at the end of this book for more detailed information on any book or study mentioned in the text. With a couple of exceptions we won't use footnotes in this book, but will include all notes and citations in the back.) We can hardly summarize all the data here, but the answers to three questions are instructive.

We asked all the organizations we surveyed if they had been active in business process redesign in the mid-1990s. Of the companies responding to our survey, 49% indicated they had. (See Figure I.1.)

We also asked each organization if it was currently active in business process re-design or improvement today. The results are shown in Figure I.2. Eighty-three percent of our respondents said they had business process projects underway today. In response to another question, they indicated that they expected they would be more active in the next few years than they are today. In other words, companies are considerably more active in business process change today than they were at the height of the BPR fad in the mid-1990s. Reengineering may have come and

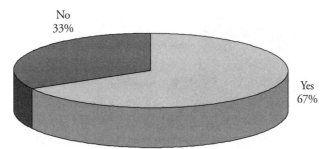

No
33%

Yes
67%

Figure I.3 Companies that indicated that their business process change efforts were being largely driven by the Internet and the need to implement e-business systems.

gone, but the need to redesign and improve processes is a perennial concern, and it's a very important concern as we enter this decade.

In the same survey, we asked all companies to speculate on the causes of today's intense interest in business process change. One specific question we asked was whether the respondents thought process change at their companies was being largely driven by an interest in the Internet and the implementation of e-business systems.

As you can see by glancing at Figure I.3, two-thirds of companies that are engaged in business process redesign and improvement efforts today believe that their efforts are being driven by e-business projects. At the same time, however, almost a third of the companies engaged in business process change projects are concerned with something other than e-business projects. We regard this as a healthy sign. It suggests a balance between integrating a new technology, like the Internet, and taking care of traditional business process concerns by increasing the efficiency of operations and automating activities that can be better done by software systems.

The overall conclusion, however, is that business process change is a growing concern of business managers and will continue to be throughout this decade. It is being driven both by new technologies, like the Internet, and by traditional managerial concerns for efficiency and productivity. Most companies learned these lessons in the 1990s, as they responded to a widespread call for business process reengineering. They are still involved and are more sophisticated than they were then.

In essence, business process redesign in the 1990s focused on improving processes within a company. Today, increasingly, business process redesign is focused on creating business processes that link groups of companies together in processes that span companies. A supply chain system that organizes dozens of suppliers, carriers, manufacturing sites, and distributors into a single process is a good example of the kinds of processes that leading companies will be developing in this decade.

This book is written for today's manager and focuses on the business process change problems today's managers face. This book was written to educate managers in the best practices available for today's challenges and to provide practical tips for anyone undertaking a business process change project.

Business Process Change and the Manager's Job

Every company wants to improve the way it does business, to produce things more efficiently, and to make greater profits. Nonprofit organizations are also concerned with efficiency, productivity, and with achieving the goals they set for themselves. Every manager understands that achieving these goals is a part of his or her job.

Consider the management of the automobile industry. The first internal-combustion automobiles were produced by Karl Benz and Gottlieb Daimler in Germany in 1885. In the decades that followed, some 50 entrepreneurs in Europe and North America set up companies to build cars. In each case, the cars were essentially built by hand, incorporating improvements with each model. Henry Ford was one among many who tried his hand at building cars in this manner.

In 1903, however, Henry Ford started his third company, the Ford Motor Company, and tried a new approach to automobile manufacturing. First, he designed a car that would be of high quality, not too expensive, and easy to manufacture. Next he organized a moving production line. In essence, workmen began assembling a new automobile at one end of the factory building and completed the assembly as it reached the far end of the plant. Workers at each point along the production line had one specific task to do. One group moved the chassis into place, another welded on the side panels, and still another group lowered the engine into place when each car reached their station. In other words, Henry Ford conceptualized the development of an automobile as a single process and designed and sequenced each activity in the process to assure that the entire process ran smoothly and efficiently. Clearly Henry Ford had thought deeply about the way cars were assembled in his earlier plants and had a very clear idea of how he could improve the process.

By organizing the process as he did, Henry Ford was able to significantly reduce the price of building automobiles. As a result, he was able to sell cars for such a modest price that he made it possible for every middle-class American to own a car. At the same time, as a direct result of the increased productivity of the assembly process, Ford was able to pay his workers more than any other auto assembly workers. Within a few years, Ford's new approach had revolutionized the auto industry, and it soon led to changes in almost every other manufacturing process as well.

Ford's success is a great example of the power of business process change to revolutionize the economics of an industry. Other examples could be drawn from the dawn of the Industrial Revolution or from the early years of computers, when mainframes revolutionized the census process in the United States and began to change the way companies managed their accounting and payroll processes.

The bottom line, however, is that the analysis of business processes and their improvement in order to increase the efficiency and productivity of companies is a perennial management responsibility. Managers, of course, have other responsibilities, but one of the most important requires that they constantly examine the processes by which their companies produce products and services and upgrade them to assure that they remain as efficient and effective as possible.

Some business process gurus have advocated crash programs that involve major changes in processes. In a sense they are advocating that today's managers do what Henry Ford did when he created the moving production line. In some cases this kind of an approach is necessary. Today's managers can often use computers to automate processes and achieve major gains in productivity. Similarly, in responding to challenges created by the Internet, some managers have been forced to create new business processes or to make major changes in existing processes. In most cases, however, gradual improvements are more effective.

There are other times, however, when a crash program is too far reaching. By the same token, a modest improvement wouldn't be enough. These are cases that we refer to as business process redesign projects. They implement a significant change without redesigning the entire process. Many projects that automate a portion of an existing process fall in this category. In some cases, redesign takes place in a series of steps in order to minimize disruption. A series of modules, for example, could be installed over the course of several months, one after another, with enough time between each change to assure that the employees can adjust as the changes are made.

The Evolution of an Organization's Understanding of Process

Managers have been thinking about business process change for several decades now. Some organizations are more sophisticated in their understanding of business processes than others. Software organizations, for example, have spent quite a bit of time thinking about the software development process. In the 1990s, the Department of Defense funded a major effort to determine how the software development process could be improved. This task was entrusted to the Software Engineering Institute (SEI), which is located at Carnegie Mellon University. The SEI/DOD effort resulted in a model of the stages that organizations go through in their understanding and management of processes.

The SEI model is known as the Capability Maturity Model (CMM). It was initially described in a book, *The Capability Maturing Model: Guidelines for Improving the Software Process,* published in 1995. In essence, the CMM team defined five stages that organizations go through as they move from an immature to a mature understanding of business processes. These stages were defined using examples from software organizations, but they apply, equally, to any large organization.

Although the CMM model is more commonly applied to large organizations, the model can also serve as an excellent reference model for small- and medium-size firms. Remember the key point of such reference models is to help you understand where you are today and to assist in developing a road map to help you get where you want to go. No one is suggesting that all companies should attempt to follow the model in the same exact way.

The key assumption that the CMM team makes is that immature organizations don't perform consistently. Mature organizations, on the other hand, produce quality products or services effectively and consistently. In the CMM book, they describe it this way:

> In a mature organization, managers monitor the quality of the software products and the processes that produce them. There is an objective, quantitative basis for judging product quality and analyzing problems with the product and process. Schedules and budgets are based on historical performance and are realistic; the expected results for cost, schedule, functionality, and quality of the product are usually achieved. In general, the mature organization follows a disciplined process consistently because all of the participants understand the value of doing so, and the necessary infrastructure exists to support the process.

Watts Humphrey, one of the leading gurus behind the CMM effort, describes it this way:

> An immature software process resembles a Little League baseball team. When the ball is hit, some players run toward the ball, while others stand around and watch, perhaps not even thinking about the game. In contrast, a mature organization is like a professional baseball team. When the ball is hit, every player reacts in a disciplined manner. Depending on the situation, the pitcher may cover home plate, infielders may set up for a double play, and outfielders prepare to back up their teammates.

CMM identified five levels or steps that describe how organizations typically evolve from immature organizations to mature organizations. The steps are illustrated in Figure I.4.

The CMM model defines the evolution of a company's maturity as follows:

▶ *Level 1: Initial.* The process is characterized by an ad hoc set of activities. The process isn't defined and success depends on individual effort and heroics.
▶ *Level 2: Repeatable.* At this level, basic project management processes are established to track costs, to schedule, and to define functionality. The discipline is available to repeat earlier successes on similar projects.
▶ *Level 3: Defined.* The process is documented for both management and engineering activities and standards are defined. All projects use an approved, tailored version of the organization's standard approach to developing and maintaining software.
▶ *Level 4: Managed.* Detailed measures of the software process and product quality are collected. Both the software process and products are quantitatively understood and controlled.
▶ *Level 5: Optimizing.* Continuous process improvement is enabled by quantitative feedback from the process and from piloting innovative ideas and technologies.

Obviously the CMM approach was very much in the spirit of Business Process Reengineering, which was popular in the mid-1990s and is also a product of an application of Total Quality Management (TQM) techniques, which were popular in engineering and manufacturing during the same period.

Every organization can be assigned a maturity level. Most software organizations studied by SEI were in either level 2 or 3. In effect, they had processes, but in most cases they weren't as well defined as they could be. Their management systems were not well aligned with their processes, and they weren't in a position to routinely improve their processes.

In this book we won't make any assumptions about where your organization is. We will, however, put lots of emphasis on how companies document processes, how they develop process architectures that describe how processes relate to each other, how they align management systems to assure that corporate goals are aligned with managerial goals, and we will stress the importance of routine and project-based process improvement. In effect, this is a book that should help managers conceptualize where their organization should go and provide the tools they need to help with the transition.

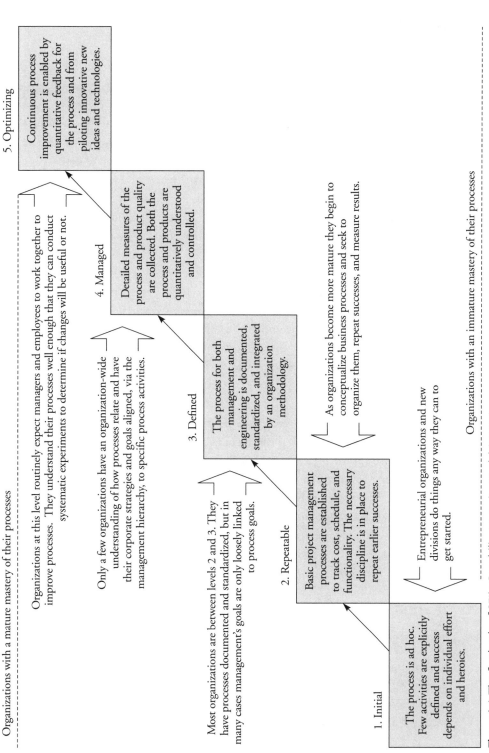

Figure I.4 The five levels of SEI's Capability Maturity Model (CMM).

The Variety of Options

If there were one way of handling all business process problems, we would be happy to elaborate it. Unfortunately, there are many different types of business process change problems. They vary by the type of work being done, by industry, and by the nature of the environmental change that needs to be accommodated. Some changes only require modest improvements in existing processes. Others require the complete redesign of an existing process or the creation of a new process. Some focus on changes in how people perform, while others involve the use of software applications to automate a process. In some cases a software application can be purchased, and in other cases it must be developed and tailored for your specific needs. In a nutshell, there are many different ways to improve or redesign business processes. Managers face options. This book will provide you with an overview of the options and describe the best practices available to help you choose the approach that is best for your situation.

Figure I.5 suggests some of the elements involved in successful business process change efforts. We refer to the entire cycle as the *business process change cycle*. It's a cycle that every organization should continuously undertake. The organization's goals and its successes must be compared with the environment in which the organization functions to determine if the organization is succeeding. As managers see the possibility of doing better, they must undertake changes in the organization to better align the organization with the opportunities and threats it faces. Internal changes begin by reconsidering the business processes that the organization currently supports. Some processes will need to be improved. Others will need major revision. Some will need to be eliminated, and new processes will need to be created to take their place or to respond to new opportunities.

Once processes are identified that need changes, some kind of process change effort must be initiated. There are different options that can be used in combination.

The Variety of Solutions

One of the problems with the business process field is that various authors and vendors use the same terms in different ways. In this book we will use certain terms in very precise ways to avoid confusion.

Process improvement refers to minor, specific changes that one makes in an existing business process. Every manager responsible for a process should always

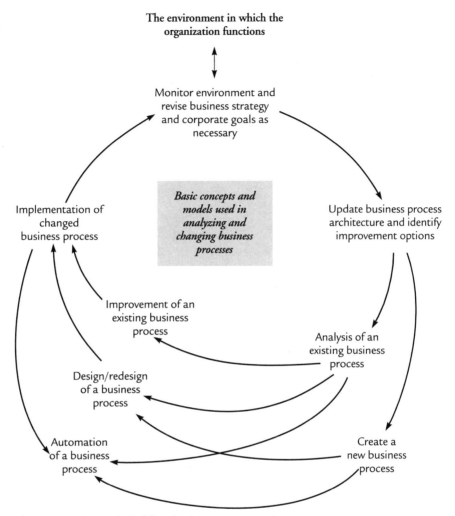

Figure I.5 Major and subsidiary business process topics.

be considering process improvements. In addition, occasionally special process improvement efforts are required to get everyone focused on improving a specific process. Six Sigma is a good example of a popular approach to process improvement.

Process design or *redesign* refers to a major effort that is undertaken to significantly improve an existing process or to create a new business process. Process redesign considers every aspect of a process and often results in changes in the sequence in which the process is done, in employee jobs, and in the introduction of automation. Business Process Reengineering, the Rummler-Brache methodology, and the Supply Chain Council's SCOR methodology are good examples of popular approaches to process redesign.

Process automation refers to the use of computers and software applications to assist employees or to replace employees in the performance of a business process. The use of workflow systems, or XML business process languages, are ways to automate processes or activities. The use of off-the-shelf ERP and CRM applications are also examples of automation. Similarly, software development methodologies like Rational Software's Unified Process or the Object Management Group's Model Driven Architecture are other examples of popular approaches to process automation.

Many authors use the term *business process management* (BPM) to refer to process automation efforts. It is used to refer to the fact that once processes are automated, they can be managed with software tools. Business executives, however, often use the term *business process management* in a more generic sense to refer to efforts on the part of business executives to organize and improve the human management of business processes. On the corporate level, *business process management* is also used to refer to the development and maintenance of a business process architecture. We will normally use the term in its generic sense, to refer to how business managers organize and control processes. When we want to use it in the more specialized sense, to refer to automated systems, we will capitalize it, or use the common acronym BPM.

In Figure I.5, we illustrate the flow of changes in strategy to changes in the business process architecture. From there, one moves to the analysis of processes and then to business process improvement, business process redesign, or business process automation. Once changes have been planned, they are implemented, resulting in updated processes. The new processes will function until the strategy committee detects new changes in the environment and decides on still newer goals. Given the rate of change that organizations face today, the business process change cycle runs continuously.

In the center of the circle are some basic concepts for modeling business processes. These graphical techniques and concepts are as important to today's manager as a knowledge of spreadsheets or the ability to read financial statements. We live in an era in which business processes are constantly being changed. Only managers equipped with the ability to quickly analyze processes can possibly understand the organizations they are asked to manage, or figure out how to effectively improve them.

In addition to the cycle pictured in Figure I.5, we will also stress the need to align managers' goals with process and corporate strategy goals and the need for an enterprise-level overview of all business processes supported by the organization. We refer to the process by which a company aligns management goals to control processes as *enterprise alignment*. We refer to the overview of its processes that is maintained by the company as a business or enterprise *process architecture.*

Finally, although it is not shown in Figure I.5, we have already referenced the fact that many companies are undertaking business process redesign, automation, or improvement efforts in order to support the Internet or implement e-business processes. Thus, we provide an overview of some of the best practices available to those engaged in e-business process change.

How This Book Is Organized

This book provides a pragmatic introduction to business process change. It's designed to provide managers with an overview of processes and to explain the options they face as they are forced to improve, redesign, or automate them. We define the basic concepts, review the steps, and describe the best practices in each area.

We could begin at any of several points in the process cycle. In fact, we will start with an overview of the kind of systematic business process improvement methodologies companies have used during the past decade. In effect, Chapter 1 will provide a brief history of business process change, just to assure we understand the basic options and are all using the same vocabulary.

In Chapter 2 we'll consider how companies develop strategies and define goals. This introduction to the strategic process will necessarily be rather general, but it will establish some important themes, including the ideas behind strategic positioning and value chains, and the importance of well-integrated processes to the maintenance of a competitive advantage.

In Chapter 3 we'll consider the nature of a business process architecture. In essence, it is the business process architecture that defines how the various business processes work together to create value. It is also the key to linking the organization's strategic goals to process goals and then to specific manager's goals. And it provides the basis for prioritizing process change initiatives. It also provides the means by which business managers and IT managers can work together to establish a corporate software infrastructure and prioritize software development efforts.

In Chapters 4, 5, and 6, we will pause to define the basic concepts and diagramming techniques used to model organizations, processes, and activities. There are lots of ways of modeling processes, and we have chosen the simplest we know about that is specifically designed for business mangers and not for software developers. As automation has increasingly become a major part of any process redesign effort, there has been a tendency to discuss processes in the more technical terms that software analysts sometimes employ. We believe this is a serious mistake, since it makes it harder for average business managers to understand the processes that they are ultimately responsible for managing. We rely on a very simple way of modeling organizations and processes that assures that business managers can stay in control of the process.

Chapters 4, 5, and 6 are necessarily a little technical. Learning the basics of modeling is a bit like learning the vocabulary used in spreadsheets or learning to operate a spreadsheet software package. A basic modeling vocabulary, however, is the key to quickly diagramming and understanding business processes and can't be avoided. Different methodologies we will discuss in later chapters use different notations and concepts. We will translate them all into the graphic concepts we introduce in these chapters to make everything that follows simpler.

So much has been written on business processes, from so many different perspectives, that inevitably there are many different terms for each basic concept. We've tried to choose the most common terms, define them, and then use them consistently throughout the rest of the book. We've included a glossary in the back of the book that provides alternative definitions for each of the basic terms and cross references them with other common business process vocabularies.

Chapter 6 also considers examples of manual processes to illustrate the points we wish to make. This is important when one considers that in most organizations, most processes are implemented by employees. It is important, when considering business process initiatives, to ensure that any approach adequately covers the human aspects of process design right along with all the other aspects. There has been a tendency among vendors and analysts alike over the past few years to focus too much on automated process. One of the reasons we like the Rummler-Brache methodology so much is because it places an equal weight on the human, or manual, aspects of business process redesign, and we have tried to maintain that balance in this book.

Chapter 7 provides an overview of how organizations can structure themselves to assure that there are clear lines of responsibility while simultaneously assuring that organizational goals are aligned with the goals assigned to specific managers. This chapter will also consider the nature of management and how managers are responsible for the ongoing control and improvement of the processes they are assigned.

Chapter 8 shifts and focuses on a specific, popular process improvement methodology, Six Sigma. Six Sigma is derived from operations research and provides a systematic way to measure and refine the output of specific processes. We do not go into the statistical techniques used in the Six Sigma process, but focus instead on the overall process and on how Six Sigma practitioners relate goals and measures to satisfying customers.

In Chapter 9 we discuss a methodology for systematically redesigning a business process. The methodology we consider is derived, in large part, from the Rummler-Brache methodology, which we consider the most manager-friendly and comprehensive of the leading methodologies. This chapter focuses on all the things that have to happen in the course of a process redesign project to assure that the project is completed and the results are implemented. Organizations tend to resist change, and they are often especially resistant to changes in well-established business processes. This chapter defines what the process redesign team must do to make sure that change happens.

Chapter 10 considers some of the popular twists on process redesign, including redesign patterns that focus on eliminating gaps and disconnects, simplifying workflow, and eliminating non-value-adding activities.

Chapter 11 is the first of three chapters that focus on business process automation. In Chapter 11 we focus on workflow modeling and on software techniques that implement workflow systems. We consider the various forms of workflow systems that are popular today, and we also consider a newer development in this area, software languages that model processes in order to facilitate the exchange of process information between company applications and between companies that are collaborating on multicompany processes, like supply chains.

In Chapter 12 we focus on ERP (Enterprise Resource Planning) applications, systems of software modules that companies can use to support or automate established business processes like inventory and accounting operations. We also consider some of the newer packaged applications used for CRM (Customer Relationship Management) automation. In addition, we focus on the modeling languages commonly used for the design of ERP and CRM systems.

In Chapter 13 we consider techniques used by software developers who create tailored applications to support or automate business processes. Most software architects and developers working within organizations rely on their own analysis techniques—notations like the Unified Modeling Language (UML) and methodologies like the Rational Unified Process (RUP) and the Object Management Group's Model Driven Architecture (MDA). Similarly, developers often use specialized CASE and software modeling software tools to facilitate their work. We discuss how business managers ought to relate to software developers, the importance of clearly defined application requirements, and how IT developers should be integrated into business redesign efforts.

In Chapters 14 and 15 we shift again and consider some of the popular e-business processes that companies are currently developing. Business managers, in surveys, suggest that the main drivers for most current business process efforts are the Internet, the Web, and email. In effect, as with other key technologies in the past, these new technologies are forcing companies to reconceptualize how they function and create and sell products. We do not attempt to explain the Internet or its related technologies, or the software systems created to support the implementation of such systems. Instead we focus on the ways in which these technologies typically impact business processes and how business analysts can go about creating processes that effectively incorporate Internet or e-business techniques.

We divide our discussion of e-business changes into two chapters. In Chapter 14 we focus on the impact of process analysis and design on portals and customer-oriented e-business applications.

In Chapter 15 we discuss the impact of Internet-mediated supply chain automation and the use of the Internet and email to change the way people and processes work inside the organization.

Chapter 16 presents a major case study of a manufacturing company that redesigns its order fulfillment process using the approach, concepts, and techniques we have discussed in earlier chapters.

Throughout this book we have used a graphical notation that a manager could draw on a sheet of paper or create in a simple graphical software application. In Chapter 17 we demonstrate the power of software business process tools by showing how we could model the case study problem we discussed in Chapter 16. Our goal here is not to advocate the use of any specific tool, but to show how features available in popular business process software tools can make the actual redesign process easier and how they can aid in maintaining process diagrams and documentation to assure that enterprise process architecture teams don't have to reinvent the wheel when they have to revise a process again in a few years.

Chapter 18 is a summary that pulls together all the main points we make in this book. It recapitulates the major options we have discussed and makes some suggestions about when each of the techniques is likely to be most effective. This book doesn't advocate a single methodology or a single set of practices to deal with business process change. Instead, we believe that business managers need to understand their options and then use the practices best suited to specific problems as they occur.

We've tried to keep each chapter as short as possible. Our goal was not to write a long book, but, instead, to create a book that a wide variety of managers could turn to when they needed information and insight on one or another aspect of their business process change. We hope this will serve as a guide and a tool for the business managers who will lead their companies through the changes that will challenge organizations in the decade ahead.

Business Process Change

THIS CHAPTER PROVIDES a brief history of corporate business process change initiatives. Individuals working in one tradition, BPR or ERP, often imagine that their perspective is the only one, or the correct one. We want to provide managers with several different perspectives on business process change in order to give everyone an idea of the range of techniques and methodologies available today. In the process we will define some of the key terms that will occur throughout the remainder of the book.

People have always worked at improving processes. Some archaeologists find it useful to divide early human development according to techniques and processes that potters used to create their wares. In essence, potters gradually refined the pot-making process, creating finer products, while probably also learning how to make them faster and cheaper.

The Industrial Revolution that began in the late 18th century led to factories and managers who focused considerable energy on the organization of manufacturing processes. Any history of industrial development will recount numerous stories of entrepreneurs who changed processes and revolutionized an industry. In the Introduction we mentioned how Henry Ford created a new manufacturing process and revolutionized the way automobiles were assembled. Ford did that in 1903.

Soon after Henry Ford launched the Ford Motor Company in 1911, another American, Frederick Winslow Taylor, published a seminal book: *Principles of Scientific Management.* Taylor sought to capture some of the key ideas that good managers used to improve processes. He argued for simplification, for time studies, for systematic experimentation to identify the best way of performing a task, and for control systems that measured and rewarded output. Taylor's book became an international best-seller, and many would regard him as the father of operations research, a branch of engineering that seeks to create efficient and consistent processes. From 1911 on, managers have sought ways to be more systematic in their approaches to process change.

New technologies have often led to new business processes. The introduction of the train and the automobile, and of radio, telephones, and television, have each led to new and improved business processes. Since the end of World War II, computers and software systems have provided a major source of new efficiencies.

Two recent developments in management theory deserve special attention. One was the popularization of systems thinking, and the other was the formalization of the idea of a value chain.

Organizations as Systems

Many different trends led to the growing focus on systems that began in the 1980s. Some of it derived from operations research and studies of control systems. Some of it resulted from the emphasis on systems current in the computer community. Today's emphasis on systems also arose out of contemporary work in biology and the social sciences. At the same time, however, many management theorists have contributed to the systems perspective. One thinks of earlier writers like Ludwig von Bertalanffy and Jay W. Forrester and more recent management theorists like John D. Sterman and Peter M. Senge.

In essence, the systems perspective emphasizes that everything is connected to everything else and that it's often worthwhile to model businesses and processes in terms of flows and feedback loops. A simple systems diagram is shown in Figure 1.1.

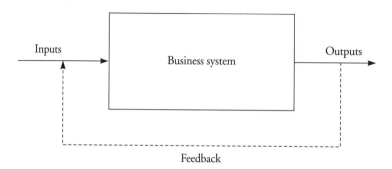

Figure 1.1 A business entity as a system.

The idea of treating a business as a system is so simple, especially today when it is so commonplace, that it is hard for some to understand how important the idea really is. Systems thinking stresses linkages and relationships and flows. It emphasizes that any given employee or unit or activity is part of a larger entity and that ultimately those entities, working together, are justified by the results they produce.

To make all this a bit more concrete, consider how it is applied to business processes in the work of Michael E. Porter.

Systems and Value Chains

The groundwork for the current emphasis on comprehensive business processes was laid by Michael Porter in his 1985 book, *Competitive Advantage: Creating and Sustaining Superior Performance.* Porter is probably best known for his earlier book, *Competitive Strategy,* published in 1980, but it's in *Competitive Advantage* that he lays out his concept of a *value chain*—a comprehensive collection of all of the activities that are performed to design, produce, market, deliver, and support a product line. Figure 1.2 shows of the diagram that Porter has used on several occasions to illustrate a generic value chain.

Although Porter doesn't show it on the diagram shown as Figure 1.2, you should assume that some primary activity is initiated on the lower left of the

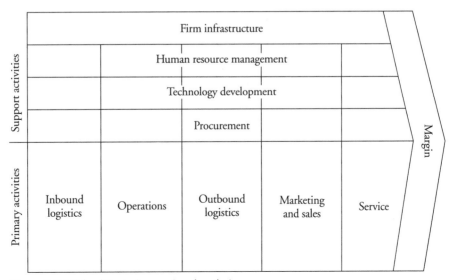

Figure 1.2 Michael Porter's generic value chain.

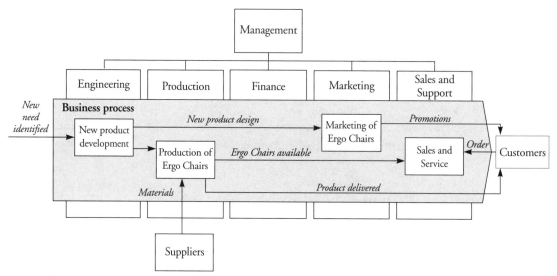

Figure 1.3 A business process cuts across traditional departments to combine activities into a single process flow. (After Rummler.)

diagram when a customer orders a product, and ends on the right side when the product is delivered to the customer. Of course it may be a bit more complex, with marketing stimulating the customer to order and service following up the delivery of the order with various services, but those details are avoided in this diagram. Figure 1.2 simply focuses on what happens between the order and the final delivery—on the value chain or large-scale business process that produces the product. What's important to Porter's concept is that every function involved in the production of the product, and all of the support services, from information technology to accounting, should be included in a single value chain. It's only by including all of the activities involved in producing the product that a company is in position to determine exactly what the product is costing and what margin the firm achieves when it sells the product.

As a result of Porter's work, a new approach to accounting, *activity-based costing,* has become popular and is used to determine the actual value of producing specific products.

When Porter's concept of a value chain is applied to business processes, a different type of diagram is produced. Figure 1.3 illustrates a value chain or business process that cuts across departments, which are represented by an organization chart. As far as I know this type of diagram was first used by another management systems theorist, Geary Rummler, in 1984.

Figure 1.3 illustrates a business process that crosses five departmental or functional boundaries. The boxes shown within the process arrow are subprocesses. The subprocesses are initiated by an input from a customer, and the process ultimately produces an output that is consumed by a customer. Prior to the work of systems and management theorists like Porter and Rummler, most companies had focused on dividing processes into specific activities that were assigned to specific departments. Each department developed its own standards and procedures to manage the activities delegated to it. Along the way, in many cases, departments became focused on doing their own activities in their own way, without much regard for the overall process. This is often referred to as *silo thinking,* an image that suggests that each department on the organization chart is its own isolated silo.

In the early years of business computing, a sharp distinction was made between corporate computing and departmental computing. A few systems like payroll and accounting were developed and maintained at the corporate level. Other systems were created by individual departments to serve their specific needs. Typically, one departmental system wouldn't talk to another, and the data stored in the databases of sales couldn't be exchanged with data in the databases owned by accounting or by manufacturing. In essence, in an effort to make each department as professional and efficient as possible, the concept of the overall process was lost.

The emphasis on value chains and systems in the 1980s and the emphasis on Business Process Reengineering in the early 1990s was a revolt against excessive departmentalism and a call for a more holistic view of how activities needed to work together to achieve organizational goals.

Business Process Reengineering

Much of the current interest in business process change can be dated from the Business Process Reengineering (BPR) movement that began in 1990 with the publication of two papers: Michael Hammer's "Reengineering Work: Don't Automate, Obliterate" (*Harvard Business Review,* July/August 1990) and Thomas Davenport and James Short's "The New Industrial Engineering: Information Technology and Business Process Redesign" (*Sloan Management Review,* Summer 1990). Later, in 1993, Davenport wrote a book, *Process Innovation: Reengineering Work through Information Technology,* and Michael Hammer joined with James Champy to write *Reengineering the Corporation: A Manifesto for Business Revolution.*

BPR theorists like Davenport and Hammer insisted that companies must think in terms of comprehensive processes, similar to Porter's value chains. If a company focused only on new product development, for example, the company might improve that subprocess, but it might not improve the overall process. Worse, one might improve new product development at the expense of the overall value chain. If, for example, new process development instituted a system of checks to assure higher-quality documents, it might produce superior reports, but take longer to produce them, delaying marketing and manufacturing's ability to respond to sudden changes in the marketplace. Or the new reports might be organized in such a way that they made better sense to the new process development engineers, but became much harder for marketing or manufacturing readers to understand.

Stressing the comprehensive nature of business processes, BPR theorists urged companies to define all of their major processes and then focus on the processes that offered the most return on improvement efforts. Companies that followed this approach usually conceptualized a single business process for an entire product line, and ended up with only 5–10 processes for an entire company, or division, if the company was very large. The good news is that if companies followed this advice, they were focusing on everything involved in a process and were more likely to identify ways to significantly improve the overall process. The bad news is that when one conceptualizes processes in this way, one is forced to tackle very large redesign efforts that typically involve hundreds or thousands of workers and dozens of major IT applications.

Business Process Reengineering was more than an emphasis on redesigning large-scale business processes. The driving idea behind the Business Process Reengineering movement was best expressed by Thomas Davenport, who argued that information technology had made major strides in the 1980s, and was now capable of creating major improvements in business processes. Davenport's more reasoned analysis, however, didn't get nearly the attention that Michael Hammer attracted with his more radical rhetoric.

Hammer argued that previous generations of managers had settled for using information technologies to simply improve departmental functions. In most cases, the departmental functions hadn't been redesigned but simply automated. Hammer referred to this as "paving over cow paths." In many cases, he went on to say, departmental efficiencies were maximized at the expense of the overall process. Thus, for example, a financial department might use a computer to assure more accurate and up-to-date accounting records by requiring manufacturing to turn in reports on the status of the production process. In fact, however, many of the reports came at inconvenient times and actually slowed down the manufacturing process. In a similar way, sales might initiate a sales campaign that resulted in sales that manufacturing couldn't produce in the time allowed. Or manufacturing might initiate changes in the product that made it easier and more inexpensive to manufacture, but which made it harder for salespeople to sell. What was needed, Hammer argued, was a completely new look at business processes. In most cases, Hammer argued that the existing processes should be "obliterated" and replaced by totally new processes, designed from the ground up to take advantage of new information systems techniques. Hammer promised huge improvements if companies were able to stand the pain of total business process redesign.

In addition to his call for total process reengineering, Hammer joined Davenport in arguing that processes should be integrated in ways they hadn't been in the past. Hammer argued that Adam Smith had begun the movement toward increasingly specialized work. Readers will probably all recall that Adam Smith compared data on pin manufacture in France in the late 18th century. He showed that one man, working alone, could create a given number of straight pins in a day. But a team, each doing only one part of the task, could produce many times the number of pins in a day that the individual members of the team could produce, each working alone. In other words, the division of labor paid off with handsome increases in productivity. In essence, Ford had only been applying Smith's principle to automobile production when he set up his continuous production line in Michigan in the early 20th century. Hammer, however, argued that Smith's principle had led to departments and functions that each tried to maximize its own efficiency at the expense of the whole. In essence, Hammer claimed that large companies had become more inefficient by becoming larger and more specialized. The solution, according to Hammer, Davenport, and Champy was twofold: First, processes needed to be conceptualized as complete, comprehensive entities that stretched from the initial order to the delivery of the product. Second, Information Technology (IT)[1] needed to be used to integrate these comprehensive processes.

---

[1] Different organizations use different terms to refer to their Information Technology (IT) or Information Systems (IS) or Data Processing (DP) groups. We'll use these terms and abbreviations interchangeably. In all cases they refer to the organizational group responsible for analyzing needs, acquiring computer hardware, acquiring or creating computer software, and maintaining the same, or to the systems created and maintained, or to both.

The Role of Information Technology in BPR

Both Hammer and Davenport had been involved in major process improvement projects in the late 1980s and observed how IT applications could cut across departmental lines to eliminate inefficiencies and yield huge gains in coordination. They described some of these projects and urged managers at other companies to be equally bold in pursuing similar gains in productivity.

In spite of their insistence on the use of IT, however, Hammer and his colleagues feared the influence of IT professionals. Hammer argued that IT professionals were usually too constrained by their existing systems to recognize major new opportunities. He suggested that IT professionals usually emphasized what couldn't be done rather than focusing on breakthroughs that could be achieved. To remedy this, Hammer and Champy argued that the initial business process redesign teams should exclude IT professionals. In essence, they argue that the initial Business Process Reengineering team should consist of business managers and workers who would have to implement the redesigned process. Only after the redesign team had decided how to change the entire process, Hammer argued, should IT people be called in to advise on the systems aspects of the proposed changes.

In hindsight, one can see that the BPR theorists of the early 1990s underestimated the difficulties of integrating corporate systems with the IT technologies available at that time. The BPR gurus had watched some large companies achieve significant results, but they failed to appreciate that the sophisticated teams of software developers available to leading companies were not widely available. Moreover, they failed to appreciate the problems involved in scaling up some of the solutions they recommended. And they certainly compounded the problem by recommending that business managers redesign processes without the close cooperation of their IT people. It's true that many IT people resisted major changes, but in many cases they did so because they realized, better than most business managers, just how much such changes would cost. Worse, they realized that many of the proposed changes could not be successfully implemented at their companies with the technologies and manpower they had available.

Some of the BPR projects undertaken in the mid-1990s succeeded and produced impressive gains in productivity. Many others failed and produced disillusionment with BPR. Most company managers intuitively scaled down their BPR efforts and didn't attempt anything as large or comprehensive as the types of projects recommended in the early BPR books.

Misuses of BPR

During this same period, many companies pursued other goals under the name of BPR. Downsizing was popular in the early to mid-1990s. Some of it was justified. Many companies had layers of managers whose primary function was to organize information from line activities and then funnel it to senior managers. The introduction of new software systems and tools that made it possible to query databases for information also meant that senior managers could obtain information without the need for so many middle-level managers. On the other hand, much of the downsizing was simply a natural reduction of staff in response to a slowdown in the business cycle. The latter was appropriate, but it led many employees to assume that any BPR effort would result in major reductions in staff.

Because of some widely discussed failures, and also as a result of employee distrust, the term "Business Process Reengineering" became unpopular during the late 1990s and has gradually fallen into disuse. As an alternative, most companies began to refer to their business process projects as "business process improvement" or "business process redesign."

Workflow and Packaged Applications

Another approach to business process improvement emerged in the mid-1990s. Some companies used software applications, called *workflow systems,* to automate applications. In essence, early workflow systems controlled the flow of documents from one employee to another. The original document is scanned into a computer. Then, an electronic copy of the document is sent to the desk of any employees who need to see or approve the document. To design workflow systems, one creates a flow plan, like the diagram shown in Figure 1.3, that specifies how the document moves from one employee to the next. The workflow system developers or managers can control the order that electronic documents show up on employees' computers by modifying the diagram. Workflow systems became a very popular way to automate document-based processes. Unfortunately, in the early 1990s, most workflow systems were limited to automating departmental processes and couldn't scale up to the enterprise-wide processes.

During this same period, vendors of off-the-shelf software applications began to organize their application modules so that they could be represented as a business process. In effect, one could diagram a business process by simply deciding how to link a number of application modules. Vendors like SAP, PeopleSoft, Oracle, and J. D. Edwards all offered systems of this kind, which were usually called Enterprise Resource Planning (ERP) systems. In effect, a business analyst was shown an ideal way that several modules could be linked together. A specific company could elect to eliminate some modules and change some of the rules controlling the actions of some of the modules, but overall, one was limited to choosing and ordering already existing software application modules. Many of the modules included customer interface screens and therefore controlled employee behaviors relative to particular modules. In essence, an ERP system is controlled by another kind of workflow system. Instead of moving documents from one employee workstation to another, the ERP systems offered by SAP and others allowed managers to design processes that moved information and control from one software module to another. ERP systems allowed companies to replace older software applications with new applications, and to organize the new applications into an organized business process. This worked best for processes that were well understood and common between companies. Thus, accounting, inventory, and human resource processes were all popular targets for ERP systems.

SAP, for example, offers the following modules in their financials suite: Change Vendor or Customer Master Data, Clear Open Items, Deduction Management, Payment with Advice, Clearing of Open Items at Vendor, Reporting for External Business Partners, and SEM: Benchmark Data Collection. They also offer "blueprints," which are, in essence, alternative workflow diagrams showing how the financial modules might be assembled to accomplish different business processes.

Davenport supported and promoted the use of ERP packaged applications as a way to improve business processes. At the same time, August-Wilhelm Scheer, a software systems theorist, advocated the use of ERP applications for systems development, and wrote several books promoting this approach and the use of a modeling methodology that he named ARIS.

Most large companies explored the use of document workflow systems and the use of ERP systems to automate at least some business processes. The use of document workflow and ERP systems represented a very different approach to process redesign than that advocated by the BPR gurus of the early 1990s. Gurus like Hammer had advocated a total reconceptualization of complete value chains. Everything was to be reconsidered and redesigned to provide the company with the best possible new business process. The workflow and ERP approaches, on the other hand, focused on automating existing processes and replacing existing, departmentally focused legacy systems with new software modules that were designed to work together. These systems were narrowly focused and relied heavily on IT people to put them in place. They provided small-scale improvements rather than radical redesigns.

Systems developed with workflow tools or ERP software modules were often called "Business Process Management" systems, to reflect the idea that one could manage the business process by making changes in the workflow diagrams. As noted in the Introduction, we'll avoid applying the term *business process management systems* to workflow and ERP systems, and call them, instead, automation systems. We do this to avoid confusing these computer-based approaches with the actual measurement and control functions managers exercise when they manage business processes.

Software Engineering

We have already considered two popular software approaches to automating business processes: workflow and the use of systems of packaged applications. Moving beyond these specific techniques, any software development effort could be a response to a business process challenge. Any companies that seek to improve a process will want to consider automating the process. Some processes can't be automated with existing technology. Some activities require people to make decisions or to provide a human interface with customers. Over the course of the past few decades, however, a major trend has been to increase the number of tasks performed by computers.

Software engineering usually refers to efforts to make the development of software more systematic, efficient, and consistent. Increasingly, software engineers have focused on improving their own processes and on developing tools that will enable them to assist business managers to automate business processes. We mentioned the work of the Software Engineering Institute at Carnegie Mellon University on CMM, a model that describes how organizations mature in their use and management of processes.

At the same time, software engineers have developed modeling languages for modeling software applications and tools that can generate code from software models. Some software theorists have advocated developing models and tools that would allow business analysts to be more heavily involved in designing the software, but to date this approach has been limited by the very technical and precise nature of software specifications. As an alternative, a good deal of effort has been focused on refining the concept of *software requirements*—the specification that a business process team would hand to a software development team to indicate exactly what a software application would need to do to support a new process.

The more complex and important the business process change, the more likely a company will need to create tailored software to capture unique company competencies. Whenever this occurs, then languages and tools that communicate between business process teams and IT teams become very important.

The Rummler-Brache Methodology

So far, we have considered approaches to business process change that were directly or indirectly driven by a concern to use IT. Hammer and Davenport both came out of consulting groups that focused primarily on IT, and Scheer was a software theorist. The fourth major business process guru of the 1990s was Geary A. Rummler, whose background was in management and psychology. Rummler had worked for years on employee training and motivation issues. Rummler's work, and the work of colleagues, has established a specialized discipline that is usually termed *human performance improvement.* His focus was on how to structure processes and activities to guarantee that employees—be they managers, salespeople, or production line workers—would function effectively. In the 1960s and 1970s he relied on behavioral psychology and systems theory to explain his approach, but during the course of the 1980s he focused increasingly on business process models.

In 1990 Rummler and a colleague, Alan Brache, published *Improving Performance: How to Manage the White Space on the Organization Chart.* Unlike the other popular business process theorists, Rummler didn't emphasize IT, but focused instead on the specifics of how to analyze processes, how to redesign and then improve processes, how to design jobs, and how to manage processes once they were in place. The emphasis on the white space on the organization chart stressed the fact that many process problems occurred when one department tried to hand off things to the next. The only way to overcome those interdepartmental problems, Rummler argued, was to conceptualize and manage processes as wholes.

Hammer and Davenport had exhorted companies to change and offered lots of examples about how changes had led to improved company performance. Scheer offered a methodology, but it was an approach that only a software engineer could understand. Rummler and Brache offered a systematic, comprehensive approach designed for business managers. The book that Rummler and Brache wrote didn't launch the BPR movement. Once Hammer and Davenport focused managers on the problem, however, they began to look around for a book that would provide practical advice on how to actually accomplish process change, and they frequently arrived at *Improving Performance.* The Rummler-Brache methodology became the most widely used, systematic business process methodology in the mid-1990s.

One of the most important contributions made by Rummler and Brache was a framework that showed, in a single diagram, how everything related to everything else. They define three levels of performance: (1) an organizational level, (2) a process level, and (3) a job or performer level. We'll refer to level 3 as the activity or performance level to emphasize that an activity can be performed by an employee doing a job or by a computer executing a software application. Otherwise, we will employ the Rummler-Brache levels in this book.

Rummler and Brache also introduce a matrix that they obtain by crossing their three levels with three different perspectives. The perspectives are goals and measures, design and implementation issues, and management. Figure 1.4 illustrates the matrix. Software architects today would probably refer to it as a framework. The important thing is that it identifies nine different concerns that anyone trying to change processes in an organization must consider. Approaches that just focus on processes or on performance level measures or on process management are limited perspectives.

Notice how similar the ideas expressed in the Rummler-Brache framework are to the ideas expressed in the SEI Capability Maturity Model we considered in the

	Goals and measures	Design and implementation	Management
Organizational level	Organizational goals and measures of organizational success	Organizational design and implementation	Organizational management
Process level	Process goals and measures of process success	Process design and implementation	Process management
Activity or performance level	Activity goals and measures of activity success	Activity design and implementation	Activity management

Figure 1.4 A performance framework. (Modified after a figure in Rummler and Brache, *Improving Performance.*)

Introduction. Both seek to describe an organization that is mature and capable of taking advantage of systematic processes. Both stress that we must be concerned with not only the design of processes themselves, but also with measures of success and with the management of processes. In effect, the CMM diagram described how organizations evolve toward process maturity, and the Rummler-Brache framework describes all of the things that a mature organization must master.

Mature organizations must align both vertically and horizontally. Activity goals must be related to process goals, which must, in turn, be derived from the strategic goals of the organization. Similarly, a process must be an integrated whole, with goals and measures, a good design that is well implemented, and a management system that uses the goals and measures to assure that the process runs smoothly and, if need be, is improved.

The Rummler-Brache methodology has helped everyone involved in business process change to understand the scope of the problem, and it has provided a foundation on which all of today's comprehensive process development methodologies are based.

ISO 9000 and the Six Sigma Methodology

For completeness, two other approaches to business process change need to be mentioned. During the same period that most managers were focusing on BPR, workflow, and ERP, operations research theorists were working on various ways of improving and controlling the quality of process outputs. Many companies expanded their Quality departments during this period.

In the area of quality, the ISO 9000 standard became commonplace. This international standard described activities organizations should undertake to be certified ISO 9000 compliant. Unfortunately, ISO 9000 efforts usually focus on simply documenting and managing procedures. Recently, a newer version of this standard, ISO9000:2000, has become established. Rather than focusing so much on documentation, the new standard is driving many companies to think in terms of processes. In many cases this has prompted management to actually start to analyze processes and use them to start to drive change programs. In both cases, however, the emphasis is on documentation, while what organizations really need are ways to improve quality.

At the same time that companies were exploring ISO 9000, they were also exploring other quality initiatives like Statistical Process Control (SPC), Total Quality Management (TQM), and Just-in-Time Manufacturing (JIT). Each of these quality control initiatives contributed to the efficiency and quality of organizational processes. In the mid-1990s, a related approach, termed Six Sigma for its statistical approach to measurement, was developed by Mikel Harry and others at Motorola. It achieved popularity when Jack Welch, then CEO of General Electric, decided to adopt it company-wide and decreed that 40% of every business manager's bonus would depend on their meeting their Six Sigma goals.

Like all of the other approaches we have discussed, Six Sigma has evolved and incorporated features of other business process change methodologies. Today, a Six Sigma theorist would argue that there are management, redesign, and improvement versions of Six Sigma. In fact, however, most Six Sigma projects are narrowly focused on process improvement rather than on large-scale redesign. In spite of that, Six Sigma theorists have made major contributions to our understanding of how to improve the consistency of processes and how to measure process success by linking activity goals to customer satisfaction.

As we shall see later, both ISO 9000 and Six Sigma can be complementary to the wider approach we describe in this book.

Changes in Business and IT in the Late 1990s

During the same period that the enthusiasm for BPR was declining, and at the same time that companies began to explore workflow and ERP approaches, new software technologies began to emerge that really could deliver on the promise that the early BPR gurus had oversold. Among the best known are the Internet, email, and the Web, which provide powerful ways to integrate employees, suppliers, and customers.

In the early 1990s, when Hammer and Davenport wrote their books, the most popular technique for large-scale corporate systems integration was EDI (Electronic Data Interchange). Many large companies used EDI to link with their suppliers. In general, however, EDI was difficult to install and expensive to maintain. As a practical matter, EDI could only be used to link a company to its major suppliers. Smaller suppliers couldn't afford to install EDI and didn't have the programmers required to maintain an EDI system. The Internet changed that.

The Internet doesn't require proprietary lines, but runs instead on ordinary telephone lines. At the same time, the Internet depends on popular, open protocols that were developed by the government and were widely accepted by everyone. A small company could link to the Internet and to a distributor or supplier in exactly the same way that millions of individuals could surf the Web, by simply acquiring a PC and a modem and using browser software. Just as the Internet provided a practical solution for some of communications problems faced by companies, email and the Web created a new way for customers to communicate with companies. Virtually overnight, in the late 1990s, customers acquired the habit of going to company Web sites to find out what products and services were available. Moreover, as fast as companies installed Web sites that would support it, customers began to buy products online. In effect, the overnight popularity of the Internet, email, and the Web in the late 1990s made it imperative that companies reconsider how they had their business processes organized in order to take advantage of the major cost-savings that the use of the Internet, Web, and email could provide.

Of course the story is more complex. A number of dot.com companies sprang up promising to totally change the way companies did business by using the Internet, Web, and email. Some have carved new niches for themselves, but most disappeared when the stock market finally realized that their business models were unsound. That process encouraged large, established companies to consider how they could use Internet technologies, but it also distracted them and encouraged some to attempt rash ventures to compete with the dot.coms that achieved extraordinary stock valuations in the late 1990s.

At the same time, other technology gurus began to warn of the approach of the end of the millennium. Too many software systems had been created in the last half of the 20th century with two-digit dates (e.g. instead of representing the year 1965 with four digits, it was represented as 65). This had been done on the assumption that the systems created in that manner would be retired well before the end of the millennium. Most hadn't, and that posed a significant problem, since it was possible that a system given the date 01 would read it as 1901 rather than 2001 and make costly, and in some cases life-threatening, mistakes. Thus, in spite of the opportunity for process improvement created by Internet techniques, many companies diverted IT resources to checking their existing software applications to assure that they didn't contain what became popularly known as the Y2K bug.

The overall result is that change that might have happened in the late 1990s was delayed, but it is now at the top of most companies' agenda as they enter the first decade of the new millennium.

Mergers, Acquisitions, and Globalization

A less discussed but still important driver of business process redesign projects in many companies occurred when one company merged with or bought another company. Throughout the 1990s there was a lot of business consolidation within the United States. Moreover, as trade barriers came down and globalization accelerated, many companies bought companies in other countries. In all cases, such acquisitions or mergers create problems because the two companies have different processes. They also have different policies, different ways of handling problems, and different ways of defining key terms, like "customer" and "account." In many cases their software applications are incompatible, and a major effort is required simply to pass data between the different systems. In other cases the differences won't go away because the companies operate in different regulatory environments.

Mergers and acquisitions usually lead to business process redesign efforts. In the easier case, one company imposes its processes and procedures on the other. In more complex cases the companies must work together to create a common process or interfaces between processes that will remain independent.

Business magazines often report that mergers have failed. In many cases it is because the companies involved couldn't figure out how to integrate their processes and failed to achieve the savings that were the justification for the merger or acquisition in the first place.

A key part of any merger and acquisition effort ought to be a detailed analysis of the business process architectures of the two companies and a plan, budget, and schedule for the process redesign that will be required to assure the merger or acquisition will actually work.

Proof of the importance that business process problems pose for mergers was nicely illustrated by a recent survey of small businesses carried out in the United Kingdom. The survey concluded that buyers were willing to pay an 86% premium for a company with well-documented processes and procedures. That would provide most small businesses with an excellent overall ROI for producing such documentation.

In a similar way, the increase in international business has led to an increased focus on complex, dispersed processes. Today's auto manufacturers, for example, have plants throughout the world. Each of those plants receives parts and subassemblies from still other plants located in other countries. Coordinating the flow of information and materials through such global processes has become a major challenge. In the past different countries used different languages, different forms, different accounting systems, and different types of computer hardware. Today the problems of coordinating international business processes have stimulated moves for standardization. And, where standardization is unreasonable, it has led to the creation of translation and integration middleware that has become a key to enabling efficient workflows.

If the Internet hadn't developed independently, companies would have needed to create it to handle the complexities they face as they try to integrate diverse systems between acquired companies or internationally distributed divisions of the same company. No one expects that mergers or globalization will decrease in the years ahead. That suggests that companies will need to be even more aggressive in using new technologies to enable them to build the large, distributed business processes that will be needed in the years ahead.

A Quick Summary

Figure 1.5 provides a summary overview of some of the historic business process technologies we have described in this chapter. Most are still actively evolving. We have pictured the Internet, the Web, and email as a very large arrow that underlies

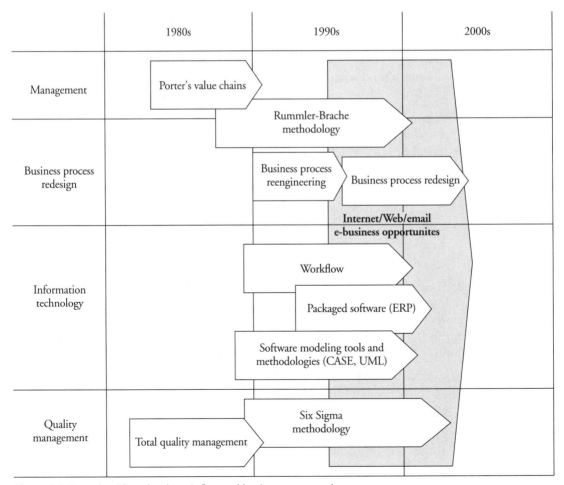

Figure 1.5 Some key ideas that have influenced business process change.

everything to suggest that it will increasingly alter all business process tools and techniques.

Business Process Change Today

Just as IT and the business environment have changed, those working on business process projects have learned important lessons. One lesson was how important it is to tie specific business improvement projects to corporate goals. Too many projects undertaken in the mid-1990s developed a life of their own and solved business problems that weren't of strategic importance. In effect, the business process redesign team maximized the effectiveness of the business process while losing sight of the broader reasons for the redesign. Several business process theorists in the late 1990s focused on how to best align individual processes with corporate strategies and goals.

During this same period, other business process theorists focused on the problems of actually implementing redesigned processes. Several companies developed new processes and then found that the line organizations responsible for implementing the new design failed to support the changes. New processes introduced with much fanfare worked for awhile, but were soon functioning as they had before the changes were introduced. It turns out that considerable attention needs to be focused on managing changes and obtaining agreement before new processes are launched. At the same time, managers involved in the process need to have their goals and incentive systems modified to align their interests with both company goals and the success of the new process.

IT automation efforts have also become much more complex. IT not only has to support specific applications and maintain databases, but it has to maintain a corporate network that connects every employee and provides email and Internet access communications. IT is also responsible for linking the business, via an external Internet system, with other businesses and with customers. To do this, IT organizations have developed a software infrastructure that is independent of any specific application and links all applications and employees, as needed. Increasingly, IT is being asked to anticipate new business goals in order to assure that its infrastructure will be ready to respond to new business initiatives when they occur. This has forced IT to develop its own strategic capabilities in order to project future corporate needs and acquire the systems and skills necessary to support possible new applications.

Thus, IT is increasingly relying on its own enterprise modeling and business process modeling techniques. It is also asking business strategists to work with IT strategists to develop an IT infrastructure and architecture that will support enterprise-wide integration.

Most businesses have not considered how to coordinate business and IT collaboration in business process design and are somewhere in the midst of a transition. Line managers still have the primary responsibility for business processes. Most companies still ask business managers to initiate process redesigns. At the same time, IT has become more aggressive in developing the tools it needs to provide the cross-process modeling and integration techniques necessary to create the new generation of e-business applications that strategies and line managers are demanding.

Large companies are increasingly automated, and business managers are being asked to know more and more about the software systems they rely upon. At the same time, most large companies still employ tens or hundreds of thousands of employees, and business managers need to be as concerned with the tasks assigned to these individuals, and the measurement of their success, as they are with the software systems these individuals rely upon. Corporate and line managers are ultimately responsible for the policies or business rules used to make decisions in business processes, and for the management of employees working in the process, and can't delegate that responsibility to IT. They are, however, increasingly delegating the communication logistics to IT, since it is the only group with the technical background to understand and manage how messages are moved from one location to another over the Internet.

The lack of overall coordination shows up in various ways. IT managers often complain that line managers don't understand the complexities they face. At the same time, business managers frequently complain that IT process modeling techniques are too focused on automation and software integration and don't pay sufficient heed to employees and other unautomated considerations. Since most companies haven't resolved how to balance these concerns, business process redesign projects often turn out to be a struggle between business managers with employee concerns, and IT managers with automation and integration concerns. In the best case the two groups continue to talk with one another and work out a mutually satisfactorily solution. In the worst case, they stop talking, since each feels the other is incapable of understanding their concerns.

In this book, we'll not only describe how to analyze and design business processes, we'll also describe a general strategy that companies can use to coordinate the work of business and IT managers. This approach, which we will refer to as *enterprise alignment,* provides a systematic way for companies to organize and transfer decisions about corporate strategy and goals to plans for redesigning processes,

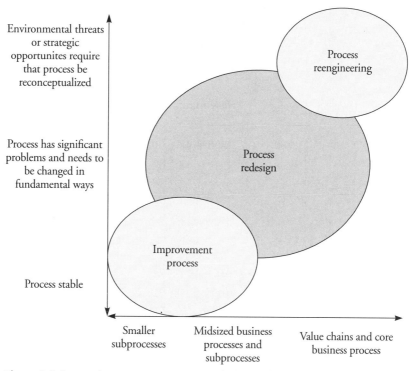

Figure 1.6 Process improvement, process redesign, and process reengineering.

initiating changes in IT infrastructure, and redefining the objectives and measures assigned to managers. Some companies will already have a portion of the cycle in place, and most companies will use different terms to describe the process. The key, however, is for every company to have a systematic, top-down approach that assures that their corporate strategies, goals, and managerial objectives, are all aligned with the goals of their business processes. Equally, since every company has limited resources, this alignment mechanism should serve to communicate priorities so that specific business process redesign efforts are undertaken only if they are likely to support high-priority corporate goals.

Figure 1.6 provides an overview of the three major terms we will use in this book to describe process change projects. If the process is relatively stable and the goal is to introduce incremental improvements, then the preferred term is *process improvement.* If the process is very large and we seek to redesign the process in a comprehensive manner, then we will use the term *process reengineering.* The key distinction is between improvement, which essentially relies on a problem-solving approach, and reengineering, which relies on reconceptualizing how a business

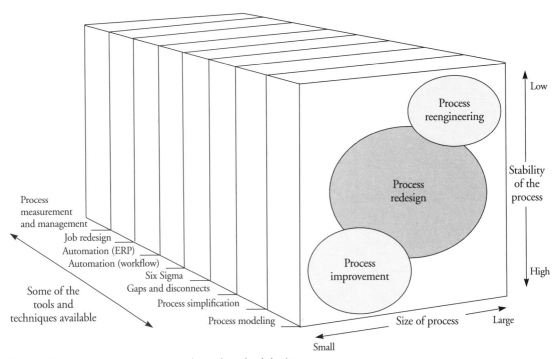

Figure 1.7 Processes, techniques, tools, and methodologies.

process should work. The first is tactical and the second is strategic. For most process change projects that fall in between these extremes, we will use the term *process redesign*.

As a general rule, large, complex projects should be rare once a company has organized around processes and given each a basic redesign. They occur when major new technologies or product lines are introduced. Linking an internal supply chain into a integrated supply chain that includes several different companies might just call for a major redesign or a BPR effort. Most automation efforts are redesign efforts. In an ideal situation, most company processes will be redesigned and thereafter, most efforts will involve process improvement efforts. In a mature process organization, the process improvement efforts will be a more-or-less continuous effort undertaken by the manager and the process team.

In Figure 1.7 we have added a third dimension to the previous figure to show how some of the other tools, technologies, and methodologies we have discussed in this chapter fit in. In effect, you could create a process model of any process, from a small, static one, to a large, dynamic one. Similarly, you could automate any of these processes or install management or measurement systems to make them more consistent and efficient.

We normally think of a methodology like Six Sigma as best for process improvement, but there are those who use it for major redesign projects. Similarly, we normally think of the Rummler-Brache methodology as best for redesign and reengineering, but some practitioners use Rummler-Brache for process improvement. Anyone seeking to manage process change projects at a company needs to learn to use all these terms with considerable flexibility.

In the remainder of this book we will look at all these theories and techniques in more detail. Our goal is to provide you with a set of tools and knowledge of their use. We hope that this will enable you to respond with flexibility to any business process challenge you encounter.

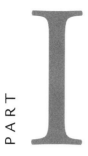

PART I

PROCESS MANAGEMENT

ANY SERIOUS BUSINESS process effort begins with the executive committee and the CEO. A commitment to conceptualizing and managing the organization in terms of processes must be a major and ongoing goal of senior management. If senior managers support the process approach, then process improvements and redesigns can become important management tools that contribute to the success of the company. If, on the other hand, senior managers are lukewarm in their support of processes, then process improvement efforts and redesign will become just another passing fad.

We have already stressed this point in our opening chapters. In this section we are going to focus on some of the key concepts and linkages that support the process commitment.

In Chapter 2 we will discuss organization goals and strategies and how they can be tied to processes and to competitive advantage.

In Chapter 3 we will consider the idea of a process architecture. Organizations that are committed to processes understand themselves in terms of processes. More importantly, a good process architecture provides the foundation required for aligning strategies and prioritizing process efforts.

2

Strategy, Value Chains, and Competitive Advantage

T HE CONCEPT OF A BUSINESS STRATEGY has been around for decades, and the models and process used to develop a company strategy are taught at every business school. A business strategy defines how a company will compete, what its goals will be, and what policies it will support to achieve those goals. Developing and updating a company's business strategy is one of the key responsibilities of a company's executive officers.

To develop a business strategy, senior executives need to consider the strengths and weaknesses of their own company and its competitors. They also need to consider trends, threats, and opportunities within the industry in which they compete, as well as in the broader social, political, technological, and economic environments in which the company operates.

There are different schools of business strategy. Some advocate a formal process that approaches strategic analysis very systematically, while others support less formal processes. A few argue that the world is changing so fast that companies must depend on the instincts of their senior executives in order to move rapidly. In effect, such companies evolve new positions on the fly.

The formal approach to business strategy analysis and development is often associated with the Harvard Business School. In this brief summary we'll describe a formal approach that is derived from Harvard professor Michael E. Porter's book, *Competitive Strategy.* Published in 1980 and now in its 60th printing, *Competitive Strategy* has been the best-selling strategy textbook throughout the past two decades. Porter's approach is well known, and it will allow us to examine some models that are well established among those familiar with strategic management literature.

Defining a Strategy

Porter defines business strategy as "a broad formula for how a business is going to compete, what its goals should be, and what policies will be needed to carry out these goals." Figure 2.1 provides an overview of the three-phase process that Porter recommends for strategy formation.

▶ *Phase 1: Determine the current position of the company.* The formal strategy process begins with a definition of where the company is now—what its current strategy is—and the assumptions that the company managers currently make

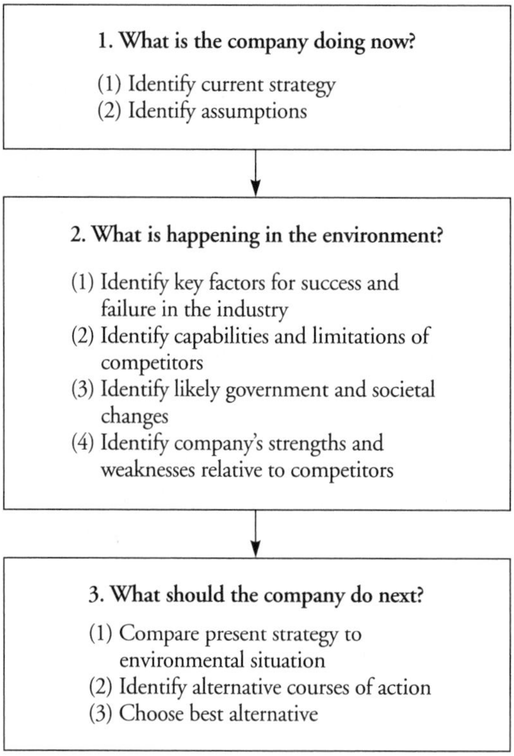

---

1. What is the company doing now?

(1) Identify current strategy
(2) Identify assumptions

---

2. What is happening in the environment?

(1) Identify key factors for success and
    failure in the industry
(2) Identify capabilities and limitations of
    competitors
(3) Identify likely government and societal
    changes
(4) Identify company's strengths and
    weaknesses relative to competitors

---

3. What should the company do next?

(1) Compare present strategy to
    environmental situation
(2) Identify alternative courses of action
(3) Choose best alternative

Figure 2.1 Porter's process for defining a company strategy. (After Porter, *Competitive Strategy.*)

about the company's current position, strengths and weaknesses, competitors, and industry trends. Most large companies have a formal strategy and have already gone through this exercise several times. Indeed, most large companies have a strategy committee that constantly monitors the company's strategy.

▶ *Phase 2: Determine what's happening in the environment.* In the second phase of Porter's strategy process (the middle box in Figure 2.1) the team developing the strategy considers what is happening in the environment. In effect, the team ignores the assumptions the company makes at the moment and gathers intelligence that will allow them to formulate a current statement of environmental constraints and opportunities facing all the companies in their industry. The team examines trends in the industry the company is in, and reviews the capabilities and limitations of competitors. It also reviews likely changes in society and government policy that might affect the business. When the team has finished its current review, it reconsiders the company's strengths and weaknesses, relative to the current environmental conditions.

▶ *Phase 3: Determine a new strategy for the company.* During the third phase, the strategy team compares the company's existing strategy with the latest analysis of what's happening in the environment. The team generates a number of scenarios or alternate courses of action that the company could pursue. In effect, the company imagines a number of situations the company could find itself in a few months or years hence and works backward to imagine what policies, technologies, and organizational changes would be required, during the intermediate period, to reach each situation. Finally, the company's strategy committee, working with the company's executive committee, selects one alternative and begins to make the changes necessary to implement the company's new strategy.

Porter offers lots of qualifications about the need for constant review and the necessity for change and flexibility but, overall, Porter's model was designed for the relatively calmer business environment that existed 20 years ago. Given the constant pressures to change and innovate that we've all experienced during the last three decades, it may be hard to think of the 1980s as a calm period, but everything really is relative. When you contrast the way companies approached strategy development just 10 years ago with the kinds of changes occurring today, as companies scramble to adjust to the world of the Internet, the 1980s were relatively sedate. Perhaps the best way to illustrate this is to look at Porter's general model of competition.

Porter's Model of Competition

Porter emphasizes that "the essence of formulating competitive strategy is relating a company to its environment." One of the best-known diagrams in Porter's *Competitive Strategy* is the one we have illustrated in Figure 2.2. Porter's diagram, which pulls together lots of information about how managers conceptualize the competition when they formulate strategy, is popularly referred to as the "five forces model."

Porter identifies five changes in the competitive environment that can force a company to adjust its business strategy. The heart of the business competition, of course, is the set of rival companies that comprise an industry. The company and its competitors are represented by the circle at the center of Figure 2.2.

▶ *Industry competitors.* As rival companies make moves, the company must respond. Similarly, the company may opt to make changes itself, in order to place its rivals at a disadvantage. Porter spends several chapters analyzing the ways companies compete within an industry, and we'll return to that in a moment.

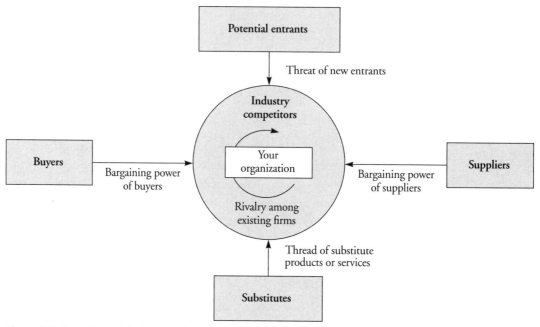

Figure 2.2 Porter's model of the five forces driving industry competition. (After Porter, *Competitive Strategy.*)

Beyond the rivalry between the companies that make up the industry, there are changes in the environment that can potentially affect all the companies in an industry. Porter classifies these changes into four groups: (1) buyers, (2) suppliers, (3) potential new companies that might enter the field, and (4) the threat that new products or services will become desirable substitutes for the company's existing products and services.

▶ *Buyers.* Buyers or customers will tend to want to acquire the company's products or services as inexpensively as possible. Some factors give the seller an advantage: If the product is scarce, if the company is the only source of the product, or the only local source of the product, or if the company is already selling the product more cheaply than its competitors, then the seller will tend to have better control of its prices. The inverse of factors like these give the customer more bargaining power and tend to force the company to reduce its prices. If there are lots of suppliers competing with each other, or if it's easy for customers to shop around, prices will tend to fall.

▶ *Suppliers.* In a similar way, suppliers would always like to sell their products or services for a higher price. If the suppliers are the only source of a needed product, if they can deliver it more quickly than their rivals, or if there is lots of demand for a relatively scarce product, then suppliers will tend to have more bargaining power and will increase their prices. Conversely, if the suppliers product is widely available, or available more cheaply from someone else, the company (buyer) will tend to have the upper hand and will try to force the supplier's price down.

▶ *Substitutes.* Companies in every industry also need to watch to see that no products or services become available that might function as substitutes for the products or services the company sells. At a minimum, a substitute product can drive down the company's prices. In the worst case, a new product can render the company's current products obsolete. The manufacturers of buggy whips were driven into bankruptcy when internal combustion automobiles replaced horse-drawn carriages in the early years of the 20th century. Similarly, the availability of plastic products has forced the manufacturers of metal, glass, paper, and wood products to reposition their products in various ways.

▶ *Potential entrants.* Finally, there is the threat that new companies will enter an industry and thereby increase the competition. More companies pursuing the same customers and trying to purchase the same raw materials tend to give both the suppliers and the customers more bargaining power, driving up the cost of goods and lowering each company's profit margins.

Historically, there are a number of factors that tend to function as barriers to the entry of new firms. If success in a given industry requires a large capital investment, then potential entrants will have to have a lot of money before they can consider trying to enter the industry. The capital investment could take different forms. In some cases, a new entrant might need to build large factories and buy expensive machinery. The cost of setting up a new computer chip plant, for example, runs to billions of dollars, and only a very large company could consider entering the chip manufacturing field. In other cases, the existing companies in an industry may spend huge amounts on advertising and have well-known brand names. Any new company would be forced to spend at least as much to even get its product noticed. Similarly, access to established distribution channels, proprietary knowledge possessed by existing firms, or government policies can all serve as barriers to new companies that might otherwise consider entering an established industry.

Until recently, the barriers to entry in most mature industries were so great that the leading firms in each industry had a secure hold on their positions and new entries were very rare. In the past three decades the growing move toward globalization has resulted in growing competition among firms that were formerly isolated by geography. Thus, prior to the 1960s, the three large auto companies in the United States completely controlled the U.S. auto market. Starting in the 1960s, and growing thoughout the next two decades, foreign auto companies began to compete for U.S. buyers and U.S. auto companies began to compete for foreign auto buyers. In the mid-1980s, a U.S. consumer could choose between cars sold by over a dozen firms. The late 1990s witnessed a sharp contraction in the auto market, as the largest automakers began to acquire their rivals and reduced the number of independent auto companies in the market. A key to understanding this whole process, however, is to understand that these auto companies were more or less equivalent in size and had always been potential rivals, except that they were functioning in geographically isolated markets. As companies became more international, geography stopped functioning as a barrier to entry, and these companies found themselves competing with each other. They all had similar strategies, and the most successful have gradually reduced the competition by acquiring their less successful rivals. In other words, globalization created challenges, but it didn't radically change the basic business strategies that were applied by the various firms engaged in international competition.

In effect, when a strategy team studies the environment, it surveys all of these factors. They check to see what competitors are doing, if potential new companies seem likely to enter the field, or if substitute products are likely to be offered. And they check on factors that might change the future bargaining power that buyers or sellers are likely to exert.

Industries, Products, and Value Propositions

Obviously Porter's model assumes that the companies in the circle in the middle of Figure 2.2 have a good idea of the scope of the industry they are in and the products and services that define the industry. Companies are sometimes surprised when they find that the nature of the industry has changed and that companies that were not formerly their competitors are suddenly taking away their customers. When this happens, it usually occurs because the managers at a company were thinking too narrowly or too concretely about what it is that their company was selling.

To avoid this trap, sophisticated managers need to think more abstractly about what products and services their industry provides. A "value proposition" refers to the value that a product or service provides to customers. Managers should always strive to be sure that they know what business (industry) their company is really in. That's done by being sure they know what value their company is providing to its customers.

Thus, for example, a bookseller might think he or she is in the business of providing customers with books. In fact, however, the bookseller is probably in the business of providing customers with information or entertainment. Once this is recognized, then it becomes obvious that a bookseller's rivals are not only other book stores, but magazine stores, TV, and the Web. In other words, a company's rivals aren't simply the other companies that manufacture similar products, but all those who provide the same general value to customers. Clearly Time-Warner-AOL realizes this and has combined companies that sell books, TV movies, magazines, and Web content in order to better serve customers and to better control the marketplace. Similarly, movies that are coordinated with books or comics also exploit the fact that they are providing a similar value to the same group of customers.

If customers ever decide they like reading texts on computer screens in some "automated book device," then companies that think of themselves as booksellers are in serious trouble. In this situation it will be obvious that the real value being provided is information and that the information could be downloaded from a computer just as well as printed in a book format. Many magazines are already producing online versions that allow customers to read and download articles in electronic form. Record and CD vendors are currently struggling with a version of this problem as copies of songs are exchanged over the Internet. In effect, one needs to understand that it's the song that has the value, and not the record or CD on which it's placed. The Web and a computer become a substitute for a CD if they can function as effective media for transmitting and playing the song to the customer.

Good strategists must always work to be sure they really understand what customer needs they are satisfying. It's only by knowing the value they provide customers that they can truly understand the industry they are in and who their potential rivals are. A good strategy is focused on providing value to customers, not narrowly defined in terms of a specific product or service.

In some cases, of course, the same product may provide different value to different customers. The same car, for example, might simply be a way of getting around for one group of customers, but a status item for another set of customers.

In spite of the need to focus on providing value to customers, historically, in designing their strategies, most companies begin with an analysis of their core competencies. In other words, they begin by focusing on the products or services they currently produce. They move from products to ways of specializing them and then to sales channels until they finally reach their various targeted groups of customers. Most e-business strategists suggest that companies approach their analysis in reverse. The new importance of the customer, and the new ways that products can be configured for the Web, suggest that companies should begin by considering what Web customers like and what they will buy over the Web, and then progress to what product the company might offer that would satisfy the new Web customers. We'll consider this in more detail when we consider customer-oriented e-business processes in Chapter 14.

Strategies for Competing

Earlier, we mentioned that Potter places a lot of emphasis on the ways existing companies can compete within an existing industry. Potter describes competition in most traditional industries when he says that most companies follow one of three generic strategies: (1) cost leadership, (2) differentiation, and (3) niche specialization.

▶ *Cost leadership.* The cost leader is the company that can offer the product at the cheapest price. In most industries, price can be driven down by economies of scale, by the control of suppliers and channels, and by experience that allows a company to do things more efficiently. In most industries, large companies dominate the manufacture of products in huge volume and sell them more cheaply than their smaller rivals.

▶ *Differentiation.* If a company can't sell its products for the cheapest price, an alternative is to offer better or more desirable products. Customers are often

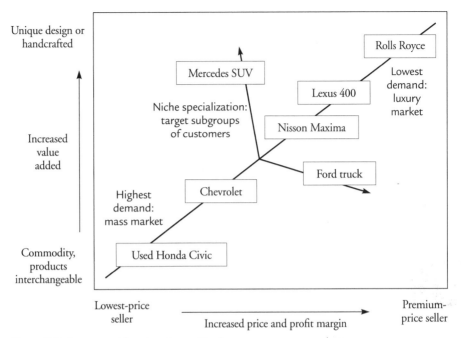

Figure 2.3 Some considerations in positioning a company or product.

willing to pay a premium for a better product, and this allows companies specialize in producing a better product to compete with those selling a cheaper but less desirable product. Companies usually make better products by using more expensive materials, relying on superior craftsmanship, creating a unique design, or tailoring the design of the product in various ways.

▶ *Niche specialization.* Niche specialists focus on specific buyers, specific segments of the market, or buyers in particular geographical markets and often only offer a subset of the products typically sold in the industry. In effect, they represent an extreme version of differentiation, and they can charge a premium for their products, since the products have special features beneficial to the consumers in the niche.

Figure 2.3 provides an overview of one way strategists think of positioning and specialization. As a broad generalization, if the product is a commodity, it will sell near its manufacturing cost, with little profit for the seller.

The classic example of a company that achieved cost leadership in an industry was Ford Motor Company. The founder, Henry Ford, created a mass market for automobiles by driving the price of a car down to the point where the average person could afford one. To do this, Ford limited the product to one model in one color and set up a production line to produce large numbers of cars very efficiently. In the early years of the 20th century, Ford completely dominated auto production in the United States.

As the U.S. economy grew after World War I, however, General Motors was able to pull ahead of Ford, not by producing cars as cheaply, but by producing cars that were nearly as cheap and that offered a variety of features that differentiated them. Thus, GM offered several different models in a variety of colors with a variety of optional extras. In spite of selling slightly more expensive cars, GM gradually gained market share from Ford because consumers were willing to pay more to get cars in preferred colors and styles.

Examples of niche specialists in the automobile industry are companies that manufacture only taxi cabs or limousines.

Within any specific industry there are usually some special circumstances that allow for other forms of specialization, or that determine what kinds of differentiation and what kinds of niche specialization will be effective.

Obviously, an MBA student learns a lot more about strategy. For our purposes, however, this brief overview should be sufficient. In essence, business managers are taught to evaluate a number of factors and arrive at a strategy that will be compatible with the company's strengths and weaknesses and that will result in a reasonable profit. Historically, companies have developed a strategy and, once they succeeded, continued to rely on that strategy, with only minor refinements, for several years.

The Unisys Corporate Strategy

Let's consider a concrete example of what a corporate strategy might look like. We attended the 2002 Unisys briefing for technology analysts in which Larry Weinbach, the chairman and CEO of Unisys, laid out the company's strategy and vision. Unisys is a $6 billion (U.S.) computer company. Since Mr. Weinbach described Unisys's position very succinctly, it provides a nice example of the issues we are discussing. We could just as well have chosen another company and derived a similar statement from their annual report.

On one slide, Mr. Weinbach summarized the Unisys Vision as follows:

Unisys Vision: Services Driven, Technology Enabled

▶ Provide total value-added solutions to client needs in focused markets
▶ Services—the driver

► Technology—the enabler
► Articulated in 1997—same vision today
► Ahead of industry shift to services-driven model

This vision statement requires a little context. Unisys arose as a computer hardware vendor and competed with companies like IBM, HP, and DEC. In 1997, the Unisys strategy team decided that computer hardware was becoming a commodity and that it wouldn't continue to command the margins Unisys was used to achieving. At that point, Unisys committed itself to a major strategy change. It decided to transform the company from a hardware vendor that incidentally helped companies build software applications, to a services company that derived its primary income from helping companies develop software and managing software applications that companies decided to outsource. In addition, Unisys decided to focus its efforts on a few industries in which it was already very well positioned, including financial services, publishing, transportation, communications, and the public sector. It also decided to focus on helping companies with e-business problems. Other hardware vendors have attempted the same transition, but Unisys clearly wants to position itself as a company that is ahead of the curve on this transition.

Weinbach put it this way in a letter to stakeholders that appeared in the company's 2000 annual report:

> Our mission in 2000 was to focus Unisys—our people, our programs, our resources, our technology—on e-business. In particular, we worked to focus Unisys on value-added, higher-margin opportunities where we can help customers design, build and manage their technology infrastructures to conduct secure, high-volume transaction processing in an e-business environment. Conversely, we worked to de-emphasize, or exit altogether, those areas of our business where we did not add value to a customer's e-business equation.
>
> We accomplished that mission through our work in 2000, and this is who we are today: We are a highly focused company. The marketplace changes I noted earlier drove a comprehensive strategic review of our business in 2000, aimed at improving our operational performance in 2001 and beyond . . .

By early 2002, when we attended the latest Unisys briefing, this transition was well underway. In a second slide, Mr. Weinbach reported that in fiscal year 2001, Unisys derived 74%, or $4.4 billion (U.S.), of its revenues from services. Specifically, they derived incomes as follows:

► Systems integration   33%
► Outsourcing   29%
► Network services   25%
► Core maintenance   13%

At the same time that he announced these results, Mr. Weinbach used another slide to announce the following strategic priorities for 2002:

- ▶ Accelerate growth in annuity-based business
  Goal: Increasing outsourcing revenue to 35% of services revenue by 2003.
- ▶ Drive profitable growth in systems integration (SI) solutions
  Goal: Refocus SI business and upgrade skills base. Shift from integrator to consultancy model.
- ▶ Expand security solutions program
  Goal: Develop integrated, lifecycle security offering.
- ▶ Accelerate marketing of Unisys hardware servers
  Goal: Focus on developing marketing and sales capabilities. Increased repeat and multiple-unit orders and 40% of sales to new Unisys customers.
- ▶ Maintain tight cost controls
  Goal: Cut SG&A expenses by 14% in 2002 by streamlining business processes and reducing discretionary spending.

Mr. Weinbach spent quite a bit of time explaining each of these priorities, and we won't do that here. Just looking at the strategic vision and priorities stated here, however, provides a good example of the kind of strategy statements and goals one normally expects from strategy committees and executives.

Obviously the strategy statement makes assumptions about the market in 2002 and in the near future. Some of the statements describe general goals. Some statements define specific goals, and some define income or expense changes as percentages of Unisys's 2001 financial results. Some statements describe principles or policies the company will seek to implement.

Some of the goals suggest that business processes will need to be changed. Others that are more generic will probably require changes in multiple business processes. Thus, for example, an improved security offering will probably begin as an R&D process goal, but the resulting technologies will eventually be incorporated into integration and outsourcing product lines and require changes in the way those services are described and sold.

In other words, Mr. Weinbach's strategy statement is really only the beginning. Many organizations within Unisys will have to work hard to determine how this strategy and these priorities are to be implemented. If Unisys followed the procedure we recommend in this book, the strategy statement would be passed to the company's process architecture committee and that committee would evolve more specific requirements and assign them to appropriate value chains and business processes within Unisys.

Porter's Theory of Competitive Advantage

Michael Porter's first book was *Competitive Strategy: Techniques for Analyzing Industries and Competitors.* This is the book in which he analyzed the various sources of environmental threats and opportunities and described how companies could position themselves in the marketplace. Porter's second book, *Competitive Advantage: Creating and Sustaining Superior Performance,* was published in 1985. *Competitive Advantage* extended Porter's basic ideas on strategy in several important ways. For our purposes, we will focus on his ideas about value chains, the sources of competitive advantage, and the role that business processes play in establishing and maintaining competitive advantage.

We've already encountered the idea of a value chain in the Introduction. Figure 2.4 reproduces Porter's generic value chain diagram.

Porter introduced the idea of the value chain to emphasize that companies ought to think of processes as complete entities that begin with new product development and customer orders and end with satisfied customers. To ignore processes or to think of processes as things that occur within departmental silos is simply a formula for creating a suboptimized company. Porter suggested that company managers should conceptualize large-scale processes, which he termed *value chains,* as entities that include every activity involved in adding value to a product or service sold by the company.

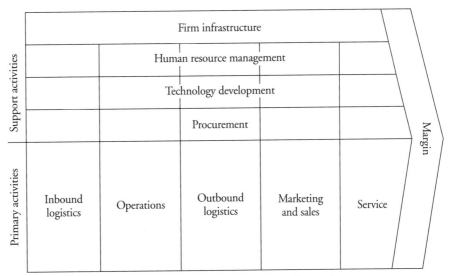

Figure 2.4 Porter's value chain. (After Porter, *Competitive Advantage.*)

We've used the terms *value proposition* and *value chain* several times now, so we should probably offer a definition. The term *value,* as it is used in any of these phrases, refers to value that a customer perceives and is willing to pay for. The idea of the value chain is that each activity in the chain or sequence adds some value to the final product. It's assumed that if you asked the customer about each of the steps, the customer would agree that the step added something to the value of the product. A value proposition describes, in general terms, a product or service that the customer is willing to pay for.

It's a little more complex, of course, because everyone agrees that there are some activities or steps that don't add value, directly, but facilitate adding value. These are often called *value-enabling* activities. Thus acquiring the parts that will later be used to assemble a product is a value-enabling activity. The key reason to focus on value, however, is, ultimately, to identify activities that are *non-value-adding* activities. These are activities that have been incorporated into a process, for one reason or another, that no longer add any value to the final product. Non-value-adding activities should be eliminated. We'll discuss all this in later chapters when we focus on analyzing processes.

Figure 2.4 emphasizes that lots of individual subprocesses must be combined to create a complete value chain. In effect, every process, subprocess, or activity that contributes to the cost of producing a given line of products must be combined. Once all the costs are combined and subtracted from the gross income from the sale of the products, one derives the profit margin associated with the product line. Porter discriminates between primary processes or activities, and includes inbound logistics, operations, outbound logistics, marketing and sales, and service. He also includes support processes or activities, including procurement, technology development, human resource management, and firm infrastructure, which includes finance and senior management activities. Porter's use of the term *value chain* is similar to Hammer's use of *core process.* Many companies use the term *process* to refer to much more specific sets of activities. For example, one might refer to the Marketing and Sales Process, the Order Fulfillment Process, or even the Customer Relationship Management Process. In this book, when we want to speak of comprehensive, large-scale processes, we'll use the term *value chain.* In general, when we use the term *process,* we will be referring to some more specific set of activities.

Although it doesn't stand out in Figure 2.4, if we represented each of the functions shown in the figure as boxes and connected them with arrows, we could see how a series of functions results in a product or service delivered to a customer. If we had such a representation, we could also ask which functions added value to the process as it passed through that box. The term *value chain* was originally chosen to suggest that the chain was made up of a series of activities that added value to products the company sold. Some activities would take raw materials and turn them into an assembled mechanism that sold for considerably more than the raw materials cost. That additional value would indicate the value added by the manufacturing process. Later, when we consider activity costing in more detail, we will see how we can analyze value chains to determine which processes add value and which don't. One goal of many process redesign efforts is to eliminate or minimize the number of non-value-adding activities in a given process.

In the case of Unisys, we might speculate that Unisys thinks of its organization in terms of five or more value chains. In the presentation we described, Unisys reported income for four general product lines. In the objectives, they also mentioned their server product line. Unisys probably has some additional product lines that it is simply maintaining. At a minimum, however, an overview of Unisys's value chains might look like Figure 2.5.

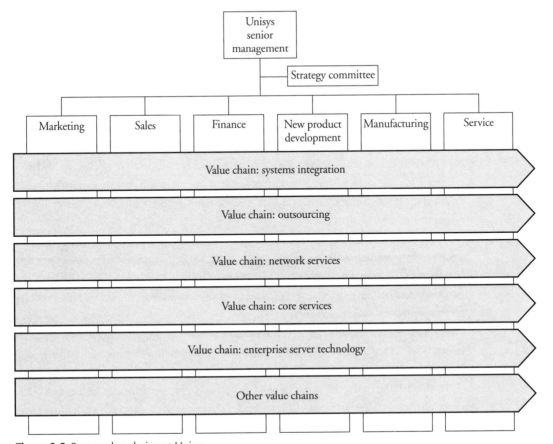

Figure 2.5 Some value chains at Unisys.

Having defined a value chain, Porter went on to define *competitive advantage* and show how value chains were the key to maintaining competitive advantage. Porter offered these two key definitions:

A *strategy* depends on defining a company position that the company can use to maintain a competitive advantage. A *position* simply describes the goals of the company and how it explains those goals to its customers.

A *competitive advantage* occurs when your company can make more profits selling its product or service than its competitors can. Rational managers seek to establish a long-term competitive advantage. This provides the best possible return, over an extended period, for the effort involved in creating a process and bringing a product or service to market. A company with a competitive advantage is not necessarily the largest company in its industry, but it makes its customers happy by selling a desirable product, and it makes its shareholders happy by producing excellent profits.

Thus a company anywhere in Figure 2.3 could enjoy a competitive advantage. Porter cites the example of a small bank that tailors its services to the very wealthy and offers extraordinary service. It will fly its representatives, for example, to a client's yacht anywhere in the world for a consultation. Compared with larger banks, this bank doesn't have huge assets, but it achieves the highest profit margins in the banking industry and is likely to continue to do so for many years. Its ability to satisfy its niche customers gives it a competitive advantage.

Two fundamental variables determine a company's profitability or the margin it can obtain from a given value chain. The first is the industry structure. That imposes broad constraints on what a company can offer and charge. The second is a competitive advantage that results from a strategy and a well-implemented value chain that lets a company outperform the average competitor in an industry over a sustained period of time.

A competitive advantage can be based on charging a premium because your product is more valuable, or it can result from selling your product or service for less than your competitors because your value chain is more efficient. The first approach relies on developing a good *strategic position.* The second advantage results from *operational effectiveness.*

As we use the terms, a *strategy,* the *positioning* of a company, and *a strategic position* are synonyms. They all refer to how a company plans to function and present itself in a market.

In the 1990s, many companies abandoned strategic positioning and focused almost entirely on operational effectiveness. Many companies speak of focusing on *best practices.* The assumption seems to be that a company can be successful if all of its practices are as good as, or better than, its competitors. The movement toward best practices has led to outsourcing and the use of comparison studies to determine the best practices for any given business process. Ultimately, as Porter demonstrates, operational effectiveness can't be sustained. In effect, it puts all the companies within each particular industry on a treadmill. Companies end up practicing what Porter terms "hypercompetition," running faster and faster to improve their operations. Companies that have pursued this path have not only exhausted themselves, but they have watched their profit margins gradually shrink. When companies locked in hypercompetition have exhausted all other remedies, they usually end up buying up their competitors to obtain some relief. That temporarily reduces the pressure to constantly improve operational efficiency, but it usually doesn't help improve the profit margins.

The alternative is to define a strategy or position that your company can occupy where it can produce a superior product for a given set of customers. The product may be superior for a wide number of reasons. It may satisfy the very specific needs of customers ignored by other companies, it may provide features that other companies don't provide, or it may be sold at a price other companies don't choose to match. It may provide customers in a specific geographical area with products that are tailored to that area.

Porter argues that, ultimately, competitive advantage is sustained by the processes and activities of the company. Companies engaged in hypercompetition seek to perform each activity better than their competitors. Companies competing on the basis of strategic positioning achieve their advantage by performing different activities or organizing their activities in a different manner.

Put a different way, hypercompetitive companies position themselves in the same manner as their rivals and seek to offer the same products or services for less money. To achieve that goal, they observe their rivals and seek to assure that each of their processes and activities is as efficient as, or more efficient than, those of their rivals. Each time a rival introduces a new and more efficient activity, the company studies it and then proceeds to modify its equivalent activity to match or better the rival's innovation. In the course of this competition, since everyone introduces the same innovations, no one gains any sustainable advantage. At the same time margins keep getting reduced. This critique is especially telling when one considers the use of ERP applications, and we will consider this in detail later.

Companies relying on strategic positioning focus on defining a unique strategy. They may decide to only focus on wealthy customers and provide lots of service, or on customers that buy over the Internet. They may decide to offer the most robust product, or the least expensive product, with no frills. Once the company decides on its competitive position, it translates that position into a set of goals and then lets those goals dictate the organization of its processes.

Porter remarks that a good position can often be defined by what the company decides not to do. It is only by focusing on a specific set of customers or products and services that one can establish a strong position. Once one decides to focus, management must constantly work to avoid the temptation to broaden that focus in an effort to acquire a few more customers.

If a company maintains a clear focus, however, then the company is in a position to tailor business processes and to refine how activities interact. Porter refers to the way in which processes and activities work together and reinforce one another as *fit*. He goes on to argue that a focus on fit makes it very hard for competitors to quickly match any efficiencies your company achieves. As fit is increased and processes are more and more tightly integrated, duplicating the efficiency of an activity demands that the competitor rearrange its whole process to duplicate not only the activity, but the whole process, and the relation of that process to related processes, and so on. Good fit is often a result of working to assure that the handoffs between departments or functions are as efficient as possible.

In Porter's studies, companies that create and sustain competitive advantage do it because they have the discipline to choose a strategic position and then remain focused on it. More important, they gradually refine their business processes and the fit of their activities so that their efficiencies are very hard for competitors to duplicate. It is process integration or fit that provides the basis for long-term competitive advantage and that provides better margins without the need for knee-jerk efforts to copy the best practices of rivals.

We urge readers to study Porter's *Competitive Advantage*. In helping companies improve their business processes, we have often encountered clients who worried about revising entire processes and suggested instead that standard ERP modules be employed. Some clients worried that we were advocating hypercompetition and urging them to begin revisions that their competitors would match, which would then require still another response on their part. It seemed to them it would be easier just to acquire standard modules that were already "best of breed" solutions. Undoubtedly this resulted from our failure to explain our position with sufficient clarity.

We do not advocate making processes efficient for their own sake, nor do we advocate that companies adopt a strategy based strictly on competitive efficiency. Instead, we advocate that companies take strategy seriously and define a unique position that they can occupy and in which they can prosper. We urge companies to analyze and design tightly integrated processes. Creating processes with superior fit is the goal. We try to help managers avoid arbitrarily maximizing the efficiency of specific activities at the expense of the process as a whole.

We certainly believe that companies should constantly scan for threats and opportunities. Moreover, we recommend that companies constantly adjust their strategies when they see opportunities or threats to their existing position. It's important, however, that the position be well defined, and that adjustments be made in order to improve a well-defined position, and not simply for their own sake. In the past few years we've watched dozens of companies adopt Internet technologies without a clear idea of how those technologies were going to enhance their corporate position. In effect, these companies threw themselves into an orgy of competitive efficiency, without a clear idea of how it would improve their profitability. We are usually strong advocates of the use of new technology, and especially new software technologies. Over the last few decades IT has been the major source of new products and services, a source of significant increases in productivity, and the most useful approach to improving process fit. We only advocate the adoption of new technology, however, when it contributes to an improvement in a clearly understood corporate position.

We also recommend that companies organize so that any changes in their strategic position or goals can be rapidly driven down through the levels of the organization and result in changes in business processes and activities. Changes in goals without follow-through are worthless. At the same time, as companies get better and better at rapidly driving changes down into processes, subprocesses, and activities, it's important to minimize the disruptive effect of this activity. It's important to focus on the changes that really need to be made and to avoid undertaking process redesign, automation, or improvement projects just to generate changes in the name of efficiency or a new technology that is unrelated to high-priority corporate goals.

To sum up: We don't recommend that companies constantly change their strategic position to match a competitor's latest initiatives. We don't advocate creating a system that will simply increase hypercompetition. Instead, we believe that companies should seek positions that can lead to a long-term competitive advantage and that that can only be accomplished as the result of a carefully conceived and focused corporate strategy. We argue for a system that can constantly tune and refine the fit of processes that are designed and integrated to achieve a well-defined, unique corporate position.

There will always be processes and activities that will be very similar from one company to another within a given industry. Similarly, within a large process there will always be subprocesses or activities that are similar from one company to another. In such cases we support a best practices approach, using ERP modules or by outsourcing. Outsourcing, done with care, can help focus company managers on those core processes that your company actually relies upon and eliminate the distraction of processes that add no value to your core business processes.

At the same time, we are living in a time of rapid technological change. Companies that want to avoid obsolescence need to constantly evaluate new technologies to determine if they can be used to improve their product or service offerings. Thus, we accept that even well-focused companies that avoid hypercompetition will still find themselves faced with a steady need for adjustments in strategy and goals and for process improvement.

Ultimately, however, in this book we want to help managers think about how they can create unique core processes, change them in a systematic manner, and integrate them so that they can serve as the foundation for long-term competitive advantage.

E-Business Strategies

Most managers realize that a major business transition is taking place. As customers begin to buy via the Internet and companies struggle to figure out how to use the Internet to create new operational efficiencies, most companies are seeking to update their business strategies. Today's business environment is suddenly much more dynamic. New value propositions are being promoted by new companies, and new technologies are being used to give companies competitive advantage. For a while, consultants argued about whether it's a matter of applying the classic models, while taking the Internet into account, or a matter of developing altogether new approaches to business strategy. In the past year or two, most large companies have concluded that Internet technologies need to be integrated with their existing processes. It isn't so much a matter of developing an e-business strategy, as figuring out how to use Internet technologies to improve the fit of existing processes.

Thus, rather than discussing e-business strategies here, we will discuss Internet technologies and e-business strategies when we discuss common patterns that companies have used to redesign their business processes. One pattern we'll consider, for example, involves creating a Web site and supporting customer sales via the Web. Another pattern seeks to increase process efficiencies by integrating with suppliers via Internet techniques. In other words, many strategy committees call for strategic goals that involve the use of the Internet. Actually figuring out what to do, however, is more tactical and involves determining how to redesign a process by means of Internet technologies. The goal shouldn't be to use the Internet, but to improve margins, reduce process times, or to increase customer satisfaction.

The Evolution of the Strategic Process

There has been a basic shift in how strategic goals are aligned with managerial goals in the course of the last two decades. This shift has been a result of the emphasis on business processes and has been driven by the work of Porter, whose books we have already discussed, by Geary Rummler, and many other business process gurus, who have all placed considerable emphasis on aligning corporate goals, business processes, and job objectives.

Before Porter's work in the mid-1980s, most strategy books suggested the following:

1. Determine corporate strategy.
2. Establish corporate goals for the strategy. (These goals were typically financial and usually had nothing to do with customer satisfaction.)
3. Convert corporate goals into functional or departmental goals.
4. Convert function or departmental goals into job objectives. These job objectives were established for everyone, from the VP on down to the lowest supervisor in the department or functional unit.
5. Establish measures to track managerial performance against job objectives.

In the 1990s, as a result of the writings of Porter, Rummler and others, a new paradigm for alignment began to emerge. The new approach is as follows:

1. Determine corporate strategy.
2. Establish corporate goals for the strategy. (Goals are more likely to emphasize customer requirements and process and employee needs, in addition to financial goals.)
3. Convert corporate goals into objectives for cross-functional processes—in other words, objectives for Order Fulfillment rather than Inventory or Service.
4. Convert process objectives into subprocess or activity objectives and assign them to the departmental or functional managers responsible for the subprocess or activity. In other words, the supervisors receive job objectives as a result of managing an activity or subprocess. Their managers receive job

objectives as a result of managing supervisors who are responsible for various subprocesses or activities, and so on, up the hierarchy.

5. Establish measures to track managerial performance against job objectives.

The difference is subtle, but very important. It shifts the emphasis from departmental success to process success. One department many perform activities that are used in multiple processes, and in this case the department is ultimately evaluated based on its support of multiple processes. Done with intelligence, this approach shifts managers from thinking in terms of departmental goals (silo thinking) to process goals. It shifts managers from thinking about how to maximize departmental performance and focuses them, instead, on how to maximize the performance of processes they support.

In either case the basic process involved in determining a corporate strategy remains the same. In either case the strategy committee and the executive committee announce the corporate strategy and define corporate goals.

The differences occur when it comes time to figure out how to implement the goals and assign objectives to managers, and those events, in our approach, are undertaken by the process architecture committee. So we'll leave strategic considerations now and consider what a process architecture committee does, once it receives a new strategic direction.

3

Process Architecture and Organizational Alignment

Most companies have an executive committee to review and make key enterprise decisions. Reporting to the executive committee, there are usually several subcommittees. One common subcommittee is the strategy committee, which surveys the environment in which the business operates to identify threats or opportunities. When it finds problems or opportunities, the strategy committee reports them and makes recommendations. Another subcommittee usually focuses on exactly what the company might do in response to the threats or opportunities identified by the strategy committee. In some companies this is called a planning committee. In this book, we will refer to it as the *business process architecture committee*. We prefer this name for two important reasons. First, we want to emphasize that this committee has the responsibility for maintaining an overview of the entire company. This committee, among other things, should know what business processes support what goals. At the same time, we use the term *architecture* because it is commonly used in IT organizations, and we want to stress that this committee should be one of the key points at which business managers interact with IT managers to plan how companies should evolve to meet new challenges. Finally, with the approval of the executive committee, the business process architecture committee should produce plans for business process redesign efforts and assign goals to processes and managers to assure that processes stay aligned with company strategies and goals.

Figure 3.1 illustrates what we call the *enterprise alignment cycle*. Obviously different companies are organized in different ways. The names aren't really important. Having a group responsible for the functions, however, is vital. Enterprise

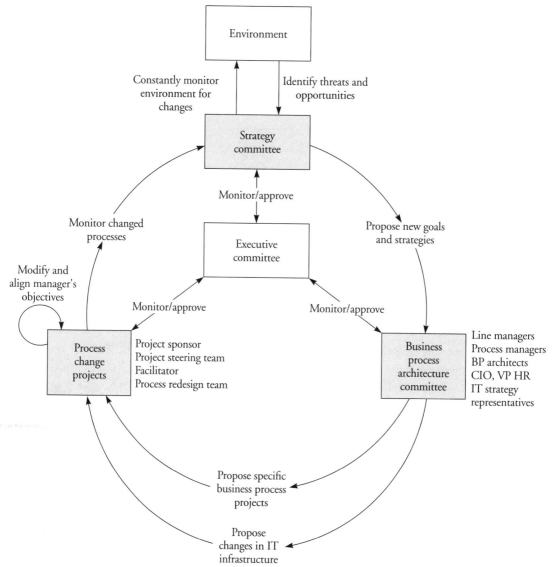

Figure 3.1 The enterprise alignment cycle.

alignment doesn't just happen. On the contrary, all kinds of forces work to move companies from alignment to misalignment. Someone has got to be constantly working to see that strategies and goals get translated into organizational structures and that processes and goals are related to managerial objectives. Whatever you choose to call it, every company needs a group of senior managers who are responsible for assuring that alignment happens.

Figure 3.1 shows the relationship between the strategy committee, the process architecture committee, and some other groups. Obviously, some of the functions could be handled in different ways, but our version emphasizes the important elements from a process analyst's perspective.

The enterprise alignment process begins with inputs from the strategy committee. The strategy committee proposes changes in corporate strategies and goals.

Statements of new strategies and goals can come in many forms, as we saw in the last chapter when we considered the Unisys strategy. They can be very general, like increase market share by 10%, or specific, like establishing a business unit in Japan, or creating a company Web site in order to sell 20% of some new product online.

Whatever the strategies or goals, the business process architecture committee begins by assessing the implications of the change. What will be involved in increasing market share by 10%? What will it take to establish a presence in Japan or create a company Web site? In many cases, the process architecture group will need to call on specialists or consultants to determine the implications of proposed changes.

Gradually, the implications will be refined into a written statement of the new assumptions, policies, and requirements. This process will normally require several iterations, as assumptions are refined and policies and requirements made more explicit.

Independent of this process, we assume the business process architecture committee will maintain a general overview of the firm that defines the major value chains and processes the company supports. Some of the documents may be in written form. Some may be high-level diagrams, and some may be very specific models. If specific models are available, this usually suggests that the process in question has already been redesigned at least once before. In some companies, process descriptions may be maintained on software tools.

We do not suggest that companies develop detailed models of all of their business processes. Given how rapidly companies are changing, few have the time required for this kind of documentation. Instead, we suggest that the process architecture committee maintain a very high-level description of the major value chains the organization supports. These high-level descriptions can be broken out into more detailed descriptions, as needed.

Once the strategy committee proposes a change, the process architecture committee reviews what it knows about the way processes currently function and determines which processes will need to be modified to meet the new goals. In some cases this may be obvious. In other cases the process architecture committee will need to learn more about specific processes before they can be sure just what needs to be changed. For example, a move to a Web portal and the sale of products online can be a relatively simple task or very complex, depending on what one decides to do. If the product is a commodity that the company simply resells, advertising it on a Web site and passing orders to the supplier may not involve many changes. If the product is a complex product that you manufacture, and you propose to allow the customer to configure the product, it may require lots of additional changes in a variety of different processes. Similarly, if you decide to integrate the external supply chain for the product, so that suppliers can make changes in response to orders, the changes can be very complex.

The effort will also vary depending on how quickly the new goals have to be met. If the changes can be phased in over the course of 2 years, that will usually be better than having to do everything within a 9-month period. Some changes, like the introduction of the euro, are controlled by external mandates and have hard deadlines. Others, like the decision to establish a presence in a new country, can be handled in phases, first working with others and providing support from the home office, and only gradually developing a complete infrastructure in the new country.

As assumptions and requirements are refined and approved, the process architecture committee gradually begins to develop a plan to accomplish the changes. The plan involves making changes in specific business processes. In some cases, the plan may call for a specific change in a specific process. In other cases—as, for example, when the euro was introduced—the plan required changes in a wide variety of processes. Several processes were affected, ranging from those that interfaced with customers to those that handled bookkeeping tasks and supplier payments. Inventories needed to be revalued, and product wrappers required reprinting. When multiple processes are going to be affected, the process architecture committee needs to develop a plan that specifies all of the changes required and prioritizes them. We are not suggesting that the business process architecture committee must determine exactly how a specific process will be changed, but only that it must determine which processes must be changed and the order or resources to be devoted to each.

Once projects and priorities are established, the process architecture committee works with the executive committee and the managers of the processes or functions involved to establish project steering teams to manage the changes. In some cases, the process architecture committee may establish several different project teams. As a generalization, however, it's better to have a single, larger steering team that oversees the entire effort and multiple redesign teams. Until redesign teams get into specifics, it's hard to be sure exactly what changes will be required.

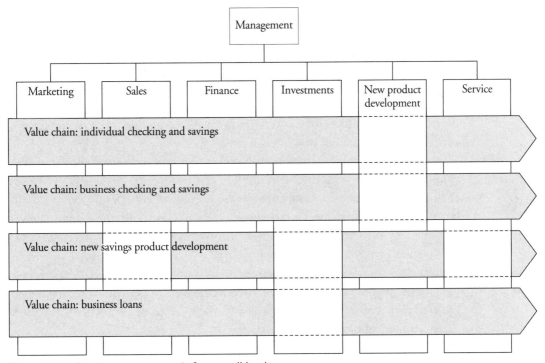

Figure 3.2 A function-process matrix for a small bank.

Moreover, as changes are made in one subprocess, new opportunities are created for improvements in other subprocesses. Thus, placing one steering team in charge of the entire redesign effort and letting them manage the coordination of all of the specific redesign efforts has distinct advantages.

This approach is especially important for companies with multiple divisions or subsidiaries operating independently. In such cases it tends to be very difficult for those at the center to control teams in subsidiaries. To facilitate coordination, they need to set documentation standards to assure that they can build a complete picture at the center and share ideas across the group of companies. The concept of a central committee with multiple project teams is especially prevalent in Europe, where companies tend to be less centralized and have multiple entities working together as a group of companies while still maintaining profit responsibility at the center.

Figure 3.2 shows the kind of matrix that the process architecture committee for a small bank might maintain. The divisions or functions of the organization are shown as on an organization chart. Major value chains or core business processes are shown as arrows running from left to right across the various functional units.

If a division or functional unit is involved in a specific value chain or process, then the appropriate intersection is highlighted. This is a very simplified example just to illustrate the concept. A real bank would have other value chains or might have them grouped into different value chains. Similarly, the departments or functional groups might be subdivided in different ways.

For the purposes of this matrix, one ignores support departments like IT and human resources, unless they are constantly involved in a process that produces a product or service sold to customers.

This analysis could be much more detailed. One could, for example, show the major subprocesses in each value chain. Or, one could enter the names of key activities that occur in each department in the respective boxes. Similarly, one could describe the goals or major requirements of each process within the process arrows.

The main purpose of such a matrix, however, is simply to provide the process architecture committee with an overview of which departments are involved in each value chain or process and, perhaps, how each process relates to the achievement of existing organizational goals. In effect this matrix provides an overview of the company and suggests which senior managers need to be involved if a given value chain or subprocess is to be changed.

The TeleManagement Forum's Process Architecture

Rather than looking at a specific company's process architecture, we are going to consider a business process architecture developed by an industry consortium, the TeleManagement Forum. The TeleManagement Forum is an organization made up of most of the major telecommunications companies in Europe and North America. One group within the TeleManagement Forum has spent several years developing a process architecture for telecom companies. It is assumed that no specific company will have exactly the same processes identified by the TeleManagement Forum, and that they will probably use different names for the various processes. Thus, this is a reference architecture rather than an architecture of a specific business. It is assumed as time passes that most members will move toward this process architecture and that, during the same period, vendors will tailor products to implement many of the processes defined by the model.

The architecture we will describe is the third iteration that the TeleManagement Forum has developed. This latest iteration, called the eBusiness Telecom Operations Map (eTOM), is based on earlier work that only sought to define the operations processes within telecom companies. As the companies began to implement e-business applications, however, they discovered that processes included in general and enterprise management had to be added to the architecture. One of the major advantages of e-business systems is that they integrate management and operations, and it's important that everyone have a clear overview of all the processes if they are to see how integration might occur.

Figure 3.3 shows the eTOM framework, using the graphic that the TeleManagement Forum uses. Figure 3.4 shows the same information, rearranged so

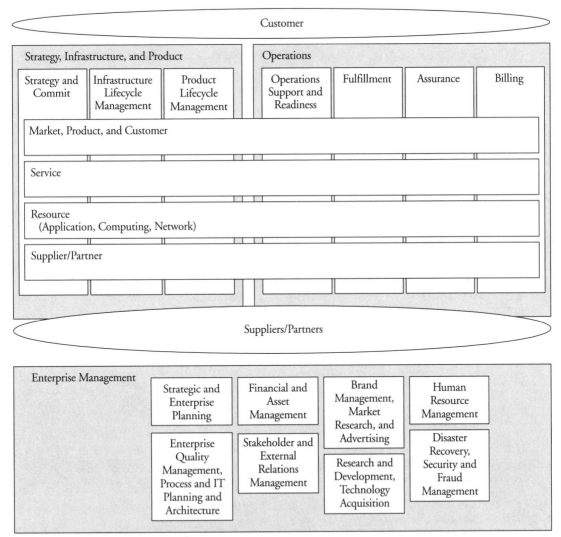

Figure 3.3 Executive-level version of eTOM business process framework. (© TeleManagement Forum October 2001).

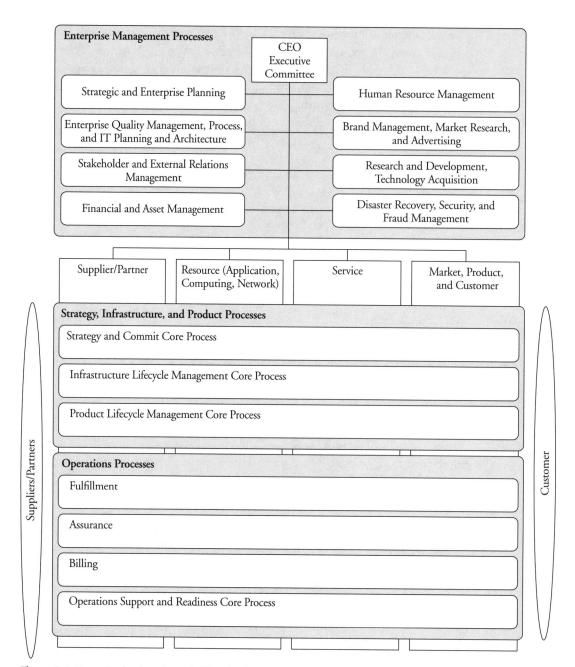

Figure 3.4 Executive-level version of eTOM business process framework rotated 90 degrees to the right and modified to use our standard notation.

that it matches the format that we use in this book. In effect, we rotated the entire diagram 90 degrees to the right. The *customer* was moved to the right side of the diagram so that *processes* now flow from left to right and functional units flow down, as organization charts typically do.

Figure 3.3 provides an idea of how a telecommunications company is organized. In essence, a telecom sells time on its network to customers. Since the time is sold and monitored by means of computers that track phone access, Service and Resource are important functions. Since almost all long-distance phone calls cross multiple networks, arrangements with other telecom companies—partners—are very important. We suspect that actual phone companies might subdivide their departments somewhat differently, placing marketing and service in separate departments, but remember that most phone sales and service requests come in through a common call center, so this high-level grouping works reasonably well. In any case, Figure 3.3 provides an idea of how a group of telecom managers felt they could represent their organizations.

When you look at the modified version of the eTOM diagram (Figure 3.4), it's clear that the three shaded blocks are groups of business processes. Within each group, there are subprocesses. By splitting up the processes in the way they have, it's unclear if Operations represents a value chain or not. The key would be if one could add the costs of all of the processes within the Operations box to determine the total cost and the profit margin on a product line—in this case phone service. If you could, that would mean that everything in the lower two shaded boxes could be grouped together as overhead and assigned to a single value chain—Phone Operations.

A minor difference between Figure 3.4 and the previous TeleManagement framework diagram is that fact that we have inserted a box for the CEO and executive committee and lines to suggest departmental linkages on the diagram. We have also rounded the corners of the boxes representing processes or activities in Figure 3.4. We will discuss specifics of process notation in the next chapter. At this point, it's sufficient to say that we use a standard notation derived from UML, an international notation standard, which is explained in more detail in later chapters. In UML all processes or activities are designated by boxes with rounded corners.

The important thing isn't the notation, however, but the fact that either Figure 3.3 or 3.4 would provide a telecom process architecture committee with an overview of the company. Every business process architecture committee needs something like these figures if they are to have a standard way to describe their company's processes and identify processes that require changes when new strategies and goals are announced.

In fact, a process architecture committee would probably want something a bit more detailed. Figure 3.5 provides the next level of detail provided by the TeleManagement Forum's eTOM model. Once again, we've transposed the subprocesses defined on the more detailed eTOM model to our preferred format. In this case, to simplify things, no subprocesses are shown within the Enterprise Management Processes box or the Strategy, Infrastructure, and Product Processes box. What is shown are the subprocesses that make up the Fulfillment Process, the Assurance Process, the Billing Process, and the Operations Support and Readiness Core Process. In each case the subprocesses have been placed so that you can see which functional area is responsible for the subprocess. Thus the subprocess Order Handling is a subprocess of the Fulfillment Process. Order Handling is administered by the Market, Product, and Customer Relationship Management function. Similarly, Supplier/Partner Settlements and Billing Management is a subprocess occurring within the Billing Process and is administered by the Supplier/Partner Relationship Management department or function.

Notice that some subprocesses occur within multiple processes. These subprocesses are marked with an asterisk to highlight the fact. Thus, the Customer Interface Management—presumably a set of customer portal management activities—is shared by the Fulfillment, Assurance, and Billing processes. Similarly, a Supplier/Partner Interface Management subprocess is shared by these same processes.

If you are not a telecom executive, you might not be familiar with some of the terms used to describe the various subprocesses. The key thing is that this business process architecture illustrates a framework that is detailed enough that a telecom process architecture committee that was familiar with its own organization could be reasonably efficient in determining just which processes or subprocesses would need to be changed to achieve specific changes in company strategy and goals. One could easily imagine an accompanying document that provided short written descriptions of each of the subprocesses.

Figure 3.5 raises two issues that we will consider in more detail later in this book. First, it suggests the possibility of a matrix management system. Someone is usually responsible for complete processes like Fulfillment. That's the person that thinks about how all the subprocesses in Fulfillment work together to deliver services to the customer in a smooth and efficient manner. Someone else is probably responsible for Service Management and Operations. The employees that work on the Service Configuration and Activation subprocess probably report to the Service Management and Operations manager. Thus, one manager works to assure that the complete process works efficiently. Another is responsible for employees

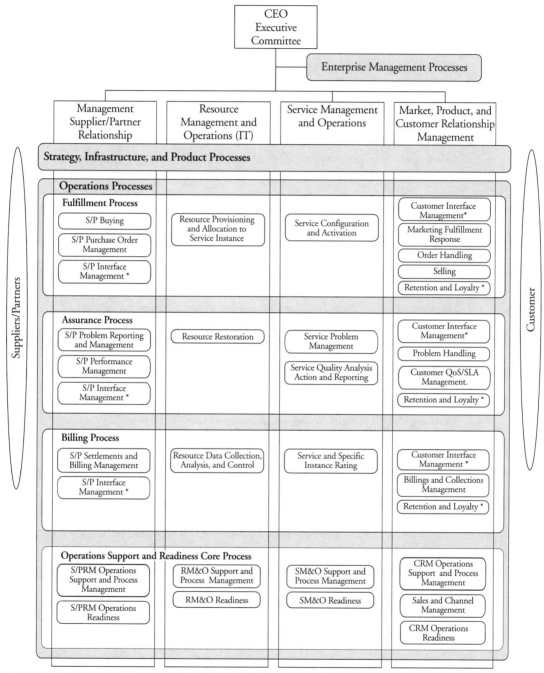

Figure 3.5 A more detailed version of the eTOM business process framework, rotated 90 degrees to the right and modified to conform with our notation.

that perform some of the subprocesses within the Fulfillment process, and within other processes as well. This is complex, but most organizations have learned to make it work, and we'll discuss this in Chapter 7.

The other issue that is obvious when we begin to discuss a framework like eTOM is how many times the word *process* appears. When the chart is as simple as the one in Figure 3.5, we can live with groups of processes, processes, and subprocesses. We have already seen how the ultimate process is a value chain. Most organizations only have a few value chains. We suspect that the entire eTOM framework really only pictures one value chain that delivers telecommunication services to customers.

Types of Processes

Several business process theorists refer to value chains as *core processes* and distinguish between core processes (which embody critical corporate expertise and produce products or services that are delivered to customers) and supplementary processes (which simply facilitate the ongoing operation of the core processes.) (Porter distinguishes between primary processes and secondary processes.) Human resources, senior management functions, and IT processes are all considered supplementary or secondary processes. These processes produce outcomes that become inputs to core processes. In other words, they don't produce outputs that are consumed by customers and generate income. In the TeleManagement Forum framework, Enterprise Management Processes and Strategy, Infrastructure, and Product Lifecycle Management Processes are good examples of supplementary processes. Similarly, one might argue that the Operations Process: Operations Support and Readiness is a supplementary process.

More to the point, almost all of the smaller processes within the Fulfillment, Assurance, and Billing processes don't produce outputs that go directly to customers. We refer to them as subprocesses. As with any hierarchical set of systems, any given system is usually the subprocess of some larger system and is a supersystem of some smaller system it contains. Similarly, if you examine any specific process, then the larger process it contains is the superprocess, and the smaller processes that are contained within the process are subprocesses.

Today, when most analysts use the term *process,* they use it to refer to something like what we called subprocesses in Figure 3.5, or they use it as a generic term to talk about whatever process they are focused on. Earlier we described a *process* as a sequence of activities that achieved a business goal. Some people use the terms *activity* and *process* as synonyms. We prefer to use the term *activity* to refer to the finest-grained process that we intend to include in our models. Processes can usually be broken down, but when you arrive at activities, as we use the term, you arrive at people doing jobs or software components processing information. The key, from our perspective, is that activities are the smallest processes shown on our diagrams. Thus, the key types of processes are the following:

▶ *Value chain.* The largest process we talk about is a value chain. A value chain includes everything between the initiation of the product lifecycle and orders to the sale of the item to customers as well as any support provided after sale. A value chain might be referred to as a core process, but more likely it includes several large processes, just as the eTOM framework includes Fulfillment, Assurance, Billing, and Operations Support within the Operations Process.

▶ *Process.* A process is any subdivision of a value chain. A process is comprised of business processes, which are large-scale processes, subprocesses, and activities. Depending on the complexity of the value chain or core process being analyzed, there may be many layers of sub- and subsubprocesses. Some analysts prefer "task" instead of subsubprocess.

▶ *Activity.* At some point, any modeling activity must stop. For our purposes, the smallest process that we show in our models is an activity. Activities may be large or complex chunks of performance that, for whatever reason, we have no need to analyze further in our models. Or they may be very discrete bits of performance, which we term *atomic activities.* In many cases, we will stop subdividing our processes, and then proceed to create textual descriptions of what occurs within a given activity.

Some analysts represent levels of processes in a hierarchy. We've provided a generic diagram of such a hierarchy with the nomenclature we normally use in Figure 3.6.

To sum up, the process architecture committee should develop a high-level model of the company that allows the committee to identify specific processes that will need to be changed to implement some new strategy or goal. The process they decide to change, may, in the opinion of those who are more familiar with it, be made up of still other subprocesses, and the process redesign team may drill down and isolate sub- or subsubprocesses to modify.

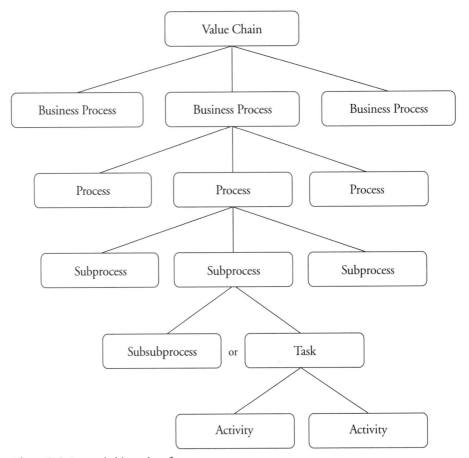

Figure 3.6 A generic hierarchy of processes.

Deciding What Kind of Process Change Effort to Undertake

Assuming your company's process architecture committee has a good description of your company's major processes, it must still decide what to do when it receives suggestions from the strategy or executive committee. Today, there are lots of different approaches one can take to process improvement. Without trying to exhaust the list, here are some of the major options:

▶ *Redesign.* This is a major analysis of the existing process followed by a redesign effort that should significantly improve the process. This kind of effort typically results in changed job descriptions and the introduction of some automation.

▶ *Automation.* This can be used in conjunction with process redesign, or it can be an independent effort to automate a specific process or activity. There are different techniques available, including workflow engines, packaged applications (ERP, CRM), and software development.

▶ *Improvement.* This is a more focused effort aimed at incrementally improving an existing process. This can be an effort a manager undertakes, or an effort undertaken by an improvement team. If the latter, it can use informal means or it can use a formal approach, like Six Sigma.

▶ *Management.* Rather than focusing on changing a process as such, one can focus on changing the way managers measure and control the process. This usually requires a management redesign or improvement effort and is often done in conjunction with a process redesign effort.

▶ *Outsourcing.* Although not a process redesign or improvement effort as such, one can sometimes decide that a process would be better run and managed if it were subcontracted to an organization that specializes in performing that kind of process.

Any of these efforts could be employed by a company considering incorporating the Internet, email, or the Web into their processes.

We'll consider each of these possibilities in more detail later in the book. At this point, however, we want to suggest a general way of thinking about these options. Figure 3.7 is a process-strategy matrix that process architecture groups can use to classify business processes. On one axis of the matrix, we consider the complexity and dynamics of the process, and on the other we consider the strategic importance of the process.

When we speak of process complexity and dynamics, we ask what types of tasks are involved in the process. Are we talking about something like sorting the mail, which is a reasonably straightforward procedure, with perhaps a few rules for handling cases when employees have left or work at home? Or are we talking about an international delivery process that involves lots of rules for dealing with different country policies, tariffs, and address systems? Or are we talking about a process that includes negotiating terms for international credit lines with Fortune 1000 companies? (To simplify things, when you think about complexity, don't ask if it could be automated, but only ask what would be involved if a human were to do the job.) Dynamics refers to the fact that some processes don't change very often, while others keep changing rapidly in response to changes in the market or regulations. Imagine, for example, being a member of an international bank loan team, whose process includes an activity that assigns risk premiums.

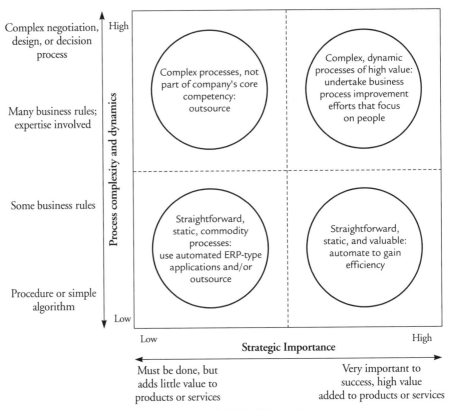

Figure 3.7 Process analysis based on complexity and strategic importance.

On the horizontal axis, we simply ask how much value the process contributes to the products or services the company sells. Is the process a core competency of your company, or simply an enabling process that needs to be accomplished to assure that you can do something else that really makes you money?

Now consider the kinds of processes we find in the four quadrants defined by our two axes. In the lower left, we have processes that must be done, but add little value, and are basically straightforward procedures. These are tasks that we want to automate in the most efficient possible way.

Processes that fall in the lower-right quadrant are high-value processes that are straightforward. An assembly process may be straightforward and involve few decisions, but the process results in the product that the company sells, and hence is very important. You want to automate these, if at all possible, to reduce costs and to gain efficiency.

Processes that lie in the upper-left quadrant are complex processes that have to be done, but don't add much direct value to your company's product or services.

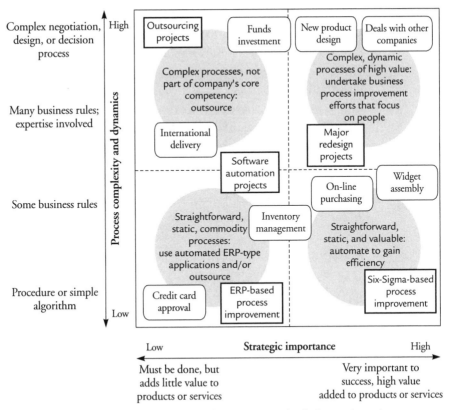

Figure 3.8 The process-strategy matrix with processes and solution options shown.

They just cause problems if they aren't done, and they are complex enough that they may be hard to automate. In most cases, these are processes that you should probably consider outsourcing to another company that specializes in doing this type of process.

Finally there are the processes at the top right that are high value and complex. They often involve human expertise—processes like new product design or negotiating partnerships—and are hard to automate.

Obviously one company's strategic process is another company's routine process. Company A may only worry about manufacturing the best widgets. For Company A, shipping is simply a process that needs to occur to assure that widgets get to customers in a timely manner. For Company B, a shipping company, their core competency is efficient, on-time deliveries. That's how they make their money. For Company B, delivery operations are a strategic process.

In Figure 3.8 we have shown some processes, based on the assumption that the processes all belong to a small hardware manufacturer, Widgets Inc. All of the processes shown in Figure 3.8 need to be done. If they don't need to be done, they have no place on the matrix. But of the processes shown, partnership deals and new product designs are really important. Widget assembly is about in the middle. Online purchasing is important but routine. International delivery is complex, but doesn't add much value; funds investment is important, but not something the company managers have any expertise in. And credit card approvals are routine.

Overlaid on the matrix are some suggestions about where major solution options are normally employed.

▶ For routine processes that you want to automate as quickly and efficiently as possible, off-the-shelf software is ideal.
▶ For complex processes that are tangential to your business, outsourcing is a popular solution.
▶ For important processes that are well understood, software development or off-the-shelf solutions are popular. You might use workflow to automate a document-oriented process, or buy a CRM package to provide sales tracking. Similarly you might undertake a Six Sigma improvement effort to assure that the process is as consistent as possible.
▶ The most important processes, however, are those that fall in the upper right. Some you can't automate at all and must simply support with education and software tools like spreadsheets and email. The important thing, however, is that these are your core processes, those that add the most value and define your company. They are the processes it is worth analyzing and redesigning very carefully. These are often processes that involve complex employee interactions that you can't automate but need to make as efficient as possible.

We'll return to the issues we have raised here. The important thing is that the process architecture committee should have some idea of the complexity and the value of processes so that they will, in turn, have some idea of priorities and the most cost-effective approach to take if a specific process needs improvement.

The Process Architecture and IT Planning

In addition to maintaining an overview of the processes that make up an organization, the process architecture group also needs to maintain a liaison with the IT organization, in order to help IT anticipate and prepare for new initiatives that may come from process improvement projects. This is represented by the lower arrow in Figure 3.1.

Most corporate IT organizations have their own strategy and planning groups. Many create their own enterprise architecture models to define the infrastructure they provide. Most probably do not organize their architecture or infrastructure models so that they are closely tied to business processes. The existence of corporate process architecture groups should change that. Once the business managers define the company's business processes, then IT should organize its own model to reflect that organization. Thereafter, IT managers ought to work closely with the process architecture committee to assure that process changes and priorities are closely coordinated with IT efforts.

Figure 3.9 illustrates a different kind of matrix. Most IT organizations conceptualize their infrastructures in terms of a series of layers. In Figure 3.9 we've shown the IT layers as horizontal bars. In this case we show business processes as vertical bars intersecting with the various IT layers. In the various intersections, we've noted the platforms (hardware and operating systems) and databases involved in supporting each process. Once again, this is a simple version just to provide an overview of the approach. Our hypothetical company is a small bank. We have only indicated a few processes and a few possible requirements.

There's nothing special about this view of IT infrastructure, and there are many other views, including more expanded versions of each of the layers shown in Figure 3.9. One might have an entire diagram just mapping the software interfaces and the middleware used to link applications across processes. Similarly, more complex diagrams are needed when one seeks to link processes running at different companies on different platforms into a common supply chain system.

Imagine that our bank didn't offer any online service and decided to offer it. In effect, there would have been no column for network servers and no online access applications. Then imagine that the corporate strategy committee decided that it was important that the company develop an online presence and allow customers to obtain information and transfer funds online. In other words, the strategy committee hands the process architecture committee a new goal: support online customer account access and transfers. The process architecture committee would need to consider each process that might need to be changed to achieve this goal. Corporate investing wouldn't need to be changed. Individual checking would. Auto loans might, depending on whether the committee committed to allowing direct transfers from checking accounts to auto loan accounts, or simply decided to let customers send transfer payments to the auto loan department. In the latter case, from the auto loan department's perspective, payments would still arrive as checks.

The key thing is that before our bank decided to support online transfers, it didn't need any of the IT infrastructure necessary to support online account access.

	Process: individual checking	Process: corporate investing	Process: auto loans	
Platform: desktop	Teller terminals Platform setup stations ATM terminals	Invester terminals	Teller terminals Platform setup stations ATM terminals	Storage: local drive
Platform: network servers	Online account access		Online account access	Storage: file and print
Platform: application servers	ATM stations		ATM stations	Storage: databases
Platform: midrange systems			Auto loan system and database Sun Unix	Storage: databases
Platform: mainframes	Checking account system and database IBM 360	Corporate portfolio tracking system		Storage: databases
	Process requirements: 24 x 7 x 365 availability, zero downtime	Process requirements: 24 x 7 availability, zero downtime	Process requirements: 24 x 7 x 330 availability, 2-hour downtime	

Figure 3.9 A process-IT matrix.

Our bank didn't need Internet servers to handle customer's access, or the network that could route information from legacy checking and savings systems to the Internet server. It takes time to develop an IT infrastructure. In many cases, 60% to 80% of the effort on a new application development project goes into infrastructure development. Thus, it's important that IT know when to prepare to support new initiatives that will require new infrastructure.

In too many organizations, infrastructure issues are associated with and charged to specific projects. This isn't a very rational procedure. It would be as if we charged a specific company that seeks to ship by train for the entire cost of the rail roadbeds. When you develop infrastructure for a specific project, you tend to get constrained infrastructure designs. Increasingly, companies need common infrastructures designed for long-term flexibility. They should be designed independent of any specific project and be designed to support the implementation of a business strategy, not a specific project. We suggest that major infrastructure issues be handled on an enterprise basis via the process architecture committee or some similar mechanism.

The Process Architecture Process

Let's see if we can pull this all together. Although the details will vary from company to company, every organization ought to have a group that is responsible for keeping track of the organization's process architecture. That group should have some means of picturing the value chains and business processes that make up the organization. They should document the corporate goals and how each value chain and business process contributes to the achievement of the corporate goals.

As the goals change, this process architecture group should assess the impact of the changes on each of the processes and determine which processes need to be changed. They should also decide on a general approach for changing each process. If specific process changes will call for a different or expanded communication or computer infrastructure, then the group should work with IT to get the new infrastructure in place before applications are created that demand the new infrastructure.

Once the process architecture group knows about the scope and nature of the changes that will be needed to implement the organization's new goals, then it should prioritize the effort. Redesign efforts are major undertakings that require lots of senior management attention and should be planned according. Several

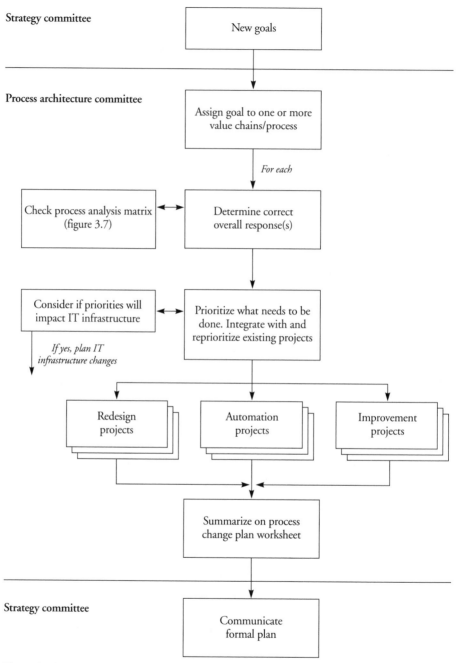

Figure 3.10 An overview of the process architecture process.

Goals, Processes, and Projects Worksheet					
Priority	Goal/Measure	Value Chain/Process Affected	Process/Subprocess Affected	Changes Needed	Change Plan
1	Create Web site and obtain 20% of industry Web sales in next 12 months.	Widget Value Chain/ Order Fulfillment Business Process	Sales Order Process	Create Web site. Develop strategy to get customers to use Web site. Change Sales Order Process to support Web sales.	Web site creation: Automation Project— assign to IT Sales Orders Process redesign: Redesign— assign to Widget Value Chain sponsor, ask her to create a redesign team.
		Widget Value Chain/ Finance and Billing Process	Order and Billing Process	Modify credit and billing process so it can be done online as customer is at Web site.	Software credit approval system to support Web site. Buy existing package or develop software to do this. Redesign—assign to Widget Value Chain sponsor, ask her to create a redesign team.
2	Create email system to get responses to customers faster.	Widget Value Chain/ Customer Support Process	Customer Support Process	Install email server in service area and train service people to use email.	Process improvement, job redesign, and training. Have service process manager undertake this in conjunction with IT and HR.

Figure 3.11 A worksheet for prioritizing process changes that flow from a new or changed corporate goal.

simultaneously. IT organizations often complain that they are given too many projects and too little guidance about the priorities of the projects they are assigned. The process architecture group ought to introduce order into organizational planning and guarantee that new processes remain aligned with new organizational goals.

Figure 3.10 provides an overview of the steps that a process architecture group might go through to arrive at a plan.

Some process architecture groups may find the task easier if they use worksheets similar to the one we've reproduced as Figure 3.11. In essence, the worksheet allows process architecture group members to organize the priority and change information all in one place.

The worksheet can provide a quick summary of the current process changes being undertaken at the company, or as the basis for a formal presentation or plan, which the process architecture group will probably have to develop for the organization's steering committee.

From Strategy Statements to Models

When we discussed strategy, we observed the sometimes vague statements that CEOs and strategy committees make. They state goals, intentions, and desired outcomes rather than practices or specific changes in processes. It is the goal of the process architecture committee, in conjunction with specific process redesign teams, to translate general goals into specific models and precise recipes for change.

Before we consider exactly how that can be done, however, we need to agree on some common ways to model organizations and processes. Once we have established some modeling techniques, we will return to the specifics involved in assigning requirements to processes and in redesigning process.

II

MODELING ORGANIZATIONS AND PROCESSES

I**N THIS PART** we will review the basic concepts and the graphical symbols that are used to describe organizations and processes. These basic modeling techniques are used in all of the various process change methodologies.

In most cases, we don't expect readers to have to draw the diagrams we describe. Usually individuals will use software tools specially designed to create organization and process diagrams. Most business architecture committees will have an individual with such responsibilities. In business process redesign, managers will generally work with a facilitator, who will actually create the diagrams on a blackboard or large sheets of paper. The facilitator will be supported by an analyst or scribe who will actually create the diagrams using a software tool.

What is important is that managers be able to read these diagrams. Organization and process diagrams are a way of documenting and communicating basic information about how a company is organized. Not being able to read these diagrams is equivalent to not being able to read financial statements: the manager has no way to gain a quick understanding of an important aspect of the business.

Diagrams, especially diagrams describing business processes and software systems, can become very complex. Some use dozens of symbols in order to describe how a computer would process each given activity. Our diagrams are considerably simpler. They use a very limited set of symbols and they focus on issues that managers are concerned with. Thus, we focus on how the business interacts with customers and which managers are responsible for which specific subprocesses and activities.

We've tried to make this part of the book as simple as possible. On the other hand, as with financial statements, it can't be too simple or it will omit important details.

In Chapter 4 we will consider basic diagrams that can be used to describe organizations, their relationships with the outside world, and their relationships with internal processes.

In Chapter 5 we will consider diagrams that can be used to describe processes.

In Chapter 6 we will consider diagrams and techniques that are appropriate for the description of specific activities.

4

Modeling Organizations

I N CHAPTER 1 we described how organizations can be conceptualized in terms of three levels. At the highest level, we think of an organization as a whole, how it relates to its environment, what divisions it consists of, and how its major processes are organized. This chapter focuses on modeling and understanding complete organizations.

The Traditional View of an Organization

In *Improving Performance,* Rummler and Brache provide a nice example of the distinction between the thinking of those who rely on organization charts and those who focus on processes. As they explain it, when asked to describe their organizations, most managers will draw something like the traditional organization chart shown in Figure 4.1. In some cases they will simply give the various groups or departments names: marketing, production, and so forth. In other cases they will detail who manages each department and to whom they report. This kind of information is often useful, of course. But it's important to notice what kinds of information a traditional organization chart doesn't provide.

First, an organization chart doesn't show the customers. Equally important, it doesn't show the products and services the company provides to customers, or where the resources needed to create the products and services come from in the first place. It certainly doesn't show how work flows from one activity to another before ultimately being delivered to a customer.

A manager might reply that an organization chart isn't expected to show such things, and we'd agree. Then we'd ask our manager to show us whatever charts he

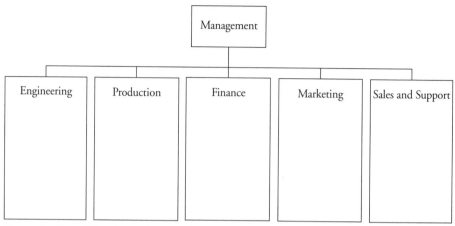

Figure 4.1 A traditional organization chart.

or she uses that do show those things. Most managers aren't prepared to create or show diagrams that provide a systems or process-oriented view of their organizations.

Traditional organizational charts are often described as a vertical view of the organization. The departments or functional groups within a department are referred to as "silos," similar to the tall, windowless grain silos one sees in farming regions. When managers conceptualize their organizations as vertical organizations, they tend to manage in a vertical manner. They focus on who reports to whom, and set goals for each group independent of the others. At the same time, *silo thinking* leads managers to focus on making their departments as efficient as possible, without much regard to what's going on in other silos. When cross-departmental issues arise, they tend to get bounced up the reporting chain till they reach a manager who is responsible for the work done in both departments. That, in turn, guarantees that senior managers spend lots of time resolving cross-functional or interdepartmental problems that could have been better resolved at a lower level by people who understood the specific problem much better. And, of course, the time that senior managers use for resolving these cross-functional disputes is time they don't have to focus on customer concerns, creating new strategies, or improving productivity.

This problem has been widely discussed since the late 1980s. Many books have been written about the problem. Silo thinking tends to lead to departmental or functional optimization. This often occurs at the expense of the whole organization. An obvious example would be a sales department that gets praised for selling products that production can't deliver in time to meet the delivery dates promised by the salespeople. Or it could be an engineering department that creates a product that is very efficient to manufacture, but doesn't quite have the feature set that marketing has promised or that salespeople can most readily sell.

Managers, like all people, tend to think in terms of their models. Physicians have a saying that, during diagnosis, physicians only find what they are looking for. Managers are the same way. To think of organizations as wholes, managers need to learn to visualize their organizations with diagrams that provide insight into how their organizations actually work. They need to think in terms of organizational systems and processes rather than thinking entirely in terms of divisions, departments, or their own functional group.

This book was written to help managers think strategically and holistically about businesses and processes. Thus, in this chapter, we will introduce some diagrams that provide a more complete view of how a company works and how a process can be analyzed. The details of diagramming may be tedious to some readers, but we urge you to make the effort. These models, ultimately, lead to new ways of thinking about your organization and how it works. We'll rely on the concepts implicit in these diagrams throughout the remainder of the book.

The Systems View of an Organization

One alternative to viewing an organization in terms of its departments and reporting relationships is to conceptualize an organization as a system that responds to inputs and generates outputs. This view is often referred to as a *horizontal* or *systems view* of the organization. Figure 4.2 illustrates a horizontal view of an organization. In this case we provide a very high-level systems view of a hypothetical restaurant, called San Francisco Seafood (SF Seafood).

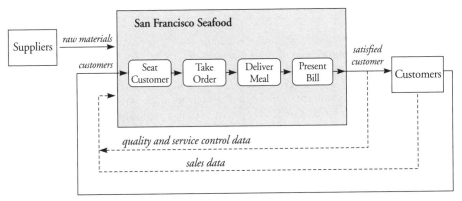

Figure 4.2 A systems view of SF Seafood.

The organization illustrated in Figure 4.2 is at such a high level of abstraction that it could be any organization. Much that could have been added has been omitted to simplify this diagram. The important thing to note is that this view provides us with lots of information that we don't get from an organization chart. First, it shows customers, products, and suppliers. Second, it shows what work actually occurs. And, third, it gives us an idea of how things are connected and flow from one thing to another—how raw materials flow to meals and how data about customer satisfaction flows back to the organization.

A systems view emphasizes process and connections, and ultimately adaptation. What would happen if the bar was closed for a period of time? You'd need to stop some supplies. You'd lose some customers. A systems diagram provides a snapshot of your organization and how it works.

Models and Diagrams

In this book we will use two broad classes of diagrams: *organization diagrams* and *process diagrams.* In this chapter we want to define the basic notation used for organization diagrams.[1]

As we have suggested, many different groups are involved in business process modeling. Predictably, different groups use different types of diagrams. Even within a relatively well-defined community, like workflow software vendors, a dozen different notations are used. Some of the notations are very different from one another, stressing very different ways to view organizations or processes. Some notations differ on such trivial matters as whether a process should be represented as a rectangle or a rectangle with rounded corners.

---

[1] Throughout the book we will use the terms *diagram* and *model* interchangeably to refer to graphical collections of boxes and arrows that convey an image of an organization or a process. Strictly speaking, a diagram is an informal collection of boxes and arrows, while a model is something more formal. A model ought to relate things in such a way that we can test assumptions about how the relationships would function in specific instances. We will see later that some diagrams can be assigned values, and simulations can be run to determine how the process will function under certain circumstances. Thus, a simulation is both a diagram and a model that we can test. In the remainder of this chapter and the next, however, we ask our readers to ignore this distinction and allow us to use both terms interchangeably to refer to pictures of graphical elements and relationships that illustrate organizations or process.

We have been active in a recent effort on the part of the Object Management Group (an international standards organization), the Workflow Management Coalition, and the Business Process Management Initiative to arrive at a common notation. The three groups weren't able to agree before this book went to press. It seems likely that they will eventually arrive at a common notation that is a subset of the Object Management Group's Unified Modeling Language (UML). Even then, many vendors will continue to support their own proprietary notations.

In this book we have tried to use a very simple set of notational elements to keep the diagramming process simple. In general we have conformed to appropriate UML 2.0 diagramming standards. The UML notation is discussed in more detail in Chapter 13. Our goal has been to provide the reader with the minimum set of notational elements needed to model organizations and processes.

The key thing to think about in selecting any notation is who is going to use it. We assume that the diagrams used in this book will be read by managers. They may also be used by software developers, but software developers are not our primary audience. Hence, we have constrained the type of things we describe in diagrams to the things most managers are interested in, and omitted notation that is only used to describe software conventions. Further, although we recommend the use of software diagramming tools for some purposes, we assume that many managers will create diagrams of their organizations and processes on drawing pads, blackboards, or relatively simple diagramming tools, like Visio or Powerpoint. Hence, we have made every effort to use simple, easy-to-understand conventions.

We started with the diagrams used in the book *Improving Performance,* by Geary Rummler and Alan Brache. We chose this book because it is almost universally regarded as the best process modeling book for business managers. Many of the software analysts we respect recommend this book as the best introduction to business process modeling. *Improving Performance* was written in 1990. It was written before the Object Management Group standardized on UML, and before companies were as automated as they are now. Hence, we have modified the Rummler-Brache notation to conform to UML (e.g., activities are represented by rectangles with rounded corners). And we have extended the Rummler-Brache notation to provide a better way of describing software systems and automated processes and activities.

Our goal was to arrive at a way of describing organizations and business processes that is as easy to understand as possible, while still making it possible to describe all of the basics that need to be described. In this chapter, as we describe the notation, we will not consider how it might be implemented in a software tool. Several tools, however, implement notations very similar to the one we use, and thus, in later chapters we will show how software tools can be used in process redesign to simplify the creation of organization and business process diagrams. At this point, however, we only want to provide readers with the basic notational elements necessary to draw models of their organizations and business processes.

Organization Diagrams

Organization diagrams are an extension of systems diagrams that are modified so that they can be used to describe the basic structure of an organization, the relationship of the organization to its external environment, and the relationships among the departmental units within the organization. In some cases they may also show the basic processes used by the organization and how those processes relate to the basic departmental units.

Figure 4.3 provides a high-level picture of an organization. Rummler and Brache refer to this diagram as a *supersystem diagram* to emphasize that it focuses on what happens outside the organization rather than on what occurs inside. This is the kind of diagram a strategy committee might use to picture the relationships between your organization and those it depends upon.

Since we are concerned with both the use of the diagrams and notation, there are two ways we could describe this diagram. We could describe what it shows, or we could focus on the generic use of boxes and arrows. We'll begin with a description of what the diagram pictures and then discuss the notation that is used.

The shaded square in the center represents the organization. We don't show any internal detail, since we want to focus on the inputs and outputs of the organization.

Suppliers of all kinds, including vendors who supply materials, research organizations that supply new technology, capital markets that supply capital, and labor markets that supply employees, are shown on the left of the business. In later diagrams, to simply things, we will often just have a single tall rectangle to the left of the organization box, and label it *Resources* or *Suppliers*.

Customers and shareholders are listed on the right. Customers order and receive products and services. Shareholders receive information and dividends. In other versions of the organization diagram, we will often place a single rectangle to the right of the organization box and label it *Customers* or *Market* to further simplify the diagram.

Below the company box, we have a rectangle for competitors, companies that compete with the organization for inputs from suppliers and for customers.

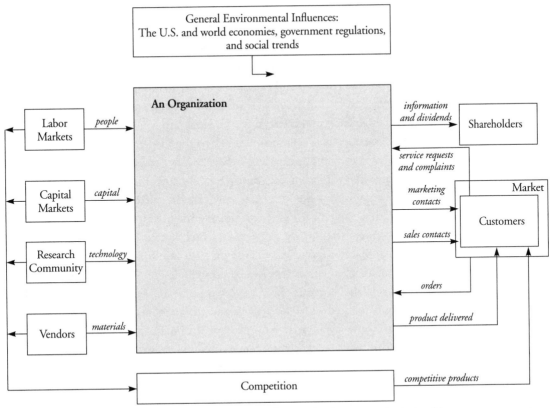

Figure 4.3 A supersystem diagram of an organization that emphasizes external relationships.

Above the company box we have a rectangle that includes more generic environmental impacts on the business. These could include government regulations, changes in the economy, or changes in popular taste. (The small right-angle arrow below the environmental influences rectangle indicates that this box would have arrows leading to a number of other rectangles. To keep things simple, when we don't want to show all the relationships, we use the small right-angle arrow. This special arrow means that this affects many other boxes on the diagram in complex ways.)

The detail one provides on this diagram depends on the purpose it is being used for. In strategy discussions, it is often important to show specific types of customers, specific suppliers, and even particular competitors. Later, when one is primarily focused on the relationships between departments and on analyzing internal processes, the external details can be removed to better focus the discussion.

We believe that the organization diagram shown in Figure 4.3 can be used to describe every possible type of organization, including monopolies and government entities. Indeed, we have used these diagrams during consulting engagements with all of these types of organizations. The names may change a little, but all organizations are systems, and they must all obtain supplies and generate products or services, just as they all have some kind of competition and operate under some general environmental constraints.

Now let's consider Figure 4.3 as a generic type of diagram. A UML modeler would refer to the diagram as a *class diagram.* It shows relationships between classes of things like your company, suppliers, and customers.

Classes or organizational entities are represented by boxes or rectangles. Classes are labeled with a name or phrase placed inside the box. Classes can contain other classes. As a generalization, the higher-level box is defined by what it contains. Thus, we have placed a box for *customer* inside a box for *market* to indicate that markets are made up of customers. We could include the names of divisions or departments inside the company box. That would be the equivalent of saying that the company is made up of its divisions and departments. Similarly, at times we might want to show several major suppliers within the supplier box.

Relationships between classes are represented by arrows. In many cases the relationships involve the transfer of items from one class to another. When it's useful we place labels over the arrows to show what is passed from one class to another. The arrowheads show the direction of the flow. Some analysts allow arrows with arrowheads on both ends, indicating that things flow both ways. We don't disallow it, but, in general, we recommend that separate arrows be used to indicate flows in both directions, as we have used to show the relationships between the organization and customers. We prefer this because it's easier to label the arrows and keep track of what's going if you use each arrow to represent a single major flow. Thus, in some cases we will show two arrows going from one box to another to indicate two major, more or less independent relationships between the two entities. Others find this awkward and put multiple labels on a single arrow.

Figure 4.4 shows how a high-level organization diagram can be used to summarize information about environmental issues that a strategy committee was concerned with. In Figure 4.4 the concerns are general. In effect, we have simply reproduced Porter's five forces model (Figure 2.2) as an organization diagram, while adding an additional note about the problem of finding skilled employees for certain tasks. A specific company, considering specific strategy changes, might find it useful to detail the suppliers or competitors and make notes on a wide variety of specific threats or opportunities.

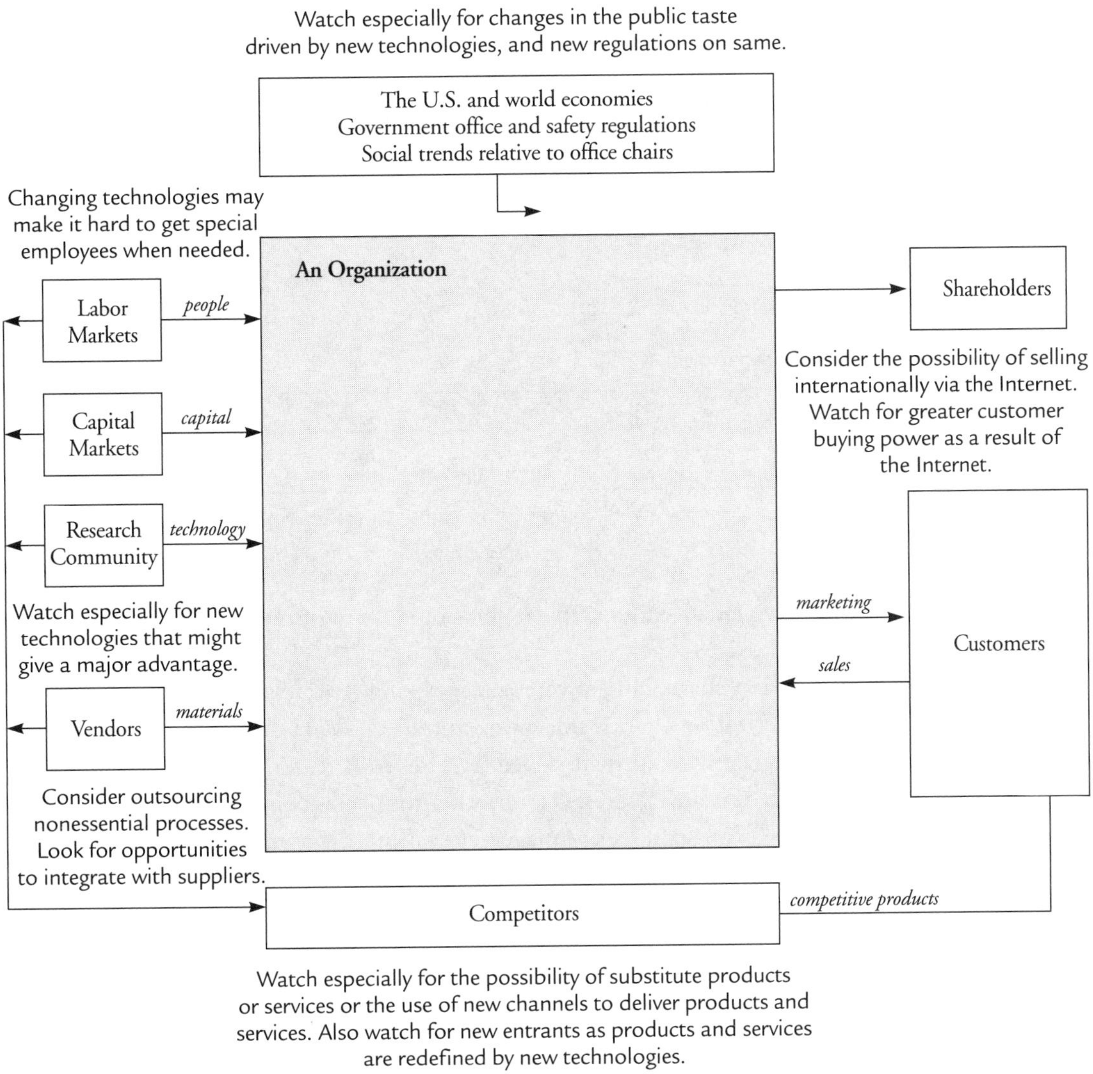

Watch especially for changes in the public taste
driven by new technologies, and new regulations on same.

The U.S. and world economies
Government office and safety regulations
Social trends relative to office chairs

Changing technologies may
make it hard to get special
employees when needed.

An Organization

Shareholders

Consider the possibility of selling
internationally via the Internet.
Watch for greater customer
buying power as a result of
the Internet.

Labor
Markets   *people*

Capital
Markets   *capital*

Research
Community   *technology*

Watch especially for new
technologies that might
give a major advantage.

marketing

sales

Customers

Vendors   *materials*

Consider outsourcing
nonessential processes.
Look for opportunities
to integrate with suppliers.

Competitors   *competitive products*

Watch especially for the possibility of substitute products
or services or the use of new channels to deliver products and
services. Also watch for new entrants as products and services
are redefined by new technologies.

Figure 4.4 A high-level organization diagram with a list of some strategic concerns.

From a notational perspective, the only difference between this diagram and the one in Figure 4.1 is the addition of free-floating text *notes,* which one can always add to a diagram.

Figure 4.5 presents a high-level organization diagram with an organization chart pictured inside the organization box. The ability to show functional units, like departments or divisions, has led some to refer to organization diagrams as function diagrams. In this case we simply show five departments and hint at the

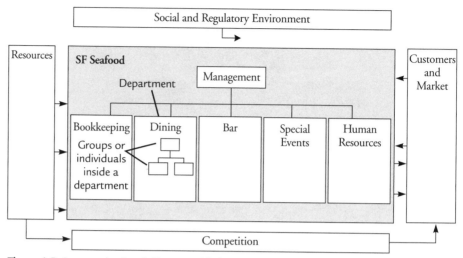

Figure 4.5 An organizational diagram with functional units or departments shown.

fact that if you had enough space you could show some of the finer structure within specific departments.

Organization charts can get very complex, and it's rarely useful to try to place a detailed organization chart inside an organization diagram as we do in Figure 4.5. It's usually better to keep them separate. The main reason one might want to do this is to represent how processes intersect with specific functional or departmental groups, as we saw in the TeleManagement Forum diagrams in Chapter 3. In that case, however, the TeleManagement Forum analysts limited themselves to four very large functional groups.

In passing, notice that when we mix organization charts and organization diagrams, we introduce a new kind of relationship—a line without an arrowhead. In effect, this relationship defines the inheritance or delegation of authority, and not any specific flow of information, money, or material between the entities. The VP of marketing, represented in this simple diagram by the *marketing* department, reports to the CEO or executive committee represented by the class labeled *management*. We hardly ever attach labels to lines that show authority or reporting relationships.

In most cases it will be more useful to represent the departments or functional groups as classes and show the flow relationships between them, as we have in Figure 4.6. In this case we picture another hypothetical organization, Ergonomic Systems, a manufacturer of high-tech office furniture.

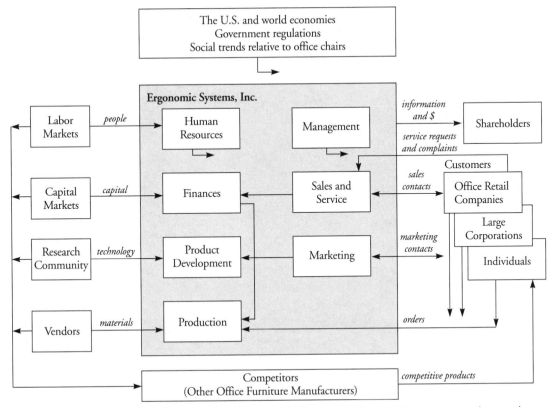

Figure 4.6 An organization diagram showing the relationships between internal departments and external entities.

From a descriptive perspective, Figure 4.6 makes it possible to show specific relationships between external entities and internal functions. To make the company's markets a little more precise, we have indicated three general classes of customers, office retailers, large corporations, and individuals, each with rather different expectations.

From a notational perspective, we have allowed ourselves to overlap the customer boxes to save some space. We have also allowed ourselves to show an arrow from marketing that doesn't touch any specific customer box but simply points in their direction to avoid multiple arrows and crossing arrows, which are always a bit confusing. Similarly, we have used the small, bent arrow to show that *human resources* and *management* would have multiple lines going to many different company departments. We wanted to show management and human resources in this

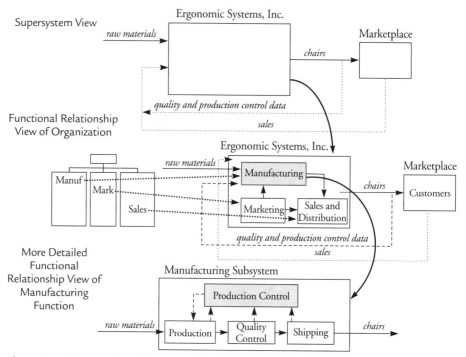

Figure 4.7 An illustration of how you can create successive organization diagrams to provide more detail.

diagram for completeness, but we didn't want to show all the detailed connections between these classes and the other functions within the company.

Just as we inserted departmental boxes inside our company box, we could show subfunctions inside the internal functions we show in Figure 4.6. If this is taken very far, it quickly results in diagrams that are too complex to read or print. It's usually best to limit high-level organization diagrams to showing major departments and, in some cases, the major functions within departments. (That would be showing three levels of detail: The company box, the departmental boxes within the company box, and one set of functional units within the departmental boxes.) If you need to show more detail, you should create a new organizational diagram that only focuses on a single department or unit within the department and then drills down from that level. Figure 4.7 shows how you can create a series of organizational diagrams, each focused on a more detailed level of analysis.

This underlines another key point. The object of our exercise is to analyze an organization and its key relationships; it isn't to create a single, all-encompassing diagram. In most cases an analysis of an organization will be made up of several diagrams. In other words, the goal is to analyze an organization by means of a set of diagrams, not a single diagram. One key to making the resulting set of diagrams more useful is to take care to use the same names for the same entities or classes as you move from one diagram to the next. This makes it much easier for everyone involved to quickly see how one diagram relates to another.

Managing multiple diagrams is much easier if you use a sophisticated software diagramming tool. Unlike simple tools that simply create stand-alone diagrams, sophisticated tools save information in a database and can manage complex relationships between diagrams. Using a sophisticated tool, like the ones we will consider in Chapter 17, you can create a high-level diagram, and then "mouse click" on a box and open a new diagram showing the boxes that are contained within the box shown on the higher-level diagram. A good tool can manage several levels of detail, so you always start with a high-level model and then just "click" your way down to the level of detail you are interested in.

Our goal in a business process analysis effort is not to define departmental units, as such. It's to describe processes, which we will consider in Chapter 5. To really understand and manage processes, however, we need to know which departmental units and managers or supervisors are responsible for each activity in our process. Thus, in effect, functional or organizational analysis and process analysis go hand in hand. In most cases companies have better-defined organizational charts than process charts. The reporting relationships of managers are usually spelled out in considerable detail, so one doesn't need to do as much to identify all of the organizational and functional levels. In any case, as we shall see in a moment, one can usually keep track of the more detailed functional units with process diagrams.

Organization Diagrams and Processes

In addition to using organization diagrams to identify external entities and to document the organizational departments or units that comprise your organization, you can also use organizational diagrams to illustrate the high-level processes your organization supports.

Figure 4.8 shows a diagram that mixes a high-level organization diagram and a high-level process diagram. Recall that we said that processes come in three varieties. Large-scale processes that include all subprocesses that contribute, in any way,

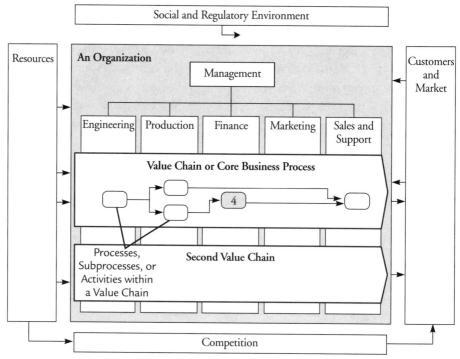

Figure 4.8 A high-level organization chart showing an organization chart and two business processes.

to the production of the product or service line are termed value chains. Recall Porter's diagram of a value chain in Chapter 1 (Figure 1.2). The most generic and comprehensive process supported by any organization is the value chain.

The key to understanding a value chain is to think of it in accounting terms. Suppose you wanted to know if it was worthwhile for a company to produce a specific line of products. Conventional financial statements might not provide much help. If you used an approach known as *activity-based costing* (ABC), you could arrive at your answer. To use activity-based costing, however, you would have to start with a value chain. In effect, you would work back from the products produced and check each step that went into their production. You would add all the costs of production and the resources consumed to arrive at the gross cost of the products. You would also need to add all the overhead costs, including a percent of the HR and IT budgets and some executive time, to arrive at a really comprehensive description of the costs. By subtracting the actual costs from the income received from selling the products, you would know how profitable the product line was.

Consider how different activity or process costing is from traditional budgets that allocate money to departments or functions. Looking at the activities that occur within a given department will never tell you if the product is making the company a profit. All they will tell you is the cost of the activities that occur within a single department. Manufacturing may be performing well and producing the product for very little money. Sales, however, may find that the product is hard to sell and may be offering incentives and discounts that result in the product actually selling for less than it costs to manufacture. It's very difficult using traditional accounting to account for the costs of delays when orders or products are passed from one department to another. Only an analysis that starts from orders and runs through to deliveries can tell you how efficient a given value chain really is. Moreover, to be really accurate, the activity analysis needs to include all of the support, overhead, and infrastructure costs associated with the order fulfillment process. The cost of designing the initial product must be included. The cost of providing employees for the fulfillment and support processes must be included, and so forth. If the TeleManagement Forum considers the processes they illustrated in their model as all contributing to a single product line—telecommunication connections for companies or individuals—then every process they included in their eTOM diagram, including both support and management overhead, would all need to be included to determine the final cost of producing the service. In effect, all the processes shown in the eTOM diagram would be included as parts of a single value chain.

Most companies talk about value chains in terms of product or service lines. Obviously you can use the term "product line" more or less broadly. You could suggest that an organization that produces a variety of chairs had a separate value chain for each of the chairs it produces. Or you could group all the chains together and say the organization has a major value chain that produces chairs. In general, it's best to lump similar products together to keep things simple. If you do lump products together, then most organizations only have a few value chains.

In the early 1990s, when Business Process Reengineering (BPR) was popular, organizations put a lot of effort into defining their value chains. We won't put so much emphasis on it in this book, but it's always important to define boundaries so that an analysis effort won't get out of hand and keep expanding. That's why we recommend that a process architecture committee maintain a high-level *value chain diagram* that shows all of the core business processes your organization supports. Then, when you decide to alter a process, you can be specific about which value chain will be affected.

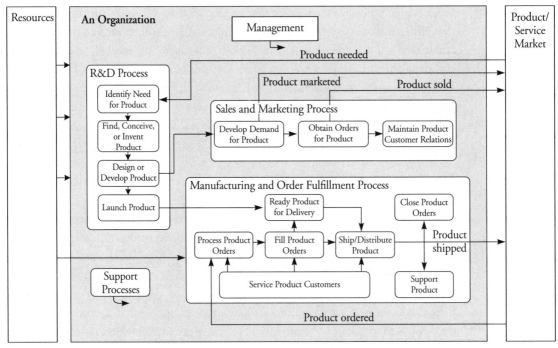

Figure 4.9 An organization diagram with major processes and sub-processes shown.

Most companies only support a few value chain processes. When they do and we want to represent a value chain, we use an arrow that points toward the customer on the right of the organizational box, as in Figure 4.8. In this case we combine an organization diagram, an organization chart, and two value chains.

This diagram is the general format we used when we wanted to translate the TeleManagement Forum eTOM diagram into something a little easier to understand. The diagram used by the TeleManagement Forum might work well enough for those who are familiar with it, but it doesn't support a focus on processes the way Figure 4.8 does. In Figure 3.5 we showed the basic subprocesses within the major processes. We didn't use an arrow because we weren't sure if any of the processes shown was really a value chain.

In most cases the business architecture committee and specific process redesign teams won't be concerned with value chains, but will instead focus on major processes and subprocesses, just as the TeleManagement Forum did. In that case a diagram showing processes and subprocesses might look like Figure 4.9.

Figure 4.9 is a popular representation of an organization, showing a few external entities and a few processes and subprocesses. In this case we left out the organization chart, so we don't know which departments or functional units are responsible for each subprocess. Usually, however, this diagram is adequate, and you can wait till you begin to create process diagrams to pin down departmental-process relationships.

The example we use here simply shows three arbitrary major processes and some key subprocesses. With the exception of value chains, all processes are arbitrary groupings of subprocesses and activities. The grouping is chosen to reflect the way a given company or group thinks about its processes, and may vary from company to company. A process can be subdivided to any level of specificity. As we indicated earlier, the smallest process we choose to picture in our models is an activity. Many activities can be subdivided into smaller steps. They are activities, by definition, simply because we decide, for the purpose of whatever project we are engaged in, not to subdivide that process any further.

Notice the notation. Processes, subprocesses, and activities are all represented by rectangles with rounded corners. This distinguishes them from classes, like departments, customers, and suppliers.

Processes are made up of subprocesses, and ultimately activities, and linked together to produce organizational outputs. It is sometimes confusing, since we could talk of the accounting department as taking financial information and turning it into financial reports, but that would confuse organizational structure with process. Functions represent the reporting relationships of the company. Divisions and departments are simply finer-grained organizations. Processes are sets of activities undertaken by employees from functional units and managed by managers within functional units. Functional units describe the flow of authority and responsibility. Processes describe the flow of work. This will all be clearer when we consider process diagrams in Chapter 5. Meantime, suffice to say that *processes* are always boxes with rounded corners and that *organizations* and *functions* are always boxes with square corners.

In Figure 4.9, management could be either. It could be a set of processes, as it was in the TeleManagement Framework, or it could be an organizational unit. In Figure 4.9, for illustrative purposes, we have arbitrarily made the *Support* box represent processes and the *Management* box represent a management function.

Systems and Processes

We began by discussing the kind of model that a manager might provide if asked to explain the organization he or she managed. The traditional organization chart that we guessed our manager might provide is a pretty static way of looking at an organization, and it doesn't provide a very good way of thinking about how things are related. It leads to silo thinking.

In this book we urge *systems thinking* and *process thinking.* As organizations become more complex, effective managers need an overview that allows each one to see how their work fits within the larger whole. Peter Senge wrote a popular book a few years ago and called systems thinking the "Fifth Discipline" and argued that every manager should cultivate this perspective. We believe that the organization diagrams that we have presented here provide an important first step toward developing a systems overview. We know that anyone involved in trying to implement strategies needs this kind of perspective. The alternative is to try to figure out how to assign strategic goals to departments without a clear idea of how the departments must work together to achieve the desired outcomes.

Process thinking is just a subset of systems thinking. Systems thinking puts the emphasis on understanding the organization as a whole. Process thinking stresses thinking about the portion of the system that produces a specific set of results. The key, again, is to think of the entire process, or to understand how a specific process fits within the larger process and ultimately within the value chain. Remember, departments don't produce profits; value chains and processes produce profits. An excellent department may not result in a great process or significant profits. Indeed, in many cases, maximizing departmental efficiency actually reduces the efficiency of the whole process. To avoid this, organizations need to focus on the flows and relationships that actually add value and produce products for customers. Older perspectives need to be subordinated to these newer perspectives if your organization is to prosper.

5

Modeling Processes

I N **CHAPTER** 4 we considered how to picture organizations, as a whole, and to show how they relate to their environment. And we considered how we can represent functions and processes on organization diagrams. In this chapter we want to consider the second major type of diagram that managers need to master in order to analyze business processes. Appropriately, these diagrams are called process or workflow diagrams.

Process Diagram Basics

Figure 5.1 illustrates the basic format of a process diagram. In this instance we are focusing on a single, high-level order fulfillment process that begins when a customer places an order and ends when the product is delivered. The example we use is a very high-level view of this process and isn't interesting in itself. It is only used to provide a starting point for our discussion of a process diagram.

Let's consider the notation used in Figure 5.1. We already know that processes are represented by boxes with rounded corners. Processes are either labeled with titles, like Manufacturing Process, or they are given names that begin with a verb, such as Manage Leads, Determine Needs, or Ship Product.

The process diagram itself is divided into a series of horizontal rows. We use the top row of the diagram to provide a context for the diagram. In this case we are told that it's the Ergo Chair value chain, and the order fulfillment process.

The rest of the diagram is divided into horizontal rows that are called swimlanes. Although there are exceptions, as a strong generalization, movement

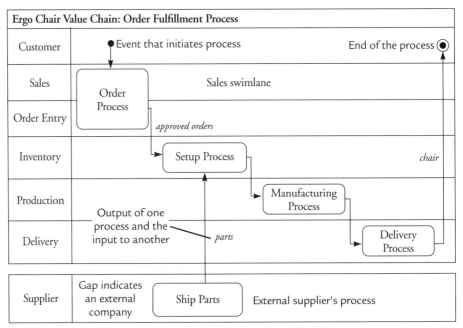

Figure 5.1 A process diagram.

from left to right indicates the passage of time. Thus, a process begins on the left-hand side of the diagram and proceeds to the right. In other words, activities on the left take place before activities on the right.

The top swimlane is always reserved for the customer, if the process links to the outside world. Otherwise the top lane is reserved for whatever entity or process initiates the processes shown on the diagram.

Sometimes we represent the initial event that starts the process as a rectangle, and at other times we represent it as a bold dot, as we do in Figure 5.1. We use rectangles whenever we want to be more specific about what the customer does.

Similarly, if there are any external processes to be shown, they are set below the basic diagram within a swimlane separated from the company's process. In the example shown in Figure 5.1, we suggest that parts are being supplied by an external vendor and show the external vendor's part shipment process.

In some organizations, a diagram similar to the one shown in Figure 5.1 might be called a workflow diagram. In a typical workflow diagram, however, we would simply represent all of the processes on a single line. The Order Process would lead to the Setup Process and then to the Manufacturing Process. In Figure 5.1, however, we want to show the functional or organizational entities responsible for the performance of each activity. Thus, the organizational departments or functions we originally identified on the organization diagram have become the swimlane labels on the left side of the process diagram. Figure 5.1 shows that there is an Inventory Department and that it is responsible for the Setup Process. Put a different way, some manager or supervisor within the reporting hierarchy of the Inventory Department is responsible for the Setup Process.

Thus, a process diagram, as we will use the term, is a workflow diagram with swimlanes. As far as we know, this approach to process diagramming was originated by Geary Rummler and Alan Brache, but it has since been adopted by a wide variety of business process modelers and by the UML software modeling language.

If we analyze large-scale processes, as we are doing in Figure 5.1, it's possible that a process will be the responsibility of more than one functional group. Thus, both Sales and Order Entry are responsible for activities that occur within the Order Process. If we analyze the Order Process in more detail, presumably we will be able to determine just which activities Sales is responsible for and which activities the Order Entry group performs.

As you can see by glancing at Figure 5.1, we can either label arrows, or not, depending on whether we think the information useful.

We usually do not represent processes and subprocesses on the same diagram. Instead, we represent a number of processes or activities that are all at more or less the same level of granularity. We usually analyze very high-level processes on an organization diagram and consider slightly more detailed processes than we show in Figure 5.1 on process diagrams. The key point, however, is that if you want to know what goes on inside the order process, you create a second process diagram with the order process on the title line and subprocesses within the swimlanes.

As we drill down, the functional groups listed on the swimlanes keep getting more specific. In effect, we are moving down the organizational chart. Initially we label swimlanes with department names. At a finer level of detail, we may only show two departments, but subdivide each of the departments into several functional units. If we continue to drill down, ultimately we arrive at swimlanes that represent specific managers or specific employee roles.

Figure 5.2 provides an overview of the way in which someone might drill down into a process. This figure shows how we use organization diagrams as a way of gathering the information we later use when we create process diagrams. In effect, the departments identified in the organization diagram become the swimlanes on process diagrams.

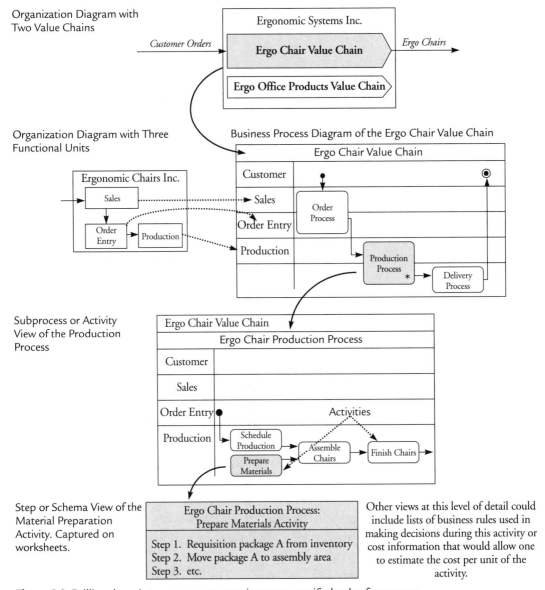

Figure 5.2 Drilling down into a process to examine more specific levels of processes.

On the initial Process Diagram, we show one process, Production Process, which we subsequently define in more detail. The asterisk (*) placed within the process box is a reminder for viewers that a more detailed process diagram is available for this process.

In Figure 5.2 we arbitrarily assume that Prepare Materials is an activity. In other words, for the purposes of our analysis, we are not going to diagram anything that occurs within the activity box labeled Prepare Materials. That is not to say that we won't gather additional information about that activity. We simply aren't going to create a diagram to describe the sequence of steps that occur within Prepare Materials. Instead, we might create a textual description of the materials preparation activity. If we want a finer definition of the process, we might type out a list of steps that occur during the accomplishment of the activity. We will certainly want to know if the activity is performed by humans or by computers or machines, or some combination of them. Similarly, if we are planning on doing simulation, we might accumulate information on the units processed in the activity, the costs per unit, time per unit, and so forth. If you are doing this by hand, you could simply write out the information on a sheet of paper and attach it to the diagram.

Later, we will provide an activity worksheet that you can use to prompt yourself in accumulating data you might need to record for an activity. If you are using a sophisticated software tool, when you click on an activity box, it opens and provides you with a worksheet in a window, and you can type in the information on your computer.

More Process Notation

In addition to the symbols we have already introduced, there are a few more symbols a manager must know in order to read process diagrams. Figure 5.3 illustrates another simple process. In this figure we are looking at a process that describes how a retail book company receives orders by phone and ships books to customers. This company doesn't manufacture books; it simply takes them from its inventory and sends them to customers.

Some of the symbols in Figure 5.3 are new, and others are simply variations. For example, instead of starting with a bold dot, we placed information inside a box that indicates that the customer placed an order. Note that the customer box is a rectangle with square corners. We aren't concerned with what process the customer goes through in deciding to order the book. From our perspective, the placement of the order is an event or stimulus that triggers the book order fulfillment process. Hence, the customer's action is handled in a special way. Some analysts go ahead and use a rectangle with rounded corners and that's acceptable. Similarly, some business analysts prefer special symbols for events or triggers—a large arrow for example. Following UML notation, however, we distinguish between processes and activities, represented by rectangles with rounded corners, and events or objects, which are placed inside boxes with square corners.

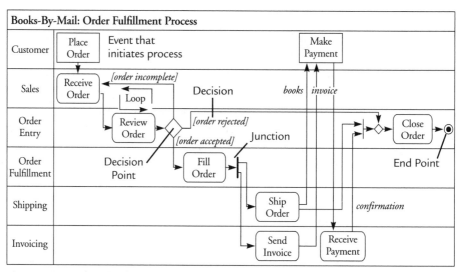

Figure 5.3 Another simple process diagram.

Business Rules

Some activities are well-defined procedures, while others involve the application of rules and decisions. Review Order is an example of a process or activity that requires a decision. If the decision process is complex, we record the decision criteria as business rules and put them on a separate piece of paper, or record them in a software tool that associates them with the activity.

Business rules take this generic form:

IF <something is the case>
AND <something else is also the case>
THEN <do this>
ELSE <do something else>

For example, we might have a rule that said:

IF the order is from a customer we don't know
AND the order is over $50
THEN check the credit card number for approval
OR wait till the check clears our bank.

Complex decision processes can involve lots of rules. In the extreme cases, there are too many rules to analyze, and we rely on human experts who understand how to solve the problem. We'll consider this entire topic in more detail when we discuss how activities are analyzed in Chapter 6.

In some cases, as in the example shown in Figure 5.3, the decision is relatively simple and different activities follow, depending upon the decision. In this case, we often place a diamond or decision point after the activity that leads to the decision. We indicate the alternative outcomes as arrows leading from the diamond to other activities. In the example shown, the order can either be

▶ *incomplete,* in which case the order is returned to the salesperson who must call the customer to obtain the needed information, or
▶ *rejected,* in which case the order is terminated, or
▶ *accepted,* in which case the order is passed on to shipping and invoicing.

In most cases a small diamond is sufficient, and outcomes are simply written by the arrows leading from the decision point. To distinguish decisions, they are usually placed in square brackets: [ ].

In some cases, you may want to describe the decision point in more detail. In that case, you can expand the diamond into a hexagon, as follows:

As in Figure 5.3, you can have multiple arrows coming from a single decision point, although in most cases, there are just two or three.

Notice that we show an arrow running *backward in time* in Figure 5.3, as it goes from the decision point, back to the Receive Order activity. This shouldn't happen too often because it runs counter to the basic idea that a process diagram flows from left to right. On the other hand, it's sometimes very useful to show *loops* or *iterations* like this rather than making the diagram much larger. We refer to it as a "loop," since we assume that once the salesperson has called the customer and completed the order, it will proceed back to the Review Order activity just as it did in the first instance.

Notice the second use of a decision diamond on the right side of Figure 5.3. In this case the diamond has two inputs and only one output. In effect, the diamond says, in this instance, that EITHER the order is going to be closed because the order was rejected OR because the order was shipped and paid for. The diamond, in this second case, is simply a graphical way of saying there are two different possible inputs to Close Order. The Close Order activity takes place whenever either one of the inputs arrives.

We also show *junction bars,* which are also sometimes called *forks* or *joins,* in Figure 5.3. In the first case an output from Fill Order is divided at a junction bar or fork and then flows to both Ship Order and Send Invoice. In the second case the information that the order was shipped and the information that payment was received both flow into a junction bar or join that then leads to the Close Order activity. In the first case the junction bar indicates that the Fill Order activity is not complete until BOTH the Ship Order AND the Send Invoice activities have been activated. In the second instance the junction bar says that the Close Order activity cannot begin until either the order is rejected, OR until BOTH the Ship Order AND the Receive Payment activities have confirmed that they have been completed. Some analysts label the junction bar with a note to indicate that the inputs have to meet some specific conditions. For example, two inputs might have to arrive at a join by a given date or might have to total to a set amount.

In effect, decision points or junction bars allow analysts to indicate the basic logic of business flows. In most cases, when you are creating a early draft of a workflow, you avoid such logical subtitles. Thus, for example, we could have shown the flow from Fill Order to Ship Order and Send Invoice as shown in Figure 5.4.

These two alternatives don't tell us anything about the logic of the flow. It might be sufficient if the information from Fill Order only arrived at Ship Order, for example. It might be that different forms were sent to Ship Order and to Send Invoice. If the second, we would probably label the arrows to tell us what went where. The point, however, is that you can define processes informally at first, and then refine the flow to capture business rules or procedural logic as you refine the diagram.

Consider the two arrows leaving Ship Order in Figure 5.5. In one case the arrow represents an object or thing—books. In the second case the arrow represents information—a confirmation—sent to the person responsible for closing orders. Some analysts use different arrows to denote the flow of information and things.

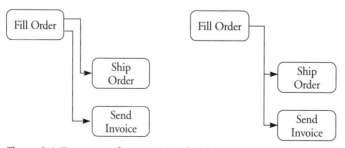

Figure 5.4 Two ways of representing flow between processes.

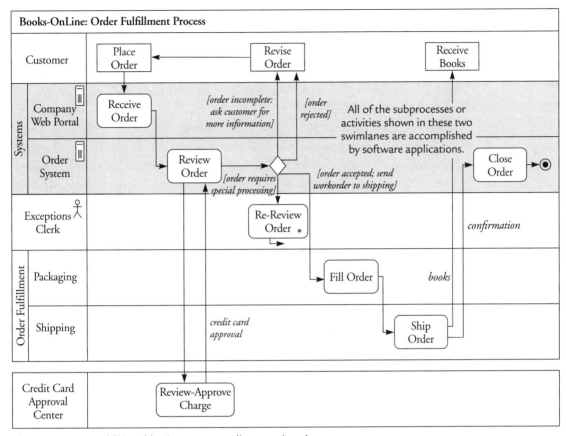

Figure 5.5 Some additional business process diagramming elements.

We don't and prefer to simply label the arrows. This usually works well enough for business analysis.

Finally, from the Close Order activity, an arrow leads to an *end point* or *sink*—a bold dot within a circle. This symbol indicates that the process ends at this point. Sometimes we also use the end point to indicate that we don't wish to pursue a given workflow any further. Thus, for example, rather than use the second diamond and create that complex bit of logic just before the Close Order activity, we might have simply let the arrow labeled *[order rejected]* lead to an end point. If we did, it would be because we thought that what happened next was obvious and we didn't want to clutter the diagram by showing the flow of that output of Review Order.

Figure 5.5 introduces some additional symbols that you may find useful. In this case we are considering a simple process that involves letting customers order books via the Web.

In Figure 5.5 we have used small symbols to distinguish various kinds of swimlanes. The default or normal condition is a swimlane that represents a department or function. We don't use any special notation for that. A special case is a swimlane that represents a role or an individual. To call attention to that we sometimes place a small stick figure near the label for that lane. We sometimes refer to this as an *actor swimlane.*

Another special case is a swimlane that represents a software application, group of applications, or a database. We use a small image that looks like a workstation computer box to highlight that lane and refer to the swimlane as a *system swimlane.*

In addition, there is the *customer swimlane,* at the top of the diagram, which is outside the organization, and a swimlane at the bottom, separated by a space, that represents a process at another company.

Occasionally in this book, we will shade lanes in light gray or use a different font in text, as we do in Figure 5.5, to call attention to the two system swimlanes. This convention is used only in this book, for emphasis and explanation, and not a formal part of our business process mapping notation.

We have also used two types of labels to identify some of the swimlanes. Both the Web Portal and the Order System are Systems. (We are avoiding the issue of whether this is a departmental-based IT group or the enterprise IT organization at this point.) Both the packaging group and the shipping group report to the Order Fulfillment department at Books-OnLine.

Some analysts make distinctions between individuals, jobs, and roles. In most cases when we speak of an activity, we speak of a role. It's something one or more people do. It may or may not be a complete job. Imagine that there are six Exceptions Clerks. There is one job description for Exception Clerk and six individuals have been hired to do the job. Next, imagine that there are 10 different activities, or roles, that are included in the Exception Clerk job description. One of the activities or roles is to re-review orders that are listed on the special processing report generated by the Order System in conjunction with the Web orders. Another role might be to handle errors generated by an accounting system. In other words, the job of the Exceptions Clerk is larger than the Re-Review Order activity. Thus, we speak of the abstract unit of work required by the Re-Review Order activity, which could be done by any one of the six Exception Clerks as a role. In other words, the little "person" symbol doesn't refer to a specific individual, but rather to any Exception Clerk who performs the Re-Review Order role.

Similarly, we might have a process that includes an activity that requires the approval of the VP of Marketing. We might show the VP of Marketing on a swimlane. Again, we wouldn't be referring to an individual because the person holding the job might change. We would simply be referring to the job or role.

Notice that the boxes in the Customer swimlane have square corners. We don't normally think of customers as performing activities. They act and create events or stimuli to which our business process must respond. This is even true when the system tells the customer that the order form they completed isn't complete and asks the customer to provide additional information, as we suggest with the loop between Receive Order, Review Order, Revise Order, and Place Order.

Notice that Figure 5.5 shows that the Exception Clerk handles orders that require special processing. In this case, we didn't want to follow the various flows that might come from the Re-Review Order box, so we used a small turned arrow to suggest that we wouldn't follow the outputs in this case. We could just as well have used an end processing symbol, as we do with the Close Order box. Notice that we placed an asterisk (*) in the Re-Review Order box. This is a symbol that shows that we have created another process diagram describing what goes on in the Re-Review Order process. You can ignore this in some cases, but its very useful to remind readers that they can go to another diagram to obtain more detail. Recall that this doesn't mean that we might not create a worksheet with a set of steps for Exceptions Clerks to follow, or a set of business rules that they should use in examining orders that show up on the special processing report. It simply means that we won't be creating diagrams of what goes on inside the box.

Figure 5.6 provides a few more variations. In this case we are looking at a small part of an auto claims process.

In most cases we indicate applications and system activities by placing them on a system swimlane. In some cases, however, it's easier to simply mark the process boxes themselves.

We occasionally use different process or activity boxes in different ways. A process box with a regular border is the default. It either means we haven't indicated how the process is performed, or that the process is performed manually by an employee. A process box with a dashed border indicates that the process involves a mix of manual and computer or machine. In our example we assume that an employee in the Claims Processing department uses a computer to enter the claim. Similarly, we assume that the Claims Approval Agent accesses the claim record and approves it via his or her desktop computer.

A process box with a bold border indicates that a software application (or a machine) performs the entire process. We could have created an additional swimlane and labeled it Payment System and placed the Create Payment Check activity within that lane to indicate it was a software process. In this case, for simplicity, we simply placed the Create Payment Check activity and the manual Mail Check activity in the same lane and used a bold border to show that Create Payment Check

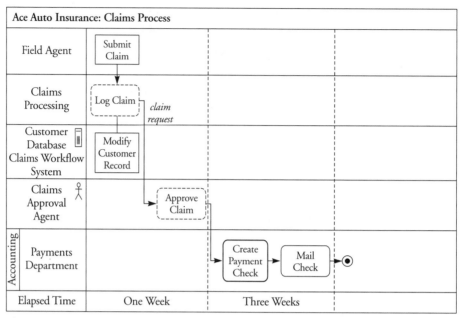

Figure 5.6 Additional symbols.

is a computer activity. In a real analysis effort, we probably wouldn't mix the two ways of notating systems activities (swimlanes and bold bordered boxes) in the same process diagram, but we could, and we did so here so we could explain and compare them.

Notice that Modify Customer Record is an event and thus is a box with square corners. This distinction is usually not worth worrying about. The activity took place at the computer of the Claims Processing Clerk, and the result was a new (modified) database record. It would be the same if a secretary had typed a document and then placed it in a file. The document itself would be represented as a square-cornered box.

We usually indicate documents and materials by simply placing the name of the item over the flow arrow. Some analysts prefer to include boxes within the flow. If you did this in a situation in which a typist passed a typed document to another clerk within the same unit, it would appear as

Finally, we added a special row at the bottom of the process diagram shown in Figure 5.6 to indicate the time involved. In this example we assume that the

company wants to get all claims processed within one week of receipt and that it wants to pay accepted claims within three weeks of claim acceptance. We usually don't indicate times for specific processes or activities, but it is occasionally useful to provide elapsed times for groups of activities, especially when the project is focused on reducing the time the process takes.

Vertical Swimlanes

So far, we've always shown process diagrams whose swimlanes run horizontally across the page. Some analysts prefer to have the swimlanes run vertically. If you do this, then the Customer lane should be the leftmost lane and noncompany functions should be shown on the right-hand side of the page. In Figure 5.7 we show the same information we pictured in Figure 5.6, arranged with vertical swimlanes. Obviously, in this case, time will accumulate from the top downward.

We have always found it much easier to picture the flow of activities and to fit the information into process diagrams with horizontal swimlanes, and we will use them throughout this book. But, ultimately, this is just a matter of personal preference, and readers can just as well draw process diagrams with vertical swimlanes if that orientation works better for them.

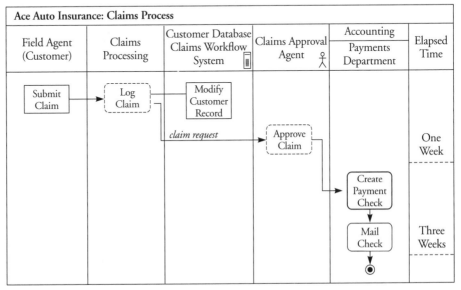

Figure 5.7 The auto insurance claims process, with vertical swimlanes.

IS, COULD, and SHOULD Process Diagrams

In analyzing a specific business process, we usually begin with an analysis of what is currently being done. We usually refer to the process diagram that documents the existing process as the *IS process diagram*. Once we understand what is currently being done, we often generate alternative workflows and compare them. When we are creating speculative alternative diagrams, we usually call them

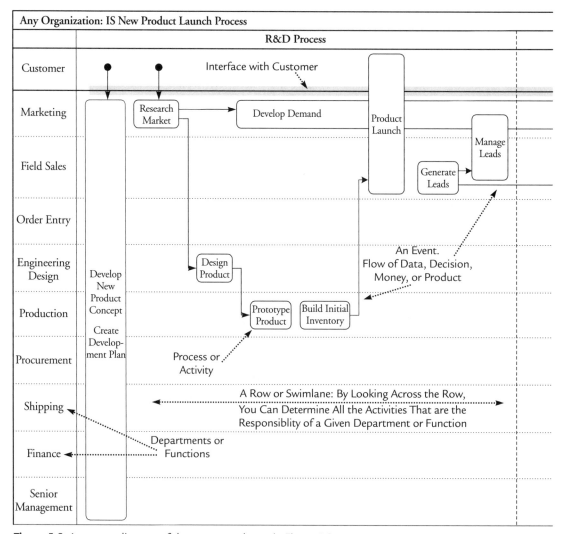

Figure 5.8 A process diagram of the processes shown in Figure 4.9.

COULD diagrams. When we finally arrive at the new process, we term that a *SHOULD process diagram.*

Figure 5.8 provides an example of a typical IS process diagram, and Figure 5.9 provides an example of a SHOULD process diagram that suggests some of the ways in which we intend to improve the process.

Figure 5.8 shows the three processes and the subprocesses we pictured in Figure 4.9. Thus, Figure 5.8 illustrates how we would represent the three processes in

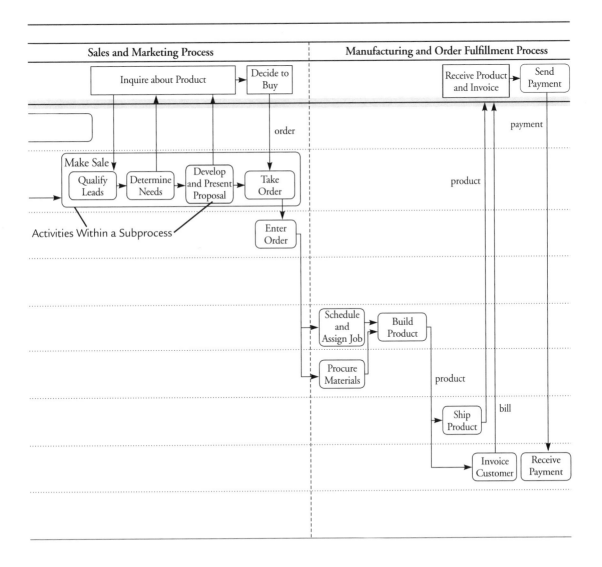

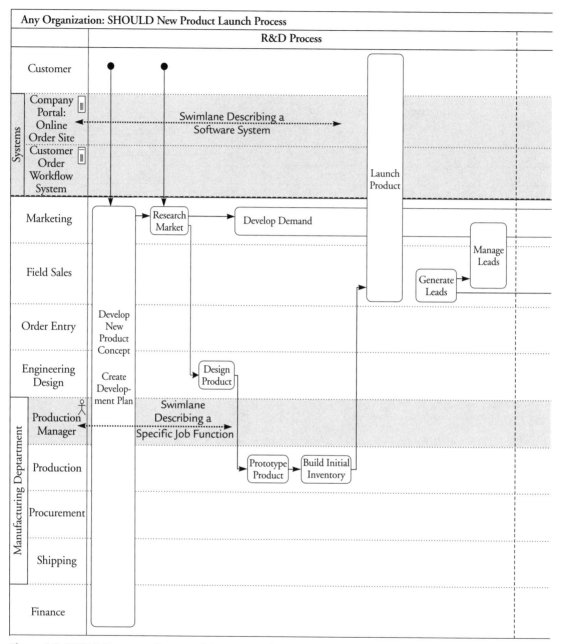

Figure 5.9 SHOULD process diagram of the New Product Launch Process.

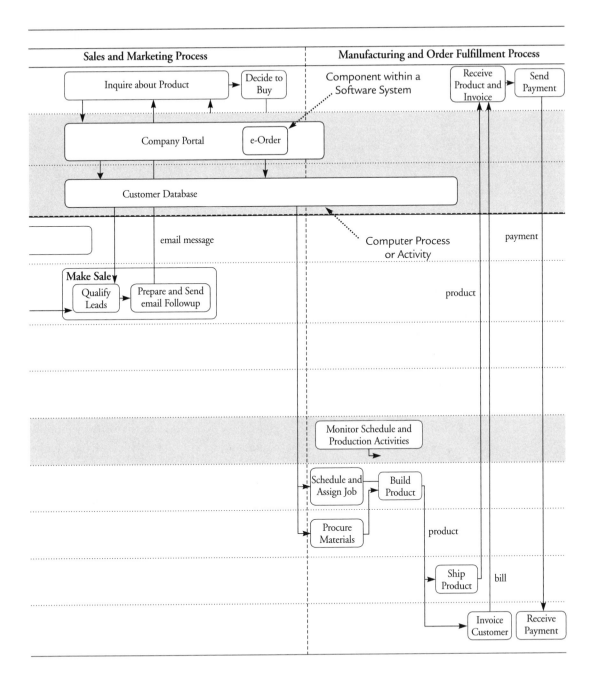

a process diagram, while Figure 4.9 illustrated the same information as an organization diagram.

In this example we added an extra line at the top of both process diagrams to indicate the three larger processes, and then we show the subprocesses below, each assigned to a functional unit. In this specific case we actually show one subprocess with activities inside it. We don't normally recommend showing two levels on the same diagram. The goal of diagnosis, however, is to help managers analyze processes, and we don't want to introduce any arbitrary rigidity. It's sometimes useful to do this when you are working with a team of managers to remind everyone of what is taking place within a specific process box.

We have made some notes on the diagram in Figure 5.8 to reiterate key features we've already introduced. We highlighted the entire line between the Customer swimlane and the Marketing function swimlane to emphasize it. Many companies today place a lot of emphasis on satisfying customers. Similarly, Internet applications often interface with customers by means of a Web site or portal that controls all interactions with the customer. By placing the customer on the top line, one can quickly scan across and see all the places where the company interacts with the customer. Some analysts make the line between the Customer swimlane and the swimlane below a bold line to emphasize this interface.

In the mid-1990s, IBM promoted a business process methodology called LOVEM (Line of Vision Enterprise Methodology) that used diagrams much like the ones used in this book. The "line of vision" referred to in the IBM methodology was the line between the organization and the customer, which we have highlighted. It provides a quick way of seeing exactly how and when your organization is interacting with its customers.

The other thing emphasized by process diagrams is the interface between departments and groups. In effect, whenever an arrow crosses from one swimlane to another, information or material is being passed from one functional group to another. As we suggested earlier and will emphasize later, many process breakdowns occur when processes cross functional lines, especially lines between departments or divisions. A process diagram makes it easy to spot where problems between functional groups might occur.

Some analysts like to keep track of the hierarchy of functional groups by listing departments at the very left edge of the diagram and grouping subfunctions, as we have done with the Manufacturing Department in Figure 5.8. Once again, it depends on who is using the diagram and whether the information is important or not. You could just as easily use two names for each swimlane. For example, you could label one swimlane Manufacturing/Shipping to document the departmental relationship. If problems between departments are a major issue to be resolved, however, more emphasis on the departmental and functional units is often useful.

Let's return to a point we made earlier. Normally, if we were going to represent the information we show in Figure 5.1, we would probably use an organizational diagram. Conversely, if we were going to show a process in the detail we show in Figure 5.8, we would not normally represent it as an organization diagram, as we did in Chapter 4 (Figure 4.9), but would use a process diagram like Figure 5.8. We have shown both simply to acquaint you with the alternatives, to let you see how the two diagrams are related, and to emphasize two different perspectives on the same process structures.

Figure 5.9 is a SHOULD process diagram. It suggests one way a team might decide to improve the New Product Launch Process.

We said earlier that swimlanes often begin as divisions or departments and can be subdivided into smaller and smaller functional groups, as we work our way down into the specifics of a process. When we first define a process, we focus on departments responsible for business processes and on how one process is related to others. That is, in essence, what we showed in Figure 5.8. Later, if it's appropriate for our analysis, we drill down through subprocesses and subsubprocesses to specific activities.

In Figure 5.9 we added one specific job title, Production Manager, and indicated one activity, Monitor Schedule and Production Activities. In this example, if the Production Manager was only concerned with activities that occurred within the value chain shown in this diagram, and our analysis were complete, we could check all of the activities assigned to the Production Manager by looking along the Production Manager swimlane. Recall that we are not focused on an individual employee, but on a job title or role. A company might have several Production Managers, one for each of several factories. We could go further and use the title of a specific individual—say, SVP for Sales—if it was really important to show what the SVP for Sales had to do during the course of the process.

Notice that we have included a generic activity, Monitor Schedule and Production Activities, in the Production Manager's swimlane. We included an arrow below the rectangle that turns right and ends, just as we did on some organization diagrams when we wanted to show generic functions. In this case we wanted to include the activity, but didn't want to define specific interactions, so we used this convention.

We highlighted two swimlanes that describe information systems on Figure 5.9. The first describes a company Web site or portal, which includes information about the company and a customer order system. When an order is placed, the

Portal system transfers the information to a Customer Database. The Customer Database stores information about customer contacts. In addition, when a customer order is placed, the database system notifies production so it can schedule jobs and update inventory. Systems is probably a support organization, so this also suggests how support functions can be integrated into processes when they have specific responsibilities. In this case they maintain the Portal and the Customer Database.

A quick glance back at Figure 5.8 will indicate that we have removed sales activities and an order entry activity. When software is introduced into business processes, lots of specific activities that were formerly done by individuals at specific points in time are done on a continuous basis by the software system. It usually isn't worth maintaining the information on the process diagram. What is important is that you show when information is put into the software process and when information is given to workers by the software application. If you need to track what goes on within the software process box, it's usually best to prepare a separate process diagram that just shows what happens within the software process. And since that gets technical and depends on the company's hardware and software architecture, it's usually best to leave that diagramming effort to software specialists.

In other words, in most cases, you should focus on inputs and outputs to software processes and ignore the internal workings. If you want to assure that everyone knows that the Customer Database is expected to maintain all information on customer contacts and orders, you can write that and other system requirements on a separate note and attach it to the diagram.

Obviously, some software processes tend to be long processes that are represented by very wide rectangles. This occurs because, in effect, a workflow or a database runs constantly, taking outputs from the processes shown on the diagram and using them to update the database from which it subsequently withdraws the data to pass to subsequent activities.

If we were really going to try to automate the New Product Launch Process, there are lots of additional things we could do. We could add a production system, for example, to automatically handle scheduling and job assignments. We might also outsource the shipping operation, and so forth. An accounting system could automatically prepare bills. In addition, there are lots of activities we didn't show. For example, we would probably add a third major software system to automate and control most of the accounting. New orders could be checked against the Customer Database as soon as they were entered, and credit checks could be handled before the order was ever transmitted to Finance. An accounting system could automatically prepare invoices when it was notified that the order was shipped.

Better, since it's an online system, we could ask the customer to pay in advance, or provide information on an account that could be automatically debited when the product was shipped. In this case, the Customer Database system would probably automatically contact an external financial institution to check the source of funds or the credit line to be debited later. In other words, we could automate this process quite a bit more. For our purposes here, however, it's enough that we've introduced the basic concepts and notation we will use when we discuss organizations, functions, and processes later in this book.

Levels of Analysis

By way of a quick summary, Figure 5.10 presents some of the diagrams we have described in this chapter and the last. It organizes them into three general layers, one within the other. Level 1 diagrams focus on the organization, its basic structure, and its environment. If you wished to subdivide Level 1, then Level 1-A

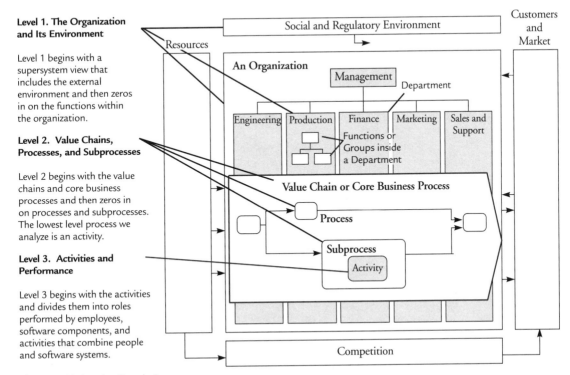

Figure 5.10 Levels of analysis.

focuses on the supersystem: the organization in relation to its external environment. Level 1-B focuses on the internal functions of the organization.

Level 2 focuses on processes. The largest processes are value chains that integrate all of the subprocesses and activities necessary to produce a major line of products or services. Value chains are divided into business processes, which are, in turn, resolved into processes and then subprocesses. Subprocesses can be subdivided as often as is necessary. We arbitrarily agree to call the smallest processes we show on our diagrams activities.

Level 3 focuses on the activities that occur within processes and subprocesses. As a default we assume all activities are done by employees. When appropriate, we can refine that and identify some activities as employee activities, some activities as software-facilitated activities, and some activities as mixed activities in which employees interact with software to complete the activity.

In the next chapter we will consider how we represent activities in more detail.

6

Analyzing Activities

IN THIS CHAPTER we will focus on activities. Activities are the smallest processes we choose to model in any given analysis effort. They are the third level of process analysis. We said earlier that the work of a business is ultimately done by the processes that make up the business. In a similar way, the actual work done by any process is ultimately done by activities.

In one sense, an activity is just a process, and we show activities on process diagrams. In another sense, however, when we try to say what occurs within an activity, we cross the line between describing process and enter into describing human behavior or the behavior of a software system. Our goal in this book, of course, is not to go deeply into the technologies used in the analysis of employee behavior or systems analysis. Business managers who specify process changes are not normally expected to develop training materials or to program software. To complete a process description, however, they are expected to describe activities in enough detail so that others can write the job descriptions, create the training, or design the software needed to assure that the activity will be properly performed. Thus, in this section and in subsequent chapters on automation, we will describe techniques that business managers can use to assure that they understand and can communicate what must be done to perform any given activity.

Since an activity is of arbitrary size, any given activity could contain lots of different steps. In some cases, hundreds of people might be employed in the accomplishment of a specific activity—say, picking grapes in a vineyard. Or an activity might be a meeting of a bank corporate loan committee in which several different people participate and discuss some complex decision.

If we are redesigning an important process, we usually refine our models to the point where each activity represents a fairly discrete set of behaviors. In some cases we will want to run simulations. In those instances we will need to be very precise about what happens in each activity.

Analyzing a Specific Activity

Let's start with an activity that is performed by a single person. To simplify things further, let's assume that the employee works full-time on the single activity. Imagine, for example, that the activity involves the entry of expense report information into a ledger. We hope no one does something like this without using a computer system today, but let's imagine that this activity is an entirely manual operation. In other words, there is a job description, describing the work of an Expense Report Entry Clerk, and there is a one-to-one relationship between the job description and the work done in the *Enter Expense Reports* activity. We might diagram the activity as shown in Figure 6.1.

If we were going to analyze this activity, we would begin by obtaining copies of *expense reports* and a correctly updated *expense report ledger.* Then we'd sit down with a skilled Expense Report Entry Clerk and watch her do the job. We'd take notes to describe the steps and actions taken by the clerk as she received the reports and then created the updated ledger. We assume the clerks would do things like stamp the incoming expense report with a date, and then examine it to see that it was complete. If it was complete, the clerk would probably proceed to copy information from various locations on the expense report to other locations on the ledger. In some cases numbers would be added and sums would be entered. After the entry was complete, the original report would probably be filed, and the ledger numbers added or subtracted to reflect a change in various balances. If the original report was incomplete, we assume the clerk would follow some alternative path. For example, the report might be returned to the sender with a note pointing out that additional information was required.

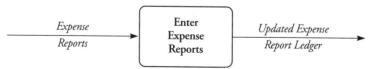

Figure 6.1 An activity.

In other words, the activity would be composed of a number of steps or tasks. The steps would be triggered by the receipt of an expense report and terminate when the report was filed and the ledger was completely updated. Obviously we could create a diagram showing each step and use arrows to show how the clerk moved from one step to the next, and where decisions and branches occurred. In this case, however, the analyst decided he or she didn't need a model and that a list of steps would suffice.

There would probably be some rules that helped the clerk make decisions. One rule would state what was required of a complete report and specify that, if reports were incomplete, they should be returned to the submitter with a note about what was missing.

There might be other rules, specifying how to deal with reports submitted over one month late, or reports submitted with or without various types of documentation. Still other rules might deal with how to handle reports that deal with expenses in foreign currencies, or with reports in which the submitter included expenses that were not permitted by the company expense policy. There might also be rules requiring the signature of a senior manager.

In addition to defining the steps in the process and the rules to be followed at each step, we might also document the time required to process an average expense report, the number of reports the clerk typically processed in a day, and the kinds of problems or exceptions that were typically encountered and the frequency of each. We would probably also determine the salary of the clerk so that we could determine the cost of processing an average report, or of handling common exceptions. We might even check on departmental overhead estimates for office space, file space, and such to obtain an even more accurate idea of the total cost of the activity.

We would also probably make some statement about the goal fulfilled by the activity—what value it adds to the production of company products or services. We would also probably gather data on how the ledgers were evaluated by the activity supervisor, and information on the rate and kinds of errors that occurred. Assuming multiple entry clerks were employed, we would develop a statement about the quality and quantity of an average clerk, and about the output typical of the best and worst performers. In other words, we would want to know how consistently the task was performed and what kind of deviation there was.

If the employee or supervisor felt that there were problems with the performance of the activity, we would ask the employee and the supervisor to suggest

Activity Analysis Worksheet

Activity: _Enter Expense Reports_   Process: _XYZ Sales Process_

Activity Performed by (✓) employee, ( ) software, ( ) a combination

Major Output of Activity: _Updated expense report ledger_

Measures of Output: _Ledger reflects all reported expenses documented in expense reports filed by sales personnel._
Ledger closed at the end of each month.

Steps in the Activity	Responsibility	Decisions/Rules	Opportunities for Improvement
1. Date-stamp each expense report when it's received. 2. Review expense reports for completeness and accuracy (return if incomplete). 3. Cross-check information on expense report with supporting documentation. 4. Enter information on expense report into ledger. 5. Update ledger. 6. File expense report and supporting documentation.	Expense Report Entry Clerk responsible for work. Work managed by Sales Accounting Supervisor	Rule 1. No expense report is processed before supporting documentation arrives. Rule 2. Incomplete reports are rerouted to submitter for completion. Rule 3. Submitter is notified whenever an item is disallowed. Rule 4. Any sign of a purposeful attempt at fraud should be brought to attention of accounting supervisor. Rule 5. Expense reports must be processed and paid in month submitted. Rule 6. If expense reports are submitted that are over 3 months old, the Sales Accounting Supervisor should be notified to approve processing.	

Figure 6.2 An Activity Worksheet.

causes of the problems and gather any data we could to support or refute those suggestions.

In this example, we are looking at a very straightforward job. In most companies, jobs like these are so straightforward that they have been automated. If they aren't, they are elementary enough that they have probably been documented for some time, and new supervisors probably simply inherited the job description and various activity measures when they were made supervisor. On the other hand, there are lots of much more complex jobs that a manager might be made responsible for supervising. The manager of sales must do something similar for his or her salespeople, and the manager of software development must analyze the jobs and performance of programmers. We are discussing a simple set of tasks, but the basic principles are the same.

In this book, to provide readers with a quick way of organizing information you might want to gather about an activity, we will use two activity worksheets: a basic *Activity Analysis Worksheet* and a supplemental *Activity Cost Worksheet*. If you were using a software tool, you would probably simply click on the activity rectangle on a process diagram and be able to enter this information. We've simply used worksheets as a quick way to summarize the kind of information you would want to record.

Figure 6.2 illustrates an Activity Worksheet we prepared for the Enter Expense Reports activity. In this case we listed the basic steps, who was responsible for each step, and some of the decision rules that control the activity.

We didn't assume the use of computers in the activity described on the Activity Worksheet in Figure 6.2. If we had assumed a computer, then one of the key variables would be the computer screens that the performer used to enter or obtain information from the computer. In that case we would have noted the name or some other reference code to identify the computer screen used in each step. Occasionally, if there are problems, they arise because the user doesn't understand the information as presented on the computer screen or doesn't understand the appropriate response called for by the computer screen, and changes in the layout or text on the computer screen can solve the problem and improve performance.

If we were interested in doing cost analysis or simulation, we would also need to gather additional information on the activity. We've provided a separate Activity Cost Worksheet for such information, and it's pictured in Figure 6.3.

In Figure 6.3 we've shown the data we gathered on the Enter Expense Reports activity. We marked it IS to indicate that this is the way the activity was performed in the existing process.

Activity Cost Worksheet				
Process or Subprocess: *XYZ Sales Process*			IS (✓) or SHOULD ( ) Analysis	
Activity	Outputs of Activity	Time/Output	Costs/Output	Problems or Decisions
Enter Expense Reports	Updated Expense Report Ledger	15 minutes/report and update, or 4 per hour.	@$24/hr (loaded with overhead) the cost per report is $6.	1 in 20 involves an exception, which takes up to 30 minutes to process.

Figure 6.3 An Activity Cost Worksheet.

Assuming that the Enter Expense Reports activity was performed by an individual, then part of the analysis effort might involve defining or redefining the job of the individual that performed the activity. In most cases this will be beyond the basic scope of the process analysis effort. Typically the process analysis team would simply define the activity and leave specialists from human resources to refine the job description of the individual who performs the job. In some cases, however, if there are problems with this specific activity, process analysts need a general approach to analyzing the performance of manual activities.

Analyzing the Human Performance Required for an Activity

When an activity is not being performed correctly, we need to analyze the situation to see what could be wrong. The best approach to this is *human performance analysis,* a technology developed by psychologists and performance analysts over the course of the last 50 years. Human performance analysis defines the variables that affect human performance and offers heuristics for analyzing any given human activity. Figure 6.4 provides a version of the human performance model used by Rummler in *Improving Performance.*

Let's consider each of the factors illustrated in Figure 6.4 in more detail.

I. Activity Standards

Do activity standards exist? If measures exist, then one assumes they measure whether the activity meets one or more standards. Obviously if you are a new manager and there are no existing measures or standards in place, then your first job is to create them. It's always useful to check to see if standards are documented and to ask performers how they interpret the standards. It's always possible that someone provided performers with standards, then established measures. Later they might have changed measures without realigning the standards that the employees are using. Similarly, it's worth checking on what standards software developers used when they created any software component used in the activity and assure they are current and aligned.

Does the performer know the desired output and standards? Once the manager knows that standards exist, he or she should next determine that the people or systems performing the activity know what the standards are. Obviously people can't systematically achieve a standard they don't know about. If performers don't know about a standard, it's the manager's job to not only assure that they learn about the

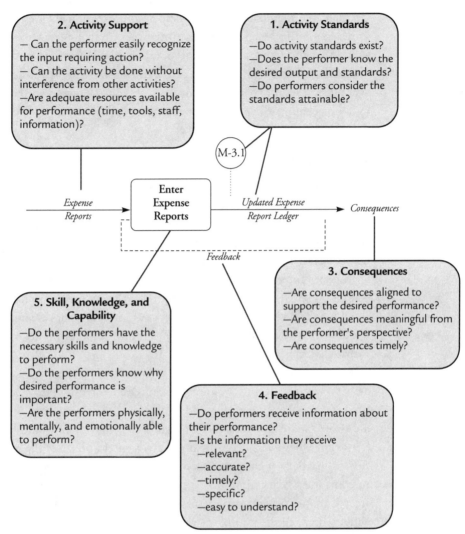

Figure 6.4 Factors affecting the performance of an activity. (Modified after Rummler and Brache, *Improving Performance.*)

standard, but also to devise an arrangement to make sure that they don't forget it and that other, new performers learn of the standard. Moving the standard from a line of text in a manual to a sign posted in the workplace is one way to accomplish this.

Do performers consider the standards attainable? Few people persist in trying to achieve something they can't achieve. When systems designers are asked to create components that are expected to achieve results the designers know they can't achieve, they tend to create components that simply do what can be done.

Unattainable standards shouldn't happen, but occasionally they are established by someone who isn't being realistic. A manager needs to check to see that everyone agrees that the standards are, indeed, attainable. If they aren't, either because no one could achieve that standard, or because an existing performer can't, the manager needs to make changes. In the first case, one changes the standard. In the second, one changes the performer or system.

2. Activity Support

Can the performer easily recognize the input requiring action? Consider a situation in which salespeople are "wasting their time on unqualified prospects." The manager should begin by determining if the salespeople know what a "qualified prospect" is. If the salespeople don't know the difference, then one step in solving the problem is to teach them how to recognize qualified and unqualified prospects. There are lots of problems that arise from similar causes. Diagnosticians don't check for certain potential problems because they don't recognize the signs that suggest they should make such a check. Developers create systems that respond to one set of inputs but don't build components that respond to other inputs because they don't realize that those situations could occur.

Can the activity be done without interference from other activities? Sometimes one activity will interfere with another. Consider, for example, a salesperson under pressure to obtain more sales and to provide documentation for past sales. These are two separate activities, and in a good situation there would be time for both. Sometimes, however, achieving one activity might preclude the successful completion of another. Or consider that one person may need to answer phones right next to someone who is trying to write a report. The report writer is constantly distracted by the person carrying on phone conversations. Or consider that a given activity may require a forklift, which someone else is always using for some other activity. In an ideal workplace none of these things happen, but in the real world they often do. Managers need to check the environment in which the work is to take place to assure themselves that one activity isn't interfering with the performance of another.

Are adequate resources available for performance (time, tools, staff, information)? Are needed resources available to those performing the activity? Do they have the time required? Do they have the tools needed for the job? If staff support is required, is it available and adequate for the job? If information is needed, is it available? These are obvious sorts of things, but more performance failures can be tracked to environmental problems than to lack of trained employees or employees who willfully choose not to perform some task. This is an extension of budgeting—assuring that employees and systems have the resources needed to perform their jobs.

3. Consequences

Are consequences aligned to support the desired performance? Motivation can be turned into a complex subject. In most cases it's really quite simple. It involves knowledge of the task to be performed, consequences, and feedback. Consequences refer to whatever follows the performance of an activity. Salespeople who make sales usually expect praise and bonuses. Every sales manager knows that a good incentive system gets good results. If people perform and only get complaints that they didn't do even better, in most cases it results in even less adequate performance. Imagine two activities: sales and entering information about sales. Imagine that the salesperson has less time than is needed to perform both tasks well. Further imagine that he or she gets a significant bonus for every sale but only gets complaints at the end of the month if all the system entries haven't been made. Which is the salesperson likely to do? It's always important to not only consider the consequences of each task by itself, but to also consider the effect of asking one individual to do several tasks with different consequences.

Are consequences meaningful from the performer's perspective? Different individuals respond to different types of consequences. It's important that the consequences be appropriate to the individual. Bonuses usually work, but in many situations, a day off will be more appreciated than a small bonus. Some employees look forward to the opportunity to do some travel, and others regard it as punishment. The good manager should have a clear idea about the consequences that will be valued by different employees.

Are consequences timely? Lots of research shows that consequences that immediately follow an activity are more likely to affect performance than those delayed. This doesn't mean that you need to hand salespeople money as soon as they return from a successful sales call. It does mean that the reward system should be clear so that the salesperson can calculate what bonus he or she made on that sales call. Making an effort without knowing if there will be consequences isn't a good practice. Giving someone a big, surprise bonus at the end of the year isn't nearly as good as giving smaller bonuses that are clearly associated with excellent performance. Best is a system that makes the consequences clear so that the employee can mentally reward him- or herself when they succeed. The same thing is true in reverse. Punishment should be closely associated with the action that deserves punishment. Waiting for a yearly evaluation to tell someone he or she is not performing up to snuff is a bad policy.

4. Feedback

Do performers receive information about their performance? Forgetting more explicit rewards, every manager should ask if employees receive information about the outcomes of their work. Assume the manager collects information about the number of chairs that arrive at the distributor's site undamaged versus with defects. As soon as the manager gets such information, he or she should pass it along to the employees involved. If defects go down, employees should learn about it (and receive praise as a consequence). If defects go up, employees should be informed immediately. Similarly, if chairs arrived damaged as a result of poor packaging, the employees in shipping should learn about it immediately, and vice versa. In too many companies, employees try to do their jobs, and month in and month out no one tells them if their work is adequate or not. After awhile, most employees will take a little less care if, as far as they can tell, no one notices or cares if they take more care. This is an area where the process sponsor plays an important role. Often the feedback needed by people in one subprocess isn't immediately available to the functional manager managing that subprocess. Care taken in packing may only pay off in reduced customer complaints, which go to sales and service and never directly to manufacturing or packaging. It's the process sponsor's job to design a process-wide feedback system that assures that subprocess managers have the information they need to provide their people with timely feedback.

Is the information they receive relevant, accurate, timely, specific, and easy to understand? As with consequences, there is more useful and less useful feedback. It's important to tell the packaging people that chairs are getting damaged in transit because chairs aren't properly packed. It's much more useful to tell them exactly how the chairs are being damaged so they will know how to change their packaging process to avoid the problem. Many companies provide managers with accounting data that is summarized in ways only accountants can understand. This isn't useful feedback. (This is one of the reasons for moving to an activity-based costing system to assure that cost information can tell specific employees about whether specific activities and subprocesses are contributing to the value of products or costing the company money.) A manager that yells that a subprocess isn't performing up to snuff without being specific about what's wrong is only creating anxiety and increasing the problems facing the people in that subprocess.

5. Skill, Knowledge, and Capability

Do the performers have the necessary skills and knowledge to perform? In many companies, the solution to all performance problems is to provide more training. For many employees, one of the worst features of a job is having to sit through training courses that drone on about things one already knows. The performance of a task requires specific information and the skills needed to evaluate the information, make decisions, and perform tasks. In most cases the place to begin is to identify the performer who is doing the job right, and then ask what is missing in the case of a performer who isn't doing the job right. If the deficient performer needs to learn specific items of knowledge or specific skills, then some kind of training is appropriate. Before training, however, be sure you really are facing a skill/knowledge problem. If employees have performed correctly in the past, it's very unlikely they have forgotten what they knew. It's much more likely in that case to be an environmental problem or a problem arising from a lack of feedback or consequences.

Do the performers know why desired performance is important? The importance and effort we assign to a task usually reflects our understanding of the importance or the consequences that result. If employees don't realize that some seemingly minor shutdown procedure can, infrequently, cause a major explosion, they might tend to skip the shutdown procedure. On most days, indeed for months or years, there may be no consequence. In these situations it's important that employees have a good overview of what's important and why it's important.

Are the performers physically, mentally, and emotionally able to perform? Finally, it's important to assure that performers can actually perform the tasks assigned. If an employee can't reach a shelf or can't read English, there are tasks they simply can't perform. In some cases changes in the environment will help. Steps can be provided or signs can be posted in another language. In some cases, however, an individual simply isn't able to perform a task. In those cases another performer needs to be put on the task.

As we suggested earlier, most of these same criteria apply to systems, although in the case of systems, the understanding and the feedback usually involve the person maintaining the software system and not the software itself.

An interesting complement to the approach we have described here is provided by the People Capability Maturity Model (People-CMM). We have already discussed the CMM model in the Introduction. It provides an analysis of the process orientation and maturity of organizations based on standards developed by Carnegie-Mellon University. When we spoke of it earlier, we emphasized the transitions organizations go through to become more systematic in their use of a process-oriented approach to management. Bill Curtis and others have created a variation on CMM that emphasizes how organizations support their workforce, and has shown cultural changes that occur in the way people are managed as organizations become more sophisticated in their use and management of processes. The People-CMM approach should be studied by any manager that wants a high-level overview of how effective organizations change their people management practices as they become more mature in their support of processes. We describe a good book on this approach in the Notes and References section at the end of the book.

Managing the Performance of Activities

Broadly, an operational manager is responsible for four things:

1. Identifying goals to be accomplished
2. Organizing activities to accomplish those goals
3. Monitoring the output of the activities to assure they meet their assigned goals
4. Diagnosing problems and fixing them when activity output is inadequate

In many if not most cases, defective output is a result of a flaw in the design of the activity or an environmental problem that prevents the correct execution of the activity. In rarer cases, the correction of the defect requires a change in the software system or one or more people assigned to perform the task.

The key, as we have stressed elsewhere, is for operational managers to organize around subprocesses and activities. Managing employees separate from the activities they are expected to perform is always a bad practice. The good manager begins by understanding the process and improves it if he or she can. Only after the process is organized does the manager turn his or her attention to the performers, and then only in the context of successful or inadequate output measures. This approach can go a long way toward taking the blame out of management, and focusing everyone instead on the problems of performing activities in ways that achieve company goals.

Automating the Enter Expense Reports Activity

As we suggested earlier, the entry of expense reports is so straightforward that it has probably been automated at most companies.

In some cases employees enter their travel expense information directly in software programs on their laptop computers and transmit it, via the Internet, to accounting. The expense reports generated in this way may be examined by a clerk or passed electronically to an application that analyzes them, makes calculations, and generates checks for the employees. In most cases, however, an employee examines the forms on a computer screen and approves the claims before they are paid. In any case the paper documentation for the expenses still has to be mailed in and needs to be filed. Most large companies conduct internal audits to compare documentation with payments.

One way we might represent this situation is illustrated in Figure 6.5. In this case we show that the entry of expense reports by the salespeople is a mixed manual/systems task. (The salesperson is completing a form managed by a software application that he or she accesses via the Internet.) Later, before a payment can be made, the report must be reviewed by an expense report clerk and approved. This is another mixed activity. The report clerk is also using a computer. The sales system sends the report to the clerk's computer and he or she approves it, after comparing it to the sales person's documentation. After the clerk indicates that the report is approved, the sales system automatically generates the payment to the salesperson and transfers the money to his or her bank account. Meanwhile, the expense report clerk files the documentation.

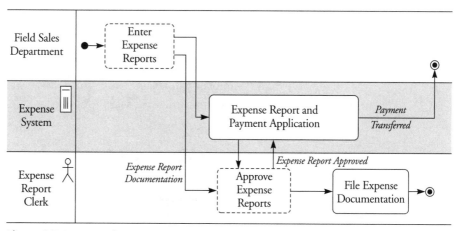

Figure 6.5 Automated expense report system.

In Figure 6.4 we assumed that the Enter Expense Reports activity was performed by a clerk. In Figure 6.5 we assume the entry activity is performed by a salesperson.

In Figure 6.5 the expense clerk has a new job. The forms now arrive by computer, and the clerk approves them online. The inputs would be computer screens rather than forms. The clerk would have to know how to use a computer, access the electronic forms, and approve them. The procedure would be different, and the clerk would need to learn the new sequence. In this case, as with most automated systems, one of the key problems would be consequences and feedback. It's easy to automate the system and forget that the performer may no longer be in a position to know about the consequences of his or her work. If we want the clerk to review and approve 50 reports a day, we might want to provide a counter as part of the software application so the clerk knows how he or she is doing. We might also want to create a way for the clerk to learn when payments are made so he or she will be in a position to tell a salesperson who inquires about the status of a check when it will likely be paid.

In effect, each time an arrow goes from a manual activity to an automated activity, there is a computer interface, made up of one or multiple computer screens that the user needs to master. The salesperson has a set of computer screens that allow him or her to create a new expense report and then fill in expense information. Similarly, the clerk interacts with the expense reports on screen. The clarity and logic of the screen layouts is a major factor in efficient processing.

We haven't shown what happens in the case of various exceptions as, for example, when the documentation is incomplete, or when the clerk needs to move an expense item from one category to another or to disallow it altogether. We might create an Activity Worksheet to document this information. If we were going to ask an IT group to create the Expense Report application, they would need answers to these questions. On the other hand, if we buy the Expense Report application from an outside vendor, they should provide documentation, and the manager and employee will need to study the documentation and redesign their activity to accommodate the new software application.

A More Complex Activity

We considered the expense approval activity because it was simple and provided us with a good overview of what was involved in analyzing an activity. Now, let's consider a more complex activity, like selling. Assume that the same company that

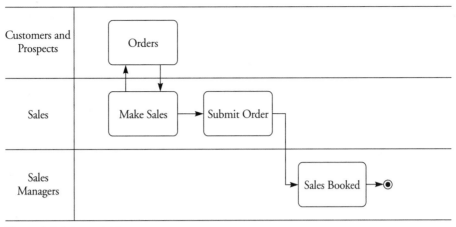

Figure 6.6 Sales activities.

employs the Expense Report Entry Clerk also employs salespeople. These salespeople sell the company's products throughout North America by calling on customers, explaining the products, and taking orders. The salespeople are divided into regions managed by regional managers, and so forth. To keep things relatively simple, we are only going to focus on the sales job in its most generic form. In a process diagram, it might simply look like Figure 6.6.

Once again, we could easily analyze the sales activities in much greater detail. For our purposes, however, it might be easier, in this case, to provide a job description in a text format. Figure 6.7, for example, is an overview of the salesperson's job description.

We could go further and write more detailed descriptions of each of these activities and assign measures to each or at least to the more important activities. For example, we could specify how many sales are expected per unit of time, how many prospect calls need to be made each month, or when expense accounts need to be submitted.

In effect, the job description in Figure 6.7 defines the salesperson's job. Assuming we only want to list two activities—Make Sales and Submit Orders—then this job description defines the steps that define those activities.

If you were the sales manager and you decided that sales were inadequate, you would need to define the tasks as we have and measure results to obtain some idea about what could be wrong. Measures of actual sales performance might reveal that most salespeople were performing in an adequate manner, but that a few weren't. In that case the sales manager would need to focus on the salespeople who weren't performing adequately. If most salespeople were performing in about the

---

Sales Activities That Define the Salesperson's Job

Selling Activities
1. Customer-Related Activities
    1.1 Prepare Account-Related Paperwork
    1.2 Prepare Cross-Selling Proposals
    1.3 Make Maintenance Calls
    1.4 Maintain Customer Contact by Phone or Email
2. Prospect-Related Activities
    2.1 Identify New Prospects
    2.2 Contact and Qualify New Prospects
    2.3 Make Sales Calls
    2.4 Develop Proposals
    2.5 Maintain Prospect Contact by Phone or Email

Overhead Activities
3. Planning and Coordinating Activities
    3.1 Time and Territory Planning
    3.2 Prioritizing Accounts
    3.3 Key Account Strategizing
4. Organizational Activities
    4.1 Meeting with Manager
    4.2 Attending Sales Meetings
    4.3 Accounting for Time and Expenses
    4.4 Preparing Special Reports
5. Product Knowledge
    5.1 Keeping Current on New Products
    5.2 Keeping Current on Competitive Products
    5.3 Maintaining Contacts with In-House Specialists
6. Self-Development and Motivation
    6.1 Keeping Current on General Business Trends
    6.2 Keeping Current on General Selling and Marketing
       Trends and Practices
    6.3 Arranging a Personal Schedule of Contingencies

Figure 6.7 Job description for salesperson.

same manner, however, then the manager would need to consider redesigning the sales job or activity to correct a more generic problem.

In either case, the place to begin the analysis would be to analyze the sales tasks and compare them with the human performance model we presented in Figure

6.4. To make this easier, we use a Human Performance Analysis Worksheet, which is pictured as Figure 6.8.

We haven't filled in the complete worksheet, but we did enter a few questions to suggest how a sales manager might begin to analyze what could be wrong with a deficient sales activity.

To analyze the sales activity, one begins by identifying the measures and examining historical records. The best performer should be compared with the average performer. That provides information on the gap between the best and the average, and provides a measurement of how much improvement could be obtained if everyone performing the activity performed as well as the best performer. Assuming the gap is worth the effort, then you need to examine the performance variables, comparing in each case the best and the average salesperson, to identify just where the differences lie. (We'll speak more of this type of analysis in the next chapter when we consider measurement in more detail.) Once the problems are identified, the supervisor can develop an improvement program.

Analyzing a Completely Automated Activity

The expense clerk's job provided a nice example of a simple job that might involve a mix of manual and computer-aided performance. The sales job is a more complex job that also has computer-aided elements, but is primarily a job performed by a human employee. In addition, the job is complex enough to assure that the manual or procedural aspects of the job are trivial compared with the analysis, decision-making, and human interaction skills required of the performer. The sales job is the kind of job that might require human performance analysts from human resources to help define and to assist in any needed training.

A third possibility is that we define an activity that will be completely automated. During the initial analysis phase of most process redesign projects, it doesn't make any difference whether the activity is performed by a person or a software system running on a computer. In both cases we need to need to determine the inputs and outputs of the activity, and measures for judging the quality of the outputs. Similarly, we need to determine how the activity relates to other activities in the same process and who will be responsible for managing the activity.

Once we decide the activity will be automated, we usually turn the actual software development task over to an appropriate IT group within the organization.

Human Performance Analysis Worksheet						
Process or Subprocess: _XYZ Sales Process_		Activity or Job: _XYZ Sales Activity_		IS (✓) or SHOULD ( ) Analysis		
Tasks Included in Activity	Measures of Task Performance	Potential Performance Problems				
		Activity Specifications	Activity Support	Consequences	Feedback	Skill, Knowledge, and Capability
1. Customer-Related Activities - Preparing account-related paperwork - Preparing cross-selling proposals - Making maintenance calls - Maintaining customer contact	Increase sales to existing customers by 12% per quarter	Does the salesperson know the goals? Does the salesperson consider the goals attainable?	Does sales-person's territory have enough prospects?	Does the current bonus system reflect the effort required?	Does the salesperson get email whenever the company gets a complaint, or a compliment from one of his/her customers?	Does the sales-person understand the new product line? Does the sales-person understand how to demonstrate the new product with his/her laptop?
2. Prospect-Related Actvities - Identifying new prospects - Contacting and qualifying prospects - Making sales calls - Developing proposals - Maintaining prospect contact	Make 20 new sales per month.		Does the salesperson get leads whenever they come to company? Does the salesperson have the new laptops with the new demo loaded?			

Figure 6.8 A partially completed Human Performance Analysis Worksheet for the Sales Activity.

In some cases we will be asking that an existing application be modified. In other cases we will be asking for the creation of a new software system. In either case, there usually isn't a one-to-one relationship between activities identified on our process diagrams and the software application to be developed. Recall Figure 6.5, where we indicated that a software application would capture expense reports from salespeople, place reports on the expense report clerk's computer, and later generate payments and transfer them to salespeople's bank accounts. In this case we were treating the software application as a black box. We really don't know or care if the application that automated the sales expense report entry activity is a single

Human Performance Analysis Worksheet (continued)						
Process or Subprocess: *XYZ Sales Process*			Activity or Job: *XYZ Sales Activity*		IS (✓) or SHOULD ( ) Analysis	
Tasks Included in Activity	Measures of Task Performance	Potential Performance Problems				
		Activity Standards	Activity Support	Consequences	Feedback	Skill, Knowledge, and Capability
3. Planning and Coordinating Activities - Time and territory planning - Prioritizing accounts - Key account strategizing						
4. Organizational Activities - Meeting with manager - Attending sales meetings - Accounting for time and expenses - Preparing special reports						
5. Product Knowledge - Keeping current on new products - Keeping current on competitive products - Maintaining contacts with in-house specialists						
6. Self-Development and Motivation - Keeping current on general business trends - Keeping current on general selling and marketing trends - Arranging a personal schedule of contingencies						

application or a combination of applications. That's a software design issue that IT will need to solve. It will depend on existing software applications being used, on the hardware used by various individuals, on the infrastructure already in place, and on the skills and software architectural strategies of the IT organization.

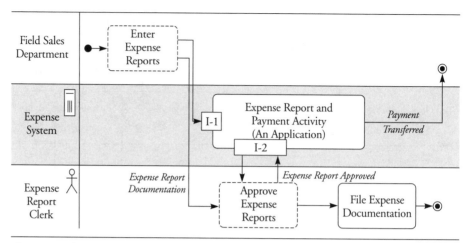

Figure 6.9 The expense system with software interfaces noted.

The important thing from our perspective is to define the inputs and outputs, and the performance requirements of the activity, as best we can, and then to turn the task over to IT. Figure 6.9 reproduces a variation of Figure 6.5. In this case we have added small boxes where the arrows from manual activities interface with a software system and labeled them, I-1 and I-2, to indicate that there are two interfaces we will need to describe. Depending on the time, we could actually sketch the screens that we imagine that would be used at each interface. Similarly, we could create lists of all of the data that is to be captured by each screen. We probably wouldn't go so far as to try to organize or structure the data to be collected, since that is usually done by the individual in IT who creates the database to store expense information. We can, however, indicate what data we know we will want to collect. (In the Notes and References at the end of the book, we suggest books on interface or Web form design.)

Predictably, IT will need more information than we will probably provide. We probably won't consider all the exceptions, and an IT analyst will surely want to work with our design team to define more exact requirements. In essence, when we seek to fill the salesperson's job, we hire for a lot of skills, knowledge, and experience. We only have to teach a new salesperson a portion of his or her job. Humans come equipped with lots of common sense and can generalize from common business practices, or ask when they run into problems. Software systems don't come with common sense or the ability to ask when they get in trouble. Hence, we need to be much more precise about defining activities that are to be performed by software systems and anticipate every possible problem that might occur. The key, from the perspective of the process designer, however, is who should do what when. We believe that the process design team should define each activity as if it were being done by an intelligent person. Beyond that, when it turns out that the task is to be performed by a software system, IT analysts should be called in to work with the process design team to define the activity more precisely, and then be allowed to develop the software application in the way that works best. IT may decide that five different activities will be part of a single software application, or should be implemented via two separate software components. The process re-design team shouldn't worry about such details, as long as IT develops a system that functions as specified on the process diagram. In other words, the IT application must take the specified inputs from the designated individuals and make the specified outputs in accordance with measures established by the process redesign team.

In a nutshell, we carefully define the inputs and outputs of activities that are to be performed by software applications and leave the actual development of the software applications to the IT folks.

Activities, Job Descriptions, and Applications

We need to clarify one final issue: the relationship between activities and the jobs or software applications that implement them. In some simple cases, a single person may be assigned to a single activity—as we assumed the Expense Report Clerk was in our first example. In such a case, an activity description and a job description would just be different perspectives on the same entity. Similarly, we later assumed that a single software application implemented the Expense Report and Payment Activity in Figure 6.9. In this latter case, the description of all of the interfaces supported by the Expense Report and Payment Activity would describe all the interfaces of the application. These examples are the exceptions rather than the rule.

In most cases a large process will support many subprocesses divided in many different activities. Some individuals will be responsible for multiple activities. Consider the example of the sales activities outlined in Figure 6.7. Each salesperson would be responsible for all of those activities. Each of those activities would have goals and measures, and each salesperson would be responsible for meeting all of the goals of all of the activities that were included in his or her job description.

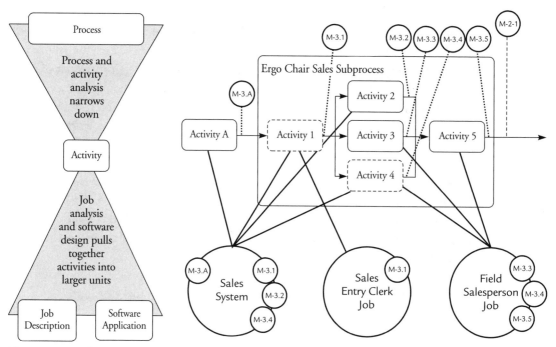

Figure 6.10 Analysis and then synthesis and the assignment of goals or output measures to jobs or systems.

Similarly, it might make sense for managers to divide a process into a sequence of activities that describe the order in which things had to happen. On the other hand, it might make sense for IT to develop a single application to support every activity in the sequence. Consider a situation where several individuals process common documents that are maintained by a workflow system. The entire process is supported by a single workflow application, and the documents being processed are maintained in a single database. In effect, each person simply edits the document in the database.

We have focused on analyzing processes and activities and defining the order in which they should occur. Once the activity or process descriptions are complete, however, we often reverse the process and lump activities together to define jobs or software applications. Figure 6.10 provides an overview of the process we are describing and illustrates how a redesign team might assign output measures to several activities and how they might be lumped as job descriptions or software applications were designed.

In Figure 6.10 we see that a sales application designed to support the Ergo Chair Sales Subprocess might end up supporting four different activities. Similarly, we see how individuals assigned to the Field Salesperson Job might be required to do some or all of the steps defined by three different activities, and be evaluated by output measures associated with the same three activities.

Assume that the manager responsible for monitoring the entire subprocess determines that the subprocess is performing in a suboptimal manner. The subprocess manager's job is to determine what is wrong. He or she will probably begin by checking each of the activities included in the subprocess, as well as the inputs received from Activity A. Once a given activity is determined to be suboptimal—say, Activity 4—the manager still has to determine if it's the sales system that is failing, or the field salespeople who use the system who are performing in a suboptimal manner.

Different organizations track these relationships in different ways. We recommend that process diagrams like the ones described in Chapter 5 be stored in databases managed by software tools and that measures and job descriptions or software systems involved in each activity be stored with the activity in the same database. We'll return to these issues after we have considered the process manager's role in more detail and when we consider the use of software tools to support business processes.

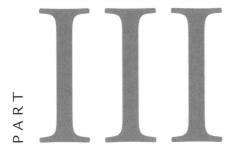

PART III

MANAGING AND IMPROVING BUSINESS PROCESSES

I N THIS PART we describe how existing processes can be managed and continually improved.

We'll begin in Chapter 7 by considering the nature of management and describing how managers are responsible for planning, organizing, and controlling the processes they manage. We'll consider how a company might divide responsibilities between a project manager who manages a business process and departmental managers who are responsible for specific activities.

Chapter 8 will describe the Six Sigma approach, the dominant approach to continual process improvement. Most Six Sigma efforts focus on creating teams to improve existing processes. We'll consider how Six Sigma projects are organized and how these establish measures for processes. You may not be interested in the rigorous statistical analysis required by Six Sigma, but learning how to measure processes will be useful to anyone involved in business process improvement.

7

Managing and Measuring Business Processes

I**N THIS CHAPTER** we want to consider how to manage business processes. As we will use the term, business process management includes the measurement and ongoing improvement of processes, and we will consider both in this chapter.

Management, like analysis, varies from level to level. Organizational management is mostly concerned with strategy and the creation of an enterprise-wide process architecture, and we treated those responsibilities in Chapters 3 and 4. In this chapter, we will focus on how companies can manage processes and activities.

In Chapter 1, when we discussed Geary Rummler's contribution to process analysis, we reviewed, briefly, the Rummler-Brache performance matrix or framework. A more detailed version of that matrix is reproduced as Figure 7.1.

As you can see in the performance matrix, there are different goals, different design decisions, and different management tasks at each level. We'll begin by considering, abstractly, the role of any manager with operational responsibilities. Next we'll consider how a company can organize to assure that processes and departmental functions are both properly managed. Then we'll consider how goals can be passed down through an organization and how they should be measured. Finally, we'll consider ongoing process improvement, as it relates to management.

	Goals and measures	Design and implementation	Management
Organizational level	Organizational goals and measures of organizational success • Has the organization's strategy/direction been articulated and communicated? • Does this strategy make sense, in terms of the external threats and opportunities and the internal strengths and weaknesses? • Given this strategy, have the required outputs of the organization and the level of performance expected from each output been determined and communicated?	Organizational design and implementation • Are all relevant departments and value chains described in a process architecture? • Are all departments and processes necessary? • Is the current flow of inputs and outputs between departments, value chains, and key processes appropriate? • Does the formal organization structure support the strategy and enhance the efficiency of the system?	Organizational management • Have appropriate department goals been set? • Is relevant performance measured? • Are resources appropriately allocated? • Are the interfaces between departments being managed?
Process level	Process goals and measures of process success • Are goals for key value chains, processes, and subprocesses linked to each other and to customer/organization goals?	Process design and implementation • Are value chains and business processes decomposed into logical and efficient processes and subprocesses? • Are these the most efficient and effective value chain, process, or subprocess for accomplishing the goals assigned?	Process management • Have appropriate process subgoals been set? • Is process performance managed? • Are sufficient resources allocated to each process? • Are the interfaces between subprocesses and activities being managed?
Activity or performance level	Activity goals and measures of activity success • Are activity outputs and standards linked to process requirements? (Which are in turn linked to customer and organization requirements?)	Activity design and implementation • Are activity requirements reflected in system or job descriptions of people assigned to the activity? • Are activity steps in a logical sequence? Have superlative policies and procedures been developed? • Is the activity environment ergonomically sound?	Activity management • Do the performers understand the activity outputs and standards they are expected to meet? • Do performers have resources, clear signals, priorities, and a logical job design? • Do performers know if they are meeting goals? • Are performers rewarded for achieving activity goals? • Do performers have the skill/knowledge to meet goals?

Figure 7.1 The Rummler-Brache performance matrix. (Modified after Rummler and Brache, *Improving Performance.*)

Managing Business Processes

Many books have been written about each of the different aspects of management. This book is about improving business processes, so we will look at management from that particular perspective. When we consider the management of processes and activities, we are primarily concerned with setting goals, assigning tasks, monitoring results, improving processes, and taking corrective actions as needed.

Many experienced business process practitioners believe that the failure to manage processes effectively is the major cause of process problems. In some cases an existing process can be significantly improved simply by installing or improving the management system used with the process. More importantly, when new processes are implemented, a good management system is the key to assuring the new process is actually implemented effectively.

The Role of a Manager

The place to start a discussion of process management is with a basic description of how managers control and are responsible for business processes. Let's start at the bottom, with a supervisor who is responsible for a single activity. Let's assume that the activity involves a single task, assembling a widget, and that it is done by a single employee. Figure 7.2 shows how we might diagram such an example.

In this instance, we assume that a process design team analyzed the widget process and established the Assemble Widgets activity shown in Figure 7.2. The design team probably didn't provide a box for the supervisor, since management is usually thought of as something rather different than the process flow. If they assumed that widget assembly was going to be done by an employee, however, they undoubtedly assumed that someone would supervise that activity. At a minimum,

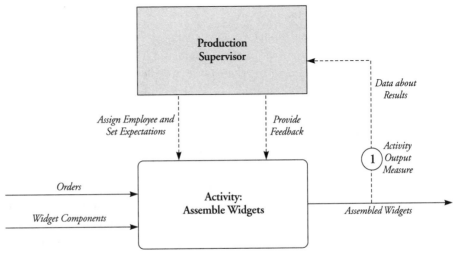

Figure 7.2 How a supervisor manages an activity.

a supervisor was going to need to hire or assign someone to the activity. This same supervisor would be responsible for training the employee, if necessary, and for establishing some expectations or goals. Similarly, the supervisor would presumably monitor the outputs of the Assemble Widgets activity to see that they were up to standard. In an ideal world, the supervisor would congratulate the employee if the work was good. On the other hand, if the output wasn't up to standard, then the supervisor would let the employee know about the problem and work with the employee to fix it.

Let's assume widgets are easy to assemble, and there are only a few orders each day that arrive in the morning. Let's further assume that the supervisor and the employee agree that every widget is to be correctly assembled and that all orders are to be complete before the employee leaves work. In other words, we have two goals, or measures: (1) all widgets assembled correctly and (2) no unfulfilled orders at the end of the day. The supervisor could measure the first by checking the widgets as they are completed, or by working out an arrangement with the next process that would notify the supervisor if any widgets were delivered that weren't assembled correctly. The second could be measured by checking with the employee to see that all orders were filled, or by arranging to monitor the number of orders received each day and comparing it with the number of widgets assembled each day.

We'll consider other tasks later, but for the moment let's assume that this simple case defines the generic relationship between a manager and a process or activity. The manager establishes expectations for the process and determines how the process is to be done and who is to do it. As the process is executed, the manager monitors the outputs to see that they are up to expectations, and if they aren't, the manager takes corrective action.

This basic model wouldn't change if the activity were done by a software system or by a team of employees. There might be special problems in determining what software element or what specific employee is responsible for specific defects, but those are details we will ignore at this time.

A Closer Look at a Manager's Job

Figure 7.3 provides a slightly more detailed analysis of a manager's responsibilities. This analysis of management is based on the ongoing work of Geary Rummler. In effect, relative to some specific process or activity, a given manager has the responsibility for setting goals and expectations, planning the process or activity, providing resources and staffing, monitoring its outcomes, and taking actions if the

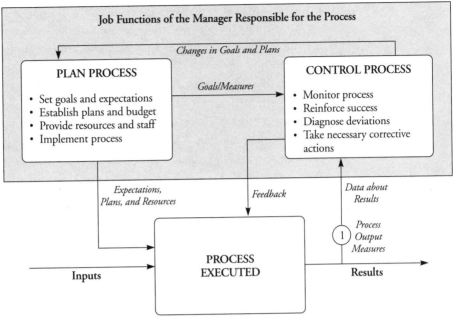

Figure 7.3 A more detailed look at a manager's job. (After Rummler.)

outcomes deviate from established goals. We can use this same basic diagram, whether we are defining the role of a business line manager, a department head, a middle-level production manager, or an accounting supervisor. Work gets done in processes. Managers are responsible to see that work gets done in the processes they manage. To emphasize our particular concerns, we have divided all managerial tasks into two broad and somewhat arbitrary processes: *Planning Processes* and *Managing Processes*. Within each of these two categories, we have listed some specific tasks.

▶ *Plan process.* In essence, a manager is first responsible for defining the process he or she is assigned to manage. Even if the process already exists and was defined by a previous manager, the new manager is responsible for understanding it and satisfying him- or herself that it is as efficient and productive as possible. This begins with a description of the scope of the process and a definition of its goals or outputs. To avoid a silo mentality, in an ideal organization the manager's manager would explain the superprocess or value chain that provides the context for the manager's specific process so the new manager can see how the specific process relates to others, and ultimately to customers. Once the process itself is defined and jobs and tasks are understood, then the manager is in a position to establish a budget. A budget requires that the manager consider the space and resources required for the process, the people or hardware needed, and a plan for how the process will be established and maintained. And once a budget and a plan are complete, the manager is able to implement the process and maintain it.

▶ *Process executed.* The process itself might be something done manually by employees, something done by a computer software system or a machine, or some combination of these. These concerns are important when one establishes a budget and a plan, but they don't really affect the overall nature of the managerial tasks. In all cases the manager must plan for the process and then monitor it and take corrective action if the process isn't producing adequate and timely results. In other words, managers are responsible for the outputs of activities, whether they are performed by employees or by systems.

▶ *Control process.* Once the process is functioning, the manager is responsible for gathering data about the outputs or results of the process. In effect, the manager turns goals into specific measures and then gathers data to see if the measures are achieved. If the measures are achieved, the manager can take actions to reward and sustain the subprocesses, activities, and individuals responsible for the success. If the measures aren't achieved, the manager must determine what is causing the deviation. This involves examining the process in detail and locating the specific reason for the deviation. Then the manager must take preventive or corrective actions to assure that the measures are met. This may require changes to software systems or changes in the way employees perform specific tasks.

If the manager is near the top of the management hierarchy, correcting a deviation will typically involve holding one or more lower-level managers responsible for deviations in subprocesses or activities they are responsible for managing. If the manager is a supervisor, corrective action usually requires holding an application, machine, or an employee responsible for the problem. If the problem involves a software or machine problem, the manager must usually consult with the software developers or engineers responsible for the system or machine. If the process is performed by an employee, then feedback, retraining, restructuring the job, or punishment are all options.

Dozens of books have been written on each the different managerial tasks described in Figure 7.3. Books give advice on planning and scheduling, on setting goals and communicating them, on staffing, on providing feedback, on diagnosing problems, and on using data to revise goals. Our focus here is on managing processes, and we aren't going into any of these managerial tasks in any more detail.

The primary interest we have here is to point out how goals and measures are used by managers to assure that processes work as they should.

How to Manage a Process

Having defined a manager's job in a very general way, we will now shift focus and consider how a company might organize its managers to plan and control a process. In essence, a process-oriented organization must shift the ultimate managerial responsibility for managing a process to an individual who can comprehend and take responsibility for the entire process. Organizations that vest primary control in the hands of functional or departmental managers can never develop the kind of comprehensive, process focus that is required if an entire process is to be integrated and made as efficient as possible. In other words, organizations that want to manage processes need to create managers for their value chains or major business processes.

Different organizations have taken different approaches, and we don't suggest there is one right way. What we suggest, however, is an overview that can be implemented in various specific ways.

In Figure 7.4 we illustrate an organization that has three functional units: Sales, Manufacturing, and Delivery, each headed by a vice president. At the same time, the organization has created a senior vice president to manage the widget value chain. This creates what companies in the 1970s referred to as a *matrix management system*. The Sales Supervisor who manages the Sales process that occurs within the overall widget value chain reports to both the VP of sales and the SVP who is in charge of the widget process.

The key to making this approach work is to think of the management of the widget value chain as a team effort. In effect, each supervisor with management responsibility for a process that falls inside the widget value chain is a member of the widget value chain management team.

The SVP for the widget process is the head of the widget process management team and sets the agenda. The team works together to see that the process works smoothly and that the corporate goals assigned to the widget process are met. The SVP for the widget process is the ultimate monitor of customer satisfaction, which is one of the key ways of determining if the widget process is succeeding.

Some organizations have managers for product lines. Imagine that the widgets produced come in two varieties, one that sells to individuals and another that is sold, in bulk, to large companies. In that case, there might be a product manager

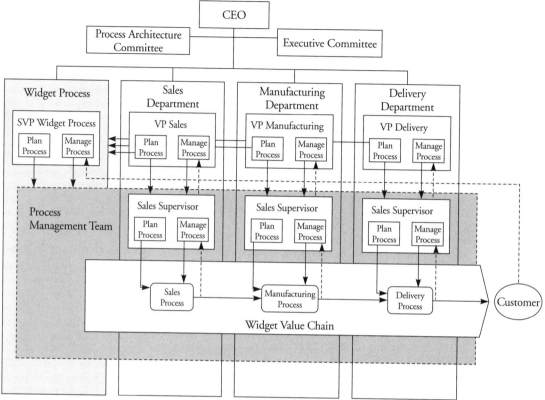

Figure 7.4 A high-level look at how processes are managed.

for individual widgets and another for bulk widgets. Some companies have experimented with splitting processes and having the product line manager manage their respective product lines. In most cases, however, it's more efficient to treat the supply chain and manufacturing operations as a single process and have a single manager responsible for the entire process. If the widget company has two product line managers, we suggest they would simply be additional members of the widget process management team.

The goal alignment process starts at the top. Depending on the organization, the executive committee, the strategy committee, or the process architecture committee assign high-level goals to the SVP for the widget process. The SVP communicates those goals to the process management team that then translates the broad goals into more specific goals and measures and determines how to achieve those goals.

If we were asked who the ultimate manager of the sales supervisor was, we'd say the SVP of the widget process.

Most organizations keep the functional or departmental units in order to oversee professional standards within disciplines, and to manage personnel matters. Thus, the VP of sales is probably responsible for hiring the Sales Supervisor shown in Figure 7.4 and for evaluating his or her performance and assigning raises and bonuses. The VP of sales is responsible for maintaining high sales standards within the organization. On the other hand, the ultimate evaluation of the Sales Supervisor comes from the SVP of the widget process. The Sales Supervisor is responsible for achieving results from the widget sales process and that is the ultimate basis for his or her evaluation. In a sense, the heads of departments meet with the SVP of the widget process and form a high-level process management team.

Departments or functional VPs can have people reporting to them that serve on different process management teams. They have their own goals and measures, but they relate to departmental discipline, sales, or accounting and not to the achievement of process goals, as such.

Most organizations are in transition from more traditional ways of organizing, to the kind of process governance we describe here. Recalling the CMM process maturity model we discussed in the Introduction, most organizations are at level 2.5. They only have some of their processes well defined and are only beginning to use process measures and process management techniques to control their organizations.

Goals, Measures, and Monitoring

Goals are general statements that describe what the company wants to achieve. They typically describe income, sales, or profits. Goals are translated into measures. *Measures* refer to how specific types of data are to be evaluated.

Functional versus Process Measures

Most organizations rely on departmental or functional goals and measures. They may talk process, but they measure silo-oriented results. Table 7.1 suggests how the measures differ.

Functional measures are usually derived from the types of measures reported to the analyst community on financial statements and on traditional ways of

Table 7.1 A comparison of some functional and process measures.

Department or function	Typical departmental measures	Typical process measures
Sales department	• Cost of sales • Revenue ($)	• Timely and accurate submission of orders • Timely and accurate entry of new orders • Cost of processing orders
Production department	• Cost of inventory • Cost of labor • Cost of materials • Cost of shipping	• Timely order scheduling • Timely and accurate production of orders • Timely shipment of orders • Cost of unit production and shipping costs
Finance department	• Percent of bad debt • Mean labor budget	• Timely and accurate invoice preparation • Timely and accurate credit checks for new accounts • Cost of processing an invoice
External organizational measures	• Gross revenue • Cost of sales • Growth of customer base • Price of stock	• Percent of on-time delivery • Percent of rejects • Customer satisfaction as measured on survey or index

measuring the efficiency of work within a department. *Process measures* derive from general measures of customer satisfaction with the outputs of a process. From these measures, we work backward to measure how each department might contribute to customer satisfaction.

Obviously they overlap in some areas, and both can be important. Managers all want their departments to be as efficient and productive as possible. And that usually means that we want to produce products and services as quickly and cheaply as possible, consistent with maintaining output standards. Similarly, customers want quality products, delivered quickly, that cost as little as possible, provided they meet the customer's standards. Where the two measures conflict, however, is when a functional measure slows or disrupts the overall speed or efficiency of the process to maximize some departmental-oriented goal. A more efficient sales process that produces more orders for products that aren't exactly like the products the company actually delivers isn't really a success. A manufacturing process that reduces inventory costs, but results in deliveries that are later than customers expect isn't a success either. Less expensive employees who can't quite do the tasks assigned to them up to the desired standard don't result in success.

We need a way to coordinate functional and process goals, while assuring that process goals always trump functional goals. The best way to do that is to assign a process sponsor whose job is to assure that there are process goals and measures, derived from continually measured external process measures, and then subdivided and coordinated with measures assigned to each department in a way that contributes to the overall production of the process outputs.

Creating Goals and Measures Hierarchies

At the top level of the organization, the goals and measures largely match the goals defined by the executive committee when they laid out the corporate strategy. As goals are delegated down in the organization, they become narrower and the measures associated with them become more specific. This happens because most organizations are made up of many different business processes, and each department or group is assigned only a portion of the overall corporate goals.

A value chain is divided into processes, which are, in turn, divided into subprocesses and subsubprocesses and eventually into specific activities. In an ideal situation, we establish one or more measures for each activity. In effect, as we analyze a process or redesign a process, we ask what that activity is contributing to the overall subprocess, process, or value chain to which it belongs. Then we establish a measure that we can use to determine that the activity is actually achieving its purpose. This approach provides a strong argument for not subdividing processes into very fine activities. As a rule we shouldn't subdivide processes any further than necessary to clearly understand what they do and how they contribute to the larger value chain.

Figure 7.5 shows one way of thinking about the way we refine goals and measures as we work our way down into a process. In this case we show how one might successively refine or subdivide goals in a sales organization, and which managers or technical people are responsible for seeing that measures are achieved. At the higher levels, we rely on more general goals that lump results together. At lower levels, however, we define the processes or activity sequences or steps within an activity that need to occur and create measures to determine if the process is working. In other words, we measure to see if steps are being accomplished correctly, in a timely manner.

In Figure 7.6 we consider the same basic idea but picture it in a different manner. In this figure we show a process with four subprocesses and several activities.

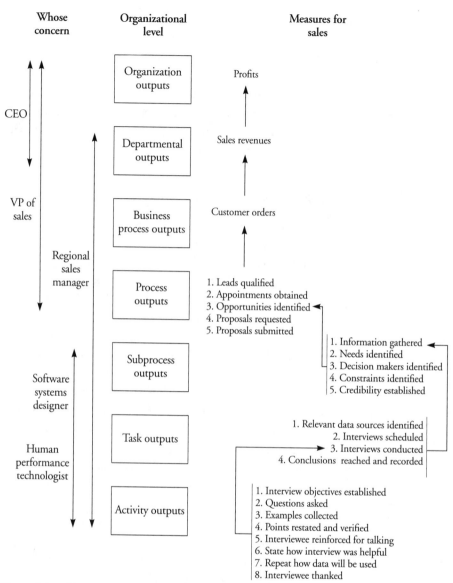

Figure 7.5 Drilling down into the goals of a sales organization.

(We have used a jagged line to reduce the size of the activities in this diagram.) At the top right, we show the ultimate measure, which is labeled M1-E (Measure 1, External). This is an external measure directly tied to customer performance. If we were selling items, it might simply be the number purchased. In the actual situation from which this example is drawn, the company relied on answers to a questionnaire that the company asks a set of customers to complete periodically.

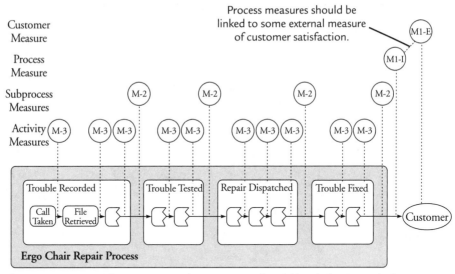

Figure 7.6 Measures for a process, subprocesses, and activities. (After Rummler.)

Specifically, it refers to the percentage of customers who say they are very satisfied with the repair and the percentage who say that the repair was done in less than four hours.

M1-E is very closely linked with the ultimate internal measure: M1-I (Measure 1, Internal). In this case the internal measure is used to determine the overall success of the process. As it happens, the internal measure checks the number of repairs that are done accurately the first time.

A third tier of measures is provided by the four M-2 measures. They check the outputs of the four subprocesses. An example is the second M-2 from the left, which measures the output of the Trouble Tested subprocess. Specifically, this measure checks the percentage of testing errors, the elapsed time in testing, and the time taken per test.

As a rule, the internal and external M1 measures are those checked by the process sponsor. They monitor the overall success of the process. The M2 measures are checked by both the process sponsor and by the manager in charge of the subprocess. They measure the success of subprocesses. In effect, well-defined subprocess measures assure that the handoffs between one subprocess and another are up to standard.

The M3 measures check the success of specific activities. They are monitored by the managers or supervisors responsible for the specific activities and by the manager responsible for the subprocess that contains each specific activity.

Process Measures Worksheet			
Process Measures: Ergo Chair Repair Process	M1-I Internal Measure: Quality: First-time accuracy of repairs.		M1-E External Measures: % yes on Q 19 "very satisfactory" % yes on Q 20 "less than 4 hours."
M-2 Subprocess: Trouble Recorded	Subprocess: Trouble Tested	Subprocess: Repair Dispatched	Subprocess: Trouble Fixed
#% of inaccurate trouble descriptions % of first-time correct trouble tickets Time per trouble ticket	#% of testing errors Elapsed time in testing Time per test	#% of dispatch (address) errors Elapsed time from testing to dispatch # of incorrect dispatches	#% of "non-fixes" to accurately record problems Elapsed time from dispatch to fix Time per fix
M-3 **Call Taken Activity:** #% of inaccurate or incomplete trouble descriptions % of trouble tickets returned due to missing/inaccurate information. Time/call Time/ticket **File Retrieved Activity:** #% of wrong files leading to inaccurate trouble descriptions % of returns due to wrong files. Time per retrieval % of "second" retrievals	*[Incomplete]*		

Figure 7.7 A Process Measures Worksheet is used to record specific measures that will be monitored.

The worksheet pictured in Figure 7.7 shows how we would record these measures. We haven't listed manager's titles or names on the worksheet, but that would probably be done on an actual worksheet.

We won't show it here, but another worksheet can be used to record what measures specific managers are responsible for, frequency and reporting responsibilities, and any incentives that are associated with the achievement of goals.

The Balanced Scorecard Approach

Many managers and organizations have embraced an approach called the *Balanced Scorecard* approach. This approach was developed at Harvard in the mid-1960s by Robert Kaplan and David Norton. It represents a major effort to link strategies to specific measures. It also represents an effort to discourage an undue emphasis on financial measures and ROI (return on investment). The Balanced Scorecard emphasizes that a company should monitor a number of key performance indicators (KPIs) that collectively tell the senior management how the organization is doing. Norton and Kaplan suggested that strategy could be conceptualized from different perspectives and that each perspective had its own KPIs. They suggest four perspectives:

▶ *Financial.* These KPIs focus on revenue growth, cash flow, and profitability.
▶ *Customers.* These KPIs focus on segments of the market and specific groups of customers and set goals and measures for each group.
▶ *Internal business processes.* These KPIs focus on measures of internal business process success.
▶ *Innovation and learning.* These KPIs focus on measuring if the technical infrastructure and employees with the required skill and knowledge are available.

Several books have been written on how one develops Balanced Scorecards and how one creates measures that tie to corporate strategies. If you haven't read one or more of these books, you should consider it. We believe that we have included everything that Norton and Kaplan include in their approach in the approach described in this book. Instead of emphasizing an approach to measurement, however, we have emphasized designing a business process and then measuring it as a whole (customer measures, financial measures). We find it easier to think of measurement in the context of processes and management practices and a hierarchy of process goals and measures, but we also feel comfortable representing those measures using Balanced Scorecard techniques.

Continuous Measurement and Improvement

If an organization establishes process measures that extend from the process to the activity, and if managers continuously check these measures and take actions when there are deviations, then process improvement becomes a part of every manager's job. In effect, measures determine how the activity should be performed. Higher-level measures determine that the outputs of the activities are resulting in the desired task, subprocess, or process outcomes. If any outputs deviate, the appropriate managers should take action.

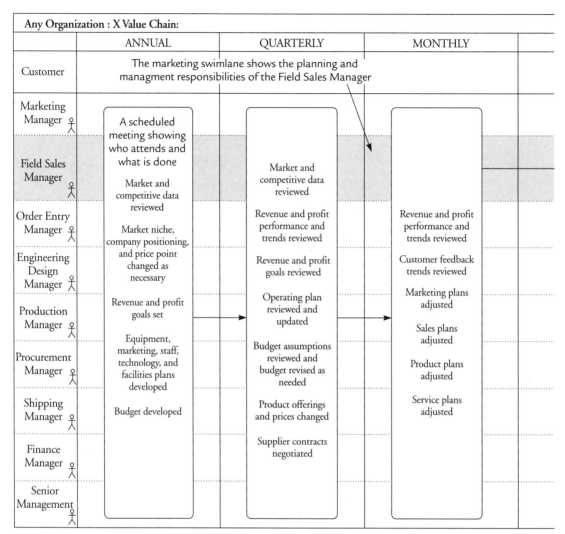

Figure 7.8 A Measuring and Scheduling Worksheet used to schedule meetings to review the success of a process. (Modified after Rummler.)

Figure 7.8 provides an overview of how a departmental group might organize to monitor the results of a given process. In this case we have used a special variant of our process diagram. On the left side we list all of the managers involved in the hierarchy. Along the top we've listed periods of time and then used rectangles to show who will be involved in review meetings and when they will occur. On the right side we have reproduced a portion of the actual process diagram to show what processes, subprocesses, and activities are being monitored. Most

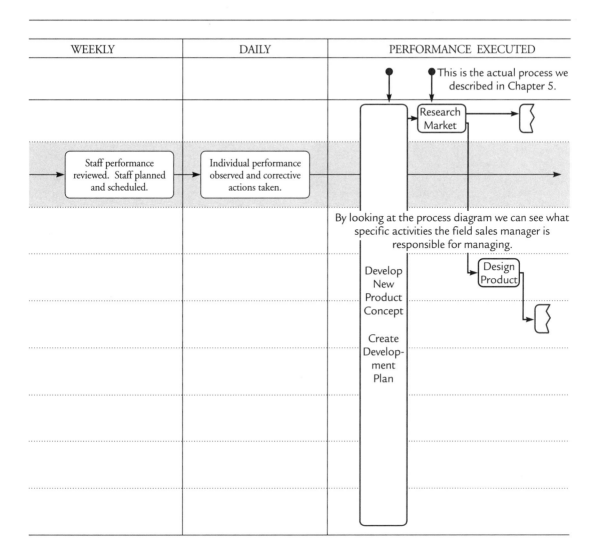

organizations won't include the process detail on the right, and most will have some other way of representing review meetings.

Figure 7.8 lays out a plan that managers can follow to assure that measures are taken and that higher-level processes meet their goals.

Any given activity may fail to produce adequate outputs for many different reasons. Some failures will be the result of a failure in process flow. The work assigned to the activity isn't appropriate or properly understood. But a flawed activity also represents a management failure. Managers are responsible for assuring that the people assigned to the activity understand what they are to do and have the resources to do it. And they are responsible for checking to see that the activity is done correctly, and that corrective feedback is provided if the activity isn't performed correctly.

Any process redesign team that is proposing a major change in the way things are done had better be sure they plan for changes in management. If a specific supervisor is to manage a given activity for new outcomes, the new outcomes need to be clearly specified. Moreover, the changes in the supervisor's job need to be incorporated in the job description of the supervisor's manager, and so on, right up the management hierarchy. If this is done during the redesign of the project, then everyone will know what to monitor, and who is responsible for what outcomes, when the new process is implemented. It may sound like a lot of work, but the alternative is to work hard on revising a process and then watch as it fails during implementation, when employees stick with previous tasks and managers don't spring into action to correct activities to assure that they conform with the goals of the new process.

Management Redesign at Chevron

A nice example of what management alignment can do is illustrated by a redesign effort undertaken by Chevron in 1995. At that time, Chevron was producing one million barrels of oil a day through six different refineries. The company was divided into three major functional units: Refining, Marketing, and Supply and Distribution. The company decided they needed to improve their supply chain system to better integrate their internal processes. According to Peter McCrea, a Chevron VP:

> We recognized that our system for planning and managing the supply chain, from crude acquisition to product distribution, was not working as well as it should. We had been working on this for a long time and were not making much progress. We decided we needed to take a holistic look at the entire supply chain.

The company called in consultants from Rummler-Brache and asked them for help. The consultants, in turn, proceeded through the steps of a process redesign, establishing a redesign team and establishing an overview of the existing process. Beyond that, however, rather than focus on redesigning the sequence of activities that made up the process, the team focused on how the process was currently measured and managed. They scrapped the old corporate operating plan and created a new plan based on linking corporate goals with process measures. Then they assigned managers the responsibility for controlling activities based on these measures. A senior manager was assigned the responsibility for the entire supply chain, and each manager who was responsible for a subprocess became part of his team.

In a report in 1996, Chevron identified savings of some $50 million and attributed a significant portion of that savings to "doing our work a different way, with common plans and measures."

We cite this example to stress two things. A good process redesign, without an accompanying management and measurement plan, often fails to get implemented. If it does get implemented, it often fails to get the desired results. A good process redesign, accompanied by a good management and measurement plan, is much more likely to be implemented and successful. And, in some cases, an existing process can be significantly improved, just by implementing a management and measurement plan that assures that the existing process works as it is intended to work.

In an ideal world, one round of process redesign would result in a nearly perfect process and appropriate goals and measures. Thereafter, managers would simply fine-tune the process by studying outputs and taking corrective action whenever necessary. In reality, of course, one round of process redesign improves the process, but leaves some problems that still need to be changed. Moreover, as time passes and employees change, new techniques are introduced, or as customer expectations rise, processes need to be further refined.

In many cases, process improvement is best undertaken by a group of employees working with the manager to refine the process. In the next chapter we will consider one of the more popular ways of handling more elaborate process improvement efforts.

8

Process Improvement with Six Sigma

I N THE LAST CHAPTER we saw how managers should be responsible for planning and controlling the business processes they manage. In a sense, planning, organizing, monitoring, and maintaining processes and activities is the everyday job of managers.

At times, however, companies undertake specific projects to improve the overall quality of an existing process or to instill employees with enthusiasm for a higher standard of performance. There are many approaches to ongoing process improvement efforts, but the most popular today is Six Sigma, which is where we will begin.

Six Sigma

At about the same time that Henry Ford created his moving production line and revolutionized auto production, other people were exploring techniques that would let other companies improve their operations. An early practitioner who got a lot of attention was Frederick Taylor, who is usually considered the father of operations research. Taylor published his classic book *Principles of Scientific Management* in 1911. Taylor was obsessed with measuring every step in every process and then experimenting with variations until he found the fastest way to carry out a process. Since Taylor, most large companies have employed engineers who have focused on improving operations. In a similar way, some individuals have specialized in catching defects by inspecting the output of processes. The latter is usually referred to as *quality assurance* or *quality control*.

Table 8.1. U.S. and Japanese auto manufacturing.

	GM Framingham plant	Toyota Takoaka plant
Gross assembly hours (per car)	40.7	18.0
Adjusted assembly hours (per car)	31	16
Assembly defects (per 100 cars)	130	45
Assembly space used (sq. meters per car)	8.1	4.8
Inventory of parts maintained (average)	2 weeks	2 hours

Source: IMVP World Assembly Plant Survey (1986)

The quality control movement got a huge boost in the 1980s after an oil embargo prompted U.S. consumers to begin to buy more fuel-efficient Japanese cars. U.S. consumers quickly discovered that Japanese cars were not only more fuel efficient, but were less expensive and better made than their American counterparts. There were fewer defects and problems, and the cars lasted longer.

Table 8.1 provides an overview of the problem that faced U.S. automakers when they began to examine the differences between U.S. and Japanese manufacturing. Clearly the Japanese companies were building cars faster (and thus cheaper) and better than their U.S. rivals.

Ironically, as U.S. auto companies began to study what Japanese auto companies were doing, they found that the Japanese companies attributed much of their success to an American quality control guru, Edwards Deming. (In Japan, the highest prize awarded for industrial excellence is the Deming prize.) Deming had been sent to Japan by the U.S. government in the aftermath of World War II and had worked with Japanese firms to improve their processes.

Deming went beyond U.S. practice and worked with Japanese companies to embed quality control programs into the very fabric of Japanese production lines. U.S. companies traditionally measured the quality of outputs by sampling the products that came off the end of the production line. Deming convinced the Japanese to go beyond that and measure quality at each step of the process. Japanese parts suppliers, for example, learned to coordinate their schedules with manufacturing schedules and to only deliver new parts as they were needed, significantly reducing inventory storage times. This technique, and others, led to improvements that eventually led to a whole new approach to mass production, often called *lean manufacturing*.

In the late 1980s, U.S. companies struggled to become as efficient and effective as the best Japanese producers. Quality control methodologies became very popular in the United States. Over the years, companies have experimented with Statistical Process Control (SPC), Total Quality Management (TQM), and Just-in-Time Manufacturing (JIT). Each of these quality control initiatives contributed to efficiency and better output if the managers of the company were willing to work at it.

Six Sigma is the latest in this series of quality control methodologies to sweep U.S. companies. The Six Sigma approach was created at Motorola in the late 1980s. It was popularized by Mikel Harry, whose work caught the attention of Motorola's CEO, Bob Galvin. Galvin, in turn, spread the Six Sigma approach throughout Motorola, applying it to a wide variety of different processes. Somewhere along the line, Six Sigma became much more than a process control technique and evolved into a systematic approach to process improvement.

In the early 1990s, companies like Allied Signal and Texas Instruments adopted the Six Sigma approach in their organizations. Then in 1995, Jack Welch, the CEO of GE, decided to use Six Sigma at GE. Welch announced that "Six Sigma is the most important initiative GE has ever undertaken. . . . it is part of the genetic code of our future leadership." More importantly, Welch decreed that henceforth, 40% of each business leader's bonus was going to be determined by his or her success in implementing Six Sigma. Welch's popularity with the business press, and his dynamic style, guaranteed that Six Sigma would become one of the hot management techniques of the late 1990s.

Six Sigma originated as a set of statistical techniques that managers could use to measure process performance. Using the techniques, a manager could then make changes in the process to see if it improved the process. Once the process was as efficient as they could get it, managers then used the statistical techniques to maintain the process. As Six Sigma became popular in the late 1990s, it was extended to improve processes far removed from manufacturing. In keeping with the then-current interest in business process reengineering, Six Sigma consultants evolved their methodology to incorporate techniques and definitions from the process reengineering consultants.

Today, for example, most Six Sigma books begin by defining three types of process change efforts: (1) process management, (2) process improvement, and (3) process redesign.

Process management, in the world of Six Sigma, means developing an overview of the company's processes, linking it with corporate strategy, and using it to prioritize process interventions. In other words, what Six Sigma folks would call *process management,* we would call *process architecture.* We prefer to use *process management* more broadly to describe how managers' jobs are organized and how managers take responsibility for the processes they oversee.

Process improvement, as Six Sigma proponents use it, refers to a set of techniques used to incrementally improve and maintain process quality. We use the term the same way, except that we would include some nonstatistical techniques as well. More importantly, we would make a distinction between *ordinary process improvement,* which every manager ought to do as a daily part of his or her job, and *process improvement projects,* which are undertaken to significantly improve the quality of a process in a short period of time.

Six Sigma practitioners use the term *process redesign* to refer to major changes in a process. In other words, they use process redesign the same way we do.

After defining the three types of process change, as we just described them, every Six Sigma book we have ever looked at proceeds to focus almost all of the remaining chapters on process improvement, on how to organize project teams, on how to measure process outcomes, and on the statistical techniques used to analyze outcomes.

None of the Six Sigma books we've seen provide nearly enough information on how to analyze processes. Most simply suggest that the project team should develop a high-level overview of the process (which we'll turn to in a moment) and then suggest the use of "workflow diagrams" if more detail is needed. What this underlines, in our opinion, is that Six Sigma works best with well-understood, currently implemented processes. If extensive analysis of a process is required, we suggest that managers look at books outside the Six Sigma tradition to find useful approaches.

What Six Sigma is very good at is describing how to think about measuring process and activity outcomes, and about how to use statistical techniques to analyze the outcomes and decide on corrective action. We believe that every process manager should study one or two Six Sigma books and use their insights to help define measures for the processes he or she manages. (We've listed several of the best in the Notes and References at the end of this book.) Six Sigma techniques are just as useful when practiced by a manager who is responsible for a process or activity as they are when they are used by a project team that is focused on improving a process or activity. A team approach, however, is often superior in situations where the manager wants to engage and motivate an entire group of employees to improve a process.

In the remainder of this chapter, we will discuss Six Sigma as it is usually presented by Six Sigma consultants—as a methodology that can be used by project teams to improve a process. Before turning to projects, however, we'll take a moment to define the statistical ideas that lie behind the name "Six Sigma."

The Six Sigma Concept

Quality control engineers have always used a number of statistical tools to analyze processes. Six Sigma is a name derived from concepts associated with a standard bell-shaped curve. Almost anything varies if you measure with enough precision. The specification might call for a car door to be 1 meter (100 cm) high. Using a standard meter stick, all of the doors might seem exactly 1 meter high. Using a laser measuring device that is more exact, however, you might find that some doors are 99.70 cm high while others are 100.30 cm high. They average 100.00 cm, but each door varies a little.

Statisticians describe patterns of variations with a bell-shaped or Gaussian curve. (Carl Frederick Gauss was the mathematician who first worked out the mathematics of variation in the early 19th century.) We've pictured a bell-shaped curve in Figure 8.1.

If the items being measured vary in a continuous manner, one finds that variation frequently follows the pattern described by the bell-shaped curve: 68.26% of the variation falls within two standard deviations. In statistics, the Greek letter

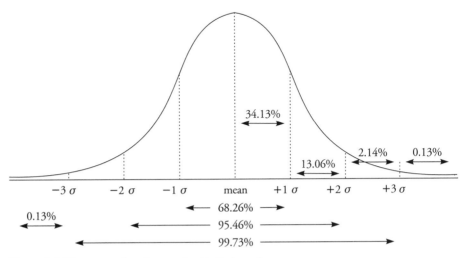

Figure 8.1 The properties of a standard bell-shaped curve.

sigma (σ) is used to denote one standard deviation; 99.73% of all deviations fall within 6 standard deviations.

In Figure 8.1 we show three sigmas to the right of the mean. Imagine that we subdivided the 0.13% of the curve out on the right and inserted three more sigmas. In other words, we would have six sigmas to the right of the mean, and some very small amount beyond that. In fact, we would cover 99.99966% of the deviation and only exclude 3.4 instances in a million.[1] Six Sigma projects rely on formulas and tables to determine sigmas. The only point you should remember is that we want to define what we mean by a defect, and then create a process that is so consistent that only 3.4 defects will occur in the course of one million instances of the process.

Returning to our doors and applying our knowledge of standard distributions, you can expect that if the shortest door was 99.70 cm and the tallest door was 100.30 cm, most of the variations in the doors would fall between 99.70 and 100.30. They might not, however, for various reasons. How they vary from a standard distribution would tell a Six Sigma practitioner something about the process. For example, if instead of one curve there were two with two different means, it would suggest that two independent variables were affecting the output. In any case, the chance that a door was more than six standard deviations to the right of the mean, using a process curve, is 3.4 in a million. The goal is to reduce clearly unacceptable output to less than 3.4 failures in a million.

At first, many managers are skeptical of the goal. It seems more appropriate for large manufacturing processes than for more complex processes that are done less frequently. Once one considers a large enough sample, however, Six Sigma isn't always that demanding. How many plane crashes, per million flights, would you accept? How many bank checks per million would you want deducted from the wrong account? How many incorrect surgical operations would you tolerate per week? In all these cases, in a week or a month or a year there are millions of events. In most cases you'd rather not have even 3.4 failures per million. The goal is rigorous, but in many situations it's the minimum that customers should have to expect.

---

[1] Technically, there is a difference between a standard normal curve, like the one in Figure 8.1, and a curve used with process analysis. There is a phenomenon called *long-run process drift*. A curve used in process work generates 3.4 defects per million, and that is defined as the instances that occur beyond six sigmas to the right or the left of the mean. In a normal curve, like the one in Figure 8.1, for reasons we won't consider, one only has to be 4.5 sigmas to the right of the curve to reach the point beyond which the 3.4 defects per million begins.

Let's consider another problem. Suppose that the hypothetical restaurant SF Seafood decided to undertake a Six Sigma project and decided to focus on the delivery of meals to diners. The team gathered data by asking customers about how quickly they liked to receive their meals and what they considered an unacceptable wait. The data suggested that half of the customers would prefer their meals in 15 minutes or less. All the customers agreed, however, that meals should arrive within 30 minutes. If a meal was delivered after 30 minutes, all of the customers were unhappy. Using this data, the SF Seafood Six Sigma team prepared the bell-shaped curve shown in Figure 8.2, assuming that they would shoot for an average time of 15 minutes and not tolerate anything over 30 minutes.

In this case Six Sigma refers to the variation on a specific process measure—time from when an order is taken to when it is delivered. The goal the team adopted was to deliver all meals as close to 15 minutes as possible. They were willing to allow some variation around 15 minutes, but wanted to assure that all meals were delivered in less than 30 minutes. In other words, they wanted to achieve Six Sigma and assure that all meals, except 3.4 meals out of a million, would be delivered in 30 minutes or less.

The goal of most Six Sigma projects is to reduce the deviation from the mean. Some projects focus on setting a more rigorous mean. Assume that we decided that we wanted to deliver half of all meals within 10 minutes and all meals within 20 minutes or less. In this case we would set 10 minutes as our target for the mean and 20 minutes at six standard deviations (sigmas) to the right of the mean. The bell-shaped curve would now be even narrower than the one shown in Figure 8.2,

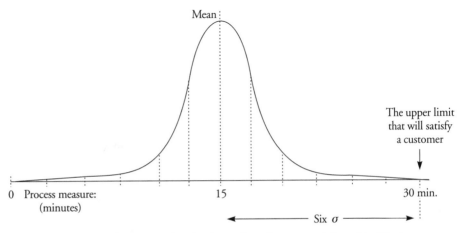

Figure 8.2 A model of a process showing how often dinners are delivered in 15 minutes.

and the deviation from the mean would be less. It would require a better controlled, more efficient process to assure that most meals arrive in 10 minutes and no meal ever arrives in more than 20 minutes.

So, Six Sigma refers to improving processes until they are so consistent that they only fail in 3.4 cases out of one million. It also refers to the idea that we establish and measure process goals and a mean and then work to reduce the deviation from the mean. In other words, we work to make the process more consistent, and we use statistical tools to test whether we are succeeding.

The Six Sigma Approach to Process Improvement

In an ideal company, every process would already be mapped and measured by those responsible for managing the process. In reality, of course, most processes aren't mapped or well understood by those who manage them. Moreover, if they are measured, then functional measures are usually the norm. In some companies, managers could read one of the popular Six Sigma books and then implement the ideas by themselves. In most cases, however, it works best if the manager involves the workers in the process of analysis and shares with them the satisfaction of achieving the goals. Six Sigma practitioners always talk in terms of process improvement projects and focus on teams, not on individual managerial efforts.

Many Six Sigma projects begin by helping a management team develop a process architecture. If an architecture already exists, then the Six Sigma practitioner focuses on helping managers identify projects that will benefit most from a process improvement effort.

Process improvement projects based on the Six Sigma methodology are usually short and typically range from 1 to 6 months. In many companies that have adopted the Six Sigma approach, the executive committee chooses two or three processes for improvement every 6 months. Some of the Six Sigma books give the impression that Six Sigma projects tackle value chains or major business processes. They reinforce this impression by discussing processes at small companies or relatively simple business processes. In reality, most Six Sigma projects focus on a subprocess or subsubprocess. Many focus on what we would regard as a single activity.

To clarify this, consider that most Six Sigma projects focus on monitoring two or three measures. If one were to try to monitor an auto production line or the insurance company sales system with two to three measures, one would not get the kind of data that Six Sigma projects need to identify causes and to check that changes are getting the desired results. Put another way, it would take at least a month just to analyze the subprocesses in a large business process like an auto production line or a large insurance sales process.

Measuring an entire value chain or business process with two or three measures is a reasonable thing for a process manager to do. Unfortunately, if the measures suggest that sales are falling or that production is down 5%, they don't usually suggest the cause. In most cases the process manager will need to examine more specific measures to determine which subprocess or subsubprocess is responsible for the problem. In other words, measures on large processes usually only provide early warning signals that a more detailed study needs to be initiated.

In most cases, Six Sigma projects are not launched to improve large-scale business processes; they are launched to improve subprocesses or activities. Importantly, however, Six Sigma always stresses that measures at any level should be tied back to higher-level processes and eventually to strategic goals.

Six Sigma Teams

Six Sigma projects are usually chosen by a steering committee that oversees all Six Sigma efforts or by the process sponsor or team sponsor. Every project needs a team sponsor or champion. This individual is usually the process sponsor or a member of the steering committee that selected the project in the first place.

The team is headed either by an individual devoted to managing Six Sigma projects or by a manager associated with the project to be improved. In Six Sigma jargon, if the leader is especially knowledgeable in Six Sigma projects, he or she is called a *black belt*. If the leader is a manager who has full-time responsibilities elsewhere and is slightly less qualified, he or she is referred to as a *green belt*. The team is often assigned an internal or external consultant who is a specialist in Six Sigma, and especially skilled in the use of the statistical tools that Six Sigma depends on. This consultant is usually called a *master black belt*. (These designations are usually the result of a combination of experience and passing examinations.)

The team members are chosen because they have expertise in the actual process that is to be improved. If the process is really an activity or small process, the team members are employees who perform the activities or steps involved in the process.

Some Six Sigma practitioners spend a lot of time talking about how good teams are formed and the processes the teams should employ—voting and so forth. We won't go into it here. Suffice it to say that the team leader should know something about team building and team processes, and should apply that knowledge to create an effective team.

The teams meet for 2–3 hours at a time. Initially they meet 2–3 times a week, but as they shift to data collection, they meet less frequently.

Phases in a Six Sigma Project

Most Six Sigma projects are organized around a pattern referred to as the *DMAIC process.* DMAIC stand for

▶ *Define* customer requirements for the process or service.
▶ *Measure* existing performance and compare with customer requirements.
▶ *Analyze* existing process.
▶ *Improve* the process design and implement it.
▶ *Control* the results and maintain the new performance.

Figure 8.3 provides an overview of these key steps or phases and the activities that occur in each step. It also suggests the time required for each step. Some overlap between phases usually occurs.

Obviously the sequence of steps and the times will vary widely, depending on the size and the complexity of the project. In the best case, one will define the goal, create measures, measure, identify some obvious improvements, implement process changes, measure again, and be done. In the worst case, you will identify multiple goals, create measures, measure, identify multiple possible improvements, try some and not get adequate results, try again, decide you need different measures,

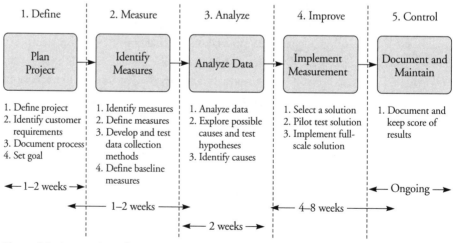

Figure 8.3 An overview of a Six Sigma project.

try again, analyze, try still another process improvement, measure some more, and finally achieve your revised goal. In other words, simple projects run straight through, as shown above. Complex projects recycle through the steps multiple times until they achieve results.

One key to accomplishing Six Sigma projects quickly is having an experienced black belt (full-time project leader) or master black belt (champion). Some elements of each project, like the steps in a process or the customers, are unique to the specific process and must be debated and analyzed by the project team. Other elements, like when to apply what measures, and how to set up certain types of measures, can be accomplished very quickly by someone experienced in the Six Sigma process and armed with an appropriate software tool that they know how to use. An experienced consultant can help keep a team moving and get them through other rough spots that would otherwise delay the project for extra weeks.

Not all projects achieve Six Sigma. As most Six Sigma practitioners explain, Six Sigma is a goal. The ultimate idea is to improve the process and to reduce the variation in the process as much as possible. It's the attitude and not a specific target that is most important.

We'll consider each phase in a Six Sigma project in more detail.

Define

In the first phase, a draft charter is usually provided by the project sponsor or team champion. The charter is a clear statement of what the team should accomplish. It should include a brief description of the process to be improved and the business case for improving it. It should also include some milestones and define the roles and responsibilities of the team members. This task is easier if the steering committee has defined a good process architecture and has already defined the scope and goals of the project. If the steering committee hasn't done this, then the Six Sigma team must make some guesses, explore the problem a bit, and then return to the charter and refine it toward the end of the Define phase.

One key to a good charter is a clear understanding of the process to be improved. Like any good contract, the charter should specify who will do what, when. Dates, costs, and a clear statement of the expected results are all important. The team shouldn't allow itself, however, to get pushed into trying to predict the exact changes they will make or exactly how long it will take to reach Six Sigma. Instead, the charter should focus on defining the process to be improved and some initial measures that can be used to judge if the team succeeds.

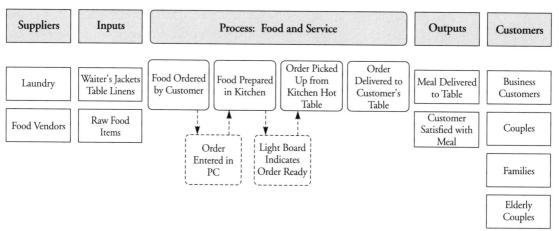

Figure 8.4 SF Seafood's Food Service Process.

Six Sigma teams usually put a lot of emphasis on who the customers are and what will satisfy them. The emphasis on the customer that occurs throughout Six Sigma is one of its more attractive features. The customer referred to, of course, is the person or group that receives the product or service produced by the process the team is focusing on. Most groups within organizations produce products for other internal groups. Thus, for example, the customer of Inventory is Manufacturing. The customer of New Product Design is Marketing and Product Engineering, and so forth. Still, it's always good for a project team to begin by focusing on the fact that they produce products or services for some person or group that functions as a customer that they must satisfy. And even when a team focuses on an internal customer, it's always good to define, if only informally, how that customer is linked to some external customer.

The Six Sigma approach to process definition is summed up in the acronym SIPOC, which emphasizes Supplier, Input, Process, Output, and Customer. Figure 8.4 is a rough SIPOC diagram of SF Seafood's Food Service Process. SF Seafood only serves dinners, so all data is based on evening dining and not on lunches. The immediate output of the food service process that we are focusing on was a meal on the table. In fact, the team was working on a broader definition of output, customer satisfaction, and a meal and its timely delivery is only one part of that overall output. We'll consider output in more detail in a moment.

Figure 8.4 shows the standard SIPOC approach that most Six Sigma practitioners use. As an overview there's nothing wrong with it, although it usually works a little better when you are describing a concrete process and is a little harder to apply when you are describing a service process. As you recall from our earlier discussion of SF Seafood, the company considers the dining area as one value chain, and the kitchen as another. We are going to focus on satisfying customers who have meals at SF Seafood; hence, in the SIPOC diagram shown we listed four major steps in the food service process. We also listed two other steps that link the waiters to the kitchen and vice versa.

In this case we are focusing on both food and service processes. We listed two inputs to the basic process we are focused on—the laundry provides jackets for the waiters and table linens, and the vendors provide the raw food used in the kitchen. We could easily list more suppliers and inputs.

In keeping with Six Sigma policy, we have divided the process—food and service—into three to seven subprocesses or steps. Luckily there are no complex branches. (If we had considered orders, and included both the delivery of food and drinks, which come from two different processes at SF Seafood, we would have had a harder time developing a neat overview.) As it is, the basic service process doesn't emphasize the food preparation in the kitchen, which is surely going to be a factor in customer satisfaction.

To simplify this case, let's assume that the food preparation process has already been the focus of a different Six Sigma project. The team determined that food was needed quickly and needed to be tasty and hot. They found that they could deliver meals in 9 minutes from the time they received the order on the kitchen PC. Six Sigma work resulted in variations of between 6 and 12 minutes. (Yes, they pre-prepare meals and sometimes use a microwave to heat them.) Thus, we know the characteristics for the Food Prepared in Kitchen activity and can focus on obtaining and delivering the order. It also means that we don't really need to worry about the raw food items delivered to the kitchen, but only about inputs to the food delivery process.

The specific output, in our example, is a meal delivered to the table. That output, however, is part of a broader goal the team is working toward—customers who are satisfied with their meals and meal service. We put most of our effort into identifying customers (or market segments) and arrived at four groups of customers who might have different ideas of what makes a satisfying meal. Customers with kids, our later research showed, prefer food much faster. Couples and elderly couples are willing to wait longer. Business people are in between—although they vary quite a bit—presumably depending on the occasion.

After the team analyzed the process and customers, they turned their attention to the kinds of things about a dinner meal that might satisfy customers. In a sense, this involves asking what kinds of needs customers have. Teams usually list potential requirements on a chart called a CTQ (Critical-To-Quality) tree, like the one

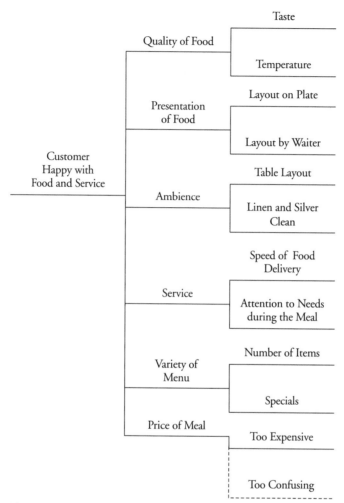

Figure 8.5 A CTQ tree for the SF Seafood Meal Satisfaction Project.

shown in Figure 8.5. One starts on the left with the overall output. Then one hypothesizes what might result in the output. If appropriate, one can move on to a third or fourth level, hypothesizing more and more specific or discretely measured requirements.

The initial list prepared by the SF Seafood Dining Six Sigma Team is shown in Figure 8.5. Once the team has arrived at a list like this, it needs to figure out how to determine the role each of these possible requirements actually plays in customer satisfaction.

One always needs to test and be prepared to revise. We added the last item (Price of Meal—Too Confusing) to illustrate something the team didn't think of, but which showed up in interviews with elderly couples. It seems that SF Seafood priced all items independently, and some elderly couples were confused about the total cost of the meal they were ordering when they had both a main item and a side order. (SF Seafood decided to change their policy and price specials, which were popular with elderly diners, as single-price meals.) The point, however, is that the team begins with a list and then gathers information to confirm or change the list.

Most Six Sigma books provide detailed discussions of the ways one can gather information from customers. We won't go into them here, but suggest that anyone interested in measuring processes consult one of the Six Sigma books for such details. In brief, most suggest surveys, one-on-one interviews, and focus groups. Other techniques include recording and studying customer complaints, or having team members act as customers and record their impressions. Restaurant Web sites often provide a mechanism that allows customers to evaluate restaurants, and SF Seafood found the local restaurant Web sites a good source of complaints and occasional praise.

Obviously the team will need to gather data about the requirements of all of the different groups or segments of customers. Different types of data-gathering approaches may work better with different groups. For example, SF Seafood found that elderly customers were happy to sit and talk with a maitre d' about what they liked and disliked about their meals. Business people and families, on the other hand, didn't want to sit and talk, although they would take survey forms and some of them would then mail them in.

Based on data gathered, the team usually identifies the most important requirements of customer satisfaction. Six Sigma practitioners put a lot of emphasis on Pareto analysis. Most of us know this mathematical concept as the 80/20 rule. As a generalization, 80 percent of customer satisfaction can be accounted for by 20 percent of the possible requirements. In other words, you can usually narrow the list of requirements that will satisfy customers down to two or three items. They may vary by customer segment, but for each customer segment, it is usually sufficient to track two or three items.

In turns out that for business customers, Taste, Temperature, Speed of Delivery, and Attentiveness during the Meal were considerably more important than the other items on the CTQ requirements tree. On the other hand, for the elderly customers, Taste, Temperature, and Specials were most important.

The team was able to ignore Taste, since that was under the control of the kitchen, but decided to gather data and pass it to the chef, while focusing on improving the dining room service.

The team ends the first phase with a refined charter—a clear idea of the scope of the project, the customers and their most salient requirements, and a set of milestones.

Measure

During the second phase of the project the team develops measures that will let them know how well each key requirement is being satisfied. Most Six Sigma books spend quite a bit of time explaining the concepts underlying statistics and measurement, and provide explanations of formulas that are appropriate for handling the different types of data one might collect. Since different types of data result in different types of curves, it's important that someone understand these things and thus know how to analyze the data and evaluate the results. In most cases this expertise is provided by a master black belt or consultant. Most Six Sigma projects rely on software tools to actually analyze the data. (MiniTab, for example, is a popular statistics analysis tool that is widely used to crunch the data and generate curves.) We are not going to go into measurement theory or discuss statistical formulas. If you need this kind of information, you will want to read a book that covers it in more detail than we can here. Once again, Six Sigma books that do exactly that are listed in the Notes and References at the end of this book.

One Six Sigma author, George Eckes, suggests three measurement principles:

▶ Measure only what is important to the customer.
▶ Only measure process outputs that you can improve.
▶ Don't measure an output for which you have no history of customer dissatisfaction.

Within these constraints, every Six Sigma team must focus on determining how to measure process effectiveness and efficiency. There are basically three things one might measure:

▶ *Inputs.* One can check what was delivered by the supplier to assure that problems do not lie with the inputs to the process. In the case of SF Seafood, there are the linen tablecloths and waiter jackets. We assume that the chef is already checking the quality of the raw food items delivered by suppliers.

▶ *Process measures.* These measures typically include cost, cycle time, value, and labor.

▶ *Outputs or measures of customer satisfaction.* In the SF Seafood case, we might stick with a survey form that we gave to customers when they left the restaurant. There might be some more dramatic form of output measure as well. Consider that some customers are reviewers or evaluators for magazines that assign ratings to restaurants. In France, every restaurant waits nervously each spring for the new Michelin Red Guide to be published so they can see how many stars they have been awarded. (A restaurant in France that moves from 2 to 3 stars—the highest Michelin gives—typically can double their prices and be assured of a full house every night! Thus, the single Michelin satisfaction rating can more than double a restaurant's annual income.)

In complex manufacturing processes the best output data is often generated by the receiving group, and the trick is to get it routed back to your group so you can use it. Our dining team, for example, is going to gather data on customers that were dissatisfied with the taste of their food, and then route that information back to the kitchen.

Another way to think about measures is to distinguish between process measures and outcome measures. You can use either, but it's usually best to start with output measures because that's what the customer is most concerned with.

If the process or activity measure is	Then an outcome you might measure is
• process with a specific goal	• strategic goals achieved
• quality of work in a specific activity	• level of customer satisfaction
• time a process takes	• on-time delivery
• adequacy of staffing	• time to answer phone or produce unit
• adequate understanding of task	• nature and number of defects produced

It all cases, it's ideal to tie the measure to customer satisfaction. This focuses everyone on the basic concept that you aren't doing the work for its own sake, but to provide a product or service that will satisfy and even please a customer. Customers buy products, and they usually have options. If they aren't satisfied, ultimately it makes no difference how the work was done. This is just as true if your customer is another process within your own organization as it is if the customer is someone outside the company. Many IT departments in large companies have learned this in recent years as companies have outsourced IT functions, applications, or entire IT departments in order to obtain more satisfactory service at a better price. Increasingly, as companies move toward virtual processes and more elaborate outsourcing arrangements, it will become clear to even support groups deep within the company that a process either provides value and satisfies customers, or the customers will end up seeking alternatives.

Some Six Sigma practitioners recommend distinguishing between output measures and service measures. In this sense, "output" refers to features of the product or service you deliver, and "service" refers to more subjective things having to do with how the customer expects to be treated and what kinds of things please the customer. Getting the hamburger, correctly assembled, quickly is an output measure. Getting a smile with the hamburger, or having the waiter remember your name and use it, is a service measure. As a company, if you want to succeed, you have to get output measures right. If you want to be really successful and have loyal customers, you have to get the service measures right as well.

Another way Six Sigma practitioners talk about this is in terms of categories created by Dr. Noriaki Kano, a leading Japanese quality control expert. Dr. Kano developed some measures that can be used to qualify data about customer satisfaction, which we won't go into here, often spoken of as *Kano analysis*. He divided customer requirements into three categories:

▶ *Basic requirements.* This is the minimum the customer expects. If he doesn't get this, he will go away upset.
▶ *Satisfiers.* The additional output or service measures that please the customer. The more of these you get, the happier the customer will be.
▶ *Delighters.* These are things the customer doesn't expect. They are usually things the customer would never put on a survey form because he doesn't even know he should want these things. Having phones available at each restaurant table, for example, might delight some business diners. Having the busboy whisk out an umbrella on a rainy day and accompany customers to their car is another.

If one is unclear, it never hurts to meet with the customer and find out how they judge the products or services they receive from your process. Every department or functional unit has some internal criteria that they measure and seek to meet. In some cases, however, departments end up maximizing goals that aren't important to customers. Imagine a sales organization that places emphasis on closing lots of sales quickly. Ordinarily it seems like a reasonable sales goal, but if manufacturing is struggling to come up to speed on a new product run, lots of sales, quickly, may only make for unhappy customers who don't receive their products in a timely manner. There's no science to choosing the right measure, but the trick is to choose one to three measures that really track quality, efficiency, and customer satisfaction in the most efficient manner. Too many measures waste time. Measures that aren't clearly tied to customer satisfaction risk maximizing some aspect of a process that doesn't really produce results that are important to the customer.

Each measure must be carefully specified so everyone understands exactly how it is going to be determined. Thus, for SF Seafood, one measure will be the time it takes to receive a meal. In this case, we would like to have someone determine the time when the waiter finished taking the order and then later determine when the food is placed on the table. Since SF Seafood uses a computer-based order system, waiters enter each order into a computer that then routes food orders to the kitchen and drink orders to the bar. The orders are placed in a queue on the computer in the kitchen. Waiters can enter a request to expedite an order, and we will need to control for that in our measurements. When the kitchen has an order ready, they enter a code and a light goes on a board that the waiters can see in the dining area. Obviously it would be easy to track when a PC order is placed and when the kitchen enters a code to indicate that the order is waiting on the hot table. The time between the PC entry and the kitchen entry, however, will only tell us how long it takes the kitchen to prepare the meal (i.e., 9 plus or minus 3 minutes). It won't tell us if the waiter went directly from the table to the PC, or went to another table before going to the PC to place the order.

Since the focus of the team's effort is the delivery itself, they decide that they will have to assign an observer to record when orders are taken and delivered. This will need to be someone not otherwise involved in any dining activities to assure that he or she has the time to watch several tables carefully and keep accurate records. Total delivery time is defined as the time between when the waiter takes the order and when he enters it into the computer, plus the time between when the kitchen indicates in their computer that the order is on the hot table and when the order is delivered to the table.

At the same time, the team created a new, simple survey form that they decided to hand out to all diners and request that they complete it and return it by mail. The survey form was on a prepaid postcard.

Without going into the details about how the team classified the various types of measures, or the formulas used to summarize the data, suffice it to say that there are lots of techniques that an experienced practitioner can use to refine the data and provide insights.

The team arrived at a variety of conclusions after looking at the data. One was the conclusion that half the customers preferred getting their meals in 15 minutes and all resented having to wait longer than 30 minutes. This resulted in the bell-shaped curve we presented earlier (Figure 8.2). Since the team was not focusing on the cooking process as such, they needed to factor out the 9 ± 3 minutes of food preparation time. That left 18 to 24 minutes that was controlled by the waiters.

(In other words, we subtracted the 6–12 minutes of food preparation time from the 0–30 minutes and arrived at a new curve that reflected the time remaining between food preparation and actual delivery.) That resulted in a new curve, and anything beyond 18 minutes was deemed unacceptable output.

If the meal was prepared in 6 minutes, and the waiter took 18 minutes to submit and deliver the order, the customer would get the meal in 24 minutes. If the meal took 12 minutes to prepare and the waiter took 18 minutes to submit and deliver the order, the order would be delivered in 30 minutes. Theoretically, if the waiter knew the meal would be prepared in 6 minutes, he or she could have up to 24 minutes to deliver the meal, but since the waiters never knew how long meal preparation would take, they had to assume that each meal would take 12 minutes. If the kitchen Six Sigma team was able to improve their process so that they could guarantee a narrower variation, then the delivery process could gain more time. But since the goal was to move toward a delivery time of around 15 minutes, this was really irrelevant.

Hence, the new bell curve for the waiters ran from 12 to 30 minutes, with a mean of 21. In other words, a waiter could use up to 18 minutes and always make the 30-minute limit. The goal the team set, however, was to come as close to 9 minutes as possible. The data suggested that it took as long, on average, to place the order as to move it from the hot table to the customer. Thus, a subsidiary goal was to place orders within 9 minutes, coming as close to 4.5 minutes as possible, and to deliver meals from the hot table to the customer within 9 minutes, coming as close to 4.5 minutes as possible.

The team proceeded to gather data on the time it took waiters to place and deliver orders. As the data began to accumulate, they moved to the analysis phase to make sense of it.

Analyze

In many cases the team members have a good idea of the cause of the problems in the process they analyze. They gather data to establish baselines and then want to jump to implementing a solution. In some cases this is reasonable. Waiters, in our example, probably know what takes time and know how they could save some. In more complex cases, however, it isn't so obvious.

Once you have some measurement data, there are lots of ways to analyze what might be causing a problem. Some of them involve defining the process in more detail. Others involve applying statistical tools to the data.

Assuming you have developed a detailed process diagram, you can establish measures for each activity on your diagram. It's also useful to consider how each activity adds value to the entire process. In essence, any given task can be classified into one of three categories:

1. The activity adds value that the customer, whether internal or the ultimate customer, is willing to pay for.
2. The activity is necessary to produce a value-added activity.
3. The activity doesn't add value.

You can always check with the customer to determine which activities add value. You normally wouldn't ask the customer to consider the activities as such, but what they add to the final product or service. This consideration takes us back to the issue of how we choose measures. You could ask, for example, if the customer likes the flowers and the white jackets the busboys wear. If the customer tells you it's a matter of indifference how the busboys dress, you might consider what the purchase and cleaning of the jackets adds to the customer's bill and consider if it might be worth dropping that aspect of the service package.

It's usually easy to identify the activities that add features that customers can identify and value. Those that don't fall in that category are usually placed in category 2. In fact, some activities do need to be done in order that other category 1 activities can be done. Each needs to be challenged, however. Often processes that have been done for a while end up supporting activities that are no longer really required. In all surveys at SF Seafood, customers indicated that napkin rings were of no value to them. Clearly the placing of napkins in rings when setting the table was an activity that could be eliminated. It took time, cost money, and didn't add any value to the customer's dining experience.

Consider a company that installed an email system that allowed salespeople to report their results each day online. For some unknown reason the company had installed the email system, but never eliminated the requirement that the salespeople fill out a Form 2B and submit it on the 30th of each month. In fact, Form 2B only provided information that the sales managers were now already obtaining via the daily emails. Filling out Form 2B was a value-reducing activity. Worse, sales managers continued to log the forms to assure that each salesperson turned them in on time. It's always wise to consider eliminating activities that don't add value. Moreover, if an activity is value reducing, one should check to be sure that no one is measuring that activity.

The analysis of waiter problems at SF Seafood seems straightforward. In fact, those familiar with a small lunchtime restaurant might be surprised that it takes as much time as it does at SF Seafood. It might seem obvious that if the waiter would simply go straight to the PC after taking an order and enter it, it would only consume a minute at the most. Similarly, it might seem if the waiter would go to the hot table as soon as he or she saw a flashing light, delivery of the food couldn't take more than another minute. That would get the total delivery time under 3 minutes. If there were only one waiter per table, they could probably come close to that. Unfortunately, in SF Seafood, each waiter is expected to cover from five to seven tables, depending on the hour. Some waiters are scheduled to begin work when the restaurant opens and there are only a few customers. Then more are added as the numbers grow toward the maximum number between 7:30 to 9:30 in the evening. Equally important, waiters not only take orders, they serve drinks and attend customers who may want help choosing a wine or other drinks, coffee, or desserts. Moreover, as every waiter learns, if you always do only one task at a time, you can never get everything done that needs doing. As long as you are going to get one meal from the kitchen, getting two is better. As long as you are taking an order, taking orders from two tables, one after the other, before placing either order, saves time.

One obvious way to analyze the process is to assign times to each of the tasks a waiter must do and multiply it by the number of tables the waiter is trying to serve. It may be obvious that a waiter should only try to serve four tables rather than five. Or, perhaps, a change that involves the busboys helping the waiters move meals from the hot table to customer tables may save time. If that's a possibility, then we would need to determine exactly what busboys do and what would remain undone if busboys began to do more to help waiters.

This isn't the place to go into such details further. Imagine if we had included the kitchen in our analysis and needed to analyze all of the steps that went into the preparation of a meal, and tried to decide if it would make a difference if the salad chef was more efficient, or if the oven was set 2 degrees higher. Or imagine we were analyzing a production line with hundreds of activities that needed to be coordinated, some of which could be rearranged. The larger and more complex the process, the more problems we need to consider. In some cases, statistical tools become an invaluable way of sorting out the seemingly overwhelming confusion about which activities are really making the most difference in the final outcome.

Six Sigma project managers usually recommend a systematic analysis process. You begin with a comprehensive look for possible causes. Then you examine the possible causes in more detail, gather data as appropriate, and apply statistical tools like regression analysis and scatter diagrams. In the most complex cases, you are forced to design experiments and vary or control one or another aspect of the problem while gathering data. In the end, you usually come back to the 80/20 rule. There may be many causes, but one or two causes (20%) usually account for 80% of the problem. Those are the causes that one initially focuses on in order to make the process more efficient.

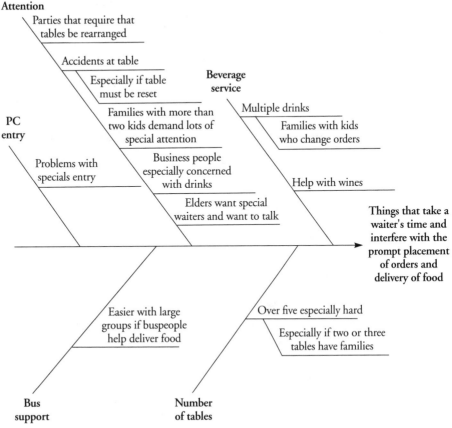

Figure 8.6 A cause-effect diagram developed by SF Seafood's Six Sigma team.

Some Six Sigma practitioners talk about problem analysis as a three-stage process:

1. *Open.* Brainstorm to identify as many possible causes as possible.
2. *Narrow.* Use tools or vote to reduce the number of possible causes to a reasonable number.
3. *Close.* Design measures, gather data, and analyze it to determine which causes in fact cause most of the deviation from the mean.

One popular tool used by many Six Sigma teams when they are trying to identify all possible causes is a cause-effect or fishbone diagram. In effect, it's another kind of tree diagram that one examines to whatever depth is appropriate. We've illustrated a cause-effect diagram for the waiting task in Figure 8.6.

The cause-effect diagram in Figure 8.6 is hardly exhaustive, but it provides an idea of how one identifies a cause, defines it further, and even further if possible.

The actual diagram for SF Seafood was much more complex than this. Also there are some overlapping categories. For example, families with more than two kids are likely to also want to rearrange tables. Moreover, these same tables are the ones that could really benefit from the extra help from a busperson.

In the end, the SF Seafood team gathered data on several causes. The team voted on the causes that were really costing the most time. They used a method in which each team member indicated which problem they thought was the worst cause of time delays, the next worst, and the third worst. The results were as follows:

Families with kids	10
Number of tables	8
Tables wanting help with wines	5
Multiple drink tables	3
Lack of busperson help	2
Elders wanting to talk	2
Accidents and spills at table	0
Problems with PC entry	0

One of the issues raised by this analysis was the control and placement of families. This is normally done by the maitre d'. An experiment was developed, and after two weeks it was determined that waiters who didn't have families in their areas definitely provide faster average service. It was also determined that a waiter with six tables that got two groups with more than two kids each was very likely to go over the 18-minute upper limit. As a result, the team decided to change the definition of the process. The new process included a new subprocess—customer seating—and it included the maitre d' placement of customers within the various waiters' areas.

At this point, a Six Sigma team usually gathers lots of data to validate the effect of the different causes identified by the team and to determine their relative salience if possible. We won't consider the various data-gathering techniques or the statistical techniques used by teams to examine the data. In the case of the SF Seafood team, the data confirmed the list that the team generated above.

Improve

As data is gathered and results accumulate, the team begins to think of ways to improve the process. In this case, they are guided by their prioritized list that tells which improvements are likely to result in the largest change.

In the case of the SF Seafood, quite a bit of effort was put into determining how the maitre d' could more effectively allocate customers to waiting areas. It was decided, for example, that two groups of families with kids would never be put in the same area. It was also decided that when families with more than two kids were placed in an area, the number of tables the waiter in that area handled would be reduced and the extra table would be reallocated to another waiter. It turned out that an additional waiter was needed for peak weekend periods to keep the number of tables per waiter below five, or four with a multikid family.

In addition, it was determined that the restaurant would hire a wine steward and have her available during peak periods. When customers requested help with wines, they were turned over to the steward, who was popular because she ultimately knew a lot more about the restaurant's wines than most of the waiters.

During this period, changes are evaluated and some are put into force. Additional data is gathered to see if the changes are resulting in a more consistent process.

In the case of SF Seafood, changes in customer placement, limits on tables per waiter, and the wine steward resulted in a two-month period in which no diner had to wait longer than 15 minutes for their food. The mean for the order and delivery aspects of the process actually dropped to 8 minutes.

Control

The last phase usually results in a plan to maintain the gains and, sometimes, in new initiatives to improve the process further. Deming, and a wide variety of other experts, has observed that what gets measured gets done.

Large manufacturing companies with production lines constantly sample and evaluate their output. Parts suppliers in sophisticated supply chain systems can only guarantee that their parts are 99.73% defect free because they maintain constant vigilance. This type of quality control costs money and is a necessary part of the process. There are statistical tools that make this kind of control more efficient. Many processes today are monitored by computer systems that derive data from sensors, automatically analyze the data using statistical tests, and report any unacceptable deviations to a human monitor.

In other organizations, once a process has identified and achieved a set of process goals, some of the measures are dropped, since they would otherwise increase the cost of the product. It's important to maintain some measures, however. As we have suggested, measurement and control are a key part of every manager's job and should be done routinely. Process managers should routinely measure customer satisfaction to assure that the process is achieving its goals. Managers responsible for subprocesses need to determine a reasonable compromise between excessive measurement and enough measurement to assure that processes remain efficient and effective. Usually this results in periodic checks, which can become more frequent if problems are detected.

In some cases Six Sigma practitioners recommend that managers develop a response plan, a list of actions tied to specific activities that the manager can take if specific activities within a process begin to deviate significantly from established measures.

The maitre d', who is the process manager for dining service, for example, began to explore ways of using the buspeople to save the waiters' time. Overall, however, everyone was happy with the results obtained from the project. The maitre d' discontinued having a person whose job was to time service, but he occasionally asked a waiter to come in 1–2 hours early and time the other waiters just to see that they continued to maintain that 8-minute average. Moreover, once every other month, a week was selected and evaluation postcards were distributed to all diners to continue to monitor their satisfaction. And the maitre d' kept scanning the local restaurant Web sites to see if any complaints showed up there.

Alternative Approaches to Process Improvement

In Chapter 7 we considered how managers could measure and control the processes they manage. Earlier we introduced a specific technique, the performance improvement potential (PIP), as a way of approaching job improvement projects. In effect, PIP is the difference between the average performer and the best performer. If the PIP is small, then a manager should probably focus on the process itself. If the PIP is large, however, it means that improving the performance of the average employee will give you a significant increase in performance. Similarly, many processes can be significantly improved by automating the task. In other words, there are alternative approaches to performance improvement. Six Sigma is only one approach, and it's an approach that requires discipline and a considerable knowledge of statistics. Whatever approach a given manager selects, he or she can probably benefit from reading one or more books on Six Sigma. The books will sharpen the manager's understanding of process measurement even if he or she never undertakes a Six Sigma project.

Although we would wish that managers were constantly working to improve processes, in the real world it is often necessary to launch a special process improvement project in order to make significant changes in an existing process. In the example in this chapter, it would be a lot easier to discuss the entire process with the waiters and enlist them in the effort to improve customer satisfaction than to try to dictate changes to them. The more sophisticated the employees, the more important teamwork and cooperation are in eliciting significant process improvements.

If one has a process that is critical to the organization and it has resisted informal approaches, a Six Sigma project can provide the techniques to systematically design measures, gather data, and measure the data to identify appropriate corrective actions. Keep in mind the major premise of Six Sigma. The approach is designed to reduce the variation in a process so that the outputs of the process are more similar and of higher quality. Our overview didn't really do Six Sigma justice because we largely avoided the dozens of charts, data analysis techniques, and pages of tables and formulas that are included in any serious Six Sigma book. We have described the process, but ducked the statistical tools that Six Sigma employs to systematically define and narrow a sequence of activities. It's expensive to undertake a Six Sigma project, at least initially, because the statistical knowledge required must be learned, and there is a temptation for managers to get lost in the details of data analysis and evaluation. Some managers dislike the focus on statistics, which they argue wastes time and restricts teams that could often move faster without it. This isn't the right approach for all processes, but when quality control and the minimization of errors are critical, it's a very powerful approach. Moreover, whether you use Six Sigma techniques or less formal ones, if you want to be sure your company's processes are performing as they should, you will have to invest in some kind of measurement effort and you will need some techniques for evaluating the data you gather.

IV

BUSINESS PROCESS REDESIGN

U NLIKE PROCESS IMPROVEMENT, which is gradual and ongoing, business process redesign methodologies focus on creating new processes or changing existing processes in major ways.

Chapter 9 describes the overall approach we recommend for business process redesign. It is based on experience and represents a synthesis of several different practices. Obviously there is no standard process redesign project. They are different in many ways. Some start with a broad mandate to make the entire process more efficient or faster. Some are begun with a very specific goal: to incorporate a Web portal, or to replace a specific software application with a newer application. Some projects focus on large-scale processes that cross multiple departments, while others are focused on very specific subprocesses that contain only a few activities. Some involve extensive job redesign, and others result in a completely automated process.

Rather than suggesting different methodologies for different types of projects, we suggest a single, general approach for all projects that emphasizes the elements that most projects have in common.

Then, in Chapter 10, we discuss some of the common variations. We refer to the different specific approaches that organizations employ when they redesign processes as *process redesign patterns.* One common pattern, for example, is what we call the gaps and disconnects pattern. The pattern assumes that inefficiencies arise because of handoffs between departments or functional groups. We'll consider several popular patterns.

9

A Business Process Redesign Methodology

I N EARLIER CHAPTERS we considered how a company might decide to modify a process or select a specific process for redesign. In this chapter we want to consider how a company might go about redesigning a business process or creating a new process. For our purpose here, we will assume that the process to be redesigned is a reasonably large process and that the company involved wants to do anything it can to make the process more effective. It other words, we will be considering a methodology for a significant business process redesign effort.

There have been a number of books published describing redesign methodologies. Some focus on major phases, as we do here, and some go into exquisite detail, defining a process with hundreds of tasks or steps. Our goal here is to describe a generic methodology that will cover all the basics.

We strongly recommend that companies use an experienced facilitator to actually manage a redesign project. The facilitator might come from a redesign group inside your organization, or he or she could be an outside consultant. In either case, the facilitator will probably have his or her own specific approach to business process redesign. What we want to do here, however, is to provide managers and redesign team members with a broad overview of what will happen in almost any large business process redesign effort.

The methodology we describe is best suited for a large-scale effort. Some changes in business processes are routine. They are adjustments made to correct a minor problem or to implement some minor change in the ways things must be done. A change in the price of an item, for example, must be communicated to salespeople, altered in sales catalogs, and changed in software systems. These changes are initiated by the process manager who is responsible for the process or by departmental managers who are responsible for the specific activities that need to be changed. We are not concerned with such routine changes. Instead, we describe an approach that can be used to undertake a major overhaul of a value chain or a major business process.

Major business process redesign projects are usually managed by a steering committee and undertaken by a team that represents all of the functional managers involved in the change. Unlike the less formal techniques used by managers who need to adjust a process, a major business process redesign effort usually requires a systematic methodology that defines phases and responsibilities and provides the basis for a project plan and schedule. A significant part of the effort will involve keeping senior managers in the loop and assuring their support when it's time to implement the process. This communication process isn't a direct part of business process redesign, but it's vital to assure that the changes get implemented. Assuring that your team has someone knowledgeable to manage the entire project, including all the communication aspects, is another reason we recommend the use of an experienced facilitator

In this chapter we will ignore the specific approaches or aims that companies sometimes employ when they undertake redesign projects. We refer to these specific approaches as *redesign patterns*. One redesign pattern, for example, looks for problems at points where departments or functions hand off products or information to each other. Another looks for human performance problems. Still another seeks to modify processes to take advantage of a Web portal. We will consider these specific patterns in the next chapter. In effect, this chapter provides an overview of the redesign process, and the redesign patterns discussed in the next chapter provide information on how to tailor the process to more focused goals.

The approach we describe here would be appropriate for most of the business process redesign patterns we discuss in the next chapter. The one exception, perhaps, might be an ERP redesign, if the company had already decided to use a specific ERP vendor. The approach we describe would work with any project that sought to develop an overview of the existing process before committing to the use of specific ERP modules. It would certainly work with patterns like Gap and Disconnects or any of today's e-business redesign efforts.

Why Have a Methodology?

Large projects take time and involve many different people. If they are well planned, they can be conducted efficiently, minimizing the time required of those involved and assuring that results will be obtained in a relatively short time. Outside consulting companies routinely analyze and redesign large business processes in 3–6 months. On the other hand, we know of projects that started off to analyze a process and were still at it 2 years later when the whole project was scrapped. Projects that lose their way usually do so because the people involved don't have a good plan, don't have concrete milestones, and don't have practical criteria that allow them to decide when a task or phase is complete.

What's even worse than a project that gets lost in the swamp of analysis is a project that completes its work and submits a good redesign that never gets implemented. Implementation failures occur because key departments, managers, or employees haven't committed to the project. A good redesign effort requires a lot more than a process redesign. It requires that the company go through a change process that systematically gains the commitments of all relevant stakeholders. At the same time, it requires that the implementation be planned with as much care as the redesign and that managers and employees involved in the process have their job descriptions and incentives changed so that they are judged, and rewarded, when the project meets its goals. If customers or other companies are involved, care must be taken to assure that they are just as committed as your company people are to the new process. Thus, the methodology we describe is not simply a plan for redesigning a process. It's a plan for both a redesign and for securing the support of all the people necessary to assure that the new process will be implemented.

How Does It All Begin?

In the earlier chapters of this book we described an enterprise alignment cycle. We argued that every organization should establish a process that linked corporate strategy with a business process architecture group. The business process architecture group, in turn, should identify process changes mandated by changes in corporate goals and then generate a prioritized list of projects. Each project should be assigned a sponsor who is responsible for undertaking the project and assuring that the scope of the redesign corresponds with the goals the executive committee and the architecture group set for the project. In this chapter, we won't concern ourselves with the strategic and architectural functions, but assume that, somehow, a senior manager has been assigned goals and the responsibility for improving a business process. Thus, for our purposes here, a project begins with a senior manager who is responsible for undertaking a business process redesign.

What Happens?

Figure 9.1 provides a very high-level overview of the phases in our redesign process methodology. The project begins, in Phase 1, when the responsible manager sets things going. Typically, the manager, who we usually call the project sponsor, retains a project facilitator who will manage the actual process analysis and redesign effort. The facilitator then works with the project sponsor to develop a plan and schedule and to select other individuals to take part in the project.

Ultimately, the planning effort results in a business process redesign team that includes a wide variety of members, including process managers, employees, IT specialists, and others concerned with the process. This team documents the current process, going into only as much detail as seems appropriate.

Once the analysis is complete, the same or a modified team considers various redesign options and arrives at the one they think best. After the redesign is approved, a development plan is created that requires efforts from everyone involved in creating products necessary for the process change.

Finally, after each of the specialized groups has completed its work, the new process is implemented. Assuming all goes well, the new process is used until managers find need to correct it, or until the strategy and process architecture committees determine that the process should be revised again, in response to still newer threats or opportunities. We'll consider each of these phases in some detail below.

To keep things simple, we are assuming that the process redesign project is confined to a single company or division. Many e-business applications, especially supply-chain-driven redesign projects, involve organizing several companies to work together. The essential process is the same as we will describe, but the establishment of steering committees and design teams can be quite a bit more complex. In some cases, goals and plans may need to be specified in legal contracts before the redesign team can even begin its work. In these cases, a strong process architecture committee is especially important.

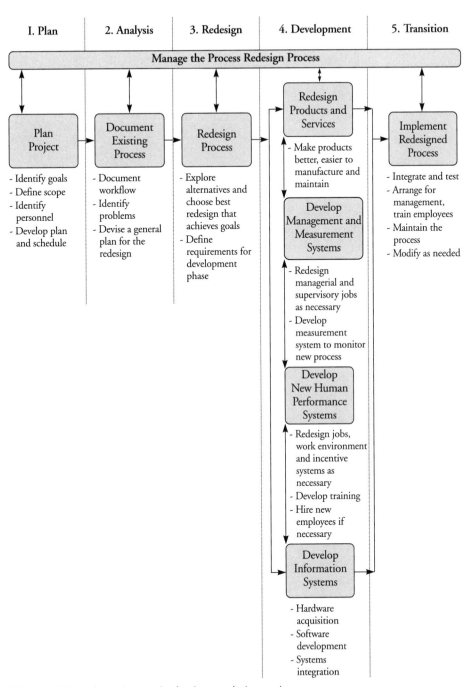

Figure 9.1 Five phases in a major business redesign project.

Who Makes It All Happen?

Obviously the names of groups and the job titles will change from one organization to the next. Broadly, however, we assume that the ultimate decisions are made by a group that we'll term the *executive committee*. The executive committee may include a strategy group and a process architecture committee, or these groups may report to the executive committee. The strategy group provides inputs to the process architecture committee, which, with the approval of the executive committee, decides what business processes need to be redesigned. However it's organized in a specific company, the executive committee is probably made up of the CEO, the COO, and the heads of major departments and business units. The executive committee is responsible for adopting new corporate strategies and setting corporate goals. Once goals and strategies are adopted, the process architecture committee is responsible for determining which value chains or business processes should be modified to achieve new strategies or goals, and developing plans to assure it happens. The process architecture committee may have many of the same members as the executive committee, or it may have more specialists and planners.

A major redesign effort takes time and consumes the efforts of lots of executives and managers. Thus, it is only justified when it is determined that minor changes won't produce the desired result. A major redesign is usually undertaken only if the organization makes a major shift in its strategic orientation, or if a major new technology is to be incorporated that will impact a number of different subprocesses and activities within a major business process.

Once the executive committee decides a process redesign effort is justified, someone must be assigned to oversee the project. If the organization already has a process orientation, and process managers, then the person responsible for the project is the process manager, and the project steering team is made up of the team of managers who normally work together to oversee the process. In this case, the project sponsor is either the project manager, or someone directly appointed by the project manager. In companies that do not currently have process managers, a project sponsor must be appointed by the executive committee. Since one of the goals of a serious process redesign effort should be to reorganize the process management system, the person appointed as project sponsor, in this case, is usually the individual who will emerge as the process manager when the redesign is complete. However it's arrived at, the project sponsor is the individual who is ultimately responsible for the redesign project. He or she does not manage the day-to-day work of the redesign team, but is responsible for approving major decisions and working with members of the executive committee to assure broad support for the work of the redesign effort.

At the same time, a *process redesign steering team* should be established. This team usually consists of high-level representatives of all of the departments or functions involved in the process. In some cases the process architecture committee serves as a permanent redesign steering team. In some cases the team is a subcommittee of the executive committee. In any case, you need to create such a team. This team has two key functions. First, it must approve the work of the redesign team. And, second, its members need to assure that the managers and employees within each of their respective organizations understand, support, and will implement the redesigned process. The work that goes on with the redesign steering team is just as important as the redesign work itself. The team members must be powerful enough to commit their functional groups and to assure that their managers will be held accountable for a successful implementation effort.

Next, an individual needs to be selected to actually facilitate the process redesign effort. In some cases this individual is a consultant who comes from outside the organization. In other cases he or she comes from a business process group within the company. In either case, it's important that this individual is neutral and doesn't have any stake in, or any commitment to, the functional groups that will be engaged in the redesign effort. The *project facilitator* should be a consultant who understands how to facilitate process redesign. The facilitator does not need to understand how the specific business process works. Instead, he or she should be skilled in working with a design team to assure that they succeed within a reasonably short time. A good facilitator is the key to assuring that the analysis and design occur on schedule and don't get bogged down in an unnecessary analysis effort.

Finally, a *process redesign team* should be established. This group will actually struggle with the details of the process and make the choices about how to redesign the process. The team is usually composed of managers or supervisors from each of the major subprocesses or activities involved in the process. In most cases technical specialists from human resources and IT should also be included on the project redesign team.

Phase 1: Planning for a Redesign Effort

Ideally, the goals and overall schedule of any specific process improvement effort should be defined and limited by a charter or plan issued by the process architecture committee. The plan may have come from the strategy committee or the executive committee. If no project plan exists, the team responsible for the specific business process improvement effort will need to develop a plan. Specifically, they will need to determine the organizational strategy and the goals that the specific process is expected to support, and they will need to define how the specific process relates to other company processes and to company customers and suppliers. In effect, they will need to generate a limited version of the company strategy in order to define and scope their task.

Assume that a process architecture committee has assigned a priority to the project, created a general plan, and assigned a project sponsor. In that case, the first task of the project sponsor is to identify a steering committee, "hire" a facilitator, and oversee the elaboration of the project plan. In most cases the project facilitator manages the actual day-to-day work of the project. In some cases the facilitator will be an outside consultant, and in other cases it may be an internal facilitator provided by a corporate business process improvement group. In either case, the facilitator will probably begin by interviewing a number of people to assure that he or she understands what everyone expects. In effect, the facilitator begins by checking the completeness of the plan.

Interactions between the project sponsor, the steering team, and the facilitator will also help refine the project plan. The same group should also work together to assemble the process design team—the individuals who will be responsible for actually analyzing the existing process and then developing the new process design.

In most cases it is the project facilitator who actually writes out a formal planning document and then modifies it after he or she receives inputs from the sponsor and other team members.

Once the project plan and a schedule are completed, they should be reviewed in a joint meeting that includes everyone involved in the project. This is a critical meeting, and the outcome should be an agreement on the scope and goals of effort to be undertaken. If someone's unhappy with the project, this is the time to deal with it. Otherwise, throughout the other meetings and later, during implementation, you are likely to have someone resisting the new process.

Major Activities

Figure 9.2 provides an overview of what's involved in the planning phase. Figure 9.2 uses a process diagram to show who is involved and what happens in what order. Most of the tall activity boxes represent meetings in which members of all the groups get together to review proposals and agree on plans. These meetings and

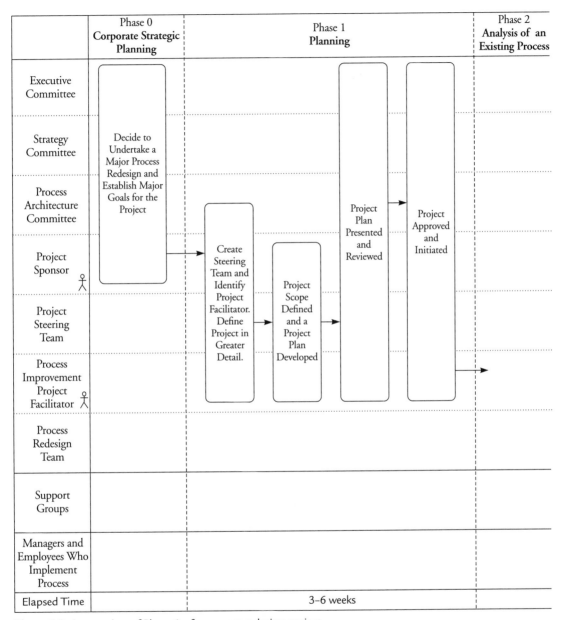

Figure 9.2 An overview of Phase 1 of a process redesign project.

the consensus-building effort that they represent are an important aspect of any major business process improvement project.

Most of the detailed work of this phase is done by the facilitator in conjunction with the steering team.

▶ The executive committee appoints a project sponsor and creates a steering team. They, in turn, appoint a facilitator and a process redesign team. Most of the detailed work is undertaken by the project facilitator, who interviews senior managers and those currently involved with the process. The facilitator creates and presents draft documents for the sponsor and steering team to review and approve.

▶ Refine the scope of the process to be analyzed and redesigned. If the corporate committee created documents describing strategy changes, goals, measures, and a description of how the process should be changed, then one begins with them. (This information can be documented on an *organization diagram* and on an *organization goals and measures worksheet*,[1] or in any other reasonable format.) The sponsor, steering team, and facilitator should begin by reviewing everything that has been documented. If no documentation of this sort has been prepared, then the team should create them. Unless the process architecture committee has already done it, the team should also review or create a *value chain* or *process relationship diagram* to assure that everyone understands how the specific project fits with other corporate processes. If the project is large, the team may want to create a high-level *process diagram,* define the major subprocesses that make up the overall process, and define their relationships. In this case, the team may also subdivide and different groups may focus on different subprocesses, or they may prioritize the analysis and improvement of subprocesses.

▶ Review project goals. The team should review the goals set for the project and explore how they relate to corporate strategy and goals. If the process is large or complex, the team may want to identify which subprocesses lead to which goals or create subgoals for different subprocesses. If a process management system is going to be created or redesigned, then managers from the different functional units should definitely be included on the redesign team.

▶ Review and document project assumptions, requirements, and constraints. The more familiar the team becomes with the specific process, the more likely it will see alternatives or identify constraints that the corporate committees overlooked. The team should document every assumption and constraint it identifies to clarify its thinking about the nature of the process. Facilities, manufacturing machines, computer hardware, and software systems are often

---

[1] In this chapter we will mention several worksheets that can be used to document a process or record decisions about a redesign. We have not introduced these worksheets yet, but they will be discussed in subsequent chapters.

sources of constraints. Changing them, or working around them, can often impose huge costs on a project and render an effective redesign impossible. It's important to find out what constraints might limit redesign as early as possible.

▶ Create a project schedule and budget. As the team learns more about the specific project it is planning, it will either create or refine the schedule and the budget developed by the business process architecture committee.

▶ Benchmark data describes industry averages for specific types of tasks. Or, in some cases, it describes what competitors have achieved. In most cases it's hard to get good benchmark data, although it's widely available for packaged applications from the vendors and in some industries from associations. If benchmark data is to be used to determine minimal goals for a redesign effort, this fact should be identified in the planning stage and a plan developed to secure it.

▶ Determine who will actually take part in the actual analysis effort. Identify the members of the process redesign team. In most cases, only some of the members of the team will actually take part in the workshops in which the process is analyzed. The overall team should determine who will take part and arrange for them to be available for the time required. The actual analysis and design work will take place during meetings, which are often called workshops. It's best to have a neutral, trained facilitator to run the actual process, and we'll assume one is available throughout the remainder of this discussion.

Outcome

This phase ends with a detailed *project plan* for a specific business process that has been approved by the executive committee, the business process architecture committee, the process sponsor, and the project steering committee. When everyone agrees on the plan, it's time to begin Phase 2.

Phase 2:   Analysis of an Existing Process

The goal of this phase is to analyze and document the workings of an existing process. Some organizations will have already done this analysis. In other cases the project team will be creating a completely new process, and there will be no existing process to analyze. Still other project teams will decide to skip the analysis of the existing process and focus on creating a new process. Most process redesign teams, however, should develop at least a high-level overview of the existing process simply to provide a starting point for redesign efforts. A few organizations will undertake a detailed analysis of an existing process and then proceed to develop a detailed time and cost model of the current process in order to run simulations to study how specific changes would improve the efficiency of the existing process.

The actual work during this phase is typically accomplished by the facilitator and during meetings between the facilitator and the process redesign team. The team that is to analyze the process meets with the facilitator. Some facilitators prefer to have the team together for several days in a row and to work through the analysis in one push. Other facilitators prefer to meet for 2–3 hours a day, usually in the morning, every other day for several weeks, until the analysis is complete. There is no correct way to do this. It depends on the company, the facilitator, and the scope and urgency of the project.

The facilitator runs the meetings and helps the team analyze the problem. The facilitator usually draws diagrams and makes lists on whiteboards or large sheets of paper that are put up around the meeting room. The facilitator is usually supported by a scribe (or analyst) who takes notes as the team makes decisions. If a process modeling software tool is used, it is usually the scribe who uses the tool. The team members don't need to use the tool or worry about it. The main goal of using a software tool is to capture the information and make it easy to print notes and create diagrams to document the process. Between team meetings, the facilitator and the scribe work together to assure that the documentation is accurate and then print documentation so that the team members will have it when they arrive for the next session. A specially designed process modeling tool makes it possible to document a morning session and then provide printouts of the resulting diagrams in the course of an afternoon. Companies that run intensive efforts, where the team meets every morning, are usually forced to rely on a software tool to assure that the documentation can be prepared promptly between sessions. Software tools are discussed in more detail in Chapter 17.

Major Activities

Figure 9.3 presents an overview of Phase 2 of the process redesign project.

The activities of this phase are undertaken by the process redesign team, guided by the facilitator.

▶ To assure that things move quickly and smoothly, the facilitator usually reviews the plan and interviews a variety of stakeholders to get up to speed on the process and the problems that call for a redesign. In addition, to assure that the process design team gets off to a fast start, the facilitator will often create a first draft version of the process. In this case, rather than having the team define the

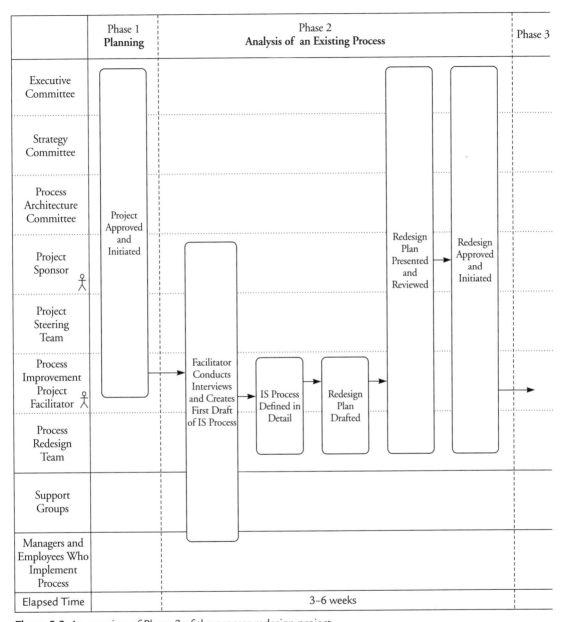

Figure 9.3 An overview of Phase 2 of the process redesign project.

process from scratch, the facilitator begins by proposing an overview of the process and then works with the process redesign team to refine the strawman version. This is a reasonably painless way to introduce *organization* and *process diagrams.* The facilitator puts up diagrams of a process the team is familiar with and talks them through it. The diagrams are easy enough to understand that the team quickly gets into identifying activities or flows that are wrong or missing.

▶ Document the current (IS) process. Use *process diagrams* to document an IS version of the process. If the process is large, begin with a high-level *IS process relationship diagram* that identifies the key subprocesses. Then develop a separate *IS process diagram* for each subprocess. Repeat this process until you arrive at an IS process diagram that shows activities and describes the process in as much detail as the team feels necessary. The goal isn't analysis for its own sake, but a diagram with enough detail so that the team can easily see what will need to be changed to improve the process and to achieve the project's goals. A good facilitator can help the team focus on creating "just enough" analysis and avoid getting lost in details.

▶ Agree on the names of processes, subprocesses, inputs, outputs, and activities. Different groups often use different terms to refer to the same processes and activities. One important outcome of a process analysis should be an agreement on what processes and outputs should be called. This is especially hard if many different functional groups are involved, and it's very hard if multiple companies are involved.

▶ Identify any "disconnects" or deficiencies in the current IS process. Record findings on a *process analysis and improvement worksheet.*

▶ Activities are linked by lines that show where inputs to the activity come from and where outputs go. The lines should be labeled. The flows between activities can be products, documents, information (data), or money. If the inputs or outputs are complex, it is probably worth describing them on a process analysis and improvement worksheet.

▶ Determine necessary characteristics of each activity. As we've said before, we use the term *activity* to describe the smallest unit of process we intend to model. Each activity needs a name, and it should probably also be given a written description to be sure everyone will know just what it entails. An activity can be performed by an individual, be automated by a software system, or performed by a combination of a person and a software system. You should note how each activity is performed. In other cases, it may be important to document how decisions are made during an activity. If the flow from an activity branches, it is often useful to include information about how it is determined which path a given output takes. If many different business rules are used to make decisions, it might be worth listing the rules that are applied. If specific goals, subgoals, or quality measures are associated with an activity, they should be defined. All of this information should be noted on an *activity worksheet* or recorded by means of a software tool.

▶ Develop a process management design. Usually a subset of the entire process design team, made up of managers, meets to document the current management process. As we have suggested, the management process involves organizational, process, and functional aspects. It also involves establishing goals and measures for the process as a whole and for each subprocess and activity. And it involves actually taking measures and evaluating deviations from the expected results. If this has been done in the past, then existing managers should be able to provide specific data on which activities and subprocesses have been performing well or failing in the recent past. Similarly there should be documentation on corrective actions that have been attempted. If this data doesn't exist, then the IS management team should at least document the structure that does exist and develop a document specifying where the management process breaks down. At a minimum, the team should develop a good idea of who is specifically responsible for managing each existing subprocess and activity.

Although we have not emphasized it up to this point, a process redesign effort typically requires changes in both the specific activities that make up the process and in the management system that monitors and controls the process in everyday use. In our examination of hundreds of business processes, we have consistently found that there were more problems with the management systems that control the process than with the activities that comprise the process. That is why the team should consider how the management system will support the process before going into the specifics of process redesign. A process with useless or poorly ordered activities will result in an inefficient process. On the other hand, even a relatively well-designed process that is managed by supervisors who haven't established clear measures or who don't reward behavior that is critical to the success of the process is just as likely to be inefficient. In reality, in any major process redesign effort, we usually find opportunities to improve both the process structure and the management system. We will devote a subsequent chapter to management and measurement problems.

▶ If the team plans to do cost studies, then each activity should be analyzed to determine its cost, the time it takes, the outputs produced per unit of time, and so forth. Time and cost can be documented on an *activity table,* but if you are really going to do cost studies and compare alternatives, then it's much better to use a software product and enter the information into tables associated with the activity on the software product diagrams. This is done on an *activity cost worksheet.*

▶ Refocus on the project goals and challenge old models and assumptions. After the process analysis is complete, it's usually useful to revisit the goals, assumptions, and constraints defined during Phase 1 and to challenge each one. Can it be achieved? Can you do better? Is the assumption or constraint valid? Is there some alternative that will ease or remove the constraint? Revise the goals, assumptions, and constraints as appropriate.

▶ Recommend changes in the effort as necessary. If, in analyzing the current version of a process, the team realizes that assumptions are wrong or that opportunities exist that weren't previously recognized, they should communicate their recommendations to the steering team or the executive committee and suggest changes in the scope of the project effort. Do not proceed to a redesign phase with flawed goals or assumptions. That's just a formula for a project that will end in acrimony.

▶ Summarize all the findings in a redesign plan. At the end of the effort, the redesign team should summarize their findings and propose a general approach to the redesign of the process. This redesign plan should take into account all of the assumptions, constraints, and opportunities the team has discovered.

▶ Present and defend the redesign plan before all of the higher-level committees and obtain their approval. Depending on the organization, this may be a public process or it make take place on a one-on-one basis. The key thing, at the end of each phase, is to obtain the approval and commitment of all those who will later have to assure that the new process is actually implemented. If an important manager doesn't accept the proposal, it's better to stop and either deal with the objections or come up with a new design. The alternative is to create a plan that will be "dead on arrival," since a key manager won't support implementation.

Outcome

The outcome of this phase is a set of documents and models describing the existing (IS) process, a draft plan for the redesign of the existing process, and the support of all key senior managers.

Phase 3: Design of a New or Improved Process

The goal of this phase is to create a design for a new or improved process. In some companies this phase is combined with the previous phase, and the design team moves smoothly from documenting the IS process to creating a new or SHOULD process. In other cases this phase is undertaken without having first undertaken Phase 2, or it is undertaken by a slightly different design team.

The actual work during this phase, as with the analysis phase, is normally accomplished during meetings between a facilitator and the process redesign team. The team that is to improve the process meets for 2–3 hours a day, usually in the morning or for several days at a time, depending on the facilitator and team member schedules, and so forth. The number of days or meetings will vary greatly depending on the scope of the project and the level of detail being created or redesigned.

Once again the facilitator runs the meetings and helps the team consider alternatives. The facilitator is usually supported by a scribe (or analyst) who takes notes on what the team decides. Between team meetings, the facilitator and the scribe work together to prepare documentation so that the team members will have it when they arrive for the next session. Many software tools include the ability to send result to team members via the Web so they can study them online between meetings.

Major Activities

The major activities in Phase 3 are illustrated in Figure 9.4.

▶ Review IS process and improvement goals, and identify specific opportunities to change the IS process. Depending on the scope of the design team's mandate and the schedule, the team may focus on very specific types of improvements, or may relax all possible assumptions and speculate about radically different ways of organizing the process.

▶ Design the new or improved process. The team's decisions should ultimately result in a new process that is documented on a *SHOULD process diagram*. In complex projects, the team may create several alternative *COULD process diagrams* and then choose among them. The new design should eliminate disconnects and unneeded activities and streamline the activities, subprocesses, and the overall process whenever possible.

▶ Design a management process to support the new SHOULD process diagram. The management process should specify who is responsible for each activity and subprocess. It should also establish measures for activities and subprocesses. This should be indicated on a *role/responsibility worksheet*.

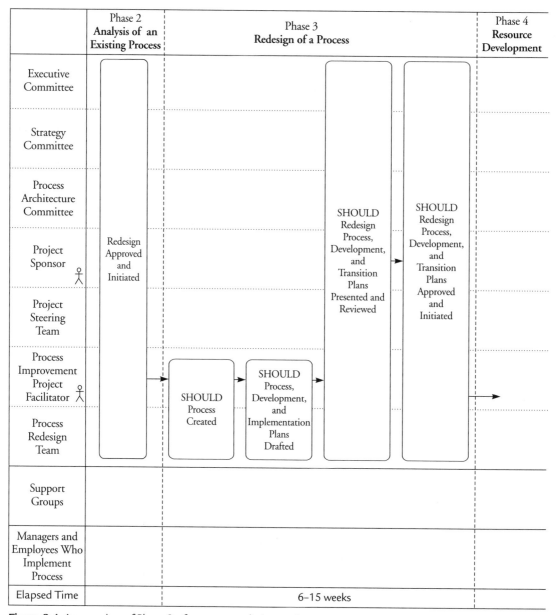

Figure 9.4 An overview of Phase 3 of a process redesign project.

▶ Rationalize reporting relationships. In some cases changes in a process may suggest a new organizational chart that regroups employees and creates reporting relationships that will allow improved accountability and efficiency. New processes will probably require that employees and reporting relationships be established. In either case, the team should prepare a new organization chart indicating the hierarchy and reporting relationships of employees involved in the new or redesigned process. When appropriate, the process redesign team should review the actual jobs or roles involved in the process, and determine which functional managers will be responsible for which of the new process activities. This information is recorded on one or more *process/responsibility worksheets.*

▶ Cost or simulate new process options. In some cases design teams will want to compare alternate COULD process options to each other or to the current IS business process. Or if the process is new, the team may want to simulate it to learn more about it. This can be very valuable, especially if the process is complex. Simulation often reveals problems that no one notices when simply looking at diagrams. To do costing or simulation, however, the team will have to use a software tool and will need the support of someone who has experience in building cost or simulation models. If the team is already using a tool like Proforma's ProVision, which is designed to represent SHOULD process diagrams and do simulation, it will simply be a matter of entering more specific information about how each of the activities will function. If a spreadsheet is to be used, then the team will want to document the costs and times involved in each activity on an *activity cost worksheet.*

▶ Provide detailed documentation of new activities. If specific activities (i.e., jobs, software systems) are being modified or created, they should be documented on an *activity worksheet.*

▶ When the team arrives at a fully documented SHOULD process design, it should arrange to present the proposal to the executive committee, project manager, and steering team. It's important that these groups not only understand the new process but approve it. These are the senior managers who will have to work to assure that the new process is actually implemented. A lukewarm approval from senior management is a recipe for a failed implementation phase.

Outcome

The outcome of this phase is documentation describing the new process and management structure that the design team proposes. This design will probably not be in enough detail to satisfy the requirements of software developers or of job analysts, but it should be sufficient to convey to business managers the exact changes that are being proposed. The redesign plan should be approved by senior managers.

Phase 4: Development of Resources for an Improved Process

The goal of this phase is to acquire the space and resources, create the job descriptions, train employees, set up management systems, and create and test software systems needed to implement the new process.

The work of this phase is handled in a variety of different ways. In some cases the design team is sophisticated enough to continue to refine the SHOULD process diagram into a detailed software requirements document that can guide software developers. In other cases, the design team that created the SHOULD process diagram and the activities worksheets will hand their work over to a new team that will develop specific software requirements. Similarly, the original design team may undertake the creation of new job descriptions, salary and incentive structures, and so forth. In most cases, however, they will pass their design on to specialists in the human resources group for detailed specification.

Major Activities

Figure 9.5 provides an overview of the activities in Phase 4.

As Figure 9.5 suggests, Phase 4 involves additional participants in the new process development effort. Although representatives of IT have probably been involved in the earlier phases, at this point they will shift and become active on IT software development teams if new software applications need to be created. Similarly, human resource specialists will probably work with other human performance specialists to redesign jobs and provide needed training if new jobs need to be created or if new skills need to be provided for those already working on the process being redesigned.

The managers on the process redesign team, working with others in their various functional areas, should refine the management systems, managerial job descriptions, and measures required to assure that all managers involved with the new process will understand the changes required and the new criteria by which their performance will be judged.

Various groups will test their work individually, and then, if it's a large process, it will probably be given some kind of field trial to assure all the pieces work together, before the new process completely replaces the old.

This phase varies in length, depending on the nature of the changes that were selected during the redesign phase. It also varies because different specialized groups may become involved in this phase. Thus, this phase usually begins with the development of a new plan by the steering team, working in conjunction with

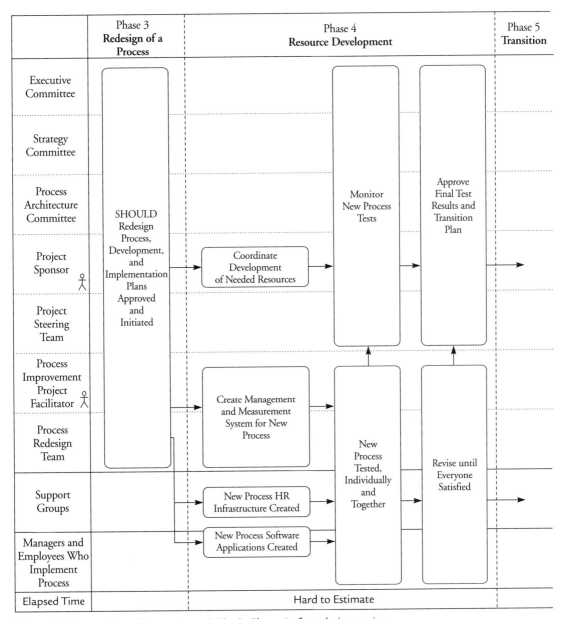

Figure 9.5 An overview of the major activities in Phase 4 of a redesign project.

the various groups that will actually develop the infrastructure needed to implement the new process.

In a typical case, IT people will be engaged to create or acquire new software to implement activities in the new process that are to be automated. In the process they will probably need to refine the SHOULD process diagrams to create more detailed *workflow models, use case models,* and any of a variety of other UML software diagrams, depending on the nature of the software application to be developed. (See Chapters 11–15 for more information on how IT might extend the work of the process redesign team.)

Human resource people will be engaged to create new or modified job descriptions and to negotiate needed changes with unions and existing employees. Training people will develop materials necessary to train employees to perform new tasks. In the course of their work, human performance analysts will probably develop *job diagrams* and prepare *job analysis worksheets.* (See Chapter 6 for a discussion of how human resources might follow up the work of the process redesign team.)

During this same period, the managers involved in the effort should create or refine their management system. If the company is already organized around processes, and the process team is headed by the manager for the process being redesigned, then it will be much easier. In this case, it is a matter of refining how the process management team functions and checking all existing goals and measures to assure that they conform with the changes in the process. If, on the other hand, the company is not organized around processes, this is the point at which they ought to consider doing so. Obviously, a shift in the management of the organization will need to involve the executive committee and cannot be undertaken lightly. A project manager will need to be appointed. Managers currently reporting to department heads will need to be reoriented to become members of the process team and to report to the process manager. Goals, measures, and incentive systems will need to be renegotiated. Some measures and incentives may continue to flow from the department structure, but most should be tied to the overall performance of the process. If a company is really converting to process management, this can easily become a redesign project in its own right.

The alternative: To redesign a process, and then leave subprocess managers responsible to department heads and not to an overall process manager, is a recipe for failure. In spite of the redesign, departmental managers will tend to manage to achieve goals chosen for departments and not for the process, and silo thinking will tend to reinsert gaps and disconnects where information and materials are passed between departmental units.

Outcome

This phase ends when the various groups developing infrastructure and materials needed to implement the new process have completed their work and tested their materials.

Phase 5: Managing the Transition to a New Process

The goal of this phase is to transition to the new process. Many companies have redesigned processes and then failed to actually implement them. This occurs for a variety of reasons. The foremost reason is that senior managers resist the change. Even managers who recognize that the old process is defective may be unwilling to endure the hassles and problems that implementing the new process will entail. Functional managers may not want to make seemingly minor changes in the way things are done within a department to support the goals of a process that's largely outside the focus of the department. Similarly, employees may resist using the new procedures or the new software systems.

The process sponsor and the steering team should plan for the transition. They should work with senior executives to assure that they have the "push" they will need to get all the relevant managers to try the new process. They should work with middle managers and employees to convince them of the advantages of the new process. In many cases, salaries and incentive systems will need to be changed to assure that managers and employees are rewarded for implementing the new procedures. And they should work with managers responsible for the process, at all levels, to assure that they have management plans in place so that the managers can measure the success of the new process.

Major Activities

Figure 9.6 provides an overview of what takes place in Phase 5.

Few people like change. We all rely on habitual behaviors to make our tasks easier, and change upsets all that. Major changes where some employees are laid off and others need to learn to use new software systems results in even more dissatisfaction. If employees, supervisors, and managers don't see the reason for the change, it's much worse. Thus, a good transition plan calls for meetings that acquaint everyone involved with the nature of the change and the reasons for it.

It also requires managerial pressure to assure there is no backsliding. Senior managers on the project steering team need to communicate to the managers below them their support for the change. The new management system needs to provide ways for senior managers to measure the results of the change, and everyone needs to understand that those measures will be carefully watched to make sure the new process works as designed.

If the change is extensive, then individuals need to be designated so that anyone having problems can get in contact with someone who can deal with the problem. Senior managers should follow up their initial meetings with subsequent meetings

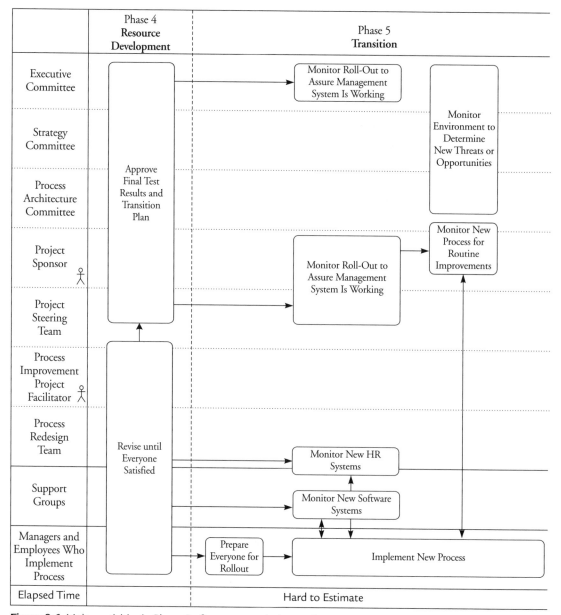

Figure 9.6 Major activities in Phase 5 of a process redesign project.

to let everyone know that the desired new results are being obtained and that management appreciates everyone's effort.

The activities of this phase vary greatly, according to the nature of the new process, the amount of change required, management support, and the resistance offered by those currently performing the process. In many cases the work of this phase will be subcontracted to a team of change management specialists.

Outcome

The outcome of this phase is a new process. Beyond the transition, managers will need to work to assure that the new process meets its goals and to identify new problems that will require subsequent changes. Maintaining a process is a full-time management job.

Summary

By way of a quick summary, the major phases in a process improvement project include

- ▶ Phase 1: Planning a process redesign effort
- ▶ Phase 2: Analysis of an existing process
- ▶ Phase 3: Design of a new or improved process
- ▶ Phase 4: Development of resources for an improved process
- ▶ Phase 5: Managing the implementation of the new process

Figure 9.7 provides a slightly different way of looking at a process redesign project. In this case, we have listed the phases as a series of boxes. Within each box we have listed the key objective and the major steps in each phase. We have also listed the diagrams and the worksheets used in each phase. We have already described the various diagrams in early chapters. We will provide examples of the worksheets in later chapters. We mention them here to lay the groundwork for their use in the case study. In most cases, companies won't use the worksheets, and we provide them only as a way of showing the kind of information that a company needs to gather and the decisions that should be documented.

This overview cannot begin to provide detailed information about what should happen in each phase of a redesign project. Hopefully, however, it provides an introduction, and it should become clearer as we consider a detailed case study in Chapter 16.

Major Steps and Objectives	*Diagrams and Worksheets That May be Used*
Corporate Strategic Planning Undertaken by executive committee, strategy committee, process architecture committee, or project sponsor	
Determine corporate strategy Identify opportunities and threats Identify corporate processes to be improved Scope projects Set general goals for project	Organization goals and measures worksheet Supersystem diagram of organization Value chain diagram
Phase 1: Project Redesign Planning Undertaken by project sponsor, steering team, and project facilitator	
Refine scope of project Establish project schedule and plan	Detailed diagram of organization Organization opportunities and threats worksheet Project plan
Phase 2: Analysis of an Existing Process Undertaken by project facilitator and process redesign team	
Define IS process Define IS activities Define IS management system Identify key disconnects and prioritize	Detailed diagram of organization IS process diagrams to various levels of detail IS process analysis and improvement worksheet IS specific activity analysis worksheet IS activity cost worksheet
Phase 3: Process Redesign Undertaken by project facilitator and process redesign team	
Eliminate disconnects and improve process fit Define COULD processes Define SHOULD process Define SHOULD activities Define SHOULD management system Define SHOULD measures	SHOULD process diagrams to various levels of detail SHOULD process diagrams with measures SHOULD process analysis and improvement worksheet SHOULD specific activity analysis worksheet SHOULD activity cost worksheet Process/responsibility worksheet
Phase 4: Resource Development Managed by project sponsor; undertaken by several specialized teams	
Create and test new software needed for new process Create new job descriptions required Develop training	SHOULD workflow model Use case and other software models Job model Job analysis worksheets
Phase 5: Managing the Transition to the New Process Managed by business managers responsible for the new process	
Manage transition and change Manage ongoing process	

Figure 9.7 An overview of process redesign.

10

Process Redesign Patterns

WHEN A BUSINESS TEAM redesigns a process, no matter what specific methodology they follow, they need an overall approach. The approach helps define the overall goal of the redesign. We call these general approaches *process redesign patterns.* One pattern, for example, is the *reengineering pattern.* Using the pattern, one ignores the existing process and sits down with a white sheet of paper to redesign the entire process from scratch, using all the latest technologies. In effect, this is what a new company must do when it sets out to create a new business. Another pattern, the *workflow pattern,* seeks to automate the flow of documents or decisions by modeling the process in a software tool that can subsequently manage the process. Still another common pattern looks at an existing process and tries to find gaps or disconnects that can be corrected.

In the last chapter we considered the overall flow of a business process redesign effort. We focused on how one organized teams and coordinated and communicated information among diverse stakeholders. In essence, we focused on the project management aspects of redesign. In this chapter, on the other hand, we will focus on the broad goals a company should set when it undertakes a business process effort. In many cases, companies don't think about their goals, and they often get in trouble. Senior management may call for a process redesign effort, hoping to significantly improve the company's competitive position. A specific team may decide that the best they can do, in the time allowed, is to simplify a given process. The software group may decide that no matter what the redesign team does, they can improve the process by substituting new ERP software applications for the current applications that are years out of date.

There's nothing wrong with using more than one pattern. Indeed, we will indicate patterns in this chapter that are often used in conjunction with other patterns. What is important, however, is to agree on the overall approach or pattern for a specific effort. Different patterns suggest different ways of organizing the effort and different techniques.

The overall approach or pattern a team uses is normally determined when the project facilitator and the steering team or the manager responsible for the process meet to determine the overall goals for the process redesign. In other words, in most cases, the overall goals of the redesign project suggest the choice of a redesign pattern.

Types of Process Redesign Patterns

In this chapter we will review some of the common patterns. Obviously many organizations routinely use more than one of these patterns in combination, but for simplicity's sake, we consider them in isolation.

We have divided the redesign patterns into two general sets. The first set, which we term *basic business process redesign patterns,* are used in almost every business process redesign, usually in combination with what we will term *specialized redesign patterns.* The basic patterns include the reengineering pattern, and three less-radical business process redesign patterns: simplification, value-added analysis, and gaps and disconnects. These patterns are described in Table 10.1, and we'll consider them in more detail in this chapter.

We refer to the second group or redesign patterns as specialized redesign patterns because they are used to extend the basic patterns or to solve specialized problems. This group includes *management alignment,* a set of software automation patterns, and patterns tailored for supply-chain design and for human performance improvement. We describe these patterns in Table 10.2. We will not discuss these patterns in this chapter, since they are treated in other chapters of the book.

Specifically, management alignment was discussed in Chapter 7. Workflow automation will be discussed in Chapter 11. Business process XML languages will also be considered in Chapter 11. ERP-driven redesign patterns will be considered in Chapter 12, and software development will be considered in Chapter 13.

The SCOR pattern will be considered in Chapter 15 when we consider supplier-oriented business applications. Six Sigma was considered in Chapter 8, and human performance improvement was discussed in Chapter 6 when we considered job design in conjunction with the analysis of activities.

Table 10.1. Basic business process redesign patterns.

Pattern	Driver	Approach	Time required	Impact and problems
Reengineering	Major reorganization desired. Major changes or new technology is to be introduced.	Start from a clean slate. Question all assumptions. Design process from ground up using best practices.	Major effort. Considerable time required.	Can achieve major breakthroughs in productivity and efficiency. Potential for disruption and risk of failure proportionally high.
Simplification	Eliminate redundancies and duplicated effort in processes.	Model IS process and ask, at each step, do we really need to do this? Focus especially on similar processes and ask if they can be combined.	Usually a mid-sized effort.	Usually results in a modest to major increase in efficiency and productivity, largely dependent on the amount of redundancy in the process.
Value-added analysis	Eliminate non-value-adding activities.	Model IS process and ask, at each step, does this activity add value or enable a value-adding activity?	Usually a mid-sized effort.	Usually results in a modest to major increase in efficiency and productivity, largely dependent on the amount of non-value-adding work in the process.
Gaps and disconnects	Problems occur when information or materials are passed between departments or functional groups.	Model IS process and ask at each point when information or materials pass between a department or function, what happens and what needs to happen? Requires a process sponsor and a matrix organization.	Usually a mid-sized effort.	Usually results in a modest to major increase in efficiency and productivity, largely dependent on the amount of problems between departments. Depends on a strong process sponsor.

In the remainder of this chapter, we describe the four classic basic patterns, beginning with the well-known reengineering pattern.

The Reengineering Pattern

This pattern is associated with Hammer and Champy and with a half a dozen popular BPR books that were published in the early 1990s. Hammer, Champy, Davenport, and others argued that large-scale business processes and value chains had been designed for a different era. To achieve radical improvements in efficiency, they believed that companies should start with a blank sheet of paper and redesign an entire value chain from scratch. This approach downplays an analysis of existing processes and emphasizes starting by asking what goals the process should

Table 10.2 Specialized redesign patterns.

Pattern	Driver	Approach	Time Required	Impact and Problems
Management alignment	The need to align strategic goals with process goals.	Examine measures used by each layer of management to assure they are all derived from the goals for the organization and the overall value chain. Assures each activity is being measured in an appropriate manner.	Can take quite a bit of time. Often done in conjunction with gaps and disconnects or simplification.	Usually increases productivity by focusing processes and activities toward company goals.
Workflow automation	Process lends itself to being controlled by a workflow system.	A workflow tool will provide the ultimate management of the SHOULD process. Usually combined with simplification process. One begins by defining the process and then determining how the workflow tools will route work between manual activities.	Usually a mid-sized effort.	Usually results in a modest to major increase in efficiency and productivity.
XML-BP languages	New approach. Focuses on automating processes and the ability to modify processes by using the XML Internet technology.	One defines processes and activities that are automated using an XML-BP language. This makes it easier for companies to exchange information about their processes. In effect, this is an Internet version of a workflow system.	New technology. Unproved. Could be significant risk.	In theory this approach ought to result in more flexible processes, but will probably prove limited to a specific subset of business processes.
ERP-driven redesign	Company wants to automate or improve a process by using an off-the-shelf application. Usually the application is part of an ERP or CRM business process suite.	Company identifies applications to be automated and then identifies vendor to provide the applications. This redesign works backwards, since you begin with the solution, and then see how the IS process must be changed to accommodate the new application interfaces.	Usually a mid-sized effort, depending on the number of applications being installed and the tailoring being undertaken.	Usually results in a modest increase in efficiency and productivity. This approach is best employed on low value-adding processes, since it guarantees your processes will be very similar to those of the competition.

Table 10.2 (continued)

Pattern	Driver	Approach	Time Required	Impact and Problems
Software development	Company wants to automate or improve a process and uses an internal or external IT group to design and develop the application.	Company identifies applications to be created and then identifies IT group to provide the applications. IT group will probably use a modeling language like UML and create a software architecture like MDA. They will probably also use a component methodology like Unified Process and software development tools.	Usually a mid-sized effort, depending on the number of applications being developed.	Usually results in a modest increase in efficiency and productivity. This approach is best employed on low value-adding processes, since it guarantees your processes will be very similar to those of the competition.
Supply-chain operations reference model (SCOR)	Company wants to create an internal or external supply chain that links departments or companies.	SCOR is a reference model developed by the Supply Chain Council (SCC), a group that promotes standards in this area. SCOR provides a common vocabulary and methodology for supply-chain process design or redesign.	Significant effort since it usually requires a major software integration effort.	Can lead to breakthrough increases in efficiency, but in most cases it leads to modest improvements. Often leads to ability to integrate with other companies more quickly in the future.
Six Sigma	Although Six Sigma is usually used for process improvement, it can be used for design or redesign. It's usually used when a manufacturing process will be created or where process consistency is very important.	Six Sigma has a lightweight process analysis component but is very good at establishing measures and refining the consistency of a process. Relies heavily on statistical methods derived from quality control methodologies.	Usually a mid-sized effort, since Six Sigma is usually used with a well-defined process.	Usually results in a modest overall increase in efficiency and productivity, but it delivers good measures and more consistent processes.
Human performance improvement (HPI)	Focuses on the design of jobs and tasks performed by employees and on motivation and the employee performance environment.	HPI has been developed by individuals associated with the International Society of Performance and Improvement (ISPI) and provides a systematic way to approach job design and improvement.	Usually a mid-sized effort, although it depends on the number of jobs involved.	Usually results in a modest overall increase in efficiency and productivity, but it delivers good measures and more consistent employee performance.

achieve and then working backward to determine the best possible way to achieve those goals using the latest technology. This approach is sometimes called *radical redesign.*

Some companies have tried this approach with great success. They have redesigned major processes and created new processes that radically change the assumptions on which the older processes were based. In some cases huge increases in productivity have resulted. In most cases, however, major redesigns have proved more difficult. They tend to cause large disruptions in the existing business and lead to great uncertainty among employees and managers as the redesign is undertaken. In many cases, especially in the mid-1990s, they relied on technologies that could not, in fact, scale up to deliver the kinds of benefits their designers hoped to achieve. By the end of the 1990s, although some companies were still tackling major reengineering efforts, most companies had shifted to less comprehensive redesign efforts.

In recent years, most BPR practitioners, including Hammer and Champy, have modified their emphasis and now often promote something closer to what we would call "redesign." In other words, they allow for modifications in business processes or subprocesses and don't always encourage redesigning comprehensive business processes from a blank sheet of paper. Still, in the minds of many managers, reengineering refers to comprehensive, complete redesign and that's the way we'll use the term here. Readers should be aware, however, that many people use BPR to refer to something more modest, like process redesign.

Case Study: TI's MMST Project

To provide a good idea of the scope of a major reengineering effort, consider the MMST project undertaken by Texas Instruments (TI) between 1988 and 1993. Hammer and Champy cited TI's work in *Reengineering the Corporation* as an example of a company that had made major improvements in the manufacturing processes in their semiconductor division, and this project provides a great example of the scope of such a major effort.

Texas Instruments is a major chip manufacturer. During the past decade, two trends have dominated semiconductor chip manufacturing. First, each new generation of chip required a more expensive facility for its manufacture. A typical manufacturing facility cost around $1 billion in 1990. To offset this, manufacturers were interested in doing larger batch runs to justify the setup costs. At the same time, companies buying chips were increasingly interested in moving away from batch production to small runs of tailored chips. Small runs minimize the problems involved in manufacturing very complex chips. The business model that dominated the industry in 1988 relied on economies of scale that were attained by large volumes with minimum product variation. The bulk of the chips manufactured were dynamic RAMS (DRAMs) that were appropriate for batch runs, but the real profits were increasingly in customer-specific or application-specific chips made in relatively low volume in a flexible manufacturing facility.

Batch production is expensive when one is manufacturing large chips because a single error can turn an entire batch of expensive chips into junk. Ideally, you would like to manufacture them one at a time, checking each chip constantly to be sure each step works correctly before moving on to the next step.

In October 1988, the Defense Advanced Research Projects Agency (DARPA) and the U.S. Air Force Wright Laboratory contracted with TI to develop a next-generation flexible semiconductor water fabrication system. The project is generally known by its contract name, the Microelectronics Manufacturing Science and Technology (MMST) project.

In essence, the goal of MMST was to redesign the chip manufacturing process, creating new hardware and software, as necessary, to make it possible to engage in cost-effective, low-volume manufacturing.

TI had been experimenting with a wide variety of new technologies for several years. The challenge for the MMST team was to decide which of the various new technologies could be made commercial in the time allowed for the project. Conventional chip manufacturing relied on clean rooms, and the manufacture of more complex chips required ever cleaner rooms. In addition, batch processing means that an error at any phase could result in hundreds or thousands of expensive but useless chips.

TI elected to create new machines that processed chips within a vacuum. To further reduce the chances of contamination, the chips were manufactured upside down. (Think of this as a piece of brainstorming. Dust is drawn to the ground by gravity. Chips were traditionally manufactured face up, exposed to any dust that might alight on them. By simply turning the equipment upside down, dust was much less likely to settle on the surface of a chip.) Since more than one machine was involved in processing a chip, a vacuum cassette was developed. Chips were processed by one machine, inside the vacuum environment maintained by that machine, then placed in the vacuum cassette, which was then moved automatically to the next machine for further processing. It sounds simple enough, but it actually required a very sophisticated effort to simply design and manufacture the hardware that would process the chips.

Another problem with conventional chip manufacturing happens when an error occurs during processing. Unless the error is detected immediately, a very expensive effort is continued that only results in a defective chip. TI elected to create hardware that would process one wafer at a time. It also arranged to monitor the production process with a number of probes that were, in effect, constantly checking to see if the evolving chip was within set tolerances and functioning correctly. This monitoring process could only be cost-effective if it could be completely automated. Thus, TI elected to create a fully automated, real-time control system. The software system was designed to plan and schedule the production of chips and then monitor each chip, determine if any errors had occurred, and take appropriate action.

Obviously, replacing a manual batch operation with an automated system was going to require changes in the human support operations. Although jobs changed, the automated system still required people to set up and monitor the new system. One of the goals of the MMST effort was to provide terminals that would provide employees with all the information they needed. In addition, IT elected to create a system that would let the monitors modify their terminal displays to suit their preferences.

TI designed and manufactured machines that could process wafers in a vacuum. In a similar way they designed and manufactured cassettes to move chips between machines. The process required experimentation, hand-assembled prototypes, testing, and finally the actual manufacture of a new chip fabrication factory. TI also created a large, real-time software system to run the new factory. TI elected to use new software techniques (object-oriented software design and development in Smalltalk). The overall design of the MMST CIM software was divided into several phases, including an architectural analysis phase, a prototyping phase, a design phase, and an implementation phase.

Even in a fully automated wafer fabrication facility, a number of people are needed to monitor the process, including production managers, engineers responsible for the actual process sequence, hardware maintenance engineers, and so on. Thus, in addition to providing the software to run the machines involved in the processing, the CIM system supports a number of workstations, each connected to a network that links the workstations to the manufacturing machines. Different modules (e.g., factory planning, factory simulation modeling, factory performance monitoring) provide interfaces and facilities for the different people who must interact with the system. The heart of the system is a scheduling or workflow system that processes orders by selecting machines and directing material movement for each step to be taken as a wafer is processed.

TI completed the redesign in 1993 and installed the MMST system in its new plants. In the process it developed the ability to manufacture application chips in low volume in a cost-effective manner. TI developed a new line of semiconductor manufacturing devices, ranging from large machines that process wafers to vac-uum cassettes that are used to transport wafers from one machine to another, and all of that hardware is now sold to other semiconductor manufacturers. In addi-tion, TI had developed a modularized software system that controls the manufac-ture of chips. The software was developed using new techniques that make it especially easy to modify and extend so that it can be used by others in related semiconductor manufacturing operations. Sematech, a consortium of semicon-ductor manufacturers, standardized on the new framework, and it is now used by other companies in the consortium.

TI's MMST project represents a complete redesign of a process. The develop-ers began with a blank sheet of paper and asked themselves how they could de-sign custom chips, using new technology. They arrived at a completely unique solution and created the hardware and software to support their new con-cepts. They reengineered the jobs of the people involved, replaced many jobs with software systems, and developed software systems for the new jobs that were created.

The MMST project completely changed the economics of small-scale chip manufacturing, making it possible for TI to dominate a new field for years, and to sell its expertise to those who wanted to compete with it. Thus MMST represents the ideal of reengineering—the complete redesign of a process and the heavy use of computer technology to revolutionize the way the process is accomplished.

Reengineering Today

In a study published in 2002, Cutter Consortium reported that 49% of a sam-ple of some 230 organizations from throughout the world reported that they had been involved in business process redesign in the mid-1990s. When that 49% was asked if they undertook large, reengineering projects, 25% reported that they did and were happy with the results. Another 19% reported that they had tried reengineering and found it too disruptive. The rest, 56%, reported that they only undertook limited redesign projects. Eighty-three percent of the organizations re-ported they were involved in redesign or improvement today, but only a small per-cent reported that they were focusing on large-scale reengineering projects. In essence, there is a role for large-scale projects, but they are costly in terms of time and disruption and should only be attempted when there is a major strategic need for a complete process redesign.

Hammer, Champy, and Davenport, each in slightly different ways, would all agree with this assessment. Hammer has focused on smaller efforts, Champy has written a book on aligning management, and Davenport has written on integrating corporate redesigns with ERP systems.

The Simplification Pattern

By the mid-1990s, most companies had decided that the radical reengineering pattern was too risky and disruptive to use in most cases. As an alternative, business process redesign practitioners developed several less radical patterns. One of the most popular is the pattern we term the *simplification pattern.*

In essence, the simplification pattern assumes that most established processes include redundancies and duplicated activities and that the processes can be improved by simply streamlining the activities. This approach can be used on large-scale business processes, or more limited subprocesses. It works best if it is used on large-scale processes, since you are more likely to identify redundancies if you look at a larger unit of process. One usually begins at the business process level and drills down. In some cases it's possible to eliminate entire subprocesses and consolidate their activities.

To apply this pattern, one starts by identifying all of the processes, subprocesses, or activities in an existing business process. Then, one begins where the process begins and challenges each subprocess or activity in the sequence. Is this activity really necessary? What information is obtained from this activity that couldn't just as well be obtained elsewhere? Is this subprocess a bottleneck? Could things be done in parallel? Do things go through unnecessary loops? Whenever an activity is identified that introduces an unnecessarily complex flow or seems to largely duplicate the work of another activity, one of the activities is eliminated and any work done by one and not the other is added to the remaining activity.

The process redesign team needs to be flexible as it considers each activity. Members from one department may argue that an activity has unique characteristics or needs to be done by members of their department rather than another. These claims need to be carefully weighed. In general, however, the group should opt to eliminate activities if at all possible.

Case Study: Xerox Non-Production Procurement

A good example of a large-scale simplification effort is the process redesign undertaken by Xerox Corporation in 1994. Non-production procurement (NPP) covers all purchases of supplies other than supplies used in the actual production of Xerox machines. Thus, all office supplies, from desks and personal computers to pencils and stationery, come under the category of non-production procurement.

In early 1994, Xerox was spending about $4.3 billion dollars a year on NPP. Xerox realized that the redesign of this process represented a major opportunity to save money. A business process (BP) redesign team was created that included managers, supervisors, and clerical personnel from the various organizations involved in NPP. We interviewed the people involved in this process and reported on it in 1996. The team members involved in the work explained how procurement had initially been spread throughout the various corporate departments and groups. Moreover, different groups had been established to handle expensive items like desks or complex items like computers, while other groups handled more routine items like paper and pencils. Specialists had been established to handle exceptions and rush orders.

The group approached the redesign by trying to think of major changes and simultaneously trying to document what was currently being done to assure that all aspects of the problem would be covered. At the same time, Xerox contracted with an outside consulting group to survey other organizations to determine the best procurement practices at companies that had a reputation for doing things efficiently. The redesign team studied the results and set its own goals accordingly.

The outside consulting group was also involved in helping the redesign team create a process diagram that described all of the activities of all of the groups involved in the NPP process. The consultants used diagrams similar to those described in this book, listing customer contacts at the top and departments along the side. Databases were listed on separate swimlanes at the bottom of the chart. The initial chart was huge and identified hundreds of different activities. Most were found to be non-value-adding activities and were eliminated.

In hindsight, the redesign team spoke lightly of the struggles between different groups as they worked to consolidate activities. Initially, each team member tried to explain why a specific sequence was necessary for handling the unique types of problems faced by his or her specific group. As time went on, however, the team members gradually agreed that most of the activity sequences were really just variations on a few basic themes. One recurring sequence, for example, involved letting contracts to vendors who would then supply items at a set price.

By mid-1996 the entire NPP process had been reduced to three sequences, each comprising a few activities. The redesign team also implemented several radical changes in the NPP process. For example, credit cards were issued to all managers. The credit cards had established limits, and managers were encouraged to use them when they needed to acquire something quickly. By shifting decision-making and responsibility for these unique, rush purchases to departmental managers, a large portion of the NPP bureaucracy was eliminated. American Express agreed to provide reports to Xerox that summarized the use of the credit cards, thereby eliminating the need for new software to monitor the small purchases.

Xerox also decided to identify and negotiate mega-purchasing deals with very large suppliers who could support Xerox throughout the world. By replacing numerous small contracts with a few very large contracts, the team eliminated most of the people involved in contract negotiation, as well as the numerous people previously required to monitor many small contracts.

The team also decided to completely automate access between Xerox managers and the suppliers so that all paperwork would be eliminated. Each manager can now use his or her PC to access the supply system and complete orders online. Departmental limits and constraints are all handled by the computer system without any need for intervention by accounting personnel.

Once the team created its SHOULD design, it began to meet with IT people to define the nature of the software system they would need to support the new process. The IT team that joined the BP redesign team preferred using object models. They converted specific activities to use case diagrams and eventually developed object models for each of the major transactions. They then used an object-oriented modeling tool to run simulations on each major set of activities defined by the BP redesign group to see if the new processes would work smoothly. This also allowed the IT team to develop a detailed cost analysis of the various sets of activities. This work impressed the BP redesign team, who said, in retrospect, that they thought the simulation had significantly improved their understanding of some of the changes they had proposed. One subprocess, in particular, turned out to have several bottlenecks that rendered the new process very inefficient. By playing with the simulation, changing the flow, and adding more positions to handle exceptions, the BP redesign and IT teams, working together, were able to make the subprocess much more efficient.

After the Xerox IT group and the BP redesign team had drawn up a complete set of IT requirements for the new NPP process, the IT group turned the requirements over to the BP redesign team that then put the software development effort up for bid.

When it was finally completely implemented, the new Xerox NPP process reportedly saved Xerox a very significant portion of the money formerly spent administrating purchasing. Hundreds of activities had been reduced to dozens and numerous redundant subprocesses were now combined into three major subprocesses. Hundreds of suppliers, with all the overhead involved in managing them, had been reduced to four major suppliers, and emergency purchases had been delegated to departments that now relied on credit cards. A complex system of dozens of paper forms had been eliminated, and the entire process was now handled online by a new NPP software system.

The Xerox NPP process improvement effort is a great example of what you can do when you simply look for redundancies and duplications and simplify down to the really basic activities you actually need. In this case the company didn't completely reinvent the process, but they simplified it and improved it in many different ways.

The simplification pattern is often combined with the value-added analysis and the gaps and disconnects patterns that we describe next.

The Value-Added Analysis Pattern

Value-added analysis looks at a process, subprocess, or activity from a customer's perspective. This can be very enlightening for a department that has been doing things without considering this perspective for some time. The customer, in this case, is whoever receives the output of the process being studied. In an ideal case it's the ultimate customers of the organization, but it could just as well be an internal customer. Manufacturing and marketing are the customers of new product design. Inventory is the customer of some manufacturing processes, and so forth.

A process or activity is said to add value if it meets three criteria:

1. The customer is willing to pay for the process or activity.
2. The process or activity physically changes or transforms a product or service.
3. The process or activity is performed correctly on the first try.

Inversely, a process or activity is said to be non-value-adding if it involves preparation or setup, if it's focused on control or inspection, if it simply results in a product being moved from one place to another, or if the process or activity results from an internal or external failure or from delays.

Many studies suggest that a typical process is made up of 20% value-adding activities and 80% of other activities. Other activities are usually subdivided into value-enabling activities and truly no-value activities. In a typical process, most of the non-value-adding activities fall in the value-enabling category.

In essence, you begin by looking at each process, subprocess, or activity in a process to see if it meets the three criteria of a value-adding activity. If you have developed an IS process diagram, you might simply color all of the processes or activities on the diagram that are clearly value-adding activities. (If you are unsure, ask the customer!) What's left are the activities that you want to consider much more closely. If it's obvious that an activity must be done to make it possible to do a value-added activity, then mark it as a value-enabling activity, using a second color.

Then consider each of the remaining activities even more closely. Obviously some control and inspection needs to be done, but how much and when? Obviously products need to be moved from one place to another, but is there any way the environment could be changed to minimize such moves?

You should focus on the activities and on the flow between the activities. You might try marking each arrow that indicates a nearly instantaneous transfer with the same color you mark value-added activities, and then examine each arrow that remains.

The main impetus behind early workflow systems was to eliminate the time that documents spent traveling and sitting in in-baskets and out-baskets. A document-handling workflow system takes each electronic document, the instant one employee clicks to say he or she is done with the document, and places it on the queue (digital talk for an in-box) on the PC of the next person that needs to look at the document. In other words, document workflow systems virtually eliminate the time that was formerly involved in moving documents about.

One automobile company has created a new automobile plant that is long and thin and has truck-sized doors behind virtually every location on the moving production line. Formerly, an employee had to be constantly moving door assemblies to the people who were installing doors. Now, the door installers simply turn about and walk into a semitrailer to grab the next door. As quickly as one truck is emptied, the trailer is hauled away and another truck backs up to the door. Once again, moving has been virtually eliminated from the production line. As an aside, forklift trucks that used to move materials on pallets were a major source of accidents in the plant, and those accidents have been eliminated as well. Of course, building a tailored assembly plan of this kind is only cost-effective when one is working on a very large-scale product process and determined to cut margins as low as one can, but the same idea can often be applied to other processes on a smaller scale, simply by rearranging desks or using email to move items from one place to another more quickly.

Obviously, whenever something has to be redone, either because it was done wrong and was caught by the employees working on the process or because it was returned by the customer, you are looking at a problem. Exception handling is another sign that you should look closely. Situations in which one employee has to refer the customer to someone else, who—horrors—has to refer the customer to still another person, is another signal. As a generalization, employees need to be empowered to handle the queries they receive, even if it means giving the employee the power to return money or send the customer a new item. If you take a customer focus, not dealing with problems or complaints as quickly as possible is about as non-value-adding as you can get.

Value-added analysis is a powerful way to organize a review of a process, and it often identifies activities that have been added for departmental purposes that have no value to customers. In some cases those non-value-adding activities are value enabling, but in other cases you can identify activities that can be eliminated.

The Gaps and Disconnects Pattern

This pattern was initially popularized by Geary Rummler and Allan Brache in their 1990 book, *Improving Performance: Managing the White Space on the Organization Chart*. Rummler and Brache pointed out that many of the major problems one finds in any process result from a failure of communication between business silos. Marketing fails to hand the new product specifications to manufacturing in time. Manufacturing makes changes in the product that will save production costs, but prove unpopular with customers and Sales feels it has been blindsided.

Rummler and Brach were, as far as we know, the first to introduce the use of swimlanes on business process diagrams. We have used swimlanes in this book. They provide managers and design teams with an easy way to see where a process flow crosses a departmental or functional group line. In effect, when a facilitator is working with a redesign team and they focus on gaps and disconnects, they focus on handoffs, coordination, and feedback problems.

The gaps and disconnects approach puts a lot of emphasis on carefully analyzing how the existing process is done before beginning to look for ways to improve the process.

Rummler and Brache also put a lot of emphasis on aligning the goals and measures managers use when they evaluate activity outcomes and on the people who perform the manual activities. Thus, for example, they often find as many disconnects in the management of processes as in the processes themselves. We treat the analysis and improvement of management alignment as a separate pattern, but it is often combined with this pattern. The emphasis on performers usually results in checking for feedback and consequences to assure that workers learn about inappropriate handoffs and that there are consequences for individuals, managers, and departments for the failure to coordinate their efforts.

Table 10.3 summarizes some of the potential disconnects that Rummler suggests organizations look for when they analyze a process.

Table 10.3 Sources of gaps and disconnects. (After Rummler.)

Potential disconnects	Process designed	Process managed	
		Process Planned	Process controlled
Organizational level			
1. Organizational goals			
2. Organizational business model		●	
3. Organizational strategy		●	●
4. Process goals and requirements		●	●
5. Organizational priorities		●	●
6. Value chain alignment		●	●
7. Operating policies		●	●
8. Functional measures, goals, and rewards		●	●
9. Reporting relationships and organizational structure		●	●
10. Business values and practices		●	●
11. Resource availability and application		●	●
12. Accountability for results		●	●
Process level			
1. Process strategy		●	●
2. Process priorities		●	●
3. Process flow simplified and straightforward	●		
4. Missing or substandard input from another process	●	●	●
5. Unclear or conflicting specifications of process or subprocess output	●	●	
6. Underlying business models	●		
7. Decision rules	●		
8. Lack of information on process or subprocess performance	●	●	●
9. Resource availability and allocation for process or subprocess	●	●	●
10. Not clear who is responsible to perform process, subprocess, etc.	●	●	●
11. Accountability for results	●	●	●
Activity level			
1. Activity outcome not clear	●	●	
2. Job/system not supportive	●		
3. Job/system support inadequate	●	●	●
4. Job/system consequences not supportive	●	●	●
5. Job/system feedback not adequate	●	●	●
6. Performer not adequately trained	●	●	●
7. Performer lacks basic capacity to produce required outputs		●	
8. System outputs not timely	●		
9. System outputs not useful	●		
10. System output access difficult or not understood	●		

Checks have been placed in one of three columns. The first column, process design, refers to the actual workflow and the activities performed by systems or employees. The second two columns refer to activities that managers are responsible for—the planning of processes and the monitoring of process outcomes. As you can see, at the organizational level, all of the problems are management problems. Even at the process and activity levels, many of the gaps and disconnects are caused by management failures.

Obviously, the gaps and disconnects approach includes simplification and some elements of value-added analysis, but it also includes more since it focuses everyone on the difference between the activities in the process itself, and the activities that managers do that enable the process. It's often possible to begin an analysis and quickly discover that the process itself is reasonably well designed and that all the real problems result from managerial problems, a lack of clear goals, a lack of feedback, a lack of needed tools and supplies, measures that measure the wrong thing, or corrective actions that make matters worse.

Similarly, it's not uncommon to begin the analysis of a process and determine that departments aren't communicating. In value-added terms, the customer department doesn't value the product that they are being given.

A process diagram is designed to accentuate potential gaps and disconnects problems. First, by looking at the departments and functional groups on the left side of a process diagram, one can easily see where products or services are passed between departments. Figure 10.1 reproduces a process diagram we used earlier.

We began by highlighting the lines between major departments and then circling places where an activity in one department passed something to an activity in another department. If you are undertaking a process analysis, you will want to have the people in the respective departments review the handoff and determine if it's a problem or not. If the receiving activity is very unhappy, why are they unhappy?

Obviously once you have cleared up any problems with departmental handoffs, you can move on to the handoffs between groups within a department.

The customer is always placed at the top of a process diagram to remind everyone to focus on every interaction with the customer, since this is the ultimate handoff and the source of all value for the process.

Each of the process redesign patterns discussed in this chapter, and in subsequent chapters, is sometimes more useful and, at other times, not very useful. Processes differ, and techniques to analyze and redesign them must differ as well. Each of the basic patterns discussed here, however, should at least be considered whenever you look at a new process and decide how to go about improving it.

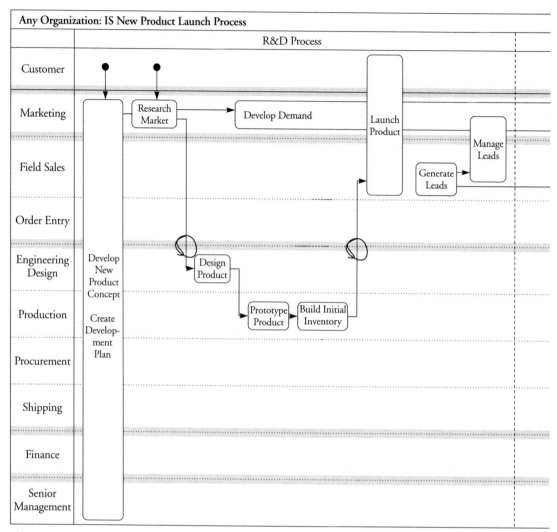

Figure 10.1 A process diagram with departmental handoffs highlighted.

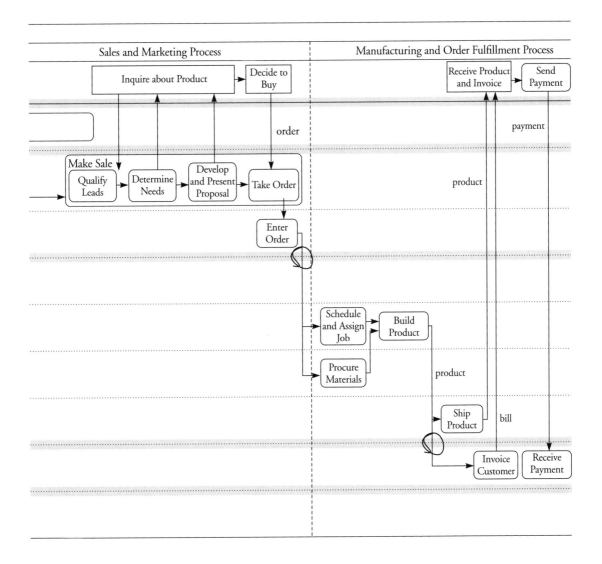

PART V

BUSINESS PROCESS AUTOMATION

Business process automation is accomplished by means of computers and software applications. It is sometimes used in conjunction with business process redesign, but it is also used by IT developers who have been asked to acquire or create software to automate a given process. There are several popular automation patterns, and we will consider the most important.

Chapter 11 describes one approach to software automation that relies on a workflow software tool that manages the flow of documents or information between a group of people working on a common process. We'll consider some common workflow systems, and then consider a recent evolution of the workflow pattern, business process languages based on XML, a popular Internet standard.

Chapter 12 describes another popular approach to software automation. In this case, vendors offer prepackaged applications, organized to reflect common business processes. Companies can assemble suites of software applications to automate all or parts of selected processes. We will consider the package software approach in general and then look at how SAP can be used for business process change.

In Chapter 13 we'll consider what problems business process managers face when they commission software developers to create custom software applications for new or redesigned processes. Most software developers use notations derived from UML, a software modeling language, and this usually means that process diagrams must be translated to use case or class model diagrams and re-quirements specified before the application software can be developed. We'll also consider some software architecture issues and how they relate to the business pro-cess architecture we discussed in Chapter 3.

11

Workflow and XML Business Process Languages

IN THE EARLY 1990S, when companies were focused on Business Process Reengineering, one popular approach was to use computers and software to automate the flow of documents from one employee to another. Systems that managed this kind of document flow were referred to as *workflow management systems* (or sometimes *workflow engines*) and were so popular for a while that many people associated early BPR automation with workflow systems. Since that time workflow systems have grown in sophistication and are today used for a wide variety of different automation tasks. We'll consider the workflow approach in general and then consider some of the different uses to which workflow has been applied.

Workflow Systems

The heart of any workflow system is a workflow engine that manages data. In the simplest workflow systems, documents are scanned when they arrive at the company. Then, following a workflow map and a set of workflow rules, the documents are routed to the computers of employees that need to see them. Depending on the rules users have built into the workflow program, documents may sit until employees have edited and approved them, or they may be automatically sent to other employees after a period of time, or to multiple employees simultaneously. If customers later request address changes or request benefit payments, employees can recall the appropriate documents to their terminals and take whatever actions are

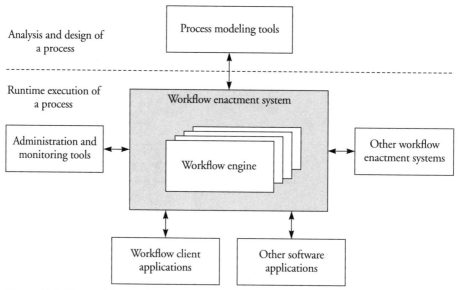

Figure 11.1 The world according to the Workflow Management Coalition. (Modifed after a model in the WfMC's *Workflow Management Coalition Terminology & Glossary.*)

required. A workflow system like this eliminates the need for employees to handle paper documents, protects the data, and automatically passes documents from one employee to another without the need of human intervention. Workflow systems of this kind routinely increase productivity when they are installed.

The Workflow Management Coalition (WfMC) is a group of users and vendors of workflow software that was founded in 1993. The WfMC describes workflow and workflow management systems as follows:

> Workflow: The automation of a business process, in whole or part, during which documents, information or tasks are passed from one participant to another for action according to a set of procedural rules.

> Workflow Management System: A system that defines, creates and manages the execution of workflows through the use of software, running on one or more workflow engines, which is able to interpret the process definition, interact with workflow participants and, where required, invoke the use of IT tools and applications.

WfMC uses the illustration we have reproduced as Figure 11.1 to show the key relationships.

The WfMC considers all of the boxes in the model shown in Figure 11.1 to be part of a workflow management system. In fact, when we have talked about process redesign, we have always distinguished between the analysis of a process (the top box) and the implementation of a process. By using process modeling tools especially designed to automatically implement a process, workflow systems move rapidly from analysis and design to implementation. This neat model breaks down in larger business process redesign efforts, when only a portion of some large process is to be implemented using workflow tools, but it will serve here.

In essence, someone using a workflow approach thinks of an activity as a set of changes to a document or form that is stored in a database. The workflow modeling tools indicate which activities occur in what order. The workflow engine keeps track of each process or set of documents and routes an electronic copy to whatever participant needs to work on them. Thus, a workflow team might describe how insurance forms are passed about at an insurance company. All of the documents used to support a given customer would constitute a single process lifecycle. The lifecycle would have different subprocesses, including Approving an Application, Notification of Late Payment, Approval and Payment of a Claim, and so forth. The initial applications would be scanned into the workflow system, and a database file would be created for each customer. Then, according to rules describing the process, electronic copies of each application would either be routed to particular participants or hold pending a request. In effect, a workflow system is an automatic, process-oriented system for managing documents.

Figure 11.2, also taken from the *Workflow Management Coalition Glossary*, defines the key business process terms, as used in workflow systems.

As you can see, we have been using most of the terms shown in Figure 11.2 to mean the same thing that the WfMC means. We haven't spoken of instances, but that simply refers to the processing of an individual case by the software system. Thus if Steven Smith submits an application to Ace Insurance, the application is scanned and becomes a file. When the workflow system begins to process Mr. Smith's application, it is executing a single process instance—Mr. Smith's application. At any point in the process, the next activity might be done by a human, or it might be an automated activity.

A Workflow Example

Let's consider how a document processing workflow system at an insurance company might work in a little more detail.

Figures 11.3 and 11.4 illustrate a simple system, before and after the introduction of a workflow system.

In Figure 11.3 we show the process as it was accomplished by people, before the introduction of a workflow system. In this case the arrows represent a paper

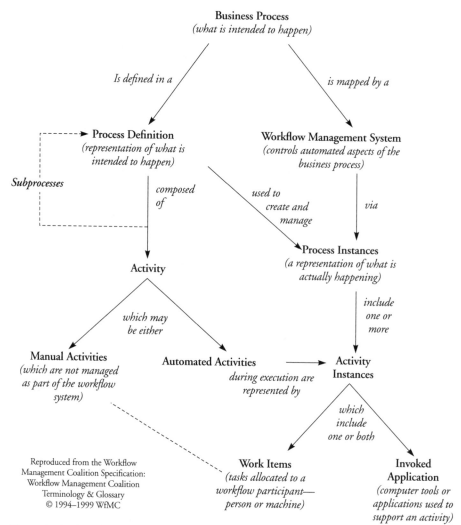

Figure 11.2 The WfMC's definition of some common workflow terms.

application being passed from one employee to another. Since employees don't normally walk applications to the next desk as soon as they are finished with them, this process is a *batch process*. The policy clerk gets a whole set of applications when he or she begins work. The clerk begins by checking the first application to be sure it is complete and then opens a file drawer to check the record of the application. Once one application is done, the finished document is put in an out-tray, and the clerk turns to the next application. Every so often a mail clerk picks up applications in the out-tray and carries them to the person indicated on a routing slip that the clerk has attached to the document, and so forth.

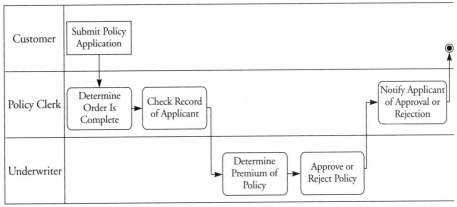

Figure 11.3 A simple insurance application process, before the use of a workflow system.

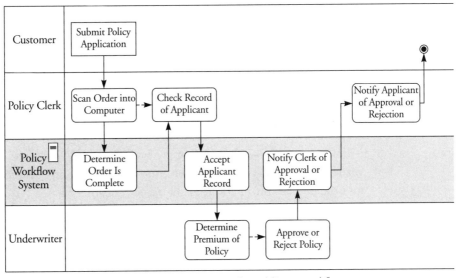

Figure 11.4 An insurance application process after adding a workflow system.

Figure 11.4 suggests how the process is changed with the introduction of a workflow system. A new activity is introduced, since the application must now be scanned so that a digital version of the application can be created for the workflow system. Once the application's electronic file is created, the computer can check to see if it is complete. Later, if it can be arranged so that the applicant or field salesperson can enter the application via a Web site, the scanning step can be skipped and the application checked for completeness as quickly as the user or salesperson can enter the data.

All workflow tools provide or link with some type of process modeling tool. Thus, the first step in creating a workflow system is to create a workflow model. If a business process redesign team had already created a detailed process diagram like those pictured in Figure 11.3, and added business rules to define how records are to be checked, premiums determined, and policies approved or rejected, they would have no trouble creating a diagram in whatever workflow tool they decided to use.

Once the workflow system has a document, it can route it according to the program described in the diagram, or simply save it for access on demand. In Figure 11.4, we show documents being routed from one employee to another. In this case, the workflow system will place the document in a virtual in-box on the Policy Clerk's computer. The Policy Clerk examines the file as soon as he or she can, and then simply drags the document image to a virtual out-box. As soon as the document is placed in the out-box, the workflow system updates its file, adding anything the clerk has added to the file, and then places the virtual document in the Underwriter's virtual input box, and so forth. If it was useful, the system could send the same document to multiple employees at the same time. Depending on the rules established when the workflow system is created, it could wait until all employees responded, or continue to move the document along if one employee was simply being given a copy as a courtesy, but wasn't expected to alter the file.

In passing, the workflow example in Figure 11.4 highlights a distinction we made earlier between the flow of control, the flow of documents or materials, and the flow of information. In the earlier document-based system (Figure 11.3), the flow of the document and the flow of control were the same. One processor passed the document and the control for the document to another processor by arranging to physically move the document from his or her desk to the next person's desk.

In a workflow system shown in Figure 11.4, in all cases the flow of documents is between the workflow system and specific PCs used by individuals. The document ceases to exist once it is scanned into the computer and is, henceforth, information or data. (In fact, the original document is probably filed, but in Web-based systems, no original paper document ever exists.) The documents only exist in electronic form and are never passed from one employee to another. Instead, a copy of the document in the database is sent to employee terminals, as defined by the workflow model that directs the workflow engine. The workflow engine contains the rules that determine who will get the next electronic version of a given document. In this circumstance, we might choose to eliminate all arrows between the activities and simply show arrows to and from the workflow system. To make the process more comprehensible to humans, however, we often show arrows between activities. The arrows between activities show the *flow of control*—they suggest who would normally be responsible for a document once a given activity is complete. In Figure 11.4 we've inserted one dashed arrow between the Scan Order activity and the Check Record activity. The dashed arrow distinguishes this control flow from the flows of information (virtual documents) that move from the workflow system to participants and back to the workflow system.

Early workflow systems were mostly concerned with automating the routing of documents from one user to another. In the course of the 1990s, however, workflow systems developers gradually realized that the real power of workflow systems wasn't in what they routed but the fact that the workflow model captured the underlying flow of the business process in a digital form. Once one had a description of a process stored as a workflow model in a computer, a manager could easily change the way a document was routed, by simply changing the model and specifying that a document go to different computer terminals in a different order. Similarly, by changing the rules applied at specific decision points, the process outcomes could easily be modified. Hence, workflow systems were soon valued more for their ability to model, control, and modify processes than for their ability to route specific types of documents. Workflow experts soon began to apply workflow engines to a very wide variety of different problems, ranging from controlling documents and machine processes to structuring the design of new products or coordinating the work of software developers.

Every workflow management system supports a computer interface for a workflow manager. Sitting at an administrative terminal, a manager can change the rules and the overall workflow specification that manages a process. Obviously there are limits. You can't cut out a necessary machine process, or the items being produced won't be ready for processing by a subsequent machine. You can, however, cut out a review cycle by clerk B on a specific type of document, if you decide it's unnecessary, and simply route the document directly from clerk A to clerk C. Similarly, you can change the rules that determine what constitutes an exception, or you can change the rules for qualifying a client.

You can also create a workflow system that manages and organizes the control of other workflow management systems. Thus, you could conceivably decide at the beginning of each specific run if the next auto was to be a red Honda Civic with the sports package or a blue Honda Civic with the regular package, and load the appropriate workflow process to assure the assembly process desired. (If you check back to Figure 11.1, you will see that the WfMC provides for administration and monitoring tools for this type of control.)

Types of Workflow Systems

Although workflow systems are most strongly associated with the automation of the flow of documents, workflow engines are used in many other ways.

Transaction or Production Workflow

Document processing workflow systems are an example of transaction or production workflow systems. One defines a process and indicates where users will interface with the workflow system. When the system is executed, it moves data from one point to another, automatically taking actions when it can, and sending information to employee computer screens when it needs manual help. This approach works well when the process is well understood and stable and the process activities can be precisely specified.

If documents are to be processed, then they must either be entered in digital form via a terminal or Web site, or, if they begin in paper form, they must be scanned and converted to a digital format.

One advantage of production workflow systems is that they can track exactly what occurs at each point in the process and record how much time is consumed in each activity. Thus, a manager can review data about the process and identify bottlenecks or sources of errors.

Ad Hoc Workflow

Ad hoc workflow systems rely on human participants to determine the sequence in which a process is executed. These systems work best when a process is dynamic and can change as new circumstances are encountered. Imagine a workflow system designed to help airplane designers create a new airplane design. Employees direct that design data be sent to other members of the team, who decide to approve or modify the diagrams and then redirect them. The employees may use conventional software packages like word processors and spreadsheets. The workflow system is concerned with routing messages between workers, with keeping track of the flow of work, and with maintaining an archived copy of the work being done.

Administrative Workflow

A third type of workflow system is based on email and assists individuals with administrative tasks. Expense approval systems, purchase requisition systems, and various HR functions like vacation and travel request processes are handled by this type of workflow system.

Administrative workflow systems are sometimes called *groupware applications.* They rely on workflow engines to pass documents or information between the members of a team that work together, while each works at his or her own PC. A simple example of a groupware application might be an application that schedules meetings. In essence, each participant has a calendar that is stored in a database. One individual initiates the program by entering a request for a 1-hour meeting between a list of individuals. The workflow engine checks each individual's calendar to determine when they all have an hour free and offers the originator the options. That person then chooses a time and the system enters the meeting on each individual's calendar, and usually sends email or some other notice to point out to each individual that a new meeting has been scheduled.

Another variation on the workflow concept is illustrated by systems that manage the work of groups of people. Consider, for example, a system to schedule the time of software developers. A database with the skills of each consultant is created. A calendar with each consultant's assignments is also created. As individual consultants finish tasks, they enter the information via their PCs, and the workflow engine determines who has available time and the skills for the next highest-priority task. This is the kind of thing that an IT manager used to do, but it can be largely automated by using a specially designed workflow system.

Generations of Workflow

Some writers discriminate between different generations of workflow systems. When they do this, they usually term the original workflow systems that focused on coordination processes within a department as *first-generation workflow systems.*

Second-generation workflow systems are designed to coordinate tasks across departmental lines. In some cases, these workflow systems control other workflow systems and can even shift work between systems according to the workload at any given point in time.

Third-generation workflow systems are just beginning to become available. These systems rely on the Internet and new Internet technologies like the Web and the XML protocols to link activities that may be distributed around the country or the world.

Redesign with Workflow

Redesign teams that decide to use a workflow system usually begin by seeking to eliminate paper documentation or to automate the flow of documents. The team begins by defining the IS process flow. Then they determine when the information will be entered into the workflow system. In some cases it's possible to ask the individual originating an order to enter the order online so that it is in electronic form from the very beginning. In other cases, the company receives paper copies, and they must be scanned into a computer database. Next, the redesign team determines who will see the documents in what order. Obviously when paper is involved, it can only go to one person at a time. Or the paper must be copied and reconciled at some point. A workflow system can route a copy of the same file to multiple individuals simultaneously, and reconcile changes made by multiple individuals so rapidly that every individual always seems to be looking at the same document. In addition, of course, a software program can do things like check arithmetic or look to see that every blank in a form is completed. Thus, once the redesign team has defined the IS process, they usually seek to automate and simplify the flow of the documents through the system. If there are security concerns, multiple, independent copies of the document can be maintained in independent databases to assure that the initial document and all changes can be tracked.

Workflow systems have been around long enough that most companies rely on standard workflow tools, and redesign efforts that automate processes using workflow tools are well enough understood that a redesign team and an IT team usually work together to design the workflow system.

Two Case Studies: Anova and iJET Travel Intelligence

Each year the WfMC gives awards to outstanding workflow applications. We'll consider two of the award winners in the 2001 contest.

Anova

The Dutch-based medical insurance company Anova completely overhauled and updated its document management and workflow system with a workflow software product from Staffware. The effort was triggered by a merger in 1998 of Anova and two other Dutch healthcare companies, Anoz and ZAO. Between them, the companies manage 1.2 million documents every month, 400,000 declarations of insurance every year, and some 1.1 million changes in existing documents every year.

The basic idea was to review the existing process, improve it wherever possible, and then move all documents to a workflow system. Staffware introduced a pilot scheme that initially involved automating over 100,000 documents that were part of Anova's insured parties operation. The pilot demonstrated that the workflow system could improve operational efficiency by 50%. The plan to automate all of Anova's document processing operations was approved.

The implementation of the system required the acquisition of workflow management software and servers, scanning hardware, laser disk storage systems, and PCs for every person who would henceforth interact with the documents.

The Anova workflow system was complete in 2001. At that time it had decreased work-in-progress jobs from 60,000 to 4,000, an improvement of 93%. The number of calls to the call center was reduced from 18,000 to 10,000 per week, and the nature of the calls had changed from concerns with problems to information dissemination. The average time it takes to process an application or claim was decreased from 16 to 2 days, and 75% of Anova's jobs are now processed within a single day. The Anova management team believes that the new system gives them a massive advantage over their competitors.

The Anova workflow system is a good example of a classic document-oriented workflow system. Anova is now thinking about migrating the system to the latest workflow technology. Thus, for example, Anova is currently exploring interfacing its workflow system to an Internet system that will give customers access to their files and information about the status of claims and other activities. Eventually, the company plans on letting customers access the company via mobile phones.

iJET Travel Intelligence

Another winner in the WfMC's 2001 contest is a new company, iJET Travel Intelligence. iJET delivers real-time intelligence and alerts to travelers and travel agents. The system runs continuously and alerts travelers to airline or hotel cancellations, political problems, transportation union problems, weather, or health problems. In effect, iJET monitors some 5,000 sources worldwide and creates small documents, usually a few lines, that are routed to or accessed by subscribers.

As the new company was created, managers analyzing what iJET was trying to do decided that the core of their business would run on a workflow management engine. In this case, since the documents were small and would be delivered via

Internet or wireless systems to computers or phones throughout the world, the workflow engine needed to be tailored for this kind of distribution.

In essence, iJET supports a library of some 50 processes, each including subprocesses. Some processes manage the routing of information from sources to analysts that study it. Other processes allow analysts to create alerts. Still other processes classify alerts and determine who to send them to. And others allow users to contact the workflow engine and request specific types of alerts.

The system was created using Java, built on an Oracle database, and relies on BEA's WebLogic application server and Fujitsu's iFlow business process management engine.

To date, iJET has consistently provided information to customers faster and more efficiently than news services and enjoys a growing customer base. iJET is an example of a third-generation administrative workflow system.

Workflow and XML

In the mid-1990s, companies began to incorporate the Internet, the Web, and email into their business processes. Toward the end of the decade, W3C, one of the major Internet standards consortia, introduced XML (eXtended Markup Language), a new format for passing data over the Internet. Companies are still exploring the uses of XML, but many companies have concluded that XML represents an ideal way for companies to pass data and to coordinate services. Microsoft's new .NET technology and IBM and Sun's Web Service offerings are all based on XML and a series of protocols that have grown up to support it.

In essence, XML is a file format. Each XML file contains data, and at the same time, it provides a way for users to include definitions of terms and processing rules within the same file. Thus, we can pass data about a part, and information about how the data is to be interpreted, over the Internet in the same package. Additional software protocols, like SOAP (a system that allows one computer to locate and send an XML file to another computer) and UDDI (a protocol that allows one company to query another company's computers to determine how they format certain kinds of data) have been introduced to make XML even more useful. (The UDDI protocol is implemented in a language called WSDL.) There are still issues to be resolved, and many standards groups are working on middleware and security standards to make XML more flexible and secure.

To make XML really useful, however, companies need to agree on how they will format or process certain types of data. Thus, for example, if two car dealerships wanted to pass information back and forth, using XML, they would need to agree on the meaning of *make, model,* and *auto type.* This information can be specified in an individual XML file, but the whole process is simpler if groups of companies agree on standards, which are usually called *XML languages.* Thus, auto dealers might want to create an XML language for communicating about autos they might want to sell or exchange.

A more technical use of XML is to allow one software system to communicate with another software system via XML. We have already mentioned that early workflow engines often had trouble communicating with each other. The initial solutions involved specific links that simply translated the output of one workflow system and converted it to a format that a second workflow machine could read. The problem of establishing that type of linkage becomes much harder if one wants to link workflow engines at different physical locations. Imagine, for example, that you were General Motors and you wanted to gather hourly data about the number of cars being sold at dealerships throughout the world. To do this, you, in fact, wanted to link the workflow systems that managed auto retailers' paper processing activities. It turns out that XML provides an ideal basis for a generic way to connect all these different workflow systems and to pass data between them, or from them to some other application residing at GM headquarters, provided the various workflow systems all support Internet and XML communication.

The Workflow Management Coalition created a workflow definition language XPDL (XML Process Definition Language). In essence, each workflow tool can define its internal concepts and constructs in terms of the XPDL common vocabulary. Then, when a user wants to link to workflow systems, they can be linked via the Internet. To pass information, workflow engine A translates its data into the XPDL XML document format, sends the XML document to workflow engine B, which then reverses the process and translates the XML data into the format used by workflow engine B. (Another protocol, Wf-XML, makes the process simpler.) It all sounds a bit complex, but it's easy for computers and provides a universal way of communicating between workflow engines—provided all of the workflow engine vendors support XPDL. Since most workflow vendors are members of WfMC, support for this XML standard has become widespread, and most workflow engines can now be connected via the Internet.

Generic Business Process Languages and Web Services

At the same time that the WfMC has concerned itself with using XML to link existing workflow systems and products, some vendors have been even more ambitious. They are working on generic business process description languages.

Companies already face significant problems as they seek to build large e-business systems. Developers find that they need to link together software applications from throughout the entire organization into a single system. Thus, a customer might come to a company portal and ask for information about a product. Satisfied, the customer might buy the product. Then, later, the customer might return to determine the status and the shipping date for the product. To find out about products, the portal probably provides the customer with limited access to a company catalog application. To buy the product, the customer probably interacts with the seller's accounting applications. The placement of the order probably sends information to a customer database and to an order entry system. It might also send messages to manufacturing and inventory or even to a set of suppliers. Inquiries could access manufacturing, inventory, shipping, or perhaps even an outside shipping company. Some of these locations may be in different states or even in different countries. If you thought of the company portal and all these various company applications as a single large workflow system, you can see how we will need to build large distributed workflow systems in the near future.

At the same time, companies are outsourcing some processes and considering building virtual processes that incorporate software components from other companies. The currently popular name for using processes provided by outside vendors is *Web services.* Web services is a term that is used in lots of different ways, but the essential idea is that you can use the Internet to access and use a process that resides at another company. In most cases, you would, in effect, be renting the use of the outside process. Some models imagine negotiating for one-time use. More commonly, companies will probably enter into long-term contracts with other companies to provide them with services (processes) they want to use. Much of the current development at large companies like IBM, Microsoft, and Sun is aimed at creating the infrastructure to make Web service processes possible.

A leading consortium, ebXML, supported by most leading companies, has created an architecture to support Web services. We have already mentioned XML, SOAP, and UDDI. These, along with WSDL and many other standards and protocols, must be combined to create a system that would allow companies to use Web services. Figure 11.5 provides an overview of the evolving ebXML architecture. The details aren't important, but the basic idea is. In essence, Company A downloads information about ebXML standards for business processes. It then builds an application (Web service) and sends information about that application to ebXML, where it is placed in a database. Later, Company B decides it would like to use a Web service with specific characteristics. Company B contacts the ebXML registry and identifies potential services. IT chooses the one offered by

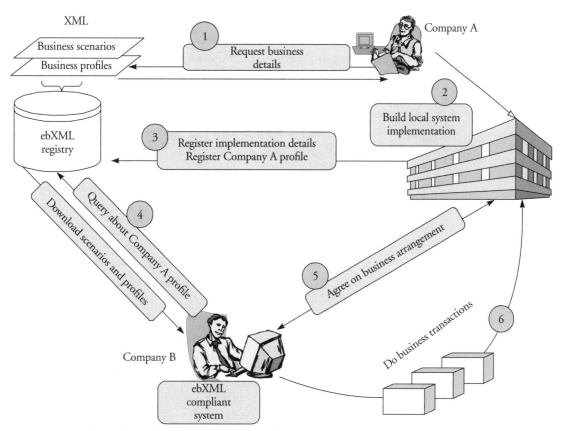

Figure 11.5 An illustration of how two companies might use ebXML to establish a relationship that allowed Company B to use a Web service provided by Company A. (After ebXML diagram.)

Company A, negotiates an agreement, and then begins to use Company A's service as a part of its own business process.

The important message here isn't how ebXML or similar systems like Microsoft's .NET work, but the fact that companies will need tools to build and manage these kinds of virtual processes.

From a programmer's perspective, a *business process language* is a formal way to describe processes, activities, relationships, and rules for the control of the flow of information and materials in code. To make such languages easier for business people to understand, they would need a graphical way of representing the workflow or business process. A workflow diagram for such a language would look like the kinds of diagrams we have used in this book, although they would probably require more precise details, at certain points, than we normally require, since the goal would be to automatically convert the diagrams into software code.

Obviously, existing workflow systems rely on business process languages. In the case of the workflow tools, however, most of the languages used by the workflow engines are proprietary to a specific vendor and are only designed to support the specific functions of the individual workflow product. What vendors and standards groups are now exploring is the creation of public business process languages that can be used by any software developer. In effect, these languages would be more like a computer language such as COBOL than the proprietary languages used in first- and second-generation workflow tools.

A generic business process language would require a workflow engine to execute. The specifications for the workflow engine, however, would be generic so that any company or tool vendor could easily incorporate the workflow engine into their computing environment. Indeed, the next generation of workflow engines will probably be called *business process servers* and will rely on XML as the mechanism for passing data via the Internet. Such a system could provide overall control for all automated aspects of a business process. It could specify activities to be carried out by employees, but would need to communicate with employees via computer screens and wait for their inputs before proceeding.

Different groups are in the early stages of formulating XML-based business process languages for general use. Many conventional workflow vendors are supporting this work, but a wide variety of other software vendors that are also interested in e-business and collaborative applications are also supporting these efforts.

Public and Private Processes

In conventional workflow systems, the workflow engine manages the activities in a process without really knowing what happens within an activity. The workflow system focuses on inputs and outputs and on moving information between one activity and another. Increasingly, however, as companies build e-business and Web service systems, they are creating complex systems that integrate the processes at two or more companies. In some cases two companies create common processes, usually called *public processes,* and each interface with the common processes. In more complex cases, however, both companies need to understand the inner workings of each other's private processes in order to really integrate their processes in a flexible manner.

Figure 11.6 illustrates this distinction. Two companies, let's say A and B again, want to buy products from each other. In this case, Company A doesn't really need to know how Company B's processes work. Company A simply wants to check a catalog, get a quotation, make a decision, order, and then pay for the product. Thus, Company A is happy to use the public processes. If Company A wanted to

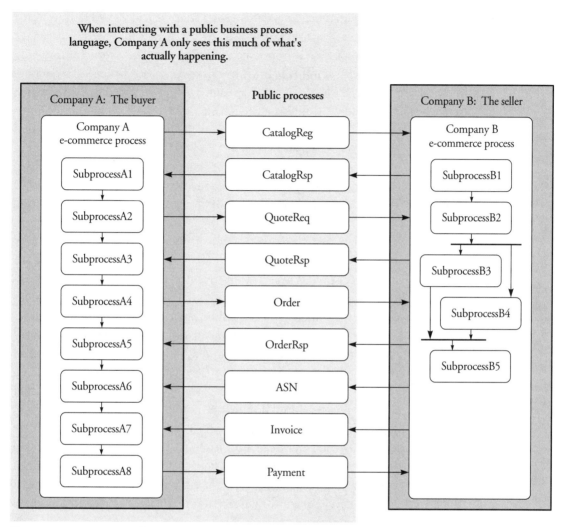

When interacting with a public business process
language, Company A only sees this much of what's
actually happening.

Company A: The buyer	Public processes	Company B: The seller
Company A e-commerce process		Company B e-commerce process
SubprocessA1	CatalogReg	SubprocessB1
SubprocessA2	CatalogRsp	SubprocessB2
SubprocessA3	QuoteReq	SubprocessB3
SubprocessA4	QuoteRsp	SubprocessB4
SubprocessA5	Order	SubprocessB5
SubprocessA6	OrderRsp	
SubprocessA7	ASN	
SubprocessA8	Invoice	
	Payment	

Figure 11.6 An overview of two companies interacting using BPSS public processes.

know how Company B handled the information it got from the public processes,
or if Company A wanted to link its processes directly to Company B's processes,
then it would need to use a language that supported the description of private
processes.

ebXML's BPSS Language

The ebXML initiative is an open, public effort that operates under the joint sponsorship of OASIS and the United Nations CEFACT standards organization.

CEFACT is the international standards group that created the EDI (Electronic Data Interface) standard that is widely used by companies that need to exchange data with other companies. Unfortunately, EDI systems are expensive to set up and even more expensive to maintain. They have been used to link large companies, but are too expensive for small companies. The Internet and XML provide technologies that should make data interchange much more common and inexpensive. OASIS and UN/CEFACT established the ebXML (Electronic Business XML) consortium to develop an architecture and standards for future business-to-business communication. The ebXML consortium is working on a wide variety of standards, including both the generic architecture we pictured in Figure 11.5, and a Business Process Specification Schema (BPSS) language, illustrated in Figure 11.6.

In effect, BPSS manages the flow of documents between the two companies by defining messages that each can exchange to accomplish a given set of goals. We speak of public processes, but in fact we are really just speaking of message standards that both companies agree to use. In effect, BPSS manages the flow of documents between the two companies using public processes. The common processes have been defined by ebXML, and each company can easily obtain descriptions of the common processes in order to determine what messages they will need to send to the common processes and what messages they will obtain from the processes. (We refer to them as "messages," but, in fact, they may be complex data files that are passed and then translated into documents or graphics, as appropriate.)

Using ebXML's public process language, which so far is focused almost entirely on e-commerce, two companies can do business without revealing or learning about the business processes of the other company. The BPSS team has defined business processes in terms of UML models (which we'll consider when we look at the use of software development for automation in Chapter 13) and a high-level model of an e-commerce exchange. They describe business processes with worksheets and use standard templates to describe how companies might communicate. Like all of the business process initiatives, however, BPSS may develop rapidly as companies build applications with it and then decide that it's valuable and request extensions.

The ebXML has a systematic approach to capturing the information used in electronic commerce-based business processes, which they refer to as the UN/CEFACT Modeling Methodology (UMM). Using this approach they are creating a catalog of common e-commerce processes. The catalog's categorization scheme is based on the idea of an enterprise value chain, as described by Michael Porter. The basic value chain business processes include Financing, Marketing and Sales,

Procurement, Transportation, Human Resources, Manufacturing, and Customer Service. (Recall that we reviewed Porter's value chain in Chapter 2 and pictured it in Figure 2.4.)

The Need for Information about Private Processes

While a public process language like BPSS works well in certain circumstances, imagine that another company was managing the sale of your products and you wanted to be able to change the product specifications and the costs of items on the fly. In effect, you would want access to the distributor's catalog application so that you could make changes whenever you needed to do so. More to the point, you would want to know exactly how changes are posted to the distributor's Web site or printed and sent to stores in order to understand when the prices would go into effect. Other, more complex operations involve the design of aircraft when those involved in the overall design and those involved in the manufacture of parts and subassemblies must work together, simultaneously, to design the entire aircraft. If all of the designers are to work together, they each need to be able to understand the design processes their partners are working through to understand the implications of a specific change.

Or imagine that your company has created a supply chain application that links your company's processes with those of several suppliers and their suppliers. One major goal of this exercise was to increase the efficiency of the combined supply chain. In this case the problem faced by those analyzing the entire supply chain is similar to managers trying to improve an internal process. A team will need to look at all of the processes and subprocesses in the supply chain to see where there are problems or disconnects and identify where changes will be necessary.

In these cases you will need a business process language that will allow you to describe the internal workings of some of your applications to your business partner, or one that would let you learn about the inner workings of some of your partner's business processes. The more ambitious generic business process languages are being designed to allow a controlled sharing of information about the private processes of companies that are working together. Some authors refer to private XML business process languages as *executable* business process languages to stress that you are actually making changes in another company's processes and databases when you execute programs written in these languages.

At the moment, there are two different, high-level private business process languages being developed to allow access to private processes. One is being developed by IBM, BEA, and Microsoft. Previously, IBM had created a language called

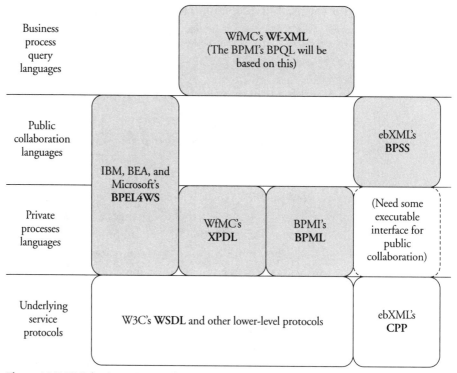

Figure 11.7 XML business process languages.

WSFL, and Microsoft had created a language called XLANG. Just as this book was going to press, however, they announced their intention to merge their two different approaches into a common language. They called this new language the Business Process Execution Language for Web Services (BPEL4WS). In spite of calling it an execution language, BPEL4WS is, in fact, designed to support either public specifications or private process descriptions. In addition, there is another private language being developed by a consortium of vendors grouped together in the Business Process Management Initiative organization, and a third being developed by the Workflow Management Coalition (WfMC), an association of companies interested in workflow issues.

Figure 11.7 provides an overview of some of the public and private business process languages currently being developed.

It's too early to say exactly how the IBM-BEA-Microsoft BPEL4WS will function. Instead, here are short descriptions of the two languages that IBM and Microsoft developed earlier. BPEL4WS will seek to merge the best features of both.

IBM's Web Services Flow Language (WSFL)

IBM originally developed a language called WSDL as a way to pass very technical information about ports or end points and messages between two companies that were using UDDI to establish online communications. WSDL is used in UDDI and in the ebXML communication process we pictured in Figure 11.7. WSDL is now an international W3C standard and underlies XLANG, WSFL, WPDL, and BPMI.

WSFL (Web Services Flow Language) extended WSDL by providing specific information about business processes, business rules, and the flow of information between specific activities within processes. WSFL was designed to support the documentation of either public processes or private processes.

WSFL was also tailored to provide an Internet interface for IBM's popular workflow product, MQSeries Workflow. In effect, each element that could be represented in an MQSeries Workflow diagram could also be represented in the WSFL language.

Microsoft's BizTalk Orchestration and XLANG

Microsoft has sponsored an initiative, BizTalk, to encourage companies to specify business software components that can be used in Web services applications. Microsoft's .NET initiative is, in effect, an XML implementation environment for BizTalk components. Microsoft's Visual Studio.NET includes a business process workflow design tool called Orchestration Designer. In effect, you create a business process workflow diagram on one side of a Visio-like environment and then specify the ports that link specific activities to COM components on the right side of the diagram (see Figure 11.8). When you are done, you compile the Orchestration diagram into XLANG—an XML schema language that captures the information from Orchestration Designer.

To date Microsoft hasn't done much to define the actual workflow notation. This isn't a tool designed for large-scale process analysis or design projects. Instead, it's designed to help software developers link and manage applications with XML messages. Like IBM's WSFL, XLANG is closely linked to WSDL.

As we will discuss briefly in the next chapter, Microsoft has announced a major initiative to develop ERP applications for midsize businesses. ERP systems, as we will see, rely on a special kind of workflow system. Assuming Microsoft does, in fact, proceed to develop ERP applications, it will undoubtedly rely on the more robust BPEL4WS standard it has just announced with IBM and BEA.

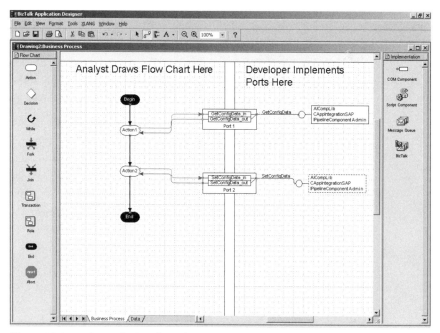

Figure 11.8 A Microsoft BizTalk Orchestration Designer screen with an XLANG diagram.

The BPMI Consortium

The Business Process Management Initiative is an open consortium that was established in 2000 and has grown to include over 100 vendors. It includes most of the business process modeling vendors and some of the major workflow vendors as well. In 2002, it enjoyed a lot of attention, but it will probably be eclipsed in the future as IBM, BEA, and Microsoft roll out their BPEL4WS and vendors switch to support it.

The first standards development undertaken by BPMI was a business process description language (the Business Process Management Language) that relies on XML to pass messages between activities. If you use a tool that supports BPML and define your business process models in the BPML language, then you could automatically transmit XML descriptions of those processes to someone else. The organization released the BPML specification in August 2002.

The BPMI is also working on a generic business process modeling notation (BPMN) that will support the language and allow business managers to create process diagrams that can be easily converted into BPML code.

The Workflow Management Coalition's XPDL

As noted earlier, the WfMC is also developing an XML language specifically designed to pass workflow descriptions between existing workflow tools called the XML Process Definition Language. It's easy to imagine, however, that XPDL could be extended to support generic process descriptions. XPDL can rely on WDSL or on the WfMC XML net protocol, wf-XML.

The Future of Workflow and Business Process Workflow Languages

Workflow tools and the systems they build have found a secure place in every large corporation. Workflow systems are designed using workflow or process diagrams that are very similar to those described in earlier chapters of this book. Accordingly, most workflow diagrams are easy for managers to understand, and many business process redesign teams create processes that are easily implemented, in whole or part by one of the popular workflow tools.

In one form or another, workflow management systems are used to automate production systems and support managers in collaborative processes. The recent efforts to extend workflow tools with XML will extend their value and make them useful for distributed Internet applications. XPDL will be widely used by companies to coordinate the work of existing workflow management systems.

At the same time, new, complex distributed applications, especially those designed to support supply chains and Web service–based processes, will require new techniques. The effort to move from proprietary workflow tools to generic business processing languages may prove very popular in the near future. At the moment, the people working on the business process languages are too technical in their orientation and have not generated the high-level generalities that will be needed to extend these efforts into the realm of business managers. Although they provide for manual activities, the current languages don't handle manual activities very well and will probably be used primarily for completely automated processes. As these languages mature and develop interfaces that business managers can use, they may prove as popular as workflow tools. Or they may simply become specialized languages used by IT developers who are asked to implement process designs developed by business managers.

Every business manager working on a business process redesign effort should be familiar with the basic idea of a workflow system, since these systems offer a simple and powerful approach to improving a wide variety of business processes.

12

ERP-Driven Redesign

I **N THE 1990S**, many companies installed off-the-shelf applications from a variety of companies, including SAP, Peoplesoft, Baan, J.D. Edwards, and Oracle. Initially, these vendors stressed that they sold applications that performed certain common tasks that companies faced, like those in accounting, inventory, and human resources. Later, in response to the widespread interest in business process improvement, these same companies began to reposition themselves. They developed templates or blueprints that showed how groups of their modules could be linked together to create business processes. In line with this transition, people began to refer to these groups of applications as Enterprise Resource Planning (ERP) applications, and recently some have added Customer Relationship Management (CRM) applications. In essence, the vendors introduced workflow-like applications that allowed companies to specify or modify the flow of control from one module to another.

One leading advocate of this approach is Thomas Davenport, one of the consultants who had kicked off the Business Process Reengineering movement in the early 1990s. In 2000, Davenport wrote *Mission Critical: Realizing the Promise of Enterprise Systems*. He argued that a packaged application approach allowed companies to integrate and improve their software systems. He was careful to qualify his argument and say that the use of software only worked within a broader business process architecture, but when implemented in such a context, Davenport believes that packaged applications can help a company to rapidly integrate diverse processes.

Processes and Packages

Vendors like SAP, Peoplesoft, and Oracle often refer to their applications as "best processes." They argue that they developed their modules after studying what worked best at several companies and that the modules represent very efficient ways of handling the processes and activities they support. In fact, of course, these modules represent "average processes." In many cases they are an advance on the applications that companies had before, but once a company decides to use SAP, Peoplesoft, Baan, J.D. Edwards, or Oracle modules in their human resources department, then their HR processes will be the same as those of their competitors who are also using modules from these vendors.

Compared to the business process improvement approach we advocated in Chapter 6, the use of ERP applications occurs in reverse order. In effect, you begin with a solution—a new inventory application from SAP—and proceed to modify your existing inventory process to accommodate the inputs and outputs of the new inventory application. It is still possible to begin by analyzing the existing process, substituting the new SAP module or set of modules during the design phase, and then making the adjustments necessary to use the modules effectively. But the heart of this kind of BPI effort is to accommodate the way your company works to the new application and not the other way around.

We think ERP applications represent a reasonable approach to improving a wide variety of business processes. If the processes are easy to automate and add little value to your overall business, then there's no reason why you shouldn't simply rely on efficient, average solutions, and focus your energies instead on core processes that do add significant value. Let's face it, managing payroll deductions or handling an office inventory database are enabling processes that need to be done, but don't add anything to the bottom line.

The problem comes when companies try to use ERP applications for tasks that are not routine and decide to tailor the ERP applications to better fit with the way your company does business. The various ERP applications are, essentially, database applications. The applications manage database operations. Each of the ERP vendors has its own favorite databases, and it's very hard to modify the internal workings of ERP applications once they are installed. If your company acquires a payroll application and then decides to tailor it, you will find that the value of buying an off-the-shelf application diminishes rapidly. Moreover, the maintenance costs will rise in the future. When new versions of the ERP application are released, they won't work at your organization until they are modified to match the previous modifications you made. If you find yourself considering ERP applications, and simultaneously planning to make lots of modifications in the ERP applications you buy, you are probably making a mistake. If the process is really a routine process and adds little value, it's probably better to change your organization and use the application in its standard version. If you really can't live with the vanilla version of the ERP application, then you ought to ask yourself if you really want to buy an ERP application in the first place.

There are vendors that sell applications or that develop applications that offer more flexibility than the standard ERP applications and in the long run don't cost as much if you want a highly tailored application or know you will want to change the application frequently. On the other hand, of course, these applications will probably not integrate with other modules as well as the standard ERP modules do, and that will add to the cost of the more specialized applications.

The ERP vendors have recently experienced problems as companies have begun to rely more on the Internet. Most ERP applications were designed to be self-contained systems, tightly linked with and relying on a proprietary database management system. The ERP systems were not prepared to support distributed data management. Most aren't especially good at working with other ERP applications, and they were totally unprepared when companies began to want to integrate applications into Web portals or into supply chains that communicated over the Internet. In the past few years most of the ERP vendors have redesigned their systems and have begun to release new ERP applications designed to communicate via the Internet. In most cases, however, this adds another layer of complexity to the problems of integrating applications into e-business systems.

A Closer Look at SAP

Let's take a closer look at SAP, the dominant ERP vendor. SAP provides overviews, which it calls *business maps,* of processes that it offers in a number of industry-specific areas. Specifically, it offers business maps, or what we would call *process architectures,* in each of these areas:

Discrete industries

▶ Aerospace and defense
▶ Automotive

▶ Engineering and construction
▶ High tech

Process industries

▶ Chemicals   ▶ Oil and gas
▶ Mill products   ▶ Pharmaceuticals
▶ Mining

Financial services

▶ Banking   ▶ Insurance

Consumer industries

▶ Consumer products   ▶ Retail

Service industries

▶ Media   ▶ Telecommunications
▶ Service providers   ▶ Utilities

Public service

▶ Healthcare   ▶ Public sector
▶ Higher education and research

Figure 12.1 illustrates one of SAP's business maps. In this case we have illustrated SAP's telecommunications business architecture. On the left side SAP lists the functional areas or, in some cases, large-scale business processes. On the right, in each row, are the processes included in the general category listed on the left.

Thus, one functional area is Service Assurance, and there are four SAP processes under that function heading: Service Agreements, Customer Trouble Reporting, Customer Trouble Management, and Trouble Resolution. Figure 12.2 shows the specific SAP components or application modules that are used to implement (automate) each process.

Notice that although the various components have different names, they often have the same component number. This suggests that the components are, in fact, subcomponents or modules of larger SAP applications, or that they rely on the same database for stored information. As we suggested earlier, SAP has reengineered its software applications to move them from a client-server architecture to a component architecture, and the original design often shows through.

We illustrated SAP's telecommunications business architecture so you can compare it with the eTOM business framework developed by the TeleManagement Forum, which is pictured in Chapter 3 as Figure 3.5. The eTOM architecture was developed by a task force of telecommunications managers and uses terms that

SAP Telecommunications Business Architecture				
Enterprise Management	Strategic Enterprise Management	Business Analytics	Business Intelligence and Decision Support	Accounting	Workforce Planning and Alignment
Customer Relationship Management	Marketing and Campaign Management	Sales Management	Dealer Management	Customer and Retention Management	Customer Care
Sales and Order Management—Standard Products	Product Selling	Contract Management	Order Management		Service Activation
Sales and Order Management—Customer Solutions	Sales Cycle Management	Site Survey and Solution Design	Contract Management	Project Management	Order Management and Fulfillment	Provisioning
Service Assurance	Service Agreements	Customer Trouble Reporting	Customer Trouble Management		Trouble Resolution
Customer Financials Management	Credit Management	Prebilling	Convergent Invoicing	eBPP	Receivables and Collections Management	Dispute Management
Supply Chain Management	Supply Network Design	Demand and Supply Planning	eProcurement	Production Planning and Execution	Supply Chain Coordination	Warehouse Management
Network Lifecycle Management	Demand Planning	Requirements Planning	Investment Management	Network Design and Build	Operation and Maintenance
Value-Added Services	Content and Intellectual Properties Management	Advertising Management	Mobile Business and Wireless ASP		eLearning
Business Support	Human Resources Operations Sourcing and Deployment	Travel Management	Financial Supply Chain Management	Treasury/Corporate Finance Management	Real Estate

Figure 12.1 SAP telecommunications business architecture.

are probably more familiar to those in the telecommunications industry. The SAP architecture was also developed by a telecom industry group organized by SAP. The resulting framework uses more generic process names since it relies on existing SAP modules whenever possible. In addition, keep in mind that the eTOM architecture was designed to describe a set of processes that might or might not be automated at any given telecom company. The SAP architecture, on the other hand, only lists software components that SAP sells or plans to sell, or that a SAP-associated vendor sells. Each software component may be entirely automated, or it may provide user interfaces, so that employees can use interface screens to monitor or control the processing undertaken by the component.

Figure 12.3 illustrates a different SAP business architecture—in this case, the architecture for insurance. Notice how similar the lists of functional areas or large-scale processes are. Also notice that functional areas near the top and bottom of the

SAP Telecommunications Business Architecture				
Service Assurance	Service Agreements	Customer Trouble Reporting	Customer Trouble Management	Trouble Resolution
SAP Components Available	- Service Contracts (C17) - Service Level Agreements (C17) - Service Event Management (C17)	- Capture of Customer Trouble Ticket (C17) - Diagnostic Engine to Aid Resolution (C6, C17) - Call Management with Front-end Close Support (C17) - Site Visit Scheduling (C17, C5) - Internet Trouble Self-Service (C17)	- Work Request Management (C17, C5) - Workflow-Based Execution and Exception Management (C5, C17) - Correlation of Customer Troubles to Network Troubles (Future) - Trouble Ticket Reporting	- Sophisticated Diagnosis Engine (C17) - Field/Mobile Service (C17) - Work Dispatching/ Scheduling (Future) - Material/Spare Part Management (C6, C8) - Capture of Resolution Data for Future Diagnosis (C17)

Figure 12.2 SAP components used to implement the four processes under Service Assurance.

SAP Insurance Business Architecture						
Enterprise Management	Strategic Enterprise Management		Business Analytics	Business Intelligence and Decision Support		Accounting
Customer Relationship Management	Customer Engagement		Business Transaction	Contract Fulfillment		Customer Service
Sales	Sales Planning	Account and Contract Management	Acquisition and Sales Management	Commission Management		Collections and Disbursements
Claims	Claim Notification		Proactive Claims Management	Claim Handling and Adjustment		Claims Accounting
Policy and Product Management	Market Research		Product Definition and Administration	Policy Management		In-Force Business Administration
Reinsurance	Reinsurance Underwriting	Reinsurance Claim Handling	Reinsurance Accounting		Retrocession	Statistics and Reporting
Asset Management	Asset Allocation		Portfolio Management	Portfolio Accounting		Portfolio Controlling
Business Support	Human Resource Operations Sourcing and Deployment		Procurement		Treasury	Fixed Asset Management

Figure 12.3 SAP business architecture for insurance companies.

diagram describe processes that are very similar to those listed on the telecommunications business architecture in Figure 12.1. Once again, the insurance architecture was developed by industry representatives in conjunction with SAP, and, as before, it relied on standard SAP modules whenever possible.

If a company decides to work with SAP, the SAP representative provides the company with a detailed description of the SAP business architecture and the processes making up each component and asks the company managers to choose which they want to use. Once a company has chosen the modules or processes they want to acquire, they can tailor them by changing names to match the terminology already in use at the company or by changing the actual processes themselves to conform more closely to practices at the specific company. It's especially difficult to link SAP components to other components that you use at your company, or to mix modules from more than one ERP vendor.

Tailoring also takes quite a bit of time. More importantly, once an SAP process is tailored, it's harder for the company to use new SAP updates. Before the company can install the updates, the company must first tailor the updates to match the existing SAP modules you have already tailored. The cost of tailoring SAP applications rapidly eats into the cost savings that one hopes to get when one buys off-the-shelf software, and raises maintenance costs. A company gets the best buy when it acquires SAP modules and uses them without tailoring, or creates add-on modules that don't change the basic SAP modules.

SAP is in the business of selling processes or components that are very similar. They have created some unique modules for each industry, but, overall, they still rely on the initial modules they introduced in the 1980s, which include core accounting, inventory, and human resource functions. There's nothing wrong with using standard modules, but any business manager should realize that many competitors are also using SAP modules. Thus, using a SAP process doesn't give a company a competitive edge, but simply provides the company with a clean, modern implementation of a software process.

So far we've looked at the business architecture view of SAP processes. Once you have settled on a specific component, you can obtain a more specific process diagram. SAP uses diagrams from the ARIS product of IDS Scheer. Both SAP and IDS Scheer are headquartered in Germany. (The founder of IDS Scheer, August-Wilhelm Scheer, is a software engineering theorist who has written several books on business process modeling and software development. He is currently on the advisory board of SAP.) The IDS Scheer annual conference, ProcessWorld 200x, is a major event in Europe each year and provides a good overview of the ERP-driven approach to business process improvement. Other process modeling vendors, like Popkin, MEGA, and CASEwise, also have relationships with SAP.

Figure 12.4 provides a process diagram of a process used by a car retailer. The diagram begins at the top of the page and flows down.

The rectangles with rounded corners represent activities. The six-sided boxes represent events or decision outcomes that occur during the process. The small circles represent decision points or describe the logic of a flow. Thus, the circle with ^ represents AND. If two events are joined by an AND, then both must occur before the next process can occur. (The circle with XOR inside represents *exclusive OR*, which means that one or the other must occur, but not both.). The person or department responsible for the processes appears at the right in an oval. On the left, in thin rectangles, are documents that are accessed, modified, or stored in a database.

SAP is widely used, and thus there are lots of programmers who understand and use ARIS process diagrams like the one shown in Figure 12.4. In addition, ARIS supports a number of other diagrams, including one that has swimlanes and is more like the diagrams we have been using in this book. The diagram in Figure 12.4, however, is the standard ARIS process diagram.

Figure 12.5 presents the same information that is shown in Figure 12.4 using the process diagram notation we have used in this book.

As you can see in Figure 12.5, there is a clearer distinction between events that a customer performs, documents that are inside the sales system, and events that define the flow of information in the process. By simply scanning along a swimlane one can quickly see all the places the retail dealer interacts with the customer. Similarly, using other swimlanes, one is provided with a better idea of who is responsible for which activities. We have represented all of the activity boxes with dashed lines since they are all mixed activities. In all cases, an employee must enter information into the sales database from a personal computer.

We have omitted most of the logic flow notation. In some cases we show two arrows arriving at a box. Our notation does not tell us if both inputs are required, if either one is sufficient to start the process, or if both are required before the process starts. These are issues that software developers must resolve before they can develop software, but they are issues that managers often ignore when they are defining business processes.

The process notation used in the SAP reference model by ARIS is designed to tell its users more about the control flow between processes. On the other hand, it doesn't emphasize the relationship between process and the customer, or make it as clear who is responsible for what activities. As a strong generalization, the diagrams

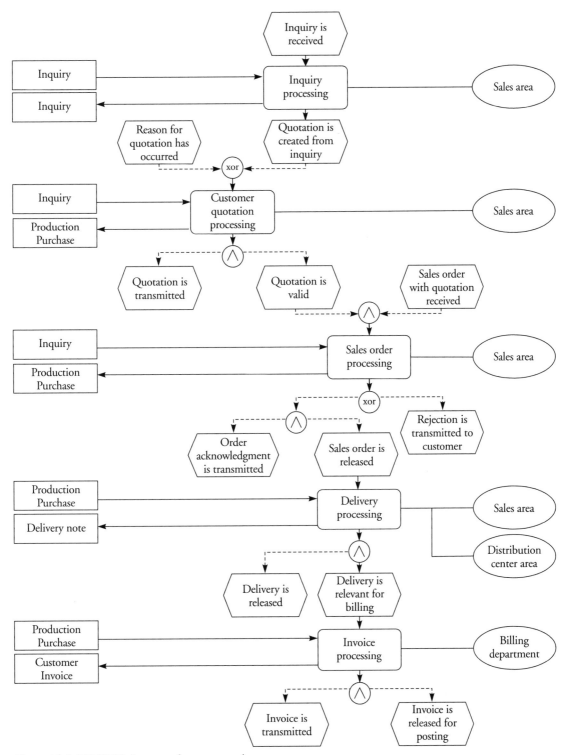

Figure 12.4 SAP/ARIS diagram of a new car sales process.

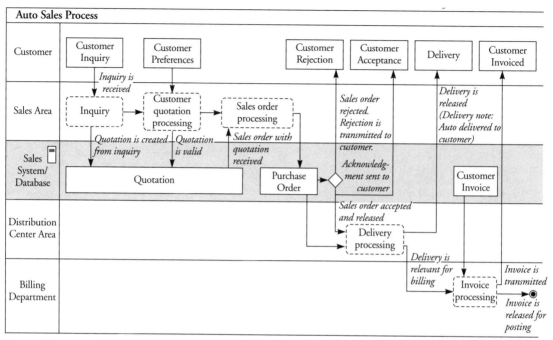

Figure 12.5 A retail car sales process in our notation.

we use are better for managers who want to analyze and design business processes. The diagrams used with the ARIS methodology are better suited for software developers who must implement a system that relies heavily on the management of documents that reside in SAP systems.

Figure 12.6 illustrates another type of SAP diagram. In this case, an e-business process that relies on the Internet to pass information between three parties—customers, an insurance company, and companies that repair cars—is illustrated. The processes or activities are shown in six-sided boxes. The flow is indicated by the fact that some boxes abut others.

SAP calls the diagrams shown in Figure 12.6 C-business maps—which stands for collaborative business maps. In essence, this is a special kind of ARIS diagram to illustrate simple e-business interactions.

What we like best about Figure 12.6 are the business benefits and value potentials that SAP includes on the right and left sides of the basic diagram. In essence, SAP lists reasons why specific activities will save or make companies money. When they have specific data, they indicate it as a value potential, and usually add footnotes to indicate the source of the data. Thus, in the example in Figure 12.6, we see that SAP predicts that approving auto repairs online will result in cost savings,

SAP Insurance C-Business Map: Loss Notification and Automated Claims Handling

This C-Business Map is designed for the insurance industry. It shows how three parties—a customer, an insurance company and a service provider—use the Internet to exchange information about an insurance claim. The map shows h the benefits of collaboration. Efficient and pro-active claims management reduces claim expenses and enhances customer service. These benefits save time and money.

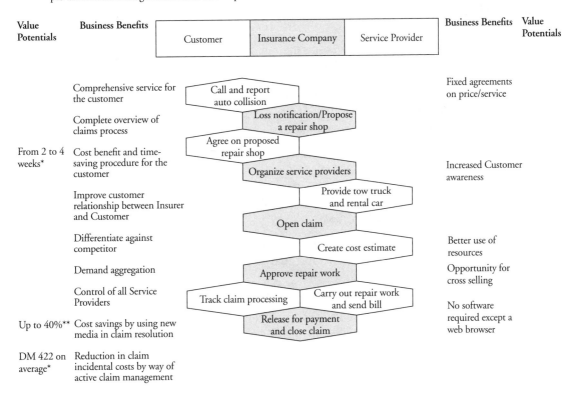

Source: *German insurance company: **Diebold Deutschland GmbH

Figure 12.6 SAP C-Business map of an Internet-based auto claims process.

and suggest that Diebold Deutschland found that it saved them 40% of the cost of the activity.

All of the business architectures and C-business maps are available on SAP's Web site: *www.sap.com.* SAP offers collaborative business maps in CRM, Supply Chain Management, Product Lifecycle Management, E-Procurement, Market-places, Financials, and Human Resources. The kind of benefits SAP lists are most reliable when a company implements a standard process. There isn't much data available on the more industry-specific processes, which only emphasizes that the ERP-driven approach is usually best employed when a company wants to automate processes where the logic is relatively simple and where the processes don't add much strategic value.

Implementing an ERP-Driven Design

In a review of ERP implementation efforts, the Gartner Group argued that the most important thing is the training of end users. This follows directly from the nature of the business process redesign efforts that are driven by ERP applications.

In essence, you begin with an architecture and choose components to use. Then you turn to specific process sequences and choose specific activities to implement. As a result, you have selected a whole set of processes and activities that you intend to install at your company with a minimum of changes. Some activities will be fully automated, but most of the activities you select will require that employees learn to use interface screens on PCs to enter or retrieve information from the SAP databases that form the core of any SAP system. That may sound simple but, in fact, depending on what your employees are doing now, you will need to teach employees an entirely new process.

Consider an auto dealer that used a less sophisticated system. The salespeople talked with customers and eventually filled out a form, which they then used when they phoned to see if a car with the desired characteristics was available. At some point, assuming the car was available, the salesperson would negotiate a price and then take a brief break to get the manager's approval of the deal being struck. The order in which the salesperson performed those tasks, and the verbal exchange with the customer, while all the details were being attended to, was probably quite specific to individual salespeople. Once the SAP system is installed, our salesperson is going to have to learn to carry on his conversation while entering information into a computer. The SAP system assumes that the manager approves online, and that the supplier determines the availability of the car online, and so forth. It's probably going to take quite a bit of training before the salesperson feels comfortable with the new process. And the auto example is relatively simple, since it largely follows the sales process already used in auto retail showrooms. Other processes that rely on the use of databases can rearrange the steps in an established process in a much more confusing manner.

SAP is not the only ERP vendor that offers architecture and business process diagrams. Oracle, Peoplesoft, and J.D. Edwards all have something similar.

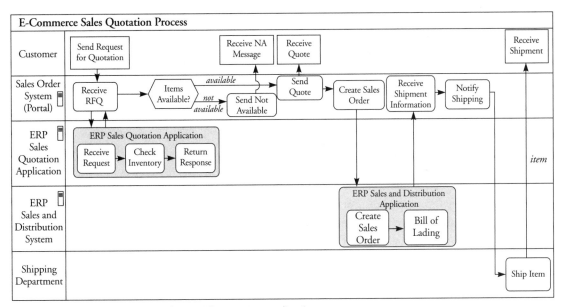

Figure 12.7 A process that interfaces with two ERP applications.

Most companies begin with an analysis of their IS process. Then they "overlay" the ERP modules they intend to install, eliminating the subprocesses and activities that the new ERP applications will replace. What one obtains is a new diagram with lots of disconnects. The interfaces to the ERP applications are PC interface screens (links to database documents). The trick is to create a new SHOULD diagram that ties each of the existing activities that remain to ERP modules that have been inserted. Once you have done that, you need to review which employees will be doing what tasks and revise job descriptions accordingly. And then you must provide the training necessary to assure that people can do their new jobs.

One technical problem involves the "translation" of diagrams. We recommend the use of the type of process diagrams we have introduced in this book. These diagrams make it easier for managers to see how processes work and who is responsible for what activities. Thus, to "overlay" a set of SAP activities, you need to do a translation of the SAP diagram, along the lines illustrated in Figure 12.5. This probably isn't something the redesign team should attempt, but something that the facilitator or someone in the IT department should be able to do for the team.

Figure 12.7 illustrates a sales order system that relies on two different ERP modules. The ERP Sales Quotation application is essentially an application that checks an inventory database to determine if ordered items are in stock. The ERP Sales and Distribution application is an application that creates a printed bill of lading. The Sales Order System is an automated system that could be on a company portal, or it could simply be an application that is accessible online to retailers who sell your company's products.

In this example, we've shown some of the activities that occur inside each ERP application. In most cases we would simply have a single process box to indicate each ERP application. The people working on the process really don't need to know exactly what goes on inside the ERP applications. What they need to know is what inputs they need to make, what outputs are made, and who has to process the inputs and outputs. In this example, since the customer is interacting with an automated system, the inputs to the ERP applications are made by the Sales Order System, which is itself a software system. If this system replaces a process that involved employees, then appropriate changes would be required. The output of this process is a request to shipping (a bill of lading) to send an item to a customer. Shipping needs to know to accept such an order and how to handle it. Assuming employees are working in Shipping, we would probably want to do another process diagram to define just what happens in the Ship Item subprocess.

The main point here, however, is that you can create swimlanes for ERP applications and indicate how the ERP applications interface with existing process flows. Preparing for a transition to the use of ERP applications means understanding exactly how the ERP applications will interact with your existing processes, and then training your people to handle the ERP inputs and outputs when the system is implemented.

Before we discussed ERP-driven redesign, we considered workflow. In essence, ERP systems are also workflow systems. Instead of designing a unique workflow system with a workflow tool, one simply chooses ERP components or processes to assemble into a system. Underneath, however, the ERP vendor provides a workflow engine that passes control from one component or process to the next. An IT manager can use the ERP management system to exclude specific documents from a particular process or to quickly modify the order in which processes are used. By combining precoded processes with workflow, companies gain considerable control over basic processes.

Microsoft recently announced that it would be entering the ERP market. Microsoft argued that existing ERP vendors had not provided for small and midsize businesses, and it hopes that it can use XML and the Internet to create a new generation of ERP applications.

Case Study: Nestlé USA Installs SAP

A good example of a company that used ERP packages to reorganize their business processes is provided by the U.S. subsidiary of Nestlé SA, a Swiss food conglomerate. Nestlé USA was created in the late 1980s and early 1990s via acquisitions. In 2002 it included seven divisions which collectively sold such popular brands as Alpo, Baby Ruth, Carnation Instant Breakfast, Coffee-Mate, Nescafe, Nestlé Toll House, PowerBar, Stouffer's Lean Cuisine, SweeTarts, and Taster's Choice. The company employs some 16,000 employees and earns about $8 billion in revenues.

In the mid-1990s the various companies that make up Nestlé SA were all operating as independent units. In 1997 a team studying the various company systems concluded that, collectively, the companies were paying 29 different prices for vanilla—which they all purchased from the same vendor. The study wasn't easy, since each company had a different number or name for vanilla, and purchased it via completely different processes. Just isolating vanilla and then determining a common unit price required a considerable effort.

In 1997, Nestlé USA decided that it would standardize all of the major software systems in all of its divisions. A key stakeholder team was set up to the manage the entire process. By March 1998, the team had its plan. It decided it would standardize on five SAP modules—purchasing, financials, sales and distribution, accounts payable, and accounts receivable. In addition, the stakeholder team decided to implement Manugistics' supply chain module. The team considered SAP's supply chaining module, Advance Planner and Optimizer (APO), but it was brand-new in 1997, and they decided to go with the better-known Manugistics module that was specifically designed to work with SAP modules.

Before even beginning to implement SAP modules, people from the divisions were gathered and spent 18 months examining data names and agreeing on a common set of names. Vanilla, for example, would henceforth be code 1234 in every division.

Somewhere along the line, the project to install SAP modules also became a Y2K program. By moving to standard software that was guaranteed to be free of bugs associated with date problems that might occur when applications started dealing with dates subsequent to December 31, 1999, the companies would avoid any Y2K problems. Unfortunately, this placed a deadline on the entire implementation effort—it had to be done before January 1, 2000.

As the various SAP applications began to roll out to the divisions, the stakeholder team managing the entire effort began to get lots of unpleasant feedback. Jeri Dunn, the VP and CIO of Nestlé USA, explained that, in hindsight, they had completely underestimated the problems involved in changing division cultures or modifying established business processes. By the beginning of 1999, the rollout was in serious trouble. The workers didn't understand the new SAP modules, and they didn't understand how the outputs they were now getting would help them do their jobs or manage the processes they were responsible for.

It was at a major meeting in early 1999 that Dunn was given responsibility for the project. Among the other conclusions reached by this executive committee meeting was that the Y2K deadline would be ignored. Henceforth, they would figure out the implementation requirements for each SAP module and then let that specification guide their schedule. They decided that it was relatively easy to install SAP modules, but that it was very hard to change business processes and to win the acceptance of the people responsible for assuring those processes operated correctly. They also decided that much more care needed to be taken to determine just how the SAP modules would interact with the processes and applications that would remain in place.

At the same time that Dunn took over, a new director of process change was hired, and a process manager (VP) for the supply chain was promoted to help Dunn on the remainder of the project. In most cases, the team now began to focus on modeling processes and defining process requirements and then creating a plan to install the SAP modules. Several installations were delayed for months or years to accommodate groups that were not prepared for the process changes required. As we go to press, the Nestlé transition is coming to an end. The company spent approximately $200 million on the transition. Dunn claims that the project has already paid for itself. The new planning processes, for example, make it possible to project Nestlé USA–wide demand more accurately and to save significant inventory and redistribution costs. The VP for Nestlé USA's supply chain, Dick Ramage, estimates that supply chain improvements have accounted for a major portion of the $325 million that Nestlé has already saved as a result of the SAP installation.

Dunn says she's happy with the SAP applications and very happy that all of the companies are now using the same basic processes. Still, in an article on the transition in *CIO Magazine* in May 2002, Dunn claimed that if she had it to do over again, she'd "focus first on changing business processes and achieving universal buy-in, and then and only then on installing the software."

Nestlé USA's use of ERP applications, and their problems, are typical of most large companies that have elected to rely on ERP applications to drive major changes. The company embraces the ERP applications in hopes that they can organize and standardize their software applications and databases across departments and divisions. Most large companies have started on this path and found that it takes much longer and is more painful than they had hoped. Few have completed their ERP transitions. The problem lies in the fact that the ERP applications aren't a solution. They are a tool to use in changing business processes. This isn't something that IT can do by itself. The transition must be conceptualized as a business process transition and guided by business managers. The ERP applications must be installed as part of the overall business process redesign effort, not as an independent activity. Used in an appropriate manner, ERP applications offer a powerful tool to aid in business process redesign.

13

Software Development

I **N THIS CHAPTER** we will consider some of the issues associated with the development of software for the automation of business processes. We have already considered the development of workflow systems and the use of business process languages that use XML. We have also considered acquiring packaged software from ERP or CRM vendors. Our focus here will be on designing and developing a tailored software application in a programming language like Java or C or with a software development tool that generates Java, C, or similar code. In most cases the developer will create an application by combining software components.

This book is not written for software developers, of course, and we will not discuss the software development process itself, but will instead focus on how business process analysts and software developers work together and on the major software development issues that managers and business process teams ought to understand if they are to work successfully with software architects and developers.

A Little Software History

The first commercial software application was a payroll application created for General Electric in 1954. Computers were used in most organizations in the 1960s. Since then, computers and the software techniques used to program them have evolved very rapidly and continue to evolve. We hardly have time to review the history of computing or the evolution of software development systems in any detail, but we want to stress a few important approaches and turning points.

In the 1970s software development relied on languages that divided applications into programs and associated databases. An analyst would create a software application by analyzing each step in a process and then create a program that would follow the same steps. As needed, data would be stored or retrieved from a database that was created just to support that application. Most of the large applications that ran on mainframes were created using this *procedural approach.* This approach worked very well when companies were creating applications for departments to do things like automating bookkeeping and payroll operations or managing inventories. The methodologies used to analyze problems suitable for this approach looked very similar to the workflow diagrams still used today by workflow tool vendors. Put another way, software developers analyzed problems in a manner very similar to the way business managers did and used techniques like the ones described in this book.

Once a process was analyzed, the specific sequence was often changed to assure that it would execute more efficiently on a computer. Once a process was recompiled to assure that it would execute more efficiently, managers usually could not understand the diagrams that described the code. During the initial phases, however, it was easy for business managers and software analysts to agree on what had to happen.

In the 1980s, however, software development began a dramatic shift. Instead of creating databases that were tailored for specific applications, database developers began to use relational databases. In essence, relational databases can support many different applications. To make this possible, a single data item is only stored once in a relational database. Imagine I have a personal checking system that organizes checking accounts by number, and that I also have a savings account system that organizes savings accounts by number. Then imagine I decide I would like to know how many checking and savings accounts Lee Jones has with my bank. Unfortunately, I can't simply go into a prerelational database and find that information. Prerelational databases are organized to support the steps in a process, and there's no step in either my checking or savings account creation process that determines if other applications know about Lee Jones. With a relational database, on the other hand, Lee Jones is only stored once, no matter how many applications use or associate other data with Lee Jones. My relational database is always up to date because each application that affects data associated with Lee Jones makes changes to the same data. Similarly, I can do a quick search and find all the accounts associated with the name Lee Jones, or with his social security number, or with any other key piece of data I might want to use.

Relational databases were a huge step forward in many ways and made it much easier for companies to link applications and to make data available for a wide variety of purposes that might not even be imagined when the data was entered into the database.

At the same time, personal computers began to be introduced and they soon offered graphical user interfaces—with buttons and icons and pull-down menus. When an application processes a payroll account, it moves through one step at a time. First it checks employee records to determine how many days the employee worked during the pay period; then it multiplies the time by a pay rate to determine a gross pay, and so forth. When a user sits down to use a word processing program, on the other hand, we can't anticipate what the user might do. The user might open a Word file with a document created earlier, or open a new file and begin to create a new document. Different users choose different type faces and sizes. Some insert graphical elements into the text. A graphical user interface requires us to think of a program as a tool or a network of options rather than a step-by-step procedure.

To build graphical applications, especially the distributed applications like those one encounters on the Web, one needs more powerful programming techniques to analyze the problem and to design how the different elements of the program will interact with each other. Indeed, software developers have gradually stopped thinking of applications as procedures or processes and have moved toward thinking of applications as a set of components that communicate with each other to accomplish a task, just as a group of people might send email to each other to determine how a specific project is to be organized. Languages like Java and Visual Basic, and software tools that support object-oriented or component-based software development and message passing, make this new approach to software development possible.

Thus, today software developers think of applications in rather different ways than business managers do. Most managers still think in terms of procedures that have steps and goals. There may be multiple paths to the final goal, but overall, business managers consistently say they prefer workflow diagrams, just like the ones we describe in this book. Similarly, they usually associate data developed during the course of a process with that process. Software developers, on the other hand, increasingly rely on object- or component-based methodologies that conceptualize applications as sets of interacting components and on relational databases that store data from many different applications in a common database.

This need not be a problem if both groups appreciate how the other group thinks. It does, however, create a translation problem. In essence, managers create workflow diagrams that software designers convert into object or component diagrams. Once the conversion has taken place, it's relatively hard for managers to see what software designers propose to do. The solution to this is for the business managers to define the requirements for any process they propose to automate in very precise terms.

Some software developers have promoted the idea that business managers should be taught to think in object- or component-oriented terms and should use software development methodologies. In our experience, this is a disaster. Managers do not naturally think in terms of objects and software components, and there is no reason to suggest they should. They have more important things to do.

One reason workflow tools have proved very popular with many organizations is that the interface on the workflow tool matches the procedural perspective that most managers naturally use. Similarly, packaged application vendors usually treat their applications as black boxes and only discuss them in terms of required inputs and the expected outputs. Of course they don't give business managers many choices in what the application does—the applications, after all, are being purchased "off the shelf."

When a company decides to create an application and relies on internal or external software developers to create a unique application, however, business managers and software architects and developers need to struggle for a common language.

Application Development

The number of software architects, designers, and programmers has increased rapidly over the last five decades. Software has evolved from simple applications that keep track of customers and parts to programs that allow managers to check on to-day's sales by querying the company's cash registers, applications that talk to users, and programs that predict sales over the course of the next 12 months. And, of course, the Internet that links computers together and lets users skim Web sites throughout the world and buy products online is also a software phenomenon.

Throughout the half century that computers and software have been available, they have been used to automate business. To provide a broad overview of the long-term trend in automation, consider what a very simple insurance company with a single business process might have looked like in 1940. There were senior managers, analysts, salespeople, and clerks. The salespeople went door to door and sold insurance policies. The analysts made decisions about underwriting the policies and determined how the company would invest the money to assure they could pay claims. The clerks processed policies and claims and mailed money to meet claims. All of the policies and all of the correspondence about them were kept in filing cabinets. There were a couple of support processes. One was the payroll system that paid all the employees.

In the early days of computing, simple processes like payroll were automated, and some of the file cabinets were replaced with databases. The initial tasks that were automated, like payroll, were numerical processes that were easy to analyze. In the 1960s, most managers thought of computers as large, fast, calculating machines.

Later, company IT groups were formed, and they began to automate more elaborate processes. Gradually, all of the sequential back-office tasks were automated. Whenever possible, forms were scanned and stored in databases.

In the 1980s, the personal computer was introduced, and employees began to use computers on their desks to aid them in performing tasks. Managers used spreadsheets, and clerks used text processing systems to handle correspondence. More information was stored on the various personal computers. During this same period relational databases were introduced, and they made it easy to consolidate lots of departmental databases while simultaneously making it possible for managers to ask for reports of all kinds. Sales managers could query the company sales database to determine just how much each salesperson sold during the past month.

The 1980s also witnessed the development of expert systems, software programs that stored the rules that experts used to analyze problems. Expert systems and their descendants have made it possible to automate a large number of analysis and decision-making tasks. Personal computers pushed computing out of the back office and into the lobby. Increasingly clerks who interacted with customers obtained data from personal computers in order to deal with customer requests.

In the 1990s, salespeople began to carry laptop computers. In the mid-1990s, with the rise of the Internet and the Web, companies began to link all their computers into networks. Employees could check their pension plans by simply going to the personnel department's Employee Portal. Customers also bought computers for their homes and began to use them to check for information about companies and products and then to buy products online. Corporate IT groups continued to work to merge data into ever larger repositories, often called *data warehouses,* to make it possible to obtain answers to more complex questions more quickly. Expert system applications, now usually called *business intelligence* (BI) systems, are used to search for patterns in data warehouses that humans might not detect—such as a particular change in buying patterns that marketing can use to suggest modifications in products.

One of the side effects of the Internet was to force companies to link applications together. A customer might sign on to a Web site and want information about her account. Once she obtained that information, she might want to make a claim against one policy and cash in another. In effect, the customer was bouncing from one application to another, using data stored in different databases. And she expected it to happen quickly, while she waited. Integrating applications—that were never originally designed to talk to one another—so they can speak to each other in this manner has become a major task of corporate IT groups.

Increasingly, everything that can be digitized and stored in a computer database is digitized and stored. Every employee is equipped with a computer so that they can stay in touch, instantly, with every other employee. Managers can use their computers to monitor activities, using data that is recorded and summarized for them nearly as quickly as it's created. An insurance company today might acquire information about new policies from field salespeople who communicate with the company via its Web site and transmit new policy applications. In most cases a computer application checks the policy for completeness and determines its underwriting status. Similarly, claims are often made by customers online and paid by transfers from the company to client bank accounts via electronic transfers.

It's hard to see why the trend toward automation won't continue in the foreseeable future. As quickly as analysts figure out how to automate one job, they move on to the next. Some theorists have begun to speak of companies as organisms that respond to their constantly changing environment, adapting to survive. The neural networks of such organisms are the Internet and the software applications that sort and store information and that make decisions. Employees are reduced in number, but they must be more skilled than ever because those that remain must use computers and manage the organization and deal with customers in real time, changing as fast as the company changes.

In spite of the amazing growth in computing technology, most companies are more reluctant to develop software than they were in the past. Software is more complex, and the risk of failure is large. Most companies have concluded that it's better to buy standard types of applications from packaged software vendors and do internal development only on applications that have great value.

Today, when a business process team sits down to redesign a major process, it's very likely they will identify new ways to automate subprocesses and other ways to link to employees to improve the efficiency of the application. In most cases, it will be a matter of the team telling IT that they need an application to do X, and IT replying that they can provide an off-the-shelf application that does XY. The business process team is then faced with adopting their process to the application on offer, or asking for a tailored application, which will be more expensive and riskier to develop. If the subprocess gives the organization a significant competitive advantage, it may be worth developing a unique application. Otherwise, the process redesign becomes a matter of give and take, as a packaged application is fitted to a process, and vice versa.

The Requirements Interface

Business managers who redesign processes are not expected to understand the intricacies of software development. They must, however, tell the software developers what the software must do to be useful. Software folks speak of this as the *requirements phase* in a software development project. The trick is for the process team to describe what they want in terms that are specific enough to define a good requirements document.

In most cases a process redesign team that has created a detailed process diagram has made a good start. They have defined the steps and the decision points. They have often defined the business rules that must be employed at each decision point. Predictably the business team has not defined the process flow in enough detail for the software designers. Things that business people normally don't worry about worry machines. What if the customer sends in too much money? What if the balance is zero? If the account is closed, do we delete the customer from the customer database? In most cases, if the business team has created a detailed business process diagram, they have provided the general requirements for the software team. It's usually a matter of the business team sitting down with the software team and answering a lot of specific questions about how exceptions will be handled.

Once the software development team has gained a clear understanding of the problem, they will usually develop their own model of the application to be developed. They will often think that they are automating a process, whereas, in fact, they are usually only automating a portion of a more complex process, but that bit of semantics need not concern anyone too much.

Software Analysis and UML

When software developers first began to transition to object-oriented languages, a variety of new methodologies and notations were proposed. In the mid-1990s, a standards consortium, the Object Management Group (OMG), issued a call for a standard notation for object-oriented development. The Unified Modeling Language (UML) was proposed by a number of methodologists, led by Rational Software, and was adopted by the OMG in November 1997. Since 1997, the OMG has managed UML as an open standard. An OMG task force works to gather information about problems and schedules revisions. The ultimate source of information on UML is the latest version of the Object Management Group's UML Specification, which is available free at the OMG's Web site. The current release of the UML Specification is Version 1.3, released in March 2000. As this book is being completed, the OMG is right in the middle of adopting a new version of UML (UML 2.0).

One of the keys to UML's rapid development and widespread acceptance was the decision to only standardize on a notation and not on a methodology. In the OMG specification, UML is defined as "a graphical language for visualizing, specifying, constructing and documenting the artifacts of a software-intensive system." UML does not define a specific, step-by-step process or methodology to follow in developing an application. Today's software developers use a variety of different methodologies, but all of the different methodologies use diagrams defined by the UML.

UML is a set of different diagrams or perspectives that are all related by a common UML core model. There are several different UML diagrams, including the following:

▶ *Use case diagram.* A use case diagram pictures a set of scenarios that collectively describe the requirements of a system or a portion of a system. The diagrams show a system as it appears to an outside user. The key graphical elements used in this diagram are "actors," "use cases" (transactions), and interactions between them.

▶ *Class diagram.* A class diagram pictures the types of objects used in a system and the static relationships that exist between them. The key graphical elements used in this diagram are "classes," "attributes," "operations," "associations," and "constraints."

▶ *Behavior diagrams.* This group of diagrams pictures the behavioral events that link states and activities.

▶ *Statechart diagram.* A statechart diagram pictures all the various states that a particular object can get into. In effect, it describes the behavior of a given object. The key graphical elements used in this diagram include "states," "activities," "events," and "transitions."

▶ *Activity diagram.* An activity diagram describes a sequence of activities and is used to describe business decision models and workflow, as well as parallel threads that one encounters in distributed systems. The key graphical elements are "activities," "transitions," "decision branches," and "forks" or "joins." "Swimlanes" are used to partition activities and indicate who is responsible for different subsets of the overall flow.

▶ *Sequence diagram.* A sequence diagram shows how objects interact. Each object is listed along the *x*-axis and lines dropped from each object define columns. Arrows running between the objects' lines (lifelines) indicate the sequence of messages passed between the objects. The key graphical elements are "objects," "lifelines," and "messages." "Conditions" indicate when specific messages will be sent.

▶ *Collaboration diagram.* A collaboration diagram provides a different perspective on the interaction of objects. Instead of arranging the objects along the *x*-axis, they are distributed throughout the diagram and connected by messages that are numbered. In effect, a collaboration diagram looks like a class diagram where the classes are replaced by specific object instances and the associations are replaced by specific messages. The key graphical elements are "objects" and "messages," which are numbered to indicate the sequence in which they are sent.

▶ *Component diagram.* A component diagram shows the components in a system, their interfaces, and their dependencies. The key graphical elements are "components," "interfaces," and "dependencies."

▶ *Deployment diagram.* A deployment diagram provides a graphical view of how specific hardware platforms (nodes) are linked together (connections). For example, such a diagram might show that a PC machine is connected to a Unix server, which is, in turn, connected to a mainframe, all via TCP/IP connections. Component and deployment diagrams are often combined. When the two diagrams are joined, the key graphical elements are "nodes" (specific hardware platforms), "components," "interfaces," "dependencies," and wire "connections."

Different methodologies use different combinations of UML diagrams. Throughout this book, we have been using a variation of the UML's activity diagram notation to represent business processes.

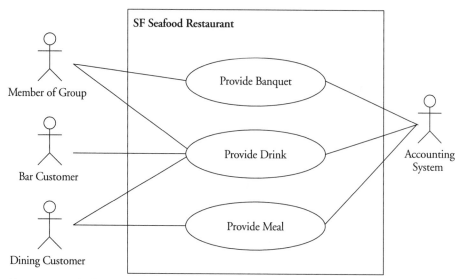

Figure 13.1 A high-level use case of SF Seafood.

In analyzing a new application, most software architects rely on two key UML diagrams: use case diagrams and class diagrams. We'll briefly consider each in turn.

Use Case Diagrams

A use case describes an interaction between actors and a system. The actors may be people or other systems. Systems may contain subsystems. A use case allows a developer to specify how a system might work without having to define any implementation details.

Consider the San Francisco Seafood restaurant example we have discussed elsewhere. We indicated that SF Seafood supported three business lines: bar service, meals, and banquets for groups. We might represent this with a use case diagram like the one pictured in Figure 13.1.

Each actor, whether a person or a system, is represented as a stick figure. The key use cases or scenarios of the SF Seafood Restaurant are described as Provide a Banquet, Provide a Drink, and Provide a Meal. A dining customer might interact with two different use cases by having both a meal and drinks from the bar. We've also pictured the accounting system used by SF Seafood as another actor. In this example the accounting system receives information whenever banquets, meals, or drinks are provided.

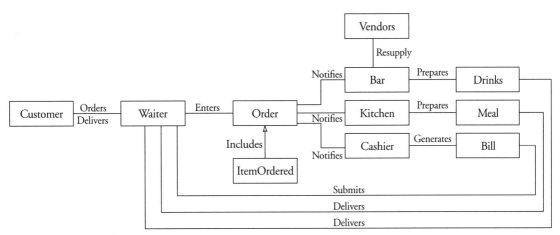

Figure 13.2 A class diagram of SF Seafood.

Use cases can become much more complex. They can also be supplemented by written descriptions of the steps in a process. For example, we could write out a script to describe how a customer obtained a meal. Software developers rely on use case diagrams when they are developing a high-level description of the classes of things that will interact and how they will interact. Unfortunately, while use cases may provide business managers with an overview of what a system will do and who it will interact with, they don't provide procedural information about who will do what, when, and who will be responsible for what is done.

Class Diagrams

A class, as used in UML, represents a concept or unit of activity. A software class has a name, attributes, and operations. The attributes specify things about which the class maintains data. The operations define activities the class could undertake to add, modify, or delete data. More generally, an operation provides a service. Class diagrams show how classes are related to each other and how they interact with each other.

Imagine that we wanted to show the various classes that might interact at SF Seafood. We would begin by thinking of the classes and how they interact. Figure 13.2 illustrates a class diagram we might create to describe the key classes involved in SF Seafood processes.

High-level class diagrams can be a bit confusing. In this case we show a number of classes that might or might not be software entities. The Customer class shown in Figure 13.2 might simply designate people and not be a part of the system, or it might represent data that we keep track of in a customer database. The lines without arrows simply show relationships. Customers relate to waiters when they place orders and when waiters deliver what is ordered. The other relationship is a class hierarchy relationship, indicated by the line with the arrowhead. A class can have subclasses. Thus, an order includes all of the specific items that are ordered.

We've tried to provide a sense of flow from left to right, but in fact, class diagrams do not normally provide an overall sense of flow. They simply define relationships. In early discussions we indicated that SF Seafood waiters entered orders on a computer that notified the kitchen and bar of each new order. Thus, this class diagram could easily represent the information that the computer system modeled and tracked, including information about when the order was submitted, when it arrived in the kitchen, when the kitchen indicated the meal was ready for delivery, and so forth.

Very high-level class diagrams can easily look like organization diagrams and picture the major divisions of a company and show how the divisions are related to each other. Software developers who are analyzing business processes often produce class diagrams to show what software objects will need to be created and how they will interact. The key thing, however, is that as class diagrams become more detailed, they increasingly refer to software details and not to the work that is performed in the workplace. If we created a process diagram to show what goes on in the kitchen, we would show the activities that occurred, including salad preparation, entrée preparation, desert preparation, and so forth. A software analyst, however, might only be interested in defining the interface screens that presented the chefs with order information and providing a button that the chefs could "push" when the order was done that would signal a waiter to come to the kitchen.

Although it is not quite the purpose of a class diagram, you could think of each class on the diagram as a set of data that any system would need to keep track of. In any case, although high-level class diagrams are sometimes useful as a way of providing managers with an overview of the elements in a process, they do not provide useful information on processes and how they work—especially if one focuses on processes that involve complex mixes of activities done by software systems and by human employees. You can model nonsoftware elements with use case diagrams, but they are primarily designed to model software elements.

UML and Business Process Modeling

Many business process redesign projects involve the automation of some or all of the business process. In most cases surveys suggest that business process redesign projects start with business managers and only devolve to software development teams after the overall redesign is defined. In those cases business managers must have tools they can use to redefine the process, and then they must pass that information on to the software developers who are charged with creating software for the redesigned process. In other cases the redesign effort is delegated directly to the software developers. In both cases the software development team must begin with a clear set of requirements that define what the software system must do when it is complete. Software requirements are usually derived from conversations with the business people responsible for the process.

In the case where business requirements are derived after a business team has redefined a process, the effort usually involves translating diagrams prepared by business managers into diagrams that software developers prefer.

If the software is to be developed with workflow tools, then there is a close match between the business process diagrams and workflow diagrams.

If the software is to be acquired from an ERP or CRM vendor and tailored, then business process diagrams must be compared with various ERP diagrams and an interface defined.

If the software is to be developed by an IT development team with a programming language, then those portions of the process diagrams that are to be automated will probably be translated into use case and class diagrams and then refined.

In all these cases, the IT development team will want to ask questions of the business managers to create a more precise specification. As we have noted before, business process diagrams rarely pin down all of the details that software developers need to develop software.

In the case in which software developers are given the responsibility for redesigning a process, they usually interview business managers and then create UML diagrams, typically beginning with use case and class diagrams. In these cases business managers may be forced to review and comment on use case or class diagrams, and the process can be frustrating for business managers, since these diagrams do not reflect the business perspective very well.

There are a number of books that describe what is usually called *enterprise modeling* or *business modeling* that rely on UML. Rational Software supports a popular Unified Software Development Process (usually called just Unified Process or UP) that is based on the use of UML to analyze and design new systems. UP begins with user requirements and generates complete software systems. UP uses use cases to capture requirements and then moves to class diagrams and sequence diagrams to analyze the needs of the software system in more detail.

There have been a number of books written on both UML development and on the analysis of requirements. We list some of the best in the Notes and References at the end of this book.

The Model Driven Architecture

A programmer can create a software application by writing lines of code in a software language like Java or C++. Today, however, most large applications are architected and designed before anyone begins writing code. A good software architecture is required because increasingly applications run on multiple machines distributed in different locations. Think of a simple Web application that supports hundreds of users who access the system via different browsers running on different types of personal computers. Since the development team can't specify the specific software that a user might use, they need to create an abstract architecture or design that can accommodate several different types of user configurations. Similarly, a company may start to develop a supply chain system only to find that suppliers use very different types of hardware and software than it uses. In all cases, the solution is to develop abstract designs that can support many different actual implementations. UML has proved the most popular approach to creating such abstract designs.

In 1999, the 800 member companies that make up the OMG began to consider if they could support abstract design in UML. After considering some of the pioneering work by member IT organizations, the OMG decided to standardize on a new software architecture, which it named the Model Driven Architecture (MDA). In effect, the OMG has decided to pop up to a higher level of abstraction and focus on describing how the system should be integrated.

A software development team using MDA begins by creating a UML class model that describes how the system should be integrated. MDA terms this a *platform-independent model* (PIM). A PIM is platform independent because it only describes how the software should work without considering any of the details about how it will be implemented on specific operating systems or on specific computers. Later, this PIM is used to generate one or more specific models, referred to as a *platform-specific model* (PSM), that define how the system will work when implemented in a specific language on a particular operating system. The OMG plans to define a set of profiles to assure that each PSM can consistently generate code for each of the popular software implementation languages (see Figure 13.3).

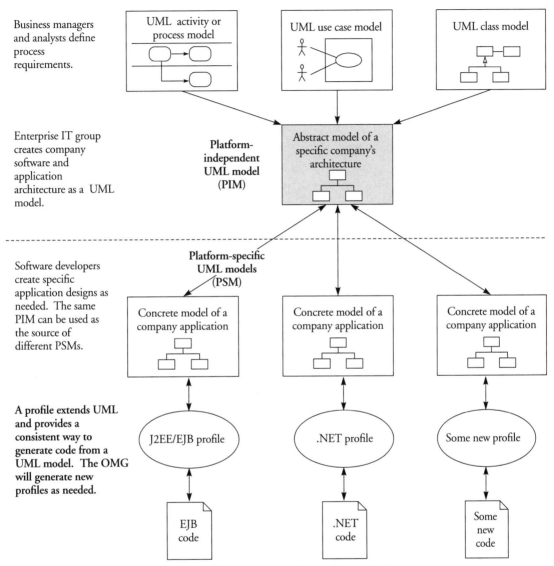

Figure 13.3 The OMG's Model Driven Architecture approach to software development.

The OMG described a set of general principles for MDA in 2001. The current revision of UML will make UML more useful for MDA. It will, for example, define utilities needed to define programming rules and to generate code directly from UML diagrams. Once MDA is complete, software developers will be able to generate code more quickly and revise applications faster by simply changing the appropriate UML models. This, in turn, will make UML models and software architectures defined in UML much more important to organizations. It will significantly increase IT's ability to reuse code from one application to the next.

MDA and CASE

Business managers who have been around for awhile will immediately recognize how similar MDA is to the Computer Aided Software Engineering (CASE) movement that dominated IT development in the late 1980s. They are alike in the sense that they both seek to improve application development by automating some code generation tasks. But consider the differences: In the mid-1980s, developers were working with much less sophisticated modeling languages. Most software development was done in COBOL and was designed to run on IBM mainframes. The best of the CASE tools let developers create diagrams of applications and then generated the COBOL code and the relational database code necessary to implement the design. Because the models were less precisely defined, it was very hard to reverse and move from code back to the model, so in most cases, once code was generated and then modified by hand, the model was out of date.

In a similar way, although there were several software modeling notations, no one had tackled the difficult problem of building a repository that could store the various modeling elements or translate one product's diagrams into models in another product's format. At the very end of the 1980s, IBM started such an effort (termed the AD/Cycle Repository). IBM abandoned that effort just as the CASE movement lost steam at the beginning of the 1990s. The CASE movement declined because companies were switching from COBOL and mainframe platforms to new languages (like C and C++), new platforms (like Unix servers and Windows), and new designs that relied on object and client-server architectures.

In effect, the OMG's Model Driven Architecture proposes that companies revive the CASE concept, with several important differences. First, a much more precise software methodology is available. The widespread adoption of UML assures that tools will use a common notation. At the same time, UML is so precise that the reverse engineering of code into UML diagrams is a common feature of several UML tools. Indeed, some products eliminate reverse engineering completely by generating a runtime application from UML and providing debugging capabilities at the model level. Another difference is that UML has already resulted in several repositories that can store UML diagrams and data. IBM, Oracle, and Unisys all offer UML-compliant repositories, for example. At the same time, a popular new Internet technology, XML, assures that UML tools can pass diagrams back and forth over the Internet, between tools, or to repositories or databases without loss of meaning. In other words, most of the problems companies faced with CASE in the late 1980s have already been overcome.

More importantly, however, in most instances, today's companies will not use the MDA approach to actually model a complete application from scratch. Component reuse or framework-based solutions, including the use of packaged ERP applications and e-commerce component frameworks, provide a more efficient way of building large portions of any new application. At the same time, the PIM model does not need to be concerned, in most cases, with which objects are distributed, parallelism and the queuing of events, transaction boundaries, or security. MDA-based application servers can support these in lower-level models or, better yet, as deployment configurations. Instead of creating complete applications, today's companies will use UML models to define how subsystems are to be linked together into an integrated whole, and then they will generate the middleware code needed for their applications. Since UML is middleware independent, the same high-level diagrams can be used to generate different middleware solutions for different aspects of a large-scale integration project. When you consider that the development of middleware and EAI code often takes well over half the time it takes to create a new application, automatic generation of middleware code could be a huge boon to enterprise systems developers.

Even though much has been done and systems have already been generated using MDA principles, there is still work for the OMG to do. In effect, MDA depends on software tools that will model distributed architectures and, in some cases, generate code from high-level specifications. To assure consistency, and hence the ability to move a model from one tool to another, the code generation process will need to be standardized. In other words, a number of profiles will need to be defined. Task forces are working on profiles that will define standard ways to generate code for various popular languages. Sun and the various other companies supporting Java are working on a profile that would generate Enterprise JavaBean (EJB) components from UML diagrams. The OMG and the Workflow Management Coalition (WfMC) are working on a profile that would allow UML to generate input for workflow tools. Similarly, while UML currently provides a complete description of structure, it lacks a complete description of behavioral semantics. Today's UML developers must currently rely on the UML Object Constraint Language (OCL), which is an incomplete way of describing what one might want a system to do. Without a complete behavioral semantics, UML cannot generate all the code needed for any possible type of application. The OMG already has a task force working on this problem. The new specification, which is termed UML Action Semantics, will be included in UML 2.0 when it is finalized in late 2002.

In a sense, MDA is a return to earlier ideas. It's a return, however, with a whole host of new standards and tools and more modest goals. More importantly, it addresses one of the key problems every company faces as it struggles to adapt to the rapidly changing world of new technologies, new business process models, and new applications. Rather than trying to standardize on one language or one middleware approach, the OMG suggests that companies standardize instead on a high-level architecture that will support the widest possible range of applications the company might want to build. After that, applications and middleware can be generated from the core architecture. As specific modules or components change, the interfaces can be regenerated from the core model, in the same language or in a new language. When companies decide to adopt the next hot thing after XML—and there will undoubtedly be yet another new API system—the OMG will prepare a profile for the new API system. Meanwhile, however, the UML architecture should last for many years.

The prospect of a reasonably stable, high-level MDA/UML software architecture, defined in terms of class diagrams, suggests that many business managers will need to be able to at least read high-level UML diagrams in the future.

Unisys and Business Process Outsourcing

In Chapter 2 we discussed the 2002 strategy of Unisys Corporation to illustrate how a company might define a high-level strategy. You may recall that growing their outsourcing business was a key goal defined by Unisys. In fact, Unisys is promoting a concept termed *business process outsourcing*. Many companies outsource applications. In most cases this means that they sign contracts with outsourcing vendors who establish data processing centers and manage the hardware and software required to provide data and applications for the client company. Only a few companies outsource all of their applications. Most outsource only well-established applications that they don't plan to change in the future. Many companies, for example, outsource suites of ERP applications. Companies tend to restrict outsourcing to stable applications because they fear that if they outsource core business applications they won't be able to change them quickly when the environment changes. Thus, it's relatively safe for a manufacturing company to outsource its accounting applications, but it's less likely that they will outsource manufacturing applications or new process development applications. Companies tend to want to maintain tighter control over strategic applications that are key to their survival as a company.

Unisys has developed many strategic applications for clients, and they understand this problem. In an effort to overcome it, Unisys became an early adopter of the OMG's MDA. In effect, Unisys plans to create new strategic applications using an MDA approach. They will begin by creating a high-level PIM model of the application. Then they will create one or more PSM models, depending on the specific code and platform that companies wants to use when they field the application. The key, however, is the PIM model, since it provides a high-level application model without any implementation details. Unisys hopes that companies will be more willing to outsource key business process applications if they know that they can quickly change them by making changes in the PIM model and then instructing the outsourcer (Unisys) to generate code in a specific PIM. Using this approach, a company could specify changes in the PIM model to comply with an upcoming regulatory change and simultaneously ask Unisys to move the entire application from Java to Microsoft's .NET environment; and Unisys could do it faster than a normal company could make the changes, let alone generate an entirely new implementation of the application.

As this kind of business process outsourcing becomes more popular, business process teams, or at least the IT members of business process teams, will increasingly find themselves examining UML PIM models to determine what changes they will want.

Software Languages, UML Modeling Tools, and CASE

Today, software developers use a wide variety of software development tools. Some tools, like Microsoft's popular Visual Studio, simply facilitate software language development. While such tools will remain popular for simple applications, enterprise applications will increasingly be developed in software modeling tools designed to support UML. Rational Rose is the most popular, general-purpose UML modeling tool at the moment, but it will probably be succeeded by a new generation of UML modeling tools that not only allow developers to model applications but also to generate code by means of MDA profiles.

The CASE tools used in the late 1980s typically relied on workflow diagrams to define applications. Some of the new MDA tools will rely on use case and class diagrams, but others will incorporate support for business process diagrams so that business managers and software developers can define applications in a common environment.

Most UML CASE or MDA tools that support a business modeling user interface support activity diagrams, which are, in effect, workflow diagrams. In this book we used an extended version of class notation to define the symbols used on the organization diagrams and a subset of the activity diagram notation to define business process diagrams—thus our square-cornered department boxes on organization diagrams and our rounded-corner rectangles to represent processes on process diagrams.

Process Architectures and Software Architectures

In Chapter 3 we discussed business process architectures. We suggested that a business process architecture showed how value chains and business processes related to each other and to business departments. A business process architecture provides business people with an easy way to see what processes the organization supports and what might be impacted by any given change.

In a similar way, IT departments and software developers rely on architectures. One of the earliest articles on what we today would call an enterprise software architecture was written by John Zachman, an IBM researcher, in 1987. Zachman proposed what is now popularly called the *Zachman Framework,* a way of conceptualizing what was involved in any information systems architecture. Zachman borrowed the term *architecture* from the building trades and discussed the various types of drawings and blueprints a building architect typically developed in order to create a house. He then suggested parallels in software development. He stressed that a project didn't have a single architecture, but a set of diagrams representing different aspects or viewpoints and different stages. An overview of the Zachman Framework is pictured in Figure 13.4. In essence the framework is a matrix. On the horizontal axis Zachman identified the three major elements that make up information systems: programs, data, and networks. On the vertical axis, Zachman described six layers. The top layer is the most abstract and focuses on the goals of the organization. The bottom layer is the most concrete and focuses on the activities of a functioning software system when it is running.

In considering Figure 13.4, note that the top two layers, the Scope/Objectives and the Business Model, are elements that are usually determined by business managers. (These are similar to the diagrams that a building architect works out in

		Function	Data	Network
Level 1	Scope/ Objectives (Ballpark View)	List of business processes (or value chains) the company supports and the goals for each process	List of things the company needs to keep track of	List of locations in which the company operates
Level 2	Enterprise Model (Business Owner's View)	Business process diagrams (e.g., workflow diagrams)	High-level database models (e.g., entity-relationship models)	Map of business units (e.g., logistics network)
Level 3	Information System Model (IT Designer's View)	Application architecture: objects, components, or data flow diagram (e.g., object models, user interfaces)	Data architecture (e.g., entities and relationships)	Distributed systems architecture (e.g., component or middleware model)
Level 4	Technology Model (Developer's View)	More detailed object or component diagrams (e.g., objects, messages)	Data design (e.g., segments, rows, keys, pointers)	Systems architecture (e.g., system software, hardware, line specifications)
Level 5	Detailed Representations	Program code (e.g., components, applications)	Data design descriptions (e.g., fields and addresses)	Network architecture (e.g., node addresses and link protocols)
Level 6	Functioning System	Programs being run	Actual data being created and used	Messages being sent between users, programs, and databases

Figure 13.4 The 1987 Zachman Framework. (Modified after a figure that appeared in J. A. Zachman, "A Framework for Information Systems Architecture," *IBM Systems Journal*, Vol. 26, No. 3, 1987.)

meetings with the people who will have to live in the house.) Actual software system design starts at level 3, the Information System Model, and becomes increasingly specific and detailed as lower levels are defined. We have emphasized this divide by shading the software development concerns. IT people often help define the business model, and business managers sometimes help refine the information model, but the distinction between what is primarily the concern of business strategists and functional managers, and the lower four layers that are mostly the concern of IT people, is an important one. As we used the term, a business process architecture falls in the cell that is highlighted by a bold border—the intersection of function and level 2 enterprise models. Of course, software developers might define this architecture with use cases or a class model, but we would define it with an organization and process diagrams.

Speaking broadly, the major concerns highlighted by the Zachman Framework are still those facing CIOs today. Zachman has gone on to identify three more columns for his framework, including People, Time, and Motivation, but these are refinements and not major changes. Information about the current Zachman Framework is provided in the Notes and References at the end of the book.

As a generalization, most corporate IT groups have several enterprise architectures to define organization-wide standards. Thus, most companies have an enterprise network or infrastructure architecture to define how all applications will be integrated together. Today that architecture is increasingly dominated by Internet standards. Similarly, most companies have an application architecture to show what software applications the IT organization must support and maintain.

Specific applications have their own architectures to show how the various components in the application will relate to each other and the corporate infrastructure. In essence, MDA PIM models fall between levels 2 and 3, while PSM models fall between levels 3 and 4. Code occurs at level 5.

The world of business and computing have both become more complex since Zachman wrote his seminal article in 1987. We have already described how a major transition has occurred in computing in the 1990s, resulting in systems that are more distributed and object-oriented. This growing complexity has resulted in more emphasis on architectures. Others, building on the work begun by Zachman and his colleagues, have created a wide variety of different ways of thinking about architectures. At the same time, companies have become more international and are relying more on information systems than they did in the past to respond to the rapid changes taking place in the world. The business process reengineering movement in the first half of the 1990s convinced most business managers that they could gain significant efficiencies by integrating and coordinating departmental activities and integrating business processes more tightly with information systems. During the late 1990s, the Internet, the Web, and related improvements in information technology offered businesses major new opportunities to improve the way they organize and conduct business. The ongoing efforts to improve business processes and integrate and coordinate them with information systems are widely perceived as a major, if not the major, determinant of corporate success in the coming decade.

Enterprise architectures reflect corporate goals and business processes and establish how software systems will help enable companies to achieve their goals. Architectures document the decisions that IT managers have made to assure that IT is aligned with and supports the corporate effort.

In most cases the business process architecture committee should be composed of business managers who are oriented toward strategic issues. IT architectures of various kinds will be developed and maintained by the IT organization. It is important, however, that the two groups talk constantly with each other to assure that IT architectures and IT priorities support business processes and organizational strategic goals.

IDEF

We have spoken of UML as if it were the only widespread notation used in software development today. As a generalization, that's true enough, but there are older notations that were originally created before UML became popular and that are still used, especially to diagram workflow systems. One example is IDEF, a system of diagramming conventions created by the U.S. Department of Defense (DOD) and widely used for DOD projects. Even the DOD is moving toward UML, but one still encounters tools and diagrams that use the various IDEF diagrams, which are numbered. Thus IDEF0 diagrams are function diagrams, IDEF1x diagrams describe data, and IDEF3 diagrams are process diagrams.

RM-ODP

Another international initiative to formalize the analysis of software systems is the Reference Model of Open Distributed Processing (RM-ODP) (or ISO 10746), which is being formalized by the International Standards Organization (ISO). RM-ODP provides a formal way to specify problems to be solved and technologies that can be used. The RM-ODP semantics are independent of any methodology, language, or vendor. They are very precise and yet abstract enough that they can be used to describe any concept found in any more specific object or component model (e.g., C++, Java, COM, CORBA, EJB). Obviously RM-ODP is not something that business managers are interested in, but something that software architects use when they are developing specifications for very complex application development efforts.

ISO RM-ODP will be used by large groups when they develop very complex applications. Thus, a U.S. Department of Defense system that is created by many different companies, each working on part of the overall project, would benefit from this type of specificity. It would take a large project, after all, to justify the considerable effort involved in learning to use the RM-ODP language. In the next decade, however, as companies create worldwide distributed systems and combine components developed in many different countries, most Fortune 1000 organizations will find themselves working on the types of projects that ISO RM-ODP was designed to facilitate.

Of necessity, RM-ODP is a very complex topic. The ODP specifications don't make for light reading. RM-ODP is, however, an effort to provide a notation that can be used to describe every aspect of a project. Rather than try to force the RM-ODP standard into a single perspective, the ISO committees divided the whole domain of discourse into five different viewpoints. Each viewpoint describes business problems and appropriate IS techniques, relevant for that viewpoint. The five viewpoints are

▶ *Enterprise viewpoint.* This view focuses on the purpose, scope, and policies for a system. It defines concepts such as "community," "actor role," "artifact role," "resource," "purpose," and so forth.

▶ *Information viewpoint.* This view focuses on the semantics of information and information processing. It defines such concepts as "invariant schema," "static schema," and "dynamic schema."

▶ *Computational viewpoint.* This view enables distribution through functional decomposition of the system into objects that interact at interfaces. It defines concepts such as "signal," "operation," "interrogation," "announcement," and so on.

▶ *Engineering viewpoint.* This view focuses on the mechanisms and functions required to support distributed interaction between objects in the system. It defines such concepts as "cluster," "capsule," "nucleus," "node," "channel," "stub," "interceptor," and "checkpoint."

▶ *Technology viewpoint.* This view focuses on the choice of technology in the system. It defines "implementation" and is used for testing.

There are annual conferences on the formal specification of business requirements, and they often focus on RM-ODP, since it provides such a precise way to define complete specifications for application development. We don't expect RM-

ODP to have much impact on business process change or software development, but those interested in business process change should be aware that there are individuals who are working on mathematically precise ways of defining business software systems and that they will probably play a larger role as companies attempt to build very complex business applications.

XML Business Process Languages

In Chapter 11, we briefly discussed XML-based languages that can be used to describe business processes. In essence, these business process languages are an evolution of the workflow languages used in workflow systems, modified to be more useful in distributed Internet environments. It's too early to determine what role these languages might play in future software development. They will probably not dominate development in the near future, but they may be widely incorporated into software development modeling tools and may play an increasing role in future UML development—primarily by encouraging developers to rely on activity diagrams more frequently as they seek to do requirements analysis.

Most UML-based business process modeling tools already support XML and will probably evolve to support whichever XML business process language proves most popular.

The Capability Maturity Model

Finally, we return briefly to the Capability Maturity Model (CMM) we considered in the Introduction. Software development is a support process in most corporations. IT develops and maintains software applications that enable core business processes. Software development is a complex business, and software developers have worked hard over the years to become more productive and to produce better software. To this end, software developers have focused quite a bit of effort and thought on how the software development process should be organized.

The Capability Maturity Model developed at the Software Engineering Institute (SEI) at Carnegie Mellon University is one result of that effort. SEI has published a number of books and articles on CMM and on the problems of defining and refining software processes. Some, like the CMM model that describes how software organizations evolve, apply to the software development process but can be readily generalized to all organizations that seek to make process improvement a major part of their culture. Any corporate manager who is primarily concerned with creating and maintaining processes at a corporation will probably benefit from studying at least an introductory book on CMM. (The current version of CMM, which incorporates a variety of different CMM approaches, is called CMMI—in essence, a newly integrated version of CMM.)

Table 13.1 summarizes the CMM model and suggests how organizations evolve. Organizations at Level 1 are preprocess. Organizations at Level 2 are just starting to get their processes identified and documented. Most organizations, software or otherwise, fall between Levels 2 and 3. Level 3 organizations have well-defined processes. In our terms, these are organizations that have process architecture committees that really understand their company's processes. Level 4 organizations have moved beyond understanding processes and have management systems that are aligned with their corporate strategies and with their processes. Level 5 organizations use the measurement information they gain from their process-oriented management systems to systematically improve their business processes. Only about 10 software organizations in the world have been identified as Level 5 organizations. The IBM software group that produces software for NASA is an example of a Level 5 software organization.

Obviously the CMM approach was very much in the spirit of this book, and we suggest that organizations that are working on business process change work closely with people in their IT organizations that are working on CMM efforts.

Companies launch business process projects all the time with little or no idea of the nature of the process they are seeking to improve. Consider a typical order fulfillment process, which would probably break down into several subprocesses, like sales and ordering, manufacturing, procurement, inventory, delivery, and billing. Senior management decides that the procurement subprocess needs to be improved. It needs to take less time and cost less money. Perhaps it should be a just-in-time system or incorporate an e-marketplace to increase competition and drive down costs. These are all important goals, and more than adequate to justify a procurement process improvement effort.

Does anyone step back, however, and ask how mature the existing procurement process is, and what level the company will be at when the process improvement effort is complete? Is the procurement process currently defined and repeatable? Is it Level 2 or 3? Or is there a management system that measures each step in the procurement process and quantitatively controls the process (Level 4)? Or is the process mature? Do the managers and employees continually seek to improve the process, using feedback and experiments to make the process ever more efficient?

Table 13.1 Features of the five CMM maturity levels.

	Level 1 Initial	Level 2 Repeatable	Level 3 Defined	Level 4 Managed	Level 5 Optimizing
Process	Few stable processes exist or are used. "Just do it."	Documented and stable estimating, planning, and commitment processes are at the project level. Problems are recognized and corrected as they occur.	Integrated management and engineering processes are used across the organization. Processes are anticipated and prevented, or their impacts are minimized.	Processes are quantitatively understood and stabilized. Sources of individual problems are understood and eliminated.	Processes are continuously and systematically improved. Common sources of problems are understood and eliminated.
People	Success depends on individual heroics. "Fire fighting" is a way of life. Relationships between disciplines are uncoordinated, perhaps even adversarial.	Success depends on individuals; management system supports. Commitments are understood and managed. People are trained.	Project groups work together, perhaps as an integrated product team. Training is planned and provided according to roles.	Strong sense of teamwork exists within each project.	Strong sense of teamwork exists across the organization. Everyone is involved in process improvement.
Technology	Introduction of new technology is too risky.	Technology supports established, stable activities.	New technologies are evaluated on a qualitative basis.	New technologies are evaluated on a quantitative basis.	New technologies are proactively pursued and deployed.
Measurement	Data collection and analysis is ad hoc.	Planning and management data used by individual projects.	Data are collected and used in all defined processes. Data are systematically shared across projects.	Data definition and collection are standardized across the organization. Data are used to understand the process quantitatively and stabilize it.	Data are used to evaluate and select process improvements.

(Modified after a table in *The Capability Maturity Model*, Carnegie Mellon University, SEI, 1995.)

(If the procurement process is already at Level 4 or 5, you probably wouldn't be asked in to improve it.)

You might apply CMM to your next internal process redesign effort. It will help you think outside the box and consider issues beyond the narrower goals that projects are usually launched to achieve. Insights that software developers have learned from CMM can help them provide insight to managers dealing with other corporate processes.

PART VI

THE E-BUSINESS CHALLENGE

WHEN YOU TALK with corporate managers today, their leading concern, at least as far as process change is concerned, is figuring out how to use the Internet, email, and the Web to improve the way their company functions and relates to customers. In this section, we review the kinds of process redesign and automation techniques that are typically used by companies transitioning to e-business.

Chapter 14 focuses on the problems and opportunities of redesigning and automating processes to incorporate portals, Web sites, and customer-oriented e-business applications.

Chapter 15 considers the problems and the opportunities implicit in redesigning and automating processes to incorporate supplier-oriented and internal-operations–oriented e-business applications.

14

E-Business: Portals and Customer-Oriented Applications

N THIS CHAPTER, and the next, we will consider some of the issues that arise when you design or redesign business processes to incorporate various e-business techniques. Our goal is not to teach you to design e-commerce or supply chain software systems, but to provide you with some heuristics about how to conceptualize how systems of this kind will change the business processes at your company. In this chapter we will begin by considering e-business systems in general and then focus on the problems involved in using Web sites and portals and in creating processes that incorporate customer-oriented e-business applications.

E-Business Applications

The Internet provides companies with a really superior way to link and integrate activities and to communicate between customers, employees, and external partners and suppliers. These are goals that business managers and IT developers have been pursuing for decades. Since 1995, however, the Internet, the Web, and email, along with a number of other Internet protocols, have made it much easier to realize these goals. Various Internet startups and a lot of media hype in the late 1990s confused things for awhile. Since the demise of most of the dot.coms, just after the millennium, most companies have settled down to figure out how to use Internet technologies, in combination with their existing strengths, to create better business processes.

The best proof of the impact of the Internet is that over 50% of the people in North America now have computers in their homes and most use them to send and receive email and to surf the Web to find information and to do business online. The possibility of online commerce and more efficient links with employees and suppliers has also changed the way business and IT managers think about what computing can do to improve business processes. Prior to the Internet, business managers used to assume that IT people would alert them to new techniques that might improve business processes. Similarly, IT people tended to focus on tactics and technologies and not on business strategies. Today, however, both business executives and IT managers are more interested in the potential of the Internet and in strategic issues. A focus on customer relationship management (CRM) and supply chain management (SCM) represents a more strategic and comprehensive perspective than IT managers typically displayed in the past. Similarly, business managers who have experienced home email and have used the Web are more likely to insist on getting involved in determining how to use these techniques to improve processes than they might have in the past. In effect, everyone is learning more about how business and technology can interact, and everyone wants to be involved in using these new technologies to make their companies more effective and efficient.

Internet-Driven Changes in Business Processes

People use the term *e-business* in a variety of different ways. There isn't even any agreement on whether it's *e-business* or *ebusiness,* or whether e-business is an appropriate term at all. In 1998, when everyone dreamed of how businesses would be totally transformed by the use of the Internet, email, and the Web, many spoke of the transition from businesses based on bricks and mortar to e-businesses. Another popular term at the time was to refer to companies that were designed to do business on the Web as *dot.com* companies. Today, after the dot.com crash, some managers still associate the term *e-business* with dot.com companies and prefer not to use the term. We still find the term useful. We use the term to describe any use of the Internet, email, and the Web to improve business processes. In the sense in which we use the term, companies that use the Internet and Web sites to allow customers access or use the Internet to facilitate the development of supply chains and other cooperative relationships with suppliers or partners are e-businesses. In spite of the failure of many dot.com companies, most companies are still moving toward new business models that incorporate Internet technologies. In most cases, we no longer contrast Internet companies and bricks and mortar companies, but focus instead on how to combine the best of both.

In the late 1990s, it was popular to try to distinguish different types of e-business applications. Some preferred the terms business-to-business (B2B) and business-to-customer (B2C), while others focused on tasks like automating customer relationship management (CRM) or the supply chain. Others focused on portals, Web sites that organized other Web sites so customers or employees could find things quickly, or e-procurement. Recently lots of people have begun to talk of collaborative computing and Web services.

We spent quite a bit of time covering developments in e-business from the late 1990s through to the present. We have always believed there were two separate drivers for e-business:

▶ *Customer-driven.* First, there is the fact that customers have embraced email and the Web and are willing to seek information about and, in some cases, buy products via the Internet. Few companies can afford to ignore this source of customers. Just as many companies have always sold a significant portion of their products via catalogs or via newspaper advertising, so in the future many companies will sell a significant portion of their products to online customers via Web sites or via email solicitations.

▶ *Integration-driven.* Second, companies have always sought to improve the efficiency of communications within their organizations and between themselves and their suppliers and partners. Telegraph, telephones, and faxes were embraced as they were introduced, and, since the 1970s, companies have been trying to use computers to provide better communications. In the late 1980s and early 1990s, most large companies explored EDI Systems. Unfortunately EDI relied on expensive, proprietary technologies, and only large companies could afford to use this approach. The auto companies were connected to major suppliers in the 1990s with EDI, but never tried to extend the system to smaller suppliers because the small companies simply couldn't afford to create or maintain EDI systems. The Internet, email, and the Web have changed corporate communications.

The Internet was first introduced in the 1970s, but didn't become really popular until the mid-1990s when graphical browsers were introduced that made email activities much easier and allowed everyone to browse the Web. The Web is a way of posting pages on an Internet server (a Web site) that others can access and read. The Web not only introduced an easy way to post pages on Web sites, but it provided an easy way to navigate by simply clicking on buttons or highlighted phrases to move to new sites or by clicking on BACK to return to previous pages. Equally important, especially for business systems developers, the Internet is based on a set of open, international protocols that use the existing telephone lines without interfering with other uses of those same lines. The Internet and associated technologies, like email and the Web, have provided companies with a cheap, easy-to-use alternative to EDI. Suddenly, projects that companies had only dreamed of became easy to accomplish. Most companies have now created email systems that link all employees. Moreover, as a free side effect, most employees have acquired personal computers and can receive email at home. Today, passing information around your organization is easier and faster than it ever was before. Similarly, linking your company to partners and suppliers is also much easier.

In our experience companies begin by thinking of a single use of the Internet. Some want to provide information for customers via company Web sites. Others want to link with suppliers. Most simply want to use email for internal communications. Wherever they start, they soon realize that they can link and integrate additional things into their Internet system and make it more effective. Sooner or later, everyone realizes that the Internet will evolve into an integrated network that will wire everything in a company together and link the company to the rest of the world. Thus, it doesn't matter if you start with a B2C system or a portal or a B2B system or a CRM system. In fact, most of these terms don't mean much. They don't refer to specific technologies or even to specific types of applications. Instead, they refer to general goals. They translate into statements like these:

▶ *B2B.* We want to link our company to partners or suppliers to increase efficiency.

▶ *B2C.* We want to let customers obtain information about our company via the Web. Or we want to let customers buy things from us over the Web.

▶ *CRM.* We want use the Internet to keep better track of our customers. Or we want to use the Internet to identify high-profit prospects or customers.

▶ *Collaborative computing.* We want to link our company to partners or suppliers to increase our efficiency.

▶ *Supply chain.* We want to link our company with our suppliers to increase our efficiency.

Behind all these general terms are the details. You need to change your business processes to take advantage of the Internet and its associated technologies.

We've divided all uses of the Internet and its associated technologies into three broad categories. There are (1) customer-driven changes to business processes, (2) integration-driven changes to business processes, and (3) changes in business process to link employees and facilitate internal information sharing. In this chapter we'll focus on customer-driven changes. We'll consider the other two types of change in the next chapter.

A Customer Focus

Companies have always focused on customers, but today the focus is much more intense. In part this results from globalization and the fact that, in many industries, more companies are competing for customer attention. In part it's a result of the fact that customers are better informed and more likely to analyze their options more carefully. The Internet provides customers with more information about products and options, more quickly, than any past technology. On top of that, a dozen management books in the past decade have argued that the most successful and best-run companies focus on satisfying customer needs.

Business process analysts have spent the past decade trying to get companies to think of processes as integrated sequences of activities. In the worst case, process analysts tend to focus on activities and sequences and miss the big picture. In many cases, process analysts focus on the products the company makes and how to improve the efficiencies or productivity. In other words, they begin by focusing on the initial design of the product and then work their way through the sequence to the customer, who lies near the end of the process sequence.

In the best case, however, an emphasis on process begins with an emphasis on the customer. Most company strategies focus on customer-oriented goals. And all value chains are represented as arrows that point to the customer. Good business process analysis begins by defining what the customer wants and then backs up to establish process measures tied to customer needs. The use of the concept of value-added activities, and the elimination of activities throughout the process that don't add value for the customer, is another way that process analysts emphasize the importance of satisfying customers.

We don't think the term *customer relationship management* (CRM) is a very descriptive term. A typical group of CRM applications will include everything from programs to manage field salespeople, to applications that field salespeople can access for information, to applications that track users on Web sites, and programs that search databases for customer buying patterns. Telling someone you are going to develop or use a CRM application doesn't give them any specific information. On the other hand, the term is very popular and we understand why. The Internet empowers the customer. In Porter's terms, customers have more buying power today. The Internet makes it easier for customers to survey what's available at what price. It gives them access to sellers located throughout the world, including discounters in large metropolitan areas that sell at very small margins. Changing from one vendor to another requires only a mouse click, and the Internet makes it all impersonal. Sales are more likely to be based on price or features and less likely to be based on a personal relationship between the customer and a salesperson. The increased power of the customer has been widely acknowledged. In response, software vendors have focused on developing applications that help companies stay focused on customers and customer concerns. Thus, although CRM may not refer to any specific type of application, it certainly does point to the fact that companies want to incorporate a greater customer focus into their business processes.

The introduction of company portals and e-commerce applications of various kinds has increased the focus on customers and provides new ways to assure that processes support customers. At the same time, it has also placed a new emphasis on integrating processes and thinking about how processes work together to satisfy customers.

We'll return to these ideas after we spend a few minutes examining how we might create a portal for a company.

Web Sites and Portals

Portals are very hot topics among those who talk about e-business systems. As far as we can tell, it means whatever the writer wants it to mean and is usually synonymous with a Web site. A Web site or portal is an access point, represented by an Internet URL like *www.portalname.com.* Individuals who want to access the Web site or portal enter the URL into a browser, and a server, somewhere in Internet space, sends a page or screen that is associated with that URL. If an individual creates a small Web site on one's own, the main page is generally referred to as the *home page.* Companies that build larger sites tend to refer to the home page as a *portal.* Some people speak of a *company portal*—the URL one enters to access a page that will then let one find any other Web sites supported by that company. *www.ibm.com* is a good example of a company portal. From the *www.ibm.com* home page you can gain access to thousands of pages on IBM and its products, publications, and services. Others refer to *internal portals,* like the Web page supported by the company human resources department that any employee can go to and obtain information about employee policies, one's pension plan status, or to enter changes in a home address or withholding information. In this book we treat Web sites and portals as synonymous, but will usually use "portal," since it's the more popular term among business people.

In most cases, a portal is simply an interface between customers, suppliers, or employees. We'll consider the development of portals first because understanding them will help us when we begin to think of the more complex e-business applications.

Let's imagine we run a small travel agency, Travel-Is-Us, and want to transform our company from an office accessed by phones to an online company that customers can access via the Web. To do this we need to create a portal that customers can come to when they want to do business with our company.

A first step is to acquire a URL domain name like *www.travel-is-us.com* and to determine how our site will be hosted on a server, but we are going to ignore all such details. Our concern in this book is the design of the site and how it interfaces with the processes at a company. Let's assume that the folks at Travel-Is-Us developed an IS process diagram of their current operations. We've pictured such a diagram as Figure 14.1.

In essence, a portal is a set of Web pages or computer interfaces that a client uses to interact with a process. Thus, as a first approximation, we might create a COULD diagram like the one shown in Figure 14.2.

Figure 14.2 is a COULD process diagram of Travel-Is-Us with a swimlane added for a portal or Web site. In effect, we've inserted one box for each customer-agency interaction. As a designer, you could think of each box as a Web page or user interface screen that the user might access to accomplish some interaction with the agency.

Figure 14.3 provides a slightly different look at the portal. We are using shaded boxes to represent the Web pages that make up the portal. In this case, we've inserted a single screen as the first screen that a user arrives at when he or she enters *www.travel-is-us.com* on a browser. The top screen is a home or index screen that will somehow list the other screens the user can access. The screens below are other Web pages or Web sites the user can reach by clicking buttons on the home screen.

The process redesign team probably does not want to get into designing interface screens, but there's no reason why they can't create a picture of a basic set of screens and imagine what processes might lay behind each screen. (We've grouped the three rejection screens together to save space.)

The redesign team might decide to add screens to provide additional services, but that is beyond what we want to consider here. The key point is that, without getting into the details of the design of the Web site, there's no reason why the redesign team can't consider, in general terms, the functionality they would want from the Web site. And the easiest way to describe the functionality is probably in terms of the information and options the team would like to see on a set of Web pages.

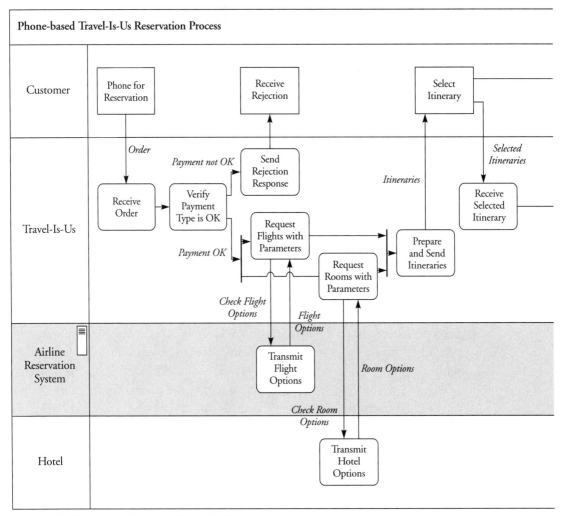

Figure 14.1 IS process diagram of Travel-Is-Us reservation process.

Returning to the Travel-Is-Us process, it's unlikely that the redesign team would stop after simply inserting a Web portal into the process, as we did in Figure 14.2. The original process assumed human travel agents interacting with customers over the phone. The COULD design assumes that customers interact with a Web portal, but that people still take the information the customers enter via Web screens and do the work. That approach wouldn't work because agents could not do it fast enough and customers wouldn't wait at the Web site for the results. To make the

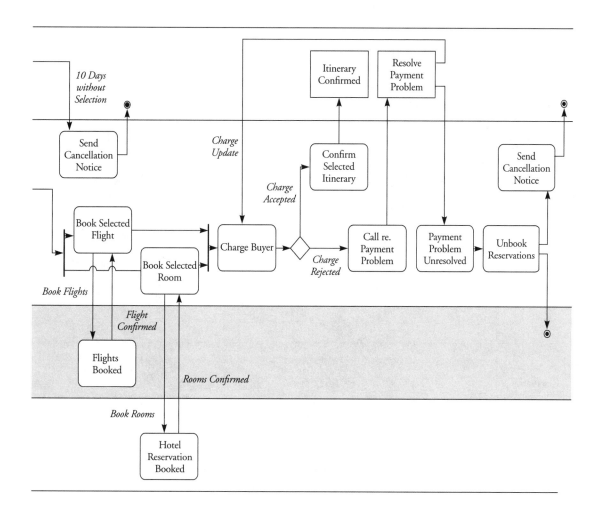

Web site work, we would need to create a software application, which for conceptual purposes we'll consider independent of the portal that would automate much of the process. (IT developers often refer to the Web page hierarchy as the *presentation* and the applications that support and provide functionality as *applications*.) Travel-Is-Us could either have their own software developers create the software application, or they could acquire it from software vendors who sell applications of this nature. One way or the other, Travel-Is-Us should be able to automate checking with the airlines and hotels to develop an itinerary list and making

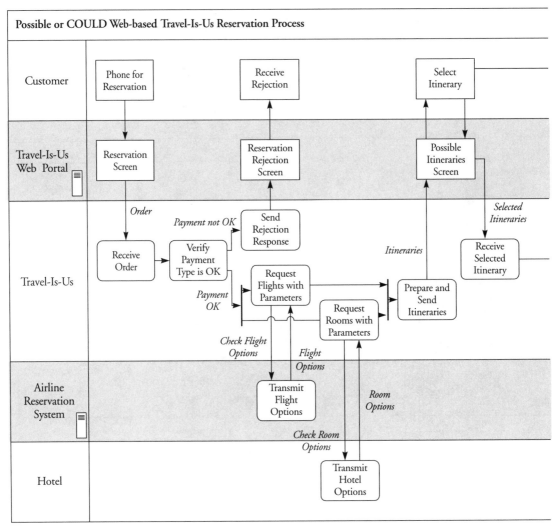

Figure 14.2 COULD process diagram of Travel-Is-Us with portal added.

reservations, checking with the credit card agency to validate the card, and generating an itinerary from the Web site (and perhaps printing one to mail to the customer), and it should be able to cancel reservations if the credit card is rejected. Depending on the nature of Travel-Is-Us customers, agents might decide to phone customers about rejected cards rather than simply rejecting them online. In any case, it's clear that adding a portal is only the beginning step in revising the Travel-Is-Us process. Adding a portal swimlane and creating an initial list of possible

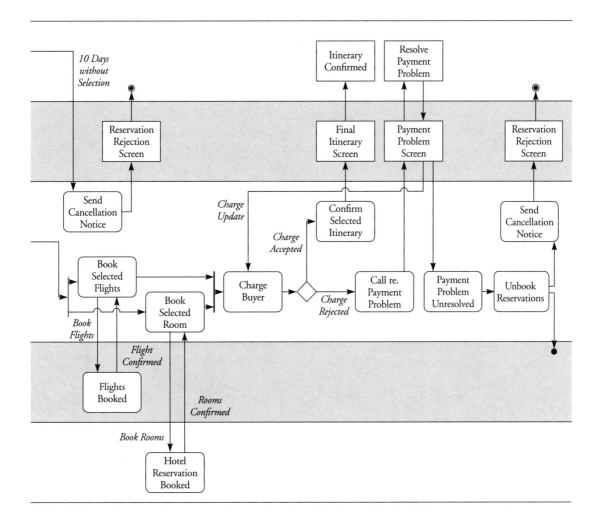

customer screens for the Web site is only a way of starting and stimulating the more detailed redesign and automation of the process that will support the new portal.

Figure 14.4 shows one possible solution for Travel-Is-Us. In this case, we assumed that everything is automated.

We are not going to go into any of the technical details of what's involved in the creation of a Web site or portal. Suffice it to say that either is a collection of Web pages or interfaces. For a business manager, the key thing is to assure that the Web pages make up a logical hierarchy and that all the information the potential users

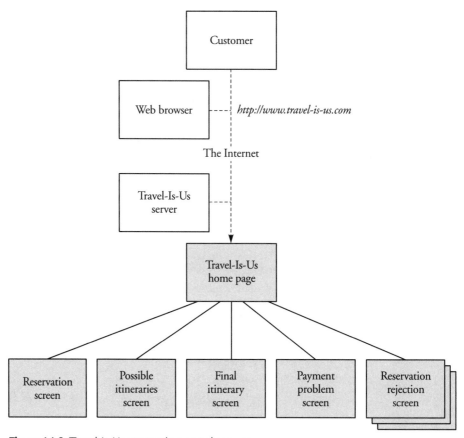

Figure 14.3 Travel-Is-Us reservation portal screens.

need can be easily found. We strongly suggest creating the initial Web pages on 8½ by 11–inch paper and testing them with potential users to make sure that they are easy to understand.

Beyond the portal, which is easily represented as a swimlane on a process diagram, there is the issue of who responds to specific requests. Keep in mind that a company can create a portal, launch it, and quickly find that 10–30% of its requests come via the portal. Moreover, they may come at odd hours and bunched up in various ways. Banks, for example, get lots of information requests on Friday afternoon just before people withdraw funds for the weekend. In most cases, inquiries via the Internet would overwhelm all but the largest manual operations, and their periodicity would make manual operations very inefficient. In other words, the responses to portal screens should almost always be automated.

If you have a diagram on an IS process and insert a portal and screens—as we did in Figure 14.2—you can quickly check to see how you currently respond to each screen. If you have a complex process, you will probably already have several software applications and the portal screens will link to existing applications. The actual linkages between the portal and existing applications can be quite complex to implement. In many cases, the existing applications were never designed to accept inputs and make responses as quickly as Internet customers expect. The linkage problems, however, are technical matters that IT systems analysts will need to work out. The redesign team should focus on the manual IS activities that support Web screens. How can they be automated?

If they can't be automated, then they probably need to be isolated and disconnected from the Web interface. You can let customers create emails, for example, that request information and promise that an employee will return an email within 24 hours. This is done by simply building a button into a Web page that triggers an email message window. The customer clicks on the button, then types out an email message and clicks another button to send it.

In most cases the activities can be automated. In that case you need to consider if you want to buy a popular ERP or off-the-shelf application, or create your own. Here the answer depends on how unique the activity is. If the activity is something that adds great value to your company's service, you may want to create a unique application to support the activity. Otherwise, it would probably be cheaper to acquire an application.

At this point, we'll leave Web sites and portals, step back from the specifics of creating a customer-oriented e-business process, and see what we can say about the overall process.

Analyzing Customer-Oriented Processes

We have used process diagrams with swimlanes throughout this book. We have used horizontal swimlanes to emphasize the flow of processes from suppliers on the left to customers on the right, an overall pattern that matches the organization diagrams that locate suppliers and customers in a similar manner. And we have always inserted a customer swimlane at the top of the diagram to emphasize the interactions between the customer and the process. (The customer represented on that top swimlane may, of course, be the ultimate customer or another process that is receiving the outputs of the process we are focusing on.)

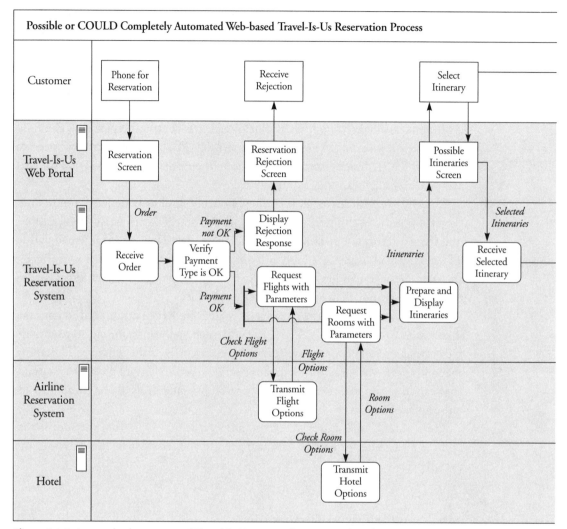

Figure 14.4 A completely automated Travel-Is-Us reservation system that the customer accesses via a Web portal.

When we analyze customer-oriented e-business systems, this approach is useful because it allows us to insert a swimlane that lies between the customer and the company, and add Web pages or Web sites that the customer can use to gain information or to interact with company processes. As we explore customer-oriented applications in more depth, we find that this arrangement also emphasizes a new way to think about how processes can be integrated to provide better support for our customers.

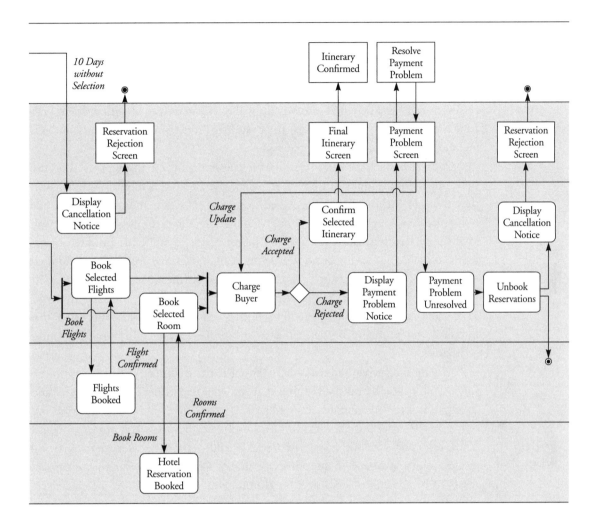

In analyzing large companies, the place to begin is with an analysis of the entire company portal. In other words, you need to create a high-level portal model like the one we created for Travel-Is-Us, but you need to do it in such a way that it emphasizes value chains and high-level business processes.

In Chapter 5, when we considered modeling the processes of an organization, we considered how we could use a process diagram to picture the value chains and major processes in a company. By inserting a portal swimlane on such a diagram, we can obtain an overview of what processes will be linked together in the company portal. (See Figure 14.5.)

A quick glance at the portal described in Figure 14.5 suggests that the portal will interact with more processes than the average process redesign team will consider in a single redesign effort. In other words, portal design is something best handled at the process architecture level. You don't start to redesign the company sales process, or even the order fulfillment business process, and then ask about the portal to be developed. The portal is more comprehensive than the existing processes. In fact, it's likely that one process will only be concerned with a single Web page or suite of Web pages. Thus, the customer service process supports the Service and Help pages on the company portal.

Notice also that the steps customers will probably go through as they use the company portal may not be the sequence that managers might think of when they think of their company processes. Company managers might think that one only warehouses a product after it has been manufactured. Thus, warehousing follows manufacturing. But the customer might check to see if the product is currently available and only consider ordering it manufactured if it can't be acquired from a warehouse. Increasingly, those thinking about processes will need to shift their thinking to match the "customer's process" rather than thinking in terms of the company's internal production sequence. As we have already suggested, this interface will probably be delegated to the process architecture group at most companies.

Next, consider what happens where more than one company process supports a single Web page. We normally think that the sales department takes an order and then passes it to someone in accounting for approval and billing. Most portals not only take the order but ask for credit card or invoice numbers and process the sale. Thus, sales and accounting, as well as an outside supplier and a credit approval agency, all get involved in supporting a single Web page. Moreover, the process needs to be automated because no customer would wait online while employees within a company processed an approval. This raises issues about which process managers will ultimately be responsible for specific Web site pages. In the long run, it may even lead to new ideas of how one thinks about processes. We may increasingly orient business processes to Web sites. It won't happen too quickly in most cases, however, because most companies are only doing about 15–30% of their business via the Internet. Thus, Widget Manufacturing is probably maintaining a field sales force, as well as taking orders online. Many manufacturers are providing portals to let customers order, but are delivering the product to an existing store or warehouse where the customer goes to actually pick up the product. (Assume, for example, that widgets weigh 2 tons each.)

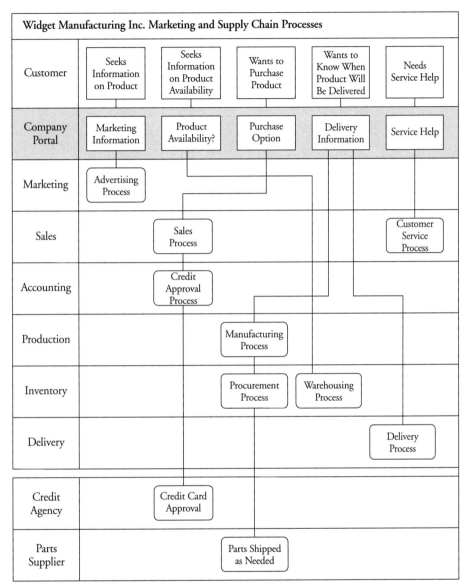

Figure 14.5 Widget Manufacturing's portal and its relationship to company processes.

Finally, assume that our Widget Manufacturing customer decides to order a tailored widget and wants to know how quickly one can be manufactured and delivered. At this point, we need to coordinate manufacturing and delivery processes. We may also need to access information at part supplier Web sites in order to provide the information our customer wants. And, once again, we have the question of which manager is ultimately responsible for this part of the Web site.

Clearly, customer-oriented e-business raises a host of new questions about how we scope business process redesign efforts. No business process team should begin a redesign effort without having a clear idea about the nature of the company portal and what aspects (pages) of that portal will likely need to be linked to the process the team is redesigning. Assuming the process architecture group has this information, the process team can begin its redesign efforts by assuming the new process will support a suite of Web pages on the company portal.

Once a team decides that it needs to redesign a given process to support portal pages, it must first consider if it has to support both online and parallel manual activities. If it does, it will need to improve the existing manual activities (field sales) while simultaneously creating an automated process to support the Web pages.

In some cases, activities that need to support Web pages can be completely automated. In other cases, they must mix some automation and some manual support. Consider how Widget Manufacturing might support customer service. It might post the answers to frequently asked questions on the Web site and then provide a phone number or an email generation module to provide customers with a way to get more personal service.

The fact that portals often lead to automation is no reason for a process redesign team to pay less attention to the details of the process. Automation must still begin with a process, and efficient and well-conceived processes are always easier to automate than confused processes.

In all cases, when designing processes to support portals, consider what happens when exceptions occur—as they almost always do. If employees are needed to handle exceptions, they probably need to be given more authority. There's nothing more frustrating than to try to use an online process, run into a problem, and then call and find out that the employee who answers the phone can't help. Remember that we are creating online systems to improve the customer's experience and make things easier. If they are poorly designed, online systems can easily prove more frustrating and unpleasant. Consider your own experience with phone answering systems that lead you down a long series of choices between 1, 2, and 3, only to end some place you don't want to go and offering you no way out but to hang up and start over.

As a strong generalization, if you automate via phone answering systems or online portals, you need to provide for exceptions and you need to structure employee jobs so that the employees who interface with customers are empowered to make the decisions necessary to help customers when exceptions occur.

Luckily, since many of the activities supported by portals are generic in nature, ERP vendors and software component vendors have developed reusable modules that can be used to automate many of the standard tasks companies must create to support their portals. SAP, for example, sells a suite of customer relationship management components or processes and includes the following in its CRM category:

- B2B Sales
- Collaborative Complaint Management
- Collaborative Sales Process
- Collaborative Announcement on the Marketplace
- Collaborative Internet Customer Self-Service
- Key Account Management
- Collaborative Campaign Planning and Management
- Collaborative Internet Customer Self-Service with Subsequent Service Request
- Product Launch
- Mobile Sales—Opportunities
- Mobile Sales—Campaigns
- Internet Sales—Business-to-Business
- Mobile Sales—Customer Visit with Order Entry
- Internet Sales—Business-to-Consumer

Customer-Oriented E-Business Redesign

Customer-oriented e-business redesign patterns include all the e-business redesign efforts that aim at increasing communication with prospects or customers, providing them with information, selling products online, or providing them with services. They also include a variety of techniques for learning about customer or prospect concerns in order to market more effectively. Early on, many writers referred to customer-oriented patterns as business-to-customer applications, or B2C. Recently, it has been more popular to refer to them as portal applications or customer relationship management (CRM) applications.

Different companies with individual needs will emphasize different reasons for developing customer-oriented e-business systems. Here are some of the common reasons cited by companies:

- To reduce time to market
- To improve organizational efficiency
- To reduce the latency of business events

▶ To make it easier to create a common presence after a merger or acquisition

▶ To integrate multiple delivery channels

▶ To provide the customer with a unified view across the company's lines of business

▶ To support effective cross-selling

▶ To maintain better, more current data on customer interests

▶ To support mass customization

IBM, as part of their analysis of customer sales, provides the following list of typical applications developed within specific industries for customer-oriented Web sites:

Insurance Industry

Locate a nearby office

Locate brokers or agents

Financial planner and insurance needs analysis tool

Portfolio summary

Policy summary and details

Claims submission and tracking

Online billing

Discount Brokerage

Portfolio summary

Detailed holdings

Buy and sell stocks

Transaction history

Quotes and news

Convenience Banking

View account balances

View recent transactions

Pay bills/transfer funds

Stop payments

Manage bank card

Telecommunications and Wireless Industry

Review account statements

Paying bills online

Change personal profile

Add/change/remove services (e.g., call waiting or caller ID)

Submitting service requests

Government

Submit tax returns

Renew automobile licenses

Download forms/applications

Submit forms/applications

Manufacturing

Review required parts/services

Locate service centers

Submit/track orders

A quick glance at the types of customer-oriented applications described by IBM suggests that adding a customer interface to major business processes will not occur overnight. Adding and then improving customer interfaces will occur over the course of the rest of this decade. Moreover, as we have already suggested, most companies will find that a serious customer-oriented e-business initiative will quickly evolve into supplier and internal e-business applications as well. Someone in the company needs to think hard about these issues and develop a plan to gradually evolve business processes to take advantage of e-business opportunities. We would suggest the process architecture committee, but many companies have created separate committees or managers to oversee e-business development. However it's managed and planned, it's clear that major business processes are going to need to be changed, and then changed again and again before it's done. We are in for a decade of business process change as companies come to grips with the opportunities offered by the Internet, Web, and email and a whole collection of associated technologies.

15

Supplier and Internally Oriented
E-Business Applications

N THE LAST CHAPTER, we considered how one might approach the analysis and design of business processes that incorporate customer-oriented e-business applications. The key in that case was to focus on the portal interface between the customer and the process. In this chapter we shall consider process development issues that arise when the process design team needs to incorporate supplier-oriented e-business applications. We will also consider some of the issues that arise from the internal use of e-business techniques. Our goal here, as in Chapter 14, is not to teach you to design supply chain or internal e-business software systems, but to provide you with some rules-of-thumb about how to conceptualize how systems of this kind will change the business processes at your company.

Supplier-Oriented E-Business Redesign

Supplier-oriented e-business redesign applications are used in process redesign efforts that aim at increasing communication with partners or suppliers, providing them with information, ordering products online, paying them for shipments, or collaborating with them on the design or tailoring of new products. A few years ago, many people talked about e-marketplaces and supply chain systems. Recently, it has been more popular to speak of collaborative applications to emphasize that, in many cases, companies are restructuring and outsourcing processes. In the latter case an outsourced subprocess may be a key part of the company's virtual order fulfillment process, even though it's done by an outsourcer. Similarly, many companies are creating processes that allow companies to work together on large projects, like designing aircraft for defense, or that coordinate the work of federal, state, and city welfare systems.

Unlike Internet-based customer response systems that are truly a new way of doing business, companies have been working on systems to integrate with suppliers and partners for at least two decades. Most large companies already employ EDI systems that link them with key suppliers. The problem with these older systems is their expense and the fact that they can't be extended to smaller suppliers or easily integrated with other company processes. Thus, Internet-based supply systems aren't really a new approach to business. Instead they are a more efficient approach to a problem that is already well understood. The Internet facilitates more extensive and more flexible supplier- and partner-oriented coordination.

Of all of the Internet processes we have considered, however, supply chains seem most likely to result in the most significant business process changes in the remainder of this decade.

In the 1990s when companies worked to improve their business processes, they focused on internal business processes. Their scope was largely limited to the organization diagrams that we presented in Chapter 4. And, in fact, most organizations are still focused on internal process improvements. Cutting-edge companies, however, have begun to think about creating business processes that cross organizational boundaries and create cross-business processes. There is no widely accepted name for this kind of process yet, but it is clearly larger than the value chain, as Michael Porter conceived it in the 1980s. Supply chain analysts speak of *traditional* or *internal supply chains* and *integrated supply chains.* An integrated supply chain combines the supply chain processes in several different businesses and seeks to manage them as a whole.

One of early examples of an integrated supply chain was created by Procter & Gamble and Wal-Mart. Ralph Drayer, the former VP of Customer Services at Procter & Gamble who oversaw the creation of the system, remembers Sam Walton sitting in a meeting and saying, "The way we do things is way too complicated. You should automatically send me Pampers, and I should send you a check once a month. We ought to get rid of all this negotiation and invoicing."

Several business theorists have argued that in the near future, the real competition will be between supply chains rather than individual companies. To put it a different way, to increase efficiency, companies have to move beyond their boundaries. Retailers, who are close to customers, are the first to learn about changes in customer preferences or a slowdown in purchasing. This information is exactly the information needed by all the upstream companies to improve their efficiencies. Similarly, changes in the availability of raw materials or the costs of making specific parts or products available is exactly the kind of information that upstream companies have, and it's the information that downstream companies need to make their pricing and stocking decisions.

Integrated supply chain models focus on inventory, transportation, availability of resources, and locations for manufacturing. An analysis of a typical supply chain today, taken as a whole, usually reveals that it has twice as much inventory as required, if everyone knew what everyone else knew. The problem, of course, is that everyone doesn't know what others know and thus tend to store extra inventory to avoid unforeseen problems. Inventory, of course, is a major source of expense in supply chain systems. In different words: What every retailer desires is the minimum number of items necessary to meet customer demand. What every manufacturer desires is to produce items in the highest volume possible to keep unit costs down. Inventory is the result of this conflict of interest.

Similar problems occur in transportation. The most costly transportation occurs when items must be shipped in small volume at short notice. The most efficient transportation occurs when companies can anticipate where items will be needed and ship in volume.

Just as companies have created internal supply chain models to minimize the costs while maximizing returns, integrated supply chain models can organize a complete supply chain, determining the idea flow, and locating plants and inventories in the most desirable locations. Of course it requires a bit of cooperation. We have already discussed the problems companies have endured shifting the management from functional managers to process managers. In effect, it requires a process orientation and teams that work together to create efficient processes. In the decade ahead, cutting-edge companies will work to master similar skills across large groups of companies.

Obviously, the integrated supply chain pictured in Figure 15.1 is a rather simple chain. In an actual situation, there would probably be multiple suppliers, multiple carriers, multiple distributors, and a wide variety of retailers. In addition, there might be a number of different manufacturing sites. A more accurate picture of an integrated supply chain might seem like a complex network.

Making an integrated supply chain a reality in the first place and keeping it running for everyone's mutual benefit, in the long term, requires lots of executive effort. It requires negotiations, contracts, and teams that operate outside traditional company management structures. The only way to integrate and distribute the information and assure timely decisions is to rely on software systems. Just as ERP

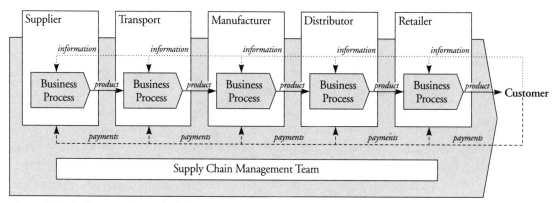

Figure 15.1 An integrated supply chain.

vendors created packaged back-office applications in the 1990s, companies like SAP and I2 are busy creating a new generation of Internet-based supply chain management (CSM) applications that will be used to manage integrated supply chains in the decade ahead.

Most companies, however, are only beginning to explore the possibilities of integrated supply chains. Instead, they are working on improving their internal supply chain processes and approaching integrated supply chain systems by means of approximations.

How Do Companies Structure Supply Chain Applications?

There are, broadly speaking, three ways that companies have approached the design of supply chain systems:

▶ *E-marketplaces.* This approach relies on a common market that an entire industry can use. The e-marketplace functions like the stock market. Companies that want to buy make bids, and companies that want to sell respond to bids they can fulfill at a given price. Someone, like NASDAQ, who sits in the middle, defines the rules and maintains the market.

▶ *Public processes.* This approach relies on two or more companies linking their internal processes via a common public process that the companies themselves develop or buy from a third party. Typically the public process is maintained by one or all of the participants.

▶ *Integrated processes.* This approach requires that two or more companies link their internal processes together, creating a new process that spans the companies. The processes of all the participants are treated as if they were simply parts of a large distributed process. This is sometimes described as integrating private processes, since each company knows how others carry on internal processing.

We have considered some of these issues before when we discussed XML-based business process languages and workflow in Chapter 11. Supply chain and other collaborative e-business systems can be developed using a variety of technologies. A company can develop an e-marketplace and offer its services to other companies, or a group of companies can join into a consortium to develop their own e-marketplace. Similarly, companies can use workflow tools or XML languages to build public processes or integrate processes. They can also use conventional software development techniques, or they can buy supply chain modules from packaged software vendors like SAP and Oracle.

SAP, for example, sells a suite of e-marketplace components or processes and includes the following in its Marketplaces category:

▶ SAPMarkets: Collaborative Demand Planning
▶ SAPMarkets: MRO Procurement
▶ SAPMarkets: Request for Information
▶ SAPMarkets: Collaborative Engineering
▶ SAPMarkets: Procurement of Direct Material
▶ SAPMarkets: Request for Quotation
▶ SAPMarkets: Collaborative Supply Planning
▶ SAPMarkets: Procurement of Direct Material with Tendering
▶ SAPMarkets: Reverse Auction
▶ SAPMarkets: Forward Auction

Figure 15.2 provides a graphical overview of the three basic design options.

E-Business Marketplaces

NASDAQ is an e-marketplace designed to facilitate the sale and purchase of stocks. As with NASDAQ, an e-marketplace requires an organization to create the application, manage it, and establish and enforce rules concerning its use. Similarly, once the Internet made the cost of developing trading systems relatively inexpensive, a number of groups decided to build e-marketplaces for specific industries.

Supply chain using e-marketplace approach

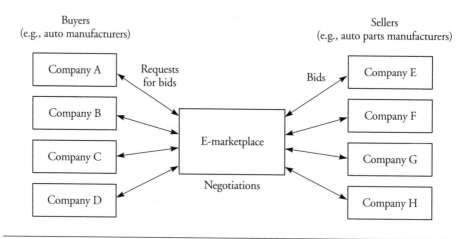

Supply chain using public process approach

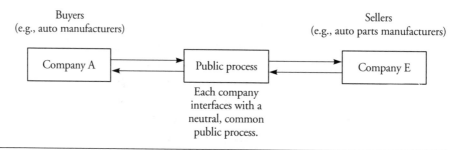

Supply chain integrating two private processes

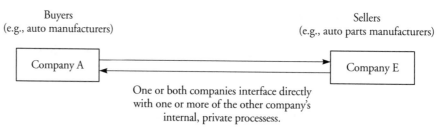

Figure 15.2 Three basic approaches to integrating supply chains or designing collaborative Web processes.

One of the first was an e-marketplace for steel. The U.S. steel market today is characterized by a number of small steel mills that produce specific types of steel in job lots. Large companies lock in major purchases with long-term contracts. At the same time, however, they often need to buy small runs of specific items—ranging from small lots of I-beams, rods, wire, or sheets, to more tailored items. It was hard for companies to determine which steel mills were available to do specific types of jobs at any given time. An e-marketplace simplified the process. Now, manufacturers needing specific types of steel can request bids, and mills with capacity and capability can bid. The steel e-marketplace functions to make the entire steel industry more efficient by facilitating communication and lowers prices by making it possible for all mills, especially smaller ones, to take part in the bidding process without spending large amounts of money to get the attention of potential buyers.

Automotive E-Marketplaces

Another well-known e-marketplace has been established by several major automakers. In the late fall of 1999, both Ford and General Motors announced that they were preparing to launch auto part exchanges or e-marketplaces in the first quarter of 2000. Both companies already had EDI systems that linked the companies to specific suppliers, so that whenever inventory drops, orders are generated. What Ford and General Motors proposed was a more generic solution. They would use the exchanges to buy parts as needed. Ford, for example, planned to conduct purchasing transactions with most of its 30,000 part suppliers via its AutoXchange system. Ford suggested that it would spend some $80 billion dollars via its exchange. At the same time, any part suppliers that are part of the Ford network would also be able to buy and sell parts to other companies on the network. Ford announced that it would be partnering with Oracle and forecast savings of 10–20% for exchange members.

General Motors announced that it intended to procure all its parts over its own exchange, TradeXchange, by the end of 2001. GM claimed that its system would cut purchase order costs from $100 an order to about $10 an order. GM was to be the major owner of the exchange and charge a fee for each transaction. GM announced that it would be partnering with Commerce One. Federal Express would handle the logistics for GM's exchange. (Commerce One announced that it would acquire CommerceBid, an auction services vendor, to acquire technology for its joint venture with GM.)

A company like TRW, which sells some $11 billion worth of parts to both Ford and GM, figured it would need to participate in both exchanges. Bill McCreary, the CIO of Pilkington Holdings, a supplier of auto glass for both GM and Ford, explained that there would be a lot of "aggressive reengineering" going on as parts companies prepare to take part in the GM- and Ford-led ventures. Clearly each parts supplier would have to build an application that can go online and participate in an exchange. They would also have to build another application to manage the various applications that were taking part in various exchanges to be sure that some eager agent doesn't sell the same parts twice, and so on. Moreover, since different protocols and techniques would likely be involved in each auto e-marketplace, parts dealers faced the prospects of creating multiple applications. The smaller parts dealers began to complain as soon as the auto companies announced their competing parts e-marketplace plans.

It isn't as if the major auto dealers had never tried to create a distributed supply chain in the past. Most of the leading parts vendors were already working with an auto company EDI system that ran over a value-added network that was integrated with their production and accounting systems. The auto EDI system is known as the Automotive Network Exchange (ANX). ANX is already supported by Ford, GM, and DaimlerChrysler and has some 300 trading partners, with another 150 more waiting to join. ANX had been developed over a 5-year period. ANX is controlled by the Automotive Industry Action Group, a nonprofit consortium that built and runs the system, and the group has indicated that it hopes to continue to offer its services.

ANX is too expensive for the small parts dealers to join, and it would be very expensive to extend it to parts dealers in remote countries. Moreover, to date, ANX has primarily been used for CAD/CAM transfers. Put another way, ANX is like all EDI systems. Since it relies on a proprietary network and specialized protocols, it was hard to create and it's even harder to change. It's hard to imagine that ANX would ever be extended to create support for the tens of thousands of vendors that the auto companies hope to support with their new Internet-based e-marketplace. On the other hand, major parts dealers have already invested years in its development. They have agreed on standardized nomenclatures for communication and have acquired the hardware and software needed to support the existing system. Now, in effect, the auto companies were asking their leading parts dealers to start to phase out ANX and move to a new system that would be based on the Internet and XML. Understandably, the leading parts dealers were upset. Few were willing to talk about ripping out mission-critical EDI systems, overnight, to help the auto companies move to competing e-marketplaces that used untested technologies.

In February 2000, the large auto companies switched direction and announced that they were negotiating to create a joint parts market. The new company was named Covisint (covisinet.com). General Motors, Ford, and DaimlerChrysler announced that they would merge their efforts and spend $200 million to build a single auto exchange that would support $50 billion in transactions in the year 2001. By merging their efforts, they could at least assure their parts dealers that they would only have to support one e-marketplace. Nissan and Renault announced that they would also join the exchange. Covisint opened temporary offices in Southfield, Michigan, but announced that it would establish offices in Europe and Japan in the future.

No sooner had the auto companies announced their new plans than rumors began to circulate that Oracle, who was working with Ford, Commerce One, who was working with GM, and SAP, who was working with DaimlerChrysler, were having lots of problems agreeing on which of them was going to provide what technologies under what kinds of licenses. It turns out that the Internet technology companies were even more competitive than the auto dealers that they had agreed to help in the first place.

Several parts dealers complained that the technology vendors were charging too much for their work and that, in the end, the new system probably wouldn't improve their profit margins nearly as much as the auto companies had originally proposed.

Figures 15.3 and 15.4 were derived from a Goldman Sachs Investment Research Report released in the spring of 2000. They suggested where savings might result from linking suppliers and automakers in a single e-marketplace.

Within a month of the announcement that the three largest U.S. auto companies would build a common auto parts e-marketplace, the U.S. Federal Trade Commission announced that it would investigate the proposed arrangement to assure itself that the e-marketplace wouldn't give the automakers undue control over prices or allow them to indirectly signal prices to each other. (The FTC was already investigating several other e-marketplaces and wanted to come up with generic rules to guide e-marketplaces owned by large companies who would be involved in the trading.) The FTC's investigation lasted throughout the summer and was only concluded in the fall of 2000. In the end, the auto companies satisfied the FTC that the marketplace would be fair, and they were given permission to proceed.

The auto companies have built a parts exchange that spans the world. They propose that parts vendors from throughout the world will be able to use the e-marketplace to respond to orders from auto factories located throughout the world. In other words, the exchange will cross dozens of different country boundaries and could easily be challenged by any of dozens of different legal entities. The

Total auto supplier savings per vehicle: $593

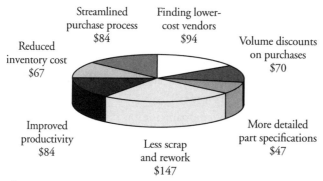

Streamlined
purchase process
$84

Finding lower-
cost vendors
$94

Reduced
inventory cost
$67

Volume discounts
on purchases
$70

Improved
productivity
$84

Less scrap
and rework
$147

More detailed
part specifications
$47

Figure 15.3 How auto suppliers can cut their costs by going online. (After Goldman Sachs Investment Research: E-Automotive Report by Gary Lapidus.)

Total automaker savings per vehicle: $368

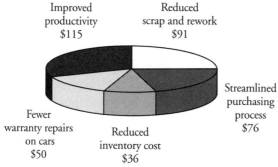

Improved
productivity
$115

Reduced
scrap and rework
$91

Streamlined
purchasing
process
$76

Fewer
warranty repairs
on cars
$50

Reduced
inventory cost
$36

Figure 15.4 Auto manufacturers save less online than suppliers. (After Goldman Sachs Investment Research: E-Automotive Report by Gary Lapidus.)

European Union, for example, might have its own fair trade concerns. Or the EU might wish to determine if various part vendors followed EU labor or safety regulations. Similarly, any country with a parts vendor participating in the exchange could decide to tax the exchange in some manner. There have already been a number of legal challenges to Internet and Web practices from a wide variety of different legal entities. The huge auto exchange, with its cross-national distribution, will be a lightning rod that will undoubtedly draw all kinds of future legal and regulatory challenges.

In the United States, at least, the auto exchange was now back on track, the fighting technology vendors were tamed, and the e-marketplace was given its first field test. On October 3, 2000, ArvinMeritor became the first company to make a deal using Covisint's exchange. ArvinMeritor is a supplier of suspension components and exhaust systems. It held a 2-hour online auction and chose a supplier for an injection-molded plastic part. It held a second auction for a related part on October 5. By the end of 2000, some 40 companies, including DaimlerChrysler, Ford, GM, Nissan, and Renault, all conducted auctions or used the collaborative product development and supply chain management tools that are included in the site.

Covisint opened the site to thousands of suppliers and other automakers on January 1, 2001. In 2002, Covisint announced that the company had done roughly $100 billion in auctions during 2001, achieving a reduction of 3% on the overall transaction costs for the deals that were done.

Keep in mind that the dot.com collapse was making many companies more cautious about Internet investments in 2001 and that the United States entered a recession as well. Many of the e-marketplaces launched at the same time as Covisint scaled back in 2000 or closed down in 2001. Like Covisint, however, the e-marketplaces that are best positioned to solve industry trading problems are still in business and growing as buyers and sellers learn of their value and how to use them.

During 2001, for example, DaimlerChrysler, Ford, General Motors, and eight other auto companies banded together to create a second procurement and supply chain trading exchange—this one for replacement parts and services. The new venture, which doesn't have a name yet, will not be part of Covisint. The new exchange will focus on providing real-time quote and catalog services for collision repair parts. The initial customers will be dealerships, fleets, and third-party collision repair shops. Eventually the exchange will be open to handle all repair and service parts and be open to any repair shop serviced by a dealership's parts department.

Chuck Rotuno, the CEO of the new joint venture, explains that automakers currently win only $30–$40 billion of the $100–$150 billion replacement parts and services business. Third-party manufacturers win the rest. Repair shops explain that they usually choose third-party manufacturers because they are cheaper and more readily available. The new dealer exchange will attempt to assure that automaker parts are easily available and hopes that consolidating orders can reduce the prices in many cases. The new exchange is owned by DaimlerChrysler, Ford, GM, and Bell & Howell, who each have 25% of the stock. The exchange was made available to dealerships and repair shops in the first quarter of 2001.

Unfortunately for the automakers, the third-party manufacturers are already selling parts by means of a similar system. An Internet startup, iStarXchange, currently links buyers and sellers of auto replacement parts. The iStarXchange system relies on I2 technology, and its e-marketplace is hosted by IBM Global Services. (For more information, check *www.iStarXchange.com.*) The iStarXchange was launched in February 2002 and hopes to capture a significant proportion of the $150 billion replacement parts business in the United States. Clearly the automotive companies are in for some competition as they get ready to roll out their replacement parts e-marketplace.

During the same period, each of the major vendors launched e-marketplaces for their dealers to facilitate the location of specific types of cars and the exchange or sale of cars among dealers. Dealers have always done this, but the exchange is much more comprehensive and makes it much easier for a dealer to quickly identify where a specific make or color of car can be found to satisfy a waiting customer.

From a process designer's perspective, the main issues are the same, no matter how the e-marketplace is constructed. One needs to be very clear about what types of products will be obtained from the marketplace and what rules will govern the purchase of such products. Then one needs to develop a procedure with automated and manual activities to interface with the e-marketplace's software.

Directly Linked Supply Chain Systems

E-marketplaces will play an important role in some industries. Most supply chain systems, however, will involve direct links between specific companies. These links will be facilitated either by indirect links via public processes, or by direct links between one company's processes, subprocesses, and activities and some other company's private, internal processes.

Links via Public Processes

If two companies don't need to know what goes on at the other company when they exchange information, they will probably elect to use public processes. In this case, each company simply has to interface to a single public process. Obviously

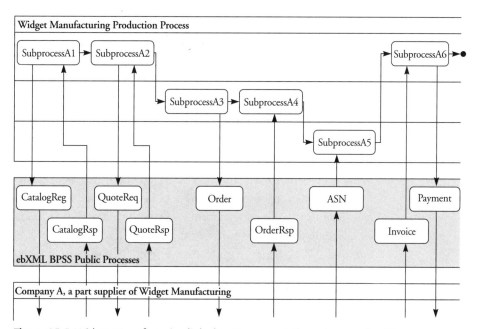

Figure 15.5 Widget Manufacturing linked to Company A through a set of public processes.

the public process may contain several subprocesses. In Chapter 11 we illustrated the ebXML public processes for business-to-business commerce (Figure 11.6). We've illustrated the ebXML BPSS public processes in Figure 15.5 using a process diagram.

The key things illustrated by Figure 15.5 are, first, that Widget Manufacturing doesn't know how Company A's processes work as they respond to inputs from Widget. All it knows is that Company A gets messages from the public processes and makes responses via the public processes, including a delivery of parts. The other important observation is that the interfaces of the public processes become inputs for Widget Manufacturing's processes.

Someone has to create the public processes and host them. It could be a consortium, or the processes could be created by Widget, by Company A, or by both working together. In any case the interfaces of the public processes are known to both companies. In the case illustrated in Figure 15.5, the public processes were developed by ebXML, an open consortium that is supported by a wide variety of companies. Assuming that Widget and Company A met and decided to use the ebXML BPSS public processes, one company or both would need to load the processes on their computer, since these are automated processes. Similarly, both companies would need to support XML, since that's the Internet protocol that ebXML

BPSS processes use to send messages. Finally, each company would need to develop software applications that would recognize messages from BPSS process modules and relay them to appropriate activities within each company.

The Widget business process design team would need to determine just which Widget processes would interface with which of the public processes and then assure that the Widget processes knew how to create the messages or interpret the responses from the BPSS processes. In most cases the Widget processes will be specified in abstract terms since they will be automatic processes created by the Widget IT department. In some cases, however, the Widget processes will interface with other processes or activities that will be manual or not part of the automated system, and those links will need to be tailored to assure that they accommodate the Widget processes that are interfacing with the BPSS processes. For example, Widget may require that a senior accountant double-check payments over a certain amount. If bills generated by the BPSS process occasionally exceed that amount, they will need to be routed to the accountant's computer for approval. The accountant will need to understand the nature of the BPSS arrangements and how to double-check them in order to do his or her job and support the supply chain system being installed in this example.

As a generalization, the main role of the business redesign team faced with a redesign driven by public processes of this nature will be to determine the business rules that will apply to each possible transaction.

Increasingly, companies will create process teams that will need to work with team members from other companies to design a public business process that both companies can use as they interact with each other. Although such designs will tend to be heavily weighted toward IT concerns, they will have business elements, and business managers will also need to be involved in negotiating what the common process will be like. From a modeling perspective, we suggest that process diagrams, like the ones we described in Chapter 5, are an excellent starting point for analyzing such joint efforts.

SAP sells a suite of supply chain management (SCM) components or processes and includes the following in its SCM category:

▶ Collaborative Planning, Forecasting, and Replenishment
▶ Collaborative Supply Management
▶ Vendor Managed Inventory
▶ Foreign Trade—Collaborative Preference Processing
▶ Foreign Trade—Importer's View
▶ Foreign Trade—Exporter's View

▶ Foreign Trade—Sanctioned Party List
▶ Proof of Delivery
▶ Plan and Process Shipments
▶ Advanced Shipping Notification
▶ Shipment Tendering
▶ Transportation Marketplace
▶ Sales and Operations Planning
▶ Supplier Managed Inventory
▶ Supply Chain Planning
▶ Collaborative Order Promising

Integrated Private Supply Chain Processes

In many cases companies will have to go beyond public processes and integrate their processes directly with the processes of another company. This will be necessary in order to make the combined process more efficient. Thus, one could use an intermediate, public process to link Widget Manufacturing and Company A, but you could create a smoother, faster overall process if you could establish a direct link between the Widget subprocess that tracked the use of Company A parts and the inventory system at Company A, so that whenever Company A parts at Widget fell below a fixed point, more could be shipped, and if there was insufficient inventory, more could be manufactured. Of course, to establish that kind of link, both Widget and Company A would need to know more about how each of their respective processes operated.

In an ideal world, Widget and Company A would have accurate process diagrams and software documentation and they would exchange them. More likely, the Widget business process redesign team would need to meet with a Company A team to work out the virtual process, creating a diagram that showed how the process would work in both companies. Then the IT groups of Widget and Company A would need to meet to work out the details so their software systems could communicate effectively.

The business process XML languages, like BPML, that we discussed in Chapter 11 are being designed to assist companies in the creation of multicompany business processes.

Coordinating public and private cross-company business process integration efforts has become a major new challenge for those engaged in architecting and documenting processes at organizations. Evidence of this is provided by the fact that today some 700 companies from throughout the world are working on a joint approach to supply chain analysis and design.

The Supply Chain Council's SCOR Approach

The Supply Chain Council (SCC) was established as a nonprofit consortium in 1996. Today, it is a worldwide organization with over 700 members. The Council conducts meetings that allow companies to gather together to discuss supply chain problems and opportunities. In addition, it has been working on a standard supply chain framework or reference model. This Supply-Chain Operations Reference (SCOR) model is, in essence, a horizontal process architecture and methodology for companies that want to develop supply chain applications. Considering the companies involved in the development of SCOR and some of the impressive applications that have been created using the SCOR reference model, any company considering developing a supply chain system should examine SCOR carefully and would probably be wise to join the Supply Chain Council.

SCOR uses its own vocabulary to describe the steps in its methodology and the elements in its process model, but the approach is largely compatible with the generic methodology we have advocated in this book.

By way of an overview, the SCC booklet *Supply-Chain Operations Reference-model: Overview of SCOR Version 5.0* describes three broad goals of the reference model as follows:

1. Capture the "as-is" state of a process and derive the desired "to-be" future state.
2. Quantify the operational performance of similar companies and establish internal targets based on "best-in-class" results.
3. Characterize the management practices and software solutions that result in "best-in-class" performance.

The SCOR reference model provides an overall architecture for supply chain systems, high-level processes and subprocesses, and management goals and measures that companies can tailor to create their individual supply chain systems.

The SCOR model is a three-level model. At the top level, SCOR defines five process types. We would say that the entire supply chain was part of a single value chain. Thus, for us, the five SCOR process types are business processes. Figure 15.6 illustrates the overview that SCOR normally uses.

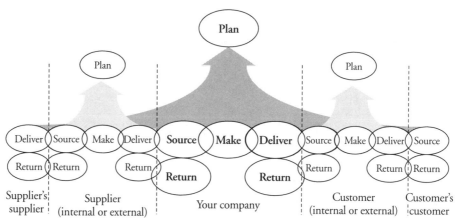

Figure 15.6 The five top-level SCOR business processes. (After the Supply Chain Council.)

What SCOR calls Plan, we would call the planning aspect of Management. SCOR associates measures with specific processes, and we would usually include them in the monitor aspect of Management. The actual core processes are Source, Make, Deliver, and Return.

SCOR defines each of the processes shown in Figure 15.6 in terms of optional subprocesses that could be included in them—and refers to the subprocesses as configuration-level process categories. It doesn't assume that every company will use all of the subprocesses. Instead, it assumes that companies will choose those subprocesses they need for their specific supply chains.

Figure 15.7 shows how SCOR conceptualizes the three levels of their reference model.

Figure 15.8 illustrates the first- and second-level SCOR model. The SCOR notation continues to use arrows until it arrives at subsubprocesses, which they call *process elements*. In Figure 15.8 we have redrawn the standard SCOR model using the notation used throughout this book.

Figure 15.7 shows the five basic SCOR process types: Source, Make, Deliver, Return, and Plan. (It also shows Enable, which isn't regarded as a process.) Each of the five basic processes include subprocesses, which SCOR calls *process categories*. Enable also includes 11 processes or databases.

The process categories Source, Make, Deliver, and Return each include three different types of process categories (or subprocesses). A designer might have a supply chain that would require different types of supplies and might have more than one Source subprocess, but it's more likely that only one subprocess would be appropriate to a given supply chain.

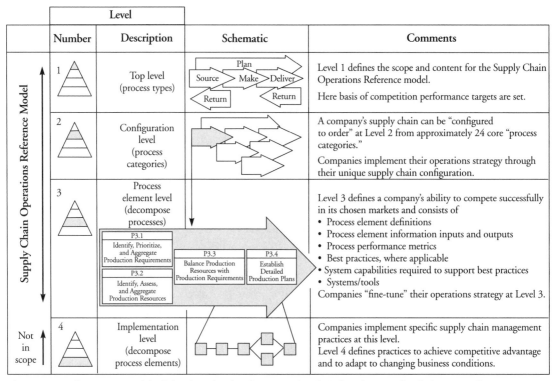

Figure 15.7 The SCOR model of the three levels of process detail. (After the Supply Chain Council.)

Planning and Management

In our opinion, by treating Plan Source and Plan Supply Chain as processes similar to Sourcing Stocked Product and Delivering Stocked Product, and associating monitoring with processes like Sourcing Stocked Product and not with Plan Source, SCOR has introduced a source of confusion. Their approach may make more sense to those planning the software systems to implement the supply chain, but it doesn't emphasize the role of management and the need for managers to monitor and take corrective actions when outputs are deficient. In fact, SCOR specifically states that they ignore training and corrective actions, which our approach to management is designed to focus upon. Hence, we prefer clustering planning and monitoring in management processes and associating them directly with the specific processes the manager controls, as we illustrate in Figure 15.9.

For those using SCOR as a source of information about how to design a supply chain system, however, our concerns are secondary. It's easy enough to see where the SCOR reference model locates the information needed and simple enough to move it as we have in Figure 15.8.

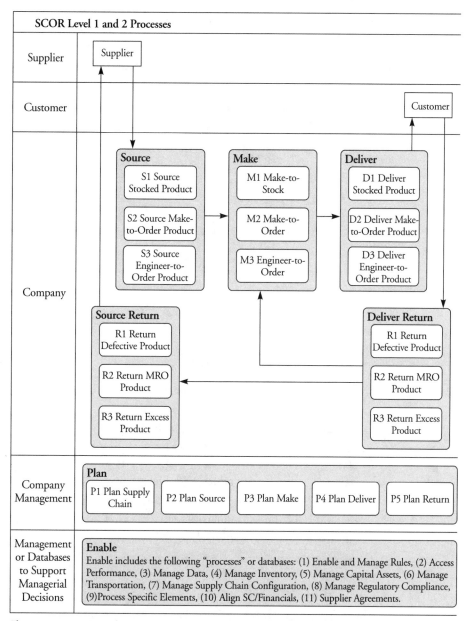

Figure 15.8 SCOR reference model with the process categories shown.

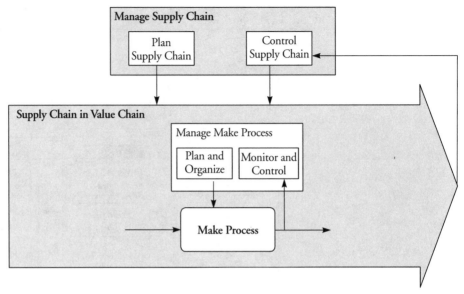

Figure 15.9 Another way of thinking about the role of planning in the SCOR methodology.

Measures and Best Practices

While SCOR may not cover all the management functions, as we prefer, it does do a nice job of defining process goals and measures and of defining benchmark information for the processes it defines. Table 15.1 provides an overview of the process goals and measures that SCOR uses for each process.

For each process category described in Figure 15.7, the SCOR model proceeds to define the next level of detail, which they refer to as process elements. At the same time, they are very precise about the inputs and outputs. What they do not specify precisely is which functional unit or manager is responsible for each process element. They show process elements as rectangles inside a large arrow, but we have converted them in Figure 15.10 to our standard notation.

The various letter-number combinations refer to other process elements defined by SCOR. SCOR distinguishes between inputs and outputs, but often isn't clear about what goes where. Thus, some of the process outputs indicated in Figure 15.9 go to the next process and some go to databases.

For each process element that SCOR has defined, it has also defined a set of measures. Thus, for the process element Schedule Product Deliveries, SCOR provides the measures in Table 15.2.

Table 15.1 SCOR Level 1 process measures. (After the Supply Chain Council.)

Process Measures	Customer-facing			Internal-facing	
	Reliability	Responsiveness	Flexibility	Cost	Assets
Delivery performance	●				
Fill rate	●				
Perfect order fulfillment	●				
Order fulfillment lead time		●			
Supply-chain response time			●		
Production flexibility			●		
Supply chain management cost				●	
Cost of goods sold				●	
Value-added productivity				●	
Warranty cost or returns processing cost				●	
Cash-to-cash cycle time					●
Inventory days of supply					●
Asset turns					●

Table 15.2 SCOR S1.1 Schedule of Product Deliveries.

Definition: Scheduling and managing the execution of the individual deliveries of product against an existing contract or purchase order. The requirements for product releases are determined based on the detailed sourcing plan or other types of product pull signals.

Measures	Metrics
Reliability	% schedules generated within supplier's lead time
	% schedules changed within the supplier's lead time
Responsiveness	Average release cycle of changes
Flexibility	Average days per schedule change
	Average days per engineering change
Cost	Product management and planning cost as a % of product acquisitions costs
Assets	None identified

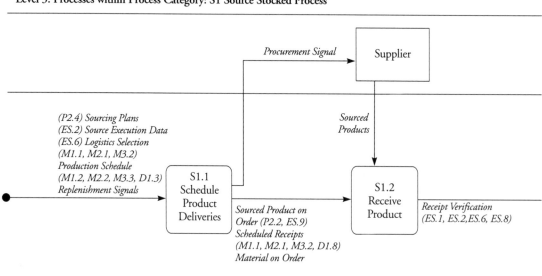

Figure 15.10 Level 3 process elements that define the Level 2 process category S1 Source Stocked Product.

SCOR also provides a list of best practices associated with each process element and metrics that show what the average company in a given industry managed to achieve against these metrics.

Among the best practices defined for S1.1 Schedule Product Deliveries are

▶ Utilize EDI transactions to reduce cycle time and costs.
▶ VMI agreements allow suppliers to manage (replenish) inventory automatically.
▶ Mechanical (Kanban) pull signals are used to notify suppliers of the need to deliver product.
▶ Consignment agreements are used to reduce assets and cycle time while increasing the availability of critical items.
▶ Advanced ship notices allow for tight synchronization between Source and Make processes.

Benchmarking SCOR Projects

In business process circles, a *benchmark* refers to a data point that one company can use to determine how well it is doing, in comparison with others in the same industry or others who undertake similar tasks. Some consulting companies that

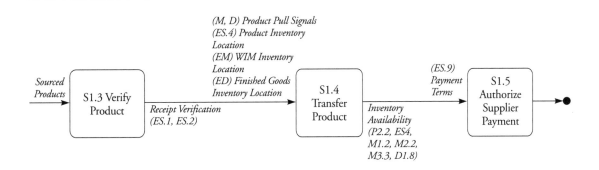

work with lots of companies within the same area gather data, compute statistical averages, and publish benchmarks. Thus, for example, a company developing a customer service process might want to know how long their competitors typically take to answer their support line phones. In most cases, good benchmarks are hard to come by. The Supply Chain Council, on the other hand, with over 700 members, is in an ideal place to gather data and generate good benchmarks for supply chain processes. The council keeps benchmarks for all of its processes and sorts them by industry. This provides companies with hard data on what kinds of savings they might be likely to obtain if they implement one or another supply chain system.

SCOR leaves the final level of analysis, which it refers to as Level 4 (Implementation Level), out of its reference model. It assumes that companies will use the SCOR model to identify process categories and elements they need and then implement them in a manner best suited to the specific company.

Several SCOR models deal with the movement of parts from suppliers to manufacturing sites to warehouses in various locations around the world. The SCOR notation provides various ways of indicating this. We prefer to use process diagrams and to label the swimlanes with the locations of various sites. If this is inconvenient, one can always put the information in the process or activity box. Figure 15.11 provides an overview of a supply chain example considered in the SCOR documentation that is widely distributed.

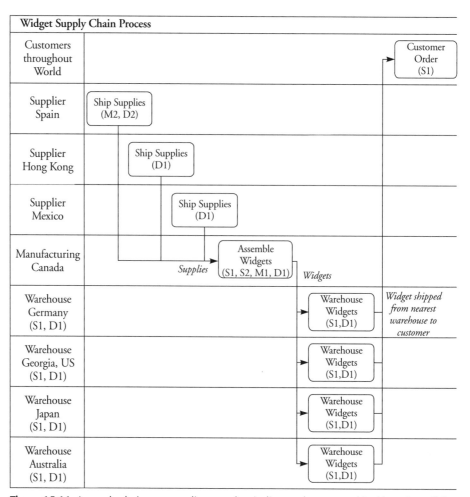

Figure 15.11 A supply chain process diagram that indicates the geographical location of the functional units.

SCC provides courses in which certified instructors teach the entire SCOR methodology and provide detailed documentation for SCOR. We describe how to obtain information on this in the Notes and References at the end of the book. In addition, several of the leading modeling tools provide implementations of the SCOR system. Starting with such a tool certainly makes it easier to quickly modify SCOR models for your company. On the other hand, most of the problems you will face will involve determining how your supply chain system should be organized and what rules will be needed. The diagrams may be less important than the ideas that simply reading about the SCOR approach will bring to mind.

Your company may or may not decide that the SCOR system is appropriate for your e-business development effort. It's hard to imagine, however, that a careful review of the SCOR approach, metrics, and performance data wouldn't give your company some good ideas about the design or improvement of a supply chain process.

Internally Oriented E-Business Redesign

Internally oriented e-business redesign patterns include all the e-business redesign efforts that aim at increasing communication with employees or managers, or providing them with information or services. It also includes a variety of applications designed to automate internal processes and to gather data and distribute it to managers who need to monitor processes. Early on, many writers referred to customer-oriented patterns as business-to-employee applications, or B2E. Historically, they have been referred to as Computer Aided Design (CAD) and Computer Automated Manufacturing (CAM) applications and groupware. Any of these older applications can usually be improved by using the Internet to link the application with other applications or sources of data. Other internally oriented applications are called e-procurement or e-ERP applications. Some CRM applications that link salespeople with sales managers or sales databases fall in this category. New workflow systems that rely on the Internet also fall in this category. Similarly, a variety of management decision-making and analysis applications can be classed here.

SAP sells several suites of applications for internal use, including:

Product Lifecycle Management

- ▶ CAD Driven Design Process
- ▶ Claim Management
- ▶ Collaborative Engineering and Project Management
- ▶ Collaborative Engineering via Marketplaces
- ▶ Collaborative Engineering with cFolders
- ▶ Customer Specific Engineering
- ▶ Document Management
- ▶ Exchanging Quality Certificate Data
- ▶ Engineering Change Management
- ▶ Environmental Vendor Managed Inventory
- ▶ New Product Development
- ▶ Order Change Management (OCM)
- ▶ PLM Data Replication in a Distributed Environment

E-Procurement

▶ Procurement of Direct Materials

▶ Procurement of Indirect Materials

Financials (ERP)

▶ Change Vendor or Customer Master Data

▶ Clear Open Items

▶ Deduction Management

▶ Payment with Advice and Clearing of Open Items at Vendor

▶ Reporting for External Business Partners

▶ SEM: Benchmark Data Collection

▶ SEM: Collaborative Planning and Performance Management

▶ SEM: Investor Relationship Management

▶ Real Estate Marketplace

▶ CFM: Foreign Exchange

▶ CRM: Central Payments

▶ Employee Self-Service Travel Management

▶ Electronic Bill Presentment and Payment

▶ CFM: External Incoming Payments

▶ CFM: Internal Payments

▶ Integration of Orbian in mySAP Financials

Human Resources (ERP)

▶ Job Exchange

▶ Benefits Marketplace

▶ Training Marketplace

▶ Talent Marketplace

▶ Services Marketplace

▶ Life Events

▶ Salary Survey Participation

▶ Salary Benchmarking Services

▶ Remote Training Registration

▶ Job Opportunities

▶ Benefits Provider

▶ Employee Self Service Travel Management

Email Systems

Most companies are firmly committed to email. The use of email has driven the growth of PCs in most companies, and leading-edge companies are rapidly approaching the point where every employee has a PC. Email, of course, is an Internet protocol, and the availability of email usually entails an Internet network at the company. Similarly, most employees access email by means of an email browser like Microsoft's Outlook Express, AOL's mail program, or Netscape's Communicator. And, while one does not require the other, most employees who have email also have a Web browser and are able to browse the Web.

As someone interested in process analysis, you might ask yourself which business process in your company uses or supports email. An easy answer would be to say it's an infrastructure service, like electricity or the telephone, and it's managed by a support group, usually the IT group. On the other hand, most business processes rely on email, just as they do phones. At its most generic, email usually functions as the most basic form of groupware used by any business process. If employees working together on the same process need to communicate or exchange information, they probably use email. If you look at most business process diagrams, however, you won't find email links on the diagram. Of course you don't see the use of phones in most process diagrams either. We tend to take infrastructure for granted.

We considered marking some very detailed process diagrams to show where the information passed was transmitted by phones or by email and decided it wasn't worth it. Still, it's worth thinking about how email is different from phone systems. It can certainly be used like a phone to transmit messages between two individuals. But it can also be used by a manager to send a message to everyone in a unit, or by a process manager to transmit a questionnaire to everyone working on a single business process. It can also be used to forward a senior manager's message or a customer complaint to everyone in the company.

We won't say more about email at this point, precisely because it is an infrastructure issue rather than a process technology as such, but in leaving, we suggest that it is making it possible for companies to wire together processes, customers, and suppliers in more complex networks than ever existed in the past, and it will certainly change the nature of process designs in the future.

Employee Portals

Employee portals and other internal company portals work just like portals for customers. They provide a Web address that employees can go to in order to find information or to transact certain kinds of business. In effect, they provide a new, and in many cases better, way to access processes. Human resources groups, in the past, have used various techniques to explain employee benefits, vacation policies, and pension plans. They have usually relied on paper forms to document employee requests for vacations and changes in their benefit fund allocations. Today, most of this is handled online by employees who link directly to the employee portal. As a generalization, employee benefits are not a value-added activity for customers. They are necessary to support employees, but they aren't unique from company to company. Thus, if they can be done by ERP applications, or via the Web, more efficiently and less expensively than previously, then it's an advantage.

Decision Support

In the past, when a manager needed information in order to make a decision, he or she asked a subordinate for it. In some cases the subordinate was a manager who gathered data from his or her subordinates and tabulated it in order to provide an answer for the boss. In other cases whole teams of employees were set to work gathering and collating information in order to provide an answer. In the recent past, data was placed in databases and accessed by means of programs that made database queries easy. Similarly, programs were designed to generate reports on demand. All of the software systems used to facilitate this kind of activity are collectively known as *decision support systems*. Over the past decade these systems have been getting better, and increasingly companies are able to eliminate the middle managers who formerly gathered and summarized information. Today, sensors input production line information, which is then summarized by software applications and converted into reports for senior managers. Today, a senior manager can go to a company Web site that provides tools that allow the data to be queried and arranged to facilitate decisions.

A nice example of this is provided by a system developed by United Artists. In the past, when they wondered about marketing issues, a team would develop a survey or plan experiments and then delegate employees to carry them out. In the mid-1990s, United Artists installed a system that let marketing people sit at a terminal and design an experiment. The marketing manager might wonder, for example, if teenagers were as sensitive to price increases as older moviegoers. To test this, the manager could quickly check all United Artists theaters and identify those theaters showing films targeted for teenagers and others showing films targeted for older viewers. Next, with the system's help, the marketing manager could select 10 theaters in each category and send a message to the managers of the respective theaters for changes in the price of soft drinks or specific types of candy. By increasing the cost of an item by a penny or two at some theaters and not at others, one could devise an experiment that would answer the question. Since the United Artists theaters' cash registers automatically send data to a central computer, the marketer could gather daily sales information for the following two weeks and reach conclusions about potential systemwide changes. In other words, because of the links between computers and the fact that the marketing manager had a decision support system that could access theater programs and analyze statistical data, a single marketing manager was now in a position where he or she could run experiments in a matter of weeks, while sitting at a desk in the corporate office, that formerly required a half dozen people to coordinate and evaluate.

Email, the Internet, and the Web are all being integrated with decision support tools and databases to create ever more powerful decision support systems. Organizations are being flattened as managers at the top of organizations increasingly interface, electronically, with employees facing customers across counters. Equally important, the Internet and more powerful computers are making it possible for companies to gather data many times a day, making it possible to refine or change decisions on an hourly or daily basis.

Many business process gurus have suggested business process dashboards. The idea here is that one creates a model of a business process and ties the measures one takes of activities or subprocesses and displays that information on dials or other devices similar to those a driver might see in a modern car dashboard. In this case a process manager might monitor an entire process as quickly and as frequently as he or she might check the stock market to see what selected stocks are doing.

It will take awhile for this to happen in many companies, but leading-edge companies that compete on price and are very sensitive to the efficiency of their key production processes are already moving in this direction. Increasingly, business process redesign and improvement teams will be asked to design measures for processes and go beyond that and design systems to collect and collate the measurement data for senior management.

Business Intelligence

Business intelligence (BI) refers to a collection of software techniques that can be used to analyze data to identify patterns. In some cases the systems simply do what a person might do, but much faster. In other cases the systems can find patterns that very few people would be able to detect. In many cases these systems are used on conventional databases. For example, a department store might record each sale via a cash register system that scanned each customer's purchases. Later, the store might ask if people who normally bought soft drinks also bought potato chips. By reviewing the purchase records, a BI system could answer such a question. That, in turn, might lead stores to rearrange their shelves so that soft drinks were closer to potato chips to make it even more likely that customers might combine those purchases.

When a customer accesses a portal to check for information or to buy something, or when a company interacts with suppliers online, data on each online event can be recorded. This can create huge amounts of data. Imagine that thousands of customers visit your company Web site each day and each generates hundreds of bytes of information, which is all placed in a database. Some companies don't bother to gather this data because it accumulates so fast and is so hard to understand. Once again, a BI system can be used to examine the data and identify patterns. Perhaps a significant percentage of the customers who buy red widgets also buy widget oil. The Widget Company could modify its Web site to have a pop-up window open whenever a customer bought a red widget to ask if the customer would also like to buy oil. This kind of research is undertaken by companies that want to design user-friendly Web sites. If you want a good example of this kind of thing, you need only shop at Amazon.com, an online retailer that sells books, CDs, and many other things. Amazon is always tracking what its customers do. It recommends books similar to books you have purchased recently. It recommends CDs that people who bought the same books also bought, and so forth. These systems aren't perfect, but they can go a long way toward making customers think that the company really is trying hard to please them.

Knowledge Management

Knowledge management means very different things, depending on whom you ask. We'll use it to refer to software systems that encode knowledge that people need to do their jobs and that display knowledge or recommend actions on demand. Increasingly companies are trying to be more efficient in capturing knowledge and making it available to employees charged with making decisions.

Let's begin with three definitions:

▶ *Data* refers to specific items, like 5 and NO.
▶ *Information* refers to propositions (or tables) that link data into meaningful patterns. Thus, the sentence "Only 5 parts in shipment 18 were defective" is information.
▶ *Knowledge* is sets of propositions, linked together to form rules. Rules suggest evaluations or actions.

Thus, the proposition "Only 5 parts in shipment 18 were defective" is just information. But the set of propositions

> If more than 2 parts in any given shipment are defective,
> then the unit producing the shipment should suspend shipments until the cause of the defect is identified and corrected

is knowledge.

Historically databases have stored data and information. Software applications use rules and hence contain a limited amount of knowledge. Humans, however, do things systems can't do today because they can evaluate large amounts of information and then use knowledge to make decisions and take actions.

Knowledge management systems aim at capturing the knowledge used to perform company activities.

In the 1980s, many companies tried to build expert systems—software systems that used knowledge to automate decisions. Some very powerful systems were built, and some are still in use today. Credit decisions at American Express and at other credit card companies are initially screened by such systems. Expert systems failed to be as extensively used as their promoters hoped, however, for a very simple reason. Knowledge is very hard to collect, and it changes very rapidly. People are constantly learning. Experts read books and go to conferences to learn the latest ways of solving problems. People talk together at lunch and suddenly realize that, because they installed a new system yesterday, they can now change another activity and be more efficient. Today, companies are more likely to focus on trying to collect knowledge and make it available for employees than to use it to automate decision making.

Once again, email and the Web are making it easier to gather knowledge and make it available for employees who need it.

It's easier to talk about e-business processes that focus on customers or suppliers. It's harder to think about how the Internet will be used to improve internal processes because they are so pervasive. Every business process team that tries to improve a major process in this decade, however, is going to change aspects of the process to take better advantage of email and the Web, and will use the ability of these communication media to let employees access data, information, and knowledge from throughout the company and beyond.

Using Processes to Organize Knowledge Management, Decision Support, and Training

Decision support is usually a concern of IT. Knowledge management may be a concern of IT or of human resources. Training and job design are usually concerns of human resources. A business process redesign or a mature process architecture provides a way of organizing all these efforts.

Rather than thinking of knowledge management in the abstract, focus on the knowledge that is required to handle a specific activity or process. Some of that knowledge will involve knowing company policies. Some involves knowing the business rules required to make decisions required during the process. Some of it may involve knowing what data to access or what software applications are available to aid in the performance of specific activities.

Decision support systems also involve knowing the policies and rules that apply to specific activities and having access to data used by or generated by the activity. Training development requires an analysis of the activities that need to be performed, and a knowledge of the policies employees must follow and the rules that employees must use to make required decisions.

Suffice it to say that all of these types of analysis overlap, but the results are usually stored in different ways in different databases. A better-organized company that has a well-established process architecture is in the position to store all the information about the Setup Process in a single location, or at least to cross-reference data, information, and knowledge about the Setup Process so that anyone interested in that specific process can access the data in an efficient manner.

Obviously organizing corporate data, information, and knowledge around processes and activities will take time and require changes in the way different departments and groups think about what their responsibilities are. In the long run, this will be one of the benefits of the Internet and the evolving corporate network. In time, as people increasingly organize around processes, all the data, information, and knowledge about the process will tend to be stored together to facilitate future changes or improvements in the process or activity.

Figure 15.12 suggests how different systems, like knowledge management, decision support, and training, keep overlapping information about a Setup Process.

An E-Business Is a Network

As a summary of our discussion of e-business, we want to return to a point we made early in Chapter 14. The Internet will increasingly serve as the nervous system of your company and eventually reach out to integrate your business processes with other companies' processes. It makes no difference where you start; as you use the Internet and its associated technologies to develop more efficient processes, you will find yourself moving from customer links to supplier links to employee links and back again. As you do this you will find your older ideas about processes being relaxed. Processes will seem less and less like sequences that begin and end and more and more like a nervous system that responds to external stimuli by reconfiguring the entire corporate system in order to respond effectively. Few companies have begun to explore the implications of this kind of integration. For

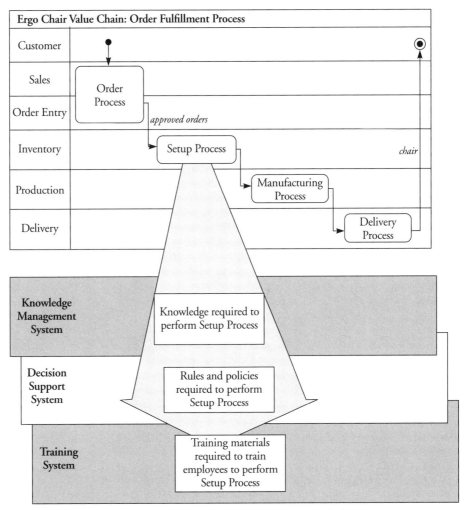

Figure 15.12 Business processes can be the way to organize knowledge management, decision support, and training efforts.

today, most companies have their agendas full analyzing and improving their existing processes and incorporating Internet elements to solve obvious needs.

As time goes on, however, we will come to realize that the whole company is a single process, and the Internet will be the network that we must study to understand how it is all tied together.

In the meantime, we recommend that IT and more technically inclined managers study a book written by an IBM group that has focused on different kinds of e-business processes. The book, written by Jonathan Adams, Srinivas Koushik, Guru

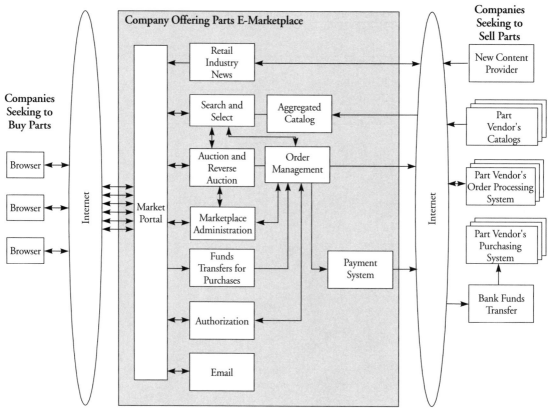

Figure 15.13 An overview of the process architecture of a company that provides e-marketplace services. (After Adams et al., *Patterns for E-Business.*)

Vasudeva, and George Calambos, is *Patterns of E-Business: A Strategy for Reuse,* and it largely focuses on issues involved in building today's e-business applications. Focus as you read it, however, on the fact that they use a single case study throughout the book and note how each new system just becomes an extension of the previous system. In the end, drawing arbitrary lines between the customer application and the supply chain application is just an exercise in nomenclature and doesn't alter the fact that the applications stretch throughout the company.

Near the end of the book, the IBM team considers a new company case study, a startup company that creates an e-marketplace system for an industry. Figure 15.13 provides the final diagram that the IBM authors use to show how the company is structured.

Both the buyer and the seller interact with the e-marketplace over the Internet. The sellers provide information, usually in the form of links to their databases or applications, to the e-marketplace so it can make the information available to potential buyers. The buyers access the site via a portal that presents options to them. The company doesn't offer a classic company portal—it offers an e-marketplace that companies can come to when they want to bid for parts. Yet it is a portal and it's the essence of the business the company provides. And it's linked to parts companies so that buyers can obtain information about the parts the various sellers have on offer. It's easy to imagine how the company might be broken up into departments or business processes, but in fact it's a single value chain and all of the processes are integrated via the Internet into a web. We suggest that as we move into the future, more and more companies are going to look like this. As we modify our processes today to incorporate Internet applications, we are taking the first steps toward this more integrated type of organization.

PART VII

PUTTING IT ALL TOGETHER

CHAPTER 16 DESCRIBES a process redesign effort that takes place at an office furniture manufacturer, Ergonomic Systems. We'll follow the management and the business process team as they modify Ergonomic's order fulfillment system, using the methodology, diagrams, and worksheets we have introduced in this book.

In this book, we have described techniques that can all be executed with a pencil and a sheet of paper. Chapter 17 discusses software tools that can make a business process redesign or improvement effort a lot simpler. We will consider the types of tools that are available, and then see how such tools could have helped us on the Ergonomics Systems case.

16

The Ergonomic Systems Case Study

THE ERGONOMIC SYSTEMS, INC. CASE STUDY is hypothetical. We did not want to describe problems associated with any specific client. At the same time, we wanted a case that would give us an opportunity to cover the full range of techniques we have discussed in this book. Thus, we created a case study that blends the characteristics and problems faced by several companies we have worked with in the past several years. (We've never worked with an office furniture company.) With those qualifications, we have tried to make the case study as realistic as possible so that readers will get a good idea of the problems they will face when they seek to implement the concepts and techniques we have described.

We will consider the case study in four parts. First, we will consider how the strategy committee of Ergonomic Systems analyzed their position in the market and arrived at a new position and new goals for the company. Next, we will consider the redesign effort that Ergonomic Systems undertook. To simplify our discussion, we will focus on the redesign of the key Ergonomic Systems Ergo Chair Value Chain. We will also consider how Ergonomic Systems redesigned their Ergo Chair management system to support the new process design. Finally, we'll comment on the actual transition process and the implementation of the new Ergo Chair process at the company.

Ergonomic Systems, Inc.

Ergonomic Systems, Inc. is a midsize company with sales of approximately $646 million in 2000. It is a subsidiary of a larger company, but it operates independently, and we'll focus only on Ergonomic Systems in this study. The company was initially built around a new design for executive office chairs for high-tech environments. The Ergo Chair is a chair especially designed for executives who spend a significant proportion of their time interacting with computers. It's comfortable, has an impressive appearance, and has proved popular with high-tech companies throughout the 1990s. The company has since created a number of other more specialized lines of Ergo Chairs. Recently it has also begun to sell "office environments"—modular units that can be assembled into work areas with features especially useful for workers who are using computers. Indeed, in a major reorganization just after it was acquired in 1999, it changed its name from Ergonomic Chairs to Ergonomic Systems to emphasize its commitment to provide complete office environments and not just chairs.

In addition to chairs and modular office units, the company sells a variety of other high-tech office products, including some desk lamps and several devices to hold and connect computer systems together and power them up or down with a single switch. Throughout the 12-year life of the company, the executive chair line has always been the company's best-known product line. Since 1999, however, the company has begun to reposition itself as an office systems company, stressing its ability to create entire office suites. Meanwhile, larger, more established office furniture companies have introduced lines of executive chairs that have many of the features of the Ergo Chair, and the competition has begun to cut into Ergonomic Systems' growth.

Figure 16.1 provides an organization chart that shows how Ergonomic Systems is organized. It has functional departments, which are subdivided into North American and European groups, and it has vice presidents for each of the company's three major value chains. All VPs and SVPs shown in Figure 16.1 are on the executive committee, along with the CEO. Three of them, including the heads of marketing, engineering and design, and finance, are also on the strategy committee, which has its own research staff. Three others, including the VPs for engineering and design and IT, are on a technology subcommittee that is charged with exploring the latest technological options. The business process architecture committee includes the three VPs for product lines and the head of IT.

Ergonomic Systems is a process-oriented company and has been since before it was acquired. The company did Business Process Reengineering (BPR) in the mid-1990s and uses a variety of ERP applications they acquired in the late 1990s. It has a matrix organization in which business line managers are responsible for processes, while departmental managers are responsible for activities performed by people in their departments. Ergonomics' business process efforts have recently

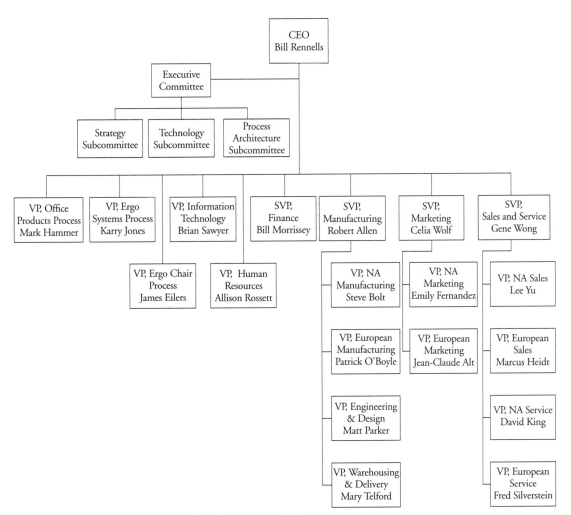

Figure 16.1 High-level organization chart for Ergonomic Systems.

been revitalized as the company begins to think about how its processes will be changed by the Internet.

Figure 16.2 provides an overview of the company's process architecture. Ergonomic has three value chains, each divided into major business processes. The various support processes, like IT and human resources, aren't shown in the diagram.

Ergonomic Systems manufactures and sells a high-quality line of office chairs and system modules. They are well regarded in the industry and by high-tech companies and have won several awards for their products. An Ergo Chair has

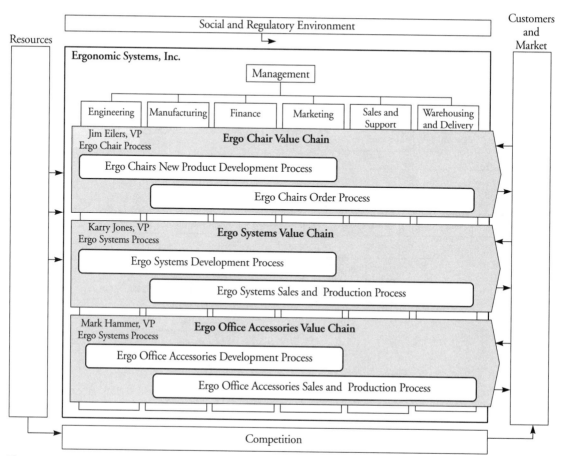

Figure 16.2 Process architecture diagram for Ergonomic Systems.

been acquired by the San Francisco Museum of Modern Art for its permanent design collection. The company charges a premium price for its products. The company believes that it has about 5% of the market for business and institutional furniture in the United States and slightly less in Europe. The company's sales grew by 5% last year—during a period in which the Business and Institutional Furniture Manufacturers Association (BIFMA) reported that total U.S. sales grew by 4.4 percent. Ergonomic Systems hopes its office systems products will allow it to continue modest growth. The company's overall strategy, however, is not to become a dominant vendor, but to remain a specialized, high-quality vendor that can maintain a high profit margin. Ergonomic Systems currently has the highest after-tax return on net sales in the industry—12.4%. It has consistently

Organization Goals and Measures Worksheet			
For the Organization as a Whole			
Organization Goals	Measures	Desired Performance	Actual Performance
Ergonomic Systems will sell the best-designed and manufactured office systems for high-tech environments. Our products will consistently command the best prices for high-tech office and industrial settings. We will maintain the highest profit margins in the industry. We will maintain modest growth.	Comparison of sale price of Ergo Chair and two closest competitors After-tax return on net sales Sales growth judged by BIFMA and EuroFMA	Our products will sell for at least 5% more than competitive products. Our after-tax returns on net sales will exceed 10%. Our growth in chairs will be 3% NA and 5% Europe. Our growth in office systems will be 5% NA and 8% Europe.	Results, Fiscal Year 1999: Our products sold for 5.6% more than competitive products. Our profit margins were 12.4%. Our growth in chairs was 4.3% in North America and 4.7% in Europe. Our growth in office systems was 5.2% in North America and 9.3% in Europe.
As Assigned to Specific Value Chains or Processes			
Value Chain	Assigned Goals	Measures	Desired Performance	Actual Performance
Ergo Chair Value	Best-designed chairs Command best price Maintain highest margins Maintain growth goals	Design reviews Sale price comparisons Profit margins Sales growth	Win design competitions, mentions in design press. Chairs will sell for at least 5% more than competitive products. Our profit margins will exceed 80%. Our growth in chairs will be 3% NA and 5% Europe.	New Ergo Conference Chair won gold star in Business Week design awards. Original Ergo Executive Chair added to SF MOMA design collection and given award. Results, Fiscal Year 1999: Our chairs sold for an average of 6.8% more than competitive chairs. Our profit margins were 89%. Our growth in chairs was 4.3% in North America and 4.7% in Europe.
Office System Value				
Office Accessories Value Chain				

Figure 16.3 Existing Ergonomic Systems goals and measures worksheet.

paid its stockholders the highest dividends of any BIFMA member for the past six years.

Figure 16.3 illustrates a worksheet that the executive committee completed at the end of last year, after reviewing Ergonomic Systems' strategy, goals, and performance as part of an annual review.

An E-Business Strategy

When the Internet first burst on the business world in the late 1990s, Ergonomic Systems, Inc. initially decided to ignore it. They had always stressed sales through distributors and targeted ads in high-tech magazines and thought it unlikely that they could sell their expensive chairs online. Within two years, however, they realized they had made a serious mistake. Their leading customers were companies that rapidly adopted new computer technologies and were willing to buy expensive systems online. In fact, they soon began to insist on buying online. In 1999 the Ergonomic strategy committee proposed that Ergonomic Systems make a major effort to transition to an e-business company.

Ergonomic Systems' CEO, Bill Rennells, rejected the initial strategy committee note about e-business and sent a memo to all of the members of the executive and strategy committees. In essence, Rennells said:

> Your e-business proposal sounds too much like a popular magazine article that argues that we must all become e-business companies or die. I don't run a company that responds to fads like that. This company is driven by a strategy and by specific goals derived from that strategy. At the moment, our strategy calls for us to sell well-designed, premium-priced office systems to companies whose workers spend a lot of time using computers. We have a well-developed and loyal group of distributors and I'm not sure how using the Internet would play with them. If the Internet or any related technologies can help us achieve our goals more effectively or more efficiently, I'm all for considering how to use them. If we need to have a Web site to sell to our customers, I'm certainly in favor of that. But I don't want to adopt technology for its own sake, or just because other companies are. I'm certainly not interested in changing this company from an office systems vendor into an "e-business company"—whatever that is. We've put a lot of effort into refining our market position and integrating our processes so that they efficiently generate our products. Please reconsider your report carefully, and only resubmit it when you can show how the Internet can help us implement our overall business strategy.

For a while nothing was done because this happened just before talks were initiated that led to Ergonomic Chairs being acquired and repositioned as Ergonomic Systems. Adding new lines kept everyone busy. In 2000, however, even Bill Rennells had become concerned about the Internet. Key distributors had begun to tell Ergonomic Systems that they wanted to buy and obtain information online. This time it was the executive committee that asked the strategy committee to review Internet and Web technologies in the light of what customers were asking for and competitors were doing and make suggestions about how these new technologies might result in an implementation of the company strategy.

Since the Internet was deemed both a strategic issue and a technological issue, the two subcommittees met together to analyze the potential of the technology and how any use of it might support or change the company's strategy.

The Joint Subcommittee's Review of E-Business

As requested, the joint subcommittee met, assigned research to staff, reviewed the results, and prepared a new report on the opportunities and threats posed by the Internet, Web, and online business activity.

The subcommittee began its report by reviewing the company's existing goals and concluding that none of them would need to be altered in any major way. The goal would still be for Ergonomic Systems to focus on the quality producer and premium-price niche in the office chairs market. The Internet and associated technologies would enable the company to better implement its existing strategy, however, by providing better service to some customers while simultaneously improving the coordination of internal process and developing tighter and more efficient relationships with suppliers. By selling online, the subcommittee suggested that margins and growth could be improved. By modifying the Ergo Chair business process, the subcommittee argued that Ergonomic Systems could save money and thereby increase profit margins. The subcommittee projected that growth could be increased in North America from the current target of 3% to 4%. At the same time, they suggested that sales order cycle time could be reduced by an average of 3 days. All of these assumptions were based on the root assumption that they would be selling 25% of their chairs via the Internet by the end of the year. Online sales of 25% is high for a company switching to the Internet, but several of their key distributors had already indicated that they would switch to Internet orders. In addition, the company decided to reach beyond its distributors and try for direct, or individual, small business sales.

The report noted that everyone was talking about the recent bankruptcies of several dot.com companies, but it also pointed out that Ergonomic has lost two major distributors as a result of Ergonomics' lack of an Internet sales system. It also pointed out that all their leading competitors were continuing to develop their Web sites and stressing online sales, in spite of the dot.com crash. Finally, the report stressed that a survey suggested that the company's image as a company that sold high-tech products to high-tech companies was being undermined by its lack of a Web site.

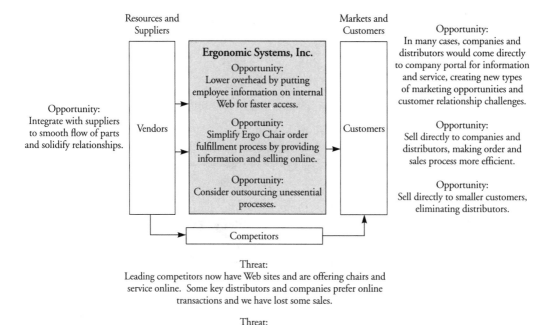

Figure 16.4 Threats and opportunities facing Ergonomic Systems.

The strategy committee summarized the opportunities and threats they perceived in Figure 16.4. They realized that some of the opportunities and threats cut across process lines, while others were more specific to the Ergo Chair process that they had been tasked to examine in more detail.

The strategy committee also prepared an opportunities and threats worksheet (Figure 16.5) and wrote a report that explained their findings and suggested initiatives in keeping with the company's strategy. In effect, they urged several changes in the company strategy, although not in the company's overall focus.

Ergonomic Systems Adopts Some New Goals

Two days after Ergonomic Systems' CEO received the report and recommendations of the strategy committee, he scheduled a special meeting of the executive committee. Bill Rennells asked all of the heads of the company's departments who are members of the executive committee, as well as a number of technical specialists, to join him at a nearby resort where they would be isolated from other concerns during the course of their 3-day meeting.

A week later, with everyone gathered at the resort, Mr. Rennells began the meeting by asking Matt Parker, the head of the strategy committee, to summarize their recommendations. Following that, given that so many of the recommendations involved the use of information systems, Rennells asked Bryan Sawyer, the VP of IT, to add any comments.

Matt Parker, the head of the strategy committee, began by emphasizing what he considered the main points. There were, he argued, two key things to consider. First, some distributors were buying online, and many more were considering it. Second, the Internet made it possible to increase productivity by improving the flow of communications and data within the company and between the company and its suppliers. He went on to say that several customers, office wholesalers and end users who had previously bought chairs from the company, had inquired about buying online. Second, he pointed out that human resources was now getting more email requests for information about employee pension, health, and benefit plans than phone calls or memos. Next, he pointed out that there was a move afoot by several of the parts vendors who supplied Ergonomic Systems to create an online e-market for ordering parts. He also pointed out that their main competitors, the larger office equipment manufacturers, had introduced Web sites and seemed to be moving to selling online. Finally, he explained that, when marketing and sales costs, discounts, and commissions were added together, it currently cost Ergonomic 22% to sell a $700 chair. By making some assumptions about the cost of doing business over the Internet, he estimated that it would only cost 12% to market and sell a chair online.

At this point the meeting broke up into a heated discussion as different managers challenged Mr. Parker's assumptions. Gene Wong, the head of sales, argued that he was ignoring the fact the most sales were bulk sales and that, in any case, the overhead for maintaining the sales force couldn't be cut the way Parker proposed, since most sales would still come from sales calls and the cost of the sales infrastructure would be almost the same, even if online sales eliminated 20% of the sales force.

Brian Sawyer, the VP of information technology, suggested that if the company was really going to embrace the Internet, it should probably consider pushing direct sales to individuals, something it didn't do at that point. Moreover, he suggested that if they did begin to sell online, they might get more sales overseas and that would create lots of shipping problems that they didn't currently face.

In response to questions about the costs and problems of supporting online sales, Mr. Sawyer explained that they wouldn't be that great. Ergonomic didn't have a very extensive product line, and it wouldn't require a very elaborate

Organization Opportunities and Threats Worksheet				
Supersystem	Opportunities	Problems/Threats	Action Required	Value Chains or Processes Involved
Customers, Distributors, and Markets	B2C: Improve support to customers that want to use Web and email. B2C: Acquire new customers that will buy online. B2C: Reduce costs of providing support to customers by using email and putting support materials online.	B2C: Losing customers by not providing online access. B2C: Reduce costs of providing support to customers by using email and putting support materials online. B2C: What do we do about shipping single chairs to individuals or small companies? B2C: How much will it cost to produce single chairs on demand?	Major revision of Ergo Chair Value Chain/Order Process to incorporate a Customer Portal or Web site.	Ergo Chair Value Chain/Order Process
Suppliers	B2B: Improve efficiency and smoothness of supply chain system by extending it to all suppliers (reduce inventory). B2B: Improve costs by eliminating existing EDI system. B2B: Make it possible to adjust more quickly to requests for small runs. B2B: Link in key suppliers with supply chain coupled with a more efficient, automatic payment system.	B2B: How do we convert all suppliers to a common set of standards to describe parts?	Major revision of Ergo Chair Value Chain/Order Process/Manufacturing Subprocess to incorporate a Supply Chain System that links Ergonomic Systems to all first and second tier suppliers.	Ergo Chair Value Chain/Order Process

Figure 16.5 Opportunities and threats worksheet for Ergonomic Systems.

application to support online sales. He pointed out that most of Ergonomics' software applications had been created by outside vendors and that they were now offering links to the Internet. In addition, other vendors offered packages that Ergonomic could use to develop a Web presence with a minimum of fuss. He suggested that the company could be ready to sell online within 6 months, if they really decided they wanted to move in that direction. At the same time, he urged the group to consider that they might get a greater return by simplifying their supply chain systems and integrating their existing production system using the Internet.

The VP of marketing, Celia Wolf, argued that Ergonomic was experiencing growing difficulties in expanding their customer base. She argued that the problems resulted partly from their high-end positioning and partly from the fact that the wholesalers they dealt with were increasingly favoring contracts with the larger

Organization Opportunities and Threats Worksheet (continued)				
Supersystem	Opportunities	Problems/Threats	Action Required	Value Chains or Processes Involved
Competition		B2C: Leading competitors already offer online sales and have taken key customers. B2B: Leading competitors have already started to link with suppliers and may develop better relationships with our key suppliers. B2B2C: Some of our systems suppliers may begin to sell directly to potential clients, undercutting our prices.	See above.	Ergo Chair Value Chain/Order Process
Resources and Technologies				
Government Regulation and Social Trends				
Organizational Improvements and Operational Efficiencies	B2E: Employee Web site: Provide more information to employees while reducing cost of doing so. B2E: Email: Make it possible for everyone in the company to communicate more efficiently. B2E: Email: Make it possible for management to get information more quickly.	B2E: Email: Company is less secure if company doesn't get involved and set standards and create firewalls for employees already using email.	Develop company-wide email system. Develop a new email-based management information system for Ergo Chair/Order Process. Develop Human Resources Internal Portal or Web site. Create groups in IT to support internal and external portals and company-wide email system.	Ergo Chair Value Chain/Order Process Human Resources Support Process Management Process IT Support Process

office equipment companies that could offer them packaged deals across entire lines of office furniture. If they wanted to maintain their current positioning, Ms. Wolf argued, they needed to find a way to significantly increase their market. She suggested that a major move into the European market and sales to individuals who work at home were both priorities. Moreover, she believed that both could be significantly helped by an Internet presence and online sales.

The discussion raged for most of the entire first day. In the late afternoon, Mr. Rennells and the managers created a list of topics to try to resolve and set up groups that would work on each topic during the evening and the following morning. Tomorrow afternoon, after they had heard from the various groups, they would pull everything together, identify action items, and prioritize them.

Without following the twists and turns of the next 24 hours, suffice it to say that by the afternoon of the following day the executive committee had decided to embrace the Internet. They concluded that they wouldn't try to completely change the company overnight, but that they would prepare to support four changes in the way the company did business.

1. They would create a portal that would allow customers and prospects to contact the company via the Web. On the portal they would provide information about the firm, a product catalog, the ability to order either wholesale or retail, and support for products. They decided to initially only support the sale of Ergo Chairs on the Web and only sell chairs online to those who paid in advance or had established credit lines.

2. They would create a new supply chain system with all first-tier Ergo Chair parts suppliers. The supply chain would be linked to the existing production system so that it would automatically generate orders as supplies dropped. The system would also be linked to the company's accounting system so that payments would be transferred to vendors as soon as new parts arrived.

3. They would examine their Ergo Chair Value Chain to see where they could improve productivity by relying more heavily on the Internet, and they would begin offering chairs for sale online, via a portal that would also provide marketing information and service support.

4. In addition, they decided to create an internal employee Web site that human resources would manage, to make it easier for employees to obtain information from human resources.

The executive committee decided that the highest priority goal was to develop a portal and begin selling to selected distributors on the Web. Given the key role of the Ergo Chair Value Chain in achieving this goal, the executive committee decided to set up a task force to review the entire process by which chairs were manufactured, sold, and delivered. In effect, they decided that they were going to redesign the Ergo Chair Order Fulfillment process, and in the process they were going to design and integrate a portal into that process. They also decided they weren't in a position to decide how much change the production process could absorb without thinking about it in a lot more detail. Jim Eilers, the VP of the Ergo Chair Process, was designated sponsor of the Ergo Chair redesign effort. He was asked to create a business process redesign task force that would be charged with developing several alternative options and estimating the risk and disruption involved in each and then report back. This task force was to pay special attention to the portal the company would develop to sell chairs online.

Separate task forces would be charged with planning the changes in human resources and in planning the new supply chain system.

To help Eilers with the Ergo Chair Value Chain redesign effort, Mr. Rennells appointed several members of the executive committee to serve on a steering team to oversee and evaluate the proposed changes.

Phase 1: Planning for the Redesign of the Order Process

The day after the executive committee concluded its meeting, James Eilers phoned David Sutton. He'd met Dr. Sutton when he'd headed production at Computec, Inc. several years ago. Computec had completely redesigned its Order Fulfillment Process with Dr. Sutton's help, and Mr. Eilers remembered how smooth and systematic the effort had been. Eilers wasn't at all sure this effort would be as smooth, since the Internet seemed to impact more aspects of the Ergonomic operations and to raise a lot more questions and controversy about what should actually be done. That, however, in Mr. Eilers' mind, made it even more important that Ergonomic follow a systematic methodology that would give everyone a say and proceed in a manner that everyone could buy into.

Dr. Sutton agreed to facilitate the Ergonomic Systems business redesign process. Dr. Sutton and his associate, Mrs. Lee, arrived at Ergonomic Systems 3 weeks later, and he and Jim Eilers kicked off the redesign planning phase of the project.

The redesign planning effort took 3 weeks. The steering team had already been appointed and a considerable amount of work on identifying the opportunities and threats had occurred. In this case the redesign planning effort focused on defining the scope of the project and on preparing a report for the steering committee.

The process sponsor and the facilitator reviewed the value chain diagram provided by the process architecture subcommittee and the opportunities and threats worksheet to assure that they had a clear idea of the scope of the project. At the same time, in conjunction with the process sponsor, the facilitator prepared the detailed organization diagram shown in Figure 16.6 to document how Ergonomic Systems conceptualizes the key relationships between internal functions and its environment.

The steering team was asked to identify individuals who could serve on the process redesign team and assure that they would have the time needed to work on the

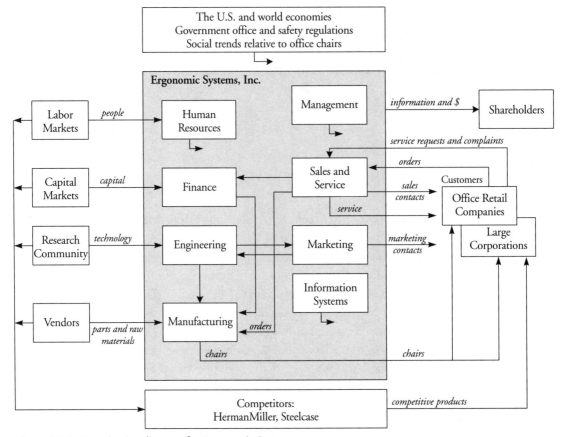

Figure 16.6 Organization diagram for Ergonomic Systems.

project. Individuals from each department involved in the process were assigned. Similarly, a mix of managers, supervisors, and workers were assigned to assure that the redesign team had a broad perspective. Individuals from IT and human resources were also assigned.

One of the key decisions that Eilers and Sutton agreed to was that the redesign effort would attempt two things. First, without regard to the Internet-based changes they were mandated to attempt, they would review the current process and look for ways it could be made more efficient. Then, they would see how the mandated Internet changes could improve the process beyond that.

Eilers and Sutton developed a plan that reviewed the goals of the project and established a schedule that would result in a redesigned process in just under 3 months. They presented their plan to the steering committee, received approval, and proceeded to Phase 2.

Phase 2: Analyzing the Current Order Fulfillment Process

The week after the steering committee approved the plan for the redesign effort, David Sutton began work on the second phase of the project.

The key to the analysis of the IS version of the Ergo Chair Order Fulfillment Process was to develop a detailed understanding of how the existing process currently worked. Sutton interviewed each of the process redesign team members to see how they would describe the process and what kinds of problems they would identify. Sutton also talked to a number of managers and supervisors who weren't on the process redesign team to gain a broader understanding of the process and any problems that it might have.

When all the interviews were completed, Sutton and his assistant, Mrs. Lee, worked up a rough overview of the Ergonomic Chairs Order Fulfillment Process. Sutton presented this on the first day the process redesign team met to provide everyone with a way of understanding of how they would be documenting the process. He had two versions of the "strawman" process—one printed on 8½ by 11–inch paper for each team member, and another larger version drawn on a whiteboard that covered one wall of the meeting room.

After introductions and a description of the process they would undertake, Sutton began to walk the team through the diagrams. The first diagram was of the entire Order Fulfillment Process divided into six subprocesses (see Figure 16.7). The second diagram was a more detailed look at just the Sales and Order Entry subprocess, which they considered in more detail.

Predictably, Sutton was interrupted by members who saw problems with the "strawman" diagram. In some cases activities had been omitted. In other cases members wanted decision points made more explicit. Much of the discussion simply involved settling on the level of detail that the first process diagram should include. Once everyone understood that subsequent groups would define each subprocess shown on the high-level process diagram in more detail, things began to move more quickly.

After agreeing on the high-level diagram, the team begin to drill down and refine some of the details of how an order would flow through the various order fulfillment processes. By the end of the first week, the team arrived at a first version of the IS diagram. We have shown a portion of that diagram in Figure 16.8. This diagram shows specific activities and identifies the two major software systems used in the Ergo Chair Order Fulfillment Process: the Customer Order and Credit System owned by Finance and shared with Sales, and the Production Management System used by Manufacturing.

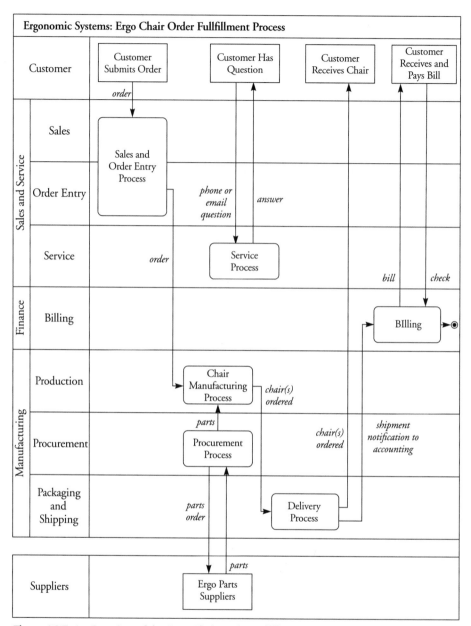

Figure 16.7 An Overview of the Ergo Chair Order Fulfillment Process.

At this point groups were set up to examine specific subprocesses in more detail. One group from Manufacturing wanted to analyze the Production Scheduling Process in more detail, while another group, mostly from Finance and Sales, chose to examine the Credit Check Process in more detail. Still another group, made up of managers, focused on describing the measures currently used by managers to evaluate the existing process. Although the process and the management evaluations took place in parallel, we'll ignore discussion of the results of the management subcommittee until a later chapter. We will also ignore the fact that the Order Process was slightly different at different locations and that the team designed slightly different processes to describe site variations. In addition, we have also omitted Marketing and Support activities that would occur beyond the edges of the diagram shown.

Since the next diagram gets quite a bit more complex, we'll shift and only focus on the activities in the Sales and Service Order Entry Process and the Finance Process as it relates to the Customer orders. (In other words, we'll ignore the Manufacturing Process, since it quickly evolves into a supply chain design problem.)

Consider Figure 16.8. It suggests that three departments are directly involved in the Ergo Chain Order Process: Sales, Finance, and Manufacturing. Functional groups within each group were identified to make it clear which managers, supervisors, and employees would be responsible for the subprocesses and activities shown on the diagram. Thus, for example, three functions within the Manufacturing department were identified: Production Management System, Production, and Packaging and Shipping. In addition, it was decided that the existing production management software system should be represented as a function since so many different management activities interacted with this system.

A swimlane for customers was placed at the top of the chart. No effort was made to discriminate between customers that were wholesale distributors and those that were the purchasing managers of large companies, although more detailed process descriptions might drill down into that distinction. No individuals were shown on the vertical axis, but two functions were represented by software systems.

Both software systems had been developed in the past and have been in use for several years. One was a financial application that maintained records of customers, undertook credit checks, and prepared invoices. This application had been acquired from an ERP software vendor that specialized in financial packages. The system ran on a mainframe and relied on a database that was an integral part of the application.

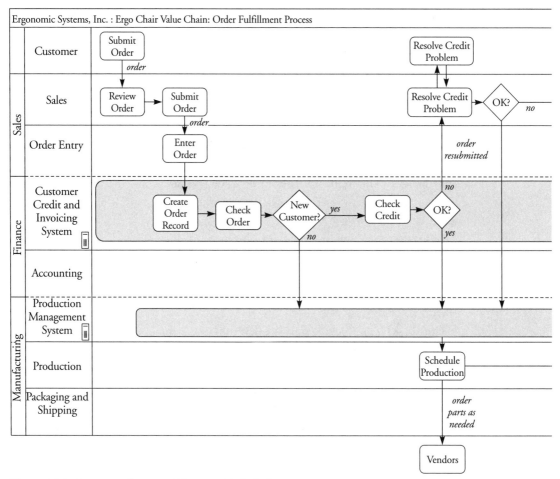

Figure 16.8 IS process diagram of the Ergo Chair Order Process.

The other application had been developed internally by the Ergonomic Systems IT group. It controlled the inventory and production process. This system ran on a linked set of Unix platforms located at the various manufacturing sites. As each order was entered into the system, a record was created. When the order was approved by Finance, the production of the order was scheduled. When the schedule was created, inventory was checked to see if additional parts would be needed for the specific order. If parts were needed, that information would show up on a report. The individual responsible for monitoring inventory would prepare and mail purchase orders to the appropriate parts vendors.

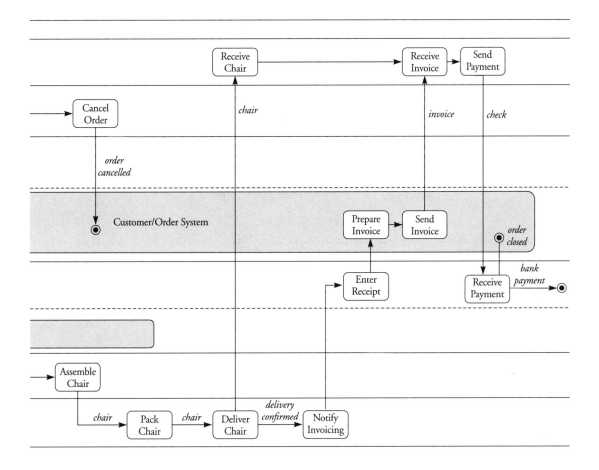

If the customer was new, and especially if the order was large, Finance would ask the salespeople to request an advance payment for some or all of the order. Since orders tended to be large and Ergonomic Systems had multiple plants and warehouses located close to major metropolitan areas, most shipping was undertaken by trucks owned by Ergonomic Systems. Once orders had been delivered, the Shipping group would transmit the customer receipt to Finance and they would initiate billing and handle the payment.

Once the basic diagram was complete, the redesign task force considered how it might be improved. Before considering any of the Internet features that the executive committee had mandated, the team discussed disconnects or gaps in the current process. They referred to the gaps and disconnects checklist that we considered in Chapter 10 (Table 10.3).

Process Analysis and Improvement Worksheet							
Process or Activity: *Ergo Chair Order Process*						IS or SHOULD	
Process or Activity Outputs	Desired Performance (Measures)	Actual Performance	Gap (If Any)	Impact of Gap	Cause of Gap	Organization Improvement Action	Activities Which Influences Gap
Salespeople take too long to submit orders.	All orders submitted on day they are signed.	10% submitted 1 day late; 2% submitted more than 2 days late.	12% not submitted on day order obtained.	Order delivery delayed; customer dissatisfaction.	Salespeople too busy. Managers don't stress importance. Delays due to location of salespeople.		
Order details misentered by entry clerks.	All orders entered as submitted by salespeople.	5% misentered.	5% misentered.	Customer dissatisfaction, service calls, delays.	Entry clerk inattention. Nature of transcription process.		
Process measures stress wrong things.	All process measures should be related to value chain and company goals.			Frustration on part of senior managers and employees.	Need to align measures used by managers with corporate goals.		

Figure 16.9 IS process analysis and improvement worksheet for Order Entry.

The group agreed that there were three major problems with the Sales and Order Entry Process. Salespeople were sometimes late in submitting new orders, causing delayed delivery. Order entry clerks sometimes misentered orders, causing problems and delays for reentry. And, finally, everyone believed that some of the existing measures were out of line with stated company goals and that managers' measures should be reassessed to assure that they were measuring the right things. The team documented these problems on a process analysis and improvement worksheet (see Figure 16.9).

The redesign team suggested that they should not only incorporate a portal into the Order Entry Process, but should also equip salespeople with laptop computers and let them enter orders directly. It would eliminate the entry clerk's job and avoid transcription problems. And it was hoped that it would allow salespeople to submit all orders on the day they were received.

The recommendations of the entire order fulfillment team, when complete, were submitted to the steering committee. Once approved, the team was asked to prepare a detailed model of the revised process.

Phase 3: Designing the New Order Process

Once the steering committee approved the report and proposal of the process redesign team, they set to work creating a new process map to reflect all of the changes they proposed.

Following the identification of disconnects, the team considered each of the proposed Internet interventions to see if they would eliminate or alleviate the perceived disconnects. In each case there was quite a bit of discussion about how a specific Internet intervention would change things. The IT representatives were often called upon to discuss what could and could not be done, relative to any specific change. In additional to technical considerations, involving an estimate on the part of IT about their ability to implement the software required for the change, there were concerns about the number and scope of changes being proposed. Everyone agreed that the greater the number of changes, the more difficult it would be to transition the process without significant disruption. Thus, the team decided to divide changes into (1) nice to do and (2) necessary. Only necessary changes would be considered initially. Afterwards, nice-to-do changes would be considered and either included or placed on a list of changes that might be made in the future.

At some point the team also decided they wanted all changes made in 6 months. Thus, if a change could be implemented, in the opinion of IT and the functional managers, within the next 6 months, it was considered a part of this redesign effort. If it would take longer than 6 months, the team decided to place it on a list of things to be considered for a subsequent process improvement effort.

Creating a Portal

The first major change they considered was the creation and incorporation of a Web site or portal. (A portal is really just a set of coordinated Web sites. Thus, rather than having one Web site for prospects that want to learn about company products and another for customers that want to check manuals about specific

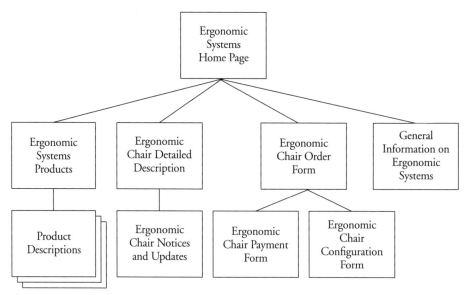

Figure 16.10 A sketch of the Ergonomic portal as sketched by the redesign team.

product features or buy additional chairs, all of the Web sites were clustered behind a single interface that all users arrived at when they entered *www.ergonomicsystemscorp.com* into their browser.)

The team agreed that the Ergonomic Systems portal should support these activities:

▶ General information about ergonomic systems
▶ A catalog of all Ergonomic Systems products
▶ A module that would allow prospects to specify Ergo Chair configurations and then buy Ergo Chairs online
▶ A page that would list announcements about part changes and answer frequently asked questions about Ergo Chairs

Each of these features required considerable discussion, since each had significant process implications. A sketch, developed by the task force, of the basic screens to be included in the initial Ergonomic Systems portal is shown in Figure 16.10.

It was decided, for example, that the general information about the firm would require the creation of a committee with people from the executive committee, marketing, the process managers, legal, and IT. This became a recommendation of the team, since it didn't directly concern the Ergo Chair process.

It was also decided that the catalog of Ergonomic Systems products should include information about all company products, and hence there were recommendations that individuals from the systems group join with the people from the Ergo Chair catalog group to develop this information.

The module that would allow companies and individuals to buy chairs online received a lot of attention. It was decided, for example, that individuals shopping online should pay in advance for chairs they ordered. Since Ergonomics was used to working with established distributors and large companies, it was felt that extending credit to unknown individuals throughout the world was too risky for the systems Ergonomics had in place. Companies and distributors with established credit would be able to buy on credit, but any new individuals or companies would need to provide a credit card or transfer funds before the chair was assembled.

They also decided that the purchase module would be designed to allow the customer to configure exactly the Ergo Chair he or she wanted. This, in turn, would require production to revise their procedures so that they could insert single or small orders within their schedule. The production members of the team suggested that they had already been moving in this direction and it could be achieved.

The team decided that they would need to contract with a delivery service to handle individual deliveries, since it would never be cost-effective to use their own trucks to make individual or even small deliveries outside of the major metropolitan areas close to their existing warehouses. They already use UPS to deliver special items, and it was recommended that Shipping negotiate with UPS to arrange to handle worldwide delivery of limited runs of Ergo Chairs. At the same time, it was hoped that they would be able to link with Production's scheduling system and UPS's tracking system so that online customers could determine when their orders would arrive and track their progress and delivery from the Web site.

It was decided that the Web site should be introduced in an English-only version and that later French and German versions should be developed to support their marketing organizations in those key European countries.

In addition to a discussion of the structure of the portal, the team recommended that an incentive system be developed to compensate salespeople who lost sales to the Web site. In the long run, everyone agreed that if they could convert distributors and large companies to Web site use, the company would save money. In the meantime, however, it was determined that the existing field sales organization should remain in place. That, in turn, meant that salespeople would need transfer payments to assure that they still made reasonable salaries during the transition. The alternative was to have resistance from the field sales staff to use of the Web site by existing customers, and to lose good salespeople who lost income as customers switched to the Web site.

The redesign team also suggested that management consider working out an arrangement with distributors to point their customers to the Ergonomic Web site. In effect, income from sales made through the Ergonomic Web site from transfers from distributor Web sites would be shared with the distributor for 6 months. The team recommended that the systems group considered a similar arrangement with suppliers of items like desk lamps, sold in conjunction with environmental systems. It was thought likely that some of the suppliers used by the systems group would create their own Web sites and that Ergonomic Systems ought to anticipate conflicts and work out a win-win strategy with its suppliers.

Modifying the Sales and the Finance Processes

Since the Web site would allow customers to buy online, everyone agreed that the existing Customer Credit and Invoicing System would need to be extended. In effect, the customer would be creating his or her own order and entering it into the customer database. At the same time, the credit system would need to be extended to allow it to automatically check credit information online. The IT team member explained that all of the major credit card companies already offer the services required. It would only be a matter of generating requests for approval and transmitting them via the Internet to the credit card companies, and then using the responses to confirm the purchase, or trigger an order reversal and an email or letter to the customer indicating that his or her credit card had been rejected. IT believed that the software vendor that had sold them the accounting system in the first place offered modules to do this and that incorporating them wouldn't be too difficult.

The SHOULD Process Diagram

Figure 16.11 provides an overview of a portion of the modified or SHOULD process that the redesign team arrived at for the Sales and Finance Subprocesses. Ergonomic Systems plans on supporting both a manual sales system and an online system. We focus on the changes made to support the online system and only just indicate the manual system that was shown in the IS diagram (Figure 16.8). Obviously Figure 16.11 only provides an overview of the changes to be made. The IT group decided to buy a CRM package to manage the online sales and simply described the outputs that the people in the Ergo Chairs processes would need to support. We show two swimlanes for the portal, one for the interface (the Web pages), and one for the software applications that actually do the work once the customer has made an entry on a Web page.

Figure 16.11 incorporates a number of changes in a revised SHOULD process. It adds a portal for those who want to use it and incorporates changes in software systems to support that path. It also provides for salespeople to use computers and enter orders directly into the customer system via the Internet.

Notice that Accounting no longer needs to make an entry into the order system to generate invoices. The task force working on the Manufacturing Process decided to outsource delivery and initiated a contract with UPS. UPS provides automatic electronic notification when chairs are delivered, and that information is now automatically input into the order system. Obviously customers that pay by credit cards don't get bills. Only established customers are allowed to order with purchase orders, and they are billed after the orders are received. If we had shown a swimlane for the deliver subprocess, we would have included a feedback loop running from the online customer who received chairs via the deliver system's computer to accounting that would have led to a closed order, just as information from the credit card agency provides the accounting group with information about funds transfers.

Obviously Figure 16.11 will need to be defined in still more detail, but we won't go into the additional detail to keep this example limited to a manageable size. Suffice it to say that the redesign team kept at it until they had worked out all the details.

This is more or less the end of our discussion of the process redesign effort, and at this point the facilitator and the redesign team might prepare a report for the steering committee. Similarly, it might draft a plan to show what kinds of development effort would be required before the changes could be implemented. Before that, however, we need to return to the issue of management redesign, which we set aside at the beginning of Phase 2.

Refining the Management System

At the same time that the various teams were discussing processes and designing the new portal interface and the supply chain that now links manufacturing to its parts suppliers, a group of managers was formalizing the new management system. Like most companies, Ergonomics had always spoken of aligning its corporate goals to process and departmental goals. Similarly, as at most other companies, the

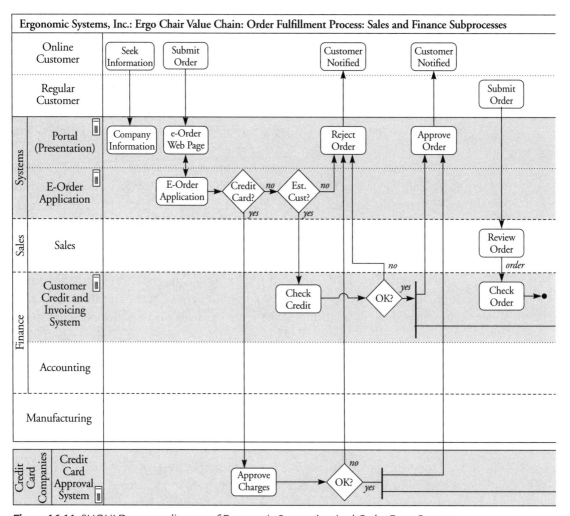

Figure 16.11 SHOULD process diagram of Ergonomic Systems' revised Order Entry Process.

alignment had always been an informal process. As part of the overall Ergo Chair process redesign, management made a commitment to create a more formal management system.

Figure 16.12 looks only at the Sales, Systems, and Finance functions as they relate to the new Ergo Chair Order Process. To keep this diagram simple, we've collapsed several of the activities to make it easy to see what managers are involved in this process.

In the simplified view shown in Figure 16.12, we see that the source of all goals for Ergonomic Systems is the executive committee and the CEO. Bill Rennells

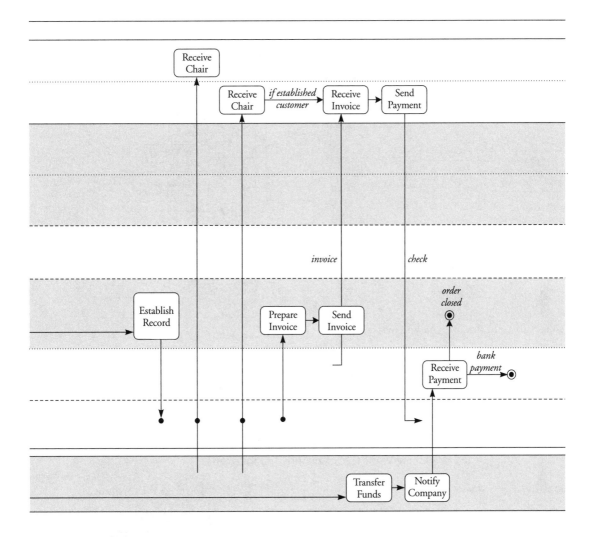

delegates two types of goals. Some goals are established for department heads and relate to the performance of the functions themselves. Things like profitability per salesperson, cost per sale, and sales reports might be delegated directly. Similarly, accounting standards and the ability to pass standard audits would be delegated to the SVP of finance. Data security requirements would be delegated to IT.

When it comes to the Ergo Chair Order Process, however, goals for the whole process ought to be established by the executive committee working with the process manager, Jim Eilers. Those goals, in turn, should be turned into broad process measures that Eilers is responsible for monitoring and controlling.

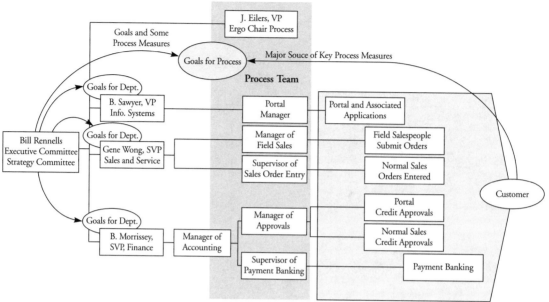

Figure 16.12 The flow of goals and measures.

Eilers then delegates subgoals for the process to function managers who are responsible for specific subprocesses or activities within the process.

Recall that Ergonomics already has an organization goals and measures worksheet (see Figure 16.3). The goals and measures listed on that worksheet for the Ergo Chair Value Chain include the following:

Goals	Measures	Desired Performance
1. Best-designed chairs	Design reviews	Win design competitions and mentions in design press
2. Command best price	Sale price comparisons	Chairs will sell for at least 5% more than competitive products
3. Maintain highest margins	After-tax returns on net sales	After-tax return on net sales exceeds 10%
4. Maintain growth goals	Sales growth	Growth in chairs will be 3% NA, 5% Europe

When Sutton and the managers on the Ergonomics redesign team sat down to discuss goal alignment, they sorted out the corporate goals as follows:

1. This goal was for the new product development process. It didn't apply to Ergo, except as the Ergo marketing communications people worked to bring the chair line to the attention of editors and juries.

2. This goal was used to set the prices, after comparing Ergo's price with other chairs.

3. This goal directly applied to the Order Fulfillment Process and required that the process be as efficient as possible. The process was currently efficient, but changes to incorporate a portal should increase the efficiency of the process, not decrease it. Thus, proposed changes would be carefully evaluated to see if they helped maintain efficiency.

4. This goal applied to the Ergo sales manager and his team and was delegated directly to the respective sales groups.

As a part of their planning for the conversion to the use of a portal, the executive committee established a corporate strategy that entailed providing information about and accepting orders for Ergo Chairs via an Internet portal. The executive committee also set goals. The process was to be redesigned and the portal was to be up and running in 8 months. In the following 12 months, 20% of the orders for Ergo Chairs were to be taken via the portal. It was hoped that online orders were to reduce the cost of sales by 3%. Customers were to indicate their satisfaction with the availability and ease of use of the portal on surveys.

As the team approached these ideas, they formalized two additional goals:

5. Assure that customers are happy with Ergo chairs.

6. Assure that customers who use the portal are happy with the experience.

Both of these goals were going to be measured by surveys that Ergonomics planned to undertake periodically.

In order to clarify their thinking about these goals, the management team developed Critical-to-Quality trees for each goal. (CTQ trees, Sutton explained, are a popular Six Sigma tool that can be used on any goal-setting project.)

The team decided that customers were pleased when they got the chairs they ordered quickly and exactly as ordered, and with a correct bill (see Figure 16.13).

Some of these goals reinforced the concerns the team had already uncovered as regards occasional misentry of order information. The team was satisfied that its billing system generated accurate and complete bills, provided it got an accurate order. The rest of the items were passed to the group that was working on the manufacturing process.

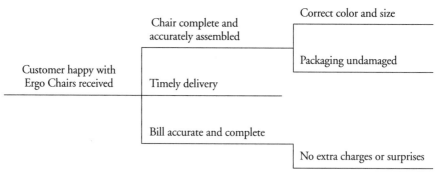

Figure 16.13 A CTQ tree for the Ergo Chairs Order Fulfillment Process.

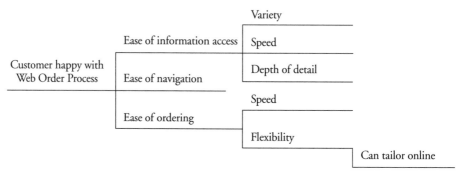

Figure 16.14 A CTQ tree for the Ergo Chairs Sales and Order Entry Process.

The team then proceeded to focus on a CTQ tree for the Sales and Order Entry Process, since that would be the process affected by the new portal. In this case, they came up with the CTQ tree shown in Figure 16.14.

The team realized that most of these would depend on the work of the software developers who created the portal. For the purposes of measurement, however, the team considered their goals, and then created some measures that they figured would allow the process manager to know if the portal succeeded.

They created a survey form that asked questions about the various items on the CTQ tree and suggested that someone be assigned to email copies of the survey to all of their customers for the first 2 months after their site was launched to determine if they were meeting these goals.

Eilers had to sit down with the various senior managers involved in the redesign and allocate subgoals and agree with the managers on measures. All the managers, for example, committed to providing the people needed to get the redesign done on schedule. The IT group was given the responsibility for creating a high-quality site. They agreed to work with Eilers to interview leading customers to determine what they wanted on the portal. Eilers would turn the customers' requests into a survey that would be used, in the future, to measure customer satisfaction with the site. The survey would not only ask questions about the overall content and ease of use of the site, but it would also ask about the speed of approvals, responses to on-line inquiries, time to delivery, and so forth.

Most of the redesigned site depended on software automation, and thus IT took a particularly heavy responsibility for the effectiveness and efficiency of the new process. At the same time, however, the SVPs of sales and service and finance agreed to performance measures for the processes that were performed by employees reporting to their departments. In each case, the SVPs, in turn, delegated specific measures to subordinates, and ultimately measures were established for each activity and for the employees who performed the activity.

In the future, when Eilers or any of the SVPs responsible for portions of the Order Fulfillment Process undertake a process improvement effort, they will already have the goals and measures needed to judge how well they are doing. They may decide to use a program like Six Sigma to try to refine the process and narrow the variation in performance, but they won't need to start from scratch. In fact, given the use of off-the-shelf software for much of the IT aspects of this effort, a Six Sigma would more likely be applied to the manufacturing assembly process, which includes more manual effort and is more susceptible to the kinds of techniques that a Six Sigma effort would employ.

Figure 16.15 shows how the measures that the management team developed were ultimately assigned to specific subprocesses within the Order Fulfillment Process.

This same exercise was repeated and specific goals were associated with each activity in each of the subprocesses.

Most organizations develop role/responsibility worksheets to show how each manager's goals will be aligned with the process goal. In Figure 16.16, we have reproduced a worksheet that the process sponsor, Eilers, and the North American sales manager, Lee Yu, prepared for a meeting of the task force. This worksheet was refined by the managers, and then other versions of the worksheet were employed by each manager to establish goals for their subordinates. Ultimately, each employee's job description was checked against the activity manager/supervisor's goals and measures to assure that employees understood how their work related to activity outcomes and thus, ultimately, to the achievement of process goals. In the end there was a set of 24 role/responsibility worksheets defining every manager's and employee's goals for the Chair Order Fulfillment Process.

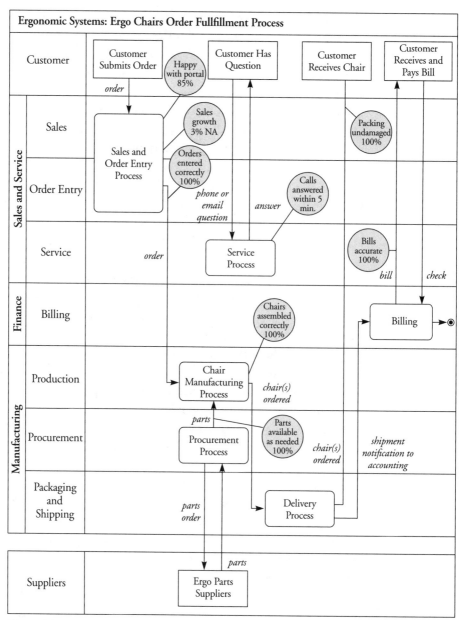

Figure 16.15 Measures established for each subprocess within the Order Fulfillment Process.

Process/Function Role/Responsibility Worksheet

Function: _Sales and Service_   Process: _Ergo Chair Order Process_

Process	Subprocesses	Activity, Job, System Responsibilities, and Goals					
		Role: _Field Sales Manager—NA_		Role: _Order Entry Supervisor_		Role: _Sales Support Manager_	
		Activity or Step	Goals	Activity or Step	Goals	Activity or Step	Goals
Sales and Order Entry	Sales and Order Entry	Sales	3% Growth in NA	Order entry	Entered on day received. Entered 100% correctly.		
Service Process						Service calls answered.	Calls answered within 3 minutes.
						Service call follow-up.	Any promised materials mailed within 24 hours. Other material mailed within 3 business days.

Figure 16.16 Process/function role/responsibility worksheet.

Phase 4: Resource Development

Once the steering committee had approved the revised Ergo Chair Value Chain design and plan, the process supervisor appointed his assistant to coordinate the implementation phase effort.

A major part of the effort involved the Information Technology (IT) department, which was going to have to develop the new company Web portal and revise the existing finance and manufacturing systems. IT had had representatives on the redesign team, and they believed that they could extend the redesign documents developed during Phase 3 to provide the requirements document that IT needed before they could begin their work. The IT members drafted the requirements document, and then the entire redesign team met again to review the requirements and sign off on them.

For many organizations the requirements definition phase is fraught with danger. In Ergo's case, however, since it had already produced process diagrams, it was much easier for the Ergo business and IT people to agree on the requirements document. Most organizations spend a significant amount of time and money defining requirements. Organizations that have already defined their processes will usually spend much less and will produce a better quality system.

Teams of senior managers from various departmental groups were assigned the responsibility for meeting with credit card companies, parts vendors, and UPS to work out contracts for the new relationships that Ergonomic Systems proposed to enter into with them.

Human resources was assigned the task of modifying or developing new job descriptions where jobs had changed and developing new compensation and incentive plans to accomplish some of the specific changes required by the new design.

The group whose efforts would take the most time was IT, which figured it would need a full 6 months to create and test the new software. Thus, everyone else was assigned tasks within that overall framework, and the rollout was scheduled to begin 7 months hence.

Phase 5: The New Order Process Goes Online

Some organizations revise processes and then, when they try to implement them, find it impossible. The new process is introduced, but within weeks or months everyone is back to the old way of doing things. The revision effort has seemingly disappeared without any effect. When this happens, organizations tend to play the blame game: The supervisors didn't support it, or the workers simply sabotaged the effort.

We have not experienced significant difficulty in implementing redesigned processes. We attribute our success to four factors.

First, we don't undertake a project unless we have a steering team and a process sponsor. We explain to those individuals, up front, that their job is to make the change happen. If they can't commit to the changes, we want to know early. If they sign off on the phase reviews, then we expect them to apply the pressure required to get their folks to implement the resulting process redesign.

Second, we don't undertake a problem without a clear statement of the scope of the project. If a company has a good process architecture and can pinpoint the process or subprocess to be changed, that's good. In most cases they don't, and we need to spend some time defining what will and won't be included. First, you need to agree on the activities that are to be included. Then, you need to decide if you are only going to work on the flow, or if you can also change management systems and jobs. Similarly, is the redesign team able to designate the use of automation and other technologies? You need to be clear on any limits on the nature of the redesign. All these issues will get resolved if you work through the phases we recommend and have the meetings we suggest to assure that all the issues are aired with everyone who is a stakeholder. If you reach a point in the process where you can't get agreement on scope, or if management or employee jobs get excluded, then you really want to examine if the project should proceed. Nobody likes to drop a project, but it's better to drop one and shift to something else than proceed when you don't have agreement. If you go past Phase 2 and don't have agreement, you can be pretty sure that implementation is going to be rocky, and there are going to be problems and recriminations in the end.

Third, we don't believe that process redesign should be undertaken separate from management system development. A sure recipe for disaster is to introduce a new process while managers are still being judged by older criteria or are using older measures to judge employee success. The whole system has to be integrated. A major redesign should always be accompanied with a goals and measures alignment effort. When the new process is rolled out, usually on a trial basis and then fully implemented, managers are measured on criteria developed to assure that the new process works as it should. Measures are taken more often during the initial months, and managers are provided feedback. Assuming that senior managers are committed, it is quickly obvious which junior managers are meeting their goals and which aren't, and corrective action is taken.

Fourth, we don't believe that process redesign should be undertaken separate from the people who must implement it. The redesign team ought to have employees (and people from other companies when a multicompany process is being designed) on the design team who represent all major groups whose work will be changed. When jobs are being changed or eliminated, plans must be established to handle the changes in a fair manner. Employees should understand the goals and measures and how they relate to company success, and should sign off on them just as the managers do.

We aren't suggesting that meeting all four of these criteria is always easy. We do insist, however, that they are as much a part of the process as any new software or any new process model. Ultimately people do the work. And ultimately managers are responsible for seeing that the work gets done. Process redesign requires the active help and consent of these individuals, or it won't get done. A good bit of any redesign effort involves selling the new process to everyone involved and getting their commitment.

Ergonomic Systems did all these things. They had the full support of senior mangers and prepared a management measurement plan that provided specific measures and linked 40% of managerial bonuses to meeting the new goals. They obtained the commitment of employees. Some salespeople were laid off, but not many, since the portal was only going to generate about 20% of the company's sales in the first few years. The salespeople realized that a portal was inevitable and liked the way Ergonomic Systems approached it gradually. They liked the fact that Ergonomics provided them with laptops and provided training to make them more skillful and efficient. Some clerical jobs were eliminated, but most of the clerks were assigned to other jobs within the company.

The software was ready on time, and the new process was implemented 8 months from the day the redesign started, just as management requested. There were some problems in the first few months, but by the end of 12 months everything was running smoothly and the new goals were being met. They actually achieved a slightly larger conversion to portal use and a 4% reduction in overall process costs. Management was happy with the results and began to think of what other lines they could sell online.

17

Software Tools for Business Process Development

THIS CHAPTER BRIEFLY DESCRIBES the range of business process software tools and then shows how one software tool can be used in the development of the Ergonomics case study.

Why Use Business Process Tools?

We have already suggested that a wide variety of people are engaged in different aspects of business process change. For those involved in software development, for example, this question would be moot. Everyone involved in software development uses software tools to aid them in their work. They use modeling tools to define and document requirements. They use UML, MDA, or CASE tools to generate code. Those involved in workflow systems development use workflow tools to model applications and then rely on those same tools to implement the results.

Business managers engaged in business process analysis and redesign, on the other hand, are less likely to use software tools. Many managers prefer written descriptions. Many use simple graphical or illustration tools, like the introductory version of Microsoft's Visio, to quickly create flow diagrams.

Professional business process practitioners usually rely on tools especially developed to support business process modeling and redesign. We refer to these tools as *professional business process modeling tools*.

In redesign a facilitator usually works with a business process redesign team to analyze the existing or IS process and then to conceptualize a SHOULD process. These sessions usually take place on two or three mornings during each week of the project. The facilitator usually stands in front of the group and makes notes on a whiteboard. Thus, each day the newly modeled process needs to be documented and changes need to be incorporated in earlier models. A tool makes it easy to record the results of a morning session and to print out neat versions of the organization and process diagrams for the participants. Some facilitators work with an associate who sits at the back of the room and records the session in a BP modeling tool. Others simply use the tool themselves to record the results in the afternoon following the morning session. Since modeling tools can save versions, it's easy to record different proposals so the group can document alternative versions of a solution.

Integrating paper documentation that shows processes and subprocesses, goals and measures, and the cost and capacity assumptions made about activities can be quite complex, but a tool makes it easy to keep all the information in a single file, providing a huge increase in the efficiency and productivity of the documentation process.

Some tools make it possible to simulate processes so teams can study alternatives or check to see how the process would perform under different flows or constraints. Some managers use tools to track results of measures, and in these cases the tool becomes a management aid.

Finally, if a company is serious about developing a process architecture and expects to keep track of ongoing changes in processes and subprocesses, they need a tool to manage all of their process descriptions. Ideally, the company should agree on modeling standards so that the outputs of business process redesign teams can be smoothly integrated into the overall model maintained by the process architecture committee.

The Variety of Business Process Tools

There are dozens of different software tools that can be used for business process change projects. Table 17.1 suggests some of the different types of tools and who might use them. We have provided generic names although, in fact, the various tools go by a wide variety of different names.

Table 17.1 An overview of the range of software tools that can aid in business process change.

	Users		
Software products	Executives, business and line managers engaged in informal business process improvement	Executives, business and line managers, BP team leaders, and employees engaged in business process redesign or improvement projects	Software analysts and developers engaged in developing applications to improve business processes
Software tools that aid in the analysis of corporate strategy, competitors, customer needs, and threats and opportunities for process improvement Tools that maintain enterprise process architectures.		Professional BP modeling tools	
Software tools that aid business teams in the analysis, modeling, and redesign of business processes. Includes methodologies, modeling tools, activity documentation, simulation, and costing tools.	Graphic and illustration tools	Professional BP modeling tools	Professional BP modeling tools
Software tools that aid business teams in defining business rules for processes.		Business Rule Tools	Business Rule Tools
Software tools that aid in creating management measurement systems for business managers responsible for managing or implementing new business processes. Includes tools that monitor ongoing business processes.		Process monitoring and measurement tools	
Software tools that aid in process improvement projects.		TQM tools, Six Sigma tools, professional BP tools with statistical utilities	
Workflow tools that can analyze and implement workflow systems. Tools that support XML business process languages.			Workflow tools, professional BP modeling tools extended to support BPMI, XLANG, etc.
Software applications that actually automate business processes. Includes ERP, CRM, and other packaged applications organized to support process automation. Tools that are tailored to help tailor ERP and other packaged applications.			Packaged applications from ERP and CRM vendors, tools from ERP and CRM vendors, professional BP modeling tools with extensions to support ERP development

Table 17.1 (continued)

Software products	Users		
	Executives, business and line managers engaged in informal business process improvement	Executives, business and line managers, BP team leaders, and employees engaged in business process redesign or improvement projects	Software analysts and developers engaged in developing applications to improve business processes
Software tools that allow software developers to model processes and create software applications.			UML modeling tools, MDA tools, CASE tools
Software tools that support the development of specific types of applications (e.g., tools that support the use of the SCOR supply chain framework and methodology).		Professional BP tools with extensions to support SCOR or other frameworks or methodologies.	
Software tools that support the redesign of employee jobs, the creation of job descriptions, knowledge management tools, and tools that track employee performance.		HR tools that help with job design, training, and performance documentation	

Some of the tools described in Table 17.1 are narrowly focused. Others fulfill more than one function. Thus, for example, there are business process modeling tools that are simply designed for that purpose. There are also UML, MDA, or CASE tools that include business process utilities so business managers can develop process diagrams that can then be converted to UML diagrams for software development. There are workflow tools that combine business process modeling and the actual execution of a workflow application.

There are well over 100 business process software tools on the market at the moment. In part, that reflects the variety of ways that companies are approaching business process change. It also reflects the immaturity of the market. We predict that in the course of the coming decade a few business process modeling tools will emerge as the most popular, and most of the other vendors will disappear. At the moment, however, since companies cannot know for certain which vendors will prosper and which will fall by the wayside, companies would be wise to approach standardizing on any one tool with considerable caution.

A Professional BP Modeling Tool

In the remainder of this chapter, we'll only focus on the more sophisticated business process tools.

Earlier, when we discussed software development in Chapter 13, we mentioned CASE (Computer-Aided Software Engineering) tools. CASE tools are professional tools designed to help software developers model software applications and then generate code. Some CASE vendors have add-on products that support business process analysis, but many don't. To clarify the distinction, we believe that business process tools must support workflow diagrams similar to the ones we have described in this book. Tools that expect users to do analysis with use case or class modeling diagrams are software development tools, not business process tools.

Figure 17.1 provides an overview of the key features we expect from a professional business process tool. It provides interfaces in which users can create organization and process diagrams. Unlike the simpler tools that only create diagrams, professional tools store the model elements in a database, usually called a *repository,* so that any information gained can be reused. Similarly, whenever a user creates a modeling element on a diagram, the user can click on the modeling element and enter information about the element. Thus, if we create an organization diagram

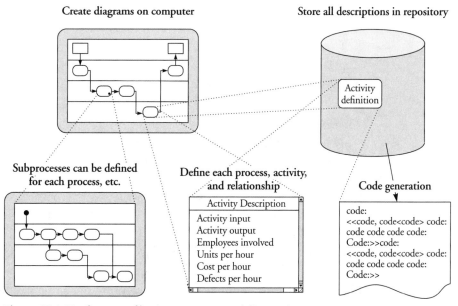

Figure 17.1 Key features of business process modeling tools.

and name six departments, we can later create a process diagram and have those six department names inserted on the vertical axis of a process diagram. Similarly, if we create a process called Sales, and then define a number of activities that occur within the Sales process, we can click on the Sales process in any diagram it occurs in and get to the diagram that shows the activities within Sales.

In other words, the heart of every professional business process tool is a database or repository in which all elements of a business process and all of the relationships between those elements are maintained. Graphic tools that only support diagrams are equivalent to pages of paper that have a process diagram on them. Each page or diagram is a thing in itself. Creating one diagram doesn't help you create the next. A professional business process modeling tool stores each element in a database and thus, as you create one diagram, you are storing information about processes and relationships that you can use on subsequent diagrams. As you proceed, you rely less and less on drawing new elements and more and more on telling the database what previously entered elements you want to place on your diagram.

Most business process tools support some kind of code generation, if for no other reason than to allow users to pass information about a process to other process tools. Increasingly business process tools will support an XML business process language. Most also support UML or some software language so that software developers can begin where business managers leave off. Code generation isn't a feature that business process redesign teams need, but it can certainly make it easier when a business process team wants to hand off a redesigned process to a software development team.

There are a number of other features that we don't show in Figure 17.1. For example, if the tool is going to be used for Six Sigma projects, it's nice to have statistical utilities or a clean interface to a popular statistical package. If the tool is going to be used with a methodology like the Supply Chain Council's SCOR methodology, the tool should probably offer frameworks for templates for SCOR models.

Similarly, many of the more powerful business process tools offer simulation. Simulation means that you can enter information about how activities will process throughput and then introduce inputs into a process and see how they are handled. You might specify, for example, that a given activity, Activity C, with one employee can tune 12 widgets an hour. If you find that the typical throughput is 20 widgets, you are either going to have to add an employee to that activity, or the simulation system is going to show widgets piling up and waiting to be processed by Activity C. The analysis of simple systems rarely demands simulation, but complex processes, with multiple paths and loops for exception handling and product tailoring, usually benefit from simulation. Most supply chain developers can benefit from tools that support simulation. Similarly, creating customer-oriented e-business systems usually benefits from simulation. It's one thing to track four or five requests through a process, and it's another thing to go online and have hundreds of requests come in more or less simultaneously. If your processes are going to respond to varying levels of customer demand and require the support of a wide variety of subsystems, depending on the nature of the customer request, then you should be doing simulation during process design.

As important as simulation can be, teams must be aware of the time and effort required to enter all the data required for a major simulation. The world's leading auto manufacturers use simulation all the time to refine their manufacturing processes, but to do it, they employ teams of simulation experts with strong mathematical and statistical backgrounds. On the other hand, if you use a tool that supports simulation and only want to check how a specific subprocess will work under some specific set of circumstances, it need not be too tedious. We generally urge clients to consider simulation. But we also suggest that they make sure that the cost of any simulation effort will justify the time and cost of formalizing a model and providing sufficient detail for effective simulation.

Modeling the Ergonomics Case

Now let's consider how using a professional business process modeling tool would have helped us as we analyzed and designed a new order fulfillment process for Ergonomic Systems, Inc. In this example, we'll assume that the facilitator is working with the Ergonomics process redesign team. The facilitator is aided by an assistant who sits at the back of the room and constantly creates models in the business process modeling tool.

We could have used any of a dozen tools to illustrate how the Ergosystems' example could have been implemented. A recent report on Business Process Modeling Analysis tools by Gartner Research identified 33 tools and placed 6 in the upper right quadrant as leaders. They included CASEwise's CASEwise, IDS Scheer's ARIS, MEGA International's MEGA, Meta Software's MetaSoft Works, Popkin Software's System Architect, and Proforma's ProVision Workbench.

In this chapter we will use two of these tools: ProVision Workbench, a tool sold by Proforma, and System Architect, a tool sold by Popkin Software, to illustrate how software tools can help. Both tools have been on the market for a decade and are among the more popular professional business process modeling tools.

ProVision was recently adopted as the standard modeling tool by General Motors after looking at over 40 tools and evaluating several in considerable detail. One of the reasons that we choose ProVision is because the tool uses a notation very similar to the notation we have used in this book, which is a cross between the Rummler-Brache notation and UML activity diagrams. In fact, ProVision supports several different notations, and you can change the notation that appears on the screen by simply pulling down a menu and selecting another notation. We chose ProVision's version of the Rummler-Brache notation so that you would have no trouble understanding their diagrams.

System Architect is used throughout the world, and the company has sold some 60,000 licenses. Like ProVision, the tool supports a wide variety of notations and is particularly strong as a tool that supports business process architecture, business process modeling, and the generation of application and database code. System Architect is used extensively by the U.S. Department of Defense to support their enterprise architecture initiatives.

An Organization Diagram

Let's assume that when the Ergonomics business process redesign team started, they created a supersystem diagram, showing how Ergonomics related to the environment outside of Ergonomics. Then they refined the diagram to show the major departmental units or functions that occur within the company.

In Figure 16.6 we pictured an organization diagram for Ergonomic Systems. Figure 17.2 shows how that same diagram would be pictured in ProVision.

If you compare this diagram to the one shown in Chapter 16 (Figure 16.6), you will see only minor differences. Notice, for example, that instead of having a small right-angle arrow (under functions) that doesn't go anywhere to indicate that we don't want to picture all the relationships on this diagram, ProVision links the arrow to the inner edge of the Ergonomic Systems box. ProVision provides pop-up windows with symbols like the rectangles shown on the screen in Figure 17.2. A developer simply clicks and drags to place one on the diagram. Then, the analyst types a name for the function. This seems simple, but in fact, once you have placed the Manufacturing box and labeled it, you have also created an entity in the database, called Manufacturing, which knows what other entities it is related to as you link that rectangle to others with arrows.

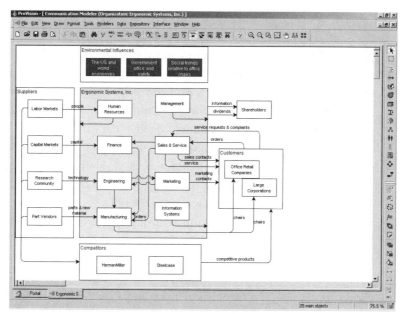

Figure 17.2 ProVision screen in which an analyst has created an organization diagram of Ergonomic Systems.

Process Diagrams

Let's assume that our business process team now turns to defining the existing order fulfillment process. In this case, our analyst would open a new window for a process diagram. ProVision would prompt the analyst to see if he or she wanted to use the departments defined in the organization diagram to create swimlanes on the process diagram. Assuming the analyst clicked YES, a process diagram with labeled swimlanes would appear. The analyst might want to rearrange the order of the swimlanes by dragging some up or others down, but the basic structure of the process diagram would be in place.

Assuming the business process team went through the same process they did in defining the IS order fulfillment process in Chapter 16, our analyst would end up with a similar process diagram. Figure 17.3 shows the diagram created in ProVision for the Ergonomic Systems IS process. In this case we reproduce the diagram that ProVision would print on demand. On the screen, we would only see a portion of the entire diagram. By printing it, however, we create a diagram that is as wide as needed.

You can compare Figure 16.8 to 17.3 to see the slight differences. ProVision uses a slightly different set of symbols to label swimlanes. The globe indicates that the function described in that swimlane is outside the organization being analyzed. Thus, both the customer at the top and parts vendors at the bottom are tagged with globes. A small PC icon is used to mark systems functions, and an organization hierarchy icon is used to mark swimlanes that describe departmental functions. Otherwise, the two diagrams are remarkably similar.

Just as we created departments on the organization diagram, we create processes and decision points on the ProVision process diagram by selecting elements from a pop-up window and dragging them to a location. Similarly, as we give names to the processes, we create database entries. In this case, the database not only knows of the existence of a process, and relationships between that process and others, but knows which department is responsible for the process.

In our Ergonomics case study, the business process redesign team created a diagram of the Web portal screens in order to figure out what the Web site would do. ProVision supports a similar function, and Figure 17.4 shows the way a portal screen hierarchy map would appear in ProVision. (Compare Figure 17.4 with Figure 16.10 in Chapter 16.)

ProVision uses arrows instead of simple lines and rounds the corners of the screens, but the diagram is otherwise the same.

In Figure 17.5 we reproduce the SHOULD diagram that was created in ProVision. In this case, the analyst started by creating the IS diagram. Later, as the team

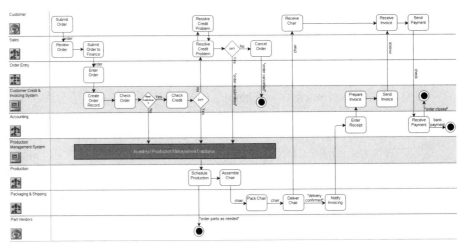

Figure 17.3 IS process diagram of the Ergonomics Order Fulfillment Process created by ProVision.

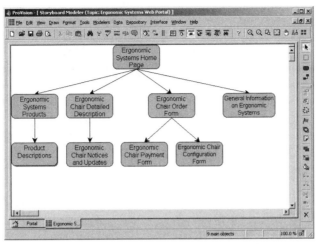

Figure 17.4 ProVision screen showing a hierarchy of Web interface screens.

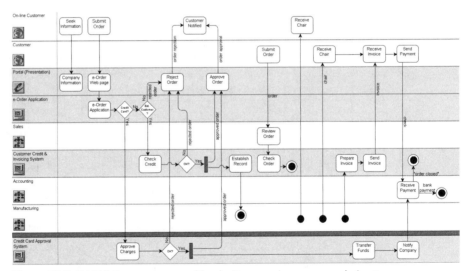

Figure 17.5 SHOULD process created by the Ergonomics process redesign team.

began to change the process, the analyst saved the IS diagram and then took a copy of that diagram and modified it as the team modified the process in their meetings. Once again, we have reproduced the printed version of the SHOULD diagram to make it easier to see the entire SHOULD process diagram. You can compare this with the SHOULD diagram in Figure 16.11 in the last chapter.

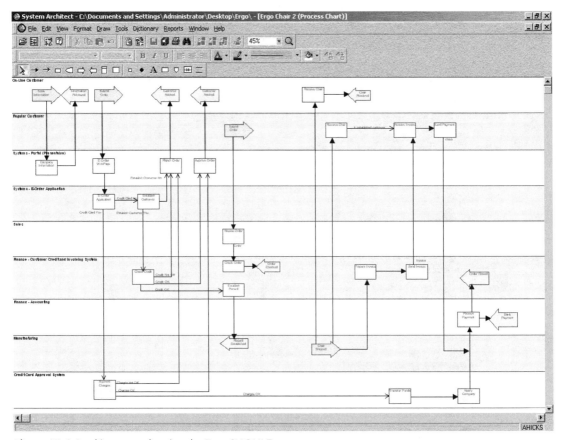

Figure 17.6 Popkin screen showing the Ergo SHOULD process.

Once again, Figures 17.5 and 16.11 are very similar. We didn't develop any diagrams that showed the details of what happened inside the boxes shown in Figure 16.11. If we had and we wanted to represent them in ProVision, we would click on one of the boxes in Figure 17.5 and indicate we wanted to do an detailed diagram. At that point, ProVision would create a new diagram, and we could create a subprocess diagram. ProVision would then mark the box on Figure 17.5 with an indicator to show that a more detailed description was available if we double-clicked on that box.

Figure 17.6 shows how our SHOULD process would be represented in Popkin's System Architect. Unlike the notation we have used in this book, System Architect diagrams do not use rectangles to represent events that start or end process sequences. Instead they use a right-facing arrow to represent an event that begins a process and a left-facing arrow to show that a sequence has ended. Similarly, instead of representing subprocesses and activities as rectangles with rounded corners, they simply use square-cornered rectangles. As we have noted before, there is no universal standard for workflow notation, and each vendor supports slight variations. In spite of the differences, it's easy to see that the same general information is captured in the Popkin diagram.

Other Diagrams

Both tools support a wide variety of specialized diagrams. For example, in the case study we assumed that the redesign team created a CTQ tree to better define the qualities that would satisfy a customer who received an Ergo Chair. Figure 17.7 illustrates a similar CTQ tree created in ProVision. Compare it to Figure 16.13 to see how it differs from the one the Ergonomics team drew on the whiteboard.

In the text, we have used a variety of worksheets to capture more specific information. In either System Architect or ProVision, one simply clicks on a given box, opens a window, and enters more detailed information on forms associated with each diagramming element. Figure 17.8 shows a window opened for an activity and information that we've entered.

Figure 16.15 in the last chapter illustrated how measures could be associated with each subprocess in the Order Fulfillment Process. It would be easy to associate those measures with subprocesses in ProVision simply by opening each subprocess box and inserting the measurement information. It would also be possible to print out lists of the measures assigned to each department or functional group.

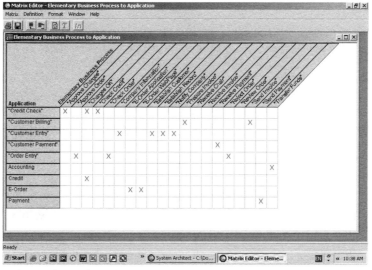

Figure 17.7 A System Architect screen showing a matrix that indicates which applications are used by specific processes.

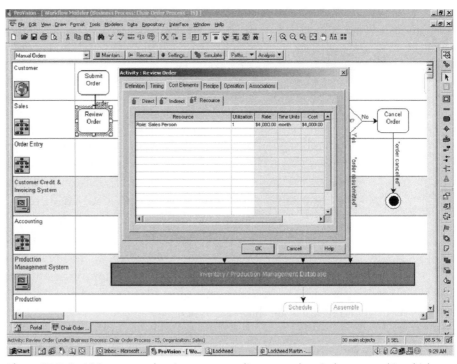

Figure 17.8 ProVision screen showing a process diagram and a window opened in which a developer can record information about a specific process.

In addition, ProVision supports almost any matrix an analyst can think of, all driven by information accumulated in the repository. Thus, for example, when we have entered as much as we want, we could ask for a matrix that showed us which departments were responsible for which activities, and ProVision would offer us a matrix.

Process Simulation

Another important feature that ProVision and System Architect supports is process simulation. The Ergonomic Systems team in the last chapter could never have simulated their redesigned process without using a software tool.

To illustrate simulation, we started with the IS diagram of the Ergonomics sales process. The IS diagram had already been created, and we didn't need to change the diagram in order to run the simulation. We did have to open each activity box that would be involved in the simulation and provide information about what would occur in that activity and how long it would, on average, require. For each activity shown in Figure 17.9, we entered data and assumptions. Thus, for example, we assumed that there were only two salespeople available for the Review Order activity and that they were also responsible for calling customers about credit problems. Ask yourself if you thought of this as a problem when you looked at this diagram in the previous chapter.

In Figure 17.9 the Review Order activity is black, indicating that it is active. Making only modest assumptions about the number of orders coming in and the number that need to be checked for credit problems, and how long each activity takes, our process quickly grinds to a halt. Basically, when one salesperson is checking a credit problem, the other salesperson, alone, can't keep up with the orders. We would need more salespeople, or we would need someone else assigned to handle credit problems if we wanted this process to run smoothly.

Figure 17.10 illustrates the matrix we created in ProVison that shows the data collected from the simulation. We highlighted the column labeled Postponed Time. Postponed time is the amount of time the activity spent waiting for resources (in this case salespeople) to become available. So, out of the 80-hour simulation duration (we ran the simulation for ten 8-hour days), the first two sales activities were waiting for available salespeople for a total of 24 and 28 hours.

This quick and trivial illustration points to the value of simulation. Increasingly companies will want to run simulations on processes they are redesigning and then maintain the simulations so they can use them in the future to test any proposed changes in the existing processes. Mature process companies will maintain simulations and routinely use them for process improvement projects.

Figure 17.11 shows how the same simulation would look on Popkin's System Architect. Just as with ProVision, the facilitator has entered information for each activity and then simulated a set of orders being processed. Here, the orders that are accumulating to be processed are shown as small pages on the diagram so you can see where there are bottlenecks.

Using Tools to Maintain Architectures

So far we have spoken of using a modeling tool to help in analyzing and redesigning a process. In Chapter 3 we spoke of business process architectures and the need to maintain an overview of all the processes supported by a company. This task would be nearly impossible without the use of software tools. In effect, a tool like System Architect can store one business process after another, keeping track of the individual processes, and holding them ready for simulations to check possible changes. At the same time, it can examine multiple processes to identify where

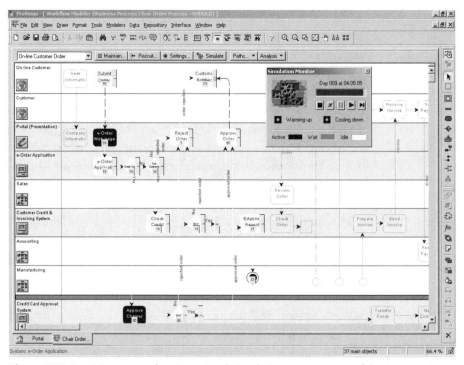

Figure 17.9 ProVision screen showing a simulation being run on a part of the Ergonomic Order Fulfillment IS process.

	Activity	Occurs	Idle time	Work time	Delay time	Pending input time	Stall time	Postponed time	Congested time
1	**Chair Order Process - IS(Manual Orders)**	1.00	401.20	96.00	73.33	0.00	0.00	57.13	0.00
2									
3	**Sales**		124.66	66.50	60.50	0.00	0.00	55.63	0.00
4	Cancel Order	2.00	53.20	0.50	0.00	0.00	0.00	1.48	0.00
5	Resolve Credit Problem	7.00	28.59	7.00	21.00	0.00	0.00	1.62	0.00
6	Review Order	79.00	5.42	39.50	39.50	0.00	0.00	24.55	0.00
7	Submit Order to Finance	78.00	37.45	19.50	0.00	0.00	0.00	27.99	0.00
8									
9	**Customer Credit & Invoicing System**		235.35	3.83	0.00	0.00	0.00	0.00	0.00
10	Check Credit	38.00	78.49	1.27	0.00	0.00	0.00	0.00	0.00
11	Check Order	77.00	78.44	1.28	0.00	0.00	0.00	0.00	0.00
12	Create Order Record	77.00	78.42	1.28	0.00	0.00	0.00	0.00	0.00
13									
14	**Order Entry**		41.19	25.67	12.83	0.00	0.00	1.50	0.00
15	Enter Order	77.00	41.19	25.67	12.83	0.00	0.00	1.50	0.00

Figure 17.10 ProVision screen showing grid with information on the wait time for each activity in the simulation.

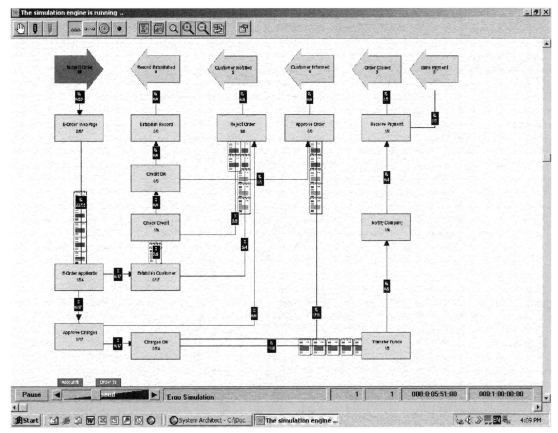

Figure 17.11 Popkin screen showing a simulation being run on the Ergo example.

common activities occur in more than one process. The amount of detail involved in this effort could overwhelm a Business Process Architecture committee if it didn't have a way of automating the task.

In Chapter 13 we talked about the Zachman Framework, a popular way of organizing all of the different kinds of plans, diagrams, and models a company might wish to maintain. Items on the top level are of interest to senior managers, while items on the second level are of more interest to process managers. Items on the lower levels are of more interest to IT managers or developers. Popkin's System Architect allows a company to implement a framework that, in turn, organizes all of the information in the repository into groups. In Figure 17.12 we show a System Architect screen that pictures the Zachman Framework. By clicking on any cell in the framework, one accesses a table that shows all of the kinds of information one has stored relative to that perspective. We have clicked on the Business Process cell

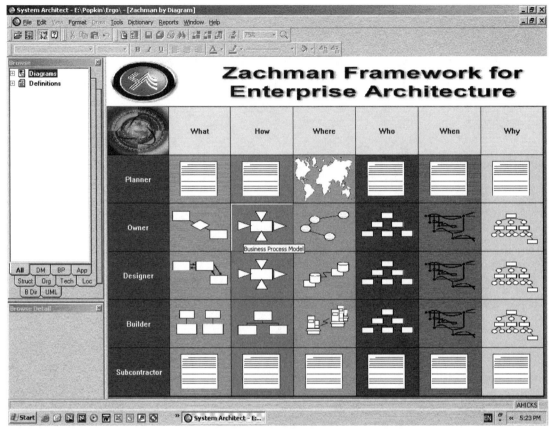

Figure 17.12 A System Architect screen showing how it organizes its repository to support the Zachman Framework.

to suggest where one would go to access business process diagrams. Companies can create whatever architectures they want in System Architect and organize their diagrams, documents, and models accordingly.

The Use of a Software Business Process Tool

The Ergonomic process redesign team would probably not have finished much faster using tools like System Architect or ProVision. If the team only met every other day for half a day, the analyst would be able to create the needed diagram by hand or in a simple diagramming tool. The tool would probably have made the facilitator's job easier and might have resulted in nicer diagrams, but it would not have changed the overall time required for the redesign. Without the tools, however, the team could not have run a simulation, and that might have changed the ultimate design assumptions.

On the other hand, once the Order Fulfillment Process had been redesigned in either System Architect or ProVision, all of the information about the process would be stored in a single software file. Future changes in the process would be easy to effect. A manager could quickly record any improvements made in the process. More importantly, a tool would allow the team to undertake simulations to answer a variety of questions. How many additional employees would need to be assigned to assembly if we were to double the number of orders each month or each week? Would bills still arrive at customer sites at the same time, and so forth?

When the Ergonomic redesign team was done, the managers responsible for the process could each place a copy of the process on their computers so that they could answer questions of that kind for themselves. A copy could also be provided to the Ergonomics business process architecture group so they would have an up-to-date, detailed description of the Order Fulfillment Process and could run their own simulations in the future when other changes were proposed.

While we don't recommend any specific business process redesign tool, we would never undertake the facilitation of a major process redesign effort without using a business process modeling tool, and we wouldn't recommend anyone else do so either. Different facilitators or analysts with different goals will prefer some tools over others. This is a matter of pragmatics and individual taste. Overall, however, any company that seeks to incorporate process into their culture should regard a process modeling tool as a tool that every manager should use, just as they use spreadsheet software or word processing programs.

In the late 1970s, we worked on a project that introduced spreadsheets in one of the largest banks. At the time, we used mainframes and the interfaces weren't very good. We developed a system that would support 12 individuals, the heads of the bank's 12 divisions, who had to prepare quarterly projections. The project met a surprising amount of resistance. Each of the 12 senior vice presidents had a person who reported to them whose primary function was to prepare spreadsheets. Those individuals worked on large pads of paper and used adding machines to crunch numbers. It would take hours to work out a spreadsheet describing a set of assumptions for a division for the next quarter. You can imagine the assistant taking the results to the SVP, who would look at it, consider the results, and then suggest that they change two assumptions. "Assume we have a 6% turnover instead of 5% and let's assume we get 25 new loans at each branch rather than 24." At this point the faithful assistant would trudge back to his or her desk and start the process over again. Don't think about the huge amount of time used by this manual process, however. Focus instead on how often the SVP would change his or her assumptions. Everyone is always under pressure, and no one has time to go through laborious cycles like this for weeks on end. The SVP would make some changes, check the results, suggest a few more changes, and then go with one of the spreadsheets.

The availability of software spreadsheet programs with relatively friendly interfaces that run on personal computers has changed all that. Today, on SVP can sit at his or her desk and make one change after another. In the course of an hour or two, an SVP can examine the impact of hundreds of different assumptions. It's hard to imagine that SVPs don't understand their financial operations a lot better today than they did in the 1970s. Moreover, it's safe to assume that an SVP can make changes much quicker when things change. You can imagine an SVP checking loan sales data each day and making changes in assumptions and revising estimates that same day.

What spreadsheets have done for the way business managers think about their cash flow, process modeling tools will do for the way business managers understand and manage business processes. This change is just beginning, but it will gain momentum throughout the decade. A manager with a process description on a software tool not only understands what is happening, he or she can make changes and run simulations to see how things can be changed or improved. In the near future managers will need to modify business processes much more frequently than they do today to keep up with environmental and technological changes. Business process modeling tools will make that possible.

chapter

18

Conclusions and Recommendations

THIS BOOK WAS WRITTEN to provide managers with an introduction to the concepts and techniques needed for business process change and to provide them an overview of some of the options they will have when they undertake business process change. In keeping with this goal, we have considered a wide variety of different business process topics. Complete books have been written on several of the topics we treat in a single chapter. We have provided references to books and Web sites in the Notes and References and in the Bibliography that will help interested readers pursue various topics in more detail. Our goal here was not to make readers into masters of tactical details, but to give them the basics they need to think strategically about how they should use business process redesign and improvement techniques in their organizations.

In this chapter we want to briefly reiterate the major themes we have emphasized in this book.

First, there is the idea that organizations are systems. Things are related in complex ways, and we only understand organizations when we understand them as wholes. We believe that every manager should be able to draw an organization diagram of his or her organization at the drop of a hat. That would demonstrate at least a high-level acquaintance with how various functions relate to each other and to suppliers and customers.

Second, we believe that the best way to understand how things get done and how any specific activity is related to others is to think in terms of processes. Process diagrams provide a good basis for demonstrating that one understands how things flow through an organization, from supplies and new technologies to products and services that are delivered to customers. In an ideal world, we'd like every manager to have a process modeling tool on his or her computer with a model of the activities he or she manages, contained within a diagram of the process they support. We believe that acquaintance with process diagramming techniques is just as important for today's manager as familiarity with spreadsheets and organization charts.

Figure 18.1 shows how processes can be the key to understanding and organizing what is done in a company. A business process architecture provides everyone with an overview of how all the activities in the organization relate to one another and contribute to satisfying customers. A well-understood process shows how each activity relates to every other and where departments must interface in order for the process to be effective and efficient.

The same process diagram provides the basis for defining measures and aligning those measures with organization strategies and goals, departmental goals, and process and activity measures. This, in turn, defines the responsibilities of individual managers and supervisors. Each manager should know exactly what processes or activities he or she must plan and organize and just which measures to check in order to monitor and control the assigned processes and activities.

Drilling down in the diagram, well-defined activities provide the framework on which a whole variety of organizational efforts can be hung. Each activity should generate data on inputs and outputs, on time and cost. Activities are the basis for cost-based accounting systems. They are also the key to analyzing jobs and developing job descriptions and training programs.

Activities also provide a framework for organizing knowledge management efforts, feedback systems, and decision support systems. And they also form the basic unit for the database systems and for defining requirements if the activity is to be automated.

As enterprises become more mature in their understanding and use of processes, they learn to constantly adjust their processes and to align the activities within a process in response to changes in their external environment. As each strategy change results in a process change, it also results in changes in the management and measurement system and in all of the other support systems that are tied to the processes and activities. Thus, the process architecture becomes the heart of enterprise alignment and organizational adaptation.

Beyond these two basics, we urge organizations to approach processes in a mature way. Following the work done at Carnegie Mellon University by the SEI group, we suggest that every organization should locate itself on the CMM maturity scale illustrated in Figure 18.2.

Organizations achieve their strategic goals by means of processes.

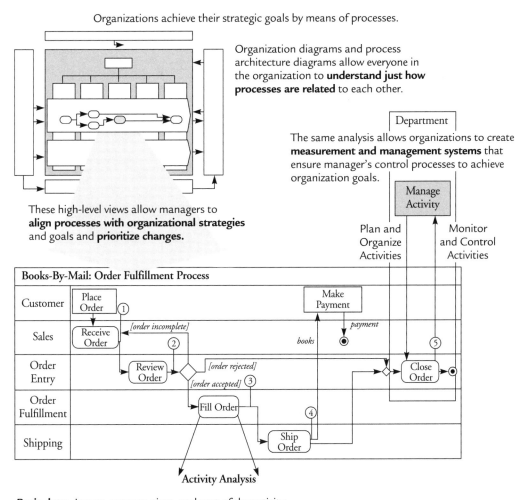

Organization diagrams and process architecture diagrams allow everyone in the organization to **understand just how processes are related** to each other.

The same analysis allows organizations to create **measurement and management systems** that ensure manager's control processes to achieve organization goals.

These high-level views allow managers to **align processes with organizational strategies** and goals and **prioritize changes.**

Activity Analysis

Basic data: Inputs, outputs, time, and cost of the activity.

Job analysis: Employees involved in activity. Job descriptions and performance support system. Training available to support employees engaged in this activity.

Communications: Feedback that should flow from this activity to other activities or to senior management.

Knowledge management and decision support: Business rules used to make decisions required for this activity. Other knowledge required by those performing this activity.

Automation and IT systems support: Data required to perform this activity. Requirements for automating this activity. Software applications and components that automate this activity.

Figure 18.1 Processes are the key to understanding an organization.

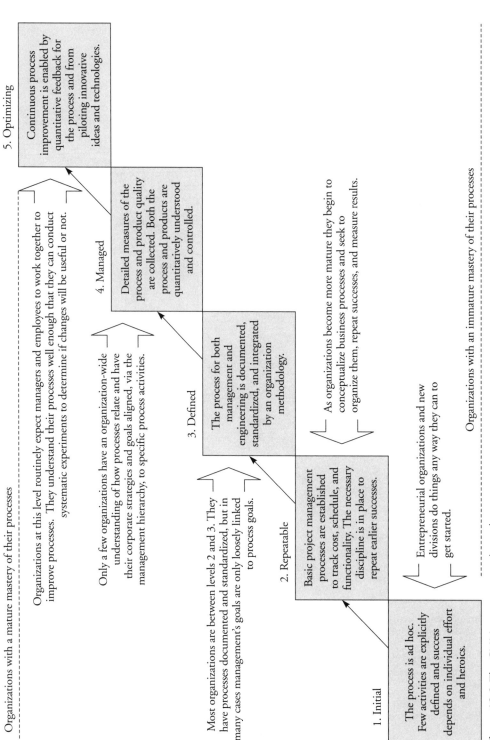

Organizations with a mature mastery of their processes

5. Optimizing

Continuous process improvement is enabled by quantitative feedback for the process and from piloting innovative ideas and technologies.

Organizations at this level routinely expect managers and employees to work together to improve processes. They understand their processes well enough that they can conduct systematic experiments to determine if changes will be useful or not.

4. Managed

Detailed measures of the process and product quality are collected. Both the process and products are quantitatively understood and controlled.

Only a few organizations have an organization-wide understanding of how processes relate and have their corporate strategies and goals aligned, via the management hierarchy, to specific process activities.

3. Defined

The process for both management and engineering is documented, standardized, and integrated by an organization methodology.

As organizations become more mature they begin to conceptualize business processes and seek to organize them, repeat successes, and measure results.

Most organizations are between levels 2 and 3. They have processes documented and standardized, but in many cases management's goals are only loosely linked to process goals.

2. Repeatable

Basic project management processes are established to track cost, schedule, and functionality. The necessary discipline is in place to repeat earlier successes.

Entrepreneurial organizations and new divisions do things any way they can to get started.

1. Initial

The process is ad hoc. Few activities are explicitly defined and success depends on individual effort and heroics.

Organizations with an immature mastery of their processes

Figure 18.2 The CMM process maturity scale.

The scale was developed to evaluate how software organizations handle processes, but it can be generalized to describe how entire companies deal with processes. Most organizations are somewhere between levels 2 and 3. They are working at defining processes. Most do not have all their processes defined. They simply define a specific process in order to improve or redesign it and then move on. The challenges that most organizations face are well described by the CMM scale. Organizations need to define all their core processes. They need, in fact, to create a business process architecture that defines all of the basic processes of the organization and shows how they all fit together and what each provides for customers.

Once organizations have achieved level 3, they need to press on to level 4. They need to establish systems of measures that tie organizational strategies and goals to processes, subprocesses, and activities. And they need to create management systems that work with these measurement systems to assure that each manager knows how to manage the activities he or she is responsible for controlling.

Beyond process management, there is level 5, where managers and employees work together to constantly improve processes, making them ever more productive and consistent.

Moving up the CMM scale requires a major commitment on the part of an organization's executives. It isn't something that can be spearheaded by a departmental manager or a business process committee. It requires the active support of the CEO and the entire executive committee. Moreover, it isn't something that can be done in a single push or in the course of a quarter or even a year. Business process management and improvement must become part of an organization's culture. Process improvement must become something that every manager spends time on each day. It must become one of the keys to understanding how the entire organization functions.

If business process improvement is to be ingrained in the organization, then improvement must, itself, become a systematic process. Every organization needs a business process architecture committee—available to support senior management just as the financial committee is available to provide financial information. The process architecture committee should be constantly working to align and realign corporate processes to corporate strategies and goals. As goals and strategies shift, process changes must be reprioritized and new process redesign or improvement projects must be undertaken. Just as senior executives receive daily or weekly reports on financial results, they should receive daily or weekly reports on how the various processes are achieving their assigned measures and what efforts are being undertaken to improve processes that fail to meet their goals. This kind of reporting assumes a matrix management structure where there are managers with specific responsibilities for seeing the processes perform, as wholes.

At the tactical level, process redesign and improvement have changed and will change more in the near future. In the early 1990s, when most managers first learned about process redesign, the organization and improvement of processes were regarded as tasks that should be handled by business managers. In effect, a redesign team determined what needed to be done. They only called the IT organization in when they decided they needed to automate some specific activities.

Today, the use of IT and automation has progressed well beyond that early view of business process redesign. Increasingly companies and information systems are so integrated that every process redesign is also a systems redesign. Today every IT organization is heavily involved in business process redesign. The Internet, email, and the Web have made it possible for IT organizations to achieve things today that they could only dream of in the early 1990s. Information systems are making it possible to integrate suppliers and partners—and in many cases, customers—in networks that are all made possible by software systems.

As we suggested earlier, the most important business processes being developed in this decade will be cross-company processes, like the integrated supply chain shown in Figure 18.3. The creation of these systems will involve all of the problems faced by companies that created large internal supply chain processes in the 1990s, and lots of new elements besides. Business managers will be heavily involved in negotiations and arranging for the ongoing management and measurement of these cross-business processes. IT people will be heavily involved in the creation of the infrastructure and the applications that will allow such a process to function efficiently.

The creation of cross-company processes will be a challenge to everyone involved in process design and development. Business managers must retain the primary responsibility for planning and controlling these systems. Determining corporate strategy and positioning the company to achieve a sustained competitive advantage remain executive responsibilities. The overview and the initiative must remain with business managers. Increasingly, however, business managers must work with teams of IT managers to realize the full potential of new technologies to create improved processes. Indeed, today corporate strategies often represent bets on how new information systems will position the company in the next few years.

At the same time, business managers must allow IT managers a larger role in business process change, since most process changes now depend on new IT technologies. There are lots of options and there will be more in the near future. Older IT techniques, like workflow management systems, are being supplemented by

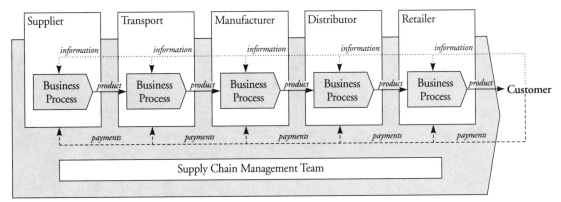

Figure 18.3 An integrated supply chain process that integrates the subprocesses of several companies.

newer techniques based on XML-based business process languages, and by the OMG's Model Driven Architecture that offers to model the core software components used by an organization and then manages them in a systematic manner.

There are no correct solutions that can be recommended for all problems. Instead, business and IT managers must struggle with specific processes and subprocesses and specific technologies, evaluating risk and giving due weight to constraints, and come up with a solution that is, hopefully, the best that can be achieved at a given moment in time.

It would be nice if all companies could simply adopt packaged solutions, but we are convinced that Porter's arguments about competitive advantage are true. Sustained competitive advantage results from tightly integrated processes that implement a unique strategy. It isn't something a company can buy or copy. Components and subprocesses may be acquired in whole or part from others, but the overall process and the unique integration will remain the responsibility of the senior managers of the organization. Good processes reflect the effective implementation of the vision of the senior executives of the firm.

To create unique and well-integrated business processes, managers must make choices. Figure 18.4 provides an overview of the range of options we have described in this book. In this case we have pictured the options in a decision tree. One starts from the top with changes in the environment and moves to the second box and asks if the organization needs to change in response.

If an organizational change is required, then new strategies and goals need to be enunciated. Once they are, the process architecture committee must determine what processes will be impacted by the new strategy and what process goals will need to be altered. If a major set of changes is required, a process redesign should

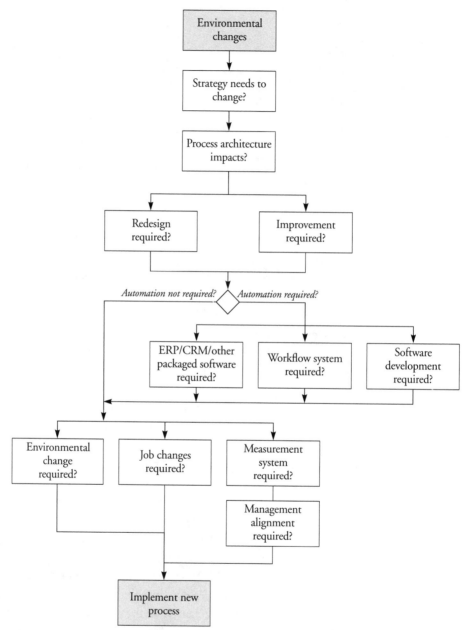

Figure 18.4 A process change decision tree.

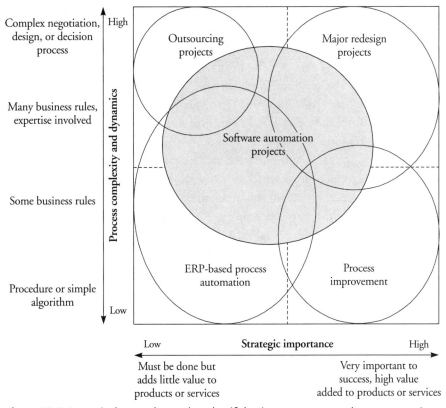

Figure 18.5 A matrix that can be used to classify business processes and some suggestions on what kind of change works best with each type of process.

be planned. If minor changes are required, a process improvement effort should be scheduled. In either case, once one has decided on change, specific techniques must be considered.

Is automation possible and appropriate? If it is, can off-the-shelf software be used? Can a workflow engine be used? Or will you need to develop a new software system to provide the needed automation? Will some combination be required?

Whatever you decide about automation, you still have other important considerations. Will environmental changes be required? Will new factories need to be built or new machines required? Will jobs need to be redesigned? Will employees need to learn new skills? Will managers need to change the measures they use to control the activities they are responsible for managing? Will the entire management hierarchy need to realign the measures it uses?

The matrix shown in Figure 18.5 is similar to the one we discussed in Chapter 3 when we considered how a company might organize and prioritize its business process architecture. Increasingly, companies will want to think of their processes as a portfolio. Each has a value, which may shift as the company strategies and goals shift. The value determines what kind of effort is appropriate for each process and how one might prioritize the process change projects.

The suggestions overlaid on the matrix in Figure 18.5 are just that. Each company's situation is different. Some companies can automate nearly everything. Other companies can outsource much more than others. Each company must determine which processes are most important to its success, consider the options, and then determine what architecture is best for their specific situation.

Once all these decisions are considered and decided and a new process is created, there is still the problem of implementing the new process. And there is always the possibility that even as you are working to redesign one process, some new environmental change may require a new initiative to change the process further.

To commit to managing an organization in a process-oriented manner requires that you commit to an ongoing process of change and realignment. The world keeps changing, and organizations must learn to keep changing as well. We have pictured this commitment as a cycle that never ends and is embedded within the core of the organization. We term it the *enterprise alignment cycle*. (See Figure 18.6.)

The process organization is constantly monitoring its external environment for changes. Changes can be initiated by competitors, by changes in customer taste, or by new technologies that allow the organization to create new products. When relevant changes occur, the organization begins a process that results in new processes with new characteristics, and new management systems that use new measures to assure those processes deliver the required outputs. Organizations can only respond in this manner if all the managers in the organization understand processes. We hope this book will have done a bit to make the reader just such a manager.

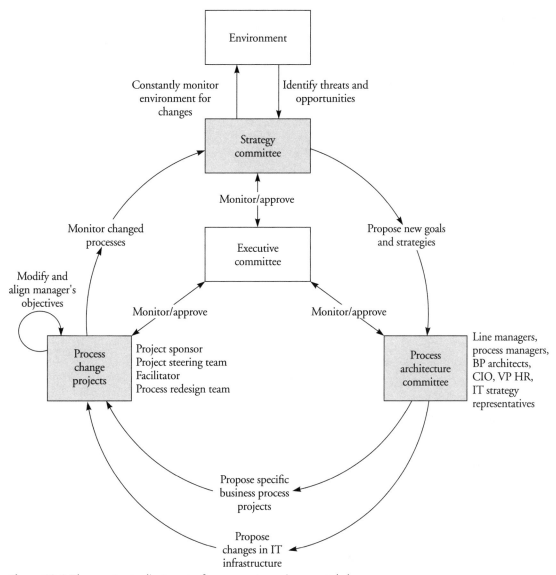

Figure 18.6 The constant adjustment of processes to environmental changes.

Glossary

WE HAVE TAKEN A BROAD VIEW of business processes, considering, among other things, strategies, process architectures, the management of processes, the redesign and improvement of processes, and the automation of processes. Some groups like the Workflow Management Coalition (WfMC) have published formal glossaries. Other communities of practice, like Six Sigma, use terms in specialized ways. Several business process methodologies use terms in specific ways. Formal business process languages, like BPML, have semantic definitions that are enforced by the language. Unfortunately, many of these different sources use terms in slightly different ways. We have tried in this book to use terms in the most generic manner. We have defined them in the text and define them again here. In cases where different significant groups or key sources use the terms in a different way than we do, we have indicated that fact.

activity. Processes can be subdivided into smaller and smaller units or subprocesses. We define *activity* as the smallest subprocess that a given business process team decides to illustrate on their process diagrams. (We could reverse that and say that a process is made up of one or more activities.) Activities can consist of a single step, like approving a purchase request or placing a cap on a bottle passing on a production line. Other activities involve multiple steps, like filling out a form or assembling a chair. There is no consistency about how the various methodologies use terms like *task* and *step,* but, increasingly, the term *activity* is reserved for the smallest unit of analysis. A given activity could be performed by one or more employees, by a software system, or by some combination. In the UML notation, both processes and activities are represented by rectangles with rounded corners. (*See also* **business process hierarchy.**) We sometimes indicate if activities are manual (normal line around rectangle), automated (bold line around rectangle), or mixed activities that involve both manual activities and systems (dashed line around activity rectangle).

activity analysis worksheet. A grid or matrix that one can use to analyze the relationships between the steps in the activity, listed on the vertical axis, and who performs the activity, who is responsible for the performance of the activity, decision rules used, and opportunities for improvement.

activity-based costing (ABC). As used in process redesigns, an approach to accounting that starts by determining how much it costs to perform each activity and then adds up activity costs to determine process costs, and so forth. The idea is that you add together all the costs in a complete value chain, subtract the costs from the income for the product or service produced by the value chain, and determine the profit on the process.

activity cost worksheet. A grid or matrix that one can use to analyze the various costs of a set of activities. Activities are listed on the vertical axis, and data about outputs, costs, times, and problems are described for each activity.

ad hoc workflow systems. Workflow systems that wait on users to indicate what should happen next. An insurance system might pull up documents for an underwriter only on request. (Contrast with **administrative workflow systems** and **transaction or production workflow systems.**)

administrative workflow systems. Workflow systems that keep track of what individuals are doing and assign new tasks according to some set of rules. (Contrast with **ad hoc workflow systems** and **transaction or production workflow systems.**)

ARIS. A business process modeling tool and a methodology for business process redesign. Created by A.W. Scheer, sold by IDS Scheer, and used extensively to link and tailor SAP applications.

asynchronous process. In an asynchronous process, one activity sends a message to another, but does not wait until it gets a response. A phone call to another person is a synchronous process—it can't go forward if the person you want to talk to doesn't answer the phone. Leaving a message on an answering machine turns it into an asynchronous process. You leave your message and go on with your business, figuring the person will respond when they get the message.

atomic activity. An activity that cannot be subdivided. An activity that consists of a single step or action.

Balanced Scorecard. A movement, method, and technique for aligning measures from an organization's strategic goals to specific process measures. It stresses measuring a variety of things to obtain a good overview of what's actually happening. A complementary approach to what we recommend. Usually associated with Robert Kaplan and David Norton.

batch processing. In either human or computer processes, a step where lots of items are accumulated and then processed together. In contrast to continuous processing, where items are processed as soon as possible.

benchmarks. As used in business process redesign, data about process measures obtained for specific types of processes. Many companies seek benchmark data on processes they seek to redesign in order to determine how well other companies manage the process.

BizTalk. Standards, protocols, tools, and a program of Microsoft Corporation to facilitate the exchange of information between companies and their business processes. (*See also* XLANG.)

BPEL4WS (Business Process Execution Language for Web Services). In the first draft of this book, we described two alternative XML business process languages, WSFL from IBM and XLANG from Microsoft. As this book goes to press, IBM, Microsoft and BEA have announced that they will be combining WSFL and XLANG to create a common XML business process language that will support both public (protocol) and private (execution) languages. It will probably become the Web standard and the acronym will probably be shortened to BPEL.

BPMI (Business Process Management Initiative). Consortium of business process modeling tools vendors and user companies that are working together to develop an XML-based business process language (BPMI), a notation for the language (BPMN), and a query language (BPQL). The idea is that companies would model their automated processes in BPMI and then be able to monitor and change the processes as needed. BPML would primarily be used by those who want to create collaborative Internet or Web service systems. For more information, check *www.bpmi.org.*

BPSS (Business Process Specification Schema). An ebXML specification that defines public processes for exchanging documents about buying and selling products over the Internet by means of choreographed transactions.

business intelligence (BI). Software systems and tools that seek to extract useful patterns or conclusions from masses of data.

business process. At its most generic, any set of activities performed by a business that is initiated by an event, transforms information, materials, or business commitments, and produces an output. Value chains and large-scale business processes produce outputs that are valued by customers. Other processes generate outputs that are valued by other processes.

business process automation. Refers to the use of computer systems and software to automate a process. Processes can be completely automated, so no human intervention is required, or semiautomated, where some human intervention is required to make decisions or handle exceptions. Techniques used for BP automation include workflow, BP-XML languages, ERP, and software development and EAI.

business process change cycle. A general description of the lifecycle of business processes. The environments in which companies operate change, and companies respond by changing their strategies and goals. Those changes drive changes in processes. In the most extreme case, a process must be retired and replaced by a new process. In most cases existing processes are redesigned or gradually improved to conform with new corporate strategies and goals. Environmental changes keep occurring, and this cycle keeps going, leading to a continuous business process redesign and improvement effort.

business process design or redesign. Business process redesign focuses on making major changes in an existing process or creating a new process. Depending on the size of the process, this can be a major undertaking and is done infrequently. And, once done, it should be followed by continuous business process improvement. Compared with BPR, as defined in the early 1990s, business process redesign usually focuses on smaller-scale processes and aims for more modest improvements. Redesign focuses on major improvements in existing processes. Design focuses on creating entirely new processes.

business process hierarchy. Everyone has a slightly different way of ordering the various levels of processes. The one we use is illustrated below.

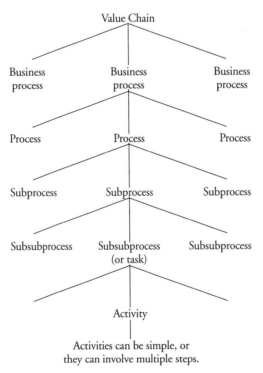

Value Chain	A value chain usually describes a major line of business. An organization has from one to a few value chains.
Business process — Business process — Business process	A value chain is usually decomposed into three to seven business processes.
Process — Process — Process	Depending on the nature of the business process, it can include a few to dozens of processes.
Subprocess — Subprocess — Subprocess	Processes usually contain three to seven subprocesses.
Subsubprocess — Subsubprocess (or task) — Subsubprocess	Depending on the nature of the subprocess, it may contain subsubprocesses and even subsubsubprocesses to any arbitrary depth. (Sometimes called *tasks* to simplify things.)
Activity	Activities are the lowest-level process we show on our diagrams. They are, in essence, the smallest subprocess we want to describe.

Activities can be simple, or they can involve multiple steps.

business process improvement (BPI). Business process improvement focuses on incrementally improving existing processes. There are many approaches, including the currently popular Six Sigma approach. BPI is usually narrowly focused and repeated over and over again during the life of each process.

business process language. *See* **XML Business Process Language.**

business process management or **Business Process Management (BPM).** In this book, we use *business process management* (lowercase) to refer to aligning processes with the organization's strategic goals, designing and implementing process architectures, establishing process measurement systems that align with organizational goals, and educating and organizing managers so that they will manage processes effectively. We occasionally use *Business Process Management* or BPM to refer to various automation efforts, including workflow systems, XML business process languages, and packaged ERP systems. In this case the management emphasizes the ability of workflow engines to control process flows, automatically measure processes, and to change process flows from a computer terminal. Business Process Management is a tricky term in the sense that two different groups within the business process community tend to use it in different ways.

business process modeling tool. A software tool that lets managers or analysts create business process diagrams. Simple tools only support diagramming. Professional business process modeling tools store each model element in a database so that they can be reused on other diagrams or updated. Many professional tools support simulation or code generation.

business process outsourcing. Many companies outsource business processes to other companies to manage and execute. Few companies outsource core business processes that they depend on for their unique position in the market. They fear that the outsourcer won't be able to improve the process quickly enough to respond to market changes. Some companies are now offering to outsource such processes, arguing that they have an approach that will let the owner make changes in the process as needed.

Business Process Reengineering (BPR). A term coined by Hammer and Davenport in the early 1990s. As originally defined in their books, it emphasized starting from a blank sheet and completely reconceptualizing major business processes and using information technology in order to obtain breakthrough improvements in performance. The term became unpopular in the late 1990s, and many business people associate BPR with failures. Those who still use the term have redefined it to mean what we mean by *business process redesign.*

business process tools. Used generically this can refer to worksheets, rules-of-thumb, and software tools used to help in business process change. With reference to software, it includes a wide range of software tools that help with every aspect of process change discussed in this book.

business rules. A statement describing a business policy or decision procedure. Some programming languages run business rules together into very complex algorithms. In business process analysis, each rule is usually stated independently, in the general format "If A and B, Then C." Workflow tools and detailed process diagrams both depend on business rules to specify how decisions are made. We generally associate business rules with activities. A decision diamond is adequate to show what happens if a loan is accepted or rejected, but dozens or even hundreds of business rules may need to be defined to clarify when a loan should be accepted or rejected. Training programs, job aids, software systems, and knowledge management systems aim to document business rules either to automate the decision process or to make the rules available to other decision makers.

Capability Maturity Model (CMM). A model developed by the Software Engineering Institute (SEI) of Carnegie Mellon University that describes how organizations develop software. The model identifies five levels or steps organizations go through as they become more sophisticated in their use of process. Level 1 organizations aren't effective in using processes. Level 5 organizations are mature in their use of processes and routinely manage and improve processes. Most organizations fall between levels 2 and 3. We argue that the same general concepts that apply to software organizations apply to any organization that attempts to organize around business processes.

CASE (Computer-Aided Software Engineering). Software methods and tools designed to generate code from models. Those involved in the CASE movement have always sought to make software generation more systematic and predictable. Software developers often use CASE tools to model business processes.

cause-effect diagram. A popular diagram used to analyze the causes of problems and provides an overview of all the possible causes. One starts at the right and lists the problem, and then extends a straight line to the left. From the line, one draws tangential lines and lists causes of the problems at the end of those lines. Lines can be drawn to the subsidiary lines as more discrete causes are considered, and so forth.

CIM (Computer Integrated Manufacturing). Movement, techniques, and tools for integrating manufacturing processes with computers and software.

class diagram. A UML diagram used for the design of object-oriented software systems and, more generally, to describe any set of logical classes and their relations. The organization diagram that we use in this book could be said to be a loosely structured class diagram. Software developers sometimes speak of a high-level class diagram as a business model. (*See also* **object-oriented**.)

COBOL. The computer language in which the vast majority of mainframe applications have been written.

competitive advantage. Occurs when one company can make more profits selling its products or services than its competitors. It occurs because a company can charge a premium because their product or service is more valuable, or because they can sell their product for less than their competitors because they are a more efficient producer. Rational strategists always seek to establish a long-term competitive advantage for their company. Many managers associate competitive advantage with the description provided in Michael Porter's *Competitive Advantage* (1985).

component. Used generically, this can refer to any entity or part. In software today, it usually refers to a software module, organized via object-oriented techniques. (*See also* **object-oriented.**)

core business process. Core processes are the processes that rely on the unique knowledge and skills of the owner and that contribute to the owner's competitive advantage. Contrast with **subsidiary business processes.**

cost leadership. A competitive strategy that emphasizes offering the product or service at the cheapest price. This can be done by creating the most efficient manufacturing price, by economies of scale, or by control of suppliers and channels.

COULD process. Also sometimes Can-Be Process. Description or diagram of one of two or more alternative redesigns that are being considered.

CRM (customer relationship management). A vague term describing any of a number of packaged or tailored applications or tools designed to help with sales, tracking customers, or managing information gained from customer interactions.

CTQ tree (Critical-to-Quality). A tree that lists the most important outcome, goal, or measure for a process improvement effort on the left and then subdivides it to identify more specific considerations that contribute to the outcome.

customer-oriented e-business applications. A generic way of talking about business processes and Internet applications that use Web sites or portals to allow customers to access the company over the Internet for information or commerce. (Compare with **supplier-oriented e-business applications** and **internal-oriented e-business applications.**)

decision point or diamond. A diamond or hexagonal figure used on process diagrams to show when a decision leads to a branching in the flow of information, control, or materials. Technically, all decisions take place within activities, and arrows only show the flow between activities. As a convenience, however, if the decisions lead to branching, we often represent them on the process diagram and label them to indicate why a flow would go to one subsequent activity rather than another.

decision support systems. Software systems designed to pull together information for managers to facilitate decisions. Increasingly, applications are not simply designed to automate a process, but to provide managers with ongoing information about the process so they can make more timely and accurate decisions.

diagram. An informal, graphical picture of some set of entities and some relations between them. (Contrast with **model.**)

differentiation. A competitive strategy that allows a company to sell its products for a premium price. This emphasizes creating superior products, products with unique or more desirable features or design.

DMAIC (Define, Measure, Analyze, Improve, Control). An acronym used by Six Sigma practitioners to remind them of the steps in a Six Sigma improvement project.

dot.com company. A generic, and increasingly derisive term, for any company that was created to take advantage of the Internet and its technologies. Most dot.com companies were founded in the late 1990s and most failed when the Federal Reserve restricted money in 2000. Most dot.com companies were based on inadequate business models. Some dot.com companies, like *www.Amazon.com* and *www.ebay.com,* have proved successful. While the recession of 2000–2002 eliminated most of the "pure play" dot.com companies, it didn't dampen the interest of conventional companies that are currently seeking to integrate Internet techniques with their existing business models to gain new customers or increase efficiencies.

downsizing. Reducing the number of employees at a company. Occasionally necessary. In the mid-1990s, it was too often done in conjunction with BPR projects, and many employees now associate BPR with downsizing.

EAI (Enterprise Application Integration). As companies seek to link their existing software applications with each other and with portals, the ability to get their applications to exchange data has become critical. EAI is usually close to the top of any CIO's list of concerns. There are different approaches to EAI. Some rely on linking specific applications with tailored code, but most rely on generic solutions, typically called *middleware.* XML, combined with SOAP and UDDI, is a kind of middleware.

e-business. A vague term that embraces all of the changes undertaken at companies that seek to take advantage of the Internet, the Web, email, and a host of associated Internet technologies and protocols. At the moment companies are transitioning to e-business. By the end of this decade all companies will be more or less e-businesses.

ebXML (electronic business XML). A consortium set up by two other organizations, a United Nations (UN/CEFACT) committee and OASIS, an Internet consortium. ebXML is charged with creating an XML architecture that standardizes all of the services that companies will need to build Web services. One subcommittee of ebXML is focused on business process communication and has proposed BPSS. For more information, check *www.ebxml.org.*

EDI (Electronic Data Interchange). A pre-Internet system for exchanging data between organizations. EDI requires that organizations standardize terms and invest heavily in computers and the maintenance of the EDI software. Although some companies use EDI systems and will only phase them out slowly, EDI is being replaced by less expensive Internet systems and protocols like XML.

email. The use of Internet protocols to pass text messages from one email address (URL) to another. Facilitates communication between employees, and between employees and customers or suppliers. Not always considered in redesigning processes, but email is gradually integrating companies in useful ways not previously achieved or fully understood.

e-marketplace. An Internet system maintained by a company or a consortium that allows individuals or companies to offer products and services or make bids to buy products or services. NASDAQ is an e-marketplace for stock. Covisint is the consortium and the name of the automotive e-marketplace.

enterprise alignment (enterprise alignment cycle). The ongoing process every company goes through to keep the elements of the organization aligned with the organization's strategy and goals. Vertical alignment is used to assure that process and activity measures and the measures used to evaluate managerial performance are all aligned with corporate goals. Horizontal alignment, or process improvement, focuses on assuring that all of the activities that take place in a process are aligned with the goals of the process. In most organizations, change is constant, and thus the organization is always working to realign, vertically and horizontally, to keep everything in sync with the changing strategy and aims of the organization.

enterprise application. As used by software designers, an enterprise system is a major software application that is designed to be used or accessed by many different departments and is usually maintained at the corporate level. Payroll is a good example of an enterprise system.

enterprise architecture. A set of diagrams and documents that describe both business and IT aspects of an organization. *See* **Zachman Framework.**

ERP (Enterprise Resource Planning). *See* **packaged applications.**

ERP-driven design. When a company elects to use an ERP application, it is getting an application that already makes assumptions about the inputs and outputs it will receive. To insert such an application into an existing business process, the company must first determine where it will fit and what it will replace and redo the existing process so that it interfaces with the new ERP application. In effect, this is the reverse of what happens when a company redesigns a process and then asks an IT group to create an application that will take inputs generated by the process and make designated outputs.

eTOM (electronic TeleManagement framework). The TeleManagement Forum, a consortium of telecommunications companies, has worked to create a standard framework, called eTOM, that describes the process architecture of an ideal telecom company. In the nature of the telecom industry, companies must work very closely together. This framework would allow them to share common process names and interfaces.

feedback. Refers to passing information from one person to another person who performed some task earlier, or from one process or system or another process or system that has already occurred. When the sales department reports customer complaints about manufacturing defects to the manufacturing department, it is providing feedback to manufacturing. When a sales manager accompanies a new salesperson on a call and then critiques the new salesperson's performance after the call, he or she is providing feedback. A lack of adequate or timely feedback is a major cause of process problems.

fishbone diagram. *See* **cause-effect diagram.**

fit. *See* **process fit.**

function-process matrix. A diagram that lists functions or departments on the horizontal axis and value chains or business processes on the horizontal axis and shows which functions are involved in which processes.

functional measures. Measures assigned to departments or functional groups that focus on goals related to departmental efficiency rather than process efficiency. A sales department might measure cost of sales or the number of calls a salesperson made in a given period of time. (Compare to **process measures.**)

gaps and disconnects pattern. A process redesign pattern that focuses on checking the handoffs between departments and functional groups in order to assure that flows across departmental lines are smooth and effective.

goal hierarchy. A hierarchical tree that shows how organizational goals, pictured at the top or on the left, are subdivided into more specific goals for value chains, processes, and subprocesses, and ultimately into activity goals. For every goal there are measures—specific tests of whether the goal is achieved or not. Thus, there is also a measures hierarchy that shadows the goal hierarchy.

goals, processes, and projects worksheet. A grid or matrix that one can use to analyze the relationships between goals, listed on the vertical axis, and processes, described on the horizontal axis.

horizontal alignment. Focuses on business processes. The alignment of activities and flows of information and materials into processes that encompass everything that happens from the time an order arrives until after the customer receives the product or service. (Contrast with **vertical alignment.**)

human performance analysis worksheet. A grid or matrix that one can use to analyze the human performance requirements of a process or activity. Tasks, activities, or steps are listed on the vertical axis of the worksheet, and measures and the elements of the human performance model are listed on the horizontal axis, making it possible to identify measures and potential performance problems for each activity.

human performance analyst. Someone who uses human performance technology to help with job analysis and design or to advise on how job performance can be improved.

human performance model. An analysis of what is involved in human performance. There are different versions of this model, but all emphasize inputs, outputs, the consequences of performance, feedback, and the skills and knowledge employed by the performer. Sometimes referred to as *human performance technology* (HPT). These models and an analysis of the variables are associated with the International Society for Performance Improvement (ISPI) and with Thomas Gilbert and Geary Rummler.

hypercompetition. Occurs when all companies focus on being the low-cost producer. Each company tries to improve their processes by adopting the best practices of their competitors. In effect each company works harder and faster to be more efficient, and their profit margins keep dropping. The alternative is for some companies to adopt other strategies. Associated with Michael Porter.

IDEF. A software methodology and diagramming system developed by the U.S. Department of Defense and widely used by CASE vendors in the late 1980s. Some IDEF diagrams are still used for U.S. Government projects today.

information technology (IT). Sometimes called information systems (IS) or data processing. Generic name for department or function that analyzes, creates, maintains, and supports applications and databases used by an organization.

instance. *See* **Process Instance.**

internal-oriented e-business applications. A generic way of talking about business processes and Internet applications that use the Internet to allow companies to link with their employees or to link their internal applications to share information or data. (Compare with **customer-oriented e-business applications** and **supplier-oriented e-business applications.**)

Internet. A set of public communication and network protocols that can pass computer data over telephone lines without interfering with normal phone calls.

IS process diagram. Also commonly called *AS-IS process diagram.* A description or diagram of an existing process before changes are made.

ISO 9000 (International Standards Organization). An international standard for how organizations should document their processes. In effect, an early effort to encourage organizations to create well-defined process architectures. In practice, it's too often simply an exercise in creating documentation to satisfy a requirement for getting on a bidding list.

ISPI (International Society for Performance Improvement). A professional society made up of individuals who are interested in the systematic analysis of human performance problems and techniques for training, changing, or managing human performance. For more information, check *www.ispi.org.*

job description. A document defining the job title and responsibilities of a specific job. It may include information on the specific tasks or activities to be performed and measures by which successful performance will be judged. May include salary and bonus information. Well-organized companies create job descriptions and then hire people to do what is described by the job description. In effect it's a contract to which both the company and employee agree. More than one specific employee can be hired to undertake the same job. You might have a description of a sales position and hire dozens or hundreds of people to function in that position. A job is not equal to a task or activity. In some cases a job and an activity are equivalent; you describe the activity and hire one or more people to do just that. In most cases, a person will be hired to perform multiple tasks or activities and may only perform specific steps within any given activity. Sometimes called a *Job Model.*

junction, junction bar. On a process diagram, a way of showing that one flow (output) is divided and sent into multiple activities, or to show that multiple flows must all be complete before the activity immediately after the bar can occur.

Kano analysis. An approach to defining customer satisfaction that divides outputs, service, or product features of outputs into (1) basic requirements (the minimum a customer expects), (2) satisfiers (additional outputs or features that please customers), and (3) delighters (outputs or features that the customer didn't expect that really please customers). Associated with Noriaki Kano, a Japanese quality control expert.

knowledge. Information defines facts (A is B). Knowledge defines what one should do if certain facts apply. Thus, if A is B, then do C. There are many different ways knowledge can be encoded, but policies and business rules are popular formats.

knowledge management. Focuses on defining the knowledge employees or systems use to perform activities and saving it in some format so that others can access it. Knowledge management systems can be organized along different lines. We recommend organizing it with processes and activities.

lean manufacturing. An approach to designing and managing production processes that emphasizes minimal inventory and just-in-time delivery, among other things, to improve the efficiency of a manufacturing process.

levels of analysis. For purposes of analysis, we divide a company into three levels: (1) the organization and its environment, (2) the value chains, processes, and subprocesses, and (3) activities, including the people and systems that actually perform the activities and the costs and times associated with the performance of each activity.

measure. A specific test to determine if a goal is being met or not. High-level measures tend to focus on profits, revenues, product output figures, and growth. As measures are subdivided, they tend to focus on whether specific subprocesses are achieving their output goals. Very specific measures may check to determine if the steps within an activity are being performed correctly or if decisions are being made according to rules and policies.

measurement scheduling worksheet. A worksheet that looks like a process diagram. Functional units or managers are listed on the vertical axis. Years, quarters, months, weeks, and days are listed along the horizontal axis. Rectangles are drawn to show which managers take part in which meetings at what points in time. Sometimes a bit of a process map is pictured on the right side of the worksheet to emphasize the process being measured by those involved in this plan. We don't expect most companies to use a worksheet like this, but it's important that measures be evaluated frequently and that managers responsible for different functions meet to assure that the handoffs between processes are satisfactory.

measures hierarchy. A hierarchical tree that shows how organizational measures, pictured at the top or on the left, are subdivided into more specific measures for value chains, processes, and subprocesses, and ultimately into activity measures. For every goal there are measures—specific tests of whether the goal is achieved or not. Thus, there is also a goal hierarchy that mirrors the measures hierarchy.

middleware. Software that allows two modules or applications to exchange data. *See* **EAI.**

model. A formal set of relationships that can be manipulated to test assumptions. A simulation that tests the number of units that can be processed each hour under a set of conditions is an example of a model. Models do not need to be graphical, although that is the way we have used the term throughout this book. Contrast with **diagram.**

Model Driven Architecture (MDA). A new approach to application development being promoted by the Object Management Group. In essence, the idea is that organizations create abstract class models of their applications and then use those models to generate specific models and software code. The idea behind MDA is that the same abstract model can be used to generate different types of code. Thus, rather than creating new applications when new technologies come along, a company can have a high-level architecture and reusable components that it can use over and over again for many years. This approach is in the early stages of development, but it has attracted quite a bit of attention. (Compare with **CASE.**)

modeling. In a loose sense, modeling simply refers to creating a simplified representation of something else. A model can be a picture, a diagram, or a mathematical formula. In this book, we have used modeling in the sense of business process modeling—to create a diagrammatic representation of how work is done. In a rigorous sense, a model must specify formal relationships and assumptions that can be tested.

niche specialization. A competitive strategy that focuses on offering products to specific groups of buyers or to buyers in particular geographical locations.

non-value-adding activities. Processes or activities that neither add value to a final product or service, nor enable activities that add value. In most cases these activities are left over from older processes and somehow continue even though they are no longer necessary, or they are done because some departmental manager insists that "that's the way things are done in this department," even though they add nothing to a specific process.

object-oriented. An approach to structuring software applications. Instead of thinking of an application as a process with steps, we think of it as a set of objects that exchange messages. Now the dominant approach to software development. Java and Visual Basic are object-oriented software development languages.

OMG (Object Management Group). An international consortium of companies that work together to create standards for advanced software engineering technologies. The OMG has developed middleware standards, like CORBA, the Unified Modeling Language (UML) for diagramming software and business systems, and the Model Driven Architecture (MDA), a systematic way of maintaining reusable software components and using them to generate code for specific applications. (*See* **UML** and **Model Driven Architecture.**) For more information, check *www.omg.org.*

operational effectiveness. A strategy, or lack of strategy, that commits a company to constantly trying to improve the effectiveness of its processes. Taken to the extreme, it results in hypercompetition. (Compare with **positioning.**)

organization chart. Traditional way of showing the relationships between departmental and functional units or the reporting relationships between managers within an organization. Organization charts tend to emphasize that each department is independent and to ignore the many relationships that exist when activities in one department interact with activities in other departments.

organization diagram. One of the two basic diagrams used in this book. A system diagram that shows either functional units or processes inside the company box and shows how they link to each other and to entities outside the company. See below.

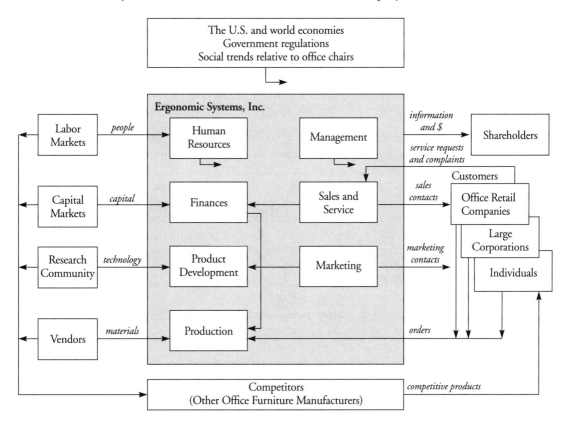

organization diagrams. Generic use of term. Diagrams that depict the organizational structure of a company or agency. An organization chart is one kind of organization diagram, but in this book we emphasize systems diagrams that show flow between entities rather than organizational charts that simply focus on hierarchical relationships.

outsourcing. Occurs when one company hires another company to manage, maintain, and run some portion of its business. A catalog company, for example, might outsource the warehousing and delivery of the products it sells to another company. Many companies outsource standard software applications. *See also* **business process outsourcing.**

packaged applications. Generically, any prepackaged software application. Normally it is used as a way of referring to vendors who sell ERP or CRM application suites that are organized to be used to integrate all of a company's main software applications. By installing a number of packaged applications, a company can assure that major business process applications in finance, accounting, human resources, and manufacturing all communicate smoothly and store data in a common database. The dominant packaged application vendor is SAP. Other well-known ERP vendors are Baan, J.D. Edwards, Oracle, and PeopleSoft.

parallel process. A process in which two or more sequences of activities are going on simultaneously. If a physical document is being passed from one person to another, the process is necessarily a single sequence. An electronic document in a workflow system, on the other hand, can be sent to several people simultaneously.

People-CMM. An adaptation of Carnegie Mellon's CMM model to the analysis of the best practices employed in the management of a workforce, as organizations move from an immature to a mature use of processes.

performance. Generically, the work involved in and the results or products that accrue from conducting a process or activity. Human performance describes how people do a task and what results. System performance describes how systems do a task and what results. Organizational performance describes what an organization does and what results.

performance framework. *See* **three levels of organization performance.**

PIP (potential for improving performance). Measure used by human performance technologists. One measures the performance of the best person performing a task and also determines the average performance of the average worker. Large differences suggest that performance can be improved by bringing average performance up closer to the best performance. Small differences suggest little potential for improvement. Term is usually associated with Thomas Gilbert. (Some other business process people use the term PIP as an acronym for "performance improvement project.")

portal. A Web site that allows the user to find other Web pages or Web sites. As a generalization, a portal is a train station. You go there in order to find out where else you can go and then to go there. Most companies will maintain one portal for their employees, where they can go to get information and to access company services, and another public portal for customers to provide them with information and the opportunity to buy products or services from the company.

Porter's model of competition. A general model of the environment in which companies operate that suggests what factors strategists should monitor. They key factors are buyers, suppliers, competitors, new companies that might enter the market, and new products or technologies that might replace those on which your organization depends. The model is defined in Michael Porter's book *Competitive Strategy.*

positioning. A synonym for choosing a strategy. A marketing concept. One should always say that one's product is the best—if not best overall, then best for the price, or best for some specific application. One positions a company by creating a strategy that allows the company to make such a claim.

private processes. A process that goes on inside a company. Most companies would rather not tell other companies how their applications accomplish things. On the other hand, certain kinds of coordination require that two or more companies know about each other's processes so that they can integrate them more effectively. Some XML business process languages are written to communicate between a company and a public process, and others are written to describe, and share, the private processes of multiple companies. Private business processes are sometimes called *executable business processes.* (Contrast with **public processes.**)

problem analysis. Six Sigma practitioners often describe problem analysis in terms of three phases: Open, Narrow, and Close. During Open, one brainstorms and considers every possible cause of the problem. During Narrow, one reduces the number of potential causes. During Close, one settles on a specific cause to focus on.

process architecture (business process architecture). A process architecture is a written or diagrammatic summary of the value chains and business processes supported by a given organization. A good process architecture shows how value chains and business processes are related to each other and to the strategic goals of the organization. Some companies use the term *process architecture* to refer to the process diagram for a single process. We refer to that as a *process model* or *process diagram.* We often add *business* or *enterprise* to *process architecture* to suggest that it's a high-level architecture of all of the processes in the organization.

process change. A purposely vague term chosen to embrace the complete range of process change methods and techniques, including the alignment of processes and strategies, the creation of a process architecture, the analysis of processes, redesign, improvement, automation, and implementation.

process diagram. One of the two basic diagrams emphasized in this book. A diagram that shows departments, functions, or individuals on the vertical axis and uses swimlanes to show which subprocesses or activities are managed by which departments, functions, or individuals. The customer of the process always appears on the top swimlane. External processes are listed below the main process. The horizontal axis usually depicts the flow of time from left to right, although informal process diagrams sometimes allow loops that violate a strict time flow. Rectangles with rounded corners represent subprocesses or activities. Arrows represent various types of flow between rectangles. See below.

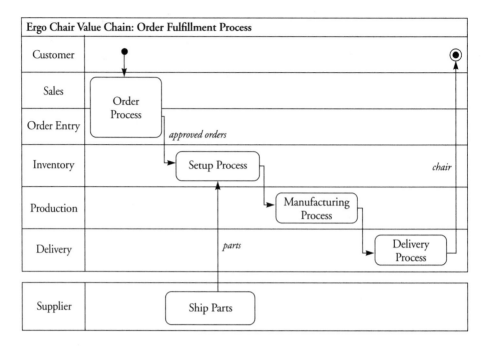

Some developers divide process diagrams into *IS process diagrams* that show a process as it is currently performed, *COULD process diagrams* that show how a process might be changed, and *SHOULD process diagrams* that show how a process redesign team ultimately proposes to change a process.

process diagrams. Used generically, a synonym for workflow diagrams or UML activity diagrams. A diagram that shows the flow of information, control, or materials from one activity to another. Any subprocess on one process diagram can become a process diagram in its own right if the designers need more details.

process fit. The way in which the elements of a business process are uniquely integrated. Companies with good process fit have worked hard to integrate everything around a specific strategic focus. It's easy for competitors to copy standard processes, but it's very hard for competitors to duplicate business process with a high degree of fit. A concept associated with Michael Porter.

process instance. A process diagram describes a generic sequence of events. An *instance* describes an actual process which includes data, real actions, and specific decisions. Workflow systems and simulation systems both keep track of the data from the execution of specific process instances in order to determine things like how long the process actually takes, who handled a specific instance, or how much it cost. In the case of simulation systems, someone has to supply information about a set of actual instances.

process-IT matrix. A matrix created by listing processes on the horizontal axis and IT platforms or other architectural elements on the vertical axis. This matrix shows what IT applications, databases, and other resources are required to support each process. If you have a clear idea of the value of your various processes, then this is an excellent tool for prioritizing IT projects.

process management. Most managers or supervisors are responsible for specific processes or activities. They are responsible for organizing the process or activity and securing the resources needed to execute it, and they are responsible for measuring the results of the activity and providing rewards or corrective feedback when necessary. They are also responsible for changing and improving it whenever possible.

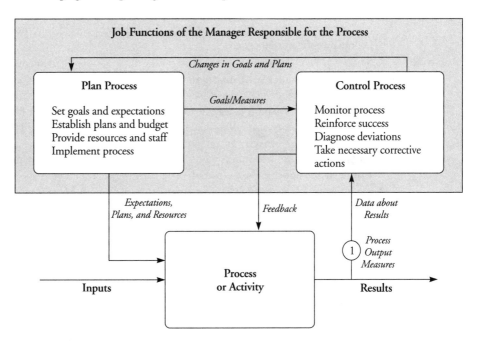

process measures or process output measures. Measures of whether a process or activity is achieving its goals. At every level, processes have outputs, and those outputs should be measured to assure that the process is functioning as it should. In an ideal organization, company goals and measures are associated with value chains and then subdivided so that, at every level, managers are measuring process outcomes that are related to the ultimate goals and measures of the organization. If vertical alignment is ignored, it's possible that activities or processes will be measured in ways that don't contribute to the overall success of the larger process or the success of the company.

process measures worksheet. A grid or matrix that one can use to analyze the relationships between measures. High-level measures are listed on the vertical axis and then successively subdivided as one moves to the right, into process, subprocess, subsubprocess, and ultimately activity measures. (Compare with the **measures hierarchy,** which is a different way of representing the same information.)

process redesign patterns. A pattern is an approach or solution that has often worked in the past. There are several patterns that have proved popular in redesign efforts. For example, one can try to eliminate all non-value-adding activities, or one can try to simplify the flow of the process.

process sponsor or process manager. Person with responsibility for the entire process. The individual who monitors the entire process and its outcome measures and provides feedback and help to departmental managers who manage specific subprocesses or activities included in the overall process.

process-strategy matrix. A matrix formed by an estimate of the strategic importance of a process on the horizontal axis and an estimate of the process complexity and dynamics on the vertical axis. Assuming that "low" is positioned at the lower-left corner of both continua, then processes that fall in the lower-left are of little complexity, don't change very often, and don't have much strategic importance. They should be automated if possible and given the minimum resources necessary for efficient functioning. Conversely, processes that lie at the upper-right are complex, dynamic, and of high strategic importance. These are usually the processes that provide your company with its competitive advantage and should be nurtured accordingly.

process thinking. A subset of systems thinking. Conceptualizing groups of activities as processes and seeking to understand how all of the processes in the organization work together to take inputs and produce products, services, and profits.

ProVision Workbench. A professional business process modeling tool sold by Proforma Corporation. We used this tool to illustrate some of the ways our Ergonomics case could have been streamlined if we had used a software modeling tool.

public processes. A business process that two or more companies use to pass messages. Both companies send messages to the public process and neither knows what the other does to generate the messages it sends to the public process. A public process simply defines a way for two companies to communicate and coordinate their processes. Some XML business process languages are written to communicate between a company and a public process, and others are written to describe, and share, the private processes of multiple companies. Public processes are sometimes called *business protocols* or *abstract processes.* (Contrast with **private processes.**)

RM-ODP (Reference Model of Open Distributed Processing). An effort to create a formal, hierarchical method for defining any type of software system. The model is being created as an International Standards Organization (ISO) specification. It is too complex for most uses, but is sometimes used in very complex projects.

Rummler-Brache methodology. Geary Rummler and Alan Brache defined a comprehensive approach to organizing companies around processes, managing and measuring processes, and redefining processes in their 1990 book, *Improving Performance.* This is probably the best-known, systematic approach to business process change, and ideas first introduced in this book have been very influential on other, less comprehensive approaches. This book draws heavily from the basic approach laid out in *Improving Processes.*

SAP (Systems, Applications and Products in data processing). Leading ERP or packaged software vendor.

SCM (supply chain management). A vague term describing any of a number of packaged or tailored applications or tools designed to help with the development or execution of supply chain systems or with managing information gained from supply chain interactions.

SCOR (Supply Chain Operations Reference) model. A method, framework, and techniques for analyzing and designing supply chain systems. Created by the Supply Chain Council.

SHOULD process. Also called *TO-BE process.* A description or diagram of the process that the redesign team proposes to create.

silo thinking. This is a metaphor drawn from the large grain silos that one sees throughout the U.S. Midwest. It is a term of derision that suggests that each department on an organization chart is a silo and that it stands alone, not interacting with any of the other departmental silos.

simplification pattern. A process redesign pattern that focuses on simplifying the flow of a process.

simulation. A technique that uses a model to make predictions about a system or process. There are different types of simulation, some more informal and some more formal. Process simulation tools normally assign values to activities and then a number of cases to see how the business process will respond. The simulation of complex processes can often reveal outcomes that the developers don't anticipate.

SIPOC (Supplier, Input, Process, Output, Customer). An acronym used by Six Sigma practitioners to remind them how to set up a high-level overview of a process.

Six Sigma. A movement, method, and set of techniques focused on improving business processes. Relies heavily on statistical techniques to measure success. There are multiple Six Sigma methods, some designed for process improvement and some for designing or redesigning business processes. Most Six Sigma books, however, emphasize incremental process improvement. Often associated with Mikel Harry and Motorola.

SOAP (Simple Object Access Protocol). An Internet protocol that is used to move XML files around the Internet.

software engineering. A movement, methods, and techniques aimed at making software development more systematic. Software methodologies, like the OMG's UML, and software tools (*See* **CASE**) that help developers model application designs and then generate code are all closely associated with software engineering.

software requirements. A more or less formal statement of what a software application should do. Sometimes business analysts create requirements and hand them to software developers. Other times software analysts interview business people in order to determine the requirements for a software application development effort. Business people invariably define requirements less formally than necessary. Business people tend to define requirements with written statements or with process diagrams. Software developers are more likely to define software requirements by means of use case diagrams or class diagrams, which often aren't that clear to business analysts. Software requirements constitute an important interface between business managers and IT organizations. If the handoff isn't clear and precise, then the resulting system is likely to disappoint the business people who requested it.

standard or normal bell-shaped curve. A statistical tool for describing variations from a mean, developed by Carl Frederick Gauss. Shows that most deviation is slight and that extreme variations are few and infrequent. Six Sigma relies on concepts derived from the standard curve, but the actual curve that is used in Six Sigma tables is a different curve defined by what is referred to as *long-run process drift*.

standard deviation. One standard deviation to the left or the right of the mean on a standard bell-shaped curve accounts for 34.13% of the variation. Two standard deviations, one to the left and one to the right, account for 68.26% of the variation. The Greek letter sigma is used to represent a deviation. One determines deviations in actual situations by gathering data and determining what actual deviation accounts for 68.26% of the deviations, and so forth. Six Sigma people rely on tables to translate numbers into deviations or sigmas.

strategic positioning. Defining a position in which an organization can achieve dominance or at least success. Common strategic positions include the low-cost seller, a premium seller with products that are better than competitive products, or a niche position in which products are sold to special segments of the market.

strategizing. The process of establishing and updating a strategy. In organizations, this is usually done by a strategy committee. In essence, the process involves determining what the organization is currently doing; checking the environment to see what competitors, customers, suppliers, and government agencies are doing; and then determining if the organization needs to change its strategy in response to changes in the environment.

strategy. A broad statement of how an organization is going to compete, what its goals are, and what policies it will pursue to realize its goals. A good strategy defines how a company can position itself to maintain a long-term competitive advantage.

subprocesses. Process analysis necessarily occurs on levels. A high-level process diagram shows major processes. Each major process is typically divided into subprocesses, which are represented on separate process diagrams. Those processes, in turn, may be subdivided into subsubprocesses. There is no logical limit to the number of times we may subdivide processes into subprocesses. We repeat it until we understand the process in sufficient detail to successfully redesign or improve it. The smallest subprocesses we identify in any given analysis effort are arbitrarily called *activities*. See **business process hierarchy** for one possible set of naming conventions.

subsidiary processes. Processes that support core business processes or processes that provide products or services that are not among the most important that the company produces. In most companies, IT and HR processes are classified as subsidiary processes because they exist to provide support services for the core business processes.

supersystem diagram. An organization diagram that represents the company as a black box and focuses on the elements like suppliers and customers that make inputs and outputs to the company. Normally we group outside elements into four groups: suppliers on the left, customers and shareholders on the right, governmental and environmental factors above, and competitors below.

supplier-oriented e-business applications. A generic way of talking about business processes and Internet applications that use the Internet to allow companies to link with business partners or suppliers to coordinate their efforts. (Compare with **customer-oriented e-business applications** and **internal-oriented e-business applications**.)

Supply Chain Council (SCC). International consortium of companies that are interested in improving organizational supply chains. SCC has conferences, publications, and training programs. They promote SCOR, a systematic process methodology for creating supply chain systems. (*See* **SCOR**.) For more information, check *www.supply-chain.org*.

swimlane. A row on a business process diagram. A way of indicating who is responsible for a given process or activity. Swimlanes are named on the left side of the process diagram. In most cases swimlanes are assigned to departments, groups within departments, individuals, applications, systems of applications, or databases. In exceptional cases, swimlanes may represent geographical regions. Processes, subprocesses, or activities that fall within a given swimlane are the responsibility of the entity named on the left axis of the process diagram. (Some workflow tools represent swimlanes as vertical rows. In effect, this would rotate the process diagrams we show in this book by 90 degrees. This is arbitrary; we simply prefer to have processes flow from left to right rather than from the top down.)

synchronous process. In a synchronous process, one activity sends a message to another and then waits for a response before proceeding. A phone call to another person is a synchronous process—it can't go forward if the person you want to talk to doesn't answer the phone. Leaving a message on an answering machine turns it into an asynchronous process. You leave your message and go on with your business, figuring the person will respond when they get the message.

system. A grouping of parts or functions that operate together for a common purpose. An automobile is a system of components that work together to provide transportation. Systems function within boundaries. They usually receive inputs from outside and, as a result of their operations, generate outputs. Systems can contain systems. Organizations, business processes, and software applications are all examples of systems.

systems analyst, systems architect, systems designer. Individuals who analyze, design, and develop software applications, systems, or infrastructure. There are different schools of systems analysts. Some emphasize relatively informal and descriptive approaches, while others emphasize formal, mathematical, and dynamic approaches.

systems dynamics. This is a specific approach to modeling systems that emphasizes the feedback loops that tie subsystems together and explain the dynamic changes that occur over the course of time. This approach is usually associated with Jay Forrester.

systems thinking. Conceptualizing sets of entities, activities, or organizations as systems. Focusing on how elements relate to each other and depend on each other. What Peter Senge refers to as the *Fifth Discipline.*

three levels of organization (performance framework). A Rummler-Brache concept. Holds that there are three primary levels of business process analysis: the organizational level, the process level, and the activity or performance level (which *Improving Performance* called the *job level*). Sometimes presented as a matrix, the performance framework, where the three levels are shown on the vertical axis and the perspectives or viewpoints are shown on the horizontal axis: Goals and Measures, Design and Implementation, and

Management. A nice way of classifying the concerns that a comprehensive business process approach should encompass.

Total Quality Management (TQM). A movement, an industrial discipline, and a set of techniques for improving the quality of processes. TQM emphasizes constant measures and statistical techniques to help improve and then maintain the output quality of processes. Often associated with Edwards Deming.

transaction processing. Refers to workflow or other software systems that make changes in databases. The most rigorous transaction processing systems make copies of everything as the transaction occurs to guarantee that it's completed correctly. If anything goes wrong, the state of all data involved is reset to its original state. Imagine you seek to move money from one account to another. The system checks to see that the money is removed from one account and placed in the other, and doesn't finalize things until it's sure that both actions have occurred.

transaction or production workflow systems. A type of workflow system that moves documents or information from one terminal to another following a workflow model. (Contrast with **ad hoc workflow systems** and **administrative workflow systems.**)

transitioning to a new process. The transition period occurs after managers and employees have been trained in the new process, when they actually start using it. A successful transition depends on having senior management support and having measurement and incentive systems in place to assure that local managers work to see that the new process is implemented correctly.

UDDI (Universal Description, Discovery and Integration). A Web protocol, based on the WSDL language, that allows one Web system to locate others and determine what format messages to that system must take.

UML (Unified Modeling Language). An international, standard notation for modeling software systems. The UML specification supports several different types of diagrams, including the activity diagram, which is used to model business processes and workflow diagrams. UML was created and is maintained by the OMG.

use case diagram. One type of UML diagram. Often used by software developers to define the software requirements for a system. Use case diagrams focus on scenarios that describe how users use the application.

value-added activity. A process or activity that adds value to a product or service. Value is judged by the customer, who can be the customer of the company or an internal customer who receives the output of the process or activity. An activity or process adds value if it satisfies all three of these requirements: (1) the customer is willing to pay for the process or activity, (2) the process or activity physically changes or transforms the product or service, and (3) the process or activity is performed correctly the first time it's undertaken.

value-added analysis. A process redesign pattern that focuses on eliminating activities that neither add value or enable value-added activities.

value chain. A very large-scale business process that is initiated by a customer request, or by the decision of the company to enter a new line of business, and results in the delivery of a process or service to a customer. A value chain includes everything that contributes to the output. By adding up all of the costs of each activity in a value chain, and subtracting the total from the sale price, an organization can determine the profit margin on the value chain. Most organizations support from 3 to 15 value chains. Many managers associate value chains with the description provided in Michael Porter's *Competitive Advantage* (1985).

value-enabling activities. Activities or processes that do not, in themselves, meet the criteria of value-adding activities, but which must be performed in order to make it possible to perform value-adding activities. The activities involved in the development of most software applications are value-enabling activities.

value proposition. A description of the value that a product, service, or process will provide a customer. Should be defined abstractly to assure that one understands who all the competitors are. Thus, rather than saying a bookstore provides customers with books, one should consider saying that the bookstore provides education or entertainment.

vertical alignment. Focuses on aligning strategic goals and measures from value chains down to activities. Sometimes includes management systems that align each manager's goals and evaluation criteria from organizational strategies to supervisor's goals.

W3C (World Wide Web Consortium). A standards consortium that develops and publishes Internet and Web languages and protocols. For more information, check *www .w3c.org*.

Web services. A vague term that refers to distributed or virtual applications or processes that use the Internet to link activities or software components. An example of a Web services application is a travel Web site that takes a reservation from a customer, then sends a message to a hotel application, accessed via the Web, to determine if a room is available, books it, and tells the customer he or she has a reservation.

workflow. Generic term for a process or for the movement of information or material from one activity (worksite) to another.

Workflow Management Coalition (WfMC). A consortium of vendors and users of workflow systems that work together on standards and to share information. For more information, check *www.wfmc.org*.

workflow model. Another name for a process diagram. Often includes both a diagram and rules that define the flow of information from one activity to the next. If used in conjunction with a workflow system or engine, a software-based process diagram that becomes the program for a workflow system that will move information from a database to one computer terminal after another.

workflow system or engine. A software tool or program that helps analysts define a process and the rules governing process decisions, and then manages the actual distribution of information related to specific instances or cases to terminals and databases. Most vendors and major users of workflow systems are members of the Workflow Management Coalition (WfMC).

worksheets. All worksheets presented in this book are simply suggestions for how an organization might want to organize information. Different companies will want to create their own worksheets to emphasize different things.

WSFL (Web Services Flow Language). Early IBM XML business process language. *See* **BPEL4WS.**

XLANG. Early Microsoft XML business process language. *See* **BPEL4WS.**

XML (eXtended Markup Language). An Internet protocol defined by the W3C. A file format that includes within a file both data and rules for how the data is to be interpreted. Using XML, one can create XML languages—in effect, sets of terms that companies agree to use in a specific way in order to facilitate the exchange of data. Emerging as the most popular way to transmit data between applications and companies over the Internet.

XML Business Process Language. A computing language in which one can describe business processes and their relationships. These languages use XML to pass messages.

XPDL (XML-based Process Definition Language). The Workflow Management Coalition (WfMC) created this standard language to describe how workflow tools can communicate information about business processes with each other over the Internet.

Zachman Framework. Zachman was an IBM researcher who outlined a framework that describes business and software architectures. On the vertical axis he describes levels of generality and specificity. On the horizontal axis he originally described three viewpoints: Data, Function, and Network. He has since set up his own company and added three more viewpoints: People, Time, and Motivation. Many regard this as the most definitive overview of architectures and seek to position any specific architecture by showing where it would lie on the Zachman Framework. For more information, check *www.zifa.com.*

Notes and References

THIS SET OF NOTES, organized by chapter, includes comments on points raised in the chapters, citations of Web sites and books mentioned in the chapters, and some additional citations that will allow readers to learn more about specific topics.

Preface

Rummler, Geary A., and Alan P. Brache. *Improving Performance: How to Manage the White Space on the Organization Chart* (2nd Ed.). Jossey-Bass, 1995. Geary Rummler started publishing articles on business process redesign in the early 1980s, but this book, originally published in 1990, provides the best introduction to the comprehensive approach to business process management, measurement, and redesign that he has been elaborating ever since. For the latest information on Rummler's thinking, check the Web site of his current company, *www.perfromancedesignlab.com*.

Introduction

Hammer, Michael, and James Champy. *Reengineering the Corporation: A Manifesto for Business Revolution.* HarperBusiness, 1993. This was the run-away best-seller that got everyone in business talking about reengineering in the early 1990s. It's still the best book if you just want to get excited about the potential for changing business processes. It emphasizes radical redesign, and that's a bit too much for most companies, but the general arguments work just as well for more modest redesigns.

Harmon, Paul. *Who's Profiting from Business Process Redesign.* Cutter Consortium, 2002. This is an expensive report that provides lots of data about what companies are doing today. To check on this report, go to the Cutter Consortium Web site: *www.cutter.com*.

McCraw, Thomas K. (Ed.). *Creating Modern Capitalism: How Entrepreneurs, Companies, and Countries Triumphed in Three Industrial Revolutions.* Harvard University Press, 1997. There are several books that describe the Industrial Revolution and the birth of modern corporations. This is my favorite, and it's where I got my basic information on Henry Ford and the Ford Motor Company.

Paulk, Mark C., Charles V. Weber, Bill Curtis, and Mary Beth Chrissis (principal contributors and editors). *The Capability Maturity Model: Guidelines for Improving the Software Process.* Addison-Wesley, 1995. This book is the easiest introduction to the concepts underlying CMM.

To access information about CMM, check *www.esi.cmu.edu/cmm.*

Bill Curtis, one of the leading thinkers behind the CMM effort, is already working on applying CMM to non-software processes in organizations. He can be contacted through his company: *www.teraquest.com.*

Chapter 1.   Business Process Change

McCraw, Thomas K. (Ed.) *Creating Modern Capitalism: How Entrepreneurs, Companies, and Countries Triumphed in Three Industrial Revolutions.* Harvard University Press, 1997. A good overview of the Industrial Revolution, the rise of various early companies, the work of various entrepreneurs, and the work of management theorists like F. W. Taylor.

Taylor, Frederick W. *The Principles of Scientific Management.* Harper's, 1911. For a modern review of the efficiency movement and Taylor, check Daniel Nelson's *Frederick W. Taylor and the Rise of Scientific Management,* University of Wisconsin Press, 1980.

Bertalanffy, Ludwig von. *General Systems Theory: Foundations, Development, Applications.* George Braziller, 1968. An early book that describes how engineering principles developed to control systems ranging from thermostats to computers provided a better way to describe a wide variety of phenomena.

Forrester, Jay. *Principles of Systems.* Pegasus Communications, 1971. Forester was an influential professor at MIT who wrote a number of books showing how systems theory could be applied to industrial and social systems. Several business simulation tools are based on Forester's ideas, which are usually referred to as *systems dynamics,* since they focus on monitoring and using changing rates of feedback to predict future activity.

Sterman, John D. *Business Dynamics: Systems Thinking and Modeling for a Complex World.* Irwin McGraw-Hill, 2000. Sterman is one of Forrester's students at MIT, and this is a popular textbook for those interested in the technical details of systems dynamics, as applied to business problems.

Senge, Peter M. *The Fifth Discipline: The Art and Practice of the Learning Organization.* Currency Doubleday, 1994. Senge is also at the Slone School of Management at MIT, and a student of Forrester. Senge has created a more popular approach to systems dynamics that puts the emphasis on people and the use of models and feedback to facilitate organizational development. In the Introduction we described mature process organizations as organizations that totally involved people in constantly improving the process. Senge would describe such an organization as a learning organization.

Porter, Michael E. *Competitive Strategy: Techniques for Analyzing Industries and Competitors.* The Free Press, 1980. The best-selling book on strategy throughout the past two decades. The must-read book for anyone interested in business strategy.

Porter, Michael E. *Competitive Advantage: Creating and Sustaining Superior Performance.* The Free Press, 1985. This book focuses on the idea of competitive advantage and discusses how companies obtain and maintain it. One of the key techniques Porter stresses is an emphasis on value chains and creating integrated business processes that are difficult for competitors to duplicate.

Hammer, Michael. "Reengineering Work: Don't Automate, Obliterate." *Harvard Business Review.* July–August 1990. This article, and the one below by Davenport and Short, kicked off the BPR fad. The books that these authors are best known for didn't come until a couple of years later.

Rummler, Geary, and Alan Brache. *Performance Improvement: Managing the White Space on the Organization Chart.* Jossey-Bass, 1990. The best introduction to business process redesign for managers. Managers read Hammer and Davenport in the early 1990s, and then turned to Rummler and Brache to learn how to actually do business process redesign. So many ideas that we now associate with business process change originated with Geary Rummler. As far as I know he was the first to begin creating diagrams that showed processes crossing organization charts. (He did it in a meeting with Motorola executives in 1984.) He was also the first to add swimlanes to workflow diagrams to show exactly what department or individual was responsible for managing a specific process or activity.

Davenport, Thomas H., and James Short. "The New Industrial Engineering: Information Technology and Business Process Redesign." *Sloan Management Review.* Summer 1990.

Hammer, Michael, and James Champy. *Reengineering the Corporation: A Manifesto for Business Revolution.* HarperBusiness, 1993. This was a run-away best-seller that got everyone in business talking about reengineering in the mid-1990s. It argued for a radical approach to redesign. Some companies used the ideas successfully; most found it too disruptive.

Davenport, Thomas H. *Process Innovation: Reengineering Work through Information Technology.* Harvard Business School Press, 1993. This book doesn't have the breathless marketing pizzazz that Hammer's book has, but it's more thoughtful. Overall, however, both books advocate radical change to take advantage of the latest IT technologies.

Smith, Adam. *The Wealth of Nations.* (Any of several editions.) Classic economics text that advocates, among other things, the use of work specialization to increase productivity.

Fischer, Layna (Ed.). *The Workflow Paradigm: The Impact of Information Technology on Business Process Reengineering* (2nd ed.). Future Strategies, 1995. A good overview of the early use of workflow systems to support BPR efforts.

Scheer, August-Wilhelm. *Business Process Engineering: Reference Models for Industrial Enterprises* (2nd ed.). Springer, 1994. Scheer has written several books, all very technical, that describe how to use IT systems and modeling techniques to support business processes.

Harry, Mikel J., and Richard Schroeder. *Six Sigma: The Breakthrough Management Strategy Revolutionizing the World's Top Corporations.* Doubleday and Company, 1999. An introduction to Six Sigma by the Motorola engineer who is usually credited with originating the Six Sigma approach.

Boar, Bernard H. *Practical Steps for Aligning Information Technology with Business Strategies: How to Achieve a Competitive Advantage.* Wiley, 1994. Lots of books have been written on business-IT alignment. This one is a little out of date, but still very good. Ignore the methodology, which gets too technical, but focus on the overviews of IT and how they support business change.

Grindley, Kit. *Managing IT at Board Level* (2nd ed.). Price Waterhouse and Pitman Publishing, 1995. This book focuses less on IT techniques and more on the advantages of different IT technologies. It's another book that managers can read to come up to speed on IT technologies and IT-business alignment.

Kalakota, Ravi, and Marcia Robinson. *E-Business: Roadmap for Success.* Addison-Wesley, 1999. There are dozens of books that try to explain the importance of the Internet and associated technologies to business managers. This is one of my favorites. It balances discussions of technology with suggestions for how they will make a difference.

CIO. "Reengineering Redux." *CIO Magazine.* March 1, 2000, pp. 143–156. A roundtable discussion between Michael Hammer and four other business executives on the state of reengineering today. They agree on the continuing importance of process change. For more on Michael Hammer's current work, check his Web site: *www.hammerandco.com.*

PART I.   PROCESS MANAGEMENT

Chapter 2.   Strategy, Value Chains, and Competitive Advantage

Porter, Michael E. *Competitive Strategy: Techniques for Analyzing Industries and Competitors.* The Free Press, 1980. The best-selling book on strategy throughout the past two decades. The must-read book for anyone interested in business strategy.

The Unisys Analysts Meeting is an annual invitational event that Unisys puts on for software and market analysts. Information included in this chapter came from presentations given at the Unisys meeting held in Philadelphia on February 20–22, 2002.

Porter, Michael E. *Competitive Advantage: Creating and Sustaining Superior Performance.* The Free Press, 1985. This book focuses on the idea of competitive advantage and discusses how companies obtain and maintain it. One of the key techniques Porter stresses is an emphasis on value chains and creating integrated business processes that are difficult for competitors to duplicate.

Porter, Michael E. "What Is Strategy?" *Harvard Business Review.* November–December 1996. Reprint no. 96608. This is a great summary of Porter's *Competitive Advantage.*

Porter, Michael E. "Strategy and the Internet." *Harvard Business Review.* March 2001. Reprint no. R0103D. In this HBR article, Porter applies his ideas on strategy and value chains to Internet companies with telling effect. An article everyone interested in e-business should study.

Chapter 3. Process Architecture and Organizational Alignment

Information about the TeleManagement Forum can be obtained from their Web site: *www.tmforum.com.* You can download publications from their site, including the specification for their eTOM framework.

TeleManagement Forum. *eTOM: The Business Process Framework: For the Information and Communications Services Industry.* Public Evaluation Version 2.5. December 2001. Document GB921. This document describes the current state of the eTOM specification and is available from the TeleManagement Forum Web site.

Proforma Corporation has a detailed version of the eTOM model, created in their ProVision Workbench tool that I studied before developing my own models. For more information, contact Proforma about their Telecomunications Industry Model at *www.proformacorp.com.*

There is no good book on business process architecture at this time, but there are several on the problems of creating and maintaining software architectures.

Bass, Len, Paul Clements, and Rick Kazman. *Software Architecture in Practice.* Addison-Wesley, 1998. This is a good introduction to software architectures.

Spewak, Steven H., with Steven C. Hill. *Enterprise Architecture Planning: Developing a Blueprint for Data, Applications and Technology.* Wiley-QED Publication, 1992. This is another popular introduction to software architecture issues.

Harmon, Paul, Michael Rosen, and Michael Guttman. *Developing E-Business Systems and Architectures: A Manager's Guide.* Morgan Kaufmann, 2001. This book in not about architectures as such, but it considers them as they relate to e-business development.

PART II. MODELING ORGANIZATIONS AND PROCESSES

Chapter 4. Modeling Organizations

Rummler, Geary, and Alan Brache. *Improving Performance: Managing the White Space on the Organization Chart.* Jossey-Bass, 1990. The best introduction to business process redesign for managers. Managers read Hammer and Davenport in the early 1990s, and then turned to Rummler and Brache to learn how to actually do business process redesign. Rummler and Brache present a detailed methodology and introduce the basic diagrams that we use in this book. The book is out of date in the sense that diagramming elements are defined in ways that are pre-UML, and we have changed various things to bring the Rummler-Brache diagrams into line with current practice.

Geary Rummler is now with the Performance Design Lab (PDL) and gives workshops on advanced process analysis and design issues. For more information, check *www .performancedesignlab.com.*

Those who have taken a Rummler workshop know that he makes extensive use of a set of organization and process diagrams of a Fine Times Restaurant he has created. In effect, or SF Seafood restaurant is a West Coast branch of Fine Times and owes much to the original in Tucson.

The official source of documentation on UML notation is the Object Management Group. You can go to their Web site and download the complete UML specification: *www.omg.org/uml.*

Fowler, Martin, and Kendall Scott. *UML Distilled* (2nd ed.). Addison Wesley, 2000. If you just want an introduction to UML, we recommend you acquire and read this book, which is widely regarded as the best, brief introduction to UML.

Chapter 5.   Modeling Processes

This chapter, like the last, is heavily indebted to the approach originated by Rummler and Brache.

Rummler, Geary, and Alan Brache. *Performance Improving: Managing the White Space on the Organization Chart.* Jossey-Bass, 1990. The best introduction to business process redesign for managers. Managers read Hammer and Davenport in the early 1990s, and then turned to Rummler and Brache to learn how to actually do business process redesign. Rummler and Brache present a detailed methodology and introduce the basic diagrams that we use in this book. The book is out of date in the sense that diagramming elements are defined in ways that are pre-UML, and we have changed various things to bring the Rummler-Brache diagrams into line with current practice.

Geary Rummler is now with the Performance Design Lab (PDL) and gives workshops on advanced process analysis and design issues. For more information, check *www .performancedesignlab.com.*

The official source of documentation on UML notation is the Object Management Group. You can go to their Web site and download the complete UML specification: *www.omg.org/uml.*

Fowler, Martin, and Kendall Scott. *UML Distilled* (2nd ed.). Addison Wesley, 2000. If you just want an introduction to UML, we recommend you acquire and read this book, which is widely regarded as the best, brief introduction to UML.

There has been quite a bit of discussion in the business and IT communities about the nature of business rules. Some business rules only specify policy actions. If X happens, then do Y. Other rules specify actions in more detail, so that the rules can be programmed into software. For our purposes in this book, we suggest that managers only focus on high-level rules that define policies and specify how decisions should be handled. Leave more precise rules for those that develop software.

A good Web site that provides information on the various approaches to business rules is the site of the Business Rule Community, a group that discusses various business rule issues and offers white papers on various topics: *www.brcommunity.com*.

Morgan, Tony. *Business Rules and Information Systems: Aligning IT with Business Goals.* Addison-Wesley, 2002. This is a good introduction to the importance of specific business rules and how they can be used to align business goals with specific processes and activities.

Harmon, Paul, and Curt Hall. *Intelligent Software Systems Development: An IS Manager's Guide.* Wiley, 1993. This is a good overview of cutting-edge technologies in the mid-1990s. This book spends a lot of time talking about expert systems and their use of rules. For a good introduction to the use of large sets of business rules, check this book.

IBM's LOVEM methodology was documented in IBM technical documents that may not be available today:

IBM. *IBM LOVEM/CABE: Methodology User's Guide,* Version 2. No document number.

IBM. *Business Process Reengineering and Beyond.* IBM International Support Organization, San Jose Center, December 1995. Document reference: SG24–2590–00.

It was the LOVEM methodology that first extended Rummler-Brache notation to incorporate swimlanes for software systems.

Tkach, Daniel, Walter Fang, and Andrew So. *Visiual Modeling Technique: Object Technology Using Visual Programming.* Addison-Wesley, 1996. This book is primarily concerned with object technology, but it does include a brief section on LOVEM and some good information on business rules.

Chapter 6.   Analyzing Activities

The behavior psychology movement in the 1960s led to the development of a general theory of how to design effective training and motivational systems, which is, today, generally termed *human performance technology* (HPT) or *human performance improvement.* The organization that serves as the meeting place for those focused on HPT is the International Society for Performance Improvement (ISPI). For more information, check their Web site: *www.ispi.org.*

Rummler, Geary, and Alan Brache. *Improving Performance: Managing the White Space on the Organization Chart.* Jossey-Bass, 1990. Rummler was a leading member of ISPI for years and introduced many HPT concepts in *Performance Improvement.* Our model of how one can analyze a job situation is derived from work done at ISPI and was especially influenced by how HPT was presented in *Improving Performance.*

Gilbert, Thomas F. *Human Competence: Engineering Worthy Performance.* McGraw-Hill, 1978. Gilbert was one of the people that created human performance technology in the 1970s, and this book provides an introduction to the field. Gilbert is extremely idiosyncratic and can be technical so you've really got to be interested in human performance issues to get through this.

Gilbert developed the idea of the PIP (potential for improved performance) as a way of measuring the possibility of performance improvement in given situations. In essence, you measure the performance of the best performer(s) and compare it to the performance of average performers. If the gap is very narrow, there isn't much potential for improvement and the variation is likely due to chance. If the gap is great, then you need to find out what accounts for the difference and train or motivate average performers to act like the best performers.

Information on the analysis of sales performance is from a sales performance workshop I gave at ISPI several years ago.

Curtis, Bill, William E. Hefley, and Sally A. Millor. *The People Capability Maturity Model: Guidelines for Improving the Workforce.* Addison-Wesley, 2002. This is a book that starts with the premises of CMM and then studies how one improves the workforce to move from one level of process maturity to another. Bill Curtis wrote that it was this book that started him thinking of applying CMM to processes other than software processes.

PART III. MANAGING AND IMPROVING BUSINESS PROCESSES

Chapter 7. Managing and Measuring Business Processes

The analysis of process management is primarily derived from the work of Geary Rummler. The basic concepts were introduced in *Improving Performance,* but have been considerably elaborated in recent lectures and workshops.

Kaplan, Robert S., and David P. Norton. *The Balanced Scorecard: Translating Strategy into Action.* Harvard Business School Press, 1996. Kaplan and Norton describe a popular approach to tying measures to organization strategies. It's good in that it gets executives thinking of a variety of measures. It's bad if it's used alone, as a measurement solution, and not incorporated into a total business process management strategy. If you want, you can easily think of the collection of measures that accumulate as a process is analyzed as a scorecard of measures.

Other business process theorists have also focused on improving the management of processes.

Champy, James. *Reengineering Management.* HarperBusiness, 1995. As with the original reengineering book, this is more about why you should do it than how to do it.

Hammer, Michael. *Beyond Reengineering: How the Process-Centered Organization Is Changing Our Work and Our Lives.* HarperBusiness, 1997. Similar to the Champy book. Lots of inspiring stories.

In the mid 1970s I worked briefly for Louis A. Allen, a then-popular management consultant. As far as I know, his books are no longer in print, but he introduced me to the idea that managers must plan, organize, lead, and control. I've simplified that in this chapter to planning and controlling.

Information on the Chevron process management improvement effort is documented in a white paper: "Strategic Planning Helps Chevron's E&P Optimize Its Assets," which is available from the Pritchett Web site: *www.pritchettnet.com/COmp/PI/CaseStudies /chevroncase.htm.*

McCormack, Kevin P., and William C. Johnson. *Business Process Orientation: Gaining the E-Business Competitive Advantage.* St. Lucie Press, 2001. This book provides an overview of some business process ideas, but is primarily focused on a methodology for developing questionnaires to evaluate the results at organizations that focus on processes. Some use in planning assessments. Not useful for e-business as such, but for any business process evaluation.

Chapter 8. Process Improvement with Six Sigma

Taylor, Frederick W. *The Principles of Scientific Management.* Harper's, 1911. For a modern review of the efficiency movement and Taylor, check Daniel Nelson's *Frederick W. Taylor and the Rise of Scientific Management,* University of Wisconsin Press, 1980. Frederick Winslow Taylor advocated the idea that managers had a responsibility to study processes and assure that they were efficient. Taylor emphasized time and motion studies, and motivational incentives to control performance. Workers, who resented being urged to work faster, called the approach "Taylorism."

The automotive data is from an IMVP World Assembly Plan Survey conducted in 1986. I discovered this data in a booklet written by Ken Orr, entitled *Creating the Smart Enterprise: Business Process Reengineering in the Real World,* which was published in 1998 and is available from the Ken Orr Institute. For more information, check *www.kenorrinst.com.*

The International Society of Six Sigma Professionals *(www.isssp.org)* sponsors meetings and training sessions in Six Sigma techniques.

The American Society for Quality *(www.asq.org)* puts on an annual Six Sigma Conference, which is a good place to meet practitioners and learn. The ASQ has a Six Sigma Forum that publishes a newsletter.

A Six Sigma consultant, Six Sigma Qualtec, has a Web site with lots of useful information *(www.ssgi.com)* and mails a monthly newsletter that lists Six Sigma events and so forth.

Eckes, George. *The Six Sigma Revolution: How General Electric and Others Turned Process into Profits.* John Wiley, 2001. A good workthrough of all the basics, for managers or practitioners. I'd recommend this be your first book on Six Sigma.

Pande, Peter S., Robert P. Neuman, and Ronald R. Cavanagh. *The Six Sigma Way Team Fieldbook: An Implementation Guide for Process Improvement Teams.* McGraw-Hill, 2001. A detailed look at what's involved in a Six Sigma improvement effort from the trainers that helped install Six Sigma at GE, Sun, and Sears. Easy-to-understand step-by-step approach. Lots of worksheets and data-gathering forms. I'd recommend this as your second book on Six Sigma.

Juran Institute. *The Six Sigma Basic Training Kit: Implementing Juran's 6 Step Quality Improvement Process and Six Sigma Tools.* McGraw-Hill, 2001. An expensive but detailed guide to Six Sigma that includes facilitator notes and training modules. For those who want to lead a Six Sigma team.

Harry, Mikel J., and Richard Schroeder. *Six Sigma: The Breakthrough Management Strategy Revolutionizing the World's Top Corporations.* Doubleday and Company, 1999. By the guy who started it. The book is too hyped and is probably best only for those who want to get an overview and some motivation.

We've stressed the use of Six Sigma for process improvement. Some Six Sigma practitioners stress design, using a slightly different model, which they call DMADV (Define Measure, Analyze, Design and Verify). For a good example of a group focused on using Six Sigma for redesign, check BlueFire Six Sigma at *www.bluefire.com*.

PART IV.   BUSINESS PROCESS REDESIGN

Chapter 9.   A Business Process Redesign Methodology

Rummler and Brache didn't describe the process redesign methodology in any detail in *Improving Performance.* It was described in more detail in workshops and publications of their consulting company, Rummler-Brache, which was later acquired by Prichett. For more information on Prichett, check *www.prichett.com.*

The methodology described here was formalized in conversations with Geary Rummler and extended by consulting some other books on business process redesign, including the following:

Manganelli, Raymond L., and Mark M. Klein. *The Reengineering Handbook: A Step-by-Step Guide to Business Transformation.* American Management Association, 1994. Lots of practical advice and a step-by-step methodology.

Kubeck, Lynn C. *Techniques for Business Process Redesign: Tying It All Together.* Wiley-QED Publication, 1995. Another good book with information on phases and what has to happen when.

Petrozzo, Daniel P., and John C. Stepper. *Successful Reengineering.* Van Nostrand Reinhold, 1994. Another good summary of successful practices.

Grover, Varun, and William J. Kettinger (Eds.). *Business Process Change: Reengineering Concepts, Methods and Technologies.* Idea Group Publishing, 1995. A book of readings. Some of the chapters are excellent and provide information on specific techniques.

Chapter 10. Process Redesign Patterns

The idea of trying to organize analysis and design by describing commonly recurring patterns has been popular in the software community since the mid-1990s and predictably will become popular in business in this decade.

Gamma, Erich, Richard Helm, Ralph Johnson, and John Vissides. *Design Patterns: Elements of Reusable Object-Oriented Software.* Addison-Wesley, 1995. This book will probably not interest managers or IT architects. It's a book for software programmers. It is, however, the book that kicked off the "patterns movement," and the first chapter lays out the history and theory of patterns.

In our own work, and in reading the following books, we kept coming across the same approaches to business process redesign, so we simply lumped these patterns under some common names: reengineering, simplification, value-added analysis, and gaps and disconnects.

Hammer, Michael, and James Champy. *Reengineering the Corporation: A Manifesto for Business Revolution.* HarperBusiness, 1993. The best source for the radical reengineering approach, although it's described in several other books cited below.

All of the following provide good examples of the simplification pattern and of the value-added approach:

Manganelli, Raymond L. and Mark M. Klein. *The Reengineering Handbook: A Step-by-Step Guide to Business Transformation.* American Management Association, 1994. Lots of practical advice and a step-by-step methodology.

Kubeck, Lynn C. *Techniques for Business Process Redesign: Tying It All Together.* Wiley-QED Publication, 1995. Another good book with information on phases and what has to happen when.

Petrozzo, Daniel P., and John C. Stepper. *Successful Reengineering.* Van Nostrand Reinhold, 1994. Another good summary of successful practices.

Grover, Varun, and William J. Kettinger (Eds.). *Business Process Change: Reengineering Concepts, Methods and Technologies.* Idea Group Publishing, 1995. A book of readings. Some of the chapters are excellent and provide information on specific techniques.

Six Sigma books tend to stress value-added analysis.

Rummler, Geary, and Alan Brache. *Improving Performance: Managing the White Space on the Organization Chart.* Jossey-Bass, 1990. The best source for a discussion of gaps and disconnects.

Harmon, Paul. "Texas Instruments' MMST Project." *Business Process Strategies Newsletter.* Cutter Consortium. Vol. II, No. 1, January 1996. This article describes Texas Instruments project to create a new process for chip manufacture.

Harmon, Paul. "BPR and Object Technology—Part II." *Business Process Strategies Newsletter.* Cutter Consortium. Vol. II, No. 2, February 1996. This issue describes the Xerox Corporation's NPP (non-production procurement) project in considerable detail.

PART V. BUSINESS PROCESS AUTOMATION

Chapter 11. Workflow and XML Business Process Languages

Recall that there is ambiguity about the phrase *business process management.* Executives tend to use it in a generic sense to refer to managing processes. People in the workflow and XML business process language area use *BPM* and *Business Process Management* to refer to systems that automate business processes.

The Web address of the Workflow Management Coalition is *www.wfmc.org.* The WfMC was founded in 1993. It's a consortium of major workflow users and workflow vendors. WfMC meets frequently to discuss key workflow issues and has developed a number of workflow standards.

Fischer, Layna (Ed.). *Workflow Handbook 2002.* Future Strategies, 2002. An annual book published in association with the WfMC and edited by the coalition's executive director. Each volume summarizes what the coalition has done during the past year, has several chapters reviewing important topics, and includes a membership list of the WfMC. An important reference book for those interested in workflow.

Workflow Management Coalition. *Workflow Management Coalition Terminology and Glossary.* Doc. No. WFMC-TC-1011. April 1999. Available from *www.wfmc.org.*

Leymann, F., and D. Roller. "Workflow-Based Applications." *IBM Systems Journal.* Vol. 36, No. 1, 1997. Reprint No. G321–5637. This article provides an excellent overview of workflow systems. It's available online from *www.research.ibm.com/journal/sj/361 /leymann.html.*

For more information on IBM's WSFL BP language, check *http://www-106.ibm.com /developerworks/library/ws-ref4/index.html.* This is a series of articles by James Snell, an IBM software engineer for emerging technologies, that was written in 2001 to describe WSFL.

Leymann, Frank. Web Services Flow Language (WSFL 1.0). IBM, May 2001. A specification that can be downloaded from IBM's WSFL Web site: *www.ibm.com.*

For more information on Microsoft's XLANG, BizTalk, and Orchestration Designer, check *www.microsoft.com/biztalk* and search for Orchestration Designer. See especially the white paper "BizTalk Orchestration: A Technology for Orchestrating Business Interactions." June 5, 2000.

For more information on the Business Process Management Initiative (BPMI) consortium, check *www.bpmi.org.*

Smith, Howard, Peter Fingar, and Ismael Ghalimi. *Business Process Management: The Third Wave.* Meghan-Kiffer Press, 2002. This book hasn't been published, as we go to the printer, but the authors are among the founders of the BPMI, and Smith has written some good reports on BPMI, so we expect that this will be a good but technical book on XML BP languages.

For more information on the ebXML business process initiative, check *www.ebxml.org.*

Khoshafian, Setrag, and Marek Buckiewicz. *Introduction to Groupware, Workflow and Workgroup Computing.* Wiley, 1995. This is an old book that is out of date in some ways, but very good on the basic concepts.

exXML. *exXML Catalog of Common Business Processes.* Document 0.91. Work in progress. March 19, 2001. Available online from the ebXML Web site.

The OMG has worked together with the WfMC on standards for workflow and business process notation. Check the OMG Web site and search on "workflow": *www.omg.org.*

Smith, Howard, Douglas Neal, Lynette Ferrara, and Francis Hayden. *The Emergence of Business Process Management.* Computer Science Corporation (CSC) Research Services. Version 1. January 2002. This report provides a good overview of the BPMI initiative and a very optimistic view of the future of BPMI. The lead author is on the board of BPMI.

For access to other Smith reports and a collection of articles on business process management, check this Web site maintained by Howard Smith, Gillian Taylor, and Peter Fingar: *www.fairdene.com/processes.*

Chapter 12. **ERP-Driven Redesign**

Davenport, Thomas H. *Mission Critical: Realizing the Promise of Enterprise Systems.* Harvard Business School Press, 2000. Having helped launch the BPR movement, Davenport noticed that by the late 1990s many companies were implementing process change with packaged applications from ERP vendors. He wrote this book to report on his investigations of the whole trend. When Davenport wrote this, he was the director of the Institute for Strategic Change at Andersen Consulting.

Davenport prefers to call these systems "enterprise systems" but that isn't a good idea, since IT people use the term in a completely different way. ERP may not make much sense, but it's the term most people use to refer to these packaged applications that are organized to solve process integration problems.

The software and business process theorist that has dominated the ERP space is August-Wilhelm Scheer, who is the head of the Institut für Wirtschaftsinformatik at the University of Saarlandes in Germany. Scheer started by developing techniques for modeling software systems and founded a company, IDS Scheer GmbH, to promote his approach and to sell a software tool, ARIS. Today, IDS Scheer is a major business process modeling and consulting company. The ARIS approach is used by SAP, the largest packaged software (ERP) vendor, which is also headquartered in Germany. Some of Scheer's books include the following:

Scheer, A.-W. *ARIS—Business Process Modeling* (3rd ed.). Springer, 2000. This book focuses on process modeling, especially as it is done with ARIS in SAP R/3. A book for IT developers, not business managers.

Scheer, A.-W. *ARIS—Business Process Frameworks* (3rd ed.). Springer, 1999. This book focuses on the ARIS approach to process redesign using SAP R/3 products and the ARIS software tool. It talks about aligning strategy and processes, but is a book for IT developers and not business managers.

Scheer, A.-W. *Business Process Engineering: Reference Models for Industrial Enterprises* (2nd ed.). Springer, 1994. The book lays out Scheer's basic approach to process reengineering. A book for IT developers, not business managers.

All of Scheer's book are very technical and written for software architects, not business managers.

For information on IDS Scheer, check *www.ids-scheer.com.*

The main source of information on SAP and the diagrams used in this chapter was the SAP Web site: *www.sap.com.*

Curran, Thomas, and Gerhard Keller, with Andrew Ladd. *SAP R/3 Business Blueprint: Understanding the Business Process Reference Model.* Prentice Hall, 1998. A good introduction to the use of SAP modules to model business processes. Lots of detailed ARIS examples. A book for IT developers, not business managers.

Conference Board Study. *ERP Post Implementation Issues and Best Practices.* December 2000.

Worthen, Ben. "Nestle's ERP Odyssey." *CIO Magazine.* May 14, 2002, pp. 62–70.

Chapter 13. Software Development

Harmon, Paul, and Curtis Hall. *Intelligent Software Systems Development: An IS Manager's Guide.* Wiley, 1993. A review of software development in the 1980s and the new techniques that changed software development in the 1990s. A good introduction to intelligent rule-based systems and CASE tools.

The best place to go for the latest version of the UML standard is the OMG Web site, *www.omg.org/uml,* where the latest version of the documentation is always available to be downloaded.

Booch, Grady, James Rumbaugh, and Ivar Jacobson. *The Unified Modeling Language Users Guide.* Addison-Wesley, 1999.

Fowler, Martin, and Kendall Scott. *UML Distilled: Applying the Standard Object Modeling Language.* Addison-Wesley, 1997 (2nd ed., 2000). The is the most popular general introduction to UML. It describes all the basic UML diagrams and how to use them.

D'Souza, Desmond Francis, and Alan Cameron Willis. *Objects, Components, and Frameworks with UML: The Catalysis Approach.* Addison-Wesley, 1999. This describes D'Souza's catalysis approach to software development, which relies on UML.

Jacobson, Ivar, Grady Booch, and James Rumbaugh. *The Unified Software Development Process.* Addison-Wesley, 1999. This book presents Rational's software development process, which relies on UML. Not as clearly written as one might wish.

Kruchten, Philippe. *The Rational Unified Process: An Introduction.* Addison-Wesley, 1999. This is a more friendly and less detailed introduction to Rational's UP.

Quantrani, Terry. *Visual Modeling with Rational Rose 2000 and UML.* Addison-Wesley, 2000.

Rosenburg, Doug, and Kendall Scott. *Use Case Driven Object Modeling with UML.* Addison-Wesley, 1999. This book provides a good introduction to using use cases for modeling requirements.

Marshall, Chris. *Enterprise Modeling with UML: Designing Successful Software through Business Analysis.* Addison-Wesley, 2000. This book describes how software developers can go about analyzing processes and generating requirements using a UML approach.

Eriksson, Hans-Erik, and Magnus Penker. *Business Modeling with UML: Business Patterns That Work.* Wiley, 2000. This is probably the most popular book that describes how software developers can go about analyzing processes and generating requirements using a UML approach.

Allen, Paul, and Stuart Frost. *Component-Based Development for Enterprise Systems: Applying the SELECT Perspective.* Cambridge University Press, 1998. An excellent book that explains how UML and component-based development can be done in conjunction with a software modeling tool.

Potter, Neil S., and Mary E. Sakry. *Making Process Improvement Work: A Concise Action Guide for Software Managers and Practitioners.* Addison-Wesley, 2002. A typical example of a book that treats process redesign as something that is done by software developers and not business managers.

Jacobson, Ivar, Magnus Ericcson, and A. Jacobson. *The Object Advantage—Business Process Re-Engineering with Object Technology.* Addison-Wesley, 1994. Read as a guide to help software developers redesigning processes, this book is useful. Read as a guide to help business managers use OO techniques to conceptualize and redesign processes, this book is misguided. It assumes that everyone will find it easy to conceptualize processes in terms of use cases and class diagrams.

There are several articles on various aspects of MDA that are available on the Object Management Group's Web site: *www.omg.org/mda.*

McClure, Carma. *CASE IS Software Automation.* Prentice Hall, 1989. CASE isn't spoken of much these days. This book, which is hard to get, provides a general introduction to CASE for managers.

Information on Zachman's current work can be obtained from the Zachman Institute for Framework Advancement (ZIFA): *www.zifa.com.*

The CMM table used in this chapter is derived from a table in Mark C. Paulk, Charles V. Weber, Bill Curtis, and Mary Beth Chrissis (principal contributors and editors), *The Capability Maturity Model: Guidelines for Improving the Software Process.* Addison-Wesley, 1995.

Kilov, Haim, and Michael Guttman. "ISO Reference Model of Open Distributed Processing: An Informal Introduction." An executive report from Cutter Consortium's Distributed Computing Architecture Advisory Service. Vol. 2, No. 4. April 1999. RM-ODP is an extremely technical effort to specify a common business language. Unfortunately, it is based on object techniques and will probably never be of interest to business people, except in very technical niches. There are reports on the specification available from ISO, but they are very technical. This report is much easier to understand.

For more on the International Standards Organization, check *www.iso.org.*

Kilov, Haim. *Business Specifications.* Prentice-Hall, 1999. This book describes an RM-ODP oriented approach to business specifications by one of the leaders in the movement. It's very difficult to understand if you aren't very knowledgeable in distributed object systems.

PART VI. THE E-BUSINESS CHALLENGE

Chapter 14. E-Business: Portals and Customer-Oriented Applications

Kalakota, Ravi, and Marcia Robinson. *E-Business: Roadmap for Success.* Addison-Wesley, 1999. A good overview of the kinds of applications companies are creating.

The IBM patterns Web site, *www.ibm.com/frameworks/patterns,* contains papers on IBM's e-business patterns approach, including detailed descriptions about how one can implement each of the various e-business patterns. A must for IT analysts.

Adams, Jonathan, Srinivas Koushik, Guru Vasudeva, and George Galambos. *Patterns for E-Business: A Strategy for Reuse.* IBM Press, 2001. This book summarizes the IBM e-business patterns approach. It's a good overview, but for detailed information about how to implement the various patterns, you need to go to the IBM patterns Web site.

McKenna, Regis. *Real Time: Preparing for the Age of the Never Satisfied Customer.* Harvard Business School Press, 1999. A nice introduction to the growing importance of the customer from a well-known marketing guru.

Evans, Philip, and Thomas S. Wurster. *Blown to Bits: How the New Economics of Information Transforms Strategy.* Harvard Business School Press, 2000. This book reflects some of the hype of the dot.com era, but it also has some solid nuggets of insight on how companies need to be very precise about what they are providing customers when they move to the Web.

Rosenfeld, Louis, and Peter Morville. *Information Architecture for the World Wide Web: Designing Large-Scale Web Sites.* O'Reilly, 1998. I don't know of a really great book on Web site analysis and design for managers. Most don't focus on the underlying processes, but focus instead on the details of the Web site as if it stood alone. This is better than most, but still primarily a book for Web site designers rather than business people. Still, if you are going to design a portal for a business process and want some ideas of what a portal might do, this provides a good overview of the options and problems.

Harmon, Paul, Michael Rosen, and Michael Guttman. *Developing E-Business Systems and Architectures: A Manager's Guide.* Morgan Kaufmann, 2001. This book focuses on how companies transition from conventional software architectures and infrastructures to architectures that support e-business development.

Allen, Paul. *Realizing E-Business with Components.* Addison-Wesley, 2001. An excellent introduction to the challenges of modeling e-business systems with UML and components.

Hall, Curt. *Supply Chain Intelligence: Technology, Applications and Products.* Executive Report. Cutter Consortium Business Intelligence Service. Vol. 2, No. 7. 2002. An excellent survey of the use of business intelligence techniques in supply chain systems.

McCormack, Kevin P., and William C. Johnson. *Business Process Orientation: Gaining the E-Business Competitive Advantage.* St. Lucie Press, 2001. Some interesting ideas about e-business processes but oriented toward assessment.

The Travel-Is-Us process described in Figures 14.1, 14.2, and 14.4 is a slight variation of a process originally described by Steven A. White, the Director of Standards at SeeBeyond, a business process company. Steve is also the chairperson of the Business Process Management Initiative's (BPMI) notation committee. As an aid to helping notation committee members think about problems, Steve developed this process, which has been used as a case study ever since. We simply adopted it as an example.

Chapter 15. Supplier and Internally Oriented E-Business Applications

The basic Web site for the Supply Chain Council is *www.supply-chain.org.* Information about the council's work and meetings is here, as well as information about their SCOR methodology.

Chopra, Sunil, and Peter Meindl. *Supply Chain Management: Strategy, Planning and Operations.* Prentice Hall College Division, 2000. This is a book written for a second-year MBA course on supply chain management. The second author, Peter Meindl, is a manager at I2 Technologies, probably the premiere company focused on creating packaged supply chain systems. This book provides a very technical introduction to all of the issues involved in creating a supply chain system.

Knolmayer, Gerhard, Peter Mertens, and Alexander Zeier. *Supply Chain Management Based on SAP Systems.* Springer Verlag, 2001. A good introduction to how SAP modules can be used to support supply chain development. Lots of good advice.

Scheer, A-W., Ferri Abolhassan, Wolfgang Jost, and Mathias Kirchmer (Eds.). *Business Process Excellence: ARIS in Practice.* Springer-Verlag, 2003. A review of some uses of ARIS, including a case study of a SCOR application.

Van de Putte, Geert, Lee Gavin, and Peter Sharp. *Business Process Management Using MQSeries and Partner Agreement Manager.* IBM Redbooks, May 2001. Document SG24–6166–00. Check the IBM Web site, *www.ibm.com,* and search for Redbooks. This paper is specific to IBM's workflow tool, MQSeries, and their Partner Agreement Manager product, but it describes the business-to-business problem well and describes how it can be conceptualized as a workflow problem.

Lapidus, Gary. *E-Automotive Report.* Goldman Sachs Investment Research, 1999.

PART VII. PUTTING IT ALL TOGETHER

Chapter 16. The Ergonomic Systems Case

This is a hypothetical case, not a specific company we have helped.

Chapter 17. Software Tools for Business Process Development

For more information on the six companies that Gartner suggested were selling the best process modeling tools, check:

CASEwise at *www.casewise.com*

IDS Scheer at *www.ids-scheer.com*

MEGA International at *www.mega.com*

Meta Software at *www.metasoftware.com*

Popkin Software at *www.popkin.com*

Proforma Corporation at *www.proformacorp.com*

Proforma Corporation created a tool that used Rummler-Brache diagrams and generated UML code. The company has since added support for many other diagramming techniques and for XML, but it can still produce diagrams very similar to what we use in this book.

For more information on Proforma or ProVision Workbench, and to download a trial version of their business process modeling tool, check *www.proformacorp.com.*

For information or to download a trial version of Popkin's Software Architect, go to *www.popkin.com.*

There are a wide variety of business process tool vendors and they keep changing. The author writes a newsletter, which is available via email without charge, and maintains a portal on business processes that provides up-to-date information on leading business process tool vendors. To subscribe to the Business Process Trends newsletter or to obtain information on the portal, go to *www.businessprocesstrends.com.*

Bibliography

BOOKS REFERENCED IN THE TEXT, as well as good books to read for more information, are listed in the Notes and References and annotated. This list simply presents all the books cited, by author, in alphabetic order.

Adams, Jonathan, Srinivas Koushik, Guru Vasudeva, and George Galambos. *Patterns for E-Business: A Strategy for Reuse.* IBM Press, 2001.

Allen, Paul. *Realizing E-Business with Components.* Addison-Wesley, 2001.

Allen, Paul, and Stuart Frost. *Component-Based Development for Enterprise Systems: Applying the SELECT Perspective.* Cambridge University Press, 1998.

Bass, Len, Paul Clements, and Rick Kazman. *Software Architecture in Practice.* Addison-Wesley, 1998.

Bertalanffy, Ludwig von. *General Systems Theory: Foundations, Development, Applications.* George Braziller, 1968.

Boar, Bernard H. *Practical Steps for Aligning Information Technology with Business Strategie*s. Wiley, 1994.

Booch, Grady, James Rumbaugh, and Ivar Jacobsen. *The Unified Modeling Language Users Guide.* Addison-Wesley, 1999.

Champy, James. *Reengineering Management: The Mandate for New Leadership.* Harper Business Book, 1995.

Chopra, Sunil, and Peter Meindl. *Supply Chain Management: Strategy, Planning and Operations.* Prentice Hall College Division, 2000.

Curran, Thomas, and Gerhard Keller. *SAP R/3: Business Blueprint.* Prentice Hall, 1998.

Curtis, Bill, William E. Hefley, and Sally A. Miller. *The People Capability Maturity Model: Guidelines for Improving the Workforce.* Addison-Wesley, 2002.

Davenport, Thomas H. *Process Innovation: Reengineering Work through Information Technology.* Harvard Business School Press, 1993.

Davenport, Thomas H. *Mission Critical: Realizing the Promise of Enterprise Systems.* Harvard Business School Press, 2000.

D'Souza, Desmond Francis, and Alan Cameron Willis. *Objects, Components, and Frameworks with UML: The Catalysis Approach.* Addison-Wesley, 1999.

Eckes, George. *The Six Sigma Revolution: How General Electric and Others Turned Process into Profits.* Wiley, 2001.

Eriksson, Hans-Erik, and Magnus Penker. *Business Modeling with UML: Business Patterns That Work.* Wiley, 2000.

Evans, Philip, and Thomas S. Wurster. *Blown to Bits: How the New Economics of Information Transforms Strategy.* Harvard Business School Press, 2000.

Fischer, Layna (Ed.). *Workflow Handbook 2002.* Future Strategies, 2002.

Fischer, Layna (Ed.). *The Workflow Paradigm: The Impact of Information Technology on Business Process Reengineering* (2nd ed.). Future Strategies, 1995.

Forrester, Jay. *Principles of Systems.* Pegasus Communications, 1971.

Fowler, Martin, and Kendall Scott. *UML Distilled* (2nd ed.). Addison Wesley, 2000.

Gamma, Erich, Richard Helm, Ralph Johnson, and John Vissides. *Design Patterns: Elements of Reusable Object-Oriented Software.* Addison-Wesley, 1995.

Gilbert, Thomas F. *Human Competence: Engineering Worthy Performance.* McGraw Hill, 1978.

Grindley, Kit. *Managing IT at Board Level* (2nd ed.). Price Waterhouse and Pitman Publishing, 1995.

Grover, Varun, and William J. Kettinger. *Business Process Change: Reengineering Concepts, Methods and Technologies.* Idea Group Publishing, 1995.

Hammer, Michael. *Beyond Reengineering: How the Process-Centered Organization Is Changing Our Work and Our Lives.* HarperBusiness, 1997.

Hammer, Michael, and James Champy. *Reengineering the Corporation: A Manifesto for Business Revolution.* HarperBusiness, 1993.

Harmon, Paul. *Who's Profiting from Business Process Redesign.* Cutter Consortium, 2002.

Harmon, Paul, and Curtis Hall. *Intelligent Software Systems Development: An IS Manager's Guide.* Wiley, 1993.

Harmon, Paul, Michael Rosen, and Michael Guttman. *Developing E-Business Systems and Architectures: A Manager's Guide.* Morgan Kaufmann, 2001.

Harmon, Paul, and Mark Watson. *Understanding UML: The Developer's Guide.* Morgan Kaufmann, 1998.

Harry, Mikel J., and Richard Schroeder. *Six Sigma: The Breakthrough Management Strategy Revolutionizing the World's Top Corporations.* Doubleday and Company, 1999.

Jacobson, Ivar, Grady Booch, and James Rumbaugh. *The Unified Software Development Process.* Addison Wesley, 1999.

Jacobson, Ivar, Magnus Ericcson, and A. Jacobson. *The Object Advantage—Business Process Re-Engineering with Object Technology.* Addison-Wesley, 1994.

Johansson, Henry J., Patrick McHugh, A. John Pendlebury, and William A. Wheeler III. *Business Process Reengineering: Breakpoint Strategies for Market Dominance.* Wiley, 1993.

Juran Institute. *The Six Sigma Basic Training Kit: Implementing Juran's 6 Step Quality Improvement Process and Six Sigma Tools.* McGraw-Hill, 2001.

Kalakota, Ravi, and Marcia Robinson. *E-Business: Roadmap for Success.* Addison-Wesley, 1999.

Kaplan, Robert S., and David P. Norton. *The Balanced Scorecard: Translating Strategy into Action.* Harvard Business School Press, 1996.

Keen, Peter, and Mark McDonald. *The eProcess Edge: Creating Customer Value and Business Wealth in the Internet Era.* McGraw-Hill, 2000.

Khoshafian, Setrag, and Marek Buckiewicz. *Introduction to Groupware, Workflow, and Workgroup Computing.* Wiley, 1995.

Kilov, Haim. *Business Specifications.* Prentice-Hall, 1999.

Knolmayer, Gerhard, Peter Mertens, and Alexander Zeier. *Supply Chain Management Based on SAP Systems.* Springer Verlag, 2001.

Kruchten, Philippe. *The Rational Unified Process: An Introduction.* Addison-Wesley, 1999.

Kubeck, Lynn C. *Techniques for Business Process Redesign: Tying It All Together.* Wiley-QED Publication, 1995.

Manganelli, Raymond L., and Mark M. Klein. *The Reengineering Handbook: A Step-by-Step Guide to Business Transformation.* American Management Association, 1994.

Marshall, Chris. *Enterprise Modeling with UML: Designing Successful Software through Business Analysis.* Addison-Wesley, 2000.

McClure, Carma. *CASE IS Software Automation.* Prentice Hall, 1989.

McCormack, Kevin P., and William C. Johnson. *Business Process Orientation: Gaining the E-Business Competitive Advantage.* St. Lucie Press, 2001.

McCraw, Thomas K. (Ed.). *Creating Modern Capitalism: How Entrepreneurs, Companies, and Countries Triumphed in Three Industrial Revolutions.* Harvard University Press, 1997.

McKenna, Regis. *Real Time: Preparing for the Age of the Never Satisfied Customer.* Harvard Business School Press, 1999.

Morgan, Tony. *Business Rules and Information Systems: Aligning IT with Business Goals.* Addison-Wesley, 2002.

OMG. *Unified Modeling Language: Specification.* The latest version of the UML software development notation is found on the Object Management Group's Web site: *www.omg.org* as a downloadable document.

Pande, Peter S. Robert P. Neuman, and Ronald R. Cavanagh. *The Six Sigma Way Team Fieldbook: An Implementation Guide for Process Improvement Teams.* McGraw-Hill, 2001.

Paulk, Mark C., Charles V. Weber, Bill Curtis, and Mary Beth Chrissis (principal contributors and editors). *The Capability Maturity Model: Guidelines for Improving the Software Process.* Addison-Wesley, 1995.

Petrozzo, Daniel P., and John C. Stepper. *Successful Reengineering.* Van Nostrand Reinhold, 1994.

Porter, Michael E. *Competitive Strategy: Techniques for Analyzing Industries and Competitors.* Free Press, 1980.

Porter, Michael E. *Competitive Advantage: Creating and Sustaining Superior Performance.* Free Press, 1985.

Potter, Neil S., and Mary E. Sakry. *Making Process Improvement Work: A Concise Action Guide for Software Managers and Practitioners.* Addison-Wesley, 2002.

Price Waterhouse Change Integration Team. *Better Change: Best Practices for Transforming Your Organization.* Irwin, 1995.

Quantrani, Terry. *Visual Modeling with Rational Rose 2000 and UML.* Addison-Wesley, 2000.

Rosenburg, Doug, and Kendall Scott. *Use Case Driven Object Modeling with UML.* Addison-Wesley, 1999.

Rosenfeld, Louis, and Peter Morville. *Information Architecture for the World Wide Web: Designing Large-Scale Web Sites.* O'Reilly, 1998.

Rummler, Geary, and Alan Brache. *Improving Performance: How to Manage the White Space on the Organization Chart* (2nd ed.). Jossey-Bass, 1990.

Scheer, A.-W. *Business Process Engineering: Reference Models for Industrial Enterprises* (2nd ed). Springer, 1994.

Scheer, A.W. *ARIS—Business Process Modeling* (3rd ed.). Springer, 2000.

Scheer, A.-W. *ARIS—Business Process Frameworks* (3rd ed.). Springer, 1999.

Scheer, A-W., Ferri Abolhassan, Wolfgang Jost, and Mathias Kirchmer (Eds.). *Business Process Excellence: ARIS in Practice.* Springer-Verlag, 2003.

Senge, Peter M. *The Fifth Discipline: The Art and Practice of the Learning Organization.* Currency Doubleday, 1994.

Smith, Adam. *Wealth of Nations.* Originally published in 1776. Available in several different editions.

Smith, Howard, Douglas Neal, Lynette Ferrara, and Francis Hayden. *The Emergence of Business Process Management.* Computer Science Corporation (CSC) Research Services, January 2002.

Smith, Howard, Peter Fingar, and Ismael Ghalimi. *Business Process Management: The Third Wave.* Meghan-Kiffer Press, 2002.

Spewak, Steven H. with Steven C. Hill. *Enterprise Architecture Planning: Developing a Blueprint for Data, Applications and Technology.* Wiley-QED Publication, 1992.

Sterman, John D. *Business Dynamics: Systems Thinking and Modeling for a Complex World.* Irwin McGraw-Hill, 2000.

Taylor, Frederick W. *The Principles of Scientific Management.* Harper's, 1911.

Tkach, Daniel, Walter Fang, and Andrew So. *Visual Modeling Techniques: Object Technology Using Visual Programming.* Addison Wesley, 1996.

Index

* (asterisk) on process diagram, 121
σ (sigma) or standard deviation,
    183–184, 478
80/20 rule, 193, 200

ABC (activity-based costing), 22,
    106–107, 458
Abolhassan, Ferri, 502
acquisitions and mergers, as business
    process redesign drivers,
    34–35, 36
activities
    analyzing a completely automated
      activity, 149–153
    analyzing a specific activity,
      134–138
    analyzing for business process re-
      design, 222
    analyzing human performance re-
      quired for, 138–144
    atomic, 79, 458
    automating the Enter Expense Re-
      ports activity, 145–146
    in business process hierarchy, 460
    defined, 79, 222, 457
    diagram, 134
    in hierarchy of processes, 80
    job descriptions and, 134,
      153–155
    levels of analysis and, 131, 132,
      133
    manager's role, 161–162
    managing performance of, 144

non-value-adding, 58, 199,
    470
notation, 109, 115, 457
in process description, 133
process diagram and, 114–115,
    120
as processes, 79, 133
processes vs., 79
as roles, 120
sales activity example, 146–149
size of, 133
software applications and,
    153–155
standards, 138–140
value-added, 481–482
value-enabling, 58, 482
activity analysis
    Activity Analysis Worksheet, 136,
      137, 458
    Activity Cost Worksheet, 137,
      458
    activity diagram, 134
    for completely automated activity,
      149–153
    complex sales activity example,
      146–149
    computer screens used, docu-
      menting, 137
    cost analysis, 135, 137
    goals statement, 135
    job descriptions and, 134,
      153–155
    observation, 134

problems, documenting,
    135–136, 138
quality analysis, 135
rules, defining, 135, 136
simple Enter Expense Reports ac-
    tivity example, 134–138
software applications and,
    153–155
steps, defining, 135, 136
time required, documenting, 135
Activity Analysis Worksheet, 136,
    137, 458
Activity Cost Worksheet, 137, 458
activity diagrams. *See* process
    diagrams
activity or performance level of per-
    formance, 31
activity standards, 138–140
activity support, 140–141
activity-based costing (ABC), 22,
    106–107, 458
actor swimlane, 120
ad hoc workflow systems, 264, 458
Adams, Jonathan, 383–384, 500
AD/Cycle Repository, 314
administrative workflow systems,
    264–265, 458
advertising costs as barrier to entry,
    50
Allen, Louis A., 493
Allen, Paul, 499, 501
Allied Signal, Six Sigma approach at,
    181

American Society for Quality (ASQ), 493

Analysis phase (business process redesign), 219–224
    activity analysis, 222
    agreeing on names, 222
    cost analysis, 223
    disconnect and deficiency identification, 222
    draft version of process, 220–222
    Ergonomic Systems case study, 403–409
    facilitator responsibilities, 220
    goal of, 219
    goals, assumptions, and constraints review, 224
    IS process documentation, 222
    labeling inputs and outputs, 222
    major activities, 220–224
    organization diagram, 221–222
    outcome (documentation and models), 224
    overview, 213, 221, 234
    plan review, 220
    process analysis and improvement worksheet, 222
    process diagram, 221–222
    process management design development, 223
    recommending changes, 224
    redesign plan creation, 224
    redesign plan presentation, 224

Analyze phase (Six Sigma DMAIC process), 198–202
    categories of tasks, 199
    cause-effect diagram, 201–202
    overview, 188
    process diagram for, 198–199
    SF Seafood example, 199–202
    systematic analysis process, 200–201
    three-stage process, 201

Anova workflow case study, 266–267

ANX (Automotive Network Exchange), 358

applications. *See* e-business applications; software applications

ARIS
    defined, 458
    development of, 28
    as market leader, 431
    SAP use of diagrams, 287, 288–290

ARIS—Business Process Frameworks, 498

ARIS—Business Process Modeling, 498

arrows
    bent, 103–104, 121
    on class diagrams, 100
    on organization diagram, 100, 103–104
    on process diagram, 113, 117, 121
    on process diagram for workflows, 259–260
    on SCOR model, 367

AS-IS process diagram. *See* IS process diagram

ASQ (American Society for Quality), 493

asterisk (*) on process diagram, 121

asynchronous process, 458

atomic activities, 79, 458

automation and automation systems. *See* business process automation

automobile industry. *See also* car sales
    Automotive Network Exchange (ANX), 358
    AutoXchange system, 357–358
    business process change example, 5–6
    competitive strategies in, 53–54
    Covisint exchange system, 358–362
    e-marketplace, 357–362
    iStarXchange system, 362
    quality control in, 180–181
    TradeXchange system, 357–358
    U.S. vs. Japanese, 180–181

Automotive Network Exchange (ANX), 358

AutoXchange system, 357–358

B2B (business-to-business), 332. *See also* supplier-oriented e-business applications

B2C (business-to-customer), 332. *See also* customer-oriented e-business applications

B2E (business-to-employee) applications, 375. *See also* internal-oriented e-business applications

Baan, ERP applications from, 281

Balanced Scorecard, 172–173, 458

Balanced Scorecard, The, 492

banking
    function-process matrix for, 71–72
    niche specialization in, 60
    process architecture and IT planning example, 85, 87

barriers to entry, 50

basic requirements in Kano analysis, 196

Bass, Len, 489

batch process, 260

batch processing, 259–260, 458

behavior diagrams, 306

bell-shaped curve. *See* standard bell-shaped curve

benchmarks
    defined, 372, 459
    in Plan phase of business process redesign, 219
    for SCOR projects, 372–374

Benz, Karl, 5

Bertalanffy, Ludwig von, 20, 486

best practices
    SCOR model, 372
    strategy approach, 63–64

Beyond Reengineering, 493

BI (business intelligence), 304, 379–380, 459

BizTalk (Microsoft), 277, 459, 496

black belt (Six Sigma), 187, 189

Blown to Bits, 500

BlueFire Six Sigma Web site, 494

Boar, Bernard H., 488

bold dot
    on process diagram, 112, 119
    within a circle, 119

Booch, Grady, 498, 499

booksellers, value proposition example for, 51

boxes. *See* rectangles

BPEL4WS (Business Process Execution Language for Web Services), 276, 459

BPI (business process improvement). *See also* Six Sigma
    BPR vs., 39–40
    business process redesign vs., 39–40, 207
    companies engaged in today, 3
    defined, 10–11, 39, 81, 460
    ERP systems vs., 282
    Improve phase of Six Sigma, 188, 202–203
    other options compared to, 80–81

Six Sigma approach, 182,
    186–187, 188–189, 202–203
systematic process for, 449–450
BPM (Business Process Manage-
    ment). *See also* business pro-
    cess management
business process management vs.,
    12, 461, 496
defined, 12, 461
development of, 289
as process automation, 12, 29
BPMI (Business Process Management
    Initiative), 278, 459, 496
"BPR and Object Technology—Part
    II," 496
BPR (Business Process
    Reengineering)
CMM and, 8
companies active in (mid-1990s),
    3
defined, 39–40, 461
development of, 23–25
downsizing and, 27
integration in, 25, 26
IT role in, 26
misuses of, 27
overview, 24–25
process improvement and process
    redesign vs., 39–40
pros and cons of, 24
radical nature of, 24–25, 26
seminal publications, 23
value chains and, 107
workflow and ERP approaches
    vs., 28–29
workflow systems and, 257
BPSS (Business Process Specification
    Schema), 273–275, 363–364,
    459
Brache, Alan P.
gaps and disconnects pattern and,
    249
Improving Performance, 30, 31,
    93, 249, 477, 485, 487,
    489–490, 491–492, 494, 495
process diagramming originated
    by, 113
Rummler-Brache methodology,
    30–32, 477
Buckiewicz, Marek, 497
Business Dynamics, 486
business intelligence (BI), 304,
    379–380, 459
business modeling, 311

Business Modeling with UML, 499
business process, 459
business process architecture. *See* pro-
    cess architecture
business process architecture commit-
    tee. *See also* process
    architecture
defined, 67
enterprise alignment process and,
    69–70
function-process matrix mainte-
    nance by, 71–72
IT planning and, 85
multiple divisions or subsidiaries
    and, 71–72
plan for business process changes
    developed, 70
Plan phase in process redesign
    and, 216
process architecture process over-
    view, 88
process redesign and, 214
process-strategy matrix and, 84
project steering teams established
    by, 70–71
business process automation. *See also*
    ERP (Enterprise Resource
    Planning) systems; ERP-driven
    redesign; software develop-
    ment; workflow systems
analyzing a completely automated
    activity, 149–153
for assembly processes, 82
defined, 12, 81, 459
for Enter Expense Reports activ-
    ity, 145–146
input and output design for,
    152–153
IT role in, 37–39
other options compared to, 80–81
precision required for, 152–153
trend toward, 304
uses for, 255
Business Process Change, 494, 495
business process change
automobile industry example, 5–6
current situation, 37–41
deciding what kind to undertake,
    80–84
decision tree, 451, 452
evolution of understanding of,
    6–9
as growing concern, 4
historic overview, 36–37

manager's job and, 5–6
process change defined, 473
senior management support
    needed for, 43
types of, 80–81
variety of options for, 10
business process change cycle, 10, 11,
    12, 459–460
business process design. *See* business
    process redesign
Business Process Engineering, 488, 498
Business Process Excellence, 502
Business Process Execution Language
    for Web Services (BPEL4WS),
    276, 459
business process hierarchy, 460
business process improvement. *See*
    BPI (business process
    improvement)
business process languages
BPSS, 273–275, 363–364, 459
defined, 271
ebXML, 270–271, 273–275,
    393–396, 459, 464, 497
future of, 279
need for, 270
for private processes, 275–276
software development and XML-
    based languages, 323
Web services and, 270
workflow systems and, 271–272
WSFL, 276, 277, 483, 496
XLANG, 276, 277, 483, 496
XML Business Process Language,
    483
Business Process Management,
    496–497
business process management. *See*
    also BPM (Business Process
    Management)
basic model of manager's role,
    161–162
Business Process Management
    (BPM) vs., 12, 461, 496
Chevron management redesign
    example, 176–177
control process task, 163, 164
correcting deviations, 164
defined, 12, 81, 461, 475
detailed model of manager's role,
    162–165
Ergonomic Systems case study,
    413–421
focus of this book, 160–161

business process management
    (*continued*)
    high-level view, 166
    job functions of the manager, 475
    manager responsibilities, 165–167
    matrix management system,
        165–167
    measures for goals, 164
    other options compared to, 80–81
    plan process task, 163–164
    process executed task, 163, 164
    redesign and management
        changes, 176, 223
    references, 492–493
    in Six Sigma approach, 181–182
Business Process Management Initia-
    tive (BPMI), 278, 459, 496
*Business Process Management Using
    MQSeries and Partner Agree-
    ment Manager,* 502
business process modeling. *See*
    modeling
business process modeling tools. *See
    also* business process tools
    defined, 461
    Web site, 502
    for workflow systems, 262
Business Process Orientation, 493, 501
business process outsourcing,
    316–317, 461. *See also*
    outsourcing
business process redesign. *See also*
    process redesign patterns; *spe-
    cific phases by name*
    in the 1990s vs. today, 3, 4–5
    BPR vs., 39–40
    Chevron management redesign
        example, 176–177
    companies engaged in (mid-1990s
        and today), 3
    crash programs vs., 6
    for customer-oriented e-business
        applications, 347–349
    defined, 11–12, 40, 80, 460
    enterprise alignment cycle and,
        211–212
    executive committee, 214–215
    facilitator for, 209, 215, 216, 218,
        220, 225, 226
    high-level overview of methodol-
        ogy, 212–213
    implementation failures, 211, 231
    implementation successes, factors
        contributing to, 422–424

for internal-oriented e-business
    applications, 375–382
Internet and, 2, 4
management and measurement
    plan needed for, 177
management changes and, 176,
    223
methodology, 209–234
multiple rounds needed for, 177
need for methodology, 211
other options compared to, 80–81
overview, 233, 234
Phase 1: Plan, 213, 215–219,
    234, 401–402
Phase 2: Analysis, 213, 219–224,
    234, 403–409
Phase 3: Redesign, 213, 224–227,
    234, 409–421
Phase 4: Development, 213,
    228–230, 234, 421–422
Phase 5: Transition, 213,
    231–234, 422–424
process improvement vs., 39–40,
    207
process redesign team, 215, 216,
    220, 225
references, 494–496
responsibilities for, 214–215
routine changes vs. large-scale re-
    design, 209–210
in Six Sigma approach, 182
steering team, 210, 215, 216,
    218, 231, 422
for supplier-oriented e-business
    applications, 351–354
with workflow systems, 266
workflow systems and larger pro-
    cesses, 259
Business Process Reengineering. *See*
    BPR (Business Process
    Reengineering)
*Business Process Reengineering and Be-
    yond,* 491
Business Process Specification
    Schema (BPSS), 273–275,
    363–364, 459
business process tools, 425–443
    for architecture maintenance,
        439, 441–442
    business process modeling tools,
        461, 502
    CASE tools, 314, 317–318, 429
    code generation, 429, 430
    defined, 461

for diagrams, 91
in Ergonomic Systems case study,
    431–443
features needed in, 429–431
for IS process diagram, 433–434
market leaders, 431
need for, 425–426
for organization diagrams, 105,
    432–433
overview (table), 427–428
repository, 429–430
for SHOULD process diagram,
    434–437
simulation, 430–431, 438–439,
    477
UML modeling tools, 314–315,
    317–318
using, 442–443
variety of, 426–428
Web portal screen hierarchy, 434,
    435
for workflow systems, 262
Business Process Trends newsletter,
    Web site, 503
business processes. *See also* processes
    in business process hierarchy, 460
    comprehensive nature of, 24
    defined, 459
    departmental boundaries crossed
        by, 22, 23
    documentation and, 69
    process-strategy matrix for classi-
        fying, 81–84
Business Rule Community Web site,
    491
business rules
    defined, 461–462
    generic form, 116
    high-level vs. detailed, 491
    for process diagram, 116–117
*Business Rules and Information Sys-
    tems,* 491
Business Specifications, 500
business-to-business (B2B), 332.
    See also supplier-oriented
    e-business applications
business-to-customer (B2C), 332.
    See also customer-oriented
    e-business applications
business-to-employee (B2E) applica-
    tions, 375. *See also* internal-
    oriented e-business
    applications
buyers, competitive strategy and, 49

CAD (Computer Aided Design), 375. *See also* internal-oriented e-business applications

Calambos, George, 384, 500

CAM (Computer Automated Manufacturing), 375. *See also* internal-oriented e-business applications

Can-Be Processes. *See* COULD processes

capability, human performance analysis and, 143

Capability Maturity Model. *See* CMM (Capability Maturity Model)

Capability Maturity Model, The, 7, 486, 500

capital investment as barrier to entry, 50

car sales. *See also* automobile industry
  C-business map with SAP, 290–291
  ERP-driven redesign implementation, 292–294
  process with SAP, 288–290

CASE (Computer-Aided Software Engineering)
  defined, 462
  MDA and, 314–316
  tools, 314, 317–318, 429

CASE IS Software Automation, 500

CASEwise, 431, 502

cause-effect diagrams, 201–202, 462

Cavanaugh, Ronald R., 494

C-business maps (SAP), 290–291

CEFACT. *See* UN/CEFACT

Champy, James
  BPR developed by, 23, 25, 26
  Reengineering Management, 492
  reengineering pattern and, 237, 243–244
  Reengineering the Corporation, 23, 240, 485, 487, 495

charter
  business process redesign, 215–216
  Six Sigma, 189, 194

Chevron
  management redesign at, 176–177
  process management improvement white paper, 493

Chopra, Sunil, 501

Chrissis, Mary Beth, 486, 500

CIM (Computer Integrated Manufacturing), 462

CIO Magazine, 488

claims process, process diagram examples, 122, 123

class diagrams
  arrows in, 100
  classes in, 100
  defined, 462
  organization diagrams and, 310
  as set of data to track, 310
  SF Seafood example, 309
  supersystem diagram as, 100
  UML, 306, 309–310

classes
  in class diagrams, 100
  notation, 109

Clements, Paul, 489

Close stage in Six Sigma Analyze phase, 201

CMM (Capability Maturity Model)
  BPR and, 8
  CMMI, 324
  defined, 462
  development of, 7–8, 323–324
  illustrated, 448
  maturity levels, 8, 9, 324, 325
  moving up the scale, 449
  People-CMM, 143–144, 472, 492
  Rummler-Brache framework compared to, 31–32
  software development and, 323–326
  table summarizing, 325
  TQM and, 8
  usefulness of, 324, 326, 446, 449
  Web site, 486

COBOL, 314, 462

collaboration diagram, 307

collaborative applications, 332, 351–352

collaborative business (C-business) maps with SAP, 290–291

company portal, 334. *See also* portals

competition
  barriers to entry, 50
  buyers as driving force, 49
  globalization and, 50
  hypercompetitive companies, 61
  industry competitors, 48
  Porter's model of, 48–50
  potential entrants as driving force, 49–50

strategies for, 52–54
substitutes as driving force, 49
suppliers as driving force, 49

Competitive Advantage, 21–22, 57, 62, 463, 487, 488

competitive advantage. *See also* value chains
  defined, 60, 462–463
  operational effectiveness, 60–61, 62
  Porter's theory of, 57–64
  profit margin and, 60
  references, 488
  strategic positioning, 60, 61–63
  sustaining, 61

Competitive Strategy, 45–46, 48, 57, 473, 487, 488

competitors on supersystem diagram, 98

complexity
  of diagrams, 91–92
  in process-strategy matrix, 81, 82–83

component diagram, 307

Component-Based Development for Enterprise Systems, 499

Computational viewpoint (RM-ODP), 322

Computer Aided Design (CAD), 375. *See also* internal-oriented e-business applications

Computer Automated Manufacturing (CAM), 375. *See also* internal-oriented e-business applications

Computer Integrated Manufacturing (CIM), 462

computer screens
  activity analysis and, 137, 152
  Travel-Is-Us reservation portal screens, 335, 340
  Web portal screen hierarchy, 434, 435

Computer-Aided Software Engineering. *See* CASE (Computer-Aided Software Engineering)

computing, corporate vs. departmental, 23

consequences, 141–142

Control phase (Six Sigma DMAIC process), 188, 203–204

core business processes. *See also* value chains

core business processes (*continued*)
defined, 463
value chains and, 58, 78
core competencies, 52
cost leadership
in automobile industry, 53–54
as competitive strategy, 52
defined, 463
COULD process diagram
defined, 124–125, 474
Redesign phase of business process redesign and, 225
Travel-Is-Us process, 335, 336–337, 338–339, 342–343
COULD processes, 463
Covisint exchange system, 358–362
crash programs, business process redesign vs., 6
Creating Modern Capitalism, 486
Creating the Smart Enterprise, 493
CRM (Customer Relationship Management). *See also* customer-oriented e-business applications; packaged applications
defined, 463
Ergonomic Systems case study, 412–413
ERP applications with, 281
goals, 332
internal-oriented e-business applications, 375
shortcomings as a term, 333–334
cross-company processes, 450, 451
CTQ (Critical-To-Quality) tree, 191–193, 418, 437, 463
Curran, Thomas, 498
Curtis, Bill
Capability Maturity Model, The, 486, 500
People Capability Maturity Model, The, 492
People-CMM created by, 144
TeraQuest Web site (Curtis's company), 486
customer relationship management. *See* CRM (customer relationship management)
customer-driven e-business, 331
customer-oriented e-business applications
analyzing customer-oriented processes, 341–347
defined, 463

ERP components, 347
exceptions and, 346
IBM offerings, 348–349
multiple processes and, 344–346
overview, 333–334
redesign, 347–349
references, 500–501
Travel-Is-Us example, 335–340
customers. *See also* value propositions
Balanced Scorecard perspective, 173
in eTOM framework, 73, 74, 75
gathering information from, 193, 196–197
internal, 190
Kano analysis categories for requirements of, 196
measuring satisfaction of, 195
need for understanding, 51–52
organization charts' lack of, 93–94
on organization diagram, 103
on process diagram, 112, 121, 341
Six Sigma emphasis on, 190
on supersystem diagram, 98
in systems view of organization, 96
Cutter Consortium Web site, 485

Daimler, Gottlieb, 5
data, defined, 380
Data Processing (DP). *See* IT (Information Technology)
data warehouses, 304
Davenport, Thomas H.
BPR developed by, 24, 25, 26, 30, 461, 489
ERP investigated by, 497
ERP promoted by, 28, 281
Mission Critical, 281, 497
"New Industrial Engineering, The," 23
Process Innovation, 23, 487
reengineering pattern and, 237, 243, 244
decision points or diamonds, 117, 118, 463
decision support systems, 378–379, 381–382, 383, 463
decision tree for process change, 451, 452
defects, Six Sigma goal for, 184, 186

Define, Measure, Analyze, Design and Verify (DMADV) model, 494
Define, Measure, Analyze, Improve, Control. *See* DMAIC (Define, Measure, Analyze, Improve, Control) process
Define phase (Six Sigma DMAIC process), 189–194
charter creation, 189, 194
CTQ (Critical-To-Quality) tree, 191–193, 463
gathering customer information, 193
overview, 188
Pareto analysis, 193
SF Seafood example, 190–194
SIPOC approach, 190–191, 478
Defined maturity level (CMM), 8, 9, 324, 325, 448
delegation of authority, on organization diagram, 102
delighters in Kano analysis, 196
Deliver process type (SCOR), 367, 368
Deming, Edwards, 180, 203, 481
Department of Defense (DOD), 7, 321
departmental measures. *See* functional measures
departmentalism
BPR as revolt against, 24–25
business processes crossing boundaries, 22, 23
evolution of the strategic process and, 65–66
value chains as revolt against, 23
departments
on organization diagram, 102–103
profits not produced by, 110
workflow system generations and, 265
deployment diagram, 307
Design Patterns, 495
Developing E-Business Systems and Architectures, 489, 501
Development phase (business process redesign), 228–230
Ergonomic Systems case study, 421–422
goal of, 228
IT involvement, 228–230

major activities, 228–230
outcome, 230
overview, 213, 229, 234
SHOULD process diagram re-
    finement, 228, 230
deviation, standard, 183–184, 478
diagrams. *See also* COULD process
    diagram; IS process diagram;
    process diagram; SHOULD
    process diagram; *specific kinds*
activity, 134, 307
behavior, 306
cause-effect, 201–202, 462
class, 100, 306, 462
collaboration, 307
complexity of, 91–92
component, 307
defined, 464
deployment, 307
levels of analysis, 131–132
models vs., 96
organization, 98–109, 221–222,
    471
organization charts, 93–95,
    470–471
sequence, 307
statechart, 307
supersystem, 98–100, 479
systems, 20
tools for, 91
UML diagram types, 306–307
use case, 306, 481
value chain, 107
diamonds or decision points, 117,
    118, 463
differentiation
    in automobile industry, 54
    as competitive strategy, 52–53
    defined, 464
directly linked supply chain systems,
    362–366
    integrated private supply chain
        processes, 365–366
    links via public processes,
        362–365
distribution channels access as barrier
    to entry, 50
DMADV (Define, Measure, Analyze,
    Design and Verify) model, 494
DMAIC (Define, Measure, Analyze,
    Improve, Control) process. *See
    also specific phases*
Analyze phase, 188, 198–202

Control phase, 188, 203–204
Define phase, 188, 189–194
defined, 464
failure to achieve Six Sigma, 189
Improve phase, 188, 202–203
keys to quick accomplishment,
    189
Measure phase, 188, 194–198
multiple iterations of phases,
    188–189
DOD (Department of Defense), 7,
    321
dot.com companies
    crash of, 329, 330
    defined, 464
    e-business and, 330
    mixed success of, 34
downsizing, 27, 464
DP (Data Processing). *See* IT (Infor-
    mation Technology)
Drayer, Ralph, 352
D'Souza, Desmond Francis, 499
Dunn, Jeri, 296
dynamics in process-strategy matrix,
    81

EAI (Enterprise Application Integra-
    tion), 464
E-Automotive Report, 502
E-Business, 488, 500
e-business. *See also* Ergonomic Sys-
    tems case study
    customer-driven, 331
    defined, 464
    differing definitions of, 330
    dot.com companies and, 330
    goals, 332
    integration-driven, 331
    as a network, 382–385
    references, 500–502
    strategies, 64–65
e-business applications, 329–332.
    See also customer-oriented
    e-business applications;
    internal-oriented e-business
    applications; supplier-oriented
    e-business applications
    customer-oriented, 333–334,
        341–349, 463
    internal-oriented, 375–382, 467
    Internet impact on, 329–330
    Internet-driven changes in busi-
        ness processes, 330–332

portals, 334–341
references, 500–502
supplier-oriented, 351–375, 479
e-business marketplaces. *See*
    e-marketplaces
eBusiness Telecom Operations Map.
    See eTOM (eBusiness Telecom
    Operations Map)
*ebXML Catalog of Common Business
    Processes,* 497
ebXML (electronic business XML)
    BPSS language, 273–275, 459
    defined, 464
    directly linked supply chain sys-
        tems and, 363–364
    overview, 270–271
    sponsorship of, 273–274
    Web site, 464, 497
Eckes, George, 194, 493
EDI (Electronic Data Interchange)
    automotive e-marketplaces and,
        357, 358
    defined, 465
    shortcomings of, 33
e-ERP applications, 375. *See also*
    internal-oriented e-business
    applications
efficiency (operational effectiveness),
    60–61, 62, 470
80/20 rule, 193, 200
EJB (Enterprise JavaBean) compo-
    nents, 315
electronic business XML. *See* ebXML
    (electronic business XML)
Electronic Data Interchange. *See* EDI
    (Electronic Data Interchange)
email
    administrative workflow systems
        and, 264–265, 458
    defined, 465
    systems, 376–377
e-marketplaces, 355, 357–362
    automotive, 357–362
    defined, 354, 465
    illustrated, 356
    NASDAQ as, 355
    process architecture, 384
    SAP components, 355
    as supply chain integration ap-
        proach, 354, 356
    U.S. steel market, 357
*Emergence of Business Process Manage-
    ment, The,* 497

employee involvement in Six Sigma, 204–205
employee portals, 377–378
end point on process diagram, 119
Engineering viewpoint (RM-ODP), 322
Enter Expense Reports activity
    analyzing, 134–138
    automating, 145–146
    overview, 145
enterprise alignment
    business process architecture committee and, 69–70
    defined, 12–13, 83–89, 465
    overview, 67–69
    strategy committee and, 69
enterprise alignment cycle
    business process redesign methodology and, 211–212
    defined, 454
    illustrated, 68, 455
    overview, 67–69
Enterprise Application Integration (EAI), 464
enterprise applications, 465
enterprise architecture, 465
Enterprise Architecture Planning, 489
Enterprise JavaBean (EJB) components, 315
enterprise modeling, 311
Enterprise Modeling with UML, 499
Enterprise Resource Planning. *See* ERP (Enterprise Resource Planning) systems; ERP-driven redesign; packaged applications
Enterprise viewpoint (RM-ODP), 322
environment. *See also* competition
    barriers to entry, 50
    driving forces for competition, 49–50
    on high-level organization diagram, 100–101
    Phase 2 of strategy process and, 46, 47
    on supersystem diagram, 98–99
e-procurement applications, 375. *See also* internal-oriented e-business applications
Ergonomic Systems case study, 389–424

architecture maintenance, 439, 441–442
business process tools, 431–443
changes agreed upon, 400
company overview, 389–393
CTQ trees, 418, 437
e-business strategy, 394–401
existing software applications, 405–406
flow of goals and measures, 414–416
goal alignment, 416–417
goals adopted for e-business, 396–401
goals and measures worksheet, 393
IS process diagram, 403, 404, 405, 406–407, 433–434
joint subcommittee review of e-business, 395–396
management system refinement, 413–421
measures, 393, 414, 416, 419, 420, 437–438
opportunities and threats (chart), 396
opportunities and threats worksheet, 396, 398–399
Order Fulfillment Process (IS version), 403, 404
Order Process (IS version), 403, 405, 406–407
organization chart, 390, 391
organization diagram, 401, 402, 432–433
Phase 1: Planning for Redesign of the Order Process, 401–402
Phase 2: Analyzing the Current Order Fulfillment Process, 403–409
Phase 3: Designing the New Order Process, 409–421
Phase 4: Resource Development, 421–422
Phase 5: New Order Process Goes Online, 422–424
portal creation, 409–412, 434, 435
previous business process efforts, 390–391
process analysis and improvement worksheet, 408
process architecture, 391, 392

process/function role/responsibility worksheet, 419, 421
products, 390
    as realistic but hypothetical, 389
sales and finance process modifications, 412
SHOULD process diagram, 412–413, 414–415, 434–437
simulation, 438–439, 440
success of company, 391–393
Zachman Framework, 441–442
Ericcson, Magnus, 499
Eriksson, Hans-Erik, 499
ERP (Enterprise Resource Planning) systems. *See also* business process automation; ERP-driven redesign; packaged applications; SAP (Systems, Applications and Products in data processing)
    advantages of, 282
    as automation systems, 29
    BPR vs., 28–29
    development of, 28
    Internet reliance and, 283
    limitations of, 282–283
    overview, 281
    portal components, 347
    process improvement vs., 282
    processes suitable for, 28
    as workflow systems, 294
ERP Post Implementation Issues and Best Practices, 498
ERP-driven redesign, 281–297. *See also* SAP (Systems, Applications and Products in data processing)
    defined, 465
    implementation, 292–294
    Nestlé USA case study, 295–297
    process redesign pattern, 238
    references, 497–498
eTOM (eBusiness Telecom Operations Map)
    defined, 466
    detailed version, 76–78
    executive-level version, 73, 75
    executive-level version rotated 90 degrees, using standard notation, 73, 74, 75
    matrix management system and, 76, 78
    overview, 72–78

process flow in, 75
as reference architecture, 72
translation into organization diagram, 108
eTOM: The Business Process Framework, 489
Evans, Philip, 500
events on process diagram, 122
executive committee
business process architecture committee, 67, 69–72, 84, 85, 88
business process redesign committee, 214–215
steering teams established by, 70–71
strategy committee, 67, 69
expense reports. *See* Enter Expense Reports activity
eXtended Markup Language. *See* XML (eXtended Markup Language)

facilitator for process redesign, 209, 215, 216, 218, 220, 225, 226
Fang, Walter, 491
feedback, 142–143, 466
Ferrara, Lynette, 497
Fifth Discipline, The, 486–487
financial perspective in Balanced Scorecard, 173
Fingar, Peter, 496–497
first-generation workflow systems, 265
Fischer, Layna, 487, 496
fishbone (cause-effect) diagrams, 201–202, 462
fit, 62, 474
flow of control in workflow systems, 262–263
Ford, Henry, 5–6, 19, 53–54
Ford Motor Company, 5–6, 19, 53–54
forks (junction bars or junctions), 117, 468
Forrester, Jay, 20, 486
Fowler, Martin, 490, 498
Frederick W. Taylor and the Rise of Scientific Management, 486, 493
Frost, Stuart, 499
functional measures. *See also* measures

defined, 168–169, 466
process measures vs., 167–169
function-process matrix, 71–72, 466
functions on organization diagram, 109

Galvin, Bob, 181
Gamma, Erich, 495
gaps and disconnects pattern, 249–253
defined, 466
described, 207
Ergonomic Systems case study and, 407
overview, 237
process diagram with departmental handoffs highlighted, 251, 252–253
simplification and, 251
sources of gaps and disconnects, 250
value-added analysis and, 251
Gartner Group, 292, 431
Gauss, Carl Frederick, 183, 478
Gaussian curve. *See* standard bell-shaped curve
Gavin, Lee, 502
GE (General Electric), 181, 299
General Motors, 54
General Systems Theory, 486
generic business process languages. *See* business process languages
Ghalimi, Ishmael, 496–497
Gilbert, Thomas F., 492
globalization
barriers to entry and, 50
as business process redesign driver, 35–36
glossary of terms, 457–483
goal hierarchy, 169–171, 466
goals. *See also* measures
alignment process, 166
of Analysis phase (business process redesign), 219
of business process redesign, 218, 224, 225
of Development phase (business process redesign), 228
e-business, 332
Ergonomic Systems case study, 393, 396–401, 414–417
functional vs. process measures and, 168–169

hierarchy, 169–171, 466
manager responsibility for measures of, 164
process redesign, 218
of Redesign phase (business process redesign), 224
SCOR reference model, 366
Six Sigma goal for defects, 184, 186
of Transition phase (business process redesign), 231
goals and measures worksheet (case study), 393
Goals, Processes, and Projects Worksheet, 89–90, 466
government policies as barrier to entry, 50
graphical applications, 301
green belt (Six Sigma), 187
Grindley, Kit, 488
groupware applications, 265
Grover, Varun, 494, 495
Guttman, Michael, 489, 500, 501

Hall, Curt, 491, 498, 501
Hammer, Michael
Beyond Reengineering, 493
BPR developed by, 24–25, 26, 30, 461, 489
core processes of, 58
reengineering pattern and, 237, 243
Reengineering the Corporation, 23, 240, 485, 487, 495
"Reengineering Work: Don't Automate, Obliterate," 23, 487
Harmon, Paul
"BPR and Object Technology—Part II," 496
Developing E-Business Systems and Architectures, 489, 501
Intelligent Software Systems Development, 491, 498
"Texas Instruments' MMST Project," 495
Who's Profiting from Business Process Redesign, 2–4, 485
Harry, Mikel J., 33, 181, 478, 488, 494
Hayden, Francis, 497
Hefley, William E., 492
Helm, Richard, 495
hexagons on process diagram, 177

hierarchy of processes, 80
Hill, Steven C., 489
horizontal alignment, 466–467
horizontal view of organizations, 95–96
HPI (human performance improvement), 30, 239
HPT (human performance technology), 491
Human Competence, 492
human performance, 472
human performance analysis
    activity standards, 138–140
    activity support, 140–141
    consequences, 141–142
    defined, 138
    factors affecting (chart), 139
    feedback, 142–143
    People-CMM as complement to, 143–144
    skill, knowledge, and capability, 143
    worksheet, 149, 150, 151, 467
Human Performance Analysis Worksheet
    defined, 467
    illustrated, 150, 151
    sales activity example, 149, 150
human performance analyst, 467
human performance improvement (HPI), 30, 239
human performance model, 467
human performance technology (HPT), 491
Humphrey, Watts, 7
hypercompetitive companies, 61

IBM
    AD/Cycle Repository, 314
    Business Process Reengineering and Beyond, 491
    customer-oriented e-business applications, 348–349
    IBM LOVEM/CABE, 491
    patterns Web site, 500
    UML-compliant repositories, 314
    WSFL, 276, 277, 483, 496
IDEF, 321, 467
IDS Scheer. *See also* ARIS
    ProcessWorld annual conference, 287–288
    Web site, 498, 502

iJET Travel Intelligence workflow case study, 267–268
implementation
    of ERP-driven redesign, 292–294
    factors contributing to success of, 422–424
    failures for process redesign, 211, 231
Improve phase (Six Sigma DMAIC process), 188, 202–203
Improving Performance, 30, 31, 93, 138, 249, 477, 485, 487, 489–490, 491–492, 494, 495
Industrial Revolution, 19
industry competitors, 48
information, defined, 380
Information Architecture for the World Wide Web, 501
Information Systems (IS). *See* IT (Information Technology)
Information Technology. *See* IT (Information Technology)
Information viewpoint (RM-ODP), 322
Initial maturity level (CMM), 8, 9, 324, 325, 448
innovation and learning perspective in Balanced Scorecard, 173
inputs
    design for automation, 152–153
    labeling in Analysis phase of business process redesign, 222
    recognizability of the input requiring action, 140
    SIPOC approach, 190–191, 478
    Six Sigma Measure phase and, 194
instance of a process, 474–475
insurance companies
    Anova workflow case study, 166–167
    generic workflow system example, 259–263
    SAP business architecture for, 285–287
integrated supply chain
    defined, 352
    design approaches, 354–355, 356
    directly linked supply chain systems, 365–366
    early examples, 352
    future of, 352–353

illustrated, 354
integrated processes, 354–355
inventory surpluses and, 353
overview, 353–354
transportation costs and, 353
integration in BPR, 25, 26
integration-driven e-business, defined, 331
Intelligent Software Systems Development, 491, 498
internal business processes perspective in Balanced Scorecard, 173
internal customers, 190
internal portals, 334
internal-oriented e-business applications, 375–382
    business intelligence (BI), 379–380
    decision support systems, 378–379, 381–382, 383
    defined, 467
    email systems, 376–377
    employee portals, 377–378
    knowledge management systems, 380–382, 383
    organizing training using processes, 381–382, 383
    redesign, 375–382
    references, 501–502
    SAP application suites, 375–376
international business. *See* globalization
International Society for Performance Improvement (ISPI), 468, 491
International Society of Six Sigma Professionals (ISSSP), 493
International Standards Organization. *See* ISO (International Standards Organization)
Internet. *See also* portals; Web sites
    application linking and, 304, 329
    business changes due to, 33–34
    business impact of, 329–330, 331–332
    business process redesign and, 2, 4
    defined, 467
    e-business as network and, 382–385
    ERP applications and, 283
    Internet-driven changes in business processes, 330–332

third-generation workflow systems
    and, 265
value propositions affected by, 51,
    52
Y2K bug and delayed incorpora-
    tion of, 34
*Introduction to Groupware, Workflow,
    and Workgroup Computing,*
    497
IS (Information Systems). *See* IT (In-
    formation Technology)
IS process diagram
    Analysis phase of business process
        redesign and, 222
    defined, 124, 468, 474
    Ergonomic Systems case study,
        403, 404, 405, 406–407,
        433–434
    example, 124–125
    notation, 128
    overview, 128–129
    in ProVision, 433–434
    Travel-Is-Us process, 335,
        336–337
ISO (International Standards
    Organization)
    ISO 9000:2000, 32
    ISO 9000, 32, 468
    RM-ODP, 321–323
    Web site, 500
"ISO Reference Model of Open Dis-
    tributed Processing," 500
ISPI (International Society for Perfor-
    mance Improvement), 468,
    491
ISSSP (International Society of Six
    Sigma Professionals), 493
iStarXchange system, 362
IT (Information Technology)
    automation efforts, 37–39
    BPR role of, 26
    business process change today
        and, 37–39, 450–451
    changes in the late 1990s, 33–34
    completely automated activities
        and, 149–153
    defined, 467
    Development phase of business
        process redesign and, 228–230
    enterprise alignment cycle and,
        68, 84–85
    history, 303–304

other terms for, 25
    portal terminology, 337
    process architecture and IT plan-
        ning, 84–87
    process-IT matrix, 85, 86, 475
    software development and, 311

J.D. Edwards, ERP applications
    from, 281, 292
Jacobson, A., 499
Jacobson, Ivar, 498, 499
JIT (Just-in-Time Manufacturing),
    32–33, 181
job descriptions
    activities and, 134, 153–155
    defined, 468
    sales activity example, 147, 148,
        153–155
Job Model. *See* job description
Johnson, Ralph, 495
Johnson, William C., 493, 501
joins (junction bars or junctions),
    117, 468
Jost, Wolfgang, 502
junction bars or junctions, 117,
    468

Kalakota, Ravi, 488, 500
Kano analysis, 196, 468
Kano, Noriaki, 196
Kaplan, Robert, 173, 458, 492
Kazman, Rick, 489
Keller, Gerhard, 498
Ken Orr Institute Web site, 493
Kettinger, William J., 494, 495
key performance indicators (KPIs),
    173
Khoshafian, Setrag, 497
Kilov, Haim, 500
Kirchmer, Mathias, 502
Klein, Mark M., 494, 495
Knolmayer, Gerhard, 501
knowledge
    defined, 380, 468
    human performance analysis and,
        143
knowledge management
    defined, 380, 468–469
    systems, 380–382, 383
Koushik, Srinivas, 383–384, 500
KPIs (key performance indicators),
    173

Kruchten, Philippe, 499
Kubeck, Lynn C., 494, 495

Ladd, Andrew, 498
Lapidus, Gary, 502
lean manufacturing, 180, 469
levels of analysis, 469
Leymann, F., 496
long-run process drift, 184, 478
LOVEM methodology, references,
    491

M1 measures, 171
M2 measures, 171
M3 measures, 171
Make process type (SCOR), 367, 368
Making Process Improvement Work,
    499
Managed maturity level (CMM), 8,
    9, 324, 325, 448
management alignment pattern, 238
managing business processes. *See*
    BPM (Business Process Man-
    agement); business process
    management
Managing IT at Board Level, 488
managing the performance of activi-
    ties, 144
Manganelli, Raymond L., 494, 495
margin, 58, 60
Marshall, Chris, 499
master black belt (Six Sigma), 187,
    189
matrix management system
    defined, 165
    eTOM framework and, 76, 78
    overview, 165–167
McClure, Carma, 500
McCormack, Kevin P., 493, 501
McCraw, Thomas K., 486
McCrea, Peter, 176
McCreary, Bill, 357–358
McKenna, Regis, 500
MDA (Model Driven Architecture),
    312–317
    CASE and, 314–316
    component reuse with, 315
    defined, 469–470
    further information, 499
    illustrated, 313
    platform-independent model
        (PIM), 312, 317

MDA (Model Driven Architecture)
(*continued*)
platform-specific model (PSM),
312, 317
work remaining for, 315–316
Measure phase (Six Sigma DMAIC
process), 194–198
inputs, 194
Kano analysis, 196, 468
measurement principles, 194
outcome measures vs. process
measures, 195–196
outputs or customer satisfaction
measures, 195
overview, 188
process measures, 195
service measures vs. output measures, 196–197
SF Seafood example, 194–198
Measurement Scheduling Worksheet
defined, 469
illustrated, 173–174
process diagram on, 174–175
using, 174–176
measures
association with processes in Pro-
Vision, 437–438
defined, 469
DMADV model, 494
in DMAIC Analyze phase, 200,
201
in DMAIC Control phase,
203–204
DMAIC Measure phase, 188,
194–198
in DMAIC process, 188,
194–198, 464
Ergonomic Systems case study,
393, 414, 416, 419, 420
functional, 167–169, 466
functional vs. process, 167–169
for goals, manager responsibility
for, 164
hierarchy, 169–171, 469
Measurement Scheduling
Worksheet, 174–176, 469
outcome measures vs. process
measures, 195–196
process, 167–169, 195, 475–476
Process Measures Worksheet, 172,
476
responsibilities for monitoring,
171

SCOR model, 370–371
service measures vs. output mea-
sures, 196–197
Six Sigma and, 182, 186–187,
188, 194–198
measures hierarchy
defined, 469
monitoring responsibilities and,
171
overview, 169–171
MEGA International
MEGA, 431
Web site, 502
Meindl, Peter, 501
mergers and acquisitions, as business
process redesign drivers,
34–35, 36
Mertens, Peter, 501
Meta Software's MetaSoft Works, 431
Michelin Red Guide, 195
Microsoft
BizTalk, 277, 459, 496
ERP market entry by, 294
Orchestration Designer, 496
XLANG, 276, 277, 483, 496
middleware, 469. *See also* EAI (Enter-
prise Application Integration)
Millor, Sally A., 492
Mission Critical, 281, 497
MMST project (TI), 240–243
Model Driven Architecture. *See*
MDA (Model Driven
Architecture)
modeling. *See also* diagrams; MDA
(Model Driven Architecture);
UML (Unified Modeling
Language)
business, 311
defined, 470
enterprise, 311
importance of, 12
levels of analysis, 131–132
references, 489–491
thinking based on, 95
tools, 461
UML and, 310–312
UML tools, 314–315, 317–318
modeling organizations. *See also* organization diagram
models and diagrams, 96–98
organization diagrams, 98–105
organization diagrams and processes, 105–109

systems and processes, 109–110
systems view, 95–96
traditional view, 93–95
modeling processes. *See* process
diagram
models
defined, 469
diagrams vs., 96
Morville, Peter, 501
Motorola, 33, 181, 478

Narrow stage in Six Sigma Analyze
phase, 201
NASDAQ as an e-marketplace,
355
Neal, Douglas, 497
Nelson, Daniel, 486, 493
Nestlé USA, SAP case study,
295–297
"Nestle's ERP Odyssey," 498
Neuman, Robert P., 494
"New Industrial Engineering, The,"
23
niche specialization
in automobile industry, 54
in banking industry, 60
as competitive strategy, 53
considerations for company or
product, 53
defined, 470
non-value-adding activities, 58, 199,
470
normal bell-shaped curve. *See* standard bell-shaped curve
Norton, David, 173, 458, 492
notation
activities, 109, 115, 457
classes, 109
functions, 109
IS process diagram, 128
methodology vs., 306
organization diagram, 100, 101,
102, 103–104, 109
organizations, 109
process diagram, 111–112,
115–123
processes, 109, 111, 115, 457
SAP notation vs., 288–290
subprocesses, 109
notes
on IS process diagram, 128
on organization diagram,
101

OASIS, ebXML sponsorship by, 273–274

Object Advantage, The, 499

Object Management Group. *See* OMG (Object Management Group)

object-oriented, defined, 470

Objects, Components, and Frameworks with UML, 499

off-the-shelf software. *See* packaged applications

OMG (Object Management Group). *See also* MDA (Model Driven Architecture); UML (Unified Modeling Language)
  defined, 470
  MDA standard and, 312, 313
  UML Specification, 306
  Web site, 470, 490, 497, 498, 499

Open stage in Six Sigma Analyze phase, 201

operational effectiveness, 60–61, 62, 470

operational managers' responsibilities, 144

opportunities and threats worksheet (case study), 396, 398–399

Optimizing maturity level (CMM), 8, 9, 324, 325, 448

Oracle
  ERP applications from, 281, 282, 292
  UML-compliant repositories, 314

Orchestration Designer (Microsoft), 496

order fulfillment process, process diagram example, 116, 119

organization charts
  defined, 470–471
  Ergonomic Systems case study, 390, 391
  illustrated, 94
  limitations of, 93–95
  on organization diagrams, 101–102

organization diagram
  Analysis phase of business process redesign and, 221–222
  defined, 471
  Ergonomic Systems case study, 401, 402, 432–433
  eTOM translation into, 108

high-level, 100–101

high-level with organization chart, 101–102

inheritance of delegation of authority in, 102

levels of analysis and, 131–132

notation, 100, 101, 102, 103–104, 109

notes on, 101

object of, 104–105

organization diagrams vs., 471

process diagram information from, 113, 114

process diagram with, 105–106

processes and subprocesses on, 108–109

in ProVision, 432–433

series of successive diagrams, 104

showing relationships between internal departments and external entities, 102–104

tools for, 105, 432–433

value chains on, 106–108

organization diagrams
  defined, 471
  high-level class diagrams and, 310
  organization diagram vs., 471
  overview, 98–105
  processes and, 105–109
  supersystem, 98–100, 479

organizational level of performance, 31

organizational performance, 472

organizations
  horizontal or systems view of, 95–96
  notation, 109
  on organization diagram, 109
  as systems, 20–21, 445
  understanding via process diagrams, 445–446, 447
  vertical view of, 94

Orr, Ken, 493

outcome measures
  process measures vs., 195–196
  service measures vs., 196–197

outputs. *See also* process measures
  design for automation, 152–153
  labeling in Analysis phase of business process redesign, 222
  process measures vs. outcome measures, 195–196

service measures vs. output measures, 196–197

SIPOC approach, 190–191, 478

Six Sigma Measure phase and, 195

outsourcing
  business process outsourcing, 316–317, 461
  defined, 81, 471
  other options compared to, 80–81

packaged applications. *See also specific kinds*
  defined, 472
  modular organization in, 27–28

Pande, Peter S., 494

parallel processes, 472

Pareto analysis, 193

Patterns of E-Business, 383–384, 500

Paulk, Mark C., 486, 500

Penker, Magnus, 499

People Capability Maturity Model, The, 492

People-CMM, 143–144, 472, 492

Peoplesoft, ERP applications from, 281, 282, 292

performance. *See also* human performance analysis
  defined, 472
  managing for activities, 144
  maturity of organizations and, 7
  potential for improving (PIP), 204, 472, 492
  types of, 472

performance framework
  defined, 480–481
  levels of performance in, 31
  in Rummler-Brache methodology, 31–32

personal computers, software development and, 301

Petrozzo, Daniel P., 494, 495

PIM (platform-independent model), 312, 317

PIP (potential for improving performance), 204, 472, 492

Plan phase (business process redesign), 215–219
  appointing sponsor, teams, and facilitator, 218, 219
  assumptions, requirements, and constraints, 218–219
  benchmark data, 219

Plan phase (business process redesign)
(*continued*)
business process architecture committee and, 216
charter, 215–216
Ergonomic Systems case study,
401–402
goals review, 218
major activities, 216–219
outcome (project plan), 219
overview, 213, 217, 234
responsibilities, 216, 217
schedule and budget creation, 219
scope refinement, 218, 423
Plan process type (SCOR), 367, 368
platform-independent model (PIM),
312, 317
platform-specific model (PSM), 312,
317
Popkin Software
System Architect, 431, 432,
436–437, 438–439, 441–442,
502
Web site, 502
portals, 334–341
analyzing customer-oriented processes, 341–347
company portal, 334
comprehensive nature of, 334
customer-oriented e-business redesign, 347–349
defined, 334–335, 472
employee, 377–378
Ergonomic Systems case study,
409–412
ERP components, 347
exceptions and, 346
hierarchy of screens in Provision,
434, 435
internal, 334
multiple processes and, 344–346
Travel-Is-Us example, 335–340
Porter, Michael
business strategy defined by, 46
Competitive Advantage, 21–22,
57, 62, 463, 487, 488
competitive advantage theory of,
57–64
Competitive Strategy, 45–46, 48,
57, 473, 487, 488
evolution of the strategic process
and, 65

generic value chain of, 21–22,
57–59
model of competition of, 48–50,
472–473
"Strategy and the Internet,"
489
"What Is Strategy?", 489
positioning. *See also* strategy
considerations for company or
product, 53
defined, 473
strategic, 60, 61–64, 478–479
strategy vs., 60
potential entrants
barriers to entry, 50
competitive strategy and, 49–50
potential for improving performance
(PIP), 204, 472, 492
Potter, Neil S., 499
*Practical Steps for Aligning Information
Technology with Business Strategies,* 488
presentation (Web page hierarchy),
337, 434, 435
*Principles of Scientific Management,
The,* 20, 179, 486, 493
Principles of Systems, 486
Pritchett Web site, 493, 494
private processes
business process languages for,
275–277
defined, 473
for directly linked supply chain
systems, 365–366
need for information about,
275–276
supply chain integration,
354–355, 356
workflow systems and, 272–273
problem analysis, 473
procedural approach
to software development, 300
in workflow systems, 302
process analysis and improvement
worksheet, 222, 408
process architecture. *See also* business
process architecture commit-
tee; eTOM (eBusiness
Telecom Operations Map)
deciding what process change to
undertake, 80–84
defined, 473

of e-marketplace services company, 384
Ergonomic Systems case study,
391, 392
eTOM, for telecom companies,
72–78
Goals, Processes, and Projects
Worksheet, 89–90, 466
IT planning and, 84–87
overview of process, 87–90
process-strategy matrix for, 81–84
references, 489
software architectures and,
318–321
process architecture committee. *See*
business process architecture
committee
process automation. *See* business process automation
process categories (SCOR), 367, 369
process change. *See* business process
change
process design. *See* business process
redesign
process diagram. *See also* COULD
process diagram; IS process diagram; SHOULD process
diagram
activities and, 114–115, 120
Analysis phase of business process
redesign and, 221–222
asterisk on, 121
basics, 111–115
business rules for, 116–117
claims process examples, 122, 123
customers on, 112, 121
decision points or diamonds on,
117, 118
defined, 473–474
departmental handoffs highlighted on, 251, 252–253
development of, 113
drilling down into a process,
113–115
end point or sink, 119
Ergo Chair examples, 112, 114
events on, 122
flow and, 118
hexagons on, 177
initial event, 112
junction bars on, 117
level of granularity, 113

levels of analysis and, 131–132
on Measurement Scheduling
    Worksheet, 174–175
notation, 111–112, 113, 115–123
order fulfillment process exam-
    ples, 116, 119
organization diagram information
    for, 113, 114
organization diagram with,
    105–106
process diagrams vs., 473–474
in ProVision, 433–437
in Six Sigma Analyze phase,
    198–199
subprocesses and, 113
supply chain process diagram
    (SCOR), 373–374
swimlanes, 111–112, 113, 120,
    123, 341
time and, 111–112, 122–123
understanding demonstrated by,
    445–446, 447
vertical swimlanes, 123
as workflow diagram with
    swimlanes, 112–113
for workflow system, 259–261,
    262
process diagrams
    defined, 474
    process diagram vs., 473–474
    with SAP, 287–291
    UML activity diagrams, 307
    understanding demonstrated by,
        445–446, 447
    workflow diagrams, 112–113
process elements (SCOR), 367,
    370–371, 372–373
process fit, 62, 474
process improvement. See BPI (busi-
    ness process improvement)
Process Innovation, 23, 487
process instance, 474–475
process level of performance, 31
process management. See BPM (Busi-
    ness Process Management);
    business process management
process manager or sponsor, 214,
    422, 476. See also project
    sponsor
process measures. See also measures
    defined, 168, 475–476
    functional measures vs., 167–169

outcome measures vs., 195–196
in Six Sigma Measure phase, 195
worksheet, 172, 476
Process Measures Worksheet, 172,
    476
process output measures. See process
    measures
process redesign. See business process
    redesign
process redesign patterns, 235–253.
    See also business process
    redesign
    basic, 236, 237
    business process redesign method-
        ology and, 210
    defined, 207, 210, 235, 476
    ERP-driven redesign pattern, 238
    gaps and disconnects pattern,
        207, 237, 249–253, 466
    HPI pattern, 239
    management alignment pattern,
        238
    overview, 210
    reengineering pattern, 235, 237,
        240–244
    SCOR pattern, 239
    simplification pattern, 237,
        244–247, 251, 477
    Six Sigma pattern, 239
    software development pattern,
        239
    specialized, 236, 238–239
    types of, 236–237, 238–239
    using multiple patterns, 236
    value-added analysis pattern, 237,
        247–249, 251, 482
    workflow automation pattern,
        238
    XML-BP languages pattern, 238
process redesign team, 215, 216, 220,
    225, 305
process reengineering. See BPR (Busi-
    ness Process Reengineering)
process sponsor or manager, 214,
    422, 476. See also project
    sponsor
process thinking, 110, 476
processes. See also activities; business
    processes; value chains
    activities as, 79, 133
    activities vs., 79
    in business process hierarchy, 460

cross-company, 450, 451
defined, 58, 78–79
in eTOM framework, 75, 76, 78
hierarchy of, 80
Internet-driven changes in,
    330–332
levels of analysis and, 131, 132
manager's role, 161–162
notation, 109, 111, 115, 457
on organization diagram,
    108–109
organization diagrams and,
    105–109
profits produced by, 110
public vs. private, 272–273
supplementary or secondary, 78
types of, 78–80
value chains as, 79
value chains vs., 58
process/function role/responsibility
    worksheet (Ergonomic Sys-
    tems case study), 419, 421
process-IT matrix, 85, 86, 475
process/responsibility worksheets,
    227
process-strategy matrix
    complexity in, 81, 82–83
    defined, 476
    dynamics in, 81
    illustrated, 82, 453
    processes and solution options
        shown on, 83–84, 453–454
    using, 81–84
    value in, 82–83
ProcessWorld annual conference,
    287–288
Procter & Gamble integrated supply
    chain, 352
production workflow systems. See
    transaction or production
    workflow systems
products
    Ergonomic Systems case study,
        390
    organization charts' lack of,
        93–94
    in systems view of organization,
        96
    value chains and, 107
professional business process model-
    ing tools. See business process
    tools

profit margin, 58, 60
Proforma Corporation
    eTOM model, 489
    ProVision Workbench, 431,
        432–436, 437–439, 440, 442,
        476, 489, 502
    Web site, 489, 502
project sponsor, 212, 214–215, 216,
    218. *See also* process sponsor
    or manager
proprietary knowledge as barrier to
    entry, 50
ProVision Workbench (Proforma)
    associating measures with pro-
        cesses in, 437–438
    CTQ tree in, 437
    defined, 476
    eTOM model in, 489
    IS process diagram in, 433–434
    as market leader, 431
    notations used in, 432
    organization diagram in, 432–433
    SHOULD process diagram in,
        434–437
    simulation in, 438–439, 440
    using, 442
    Web portal screen hierarchy in,
        434, 435
    Web site, 502
PSM (platform-specific model), 312,
    317
public processes
    defined, 272, 476–477
    for directly linked supply chain
        systems, 362–365
    ebXML BPSS for, 274
    supply chain integration, 354,
        356
    workflow systems and, 272–273

quality control. *See also* Six Sigma
    defined, 179
    lean manufacturing and, 180
    in U.S. and Japanese auto manu-
        facturing, 180–181
Quantrani, Terry, 499

Ramage, Dick, 296
Rational Software
    Rational Rose UML modeling
        tool, 317
    Unified Process, 311
Rational Unified Process, The, 499

Real Time, 500
Realizing E-Business with Components,
    501
rectangles
    with bold border, 121–122
    with dashed border, 121
    on organization diagram, 109
    on process diagram, 115,
        121–122
    with rounded corners, 109
    with square corners, 109
redesign. *See* business process
    redesign
redesign patterns. *See* process redesign
    patterns
Redesign phase (business process re-
    design), 224–227
    cost or simulation of new process
        options, 227
    COULD process diagram, 225
    documentation of new activities,
        227
    Ergonomic Systems case study,
        409–421
    goal of, 224
    IS process and goals review, 225
    major activities, 225–227
    outcome (documentation of new
        process and management
        structure), 227
    overview, 213, 226, 234
    process/responsibility worksheets,
        227
    reporting relationships rationaliza-
        tion, 226–227
    responsibilities, 225
    SHOULD process design presen-
        tation, 227
    SHOULD process diagram,
        225
Reengineering Handbook, The, 494,
    495
Reengineering Management, 492
reengineering pattern
    described, 235
    development of, 237
    overview, 237, 240
    TI's MMST project case study,
        240–243
    today, 243–244
"Reengineering Redux," 488
Reengineering the Corporation, 23,
    240, 485, 487, 495

"Reengineering Work: Don't Auto-
    mate, Obliterate," 23, 487
Reference Model of Open Distrib-
    uted Processing (RM-ODP),
    321–323, 477
relational databases, software devel-
    opment and, 300–301
Repeatable maturity level (CMM), 8,
    9, 324, 325, 448
repository, 429–430
requirements interface in software de-
    velopment, 305
Resource Development phase. *See*
    Development phase (business
    process redesign)
Return process type (SCOR), 367,
    368
RM-ODP (Reference Model of Open
    Distributed Processing),
    321–323, 477
Robinson, Marcia, 488, 500
ROI (return on investment), Bal-
    anced Scorecard approach and,
    173
roles. *See also* activities
    activities as, 120
    manager, basic, 161–162
    manager, detailed, 162–165
    process/function role/responsibil-
        ity worksheet, 419, 421
Roller, D., 496
Rosen, Michael, 489, 501
Rosenburg, Doug, 499
Rosenfeld, Louis, 501
Rumbaugh, James, 498, 499
Rummler, Geary A.
    evolution of the strategic process
        and, 65
    gaps and disconnects pattern and,
        249
    HPT and, 30, 491–492
    Improving Performance, 30, 31,
        93, 138, 249, 477, 485, 487,
        489–490, 491–492, 494, 495
    management analysis by, 162
    Performance Design Lab Web
        site, 485, 490
    process diagramming originated
        by, 113
    Rummler-Brache methodology,
        30–32, 477
Rummler-Brache methodology,
    30–32, 160, 477

Rummler-Brache notation. *See* notation

Sakry, Mary E., 499
sales activity example, 146–149
   job descriptions and, 147, 148, 153–155
   overview, 146–147
   software applications and, 153–155
San Francisco Seafood. *See* SF Seafood
SAP (Systems, Applications and Products in data processing). *See also* ERP-driven redesign
   ARIS diagrams in, 287, 288–290
   business maps (process architectures), 283–284, 285
   C-business maps, 290–291
   defined, 477
   e-marketplace components, 355
   ERP applications from, 281, 282
   financials suite, 28
   insurance company applications, 285–287
   internal-oriented e-business application suites, 375–376
   Nestlé USA case study, 295–297
   portal components, 347
   process diagrams, 287–291
   SCM components, 364–365
   tailoring modules from, 287
   telecommunications applications, 284–285
   updates and tailored modules, 287
   vendor relationships, 287–288
   Web site, 291, 498
SAP R/3 Business Blueprint, 498
satisfiers in Kano analysis, 196
SCC (Supply Chain Council). *See also* SCOR (Supply Chain Operations Reference) model
   defined, 366, 479
   SCOR benchmarks from, 373
   SCOR training from, 374
   Supply-Chain Operations Reference-model, 366
   Web site, 479, 501
Schedule Product Deliveries process element (SCOR), 370–371
Scheer, A.-W., 28, 30, 458, 488, 498, 502. *See also* ARIS

Schroeder, Richard, 488, 494
SCM (supply chain management), 364–365, 477
scope of project, 218, 423
SCOR (Supply Chain Operations Reference) model, 366–375
   benchmarking projects, 372–374
   best practices, 372
   defined, 477
   goals, 366
   measures, 370–371
   planning and management, 368
   process categories, 367, 369
   process elements, 367, 370–371
   process redesign pattern, 239
   Schedule Product Deliveries process element, 370–371, 372–373
   supply chain process diagram, 373–374
   three levels of process detail, 366–368
   top-level processes, 366–367
   training, 374
Scott, Kendall, 490, 498, 499
secondary processes, 78
second-generation workflow systems, 265
SEI (Software Engineering Institute), 7, 29, 323, 462. *See also* CMM (Capability Maturity Model)
Senge, Peter M., 20, 110, 486–487
sequence diagram, 307
service measures, output measures vs., 196–197
services
   organization charts' lack of, 93–94
   value chains and, 107
SF Seafood
   Analyze phase (Six Sigma) for, 199–202
   bell curve, 185–186, 190
   cause-effect diagram, 201–202
   class diagram, 309
   Control phase (Six Sigma) for, 204
   CTQ tree, 192–193
   Define phase (Six Sigma) for, 190–194
   Food Service Process, 190

   Improve phase (Six Sigma) for, 202–203
   Measure phase (Six Sigma) for, 194–198
   SIPOC diagram, 190–191
   Six Sigma goals for, 185–186
   systems view of, 95–96
   use case diagram, 308
shareholders on supersystem diagram, 98
Sharp, Peter, 502
Short, James, 23
SHOULD process, 477
SHOULD process diagram
   defined, 125, 474
   Development phase of business process redesign and, 228, 230
   Ergonomic Systems case study, 412–413, 414–415, 434–437
   example, 126–127
   overview, 129–131
   in ProVision, 434–437
   Redesign phase of business process redesign and, 225
   swimlanes, 129–130
sigma (σ) or standard deviation, 183–184, 478
silo thinking, 23, 94, 477
Simple Object Access Protocol (SOAP), 478
simplification pattern, 244–247
   defined, 244, 477
   gaps and disconnects pattern and, 251
   overview, 237, 244
   Xerox NPP case study, 244–247
simulation, 430–431, 438–439, 477
sink on process diagram, 119
SIPOC (Supplier, Input, Process, Output, Customer) approach, 190–191, 478
Six Sigma, 488, 494
Six Sigma. *See also specific phases*
   alternative approaches, 204–205
   Analyze phase, 188, 198–202
   Control phase, 188, 203–204
   customer emphasis of, 190
   defects per million, 184, 186
   Define phase, 188, 189–194
   defined, 478
   development of, 33, 181
   DMADV model, 494
   DMAIC process, 188–204, 464

Six Sigma (*continued*)
  employee involvement in, 204–205
  expertise designated by belt, 187, 189
  failure to achieve, 189
  focus of, 33
  Improve phase, 188, 202–203
  keys to quick accomplishment, 189
  Measure phase, 188, 194–198
  measures in, 182, 186–187, 188, 194–198
  multiple iterations of phases, 188–189
  name explained, 183–184
  process analysis and, 182
  process improvement in, 182, 186–187, 188–189, 202–203
  process management in, 181–182
  process redesign in, 182
  process redesign pattern, 239
  references, 493–494
  statistics in, 205
  teams, 187–188
  value chains and, 186
Six Sigma Basic Training Kit, The, 494
Six Sigma Qualtec Web site, 493
Six Sigma Revolution, The, 493
Six Sigma Way Team Fieldbook, The, 494
skill, human performance analysis and, 143
Smith, Adam, 25, 487
Smith, Howard, 496–497
So, Andrew, 491
SOAP (Simple Object Access Protocol), defined, 478
software applications. *See also specific kinds*
  activities and, 153–155
  for completely automated activities, 149–153
  Expense Report application, 146
  first commercial application, 299
  history, 302–305
Software Architecture in Practice, 489
software development, 299–326. *See also* MDA (Model Driven Architecture)
  application development, 302–305
  CASE tools, 314, 317–318

CMM and, 323–326
graphical applications and, 301
history, 299–302
IDEF for, 321
managers vs. software developers, 301–302
MDA, 312–317
personal computers and, 301
procedural approach, 300
process architectures and software architectures, 318–321
process for completely automated activities, 149–153
process redesign pattern, 239
relational databases and, 300–301
requirements interface, 305
RM-ODP for, 321–323
SEI/DOD effort, 7
software analysis and UML, 306–310
UML modeling tools, 317–318
XML-based business process languages and, 323
Zachman Framework, 318–320, 483, 500
software engineering, 29–30, 478. *See also* CMM (Capability Maturity Model)
Software Engineering Institute (SEI), 7, 29, 323, 462. *See also* CMM (Capability Maturity Model)
software requirements, 30, 305, 478
software tools. *See* business process tools
Source process type (SCOR), 367, 368
SPC (Statistical Process Control), 32–33, 181
specialization. *See* niche specialization
Spewak, Steven H., 489
sponsor
  process, 214, 422, 476
  project, 212, 214–215, 216, 218
standard bell-shaped curve
  curve for process analysis curve, 184, 478
  defined, 478
  illustrated, 183
  long-run process drift and, 184, 478
  SF Seafood example, 185–186, 190
  standard deviation and, 183–184

standard deviation, 183–184, 478
statechart diagram, defined, 307
Statistical Process Control (SPC), 32–33, 181
steel e-marketplace, 357
steering committee. *See* steering teams
steering teams
  need for, 422
  for process architecture, 70–71
  for process redesign, 210, 215, 216, 218, 231, 422
Stepper, John C., 494, 495
Sterman, John D., 20, 486
"Strategic Planning Helps Chevron's E&P Optimize Its Assets," 493
strategic positioning. *See also* positioning; strategy
  best practices approach, 63–64
  company organization for, 63
  competitive advantage from, 60, 61–63
  defined, 60, 478–479
  focus on fit, 62
  operational effectiveness vs., 60, 61, 62
strategizing, 479
strategy. *See also* positioning; strategic positioning
  best practices approach, 63–64
  for competition, 52–54
  cost leadership, 52, 53–54
  defined, 46, 479
  differentiation, 52–53, 54
  for e-business, 64–65
  Ergonomic Systems' e-business strategy, 394–401
  evolution of the strategic process, 65–66
  industry change and, 51
  niche specialization, 53, 54
  overview, 45–46
  Phase 1: current company position, 46–47
  Phase 2: environment analysis, 46, 47
  Phase 3: new strategy development, 46, 47
  Porter's model of competition, 48–50
  Porter's theory of competitive advantage, 57–64
  position vs., 60

positioning and specialization in, 53–54

process-strategy matrix, 81–84, 453–454, 476

recent business environment changes and, 47

references, 489

senior management responsibilities, 45

Unisys example, 54–56

value chains for, 57–60

value propositions and, 51

"Strategy and the Internet," 489

strategy committee, 67, 69

strategy group for process redesign, 214

subprocesses
in business process hierarchy, 460
defined, 23, 479
levels of analysis and, 131, 132
notation, 109
on organization diagram, 108–109
process diagram and, 113
as Six Sigma focus, 186

subsidiary business processes, 479

substitutes, competitive strategy and, 49

subsubprocesses
in business process hierarchy, 460
as Six Sigma focus, 186

Successful Reengineering, 494, 495

supersystem diagram
as class diagram, 100
defined, 479
detail on, 99
illustrated, 99
levels of analysis and, 131–132
overview, 98–100

supplementary processes, 78

Supplier, Input, Process, Output, Customer (SIPOC) approach, 190–191, 478

supplier-oriented e-business applications, 351–375
defined, 351, 479
directly linked supply chain systems, 362–366
e-business marketplaces, 354, 355, 357–362
integrated supply chain, 351, 352–355
redesign, 351–354
references, 501–502

SCOR approach, 366–375
structuring supply chain applications, 354–355, 356

suppliers
competitive strategy and, 49
on supersystem diagram, 98
in systems view of organization, 96

Supply Chain Council. *See* SCC (Supply Chain Council)

Supply Chain Intelligence, 501

Supply Chain Management, 501

Supply Chain Management Based on SAP Systems, 501

supply chain management (SCM), 364–365, 477

Supply Chain Operations Reference model. *See* SCOR (Supply Chain Operations Reference) model

supply chain process diagram (SCOR), 373–374

supply chain systems. *See also* supplier-oriented e-business applications
design approaches, 354–355, 356
directly linked, 362–366
e-business marketplaces, 354, 355, 357–362
goals, 332
history, 352
integrated, 351, 352–355
traditional or internal, 352

Supply-Chain Operations Reference-model, 366

swimlanes
actor, 120
customer swimlane, 112, 121, 341
defined, 480
passage of time on, 111–112, 122–123
on process diagram, 111–112, 113, 120, 123
process diagram as workflow diagram with, 112–113
shaded, 120
on SHOULD process diagram, 129–130
symbols and labels for, 120
vertical, 123

synchronous processes, defined, 480

System Architect (Popkin Software)

for architecture maintenance, 439, 441–442
described, 432
as market leader, 431
SHOULD process in, 436–437
simulation in, 438–439
using, 442
Web site, 502
Zachman Framework in, 441–442

system performance, 472

systems
defined, 480
diagram, 20
organizations as, 20–21, 445
value chains and, 21–23
view of organization, 95–96

systems analyst, 480

Systems, Applications and Products in data processing. *See* SAP (Systems, Applications and Products in data processing)

systems architect, 480

systems designer, 480

systems thinking, 110, 480

Taylor, Frederick W., 19–20, 179, 486, 493

Taylor, Gillian, 497

teams
process redesign, 215, 216, 220, 225, 305
Six Sigma, 187–188
steering, for process architecture, 70–71
steering, for process redesign, 210, 215, 216, 218, 231, 422

Techniques for Business Process Redesign, 494, 495

technologies
business processes generated by, 20
strategy and evaluation of, 64

Technology viewpoint (RM-ODP), 322

telecommunications
SAP business architecture for, 284–285
SAP components used in, 286

TeleManagement Forum. *See also* eTOM (eBusiness Telecom Operations Map)
eTOM framework, 466

TeleManagement Forum (*continued*)
   eTOM: The Business Process Framework, 489
   process architecture, 72–78
   Web site, 489
"Texas Instruments' MMST Project," 495
Texas Instruments (TI)
   MMST project, 240–243
   Six Sigma approach at, 181
third-generation workflow systems, 265
three levels of organization. *See* performance framework
TI. *See* Texas Instruments (TI)
Tkach, Daniel, 491
TO-BE process. *See* SHOULD process
Tony, Morgan, 491
tools. *See* business process tools
TQM (Total Quality Management)
   CMM and, 8
   contributions of, 32–33, 181
   defined, 481
TradeXchange system, 357–358
transaction or production workflow systems, 264, 481
transaction processing, 481
Transition phase (business process redesign), 231–234
   Ergonomic Systems case study, 422–424
   goal of, 231
   major activities, 231–232, 233
   outcome (new process), 233
   overview, 213, 232, 234
   responsibilities, 231
transitioning to a new process, 481
Travel-Is-Us
   completely automated reservation system with portal, 339, 342–343
   COULD process diagram, 335, 336–337, 338–339, 342–343
   IS process diagram, 335, 336–337
   portal creation, 335–340
   references, 501
   reservation portal screens, 335, 340

UDDI (Universal Description, Discovery and Integration), 481

UML activity diagrams. *See* process diagrams
UML Distilled, 490, 498
UML notation. *See* notation
UML (Unified Modeling Language)
   activity diagrams, 307
   behavior diagrams, 306
   business process modeling and, 310–312
   class diagrams, 306, 309–310
   collaboration diagram, 307
   component diagram, 307
   defined, 481
   deployment diagram, 307
   modeling tools, 314–315, 317–318
   OMG UML Specification, 306
   references, 498–499
   sequence diagram, 307
   software analysis and, 306–310
   statechart diagram, 307
   use case diagrams, 306, 308–309, 481
   Web site for documentation, 490, 498
   XML and, 314–315
UMM (UN/CEFACT Modeling Methodology), 274–275
UN/CEFACT
   ebXML sponsorship by, 273–274
   Modeling Methodology (UMM), 274–275
Unified Modeling Languages Users Guide, The, 498
Unified Process (UP), 311
Unified Software Development Process, The, 499
Unisys
   business process outsourcing and, 316–317
   corporate strategy, 54–56
   letter to stakeholders (2002), 55
   services-driven model adoption by, 55
   strategic priorities for 2002, 56
   UML-compliant repositories, 314
   value chains, 59
   vision statement, 54–55
Unisys Analysts Meeting, 488
Universal Description, Discovery and Integration (UDDI), 481
UP (Unified Process), 311

use case diagrams
   defined, 306, 481
   overview, 308–309
   SF Seafood example, 308
Use Case Driven Object Modeling with UML, 499

value
   defined, 58
   in process-strategy matrix, 82–83
value chain diagram, 107
value chains
   activity-based costing and, 106–107
   BPR and, 107
   in business process hierarchy, 460
   core processes and, 58
   defined, 21, 58, 79, 482
   enterprise alignment and, 69
   function-process matrix for small bank, 71–72
   in hierarchy of processes, 80
   levels of analysis and, 131, 132
   on organization diagram, 106–108
   Porter's generic value chain, 21–22, 57–59
   as processes, 79
   processes vs., 58
   for product or service lines, 107
   profits produced by, 110
   references, 488
   as revolt against departmentalism, 23
   Six Sigma approach and, 186
   systems and, 21–23
   Unisys examples, 59
value propositions
   bookseller example, 51
   defined, 51, 58, 482
   focus on core competencies vs., 52
   Internet effect on, 51, 52
value-added activities
   criteria for, 247
   defined, 481–482
   Six Sigma Analyze phase and, 199
value-added analysis pattern, 247–249
   criteria for value-added activities, 247
   defined, 482

gaps and disconnects pattern and, 251
  overview, 237
value-enabling activities, 58, 482
Van de Putte, Geert, 502
Vasudeva, Guru, 383–384, 500
vertical alignment, 482
vertical swimlanes on process diagram, 123
vertical view of organizations, 94
vision statement of Unisys, 54–55
Vissides, John, 495
Visual Modeling Thinking, 491
Visual Modeling with Rational Rose 2000 and UML, 499

W3C (World Wide Web Consortium), 482
Wal-Mart integrated supply chain, 352
Walton, Sam, 352
Wealth of Nations, The, 487
Web services
  business process languages and, 270
  defined, 270, 482
  ebXML for, 270–271
Web Services Flow Language. *See* WSFL (Web Services Flow Language)
Web sites. *See also* Internet; portals
  ASQ, 493
  BlueFire Six Sigma, 494
  BPMI, 459, 496
  business process management articles, 497
  Business Process Trends newsletter, 503
  Business Rule Community, 491
  Chevron process management improvement white paper, 493
  CMM information, 486
  Covisint, 359
  Cutter Consortium, 485
  e-business patterns, 500
  ebXML, 464, 497
  HPT information, 491
  IDS Scheer, 498
  ISO, 500
  ISPI, 468, 491
  ISSSP, 493
  iStarXchange system, 362

Ken Orr Institute, 493
  MDA information, 499
  Microsoft BizTalk, 496
  OMG, 470, 490, 497, 498, 499
  PDL (Rummler's company), 485, 490
  Pritchett, 493, 494
  process modeling tools, 502
  Proforma Corporation, 489
  SAP, 291, 498
  SCC information, 479, 501
  Six Sigma Qualtec, 493
  Six Sigma resources, 493, 494
  Smith reports, 497
  TeleManagement Forum, 489
  TeraQuest (Curtis's company), 486
  UML documentation, 490, 498
  W3C, 482
  WfMC, 482, 496
  Who's Profiting from Business Process Redesign report, 485
  "Workflow-Based Applications" article, 496
  WSFL information, 496
  Zachman Institute for Framework Advancement, 483, 500
Weber, Charles V., 486, 500
Weinbach, Larry, 54, 55, 56
Welch, Jack, 33, 181
WfMC (Workflow Management Coalition)
  award winners, 266–268
  defined, 258, 482
  key workflow relationships, 258
  MDA and, 315
  Web site, 482, 496
  Wf-XML protocol, 269, 279
  workflow defined by, 258
  Workflow Management Coalition Terminology and Glossary, 259, 496
  workflow management systems defined by, 258
  workflow terms defined by, 260
  XPDL, 269, 279, 483
Wf-XML protocol, 269, 279
"What Is Strategy?", 489
White, Steven A., 501
Who's Profiting from Business Process Redesign, 2–4, 485
Willis, Alan Cameron, 499

workflow
  defined, 258, 482
  references, 496–497
  XML and, 268–269
workflow automation pattern, 238
workflow diagrams. *See* process diagrams
workflow engines. *See* workflow systems
Workflow Handbook 2002, 496
Workflow Management Coalition. *See* WfMC (Workflow Management Coalition)
workflow management systems. *See* workflow systems
workflow manager, 263
workflow model, 258–259, 262, 483
Workflow Paradigm, The, 487
workflow systems, 257–269. *See also* business process automation; WfMC (Workflow Management Coalition)
  ad hoc, 264, 458
  administrative, 264–265, 458
  Anova case study, 266–267
  as automation systems, 29
  before and after, 259–263
  BPR and, 257
  BPR vs., 28–29
  business process languages and, 271–272
  defined, 483
  early use of, 27, 28–29
  ERP systems as, 294
  flow of control in, 262–263
  future of, 279
  generations of, 265
  groupware applications, 265
  iJET Travel Intelligence case study, 267–268
  insurance company example, 259–263
  large processes and, 259
  modification facilitated by, 263
  other Web site managed by, 263
  overview, 27, 257–258, 259
  procedural approach of, 302
  process diagram, 259–261, 262
  process modeling tools for, 262
  public and private processes, 272–273
  redesign with, 266

workflow systems (*continued*)
  scheduling using, 265
  transaction or production, 264, 481
  types of, 264–266
  WfMC definitions of terms, 258, 260
  WfMC model, 258–259
  workflow engine as heart of, 257
  workflow manager, 263
  workflow model for, 262
"Workflow-Based Applications," 496
worksheets
  Activity Analysis, 136, 137, 458
  Activity Cost, 137, 458
  defined, 483
  goals and measures (case study), 393
  Goals, Processes, and Projects, 89–90, 466
  Human Performance Analysis, 149, 150, 151, 467
  Measurement Scheduling, 174–176, 469
  opportunities and threats (case study), 396, 398–399
  process analysis and improvement, 222, 408
  Process Measures, 172, 476

process/function role/responsibility (case study), 419, 421
process/responsibility, 227
World Wide Web Consortium (W3C), 482
Worthen, Ben, 498
WSFL (Web Services Flow Language). *See also* BPEL4WS (Business Process Execution Language for Web Services)
  defined, 483
  overview, 277
  Web sites, 496
  XLANG merging with, to form BPEL4WS, 276
Wurster, Thomas S., 500

Xerox, non-production procurement (NPP), 244–247
XLANG (Microsoft). *See also* BPEL4WS (Business Process Execution Language for Web Services)
  defined, 483
  overview, 277
  references, 496
  WSFL merging with, to form BPEL4WS, 276
XML Business Process Language, 483

XML (eXtended Markup Language). *See also* XPDL (XML Process Definition Language)
  defined, 483
  described, 268
  development of, 268
  software system-to-software system communication using, 269
  UML tools and, 314–315
  workflow and, 268–269
  XML languages, 269
XML-BP languages pattern, 238
XPDL (XML Process Definition Language), 269, 279, 483

Y2K bug, 34

Zachman Framework
  defined, 318, 483
  illustrated, 319
  overview, 318–320
  in System Architect, 441–442
  Web site, 483, 500
Zachman Institute for Framework Advancement Web site, 483, 500
Zachman, John, 318
Zeier, Alexander, 501

Author Biography

Paul Harmon is the president and founder of Enterprise Alignment, a professional services company providing educational and consulting services to managers interested in business process options, and executive editor and founder of *Business Process Trends,* an Internet portal providing a news and information community for Business Process trends, directions, and best practices.

Prior to founding Enterprise Alignment in 2002, Paul was a noted consultant, author, and analyst concerned with applying new technologies to real-world business problems. Some of the books he has written include *Developing E-business Systems and Architectures* with Michael Rosen and Michael Guttman (Morgan Kaufmann, 2001), *Understanding UML* with Mark Watson (Morgan Kaufmann, 1998), *Intelligent Software Systems Development* with Curt Hall (Wiley, 1993), *Objects in Action* with David A. Taylor (Addison-Wesley, 1993), and *Expert Systems: AI in Business* with David King (Wiley, 1985).

Mr. Harmon has served as a senior consultant and head of Cutter Consortium's Distributed Architecture practice. From 1985 to 1994, Mr. Harmon wrote Cutter Consortium's *Component Development Strategies* newsletter.

Paul has worked on major process redesign projects with Bank of America, Wells Fargo, Security Pacific, Prudential, and Citibank, among others. He is a well-known and respected consultant, analyst, and speaker. He has been the keynote speaker and has delivered workshops and seminars on a wide variety of topics to conferences and major corporations throughout the world.